THE
WARNER BROS.
STORY

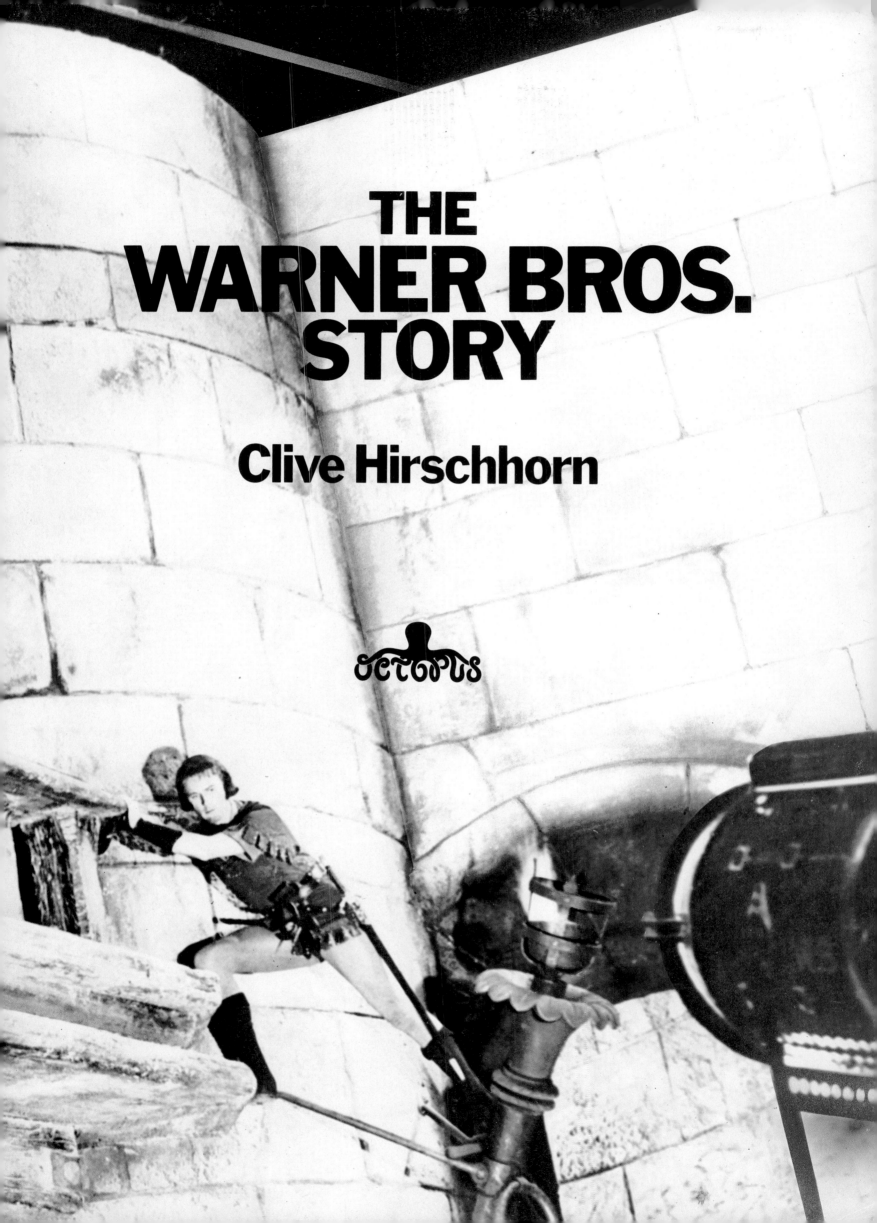

THE
WARNER BROS.
STORY

Clive Hirschhorn

OCTOPUS

Previous page: Michael Curtiz (in boots) directing Errol Flynn in The Adventures Of Robin Hood (1938). This page: preparing a camera set-up for East of Eden (1955).

CONTENTS

First published in 1979
by Octopus Books Limited, 59 Grosvenor Street, London W1

Reprinted 1980, 1981, 1982, 1983

First impression in paperback 1986

© Warner Bros., Inc. 1979 ISBN 0 7064 2757 2

Produced by Mandarin Publishers Limited
22a Westlands Road, Quarry Bay, Hong Kong

Printed in Hong Kong

To the memory of Paul Pickering

For their help and assistance on **The Warner Bros. Story**
I am indebted to Monty Arnold and the staff of the
Lincoln Centre Library for the Performing Arts, Peter
Seward, Linda Wood and Susan Julian-Huxley of the
British Film Institute, without whose patience and
assistance the book might have taken twice as long to
write; George Pratt (Eastman House, Rochester), Carol
Carey (Stills Archive of the Museum of Modern Art,
New York), The Stills Library of the British Film
Institute, Susan Dalton (University of Wisconsin), George
Nelson, Sidney Ganis, Arthur Wilson and Mort Lickter
(Warner Bros. USA), Brian Burton (Columbia-Warner,
UK), *Sunday Express*, London, and my two researchers
Sydney Rosenzweig (Rochester) and Andrew Rosner
(California).

I'd also like to thank Allen Eyles, editor of *Focus on
Film*, for bringing his eagle eye to bear on the manuscript,
ditto Robyn Karney, Dick Vosburgh, and for his
constructive comments and suggestions William Schaefer,
who, as an erstwhile assistant to the late Jack Warner,
proved to be absolutely invaluable.

Finally, a word of thanks to Miles Kreuger, Tony Slide
(of the Academy of Motion Picture Arts and Sciences,
California), Madeleine Harmsworth, Barbara Roëtt,
Ronald Bergan, Gilbert Adair, David Robinson, Rudi Fehr,
Alexander Walker, Barry Burnett, Frank Lazarus, Peter
MacKriel, and to the following people for providing the
colour material used in this book: Joel Finler for pp.
450–451, 452 above, 452–453, 456 below, 457 below,
458–459, 460 above; ITC pp. 461 below; Kobal
Collection pp. 449, 454–455, 457 above, 460 below,
464; Warner Bros. London pp. 452 below, 456 above,
461 above, (D.C. Comics Incorporated) 462–463.

Clive Hirschhorn
London, 1979.

Publisher's Acknowledgment
The publishers would like to thank John Douglas Eames
for originating the concept for this series of studio
histories.

Designers: Design 23
Photographic Consultant: Ian Cook

Preface

As **The Warner Bros. Story** began to take shape, it became increasingly clear to me that, in order to keep the undertaking manageable I would have to lay down certain guide-lines for myself. The first and most fundamental of these was to establish what, exactly, constituted a Warner Bros. film. Certainly, all the feature films to emanate from the Warner Bros. studios at Burbank would have to be included and, as such, most of the films up to 1950 presented no problems. The difficulties arose in the fifties, sixties and seventies when, with the dissolution of the studio system and the general change that was overtaking Hollywood, the kind of pictures once so easily identifiable with the particular studio that made them, were becoming increasingly rare. Instead of relying solely on home-grown product, as was generally the case in Hollywood's halcyon days, the major studios now seemed more concerned with distributing movies from elsewhere (under their own logos) than with making them. And, as many of these films were released by different companies in different parts of the world (e.g. the recent **Too Many Chefs** was a Warner Bros. release in America but the property of GTO in Britain) it was not always easy to know what, precisely, to include in the book and what to leave out.

My final decision was to describe every film released by Warner Bros. in the United States, regardless of the country or studio of its origin. Hence such titles as **The Hasty Heart** (Associated British Picture Corporation, 1950) **Look Back In Anger** (Woodfall, 1959) and **The Cranes Are Flying** (Mosfilms, 1959) – to name but three – appear.

Strictly speaking, of course, these were not Warner Bros. films in the sense that **The Maltese Falcon** (1941) and **Casablanca** (1943) were. But they were bought by Warner Bros. for release in the US and, as such, are part of the company's history.

Warner Bros. acquired First National Studios in October, 1928, and with it First National's impressive catalogue of silent films. I have not included these in **The Warner Bros. Story** for, although they became part of the studio's inventory, they were not initially released by Warner Bros. and, with the arrival of sound, virtually disappeared – as, indeed, did the bulk of Warner Bros.' own silent product.

Nor have I described in any detail the numerous films made by Warner Bros. at their Teddington Studios in England during the thirties and forties except for the handful that were given American releases (like **The Prime Minister**, 1942). I have, however, provided a year by year listing of these films together with a breakdown of the main players in each, its director, and a one-line, no comment synopsis. Denis Gifford's British Film Catalogue (1895–1970) published by David and Charles, proved invaluable for this purpose.

No feature film running less than 45 minutes has been included, hence the omission, as fully-fledged entries, of the Warner brothers' first tentative attempts at film-making with such efforts as **Passions Inherited, Perils Of The Plains, Raiders On The Mexican Border, The Lost City** and **Miracles Of The Jungle.**

I have also omitted all references to Warner Bros.' short subjects and cartoons. These, like the silent films of First National, deserve a book in themselves. But I have named, in the appropriate 'year opener' those shorts (such as the 1939 two-reeler **Sons Of Liberty**) which won Oscars.

The studio's annual profit and loss figures, a feature of every year opener from 1926 onwards (records before that no longer exist) were taken from the company's annual stockholder's reports.

Occasionally various people altered the spelling of their names during their careers, for instance Julian Josephson became Julien Josephson, Anthony Coldewey became Anthony Coldeway and Douglas Dumbrille became Douglass Dumbrille. For consistency I have adopted the spelling which appears most often (nearly always the spelling used at the end of the person's career).

Many of the movies listed in **The Warner Bros. Story** – especially those from the silent era – have been lost or destroyed and were, therefore, unavailable for viewing. In such cases the critical comments incorporated in their description were culled from a large cross-section of the major newspapers and periodicals of the time. Rather than splatter the text with a rainstorm of quotation marks or lengthen the entries unnecessarily by listing, in each case, the numerous critical sources called upon, I have simply presented a composite and, I hope, uncluttered general opinion of the film in question. The main sources used, in such instances, included *The Bioscope, The Motion Picture Herald, Kine Weekly, Variety, The Monthly Film Bulletin, Photoplay* and *The New York Times.*

The Early Years

Benjamin Warner and his wife, Pearl, were both born in 1857 in the small Polish village of Krasnashiltz near the German border. Like his father before him, Benjamin, being a Jew, was prevented by the Russians, who dominated Poland at the time, from having a formal education. Whatever knowledge he and, ultimately, his family acquired was 'stolen' in lofts and stables where the local village rabbi, forever watchful of the police, would teach the writings of the Talmud.

Benjamin Warner was a cobbler and he and his wife lived in poverty. In 1879, their first son Harry was born. Then came a daughter, Anna in 1881. By this time the ghetto conditions, aggravated by the constant harassment of the Russian police, forced Benjamin, in common with so many other Jews, to seek a future elsewhere.

America seemed to be the place that offered the most opportunities, so, shortly after Anna's birth, Benjamin left his wife and family behind and boarded a cattle boat for Baltimore, Maryland, on the advice of a friend who had gone there before him and sent back word of its golden prospects.

There was nothing golden, however, about Benjamin Warner's early days in Baltimore. He found lodgings in a clapboard and brick rooming house in Harrison Street — the Skid Row of the city — and opened a modest shoe repair shop at the corner of Pratt and Light Streets. He made two dollars a week, but didn't complain as it was two dollars more than he had made in Krasnashiltz. Sometimes he even made three dollars a week, for he soon hit on a gimmick: repairing shoes while the customer waited. The Warner pioneering instinct was already at work.

A year after his arrival in America, Benjamin had managed to save enough money to send for Pearl and their two children.

He worked hard and long, and at the first opportunity, moved out of Harrison Street, or the Tenderloin district as it was also known, to a house in South Baltimore. After that he and Pearl began to have children every other summer, thus making it impossible to save a single cent. Albert was born in 1884 and, after him Henry, Samuel, Rose and Fannie. Henry and Fannie died before they were

four years old; the others, however, were made of sturdier stuff and as soon as they were able to walk, were supplementing the family income by doing odd jobs in the neighbourhood, such as selling newspapers or shining shoes on street corners, a pattern familiar to most large immigrant families.

It was not nickels and dimes, however, that Benjamin Warner needed to keep his family housed, fed, educated and clothed, but paper money, and as his cobbling business could hardly be considered brisk, he decided on a new venture: travelling the country selling pots and pans while his wife looked after the shop in Baltimore.

But most Americans were already the proud possessors of pots and pans and he soon realized that if he wanted to make a decent living as a salesman, he would have to tap a market hitherto unexplored — such as the new, small fur-trapping communities in Canada. So he ventured northwards and, for two difficult years, he exchanged kitchenware for furs and pelts which he then attempted to sell for currency. Convinced that he was really on to something worthwhile, he sold his shop, piled his family into a wagon and bartered his way across the freezing Canadian North.

He need not have bothered. A crooked associate in the venture made off with the pelts, leaving Benjamin Warner and his family penniless. The arrival of two more children during this unhappy period — Jack in London, Ontario on 2nd August 1892, and David, in Hamilton, Ontario a year later, brought Mr. and Mrs. Warner more misery than pleasure.

In desperation, the family returned to Baltimore where Benjamin picked up his rusty cobbler's tools and once again attempted to eke out a living mending shoes while the customers waited.

In 1896, Harry Warner, who was 15, proved to be so skilled a cobbler (as, indeed, did 12-year-old Albert) that Benjamin felt confident enough to move to Youngstown, one of the toughest turn-of-the-century American cities, where he put himself and his two boys to work in a shop downtown.

The locals were impressed with the family's repairs-while-you-wait approach, supported the shop

Edison's Kinetoscope

and gave Benjamin Warner his first taste of success in America. But shoes, in those days, were built to last, and business, inevitably, dropped off. If he wanted to remain solvent, Benjamin Warner would somehow have to think of something else.

He came up with just the thing — or so he thought. As there was a fair amount of unused space at the back of the store, he would expand his business by adding a grocery section to the shop.

Youngstown, however, was not short of grocery stores, and because Benjamin Warner could not compete with the larger, better equipped premises in the neighbourhood, his idea was not a success. Competition from rival cobblers also increased and, as most of his competitors also adopted a repairs-while-you-wait system, Benjamin's takings dropped to almost nothing. He decided that things might improve if he gave up cobbling altogether and concentrated on groceries. But his existing store was far too small. He needed a much larger place if he was to make a success of this venture.

So, with what little money he had managed to save, he rented a bigger place in the Polish section of the city on West Federal Street, where he not only expanded his grocery store, but added a meat section as well. 'With nine kids to feed,' he argued, 'at least we get the menu for wholesale.' (A daughter Sadye and son Milton were born in 1895 and 1896.)

The children who were old enough to help out in the store did so — including Jack, who was put in charge of the delivery department and whose duties commenced at four in the morning. Despite the long hours he had to work, Jack still found the energy to pursue a hobby he had been nurturing since he first began to talk — performing for anyone

who would stop long enough to listen. As he got older, carnivals, fairs and neighbourhood theatres became Jack's perennial hangouts, as well as church halls, minstrel shows and benefit nights at the Y.M.C.A. He would often spend his time, and whatever spare pocket money he could save, having his photograph taken in a small photographic studio on West Federal Street. He was eight years old, and in the snapshots registered a variety of emotions, from laughter to anger. He was once even conned into parting with a fifty-dollar down payment by a bogus Italian 'maestro' in return for a series of singing lessons. The following day the maestro mysteriously disappeared.

But Jack did not need to be taught how to sing. When he warbled 'Wait Till The Sun Shines, Nellie' or 'Sweet Adeline' there wasn't a dry eye in the house. He was a boy soprano much in demand at singing lodges, clubs, churches and benefits.

Despite his lack of formal training, he was a fast sight-reader of sheet music and picked up a new tune after hearing it only once. In Youngstown, a veritable melting pot of ethnic groups, he assimilated a variety of dialects which he incorporated into his songs and routines. He even changed his name for a brief time to Leon Zuardo, which he used later when he and other members of the Warner Bros. studio performed on KFWB, the radio station they developed in Los Angeles. Eventually he was asked to sing the song slides at a new theatre in downtown Youngstown. The engagement led to a small-time impresario booking him for a 'fleabag' tour of Ohio and Pennsylvania. The show business career of Jack Warner, alias Leon Zuardo, was finally launched. The year was 1907 and he was fifteen.

Meanwhile Albert had set out from Youngstown for Chicago in 1900 where he temporarily became a soap salesman. Back at the family store, Harry began to demonstrate his ability to harness money to its best advantage and was promoted by his father from salesman to 'financial adviser' of the store. He did not much enjoy the meat and grocery side of things, but his aptitude for business negotiations was unmistakable. The market in perishable goods, however, was not something to which he wanted to devote the rest of his life, so, while continuing to work for his father, he kept an eye open for something more exciting. At one point he thought he had found it in bicycle spare-parts.

The showman's instinct was beginning to manifest itself in Sam Warner too. He became a barker at a carnival egg-throwing stall, but when the price of eggs went up, business went down and the stall closed. Undaunted, he found employment fronting for a snake charmer who left the business rather abruptly when one of his pythons nearly strangled him to death.

Out of work again, Sam looked around for something different and became an ice-cream cone salesman. But forever restless, he again changed the pace of his activities by becoming a fireman on the Erie Railroad. It was merely a temporary stint and, while shovelling coal into the locomotive's boiler, he kept an eye open for a job that would return him to show business.

The Warner Brothers West Coast Studio in the early 1920s and (inset) its main entrance

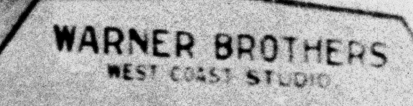

Jack Warner   *Albert Warner*   *Sam Warner*   *Harry Warner*

He did not have to look for very long. One Sunday, a friend introduced him to a piece of machinery called the Edison Kinetoscope which he taught Sam how to operate. Sam was intrigued, left his job on the railroad and became a projectionist in White City Park in Chicago where he was put in charge of screening a travelogue on Yosemite National Park.

Realizing what immense potential this new toy had, he returned excitedly to Youngstown where he managed to convince his family, who were now all together again, that moving pictures were big business. He even talked his father into pawning a valuable watch and chain, as well as their old horse, Bob, in order to purchase a Model B Projector.

Together with the kinetoscope came a print of Edwin S. Porter's **The Great Train Robbery**, the first motion picture to tell a definite story. It was only 800 feet long, but a decided crowd-pleaser, as the Warners found out when they rented an empty store in Niles, just outside Youngstown. Their shows coincided with a touring carnival and were a sell-out. Rose Warner played the piano, Albert and Harry were in charge of the box-office, Sam operated the projector and Jack sang illustrated songs during performances. Their first week's takings totalled $300, more money than Benjamin Warner made in a month selling meat.

Harry, clearly the businessman of the family, was encouraged by the success of their initial attempts and tried to find permanent premises for their kinetoscope. This proved to be a difficult task, so Sam and Albert took the show on the road instead. They played in halls throughout Pennsylvania and Ohio, scoring their biggest success in Newcastle.

There were problems, of course, the main one being the fragility of the film itself which, with constant winding and rewinding, became so worn that it snapped in dozens of places until it was beyond repair.

Undaunted, they returned to Newcastle where, in 1903, with the profits of their successful tour, Harry, Sam and Albert hired some chairs from the local undertaker and opened the Cascade Theatre which

screened films which Harry had managed to rent in Pittsburgh. As the reels were being wound back, Jack would jump up on stage and recite poems for the customers, an ingenious ploy which instantly cleared the theatre, thus freeing the seats for the second show.

Though business in Newcastle continued to be good, the brothers realized that they had merely penetrated the surface of the picture business, and that its real money-making potential lay not just in screening films, but in distributing them. So, in 1907, they left Newcastle for Pittsburgh and devised a way of entering the motion picture exchange business.

At the end of his own tour of Ohio and Pennsylvania as a performer, young Jack Warner moved to Pittsburgh to be with his brothers, two of whom – Harry and Albert – had recently married. He was, he recalls in his autobiography, too young to be allowed to operate the projector and, instead, was given the title of 'film inspector' which meant, in effect, that all the messy work, such as splicing together broken film, and checking the sprockets, was delegated to him. Another of his chores was to see that the films were successfully despatched to the theatres with whom the Warners had contracts. By 1908, the Warners had amassed 200 film titles and serviced theatres all over Western Pennsylvania.

Spurred on by their success in Pittsburgh, Sam, Albert and Harry decided to open more film exchanges in Norfolk, Virginia and Atlanta, Georgia; and Jack was sent along as Sam's assistant. The two exchanges, in the Bakewell Building, Pittsburgh and the Monticello Arcade, Norfolk, were collectively known as the Duquesne Amusement Supply. Advertising its product was a bulletin, founded by Jack and Sam, called *The Duquesne Film Noise.*

The Warner brothers were at last making money. Throughout the country, the fashion for moving pictures caught on spectacularly. Theatres proliferated and by the end of 1909, there were thousands of them across America. Every abandoned store, barn or village hall was swiftly turned into a movie house and the independent film exchanges benefited handsomely.

Then came disaster. Thomas Edison, one of the pioneers of motion pictures, upset by the huge profits being enjoyed by exhibitors throughout the country – profits in which he, unfortunately, did not share – had no difficulty persuading the major film makers of the time (Vitagraph, Selig, Essanay, Biograph, Lubin, Kalem, as well as the French companies Pathé and Méliès) to band together to form The Motion Picture Patents Company, collectively known as The Trust. The object of The Trust was clear. It prevented independent producers from making films without a licence, and film exchanges from distributing their products. Furthermore, all theatres using The Trust's patents would be licensed and charged two dollars a week for the use of each projector. And just to make quite sure that the small-time distributor was eliminated from the race, the General Film Company was formed for the purpose of buying out these exhibitors, leaving the field wide open for The Trust. Anyone who fought back or failed to pay the astronomical amounts of money demanded by The Trust had his film supply withdrawn, or was even physically attacked by hired thugs. It was as ruthless and as simple as that.

The Warner brothers, who were neither rich enough nor strong enough to combat this sort of victimization, sold their exchanges, returned to Youngstown and bided their time wondering what to do next.

It was only a matter of months, however, before Sam Warner returned from a trip to New York having bought the rights for a five-reeler called **Dante's Inferno** based on the famous poem. Sam's idea was to take the film on the road, together with

a narrator, who, while the movie unspooled, would read extracts from the original poem.

The idea worked. The film opened in Hartford, Connecticut, and, according to Jack Warner, you could hear the cash registers ringing all the way to Ohio.

The tour netted them $1,500 which Sam and Jack blew on a crap game in New York. However, after pooling their combined resources, Jack, Sam, Albert and Harry had just enough money to put into practice a suggestion of Harry's that they turn to production and make a couple of two-reeler quickies. Harry knew of an abandoned foundry in St. Louis which would be ideal for a studio. So, once again, the four brothers moved across the country in search, as ever, of something new.

En route Jack devised a scenario involving Indians and settlers and called it **Peril of the Plains.** It starred Dot Farley, a young girl from Chicago who could ride better than she could act. With Sam directing, the epic was completed in three days. It won no awards, and neither did their second effort, which was

Above: the entrance to the Warner Bros. studios in 1925
Below: Sam and Jack Warner (right and second from right) at the Apollo Theatre in Atlantic City with their first travelling road show in 1905

again directed by Sam, called **Raiders on the Mexican Border.**

At the same time as the Warner brothers were making films that nobody wanted to see, Carl Laemmle, soon to become head of Universal Pictures, made brave efforts to undermine The Trust's pernicious stranglehold on independent film-makers and distributors, and formed The Independent Motion Picture Company for distribution through his own and other private exchanges. Harry and his brothers willingly gave Laemmle their support and, in 1912, once again risked entering the exchange business. This time they decided to operate in California. Sam was accordingly despatched to Los Angeles, and Jack to San Francisco.

Refusing to be intimidated by The Trust, the Warners' Californian exchange prospered. After the tremendous success they had with a European import called **War Brides,** starring the exotic Nazimova, for which they paid $50,000 for the California-Nevada-Arizona rights, they paid twice that much to buy the West Coast rights for a Civil War drama made by the Selig Polyscope Company, called **The Crisis.**

The critics were very enthusiastic, but unfortunately the brothers' timing was wrong. The day after the film opened, April 6th, 1917, America declared war on Germany, and no one was in the mood to fuel their anxieties on a subject so near to home. **The Crisis** was indeed that and the brothers lost their entire investment in it.

While Sam and Jack were contemplating their next move, Harry, who was in New York, decided to have another go at film production and purchased the rights to a story called *Passions Inherited* from the poem by Ella Wheeler Wilcox for which he paid $15,000. He hired a director called Gilbert P. Hamilton to deliver the finished picture, which was to be shot on location in Southern California in five weeks. But Hamilton ran off with one of the extras, leaving Jack Warner the task of editing what had already been shot and, somehow, completing the film. Though Jack had never edited film before, he had duplicates made of certain early scenes which he then inserted towards the end of the film where additional footage was required. Jack claimed that nobody spotted the repetition and considered his efforts on **Passions Inherited** to be his introduction to the vital art of movie editing.

Like **Perils of the Plains** and **Raiders of the Mexican Border, Passions Inherited** made absolutely no impact on the industry whatsoever and barely recouped its production costs.

But the four Warner brothers were nothing if not resilient and although real success continued to elude them, they knew they were on to a good thing. Movies were now the country's number one form of popular entertainment, and the movie industry big business.

With a little bit of perseverance — and, more important, luck — there was no reason at all why they, too, shouldn't become a successful part of it.

The Warner Bros. studios in the late 1940s

1918

In 1918 the Warner Brothers decided to make a really serious bid for acceptance in the now fast growing movie industry. This took the form of **My Four Years in Germany**, their first attempt at a major feature film. It all came about when Jack Warner, while walking in downtown Los Angeles, spotted a copy of US Ambassador to Germany James W. Gerard's intimate account of his dealings with Kaiser Wilhelm II and his futile attempts to persuade the Kaiser to end submarine warfare. The book had become a best-seller, and both Jack and Sam were convinced that it would do equally well as a film. Harry secured the rights for $50,000 (against stiff competition) and although finding finance for the project proved difficult, their perseverance paid off. When the film was finally released (by First National), it grossed an impressive $1,500,000 leaving them with a net profit of $130,000 after all expenses and loans had been paid. At last the Warner brothers were finally on their way.

My Four Years in Germany was advertised as 'fact not fiction' and the ▷ documentary approach to the events depicted (particularly those leading to America's involvement in the war) enthralled audiences, setting an early trend for the sort of patriotic film which would reach its peak during World War II and greatly enhance the prestige of the studio. Because of its documentary format some scenes portrayed uncommon violence and brutality: director William Nigh, a Keystone Kops recruit, included footage of a young girl being kicked and maimed for life, and a Prussian officer separating a young girl from her parents with intent to commit rape. Because then, as now, violence was very popular, the film was a box-office hit and its anti-German sentiments struck just the right patriotic chord in a country which had only recently entered a major war. Most of **My Four Years in Germany** was shot on location in upstate New York, the interiors being completed at the Biograph Studios in the Bronx. In the interests of economy, props and costumes were begged, borrowed or stolen, and their eventual appearance on screen looked marvellous in Jack Sullivan's striking black and white photography. The scenario was by director Nigh with help from James Gerard himself and Charles A. Logue. Gerard also appeared in the film together with several top Broadway actors, among them Halbert Brown, William Daschiell, Earl Schenck, George Kiddell, Frank Stone, Karl Dane, Fred Herd, Percy Standing and William Bittner.

◁ The Warners again boarded the patriotic bandwagon with **Kaiser's Finish**, another World War I story (but fictitious this time) in which the illegitimate American-reared son of the Kaiser (and a double of the Crown Prince) enters Germany as a spy in order to kill both the Kaiser and his son. Actual newsreel footage showing the Crown Prince on the battlefield or just standing around looking foolish was integrated into John Joseph Harvey's scenario with such skill that it was often difficult to tell which scenes were the work of cameraman Rial Schlessenger, and which were not. Earl Schenck (illustrated) played the Prince; Claire Whitney was the female lead. Co-directors John Joseph Harvey and Clifford P. Saum kept the action going, supported by a cast including Percy Standing, John Sunderland, Louise Keene and Philip Van Loan.

1919

In 1919, encouraged by Hollywood's atmosphere of development and growth, the Warner brothers now built a studio of their own. Previously they had been renting shabby, makeshift premises, first on 18th and Main Streets, where they shot two serials, **The Lost City** and **The Tiger's Claw**, both of which starred Helen Holmes and made use of a collection of animals that was part of the studio's inventory; then at the Ince Studios in Culver City which were only marginally better. The new studio, however, was situated on Sunset and Bronson and with money borrowed from a young Los Angeles banker named Motley Flint, who had also helped to finance the serials, the Warners were now in a position to produce films as technically proficient as any being made in Hollywood at the time. The studios were called Warner Brothers West Coast Studio and extended over ten acres. The price the brothers paid was $25,000, nothing down, and $1,500 a month. Harry looked after the business end of things in New York, particularly the theatre division which was to increase throughout the next decade; Albert's official title was treasurer, though he was answerable to Harry in most business matters; while Jack and Sam (particularly Jack) ran everything on the artistic side. It all worked very well, except that, as the twenties began and for the first year or two of the decade, the one commodity lacking on the Warner lot was genuine creative talent.

Though released in 1919, **Open Your Eyes** was made two years earlier at the same Biograph Studios in the Bronx, New York, where the interiors of *My Four Years in Germany* were filmed. An educational film dealing with venereal disease, it was a cautionary tale which warned against indiscriminate wartime sex, and the often tragic outcome of such encounters. Apart from the controversial nature of its subject, the film was memorable only in that it featured Jack Warner playing a young soldier who is sold a worthless bottle of 'medicine' for ten dollars. It was Warner's first and last appearance in a feature film. G.P. Hamilton directed, and, just as he had done on *Passions Inherited*, quit halfway through, forcing Sam and Jack Warner to step in as co-directors. The cast included Ben Lyon (illustrated), Gaston Glass, Faire Binney and Emilie Marceau. Sam Warner and C.B. Mintz provided the scenario. In a deal made with the United States Signal Corps, the brothers retained the commercial rights of the film after the war was over in return for financing the production from their own personal funds.

Mr. Gerard listening to War speeches in the Reichstag.

"The British Fleet is formidable. No?" Kaiser's observation on Royal yacht during Kiel Regatta Festivities.

Hindenburg's orders regarding civilian population of Belgium "healthy ones to the farms, use your discretion with young and old" Young woman to Mr. Gerard "We are slaves"!

Mr. Gerard questioning the use of dogs in prison camp at Wittenberg.

Mr. Gerard's interview with German Foreign Minister

Mr. Gerard's inspection of Wittenberg Prison - chatting to British soldier in cage

Mr. Gerard's inspection of Prison Camps

Mr. Gerard discussing the Sarajevo incident with Sir Edward Goschen the British Ambassador.

THE TWENTIES

By now Hollywood was a boom town. The star system, with names like Charles Chaplin, Mary Pickford, Douglas Fairbanks, Harold Lloyd, Lon Chaney, Gloria Swanson, Pola Negri, Lillian and Dorothy Gish, Nazimova, Colleen Moore, Buster Keaton, Clara Kimball Young, Norma Talmadge, Blanche Sweet, John Barrymore, Wallace Reid and, most spectacularly, Rudolph Valentino, a bit player who catapulted to stardom in 1921 in **The Four Horsemen of the Apocalypse** (Metro), was creating personalities the whole world clamoured to see; and with some of the 'living legends' earning upwards of $5,000 a week, movies were bigger than ever.

As the decade began, Adolph Zukor, who had merged his Famous Players with Jesse Lasky's Feature Plays and taken over Paramount Pictures, with himself as president and Lasky as vice-president, was the dominating figure in the industry, and one of its most ruthless. Determined to crown himself emperor of Hollywood, he set out to make Paramount the most powerful and influential studio in the industry by refusing to tolerate smaller independent companies (such as First National) and bankrupting cinemas who refused to sign with him. In 1921 successful action was taken against Zukor's monopolistic practices by a group of independent theatre owners who called themselves the Motion Picture Theatre Owners, and the following year the Federal Trade Commission made quite sure that Zukor's Napoleonic tactics came to an end.

Louis B. Mayer was another force in Hollywood, having left the Metro Production Company to form his own Mayer Productions. In 1924 Mayer joined with theatre owner Marcus Loew who, in 1920, had acquired the Metro Company, and merged with the Goldwyn Company to form Metro-Goldwyn-Mayer. Samuel Goldwyn, another of the industry's giants, had no part in the running of MGM, and left to form his own studio insisting, however, that his name be retained in the masthead of the new company.

On September 5th, 1921, the comedian Fatty Arbuckle attended a party at the St. Regis Hotel in San Francisco. So did a young actress called Virginia Rappe. The couple allegedly had sexual intercourse, shortly after which she died of peritonitis. Arbuckle was charged with manslaughter (lurid rumours circulated as to the exact circumstances of her death) but after two trials in which the juries were unable to reach a verdict, he was acquitted. His career, however, was shattered. It was 11 years before he appeared in front of the cameras again and was just beginning to re-establish himself when he died aged 46 in 1933. For those 11 years Hollywood had hypocritically used his abilities as a director but denied him credit under his real name (he was billed as William Goodrich).

The Arbuckle scandal was followed in 1922 with another: the murder of director William Desmond Taylor, and the involvement in it of stars Mabel Normand and Mary Miles Minter.

As a result of these and other scandals (including the discovery of Wallace Reid's drug addiction) Postmaster General Will H. Hays (a member of President Harding's cabinet) was offered an annual salary of $100,000 to head the Motion Picture Producers and Distributors of America Inc, which took effect in March 1922. One of the first things Hays did was to establish a black-list of books and plays which were *verboten* to the industry. More positively, though, he created the actor's employment agency known as Central Casting (1925) – a boon to Hollywood's extras who hitherto had no alternative but to form vast queues outside the studios' gates each day in the hope of being called.

The early part of the decade also saw the beginning of an influx into Hollywood of top European film talent which brought directors such as Ernst Lubitsch, Mauritz Stiller (and his protegé Greta Gustafson – renamed Garbo by Louis B. Mayer), F.W. Murnau, Paul Leni and Michael Curtiz. Henry Blanke, who became an important part of the Warner Bros. story arrived as part of the Lubitsch entourage; so did writers Hans Kraly and Edward Knoblock. Their efforts could be seen in such films as Lubitsch's **Rosita** (1923, United Artists) plus those he made for Warner Bros. including **The Marriage Circle** (1924), **Three Women** (1924), **Kiss me Again** (1925) and **Lady Windermere's Fan** (1925). Murnau's **Sunrise** (1927, Fox), Leni's **The Cat and the Canary** (1927, Universal), Curtiz's **The Third Degree** (1926) and **Noah's Ark** (1928 – both for Warner Bros.) and Stiller's **Hotel Imperial** (1927, Paramount), were further notable examples of these new directors' work.

As the decade reached its half-way mark, the top stars continued to be Fairbanks, Pickford, Valentino, Chaplin, Swanson and Harold Lloyd, with Dolores Costello, Corinne Griffith, Richard Barthelmess, Richard Dix, John Gilbert, Rod La Rocque, Norma Shearer, Clara Bow, Vilma Banky and vamp Nita Naldi potent box-office fodder as well. Just starting out on their careers at this time were Joan Crawford, Clark Gable, Charles Farrell, Carole Lombard, Janet Gaynor and Gary Cooper.

By 1926 Hollywood had reached the peak of its popularity with the trade paper *Motion Picture News* issuing some statistics to prove it: over 400 feature films, it claimed, were made that year, and $120 million spent making them. There were 14,637 cinemas throughout the US, of which 7,178 were in towns and cities where the population was over

5,000 and 7,495 in towns and villages with a population of under 5,000. New York state led with a total of 1,194 cinemas, Pennsylvania was second with 1,032 and Illinois third with 1,008. Nevada came last with 23. Valentino's death in August 1926 indicated just to what extent the movies impinged on the lives of the public for, from New York to Los Angeles, thousands of fans gathered together for a final glimpse of his funeral train.

In 1924 a more sensitive film stock called Panchromatic (a vast improvement on what had been used before) was introduced, while in 1926, two-colour Technicolor was used in the United Artists release, **The Black Pirate**, starring Douglas Fairbanks. At the same time experiments were taking place with three dimensional films, as well as with films shot in 70 mm and known as 'Natural Vision'.

But undoubtedly the most important and far-reaching technical innovation of the decade was the introduction of sound as demonstrated on August 6th, 1926 by Warner Bros. with their presentation of **Don Juan** starring John Barrymore in a new sound-on-disc process known as Vitaphone (see details on pages 30–35).

Sound, of course, was not exactly new to the movies. During the war years Dr. Lee De Forest, a pioneer in sound films, developed a photo-electric vacuum cell called the audion tube which made it possible to amplify a signal from a remote point and transmit it hundreds of miles. After selling his patents to the Bell Telephone Company, he went to work on the possibilities of photographing and then reproducing sound impulses on motion picture stock and came up with his phonofilm system. De Forest first unveiled the results of his experiments – called the De Forest Phonofilm – on a synchronized musical soundtrack in New York on April 15th, 1923. The new experiment was not a success.

The Bell Telephone Company, meanwhile, were continuing their own experiments to find a way of adapting the audion tube for amplification in theatres using the sound-on-disc approach eventually adopted by Warner Bros.

The combination of moving images and sound began, long before De Forest's experiments, with Thomas A. Edison who after inventing the phonograph, worked on a machine that would produce images to accompany his early recordings. As far back as 1894, in the Kinetoscope parlours, customers could, by means of stethoscope-like ear-tubes, hear scratchy poorly synchronized sound as they watched some fleeting, flickering images.

There were other early pioneers in sound as well. At the Paris Exposition Internationale in 1900, the English comedian Little Tich could be seen and heard performing a dance. In 1904, the Chronophone of Léon Gaumont astonished London's Hippodrome audiences with Harry Lauder in action. Cecil Hepworth, a leading British film-maker, produced the Vivaphone. In 1911 King George V's coronation was not only filmed with accompanying sound, but in a colour process known as Kinemacolour.

None of these processes, however, including a sound-on-disc experiment employed by D.W. Griffith in his 1921 film **Dream Street**, were as effective as the Vitaphone system developed by Warner Bros. and Western Electric for both **Don Juan** and, a year later, the epoch-making **The Jazz Singer** in which Al Jolson spoke the first words ever heard in a feature film. The public's response to the film was overwhelming, and by the spring and summer of 1928 Paramount, MGM, Universal and Columbia were all wired for sound. By the end of 1929 hardly any silent films were being made, and those still in distribution were relegated to third and fourth run houses.

With the arrival of sound all sorts of major problems both technical and artistic needed to be overcome. Studios had to be sound-proofed and armies of technicians were engaged to operate the complicated new equipment. As for actors, directors and writers, they had virtually to learn their craft anew. Some succeeded, others did not and although the only real casualty of the new era was John Gilbert, many other silent stars, such as Vilma Banky, Norma Talmadge, Corinne Griffith, May McAvoy, Lillian Gish, Gloria Swanson, Blanche Sweet, Dorothy Mackaill and Buster Keaton declined in popularity as a galaxy of new stars emerged in the thirties to take their places.

Talking pictures gave a successful industry an added boost, as did the introduction of the Academy Awards in 1929, and by the end of the decade no fewer than 9,000 theatres across America were equipped to show sound pictures. Also, many more people were going to the movies than ever before, and going more often, with an estimated 110,000,000 admissions each week. Then came catastrophe.

On October 29th the American stock market centred on Wall Street collapsed and knocked Hollywood out of its euphoria. It was the first real crisis in the film capital's profitable history and, in an attempt to lure back dwindling audiences, Hollywood's film-makers realized that their future survival would have to become synonymous with quality and with giving the public new and original experiences in filmed entertainment.

Throughout the thirties and forties, Warner Bros., now a major force in the industry, filled the bill on both counts, consolidating its position as one of the greatest, most adventurous film factories in the world.

1920/22

The decade opened unpromisingly for the brothers Warner. Although Harry Rapf, Lewis Selznick's production manager, was recruited onto the staff in 1920 (together with a young publicity man called Hal Wallis), only one film was made that year – a serial in 15 episodes called **A Dangerous Adventure.** It was directed by Sam and Jack Warner, who, attempting to capitalize on the popularity of animal movies (and grateful for the fact that four-legged creatures couldn't read the reviews and didn't demand overtime) hired a complete travelling circus for the enterprise, as well as the acting services of Grace Darmond and Derelys Perrdue. Francis Guihan was commissioned to write a suitably exciting plot and the story he came up with involved two sisters in search of hidden treasure in the depths of the African jungle. The off-screen shenanigans turned out to be far more exciting than anything happening on celluloid. Jack Warner was attacked by a vagrant monkey, an elephant caused excessive damage and the two leading ladies threw jealous tantrums and were constantly at each other's throats. The direction of the finished film in no way undermined the talents of Griffith or Eisenstein, and, on its initial release, **A Dangerous Adventure** was a failure. Two years later, however, it was edited down from thirty reels to seven, released as an ordinary feature and cleaned up.

1921 was only marginally better for the brothers, with Harry Rapf's production of **Why Girls Leave Home** proving to be the most popular of the studio's three productions that year and its only money maker. The following year was notable only for the film debut of Wesley Barry, a child actor who went on to become Warner Bros.' first box-office attraction.

Your Best Friend, written and directed by William Nigh, was the sentimental story of a Jewish mother who finds herself spurned by her son's extravagant Gentile wife. When, however, the wife realizes that her mother-in-law's money is keeping her in a fashion to which she has not previously been accustomed, she smartly changes her attitude. Vera Gordon starred as the mother, and in her performance managed to avoid the sentimentality that ran riot in the scenario. Production values were excellent and the glimpses of Jewish family life gave the film its chief source of interest. Also cast were Doré Davidson, Harry Benham, Stanley Price, Belle Bennett (illustrated) and Beth Mason. The producer was Harry Rapf.
▽

◁**Why Girls Leave Home** starring Anna Q. Nilsson (illustrated) embraced a theme dear to Jack Warner's heart and one which would be exploited several times over in the next couple of decades: the innocent at large and the corrupting effects on him (or her) of big city life. The film appealed to almost everyone, especially those born without inherited money, and it was a popular success. Owen Davis fashioned the scenario from Fred Summerfield's play, and a cast which featured Maurine Powers, Julia Swayne Gordon, Corinne Barker and Kathryn Perry was directed by William Nigh. Harry Rapf produced this important film for the brothers.

Freckle-faced Wesley Barry's first film for ▷ Warner Bros. was **Rags to Riches,** produced by Harry Rapf, directed by Wallace Worsley from a script by Walter De Leon and William Nigh, based on a story by Grace Miller White. Barry (right) played Marmaduke Clarke, a rich kid who goes through all manner of hardships (including a kidnap attempt) before he proves his worth to the gang he has joined. Artistically, the film was of little consequence, but it did launch young Barry, who was to become one of the studio's biggest attractions after Rin-Tin-Tin, and, more importantly, its urban environment presaged the crime films and social dramas the studio was to produce in abundance throughout the next decade. Also cast were Niles Welch (left), Russell Simpson, and Minna Redman.

Ashamed of Parents was one of the first ▷
socially aware dramas to emerge from the
Warner stable (there would be many more
in the next two decades) and Adelaide
Hendricks' scenario (from a story by
Charles K. Harris) was clearly modelled on
the life and hard times of the Warner
family itself. Its chief character, Silas
Wadsworth, a shoemaker, bore a striking
resemblance to Benjamin Warner, whose
own attempts to make a decent living for
his family were parallelled in Silas's struggle
to send a son to college. Just as four of the
brothers Warner made good in the movie
industry, so Silas's son becomes a famous
football star – the pride and glory of his
family. Charles Eldridge, Edith Stockton
(illustrated), Walter McEvan and Jack Lionel
Bohn were in the cast, and the director was
H.G. Plimpton.

△
As long as director Sidney Franklin's
screen version of F. Scott Fitzgerald's 'lost
generation' novel **The Beautiful and Damned**
showed the youth of the early twenties as
an irresponsible, crazy, hard-drinking crowd,
his film, adapted by Olga Printzlau, maintained a jolly pace. But as soon as it began
to take itself seriously, it adopted a sermon-
izing quality that was as hard to swallow
as some of its sub-titles. Marie Prevost and
another former Mack Sennett girl, Louise
Fazenda, made their first film for the
Warner Bros., and were featured alongside
Harry Myers, Kenneth Harlan (illustrated),
Tully Marshall and Walter Long. Although
the film was produced in 1921, it was
not in fact released until December 1923. It
was a fairly successful production.

Inspired by a well-known Gus Edwards song,
School Days was another Wesley Barry
vehicle, this time dealing with reform. Barry
(right) played a youngster whose austere,
small town upbringing failed to prepare
him for the sophistication of New York's
elite society and drove him, instead, to an
underworld of crime. By the last reel,
however, he finds spiritual redemption,
having reformed and returned to the town
where he belongs. The same theme later
found its way into Warner Bros. pictures
again and again. The script was written by
Walter De Leon and William Nigh, the
latter also serving as director. Its cameramen were Jack Brown and Sidney Hickox,
who later became famous for his work on
such classics as *To Have And Have Not*. Also
cast were George Lessey, Nella P. Spaulding,
Margaret Seddon, J.H. Gilmore (left), Arnold
Lucy (centre), and Arlene Blackburn. The
producer was Harry Rapf.
▽

△
Though a financial failure, **Parted Curtains**
was of historical interest in that it was an
embryo of the type of hard-hitting gangster
film that would be closely associated with
the studio throughout the thirties. It
starred Henry B. Walthall (illustrated) as a
convict who, when released from jail, cannot
find a job and, in desperation, resorts to
stealing money off a painter (Edward Cecil).
The painter, however, shows compassion
and sets about rehabilitating him. James
C. Bradford directed until he fell ill and was
replaced by Bertram Bracken. Bradford
also wrote the screenplay from a story
by Tom J. Hopkins and the capable cast
included Mary Alden, Margaret Landis,
Edward Cecil and Mickey Moore.

1923

In April 1923, the Warner Brothers West Coast Studio was fully incorporated and became known as Warner Bros. The studio was refurbished at a cost of $250,000; additional dressing rooms were built alongside the existing ones, and a new stage, 113 metres by 43 metres was constructed, thus making it possible for the simultaneous shooting of six films, all of them lit by a newly installed electrical plant.

One of the films made in 1923 was the outstandingly successful production **The Gold Diggers**, which was adapted from David Belasco's hit Broadway production of Avery Hopwood's play. Harry Warner purchased two other successful plays at the same time – Sacha Guitry's *Deburau* and Belasco's *Daddies* for a total of $250,000. About the Belasco deal, the *Los Angeles Times* of 24th January 1923 wrote: 'The effect of Mr Belasco's allying himself with the silent drama will be profound among producers of motion pictures. The magic of 'David Belasco Presents' flickering in a motion picture title is expected to pave the way to greater and better things in the industry.'

Whether it did or did not, the purchase of **The Gold Diggers** paved the way for a series of musicals throughout the 1930s that, together with the distinctive crime films produced by Warner Bros. during the same period, showed the studio at its inventive best.

1923 was also the year in which Warner Bros. introduced dog star Rin-Tin-Tin to the world. The film, called **Where The North Begins**, was an instant smash, and launched Rinty, as he came to be known, on a career as spectacular as any of the major stars of the day. He was so profitable that, insuring against his demise, the studio trained no fewer than 18 other dogs, all called Rin-Tin-Tin who could, at a moment's notice, double for the original Rinty should it ever become necessary – which it often did.

In all, Warner Bros. made nineteen Rin-Tin-Tin features. Rinty's salary was $1,000 a week, and his perks included a small orchestra for mood music, a diamond-studded collar and, at mealtimes a Chateaubriand steak with all the trimmings. But it was worth it. His exploits on the screen kept the studio buoyant throughout the silent era and saved many theatres from closure.

△
The Tie That Binds was a film that failed. All about a private secretary who, instead of marrying the boss, chooses one of his staff, it starred Barbara Bedford (centre) as the secretary, Walter Miller as her husband (who confesses to a murder he did not commit in order to protect his wife on whom suspicion has fallen) and William P. Carlton as the boss. Others in the cast were Marian Swayne, Effie Shannon and Julia Swayne Gordon, though the most impressive performance was delivered by a babe in arms with a remarkable ability to laugh or cry on cue. It was adapted by Paul Keating and directed by Joseph Levering.

△
Main Street, adapted by Julien Josephson, from Sinclair Lewis's best-selling novel (and the play by Harvey Higgins and Harriet Ford) starred Florence Vidor (second from left) as Carol Milford whose arrival in Gopher Prairie and the consequent reactions of the locals was the best thing in an otherwise indifferent and often tiresome film. But it did have its moments, most of them supplied by its appealing cast which also included Monte Blue (right), now firmly launched on his Warner Bros. career, Kathleen Perry (second from right), Harry Myers (left), Robert Gordon, Noah Beery, Alan Hale (another Warner name that would crop up for the next couple of decades) and Louise Fazenda. The director was Harry Beaumont.

△
The Little Church Around The Corner was a mawkish drama with a mining background which starred Kenneth Harlan as a priest who falls in love with a tyrannical mine-owner's daughter. Good photography (by Homer Scott), a well staged pit disaster, and some pleasing performances went a long way towards syphoning off some of the syrup from Olga Printzlau's screenplay (from a play by Marion Russell and a story by Charles E. Blaney). Others cast in this story, which also had Harlan quelling a rebellion among the disgruntled miners by miraculously giving a girl born dumb the power of speech, were Claire Windsor (as the miner's daughter), Alec B. Francis, George Cooper, Wallis Long, H.B. Warner (right) and Pauline Starke (left) as the dumb girl. The director was William A. Seiter.

Both Monte Blue (left) and Irene Rich made their debuts for the brothers in **Brass**, an adaptation by Julien Josephson of Charles G. Norris's play. It was the story of the break-up of a marriage, and the attempts on the part of the wife (Marie Prevost, right) to win back the love of her husband and child. The situation failed to resolve itself with anything resembling a satisfactory ending and the characterizations were totally uncompelling. Monte Blue was the husband, Irene Rich the understanding woman to whom he turns for affection after his divorce. Sidney Franklin directed and Harry Myers, Cyril Chadwick, Frank Keenan, Helen Ferguson, Vera Lewis, Margaret Seddon and Winter Hall completed the cast. The producer was Harry Rapf.

▽

pack of wolves in the North. Reared as a wolf, the dog rescues a fur trapper and makes a friend for life. Under Duncan's supervision, Rin-Tin-Tin gave a remarkable performance, even managing to convey a range of emotions which put his human co-stars Claire Adams and Walter McGrail (illustrated) to shame. The film was premiered at Loews State Theatre in Los Angeles with Rinty on hand to acknowledge the thunderous applause of an appreciative audience. A promotional tour followed involving several personal appearances by the dog, as well as a lucrative three year contract. Warner Bros. had at last found its first big money-making star.

The Gold Diggers formed the first part of a three picture deal the brothers made with showman David Belasco, who was billed as presenting the film together with Warner Bros. It was based on the Avery Hopwood stage success which Belasco had presented on Broadway and was the first of a series of films about New York showgirls on the make. Basically the story of two sisters (Louise Fazenda and Hope Hampton, centre right), one of whom risks everything to see that her sister gets the man she loves, it was directed by Harry Beaumont, written for the screen by Grant Carpenter (whose witty captions contributed considerably to the film's popularity) and featured Wyndham Standing (centre), Alec B. Francis, Jed Prouty (in small hat) and Louise Beaudet.
▽

△

Based on George M. Cohan's 1904 musical of the same name, **Little Johnny Jones** desperately needed Cohan's cheeky score to give it zip. The story of an English earl's decision to enter an American horse in the Epsom Derby, its absurdity reduced all who were familiar with the English racing scene to helpless laughter. Johnny Hines (centre) played Johnny Jones and Wyndham Standing (enjoying himself enormously) played the English earl. Others under Arthur Rosson's direction were Margaret Seddon, Herbert Prior (right), Molly Malone (left), George Webb and Mervyn LeRoy, who, six years later, directed the sound version of the same story. Raymond L. Schrock, switching his allegiance from dogs to horses, wrote the scenario.

△

Where The North Begins marked wonder dog Rin-Tin-Tin's first association with the studio. Director Chester Franklin, working with writer Raymond L. Schrock, re-fashioned a story by Lee Duncan, the dog's trainer, and came up with a yarn about a German shepherd pup's adoption by a

Wesley Barry (centre) starred as the eldest of three orphaned brothers in **The Country Kid.** The other two were forever getting into trouble and it was big brother's lot to see that they didn't. Julien Josephson's story revolved around the antics of the kids and Barry's attempts to stop their unpleasant protector from stealing the farm they had inherited. The young star's boyish appeal was decidedly limited under William Beaudine's sugary direction; nor was there much joy to be derived from the performances of 'Spec' O'Donnell (left), Kate Toncray, Helen Jerome Eddy and little Bruce Guerin (right).
▽

△
The rugged exteriors of **Tiger Rose** photographed in the Canadian Northwest were splendid, as, indeed, was the physical production of this solidly directed (by Sidney Franklin) screen adaptation of David Belasco's play which Belasco wrote with Willard Mack. Unfortunately, its humdrum plot involving villains and heroines and Canadian mounties was too similar to *The Girl of the Golden West* (released the same year by First National) to make any real impact. Lenore Ulric (left) played the title role and, in the end, she, rather than the mountie, got her man (Theodore von Eltz). What the mountie got was a bullet in the stomach, shot by Miss Ulric to protect her lover. Others involved in the adventure were Forrest Stanley (right), Joseph Dowling, André de Beranger, Sam De Grasse and Claude Gillingwater. David Belasco presented it, and it was adapted by Edmund Goulding and Millard Webb.

◁ Wesley Barry and Harry Myers were teamed for **The Printer's Devil,** a comedy in which the protagonists become joint proprietors of a local newspaper called *The Briggsville Gazette.* They are fairly successful until Myers is arrested for a robbery he did not commit. The rest of the plot follows hero Barry (illustrated) as he accidentally tracks down the crooks. It was routine stuff, with Myers making more of an impression than its young star. Julien Josephson wrote the screenplay from his story *Ink Slinger,* and William Beaudine directed. Also cast were Kathryn McGuire, Louis King, George Pearce, and Raymond Cannon.

△
Smiling Johnny Hines (right), as an Irishman at large in the New World, became **Conductor 1492** when he took a job on a streetcar. He saves the life of the boss's child, is financially rewarded for his bravery, and wins the hand of his employer's pretty daughter. Written by its star as a vehicle for himself, it made the most out of its numerous comic situations with absolutely hilarious results. Doris May co-starred and the film also featured Dan Mason and Dorothy Burns with Byron Sage (left) as the child. Charles Hines and Frank Griffin directed.

△
A glamorous cast was assembled by director Jack Conway to give credence to the Kathleen Norris soap opera **Lucretia Lombard** in which an attractive young wife (Irene Rich, right) finds herself lovelessly married to a man twice her age (Marc McDermott). The marriage endures for seven miserable years until the old boy takes a powder (literally) and dies, thus leaving the way open for Lucretia, who once again 'knew the joy of laughter' as a subtitle put it, to marry the local country prosecutor (Monte Blue, left). But not before a purging forest fire, a powder house explosion and a massive flood enlivened the proceedings. The film also featured Norma Shearer (prior to her stellar days at MGM), Alec B. Francis, John Roche, Lucy Beaumont and Otto Hoffman. It was produced by Harry Rapf and written by Bertram Millhauser and Sada Cowan, and was also released as **Flaming Passion.**

△
Heroes of the Street was an early example of the sort of gangster drama that found its richest expression less than a decade later. It was directed by William Beaudine from Edmund Goulding and Mildred Considine's screenplay taken from the play by Lee Parker. Wesley Barry (left) played a young lad who sets out to solve the riddle of his policeman father's murder. He was supported in his efforts by Marie Prevost as a wisecracking no-nonsense chorus girl. Also among the capable cast were Jack Mulhall, Wilfred Lucas, Aggie Herring, Joe Butterworth and Phil Ford.

1924

One of Warner Bros.' most prestigious productions of 1924 was **The Marriage Circle**. It was directed by the autocratic Ernst Lubitsch, whom Jack Warner had hired, but whose insistence on doing things his way rather than the company way eventually resulted in creative stalemate. Consequently, after making a superb social comedy called **Three Women**, Oscar Wilde's **Lady Windermere's Fan, Kiss Me Again** and **So This Is Paris**, he left the studio, leaving behind his young assistant, Henry Blanke, who, in time, was to become one of Warners' most durable producers at a weekly salary escalating to $5,000.

Apart from Rin-Tin-Tin, Warner Bros.' other big star of the twenties was John Barrymore, the hard-drinking but explosively talented stage actor whose *Hamlet* on Broadway was hailed as definitive. His first film for the studio, **Beau Brummell**, co-starring Mary Astor, was so successful (it appeared, together with **The Marriage Circle**, on the *New York Times* Ten Best list for 1924) that, after a brief visit to London where he repeated his success in *Hamlet*, he was signed to a long-term contract at $76,250 per film, each film to be completed in six weeks. For every week over, he would be paid an additional $6,625. Furthermore, his contract stipulated that he was to have leading lady approval, a four-roomed suite at the Ambassador Hotel, a chauffeur-driven limousine and all meals paid for by the studio. But, like Rin-Tin-Tin, the perks were more than justified in terms of the star's box-office draw.

In 1924 – after completing the successful **Broadway After Dark** – producer Harry Rapf, who had worked on many of the studio's early films, was lured from Warner Bros. to the newly formed Metro-Goldwyn-Mayer Studios by Louis B. Mayer, who made Rapf an offer he could not refuse.

Daddies, adapted for the screen from John L. Hobble's play by Julien Josephson and charmingly directed by William A. Seiter, was a thoroughly pleasing variation on the 'Three Wise Fools' theme. This time, the neatly constructed plot foisted six children on a quintet of confirmed bachelors, turning their anti-matrimony club into a home for adopted orphans. It was beautifully handled with the children's arrival at the club particularly effective. There were excellent performances from (left to right) Otto Hoffman, Harry Myers, Willard Louis, Crauford Kent and Claude Gillingwater, as well as Claire Adams, Boyce Combe, Mae Marsh, the De Briac twins and King Evers.
▽

◁ Director Harry Beaumont, lacking a strong storyline, floundered badly with **Babbitt**, in Dorothy Farnum's adaptation of Sinclair Lewis's celebrated novel. Willard Louis (right) played the title role, and though physically perfect for it, he was unable to breathe life into a scenario incapable of restructuring for the screen Lewis's carefully modulated central character. What worked between hard covers was tedious on celluloid. Also cast were Mary Alden (as Mrs Babbitt), Carmel Myers (as the woman who tries to lure him away from his wife), Raymond McKee (left), Maxine Elliott Hicks, Cissy Fitzgerald and Clara Bow. It was remade in 1934 with Guy Kibbee in the central role.

Wesley Barry (centre) starred as **George Washington Jr.** alias George Belgrave, an idealistic young man who cannot tell a lie and who, as the comedy unfurls, exposes a bogus count (Leon Barry) as an international criminal with a price on his head. Based on George M. Cohan's 1906 play, it was written by Rex Taylor, directed by Malcolm St. Clair, and featured Gertrude Olmstead, Charles Conklin (in blackface as a servant), Otis Harlan, William Courtwright and Edward Phillips.
▽

Ernst Lubitsch's renowned touch was very ▷ much in evidence in **The Marriage Circle**, a marital comedy of manners which set a floundering marriage against a healthy one and threw a bachelor into the middle of both. Though the director and his scenarist Paul Bern (who later married Jean Harlow) thickly coated their subject in irony, the era depicted (pre-World War I Vienna) was idealized into a veritable paradise with elegance and gentility the norm; an artificial milieu whose atmosphere was to pervade many sophisticated comedies throughout the rest of the twenties and thirties. A favourite film of both Alfred Hitchcock and Charlie Chaplin (whose *A Woman of Paris* inspired it) it starred Florence Vidor (left), Monte Blue, Marie Prevost, Creighton Hale (right) and Adolphe Menjou. Critics praised it highly, but it failed to make money.

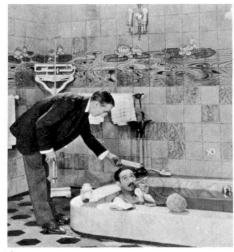

Adolphe Menjou was the debonair hero of **Broadway After Dark,** an entertaining adaptation (by Douglas Doty) of Owen Davis's play. After an unhappy love affair, Menjou (right) deserts the bright lights of Broadway for a West 47th Street theatrical boarding-house, the epicentre of the film's activities, where all sorts of events overtake him. Monta Bell, the director, did wonders with the slender material; so did a cast that included Edward Burns, Anna Q. Nilsson, Carmel Myers, Vera Lewis, Willard Louis, Mervyn Leroy, Norma Shearer and Otto Hoffman (left). It was produced by Harry Rapf.

Running a mere 53 minutes, **Lovers' Lane** was a low-budget film about a small-town doctor who rejects the advances of a wealthy young woman. All he wants is to help the local community; all she wants is a good time. Robert Ellis (right) was the doctor, Gertrude Olmstead (second from left) the woman in (and out) of his life. Phil Rosen directed from a screenplay by the prolific Dorothy Farnum (based on a play by Clyde Fitch) and the cast included Maxine Elliott Hicks, Kate Toncray, Norval McGregor, Crauford Kent (left) and Charles Sellon.

When businessman Monte Blue (right) takes the advice of Creighton Hale and enlists the service of his wife (Marie Prevost, left) in order to stimulate trade, his troubles really begin. For, in no time at all, he is jealously accusing her of 'stepping out' with a prospective client, as a result of which she leaves him. But she does not stay away long enough to do any damage, and **How to Educate a Wife** ends happily. Directed by Monta Bell, and based on a story by Elinor Glyn (screenplay by Douglas Doty and adaptation by Grant Carpenter), it was a pretty ordinary effort which featured Claude Gillingwater, Vera Lewis, Betty Francisco, Edward Earle and Nellie Bly Baker.

Critics found Monte Blue as Jean Gaspard ▷ Deburau in **The Lover of Camille** (an adaptation of Sacha Guitry's play *Deburau*, presented on stage by David Belasco) less convincing than Lionel Atwill, the beauty and melancholy of whose Broadway performance was lost on the less subtle Mr. Blue. Still, this early 19th-century romance about a pantomimist's unrequited love found favour with less discriminating audiences, and was a popular success. It also starred Miss Prevost (who seemed to go from one film to another without pause, as indeed did her overworked co-star) as the object of Deburau's love, and featured Willard Louis, (illustrated) and Pierre Gendron. Harry Beaumont directed from a screenplay by Dorothy Farnum.

Monte Blue, the hero of a routine drama, **Her Marriage Vow,** sees his wife Beverly Bayne (left) flirting with former beau John Roche and decides it is time for a separation. But, on second thoughts, and for the sake of the children, he thinks better of the idea and determines to give his ailing marriage another try. Based on a play by Owen Davis, it was written and directed by Millard Webb, and also featured Willard Louis, Margaret Livingston, Priscilla Moran, Mary Grabhorn, Martha Petelle (right) and Arthur Hoyt.

John Barrymore's first film for the studio, ▷ in a one-picture deal, was **Beau Brummell,** taken from the Clyde Fitch stage success; and, as the Regency dandy who worms his way into the Prince of Wales's good books with his wit and sartorial elegance, only to die in obscurity and poverty because of his overweening arrogance, he was sensational. A seventeen year old Mary Astor (whom Barrymore at their first meeting confessed was so beautiful that she made him feel faint) played Lady Margery Alvanley. Willard Louis was the Prince and on several occasions found himself on the receiving end of one of Barrymore's less edifying pranks. While the silent cameras turned, Barrymore, in the friendliest manner, hurled the foulest of obscenities at him. When the film was released, several outraged lip-readers protested vehemently. Harry Beaumont was responsible for the stylish direction and Dorothy Farnum did the adaptation. The film's success secured its star a handsome three-year contract with the studio. Also in the cast were Irene Rich, Alex Francis, Richard Tucker, André Beranger and Carmel Myers (left, with Barrymore).

Ernst Lubitsch held a mirror up to womanhood in **Three Women** and what he saw was not particularly flattering to those whose preoccupation with youth and beauty he severely, but wittily, condemned. Pauline Frederick played a wily widow, May McAvoy was her daughter and Marie Prevost the mistress of a personable young rake (Lew Cody, left) who at the time is wooing all three of the women in turn. Miss Frederick (right) was particularly impressive in the film's memorable opening sequence, grotesquely weighing herself and then painting her face in a desperate attempt to recapture her lost youth and beauty. Charles Van Enger photographed it dazzlingly and Hans Kräly supplied the scenario from Yolanthe Maree's's story *The Lilie*. The film also featured Willard Louis, Pierre Gendron, Mary Carr and Raymond McKee. Connoisseurs loved it, but unfortunately there were not enough to make it a hit.

△

Being Respectable found Monte Blue (centre) making the most of an unhappy marriage to Irene Rich (left). It also starred Marie Prevost as the 'vamp' he really loves, with other roles going to Frank Currier, Louise Fazenda, Theodore von Eltz, Eulalie Jensen and Lila Leslie. Phil Rosen directed from a scenario by Dorothy Farnum (story by Grace H. Landrau) and failed to generate electricity either at the box office or between his three leading players.

△

Rin-Tin-Tin's second Warner feature, **Find Your Man,** was altogether a more assured effort than his first though there was little advance in the story line. This time Rinty witnesses a murder of which his innocent master (Eric St. Clair) is accused, tracks down the culprit (Pat Hartigan at his most villainous) and ensures the film's happy ending. The dog's prowess in any number of difficult situations amazed and delighted audiences whose response encouraged the studio to churn out a string of similar adventures in the next few years. It was written in 4 days by a new Warner acquisition, 22 year-old Darryl Zanuck; Mal St. Clair directed. Also cast were June Marlowe (left), Raymond Mckee and Lew Harvey (right).

△

A light-hearted concoction, **The Tenth Woman** starred John Roche (centre) as a ranch owner who, after preventing a young woman (Beverly Bayne) from committing suicide, marries her. All goes well until a former flame (June Marlowe, right) descends on the ranch, causing the wife to pack her bags and leave. But Julien Josephson's screenplay, from a story by Harriet Comstock, provided a happy ending with the married couple reunited in each other's arms. Others cast were Raymond McKee, Alec B. Francis and Charles Post. The director was James Flood.

Straight after **Three Women**, Marie Prevost (centre) landed a dual role in **Cornered**. She played a girl from the 'Hell's Kitchen' part of town whose physical appearance was identical to a wealthy girl from the classier side of the tracks. To facilitate a robbery, the poor Miss Prevost forces the rich Miss Prevost to change places with her. Director William Beaudine neatly resolved the twists and turns of William Leighton and Hope Loring's screenplay (from a stage play by Mitchell Dodson and Zelda Sears) and saw to it that his cast, which included Rockliffe Fellowes (right), Vera Lewis, John Roche, Cissy Fitzgerald and Raymond Hatton (left) were more convincing than their material. It was predictable but entertaining.

▽

This Woman adapted by Louis Lighton and Hope Loring from a novel by Howard Rockey, was a Peg's Paper saga involving a young singing student (Irene Rich, right) who is forced by poverty to curtail her studies and return to New York from Europe. She arrives penniless, and that's when her troubles really begin. It all ends happily, however, when an impresario (Marc MacDermott) takes her on as his pupil. Louise Fazenda (left) and Creighton Hale were also cast, and the sledgehammer direction was by Phil Rosen.

▽

Elliott Dexter had his composure ruffled in **The Age of Innocence**, a psychological drama adapted by Olga Printzlau from the novel by Edith Wharton. A member of a somewhat straight-laced family, Dexter (right) finds himself courting scandal when, after marrying blue-blooded Edith Roberts (left), he meets, and falls madly in love with Beverly Bayne (centre), a Polish countess. The couple have a raging affair, and it is only when Miss Roberts gets to hear about it and quietly tells her rival that she is expecting a baby, that Miss Bayne does the correct thing and returns to Poland. More concerned with character delineation than plot (of which there was very little) director Wesley Ruggles kept the interest simmering; so did a cast that also included Willard Louis (as a professional philanderer whose presence served no purpose in the narrative other than to amuse), Fred Huntley, Gertrude Norman and Sigrid Holmquist.

△

Again relying more on character development than on plot, **The Dark Swan**, produced by Jack Warner, was a well directed (by Millard Webb) drama which starred Marie Prevost and Helene Chadwick (left) as half sisters, the former being meretriciously charming and attractive, the latter rather plain. Monte Blue switched romantic allegiance from Miss Chadwick to Miss Prevost, with disastrous results. The film ended with divorce proceedings in the offing, and with a contrite Mr. Blue turning, for comfort, to the woman he should have married in the first place. It was written by Fred Jackson from a novel by Ernest Pascal, and also featured John Patrick (right), Lilyan Tashman and Vera Lewis.

The Beginning of Sound

Although as a studio Warner Bros. was small compared with MGM or Paramount, Harry Warner's sharp business acumen impressed potential investors such as Motley Flint of Pacific South-West Savings Bank and Trust Company and A.H. Giannini, President of the Bank of Italy, and he had no difficulty raising a million dollars to increase production. In 1925, for example, the studio made thirty-one films compared with seventeen the previous year. Also in 1925, with a perennial eye on expansion, the brothers borrowed a substantial amount of money and bought the old Vitagraph studios in Brooklyn, together with its 34 exchanges throughout America and Canada. Later that year, Sam Warner, fascinated by the experiments in sound that were being carried out at the time, persuaded Harry, who was somewhat less enthusiastic, to take a chance and sign an agreement establishing a partnership between Warner Bros. and Western Electric (which then merged with Bell Telephone) for the specific purpose of furthering these experiments. With financial assistance from Waddill Catchings of the Goldman, Sachs banking group, Harry Warner arranged for the studio to underwrite a $4,200,000 note issue, and on April 20th, 1926, the Vitaphone Corporation was formed with Warner Bros. holding 70% of the stock.

Sam Warner's dream, initially, was to duplicate the sound of a full orchestra, as employed in several plush New York theatres, on special discs, enabling the most modest of theatres away from the big cities to enjoy the same aural accompaniment. Convinced that this would enhance both the quality of the film as well as its popularity at the box-office, Sam, together with Major Nathan Levinson, who became the head of Warner Bros. sound department, concentrated on synchronizing music rather than dialogue. They settled for a sound-on-disc system which was really quite simple.

A record 406 mm (16 inches) across, and revolving at $33\frac{1}{3}$ r.p.m. was played simultaneously with the film. But, in order to ensure that the mechanism did not jump out of synchronization, two motors, held at the same speed by an electric gear, were used. The motors were inter-connected by slip rings so that the necessary interchange of power between the armatures ensured correct synchronization at the start of the film. The frequency of the power source then maintained synchronization.

The film and sound machines were coupled to opposite ends of the same motor, the motor speed being held constant by a vacuum tube regulator. Mechanical vibrations and irregularities of tone were prevented from speeding up or slowing down the speed of the revolving record by a device known as the flywheel.

When Harry, Albert and Jack Warner first had this sound-on-disc method demonstrated to them, they were not convinced that it was sufficiently developed to risk incorporating into a major feature film. It was only after Sam literally tricked his brother into a further demonstration of the system's possibilities by pretending to call a meeting with some Wall Street financiers at the Bell Telephone offices, that Harry finally began to see its potential.

Not only, claimed Warner Bros. and Western Electric in a joint statement, would Vitaphone bring to audiences everywhere the greatest orchestras, and vocal entertainment by the world's greatest stars, but the system's possibilities in the fields of education and religion offered new perspectives in marketing potential as well. On June 17th, 1926 Warner Bros. bought the Piccadilly theatre in New York, wired it for sound and renamed it the Warner Theatre.

For some inexplicable reason, Sam Warner did not see the sound film as a means of putting words into actors' mouths, but only as a means of providing a musical accompaniment to silent features. He was also interested in exploring the entertainment potential of musical shorts and, to this purpose, signed a contract with the Metropolitan Opera Company in New York which gave him the use of some of its biggest stars. As these shorts (which would be shot in Oscar Hammerstein's old Manhattan Opera House in New York) would not, in themselves, attract large enough audiences to justify the expense, he decided to present several of them as the first half of a programme, the second half being a major feature film, also utilizing the Vitaphone system.

The feature turned out to be another star vehicle for John Barrymore – **Don Juan**, directed by 31-year-old Alan Crosland, and filmed in Hollywood simultaneously with the filming of the Vitaphone shorts in New York.

Although, in theory, the Vitaphone process of synchronizing sound-on-disc with film was simple, Sam Warner, who directed the musical shorts in Brooklyn, encountered unexpected teething problems, the main one being that, because the small Vitaphone stage was so sensitive to the slightest sounds, he and the technicians were forced to move around the set with their shoes off while the camera was turning. Even the barely perceptible motor-whirr of the camera was picked up, as a result of which the camera was incarcerated in a large, claustrophobic wooden booth. Fortunately, Warner Bros. had two sound experts under contract, Stanley Watkins and George Groves, whose painstaking experiments in the field resulted in as perfectly synchronized a picture as was possible at the time, skilfully varying the density and volume of sound as the performers

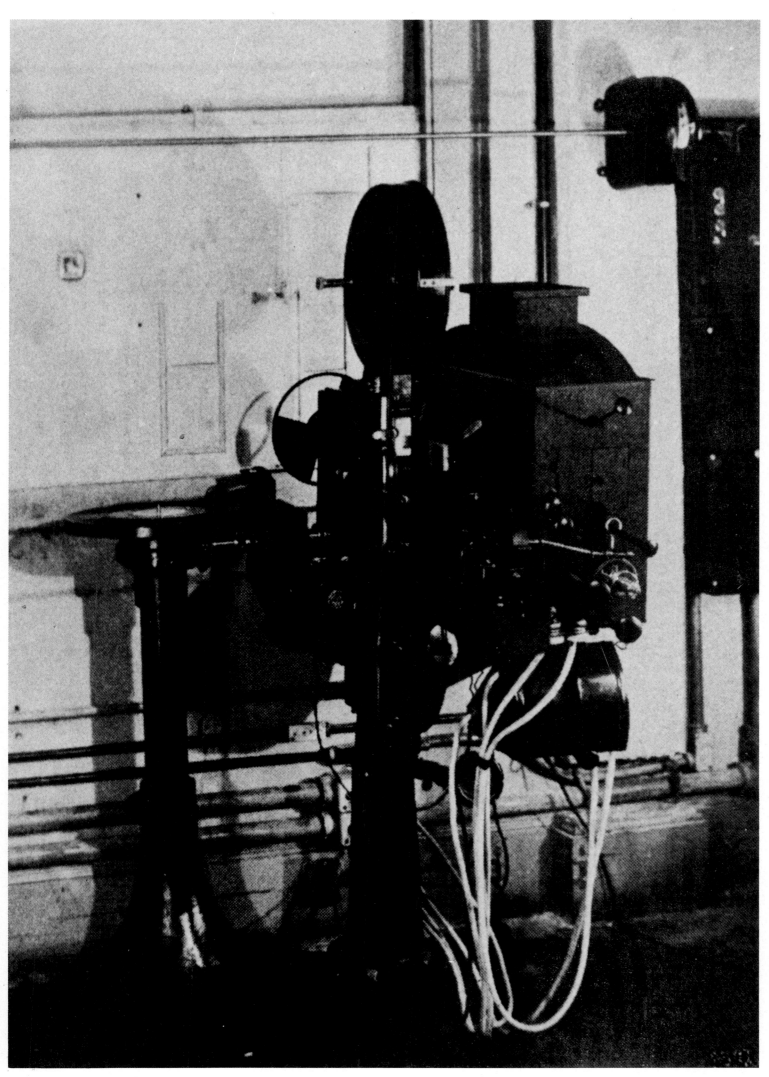

The Vitaphone sound system.

The cast of **Don Juan** *and the Warner Bros. studio technicians.*

moved from long-shot to close-up. There was one problem, however, which they were not able to overcome: editing the synchronized film. As a result, every sequence had to be shot with a full roll of film stock, each roll lasting ten minutes. And if a take was ruined by the rumble of a passing subway, or for some other reason, the entire roll of film had to be scrapped and the sequence repeated from the beginning until Sam Warner was satisfied.

When the Vitaphone shorts were completed, Sam supervised the musical scoring and recording of William Axt's score for **Don Juan** as reel by reel arrived in Brooklyn from the West Coast. Matching the images to the score was exhausting, finicky work and it took months to complete.

The premiere of **Don Juan**, Warner Bros.' most expensive film to date, starring Barrymore, Warner Oland and Mary Astor, took place on August 6th, 1926 at the Warner Theatre in New York. The studio publicity department, aware that what was being launched that night was more than just another film, was determined to provide a sense of occasion to the proceedings and, as well as an impressive front-of-house display, including large cardboard-cut-outs showing the star's renowned profile, the entire theatre staff was arrayed in some of the 15th century style costumes from the film.

The evening began with a filmed sequence showing Will H. Hays, President of the Motion Picture Producers and Distributors of America, praising the joint efforts of Western Electric, the Bell Telephone Company and Warner Bros. for making possible the magic that the assembled audience was about to witness. This was followed by a film of the New York

Philharmonic Orchestra under its conductor Henry Hadley playing Wagner's overture to *Tannhauser*.

Vitaphone was well and truly launched!

Verdi followed Wagner as Marion Talley, one of the Met's most popular stars, sang 'Caro Nome' from *Rigoletto*. She, in turn, was followed by Roy Smeck, a vaudeville comedian who played his guitar and recited a monologue called 'His Pastimes'. The parents of Rita Hayworth, the dancing Cansinos, accompanied Miss Anna Case who sang 'La Fiesta', after which Mischa Elman played the violin and Efrem Zimbalist the piano. Giovanni Martinelli, another Met star, sang 'Vesti La Giubba' from *Pagliacci*, and the first half of the evening's films closed with a rousing version of several national anthems by the New York Philharmonic Orchestra.

The audience responded warmly rather than wildly, though there was genuine appreciation for some of the sound effects, such as the clashing of swords and the pealing of bells which were incorporated into the main feature, **Don Juan**.

Despite the audience's failure to hail the arrival of Vitaphone as another Second Coming, the system found favour with the press who welcomed it most enthusiastically.

Yet, while it was rewarding to receive, the favourable critical reaction to **Don Juan** did not bring immediate wealth to the Warner brothers' coffers, and in 1926, the studio showed a loss of $279,096. Although they had equipped the Warner Theatre for sound, the brothers were hardly in a

Left: a sound control board with Paul Muni on screen. Above: shooting **The Girl From Woolworth's** *(1929) with the cameras inside booths.*

position to make similar installations in theatres all round the country, and as long as theatres remained silent there was no way they could recoup their initial investment.

In 1926 the installation of sound equipment in a theatre was an expensive business, costing between $16,000 and $25,000, depending on the size of the theatre, and Harry Warner himself became a roving salesman, wandering around the country in an attempt to talk theatre managers everywhere into investing in Vitaphone. He was only moderately successful. By the end of 1926, the brothers' financial situation seemed anything but healthy and a loss of over $100,000 had been declared to shareholders. The following year, Motley Flint opted out of investment banking, leaving Warner Bros. almost entirely dependent on Goldman, Sachs in New York.

By the end of 1927, only 200 theatres in America were equipped to show talking pictures, and even this figure might not have been reached had not studio boss William Fox boarded the band-wagon with his own sound-on-film (as

opposed to disc) process which he called Movietone. (It wasn't until 1930 that Warner Bros. decided to jettison their sound-on-disc system in favour of Fox's sound on film).

Fox concentrated mainly on sound newsreels; so that audiences, not only seeing but hearing such national personalities as Calvin Coolidge, Al Smith, Babe Ruth and Charles Lindbergh (the start and finish of whose non-stop flight from New York to Paris was recorded for posterity by Movietone), went wild. Like Warner Bros., Fox also added a musical score to some of his films, notably **Seventh Heaven** and **Sunrise** (both 1927).

By the end of 1926 Warners had produced over a hundred Vitaphone short subjects and in February 1927 with the opening of John Barrymore's **When A Man Loves,** had three successful Vitaphone features simultaneously on release in New York. By the end of 1927 the number of shorts had risen to 200. Yet, as far as the other studios were concerned, there was a certain timidity towards sound. Because there were several sound systems in the pipe-line — none of them interchangeable – studios such as MGM, Paramount and Universal decided to bide their time, and together with First National and Producers Distributing Corporation, formed the 'Big Five' agreement in February of 1927 which stipulated that they would not commit themselves to any one system until their appointed committee had decided what

specific system would best serve the industry. There was even a certain amount of caution at Warner Bros. as evidenced by the fact that, though undeniably eager to persevere with sound, Vitaphone remained a separate part of the company; and one that could easily be dropped if, in the next couple of years, it failed to find favour.

All that Jack Warner and his brothers needed at this

point was the kind of irrefutable success to help them prove to the rest of Hollywood and exhibitors throughout the country that sound pictures were more than a passing fad.

The miracle happened, and it was called **The Jazz Singer.** Based on a successful play by Samson Raphaelson, it was bought by Jack Warner for $30,000 as a vehicle for George Jessel, who originally appeared in it on Broadway playing a cantor's son who deserts his faith for show business. But when Jessel, who had made **Private Izzy Murphy** and **Sailor Izzy Murphy** for the studio learned that songs were to be added, he took Eddie Cantor's advice and doubled his fee. As Jessel was not that big a star, Jack Warner refused to meet his price.

It was Sam Warner's idea to sign Al Jolson, who was then appearing in a touring version of Raphaelson's play. Jolson was expensive. He was twice the star Jessel was, and consequently asked for twice as much money. The deal finally agreed on was $75,000, a third in cash and the rest in weekly instalments of $6,250, part of the money to be reinvested by Jolson in the film in order to secure a percentage of the profits.

The Jazz Singer opened on October 6th, 1927, at the Warner Theatre in New York and was nothing short of a sensation. All the cheers the brothers had expected, but had not received, for their production of **Don Juan** were being saved for **The Jazz Singer**, as the sound sequences brought the ecstatic first nighters to their feet in a frenzy of excitement. History was being made, and everyone privileged enough to be there knew it.

By some terrible irony, however, Sam Warner, the man who had fought so hard to turn his dream into a reality, was not one of the privileged that night. On October 5th, twenty-four hours before **The Jazz Singer's** premiere, he died in the Californian Lutheran Hospital of a cerebral haemorrhage. His brothers, on receiving the news, immediately took a train to Los Angeles, thus also missing what would have been undoubtedly the greatest night of their lives.

As it was, Jack, in his autobiography, refers to the triumph of **The Jazz Singer** as 'an empty victory'. 'When Sam died,' he wrote, 'and there is no doubt that **The Jazz Singer** killed him, something went out of our lives. The soaring shaft of sound film still stands, and brings to our lives laughter, tears and escape from daily stress. Sam brought it into the world, and gave his own life in exchange.'

All the same, for the brothers Warner there was now no question of turning back.

1925

The studio made thirty-one feature films in 1925 compared to seventeen the previous year. Though Rin-Tin-Tin starred in no fewer than four of them – all box-office successes, artistically it was Ernst Lubitsch's **Kiss Me Again** and his adaptation of Oscar Wilde's **Lady Windermere's Fan** that won the critic's accolades. By now the studio had several stars under contract who continued to prove their great popularity with audiences. Among them where Marie Prevost, Monte Blue, Irene Rich, Patsy Ruth Miller, Willard Louis, Matt Moore, May McAvoy and Dorothy Mackaill.

Over emphasis, too many flashbacks and lack of subtlety in Harry Beaumont's direction were the key flaws in **A Lost Lady**, a dramatization by Dorothy Farnum of Willa Cather's novel concerning a spoilt girl (Irene Rich, right) who is bored to distraction with her wealthy but elderly husband (George Fawcett), but doesn't know what she wants instead. Beaumont's cast included Matt Moore (left) as a friend and admirer who takes in Miss Rich after she deserts her husband, John Roche, June Marlowe, Victor Potel, Eva Gordon and Nanette Valone, all of whom responded better to the film's lighter moments than to its more serious ones.
▽

Laguna Beach provided the Maine, New ▷ England setting for another Rin-Tin-Tin money spinner, **Lighthouse by the Sea**. The story of a blind lighthouse keeper whose chores are taken over by a protective daughter (Louise Fazenda), it involved Miss Fazenda's romance with William Collier Jr after he and his dog are shipwrecked near the lighthouse. In no time at all, however, she is kidnapped by bootleggers who, in turn, are duly foiled by Rin-Tin-Tin, and everyone lives happily ever after. Though it returned a handsome profit on its $150,000 investment, it was not a happy production, as there was a great deal of bitterness among the human contingent who considered themselves grossly underpaid compared with the earnings of the four-legged star. Collier received a mere $150 a week compared to Rinty's $1000; and, as if that were not injustice enough, he and the rest of the cast had to endure the dog's aggressive, decidedly unfriendly physical attacks on them. Directed by Mal St. Clair with an embarrassed awareness of what blatant melodrama it all was, and written by Darryl Zanuck from the play by Owen Davis, it appealed to a large section of the dog-loving public, as well as to schoolboys everywhere, and helped to keep the Warners in business.

△
In **The Narrow Street**, Matt Moore (right) was given the chance to play a timid bachelor who returns home one evening to find a pretty young girl (Dorothy Devore, left) ensconced in his house, her explanation being that she was seeking refuge from a storm. The principal players did their vigorous best to get all they could out of the rather thin material, and succeeded. Irvin S. Cobb's screen-play was consistently

amusing, and director William Beaudine brought to it just the right farcical touch. His cast included David Butler, Russell Simpson, Gertrude Short, Kate Toncray and Mademoiselle Sultewan.

△
Mixing comedy, sentimentality and realism, **A Broadway Butterfly** emerged as a pulp-fiction story about a country girl with thespian tendencies who arrives on Broadway seeking fame and fortune but settles for a husband instead. It starred Dorothy Devore as the young hopeful, with Louise Fazenda, Willard Louis, John Roche (left) and Cullen Landis completing the cast of this artificial but entertaining tale. It was adapted by Darryl Zanuck from a story by Pearl Keating, and the director was William Beaudine.

On Thin Ice, written by Darryl Zanuck, ▷ skated across a feeble story by Alice Ross Colver that linked naive Edith Roberts (centre) with a bunch of unpleasant gangsters (the plot included her finding a bag supposedly containing $200,000 in stolen gold and banknotes, but when opened it was stuffed with washers). It was directed by Mal St. Clair (badly in need of Rin-Tin-Tin on this occasion) and featured Tom Moore (right), William Russel, Theodore von Eltz (left), Wilfred North and Gertrude Robinson.

The Bridge of Sighs elicited groans from the more sophisticated in the audience, who, understandably, refused to accept this trite romance between the bird-brained son of a wealthy businessman and the daughter of the businessman's manager. The basic fault in the Louis Lighton-Hope Loring scenario (from a story by Charles K. Harris) was that the spoiled son was so totally unlikeable that his childish, irresponsible behaviour simply became irksome. Creighton Hale (centre left) and Dorothy Mackaill (centre right) did their best with the wretched material but under Phil Rosen's uninspired direction were unable to rescue the film. It was, however, fairly successful at the box office. Also cast were Alec B. Francis, Richard Tucker, Ralph Lewis and Clifford Saum.

In Recompense, Marie Prevost (illustrated) played a bright-eyed single-minded Red Cross nurse and Monte Blue a clergyman who gives up his chaplaincy and goes to war. France, South Africa and England featured prominently in the narrative, and care was taken to ensure authenticity in each case. The result was solid, often stirring entertainment, marred at the last moment by an unconvincing plot contrivance to secure a happy ending. Dorothy Farnum adapted the Robert Keable novel on which it was based; Harry Beaumont directed, and the cast included John Roche, George Siegmann, Charles Stevens, Virginia Brown Faire, William B. Davidson and Etta Lee.

◁ A typical Rin-Tin-Tin story, Tracked in the Snow Country found the world's most famous hound falsely accused of murdering his master. He clears his name, however, by pursuing the real killer and bringing him to justice. Set amid the snow and ice of the frozen North, it was first-rate Boy's Own entertainment, unfolded with panache by director Herman Raymaker, and with Rinty (illustrated) doing all that could possibly be expected of a dog. The human element included June Marlowe, David Butler and Mitchell Lewis, and the story was written by Edward J. Meagher.

△ The Man Without a Conscience was a film without a sense of humour despite the presence in the leading role of comedian Willard Louis (right) who, on this occasion, changed theatrical masks for his portrayal of an unscrupulous businessman whose methods ultimately result in a jail sentence for fraud. Director James Flood, working from a story by Max Kretzer (which Louis Lighton and Hope Loring adapted) made heavy going of it all, though Irene Rich as Louis's wife retained her charm throughout. June Marlowe (left) and John Patrick were also in the cast.

◁ A high-life melodrama, My Wife and I had a father (Huntly Gordon, centre) and son (John Harron) vying for the affections of a pretty little minx (Constance Bennett) while a hapless wife and mother (Irene Rich, lying down) watched it all from a distance. It rained a great deal throughout, which served only to waterlog the already soggy plot and dampen the enthusiasm of the paying customers. Based on a novel by Harriet Beecher Stowe (but updated and set in New York) it was written by Julien Josephson and directed by Millard Webb. Others involved in this mediocre production were John Roche, Tom Ricketts and Claire de Lorez.

Helene Chadwick, Clive Brook and John Harron acquitted themselves remarkably well considering the fatuousness of the material they had to work with in **The Woman Hater.** Miss Chadwick (centre) played a great international actress ('men from all Europe crowded her dressing room', a title informed) who was prevented at the last moment from marrying million-aire Harron (left) by woman-hater Brook who, needless to say, wanted her for himself. Based on Ruby M. Ayres' novel *The Eleventh Virgin*, it was adapted by Louis Lighton and Hope Loring and directed by James Flood. Helen Dunbar and Dale Fuller (right) also appeared.

A forerunner of Walter Mitty and Billy Liar, Henry Baxter, the amiable billing-clerk hero of **How Baxter Butted In,** spends his life day-dreaming about this and that, but mainly about becoming a hero in the eyes of his boss and stenographer sweetheart (Dorothy Devore, centre). It was beautifully played by Matt Moore (as Baxter, right) and imaginatively handled by director William Beaudine. Julien Josephson adapted it from Owen Davis's play. Also cast were Ward Crane, Wilfred Lucas, Adda Gleason, Turner Savage and Otis Harlan.

The basic plot of Ernst Lubitsch's **Kiss Me Again** could not be simpler. Monte Blue is married to Marie Prevost, a fact which doesn't particularly thrill her. She thinks naught of indulging in a spot of extra-marital pleasure with her bushy-haired pianist lover, John Roche, and a perennial triangle situation ensues with the husband emerging as the victor. Lubitsch's handling of this simple romantic tale staggered the critics who hailed the film as a masterpiece and as one of the most penetrating, witty and intelligent studies of the mechanics of romantic love ever filmed. Based on Victorien Sardou and Emile de Najac's play *Let's get a Divorce*, it was written for the screen by Hans Kraly and photographed by Charles Van Enger. It also featured Willard Louis and Clara Bow. The *New York Times* considered it one of the ten best films of the year.

Director Harry Beaumont made heavy weather of Harry Leon Wilson's novel **His Majesty, Bunker Bean.** This was the quaint tale of a gullible stenographer who after being told by a clairvoyant that, in a former incarnation, he was Napoleon, and by an archaeology Professor that he was an Egyptian king, agrees to pay the professor $5000 in return for the mummy whose body he believes his spirit once occupied. Matt Moore (right) battled in vain against his director's tendency to reduce the whimsy to slapstick, with other roles going to Dorothy Devore (left), David Butler, George Nichols and Helen Dunbar.

◁ On paper, **Eve's Lover,** written for the screen by Darryl Zanuck (from a novel by Mrs W.K. Clifford) was a routine melodrama about an industrious young woman (Irene Rich) whose steel mill is coveted by a villainous business rival. The blackguard even goes so far as to arrange a romance between his victim and an impecunious baron (who had once passed him a bad cheque) in the hope that the liaison will result in his eventual ownership of the mill. By refusing to take any of it seriously, its able cast which included Bert Lytell, Clara Bow (in bath) and Willard Louis, and its talented director Roy Del Ruth managed to bring a sparkling freshness to an extremely tired plot, and scored a real triumph of style over content.

The Wife Who Wasn't Wanted was the story of a district attorney who finds himself in the awkward position of having to prosecute his own son for killing a girl in a car smash as a result of reckless driving. The boy's mother, desperate to save him from a lingering prison sentence, compromises herself with her husband's political rival on the understanding that if he, the rival, is chosen as district attorney in the forth-coming elections, he will make sure that the boy is not prosecuted. Directed with great intensity by James Flood, and neatly adapted by Bess Meredyth from a novel by Gertie Wentworth-James, it starred Irene Rich (left), Huntly Gordon (right) and John Harron with Gayne Whitman, June Marlowe, Don Alvarado and Edward Piel.

The usual dose of histrionics prevailed in **Below the Line**, a Rin-Tin-Tin epic which evoked atmosphere through heavy rainstorms and thick forests as the canine hero held back a pack of bloodhounds, jumped up and down trees, and even killed a murderer. It was directed by Herman Raymaker from a story by Charles A. Logue. John Harron, June Marlowe, Pat Hartigan and Victor Potel were the two-legged stars.
▽

△
Lowell Sherman was unable to bring much conviction to his portrayal of a Russian prince in Bradley King's **Satan in Sables,** a romance of sorts set in the South of France. On the eve of his divorce, Sherman (above) has a fling with a dancer unaware that her disapproving brother-in-law is about to make trouble. The film was directed by James Flood who clearly had no confidence in his material, and performed without lustre by Pauline Garon, Gertrude Astor, Frank Butler, John Harron (below), Francis J. MacDonald and Otto Hoffman.

Though Monte Blue (centre) was the top star in **Hogan's Alley**, the best moments were supplied by Willard Louis in a sequence which questioned his table manners. Another scene had a prize-fighter with a damaged fist resisting the temptation to use it in a fight with a villain for fear that further injury might mean the loss of the forthcoming championship. His resistance, however, was low. Darryl Zanuck (alias Gregory Rogers) wrote the script and Roy Del Ruth directed. Also cast were Patsy Ruth Miller (left), Louise Fazenda, Ben Turpin, Max Davidson, Herbert Spencer Griswold, Mary Carr and Nigel Barrie.
▽

The general consensus of opinion was that Sydney Chaplin's emphatic attempts at comedy in **The Man on the Box** in no way threatened his brother Charlie's supremacy in the field. Whether indignantly rebuking an apache dancer for ill-treating the weaker sex (a gag Charlie used to better effect in 1931 in *City Lights*) or disguising himself as a parlour maid, he proved that straining for laughs was one certain way not to get them — a lesson his brother never had to learn. Charles Reisner's direction lacked moderation, enveloping in its frenzy Chaplin (left), David Butler, Alice Calhoun, Kathleen Calhoun, Theodore Lorch and Helene Costello. Harold MacGrath provided the original story, Grace L. Firness turned it into a play, and Charles A. Logue wrote it for the screen.   ▷

△
Twenty different authors pooled their respective creative resources and came up with a novel which Lewis Milestone adapted for the screen. **Bobbed Hair** was a vehicle for Marie Prevost who played a heroine with two lovers: one who liked bobbed hair and one who did not. Miss Prevost (centre) tantalized both by wearing a nun's habit. There was a dog called Pal who latched on to $50,000 and refused to let it go, and a woman (Louise Fazenda) who dressed as a man. Kenneth Harlan was the hero. Audiences couldn't be held responsible for not making much sense of it. Alan Crosland was the director and his cast included John Roche, Emily Fitzroy, Reed Howes, Dolores and Helene Costello and Pat Hartigan.

◁ Resourcefully directed by Erle C. Kenton, **Red Hot Tires** was an unpretentious comedy that aimed merely to please and succeeded. The story was simple. Monte Blue has taken to riding a buggy ever since his car collided with a steam-roller. His girl-friend (Patsy Ruth Miller, left), however, is a speed freak who one day crashes into Monte's buggy. Both are sent to jail and put in opposite cells. Monte is released, but wishing to be near his loved one, contrives various ways of remaining behind bars. Darryl Zanuck, alias Gregory Rogers, wrote the story; Edward T. Lowe Jr, adapted it and contributing to the story's fun were Lincoln Stedman, Charles Conklin, Fred Esmelton (right) and Tom McGuire.

A climactic tornado was hardly needed to shake up the dust in **Compromise**, adapted for the screen by Edward T. Lowe Jr. There was enough hot air in Jay Gelzer's plot about a woman who sets out to ruin her half-sister's marriage to keep a dozen such soap-operas airborne. Irene Rich (right)

was the wife who discovers that life is nothing but a compromise, Clive Brook her husband. The rest of the cast included Louise Fazenda, Pauline Garon (left), Raymond McKee, Helen Dunbar, Winter Hall, Frank Butler and Lynn Cowan. Alan Crosland directed.

△

Based on a play by Elmer Vance and written for the screen by Darryl Zanuck and Charles A. Logue, **The Limited Mail** was a lightweight Western about the Limited Mail's conquest of the West. It starred the hard-working Monte Blue as an engineer who, disillusioned by the death of his best friend (Tom Gallery) in a freight train accident, becomes a hobo, regaining his dignity and the esteem of his superiors when he prevents a train smash during a landslide. Filmed on location in Feather City and Royal Gorge in Canyon City, it was a notable success for director George Hill and set a profitable trend for adventure yarns in a similar vein. Also cast were Vera Reynolds, Willard Louis (illustrated) and Master Jack Huff.

◁ In **Clash of the Wolves** Rin-Tin-Tin became the first dog ever to go about his business in disguise. Charles A. Logue's plot not only had him wearing shoes, but at one point, a beard as well! Rinty played Lobo, leader of a pack of wolves who, after injuring himself on a cactus bush goes off into the desert to die. He is rescued by David Weston, recovers and eventually manages to apprehend the film's obligatory villain. The comic scenes were embarrassingly bad, but the action scenes were fine. June Marlowe, Charles Farrell, Charlie Conklin and Pat Hartigan offered little support to Rinty, who did not really need it. The director was Noel Smith.

By inundating viewers with shoals of red ▷ herrings and extraneous clues, scenarists Louis Lighton and Hope Loring underestimated the audience's intelligence in their adaptation of the Arthur Somers Roche *Daily Express* serial **The Pleasure Buyers**. Stripped of its needless complications, the film posed a simple question: which one of half a dozen people, all with reasons of their own for wanting to do so, murdered a society crook called Cassenas? Was it Irene Rich (right)? Clive Brook? Gayne Whitman (left)? June Marlowe (centre)? Strong performances, capable direction by Chester Withey and excellent photography by Joseph Walker helped to keep the interest simmering.

Director Lewis Milestone lacked the requisite lightness of touch to give **Seven Sinners** the sparkle it demanded, but nonetheless made a pleasing job of a caper involving seven burglars who rob the same house on the same night. The story, by Milestone and Zanuck, provided its stars with all manner of comic opportunities which Marie Prevost (centre), Clive Brook (right, superb as a phoney butler) Charlie Conklin, Claude Gillingwater (left), Mathilde Brundage and Fred Kelsey pounced on with gratitude.

Rose of the World was a wearying tale ▷ about a jilted girl who marries a man on the rebound only to discover that it's her fortune he's after. In the end, she goes back to the lover who jilted her, this time with more success. Harry Beaumont directed from a screenplay by Julien Josephson (adapted by Dorothy Farnum from a novel by Kathleen Norris) and coaxed from Rockliffe Fellowes (as the fortune seeker) the most robust performance in the film. Patsy Ruth Miller (right) simpered as the heroine, Alan Forrest (left) vacillated as her lover. Others in the cast included Pauline Garon, Barbara Luddy, Alec B. Francis, Helen Dunbar and Lydia Knott.

Substituting what Ernst Lubitsch himself termed 'visual epigrams' for Oscar Wilde's verbal ones, **Lady Windermere's Fan** miraculously managed to capture the essence and spirit of Wilde's play without recourse to a single line of the playwright's dialogue. Lubitsch was greatly assisted in his endeavours by a sparkling cast which included Irene Rich as Mrs. Erlynne, May McAvoy as Lady Windermere, Bert Lytell as Lord Windermere (left), Ronald Colman as Lord Darlington, and Edward Martindale (centre). Julien Josephson adapted the play for the screen and Charles Van Enger was the cameraman. The film was on the *New York Times'* ten best list for 1925.

The Golden Cocoon did nothing for the respective careers of its star Helene Chadwick or its director Millard Webb. It told the banal story of a much put-upon heroine who becomes involved with a professor of political economy only to be thrown over by him for the daughter of a wealthy businessman. Its main purpose seemed to be to show how affectingly Miss Chadwick could suffer. Huntly Gordon, Richard Tucker, Frank Campeau, Margaret Seddon and Carrie Clark (illustrated) were also in the cast. It was adapted by Louis Lighton and Hope Loring from a novel by Ruth Cross.

1926

Of the thirty-three features made by the studio in 1926, **The Sea Beast** and the first full-length Vitaphone feature **Don Juan** – both of which starred John Barrymore (at the height of his popularity) – helped keep the studio solvent. The director Michael Curtiz was brought over from Germany by Jack Warner who, after seeing his work on an unreleased German film, **Moon Over Israel** (which Paramount bought and then suppressed because of its similarity to De Mille's **The Ten Commandments**) cabled him in Germany and offered him a contract. Curtiz accepted and arrived in New York on 4 July 1926.

Tired of playing so many 'scented, be-puffed, bewigged and ringletted' characters as John Barrymore himself put it, he asked Warner Bros. to star him as Captain Ahab in a screen version of Herman Melville's *Moby Dick*. The result was **The Sea Beast** which, in the end, bore little resemblance to the novel, retaining in Bess Meredyth's screenplay only Ahab's search for the great white whale. Love interest and a happy ending were added, with Priscilla Bonner originally chosen to supply the former. Barrymore's first choice however was Mary Astor, who was unavailable. He settled, instead, for a relative unknown called Dolores Costello, whom he considered the most preposterously lovely creature in all the world. Meantime, the thwarted Miss Bonner sued the studio and an out-of-court settlement was reached. Other problems surfaced during the shooting of the $800,000 epic, not least of which was Barrymore's heavy drinking. All the same, **The Sea Beast** was a huge success, with critics and public alike responding particularly to the chemistry between Barrymore (right) and Miss Costello (left), whose love scenes were so authentic that they gave director Millard Webb an unusual problem. He was unable to decide which of the many brilliant takes to choose, so, for the final embrace, he spliced them all together to create a love scene of unprecedented length and passion. The photographer was Byron Haskins. Also cast were Mike Donlin, Sam Baker, Sam Allen, George Burrell, Frank Nelson and James Burrows.

A motor crash, a car chase, several fights and the occasional dash of slapstick (provided by Charlie Conklin) were the chief components of **The Fighting Edge**, a melodrama in which Patsy Ruth Miller and Kenneth Harlan (centre, as a US Secret Service agent) evinced more energy than acting ability as a pair of lovers waging a war against a gang of crooks who smuggle passportless aliens into the US from Mexico. It all took place in a rambling mansion on the Mexican border, and, under Henry Lehrman's action-filled direction, maintained interest. It was written by Edward T. Lowe Jr and Jack Wagner from a story by William MacLeod Raine.

▽

△

The Man Upstairs was a comedy spiced rather confusingly with melodrama. The far-fetched but potentially amusing story of a hotel guest who in order to impress a young lady invents a murder in which he is implicated, only to find that in fact such a murder has been committed, and that he is indeed implicated, it starred Monte Blue (right) as the story-teller and Dorothy Devore as the equally inventive girl he is trying to impress. John Roche was also in the cast, so was Charlie Conklin in black-face playing a jokey servant. Roy Del Ruth directed from yet another Edward T. Lowe Jr screenplay, this time based on a story by Earl Derr Biggers. It was remade as *Passage From Hong Kong* in 1941.

△

A comedy satirizing war and monarchy, **The Love Toy**, written by Sonya Hovey from a story by Pearl Keating failed to find favour with the public and rapidly disappeared. It was the whimsical tale of a young man, who, after being jilted on the eve of his marriage, departs for the mythical duchy of Luzania in Ruritania where he is given command of a Lilliputian army. Lavishly produced, it was well acted by a cast including Lowell Sherman (as the hero), Willard Louis (as the King of Luzania, illustrated), Gayne Whitman (as the villainous Prime Minister), Helene Costello (as the heroine) and Ethel Gray Terry (as a possessive Queen whose love for the hero is unrequited). Erle C. Kenton's direction lacked the popular touch.

△

Rin-Tin-Tin was up to his old tricks again (and some new ones) in **The Night Cry**, an adventure yarn which found him being blamed for the massacre of some sheep by a giant condor. He was innocent, of course. So was everything else about this Boy's Own yarn including its climactic mountain-top rescue. Herman Raymaker directed, Ewart Adamson adapted the Phil Klein-Edward Meagher story, and the humans in the cast included June Marlowe (right), Don Alvarado (centre) and John Harron.

It must have been daunting for Sydney Chaplin to be the brother of the legendary Charlie, which is doubtless why, in a desperate attempt to be different, he resorted to wearing drag so often. For example, in **Oh, What a Nurse!** he transforms himself into a hospital nurse (left) who dances attention on one of the film's villains in a frantic attempt to keep the man away from his girlfriend (Patsy Ruth Miller). Miss Miller alone managed to keep her head when all around her the rest of the cast (Gayne Whitman, Matthew Betz [right], Pat Hartigan, Edgar Kennedy, Edith Yorke and Dave Torrence) were losing theirs. Based on a story by Robert E. Sherwood and Bertram Bloch, Darryl Zanuck's screenplay was reasonably good but Charles F. Reisner's direction was wearingly frenetic.

The raging sea was the real star of **Bride of the Storm**, a quintessential melodrama in which a wealthy mother and her young daughter find themselves washed up onto a lighthouse rock after a shipwreck. The mother dies, leaving the daughter (who grows up into Dolores Costello, left) to be reared by a family of three men — grandfather, father and lunatic son. Trouble rears its head, however, when the father attempts to thrust his son onto the girl hoping they will marry so that he can get his hands on his prospective daughter-in-law's inheritance. The over-ripe scenario (by Marian Constance from a story by James Francis Dwyer) piled one implausible situation on top of another, totally defeating its director (J. Stuart Blackton) and its cast (John Harron [centre], Otto Matiesen, Sheldon Lewis [right], Julia Swayne Gordon and Tyrone Power Sr). It was a Vitagraph picture distributed by Warners.

plunged into dire straits when they discover that it is not such a fortune after all. W.B. Maxwell's promising story (adapted by Marian Constance) was not particularly well directed (again by J. Stuart Blackton) and although the production was lavish, the film itself was hollow. Filling unsympathetic roles were Dorothy Devore and Macklyn Arbuckle with Florence Turner, John Harron, Myrna Loy (illustrated) and Andrée Tourneur in support.

In **The Sap**, although young Billy Weston (Kenneth Harlan, right) was mistakenly decorated in the war for an act of bravery that should not have been attributed to him, and returns home a hero, he is, at heart, a coward who cannot even stand up to his rival in love (David Butler). However, in the course of Edward T. Lowe Jr's routine screenplay (from William A. Grew's play), he undergoes a change of character. He sends back his medal to the War Office, leaves home and the dominating influence of his mother and wins back his sweetheart's affection by beating Butler in a fair fight, just as one would have expected. It was directed by Erle Kenton and also featured Mary McAllister (left) and Eulalie Jensen. The cast gave good performances but otherwise the film was only moderately entertaining.

The dramatic highlight of **Hell-Bent For Heaven** was a massive flood which engulfed everything in its path, including villain Gayne Whitman who engineered it all by dynamiting a dam. Patsy Ruth Miller (right) was the eternal heroine who scorns Whitman's advances in favour of hero John Harron (left). Set in the Blue Ridge mountains and again directed by J. Stuart Blackton, it was stirring entertainment. Marian Constance fashioned the scenario from a play by Hatcher Hughes and the cast was completed by Gardner James, James Marcus, Wilfred North and Evelyn Selbie.

The Gilded Highway told the story of a ▷ family of snobbish fortune-hunters who inherit a legacy from an old uncle and start to live a life of shameless luxury, only to be

Director Lewis Milestone, working from another Zanuck screenplay, this time an adaptation of Gelett Burgess's play *Lady Mechante*, came up trumps with a comedy called **The Cave Man**. All about a bored society dame (Marie Prevost, right), who cuts a $100 bill in half, writes a message on one of the halves asking whoever finds it to call at her apartment (address supplied), then lets it waft out of her window, it offered immense comic possibilities, all of them fully realized. A coalman (Matt Moore, left), finds the note, arrives at the apartment and in no time at all is transformed into a man of fashion, with hilarious consequences. Contributing to the fun were Myrna Loy (in the early days of her long and distinguished career, although at Warner Bros. she was cast in secondary roles usually playing Orientals or half-castes), Phyllis Haver, John Patrick and Hedda Hopper.

A slender comedy of marital infidelity, **Other Women's Husbands** aspired to a Lubitsch-like sophistication and, under Erle C. Kenton's direction, often achieved it. A quartet of capable players (Marie Prevost and Monte Blue [centre] as the husband and wife; Huntley Gordon and Phyllis Haver as their indiscretions) added style to the amusing and inventive proceedings, giving Edward T. Lowe Jr.'s scenario a sheen it might otherwise not have had.

The Passionate Quest was an inferior melodrama which dealt with the aspirations of three friends who desert their provincial existences for a crack at the big time in London. It starred Willard Louis in an aggressive mood as a would-be business tycoon, May McAvoy as a typist with the smell of greasepaint in her nostrils, and Gardner James as her poet boyfriend. J. Stuart Blackton directed and the screenplay, from a story by E. Phillips Oppenheim, was the work of Marian Constance. Also cast were Louise Fazenda, Holmes Herbert, Vera Lewis, Frank Butler (right) and Jane Winton (left).

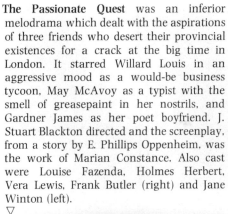

Dolores Costello fell among thieves in **The Little Irish Girl**, a drama of suspense which director Roy Del Ruth put together from C.D. Lancaster's play *The Grifters*. Darryl Zanuck did a nifty job of adapting it and although Miss Costello (right) went through most of the film with a fixed expression of despondency on her pretty face, there was compensating animation from John Harron (left), Dot Farley, Matthew Betz, Lee Moran and Gertrude Claire. In all, it was undemanding but adroit entertainment.

◁ Director Walter Morosco brought to his and Philip Klein's screenplay of Charles K. Harris's play **Silken Shackles** a sparkling surface gloss that reflected well on its participants. Irene Rich (left) played a flirtatious wife whose husband, Huntley Gordon, decides to teach her a lesson. He hires a musician (Victor Varconi, right) to woo her, then disillusion her by losing interest. Of course, the inevitable happens and Varconi finds himself smitten. Substantial performances from a cast which also included Bert Harburgh, Evelyn Selbie, Robert Schabble and Kalla Pascha made up for the insubstantial plot.

John Patrick (left) played an intrepid cub reporter called Jay Walker in **The Social Highwayman**, the main business of Elizabeth Phipps Train's plot being the tracking down of local bandit Ducket Nelson (Montagu Love). It didn't take itself seriously for an instant (sample caption: 'Evening came because afternoon had gone and morning was not due until dawn'), and was a box-office failure. It was directed by William Beaudine and written by Phillip Klein and Edward T. Lowe Jr whose scenario gave work to Dorothy Devore (right) as the heroine, George Pearce, Lynn Cowan, James Gordon and Fred Kelsey.

Marie Prevost (left) and Helen Dunbar played two spoiled, extravagant wives in **His Jazz Bride,** a comedy with dramatic undertones which ended with the deaths of Miss Dunbar and her engineer husband (George Irving) when the boilers of the steamship they happen to be travelling on explode, as a result of Irving having accepted a lucrative bribe to pass the plans of the unseaworthy vessel. A cautionary tale based on a story by Beatrice Burton and written for the screen by Charles A. Logue, it riveted attention despite the intrusion of tragedy into the basically light-hearted proceedings. Miss Prevost's husband was played by Matt Moore (right) with John Patrick and Gayne Whitman in support. Herman Raymaker directed.

Director Ernst Lubitsch more than con- ▷ solidated his formidable reputation as the most sophisticated craftsman in Hollywood with **So this is Paris,** his only money-making film for the studio. By underpinning a banal plot involving two amorous couples with elegance, wit, and satire, and imbuing the farrago with a delicious sense of gaiety and fun, the great German director guaranteed another set of outstanding

reviews for himself and a jolly time for the paying customers. The celebrated 'Lubitsch touch' was apparent in every scene, and it came as no surprise when the *New York Times* voted the film as one of the ten best of 1926. Hans Kräly again did the scenario

(from Henri Meilhac and Ludovic Halevy's play *Réveillon*) and John Mescall photographed it. It starred Monte Blue (right), Patsy Ruth Miller and Lilyan Tashman, with André de Beranger, Myrna Loy and Sidney D'Albrook.

△
Monte Blue (left) turned serious for just over an hour in **Across the Pacific.** He played a spy sent to the Philippines to locate a rebel leader, and the film was an account of his adventures there. Myrna Loy (right) co-starred as a half-caste islander with other roles going to Jane Winton (as Blue's sweetheart), Walter McGrail and Charles Stevens. Darryl Zanuck wrote it from a play by Charles E. Blaney, and Roy Del Ruth directed.

△
Why Girls Go Back Home was not a sequel to *Why Girls Leave Home* (1921), but a first-rate comedy about an arrogant actor who makes good on Broadway, allows success to go to his head, and refuses to acknowledge his one-time relationship with an aspiring young actress when she arrives in New York to try her luck on the stage. In time she, too, makes a success of her career, and determines to put her actor friend squarely in his place. Clive Brook was the actor (or 'Broadway's newest pain', as a subtitle put it), Patsy Ruth Miller (centre) the actress. They sparked each other off beautifully and under James Flood's capable direction gave two delightful performances. Sonya Hovey's adaptation from Catherine Brody's play was written with a pleasing lightness of touch, and the satirical swipes it took at self important actors were bang on target. Also cast were Jane Winton, Myrna Loy, George O'Hara, Joseph Dowling and Herbert Prior.

△
Similar to *Abie's Irish Rose*, **Private Izzy Murphy,** which marked George Jessel's debut as a screen actor, was about the relationship between a Jewish boy and a Catholic girl, except that, until the end, the girl doesn't realize Izzy (illustrated) is Jewish for he had previously changed his name to Isadore Patrick Murphy. It is only after he enlists in the army that he writes to her from France revealing his true identity. She, happily for him, couldn't care less, and on his return from the front, they decide to get married. Raymond L. Schrock and Edward Clark's story (adapted by Philip Lonergan) plumped for tears rather than laughter, and it was directed in an overtly lachrymose fashion by Lloyd Bacon. Patsy Ruth Miller played Izzy's sweetheart, with other roles going to Vera Gordon (as Izzy's mother – a performance similar to the one she gave in *Your Best Friend* in 1922) Gustav von Seyffertitz, Nat Carr, William Strauss and 'Spec' O'Donnell.

The Honeymoon Express was dogged by ▷ misfortune from the start. Ernst Lubitsch was pencilled in to direct it, but fell ill and was replaced by James Flood. Then, midway through shooting, its star Willard Louis died. This necessitated a re-jig of May O'Hara's scenario (from a play by Ethel Clifton and Brenda Fowler) which resulted in Louis being written out and co-star Irene Rich (left) finding another father for her three children. Fortunately, this made perfect sense in the plot for Louis played a philandering husband whose boozing and infidelities have an acutely disruptive effect on his family; and it is only a matter of time before his wife decides she has had enough and walks out on him. Despite the film's excellent production, Flood's intelligent, fast-paced direction, and a cast that also included Helene Costello (right), Jason Robards and Virginia Lee Corbin, Louis' death was a decided dampener and the film was never given a satisfactory release.

◁ Apart from a fur-trapper who briefly mistreats Rin-Tin-Tin, there was no real villain in **Hero of the Big Snows.** Rinty's main task in this one was to deliver a message to his master when a violent storm capsizes a tree and prevents a young girl in need of medical attention from being rushed to a doctor. Alice Calhoun (right), Don Alvarado (left), Leo Willis and Mary Jane Milliken all took secondary billing to Rinty. Ewart Adamson wrote the screenplay from a story by Darryl Zanuck, and the director was Herman Raymaker.

Another elaborate costume drama, but without the benefit of sound effects or a musical score was **My Official Wife** which starred Irene Rich (right) as a nobleman's daughter who, while on her way to a fancy dress ball as a peasant, is abducted by six men – one of whom rapes her. She vows she will be revenged, but, as the complex plot unfurls, falls in love with the brute instead. Miss Rich's performance was one of her best, though her co-star Conway Tearle (left) was miscast as the cad. Gustav von Seyffertitz also appeared as a Russian Grand Duke. His well-observed performance was in direct contrast to the rest of the aristocrats, all of whom behaved like a bunch of rowdy schoolboys. Paul Stein directed from a screenplay by C. Graham Baker, which, in turn, was based on a novel by Archibald Clavering Gunter. Also cast were Jane Winton, Stuart Holmes, John Miljan, Emile Chautard and Sidney Bracey.
▽

△
Just when you had ceased to believe a single frame of what you were seeing, and suspected you must be dreaming, it was revealed that the entire plot of **Three Weeks in Paris** was in fact a dream. It told the story of a man (Matt Moore, right), who, on his wedding night is forced to leave his wife (Dorothy Devore) to go to Paris where he is involved in a duel, jailed, and thought to be dead when the steamer on which he is due to return home sinks. However it turns out that Matt and Dorothy are really a happily but uneventfully married couple. Written by Darryl Zanuck (alias Gregory Rogers) from his own story and directed with a pleasing sense of the ridiculous by Roy Del Ruth, it also featured Willard Louis (left), Helen Lynch, Gayne Whitman, John Patrick, Frank Bond and Rosa Gore.

△
Louise Fazenda (right) and Jacqueline Logan (left) starred as two wealthy widows in **The Footloose Widow**, and, under Roy Del Ruth's crowd-pleasing direction, gave an improbable comedy a decided shot in the arm. In fact, the ladies were not widows at all. They were not even married, and, as for being wealthy, that was merely their goal in life. Adapted by hard-working Darryl Zanuck from a story by Beatrice Burton, it also featured Jason Robards (centre), Arthur Hoyt, Neely Edwards, Douglas Gerrard, John Miljan and Jane Winton. It was a well-deserved popular success.

△
Based on a play by Edward Phillips Oppenheim, **Millionaires** told the amusing rags-to-riches story of a Jewish tailor and his wife (George Sidney, right and Vera Gordon) who strike it rich when some apparently worthless oil stock turns out to be worth a fortune. They move from their humble East Side home to Fifth Avenue, and, lacking all the requisite social graces, attempt to crash the *haute monde*. Competently directed by Herman Raymaker from a screenplay by Raymond L. Schrock (adaptation by Edward Clark and C. Graham Baker) it also featured Nat Carr, Helene Costello, Arthur Lubin, Jane Winton (left), Otto Hoffman and William Strauss.

A cinematic variation on Noel Coward's ▷ song 'Don't put your Daughter on the Stage, Mrs. Worthington', **Broken Hearts of Hollywood** gave the same advice to mothers whose daughters were determined on a career in films. Its plot involved a murder, in which a protective mother shoots a man to save her daughter's honour, but it was basically a warning to young hopefuls to resist the lure of the Klieg lights. Louise Dresser was excellent as the mother, and Patsy Ruth Miller fine as the daughter. There were good performances too from Douglas Fairbanks Jr making his debut at the studio, Jerry Miley, Stuart Holmes and Barbara Worth. It was based on a story by Edward Lowe and Philip Klein, adapted by C. Graham Baker and Darryl Zanuck, and directed by Lloyd Bacon.

◁ Tired of the regulation outdoor Rin-Tin-Tin settings, Jack Warner purchased Walter Morosco's **While London Sleeps,** and engaged Howard Bretherton (who also directed) to turn the story of a murderer who stalks the back streets of London with a pet monster and a dog (Rinty) into an exciting and unusual vehicle for the studio's money-making hound. Cameraman Frank Kesson endowed the film with a look that would characterize many Warner Bros. films throughout the remainder of the decade and well into the thirties. Human interest was supplied by Otto Matiesen (deliciously sinister as the killer, right), De Witt Jennings (as Inspector Burke of Scotland Yard) and Helene Costello as Burke's pretty daughter, whom Rinty befriends.

John Barrymore (right) gave Douglas Fairbanks' reputation as the screen's foremost acrobat and lover a decided jolt with **Don Juan,** Warner Bros.' first full-length Vitaphone excursion into sound (a music track by William Axt, appropriate sound effects, but no spoken dialogue). Theatres not wired for sound screened a silent version. Whether swinging on vines, leaping on and off balconies to vouchsafe a promised rendezvous, braving the icy Tiber, scaling walls or thrusting himself bodily onto an opponent from the top of a flight of stairs, Barrymore cut a dashing figure and swashbuckled his way into the hearts of audiences across the country. A statistic-prone press agent recorded that, in the course of his romantic exploits, he favoured the women who comprised the *dramatis personae* with 191 kisses. Bearing the brunt of his adoration was Mary Astor (left) as Adriana della Varnese, with Estelle Taylor (as Lucretia Borgia), Myrna Loy, Phyllis Haver, and June Marlowe all getting their share of love as well. Also cast were Warner Oland as Caesar Borgia, and Willard Louis as Don Juan's faithful servant. Hedda Hopper appeared in a small role. Barrymore wanted Dolores Costello to play Adriana, but as Mary Astor was already signed the studio did not wish to risk a second breach of contract suit and he was forced to capitulate. Opinions about the film itself were mixed, but as the hero and heroine literally rode off into the sunset, Jack Warner knew he was on to a winner. The film made a fortune and spurred the brothers in their efforts to pioneer sound pictures. Alan Crosland directed with just the right amount of dash and bravado. It was written by Bess Meredyth and beautifully photographed by Byron Haskins.

△
Working with characters created by Bruce Bairnsfather, director Charles F. Reisner came up with the second synchronized Vitaphone feature – a screen version of **The Better 'Ole** that was undeniably funny if somewhat overlong. Sydney Chaplin (left) starred as old Bill, a jovial Limey sergeant, and his numerous experiences in World War I (including the discovery that his major is a German spy in collusion with the local innkeeper Theodore Lorch), kept audiences falling about and box-office cashiers busy. Also cast were Doris Hill, Harold Goodwin, Jack Ackroyd (right), Edgar Kennedy, and Charles Gerrard. It was written by Darryl Zanuck and Charles Reisner from a play by Bairnsfather and Arthur Eliot. Accompanying **The Better 'Ole** on its initial release were a selection of Vitaphone shorts featuring Al Jolson (making his film debut) and George Jessel.

△
The Third Degree, the last film released by Warner Bros. in 1926, heralded the American debut of the Hungarian-born director Michael Curtiz, who, in the next few years would establish himself as one of the studio's most eclectic and money-making talents. Several of his trademarks were already in evidence in this highly improbable story with its circus background – brilliant lighting effects, the imaginative use of dissolves and the fluidity of the camera movements. Though the film itself emerged as little more than a routine melodrama, it was the scenario (by C. Graham Baker from a play by Charles Klein) rather than the direction that was at fault. The story of a woman who discovers that the man she once eloped with has, years later, been hired to prevent her daughter's marriage from taking place, it starred Louise Dresser (left) as the mother and Dolores Costello (right) as the daughter with Rockliffe Fellowes, Jason Robards, Kate Price, Tom Santschi, Harry Todd, Mary Louise Miller and David Torrence in support.

1927

In the year that Al Jolson uttered the first words ever heard in a feature film, Warner Bros. made a record 43 movies. Monte Blue starred in seven of them, Irene Rich and May McAvoy in six. Warner Oland and Myrna Loy in five. Rin-Tin-Tin, Ben Lyon and Dolores Costello in four. The studio's other stars included Dorothy Mackaill, Sydney Chaplin, Helene Costello, Conrad Nagel and George Jessel. John Barrymore's single appearance for Warner Bros. in 1927 was in **When A Man Loves**, which was a great success with both critics and audiences.

In **Wolf's Clothing**, Monte Blue (left) starred ▷ as a subway station guard who has not had a night off for three years. One New Year's Eve, however, he is told that his services will not be required until the following morning, so he decides to go on the town. But he is knocked down by a large, expensive car whose driver is wearing evening clothes. In his state of semiconsciousness, Blue begins to hallucinate, and his hallucinations form the basis of the film — a rip-roaring comedy, as it turned out, with the star in fine form, ably assisted by Patsy Ruth Miller (right), John Miljan, Douglas Gerrard, Lewis Harvey, John Webb Dillon and Lee Moran. It was skilfully directed by Roy Del Ruth from the story by Arthur Somers Roche and a screenplay by Darryl Zanuck.

A comic servant, a burlesque detective, a half-witted sheriff and a mentally retarded coroner were the cast of characters in **Finger Prints**, a jokey detective yarn involving a search for hidden money by a gang of crooks. Secret panels, concealed doors and trick coffins were employed to lend an air of mystery to the plot, but the events as scripted by C. Graham Baker and Edward Clark from a story by Arthur Somers Roche, and directed by Lloyd Bacon, outstayed their welcome almost before they began. Louise Fazenda starred, with Edgar Kennedy (in coffin), Myrna Loy, Helene Costello, Warner Richmond, William Demarest (centre left), John T. Murray (left) and Franklin Pangborn (centre right) in support.
▽

Louise Fazenda (right) pulled out all the ▷ stops trying to inject laughs into **The Gay Old Bird**, a hoary old comedy in which she played a devoted maid who is forced, temporarily, to take the place of the estranged lady of the house. Several bedroom scenes in dubious taste, plus the sight of Miss Fazenda attempting to squeeze into her mistress' clothes (many sizes too small) were the comic highlights of this otherwise tedious romp. It was written by C. Graham Baker and Edward Clark (from a story by Virginia Dale), directed by Herman Raymaker, and also featured Edgar Kennedy, John Steppling, John T. Murray (left), Frances Raymond, Jane Winton (centre) and William Demarest.

△
A sort of marital La Ronde in the Lubitsch manner, but with the maestro's lightness of touch conspicuously absent, **Don't Tell The Wife** brought together a quintet of attractive performers in a Paris-based tale of extra-marital dalliance that always promised more than it delivered. Its stars were Irene Rich (right), Huntly Gordon (left) Lilyan Tashman, Otis Harlan and William Demarest. Rex Taylor wrote it and the director was Paul Stein.

△
Hills of Kentucky was the one in which Rin-Tin-Tin saved the heroine from plunging to certain death over a cataract. He did quite a lot else besides, proving, once and for all, that a dog's life is anything but dull. He was called Grey Ghost and appeared with Rin-Tin-Tin Jr, whom he managed to help out of difficulties by dislodging a piece of wood to which the pup had been chained. He also befriends a crippled youngster, and, of course, tracks down the villain. Edward Clark wrote it (from a story by Dorothy Yost) and the director was Howard Bretherton. Jason Robards (left), Dorothy Dwan, Tom Santschi and Billy Kent Shaeffer (as the crippled lad) co-starred.

What Every Girl Should Know gave Patsy Ruth Miller (illustrated) a chance to exercise her other talent — tennis. For in it she and Hollywood champion Carmelita Geraghty were seen competing in a tournament. What it all had to do with a plot

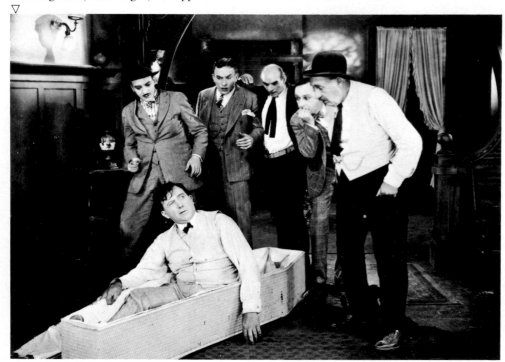

involving two child institutions to which ▷
Miss Miller and her young brothers are
confined after their older brother – who
helps to support them – is jailed, was as
much a mystery as the question implicit in
the title. Inherent in Lois Jackson's screenplay (from a story by Jack Wagner) was a
criticism of the sort of institutions that
separate brothers and sisters, but social
comment was not the film's basic intention.
Charles F. Reisner directed, and his cast
included Ian Keith, Carol Nye and Little
Mickey McBain.

White Flannels went over the top in its
telling of a trite story about a 20-year-
old boy whose possessive mother stands in
the way of his engagement to a local girl,
believing – as the wife of an ill-educated
coal-miner – that her son should receive a
college education. Possible disenchantment
with C. Graham Baker's tear-drenched
screenplay (from a story by Lucien Cary)
resulted in director Lloyd Bacon taking a
crowbar to the narrative, and hammering
exceptionally unsubtle performances out
of Louise Dresser (as the mother), Jason
Robards (as the son, centre), and Virginia
Brown Faire' (as the college flirt) as well
as Warner Richmond, George Nichols, and
Brooks Benedict, who were cast in supporting roles.
▽

△
Bitter Apples was a far-fetched drama which
starred Monte Blue (left) as a young
banker and Myrna Loy (right) as the
daughter of an Italian investor who commits suicide when the bank collapses. Blue
is blamed for the collapse, and Miss Loy
sets out to revenge her father's suicide.
But, as happened in *My Official Wife* (1926),
revenge soon turned to love and, after
being shipwrecked with Blue, she agrees
to marry him. It was written and directed
by Harry Hoyt (from a story by Harold
McGrath).

Director Byron Haskins was completely defeated by C. Graham Baker's screenplay
(from the story by Albert S. Howson and
Sidney R. Buchman) of **Matinée Ladies**, a
lightweight trifle which revolved around a
group of wives who, tired of their spouses,
seek diversion with paid dancing partners
at an afternoon club. May McAvoy (right)
and Malcolm McGregor (left) starred, with
Hedda Hopper, Margaret Seddon, Richard
Tucker, Jean Lefferty, Cissy Fitzgerald and
William Demarest in featured roles.
▽

The Brute was an entertaining enough
Western with a plot that did not bear
close examination (it pits Monte Blue
as an easy-going kind of guy against a
shady character called 'Square Deal' Fenton,
whose chief means of making money is
befuddling cowpuncher's brains with alcohol, then robbing them). Blue and director
Irving Cummings did well enough with the
material, and so, in support, did Leila
Hyams, Clyde Cook, Carol Nye and Paul
Nicholson. It was written by Harvey Gates
from a story by W. Douglas Newton.
▽

△
Irene Rich (left) played the Duchess of
Aragon in **The Climbers,** loosely based on
the Clyde Fitch play of the same name,
loosely written by Tom Gibson, and loosely
directed by Paul Stein. Miss Rich is wooed by
the King of Spain, much to the annoyance
of his mistress, who forces the Duchess out
of the country and into Puerto Rico. After
that, the Duchess is called on to behave in a
most unladylike manner, riding horses
cowboy fashion, and duelling with brigands
in true John Barrymore style. What it all
added up to was, alas, very little. Also
featured were Clyde Cook, Forrest Stanley,
Flobelle Fairbanks (right), Myrna Loy and
Dot Farley.

◁ With the hero trapped in a deep hole in the ground, and the heroine hanging on for dear life as a waterfall gushes over her, Rin-Tin-Tin had his work cut out in **Tracked by the Police**. Known by the villain of the piece as 'that devil dog', old Rinty (who, in dog calculations, must have been hitting the equivalent of almost seventy) effects all sorts of ingenious escapes, proving, in the process, that you certainly can teach old dogs new tricks. Jason Robards (pictured with Rinty), Virginia Brown Faire, Tom Santschi, Dave Morris and Theodore Lorch tried in vain to get a look in, but upstaging was probably Rinty's greatest trick of all. Gregory Rogers (Darryl Zanuck) wrote the story, John W. Gray did the screenplay and Ray Enright directed. It was, predictably, an enormous hit.

May McAvoy (centre) at her prettiest starred in **Irish Hearts**, a sob story about an Irish lass who joins her sweetheart (Warner Richmond) in America, only to discover that he has no intention of marrying her at all. Her disappointment turns to elation (though it was difficult to tell from her performance which was which) with the arrival of Jason Robards, a man altogether more worthy of her love. C. Graham Baker and Bess Meredyth adapted it from a story by Melville Crossman (alias Darryl Zanuck) and the director was former cameraman Byron Haskins. Also cast was Walter Perry as the girl's drunken father.

▽

Simple Sis was entertainment for the simple minded. It miscast Louise Fazenda (illustrated) as a laundry girl on the lookout for a lover, with a bashful Clyde Cook as the man she eventually finds. Helen Klumph's story (adapted by Albert Kenyon) involved a pathetic orphan (Billy Kent Schaeffer) as well as a fire, but nothing managed to overcome the story's tedium. Herman Raymaker directed. Also cast were William Demarest, Myrna Loy, Betty Kent and Cathleen Calhoun.
▽

A lustreless romance between Monte Blue (right) and Edna Murphy (left), plus a climax involving a runaway coach hardly gave audiences value for money, and **The Black Diamond Express** failed to gather momentum at the box office. The story of an engine driver (Blue) whose love for Miss Murphy is discouraged by her social climbing mother (Myrtle Stedman), it featured Claire McDowell, William Demarest and Carol Nye in support, was written by Harvey Gates from a story by Darryl Zanuck, and was directed by Howard Bretherton.
▽

What Happened to Father, from a story by Mary Roberts Rinehart, directed by John Adolfi, was that he changed from being a henpecked husband to a dominating one. Warner Oland, as father, headed the cast, and made a meal of his role as an absentminded Egyptologist who, unknown to his family, writes musical comedies on the side. Flobelle Fairbanks was his daughter, John Miljan the unsavoury millionaire she almost marries, Hugh Allen the decent man she ▷ finally catches and Vera Lewis the overbearing mother whose role as head of the household Oland (centre) finally usurps. There was more conviction in the performances than in Charles Condon's screenplay. Busy William Demarest was also in the cast.

Dolores Costello and Jason Robards were the star-crossed lovers in **The Heart of Maryland**. Unfortunately, she was a Southerner, he a Union man, and as it all took place during the Civil War, numerous complications interfered with the romance, ▷ until the armistice came and all was well. This could not be said, however, for C. Graham Baker's screenplay (based on the play by David Belasco) which relied heavily on coincidence. Lloyd Bacon directed (his best moment being the climax atop a bell tower) and the cast included Myrna Loy, Warner Richmond (left), Charles Bull (as Abraham Lincoln) and Helene Costello (right).

◁ Director Michael Curtiz demonstrated his whole box of cinematic tricks in **A Million Bid**, desperately attempting to salvage Robert Dillon's adaptation of the George Cameron play on which it was based. Basically the story of a woman who, acting on her mother's instructions, deserts the man she really loves and marries someone she doesn't, it starred Betty Blythe as the mother, Warner Oland (left) as the husband and Dolores Costello (right) as the daughter. The plot had Oland disappearing, presumed drowned, only to reappear suffering from amnesia. Though befuddled, he realizes that his wife still loves the man she walked out on (a surgeon, played by Malcolm McGregor) and conveniently vanishes for a second time. Audiences seemed to vanish as well. Also cast were William Demarest, Douglas Gerrard and Grace Gordon.

△
Irene Rich (right) not only had to suffer an impossible scenario in **Dearie**, but also the selfishness of a priggish son who believed he was a genius, and whom (unknown to him) she supported by performing in a night-club under the soubriquet 'Dearie', her real name being Sylvia Darling. William Collier Jr was the thoroughly objectionable son. Others involved in Anthony Coldeway's adaptation of Carolyn Wells's story were Edna Murphy, Anders Randolph, Richard Tucker (left), Arthur Rankin and Douglas Gerrard. Director Archie Mayo underlined every dramatic moment in thick red lines when what was required was an editor's ruthless blue pencil.

Sydney Chaplin (right) did much more than was required of him to secure laughs in **The Missing Link,** a trifle in which he played an impoverished poet who impersonates a big game hunter in an attempt to locate the missing link. Unfortunately the poet has an aversion to animals. Competing with (as well as dodging) a pride of lions, a chimpanzee, a leopard, and a dog, Chaplin admittedly had some funny moments. But under Charles F. Reisner's full-steam-ahead direction, it was all too frantic for comfort. Darryl Zanuck wrote the screen-play, Reisner the story. Also cast were Ruth Hall (left), Tom McGuire, Crauford Kent, Sam Baker and a chimp called Akka.

Strong production values, a capable cast and solid direction (by Ralph Graves, left, who also starred and wrote the story), gave an unlikely romance called **A Reno Divorce** a quality absent from Robert Lord's adapta-tion. May McAvoy as an attractive heiress and Graves, as a successful artist, fall in love following a motor accident. Their idyll, however, is interrupted by a misunder-standing, and only several years later, when a chance meeting brings them face to face, are they reconciled. More convincing than it sounds, it also featured Robert Ober and Hedda Hopper (right).
▽

Bess Meredyth's reworking of Abbé Prevost's *Manon Lescaut* surfaced as **When a Man Loves,** with John Barrymore (right) as des Grieux and Dolores Costello (left) as Manon. It was the third of the studio's feature films to have a Vitaphone orchestral accompaniment. The picturesque tale of a gallant hero who escapes from a French prison ship taking Manon with him, it provided Barrymore with all the scope he could possibly have wanted to demonstrate his prowess with a sword and his way with a woman. It has been said that he under-played in order to allow his real-life sweet-heart, Miss Costello, to shine. But to judge from his braggadocio histrionics, there was little evidence of dramatic reticence. There was no holding back, either, from Warner Oland, the quintessential screen villain, as Manon's brother, or Stuart Holmes as Louis XV. Others responding well to Alan Crosland's brisk direction were Sam De Grasse, Holmes Herbert, Marcelle Corday, Charles Clary, Templar Saxe, and Eugenie Besserer. It was a popular as well as a critical success.
▽

△
A.E.W. Mason's play *Green Stockings* came to the screen as **Slightly Used** and starred May McAvoy (right) who, to get round her father's insistence that her two younger sisters cannot marry before she does, invents a husband for herself called Major Smith. Needless to say, the fictitious Major materializes bringing with him chaos and confusion. Miss McAvoy was splendid as the eldest sister, so was Conrad Nagel (left) as the Major. Also cast were Bobby Agnew, Audrey Ferris (making her debut for the studio) and Anders Randolph. C. Graham Baker wrote the screenplay from a story by Melville Crossman (Darryl Zanuck) and Archie Mayo directed. The film was remade in 1930 as *Flirting Widow.*

The Desired Woman left a great deal to be desired. Directed by Michael Curtiz from a scenario by Anthony Coldeway, and a story by Mark Canfield (Darryl Zanuck) good use was made of its desert background, but nothing very satisfactory could be done with a plot involving an officer's wife (Irene Rich, left) and the havoc she causes among the men stationed in an isolated fortress in the Sahara. Competent perform-ances, however, came from Miss Rich, William Russell (her jealous husband), William Collier Jr (right), Douglas Gerrard, Jack Ackroyd, John Miljan and Richard Tucker.
▽

◁ Stunningly photographed by Hal Mohr and directed by Alan Crosland with immense assurance, **Old San Francisco** was a preposterous melodrama (with a musical sound track and appropriate sound effects) that looked a great deal better than the story warranted. All about an aristocratic family of Spanish settlers, it was given what little impetus it had by evil Warner Oland who, on revealing that his veins flowed with Oriental blood, caused a tremor which might conceivably have brought about the great earthquake of 1906. The story was by Darryl Zanuck, the screenplay by Anthony Coldeway, and Dolores Costello (left) was the star of this slick production. Also cast was Josef Swickard (right).

△
Another Rin-Tin-Tin melodrama, **Jaws of Steel**, written by Darryl Zanuck under his alias Gregory Rogers and adapted by Charles Condon, retained its workmanlike standards. This time, Rinty had to live down a rumour that he was a vicious killer, which he did by protecting a baby girl from a multiplicity of hazards. Jason Robards, Helen Ferguson and Mary Louise Miller (illustrated) were also in the cast, and the director was Ray Enright.

One-Round Hogan was a boxing drama that failed to pack a knockout punch, but could perhaps be called a win on points instead. The story of a fighter (Monte Blue, left) who, as a result of a friend's death in the ring, almost wrecks his own career by holding back, it was again written by the team of Zanuck and Condon and directed by Howard Bretherton. Though predictable, it was well structured with most of the excitement saved for the climactic match in the last reel. Leila Hyams (right) was Blue's sweetheart, with James J. Jeffries and Tom Gallery also cast.

▽

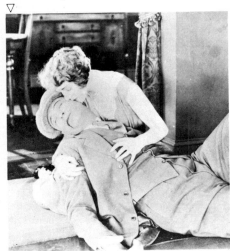

The automobile's supremacy over the horse was the theme of **The First Auto**, the sentimental tale (circa 1895) of a feud between a horse-loving father and his automobile-favouring son. Director Roy Del Ruth, not content with simply telling Darryl Zanuck's story, crammed the narrative with factual details regarding the first horseless carriages, and with humour as well as conviction, evoked the pioneering spirit that gave birth to the new invention. Russell Simpson (left) played the old-fashioned father splendidly, and Charles Emmett Mack his son. (Sadly, Mack did not live to see the film completed. He died in a car crash on his way to the studio four months prior to the film's release.) Also appearing were veteran racer Barney Oldfield, Patsy Ruth Miller, Frank Campeau, William Demarest and Paul Kruger (right).
▽

George Jessel's second Izzy Murphy comedy was a bizarre item called **Sailor Izzy Murphy** which had Jessel (illustrated), as a street vendor of scents, falling in love with the beautiful woman whose picture adorns the perfume bottles he sells. After resourcefully tracing the beauty (whose father happens to manufacture the perfume) to a luxury yacht, he finds himself in the company of an escaped lunatic who has vowed to murder the perfume manufacturer in retaliation for all the flowers that have been lost in the making of the scent. But Izzy saves the day by overpowering the lunatic, and is rewarded for his bravery by winning the love of the grateful manufacturer's daughter. Audrey Ferris was the girl, Warner Oland her father and John Miljan the loony. It was written by Edward T. Lowe Jr and directed by Henry Lehrman, who together with Lowe provided the story. ▷

△
Monte Blue (centre left) was not at his best in **The Bush Leaguer**. He played the proprietor of a small garage who deserts his business (and a new-fangled petrol pump he is in the midst of inventing) to pursue a career as a baseball player. After a few minor setbacks Dame Fortune gives him the nod. He sells his patent on the new pump, becomes a baseball star and falls in love with a rather insipid Leila Hyams (left). Harvey Gates adapted Charles Gordon Saxton's story, and Howard Bretherton directed. Clyde Cook (centre right) and William Demarest were also in the cast.

△
A Sailor's Sweetheart was low comedy at its lowest. It starred Louise Fazenda (right) as a headmistress who is left a fortune on condition that no scandal ever be associated with her name. Need one mention it, but scandal was just around the corner... Also cast were Clyde Cook (left), John Miljan, Tom Rickett, and Myrna Loy. Harvey Gates wrote the script from a story by George Godfrey and the director was Lloyd Bacon.

A vehicle for George Jessel (centre), **Ginsberg the Great** was a moderately entertaining comedy about a tailor's assistant (Jessel) whose ambition is to become a successful conjuror. He fails but not before apprehending a gang of jewel thieves. Audrey Ferris (left) co-starred as the girl he loves, with other roles assigned to Theodore Lorch and Gertrude Astor. Anthony Coldeway wrote it and the director was Byron Haskins.
▽

Effective performances from Myrna Loy (illustrated), Conrad Nagel and William Russell gave **The Girl From Chicago** what little quality it had. Written by C. Graham Baker from a story by Arthur Somers Roche, this gangland yarn had Miss Loy, aided by her detective lover 'Handsome' Joe (Nagel) outwitting the thug who murdered her brother. Director Ray Enright did his best, but almost from the beginning he failed to keep the clichés in check. Also cast were Carol Nye, Paul Panzer and Erville Alderson.
▽

Sydney Chaplin (left) starred in **The Fortune ▷ Hunter**, a rather woebegone comedy adapted by Robert Dillon and Bryan Foy from a play by Winchell Smith. A few sporadic laughs and the good looks of co-star Helene Costello hardly justified the price of admission. Sabotaged by his leading man's desperate attempts at humour, there was little director Charles F. Reisner could do with a story which had Chaplin as a cafe bouncer going respectable in a hick town in order to marry into money. Others involved included Clara Horton, Duke Martin, Thomas Jefferson, Erville Alderson, Paul Kruger and Nora Cecil.

Dolores Costello's melting good looks were put to excellent use in **The College Widow**, a nicely turned comedy about an inferior college football team whose game needs a boost. This turns out to be Miss Costello (centre), who gives each member of the team the impression that she is in love with him, and only him, knowing that her interest will spur them on to great things on the day of the big match. Inevitably, complications arise when the lads get wise to her ploy, and director Archie Mayo had a field-day resolving it all. Audiences benefited from his expertise, from the teamwork displayed by William Collier Jr, Douglas Gerrard (right), Guinn 'Big Boy' Williams (left) and Anders Randolph, and from Peter Milne and Paul Schofield's adroit reworking of George Ade's play. It was remade as *Freshman Love* in 1936.
▽

◁In **The Silver Slave** Irene Rich played a self-sacrificing mother who was quite prepared to suffer a fate worse than death at the hands of the villain rather than allow him to take advantage of her attractive daughter (Audrey Ferris). Director Howard Bretherton brought nothing fresh to the Peter Milne-Anthony Coldeway screenplay (from a story by Howard Smith) and the performances were merely adequate. Miss Rich (right) starred, with Miss Ferris (centre), Holmes Herbert, John Miljan (left) and Carol Nye in support.

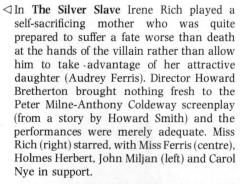

Roy Del Ruth milked a few laughs from **If I Were Single**, another comedy of marital infidelity in which a flirtatious brunette (Myrna Loy, left) does her best to break up a marriage between May McAvoy and Conrad Nagel (right), and almost succeeds, but not before Miss McAvoy has a little flirtation of her own with a rather effeminate specimen in the shape of André Beranger. It was written by Robert Lord.
▽

△
A ferocious knuckle fight between Monte Blue and William Russell was the dramatic highpoint of **Brass Knuckles**, a well mounted drama about an ex-con who, on his release from prison, 'adopts' the 17-year old daughter of a fellow inmate, is reformed by her innocence, and, in time, marries her. Betty Bronson (left) was in fine form as the girl, Monte Blue (right) turned in a more than adequate performance, but comedian George E. Stone was better than both of them as one of Blue's fellow prisoners. Harvey Gates wrote it, Lloyd Bacon was the director.

t is of no consequence at all that **The Jazz Singer** is really a rather wretched drama about a rabbi's son (Al Jolson, illustrated), whose love of show business causes a rift between him and his orthodox father; a rift which is finally resolved on the old man's death bed on the eve of the Jewish Day of Atonement. The eye-rolling, breast-beating, hair-tugging style of acting indulged in by Warner Oland (as the rabbi) and Eugenie Besserer as his wife, a woman torn between the love of a husband and the love of a son, gives the film a ludicrous aspect today which, again, is of little consequence. What is really important about **The Jazz Singer** is that it was the first motion picture in which spoken dialogue was heard. True, the words uttered by Jolson were improvised (contrast their freshness with some of the film's silent titles, a typical example being 'God made her a woman and love made her a mother') and although the words he spoke numbered only 281, plus a few astonished ad libs from Miss Besserer, they revitalized the film business and helped to turn Warner Bros. into one of the top three studios in the industry. Apart from its revolutionary aspect, **The Jazz Singer** gave a wide audience a chance to see and experience Jolson performing as he must have done in those legendary Winter Garden concerts in New York. After watching and listening to him weave his magic on the film's musical numbers it was not difficult to understand why he was called the greatest entertainer in the world. Others in this epoch-making production were May McAvoy, (in Jolson's arms) the celebrated cantor Joseph Rosenblatt, Otto Lederer and William Demarest. **The Jazz Singer** was photographed by Hal Mohr and directed by Alan Crosland. It was written by Alfred A. Cohn from a story and play by Samson Raphaelson. Songs included: Blue Skies (by Irving Berlin), Mother I Still Have You (by Al Jolson and Louis Silvers), My Mammy (by Sam Lewis, Joe Young and Walter Donaldson) and Toot Toot Tootsie Goodbye (by Gus Kahn, Ernie Erdman and Dan Russo).

Director Michael Curtiz needed more than a variety of cinematic tricks to rescue **Good Time Charley** from absurd sentimentality. The hearts-and-flowers story of an old-time actor whom misfortune stalks with cruel determination, it alternated mawkishness with misplaced bouts of humour finishing up as an impoverished variation on the Job theme. Darryl Zanuck and Owen Davis contrived the plot, Anthony Coldeway and Owen Francis turned it into a screenplay. Warner Oland, fresh from his role as the rabbi in *The Jazz Singer* starred as the put-upon actor and Helene Costello (illustrated) was his daughter. Also cast were Clyde Cook, Montagu Love, Hugh Allan and Julanne Johnston.

Released in the same month as *The Jazz Singer* but in complete contrast, was **A Dog of the Regiment,** a Rin-Tin-Tin adventure whose only element in common with the first 'talkie' was that they both made money. Set against a World War One background, the star's *pièce de résistance*

One of the studio's last silent comedies, **Ham and Eggs at the Front** (released in Britain as **Ham and Eggs**) was advertised either as 'The Big Jazz Parade of Burnt-Cork Comedians in the Trenches' or as 'Two darkies' hair-raising adventures with girls, ghosts and guns in No Man's Land'. Ham and Eggs, the two main characters, were played by whites in black-face (Tom Wilson, centre and Charlie Conklin, left) with Myrna Loy (right) on hand as a dusky Senegalese girl who uses her wiles to elicit information out of them. It was written by Darryl Zanuck, adapted by Robert Dillon and James Starr, and was directed, with many genuinely funny touches, by Roy Del Ruth.

was rescuing pilot Tom Gallery (illustrated) from a wrecked plane and helping him to escape from his rival in love (John Peters) who orders him to be shot. The object of their affections was Dorothy Gulliver. It was written by Albert S. Howson, scripted by Charles Condon and directed by D. Ross Lederman.

Husbands for Rent, the 43rd and last film Warner Bros. released in 1927, featured marriage and divorce as its twin themes, neither being taken particularly seriously in this light-hearted romp in which Owen Moore (right) and Helene Costello, after a brief six months of marriage, decide they're bored with one another and plan a divorce. Miss Costello's father (Claude Gillingwater) has other ideas, and manages to convince them that they really love each other and should stay married. John Miljan, Kathryn Perry and Arthur Hoyt were also in it; it was scripted by C. Graham Baker from a story by Edwin Justus Mayer, and directed with a pleasing sense of humour by Henry Lehrman.

1928

After the phenomenal success of **The Jazz Singer**, which cost $500,000 to make, brought Warner Bros.' investment in sound to $5,000,000, and made a profit of $3,000,000, the studio's next venture into the successful world of 'talkies' as they were called, was **Tenderloin**, directed by Michael Curtiz.

Tenderloin, which was basically a silent film with a small amount of spoken dialogue interspersed throughout its running time, was followed by two more part-talkies called **Glorious Betsy** with Dolores Costello and **The Lion and the Mouse** with Lionel Barrymore, both of which were reasonably successful.

In 1928, with talking pictures continuing to be the main topic of conversation in the industry, work commenced on the construction of the studio's fourth and largest sound stage. By the end of the year, Vitaphone sound equipment had found its way into more than 400 theatres across the country.

1928 also saw the release of the first complete all-talking feature film, another Warner Bros. triumph. It was an old-fashioned melodrama called **The Lights of New York** and was directed by Bryan Foy, an ambitious young gag writer on the lot, who had hitherto supervised the production of some 300 Vitaphone musical shorts. Originally intended as a two-reeler (Jack Warner felt that Foy, a virtual newcomer to direction, was not ready to handle something as important as the studio's first 100 per cent all-talking film) it was nonetheless shot to feature length and, with Albert Warner's approval, released as such.

The Lights of New York, which was a financial success, was followed by **The Terror** with May McAvoy and Louise Fazenda, and **The Singing Fool**, with Al Jolson. **The Singing Fool** was an out-and-out smash and the most successful film the Warners had ever made. Other talking or part-talking productions released during this busy year included **State Street Sadie, Women They Talk About, The Midnight Taxi, The Home Towners, My Man, On Trial** and the particularly successful **Caught in the Fog**.

On September 13th, 1928, as part of a massive spending spree, Warner Bros. borrowed $100,000,000 from Goldman, Sachs and Hayden, and Stone and Co., and bought out the powerful Stanley Corporation of America, one of the country's largest theatre chains (over 250 theatres in 75 cities and 7 states, including the luxurious Strand Theatre on Broadway) thus ensuring all future Warner Bros. product a nationwide distribution. As a result of the move, Warner Bros. shares rose from $28 to $130 a share.

The following month, the control of First National Pictures, which was formed in 1917 by a group of independent exhibitors in order to break Adolph Zukor's domination of the industry and which soon became America's largest theatre chain as well as an important production company with studios in Hollywood and New York, passed to Warner Bros. who had bought 42,000 of the company's 75,000 shares, the rest of the shares belonging to Fox West Coast Theatres.

Jack Warner, now the head of production for Warner Bros. with Darryl Zanuck his second in command, moved into the First National Studios in Burbank, which he wired for sound, with Al Rockett remaining as production head of First National, whose roster of stars included Colleen Moore, Douglas Fairbanks Jr, Billie Dove, Loretta Young, the Talmadge sisters, Richard Barthelmess, Harry Langdon, Basil Rathbone, Constance Bennett, Alice White and Milton Sills. Both companies would work in tandem, sharing equally the facilities offered by Vitaphone in what was a new departure for First National, who hitherto had made only silent films.

In November 1928 Warner Bros. purchased the Skouras Brothers theatres of St. Louis, and paid off all their outstanding bank loans. The year ended with publicity man Hal B. Wallis being made studio manager of First National. The year's net profit was $2,044,841.

△ The plot devised by Franz Jacques for **Beware of Married Men** and brought to the screen in a scenario by E.T. Lowe Jr, was a highly mechanical affair in which a womanizer – complete with cocktail shaker and Japanese manservant as symbols of sophistication – lures a variety of ladies to his glamorous pad. Some come to be seduced, others to prevent their sisters from being seduced, but in the end everything turns out well. The capable cast included Irene Rich (left), Audrey Ferris, Clyde Cook, Myrna Loy, Richard Tucker, Stuart Holmes (right) and Hugh Allan.

△ Heralded as the first actual talking picture in which the characters spoke their film roles, **Tenderloin**, directed by Michael Curtiz, was a murky melodrama about a dancer (Dolores Costello) accused of stealing $50,000. As a result, she receives no peace from the law nor from the crooked underworld in which she moves. Of its 88 minutes running time, 15 were devoted to actual speech, though E.T. Lowe Jr's dialogue (from a story by Zanuck under the alias of Melville Crossman) might just as well have been spelled out on title cards, so unspeakably hammy was it. However, many of the studio's gangsterland trademarks were beginning to surface – particularly in Hal Mohr's photography with its emphasis on cold, wet streets and sordid little rooms. And Miss Costello (centre), despite her tribulations, looked stunning. Conrad Nagel appeared somewhat uncomfortably as a gangster, with other parts going to Mitchell Lewis, George E. Stone, Dan Wolheim and Pat Hartigan. On the same programme at the Warners Theatre in New York where **Tenderloin** was premiered, were a series of Vitaphone short subjects featuring, among others, 'Cugat and his Gigolos', and Beniamino Gigli and Giuseppe de Luca singing a duet from *The Pearl Fishers*. Though these musical items were all warmly applauded, the feature they accompanied met with derisive laughter.

◁ Another Rin-Tin-Tin melodrama, **A Race for Life** was about a lad who runs away from home with his pet dog, and heads for a race track determined to become a famous jockey. Rinty of course comes up trumps for his young master, who in turn comes up trumps for the owner of the horse he is riding in the big race. The brainchild of Charles R. Condon, it was directed by D. Ross Lederman and also featured Bobby Gordon (illustrated), Virginia Brown Faire, Carol Nye and Pat Hartigan.

Rin-Tin-Tin, a dog of the desert, had every ▷ reason to turn his back on humanity in **Rinty of the Desert,** for, on arriving in the city where he is given a home by Audrey Ferris (centre), he finds himself badly treated by Paul Panzer, as an animal trainer. All the same, he saves his mistress from Panzer's unwelcome attentions and comes to the rescue of her grandfather (Otto Hoffman) who is being held prisoner by a gang of hooligans. D. Ross Lederman directed from a screenplay by Harvey Gates, and Frank Steele supplied the story. Carol Nye (centre left) was also in the cast.

△
Some excellent aerial photography of New York and the coast of France, plus a behind-the-scenes look at the construction of aeroplanes lent interest to **Across the Atlantic,** an otherwise routine story of a pilot (Monte Blue, right) who loses his memory in the war and is presumed dead. Years later, however, he surfaces, takes a job in an aeroplane factory and has his memory restored to him while flying at a high altitude. Scenarist Harvey Gates, working from a story by John W. Ransome, compounded the implausibility of it all by devising an ending in which the pilot flies a plane designed by his father across the Atlantic to find, on arriving in France, his wife and father waiting to welcome him. The real stars of the film were the planes, and they successfully managed to upstage Blue, Edna Murphy (left, as his wife), Burr McIntosh, Irene Rich and Robert Ober. Howard Bretherton directed.

The Lion and the Mouse, a part-talkie with 31 minutes of dialogue, demonstrated more fully than the three earlier Vitaphone productions, that most screen performers were simply not capable of acting and talking at the same time. Consumed with self-consciousness, burdened with unspeakable dialogue, and cursed with inadequate, untrained voices, many of them floundered hopelessly. An exception was Lionel Barrymore (right), the star of **The Lion and the Mouse** who bulldozed his way through the role of a powerful financier by taking sound in his stride and changing Robert Lord's dialogue (from the play by Charles Klein) to suit the character he was playing. The same could not be said for his co-star May McAvoy as the mouse who takes him, or for William Collier Jr (left) as Barrymore's son. There were also signs of insecurity in Lloyd Bacon's tentative direction. Alec B. Francis, Emmett Corrigan and Jack Ackroyd completed the cast.
▽

△
Audiences ignored the plot of an inconsequential comedy called **Pay As You Enter** just as writers Darryl Zanuck (alias Gregory Rogers) and Fred Stanley did. They concentrated, instead, on the antics of the protagonists Clyde Cook (right) and William Demarest (centre left) as a tram driver and bus conductor out to win the love of a coffee-stall owner played by Louise Fazenda (centre right). Myrna Loy (left) was also in the cast, and it was directed by Lloyd Bacon.

△
Five and Ten Cent Annie, a vehicle for the combined talents of Louise Fazenda (right) and Clyde Cook (centre), cast the latter as a streetcleaner who inherits a million dollars from his uncle on condition that (a) he retains the uncle's valet until such time as he, the streetcleaner, marries, and (b) that he appears at the lawyer's office promptly at 5 p.m. on an appointed day. Complications arise as a result of the valet's determination to ruin the arrangement, and the hero and heroine's equal determination to see that he doesn't. The two stars, abetted by director Roy Del Ruth, worked hard to keep it afloat, and the strain showed. It was written by Robert Lord and Charles R. Condon (from a story by Jack Warner alias Leon Zuardo) and, in support, featured William Demarest (left), Gertrude Astor, Tom Ricketts, Douglas Gerrard and André Beranger. It was released in Britain as **Ambitious Annie.**

◁ Snobbery may not be one of the seven deadly sins, but one would have certainly gained the impression that it was from **The Little Snob,** a preachy piece starring May McAvoy as a working-class girl who gets ideas above her station when her father, a Coney Island employee, saves enough money to send her to finishing school. Even at 52 minutes Robert Lord's screenplay (from a story by Edward T. Lowe Jr) seemed padded, though there was no denying Miss McAvoy's (centre) effectiveness in the role. John Adolfi directed the film, and his cast included Robert Frazer, Alec Francis, John Miljan, Virginia Lee Corbin (left) and Frances Lee (right).

Myrna Loy (right) once again found herself ▷
cast in the role of an Oriental in **The
Crimson City**, a picturesque, generally
successful drama of suspense and intrigue
which also starred John Miljan as a young
American on the run from the police for a
crime he did not commit, Matthew Betz
as the villainous Daggar Foo and Leila
Hyams as Miljan's sweetheart. Anna May
Wong (centre) was in attendance, too,
adding a touch of authenticity, with other
parts being taken by Richard Tucker,
Anders Randolph and Sojin. Anthony
Coldeway wrote it and Archie Mayo was
the director.

Powder My Back gave Irene Rich (left) yet
another chance to work her feminine wiles
on the opposite sex. She played a showgirl
who gets her revenge on a politician who
closes her current show (he thinks it's
immoral) by seducing and eventually marrying him. But not before she wins his son's
heart as well. Anders Randolph overacted
as the politician, but Miss Rich was fine.
Others involved in Roy Del Ruth's undistinguished caper were Carol Nye (right),
André Beranger and Audrey Ferris. It was
written by Robert Lord from a story by
Jerome Kingston.
▽

△
State Street Sadie, another faltering excursion into Vitaphone territory, was a part-
talkie in which Conrad Nagel (playing a
dual role) and Myrna Loy were given a
chance to outsmart a bunch of crooks, one
of whom ends his days by taking a flying
leap from the top of a skyscraper. Both
Nagel (left) and Loy (centre) coped with
the demands of the overhead microphone
well enough, though co-star William Russell
(right) was unhappy throughout. Archie
Mayo, clearly easing his way into new territory, was the director, and E.T. Lowe Jr wrote
it from a story by Melville Crossman (Zanuck
again). George E. Stone and Pat Hartigan
were also cast. It was released in Britain as
The Girl from State Street.

Advertised as the studio's first 100 per cent
all-talking picture, **Lights of New York** was a
catastrophe as a piece of film-making but a
landmark all the same. Battling with a
plot that would have been old-fashioned
in the early silent era, (country yokel
exploited by the wicked denizens of Broadway) Helene Costello (right), Cullen Landis
(left), Gladys Brockwell, Mary Carr and
Eugene Pallette proved they were more
intrepid than Christopher Columbus as
they gamely but unsuccessfully explored the
new world of the talking picture. Though
the sound quality itself was little better
than turn of the century phonograph
recordings (Miss Costello's voice came in
for particular censure), audiences responded
to the novelty, turning the 57 minute
feature, which had cost $75,000, into a
two million dollar hit. It was written by
Hugh Herbert and Murray Roth (from a
story by Charles L. Gaskill) and directed
by Bryan Foy.
▽

An amusing farce, **Domestic Troubles**
starred Clyde Cook (centre) as an identical
twin who, when his brother (also played by
Cook) is sent to jail, changes places with
him much to the confusion of both men's
wives who have not been told of the ploy.
The rich vein of comic possibilities were
delightfully tapped by director Ray Enright,
scenarist C. Graham Baker and a cast that
included Arthur Rankin, Betty Blythe, Jean
Lafferty and Louise Fazenda.
▽

For some reason English audiences found
it all an enormous giggle but Americans
took the creepiness of **The Terror** seriously,
thus ensuring its success at the box office.
All about an organ-playing homicidal
maniac who terrorizes the guests in a
British hostelry, it starred May McAvoy
(left), Louise Fazenda, Edward Everett Horton (who became a staple ingredient of
the Warner Bros. stock company) and Alec B.
Francis (right). It was the first feature without a single subtitle, and as in Orson Welles'
The Magnificent Ambersons (RKO) 14 years
later, the film's titles were spoken (by Conrad
Nagel) with other experiments on the Vitaphone disc in the shape of rain, thunder,
creaking floorboards and organ recitals.
Some less charitable critics also regarded
Miss McAvoy's rather squeaky voice as a
sound effect. Based on a story by Edgar
Wallace, it was written by Harvey Gates.
Also cast were Frank Austin and John Miljan,
in one of the 12 films he made in 1928.
▽

Women They Talk About, a part-talkie, did nothing to enhance the cause of Vitaphone. A comedy with more than a touch of melodrama, it pivoted on two relationships, one of which involved the mayor of a city (Anders Randolph) and his renewed friendship with an erstwhile sweetheart (Irene Rich, right) the other concerning the mayor's son (William Collier Jr) and his romance with Miss Rich's pretty daughter (Audrey Ferris, left). There was nothing exceptional about the supporting performances of Claude Gillingwater, Jack Sanford and John Miljan, Lloyd Bacon's direction or the screenplay by Robert Lord from a story by Anthony Coldeway.

The Head Man was a First National Film which Warner Bros. released after their take-over of that studio. The story of a bibulous ex-senator whose outrageous behaviour while under the influence of alcohol leads indirectly to his being elected mayor, it strained belief, and was performed by its two stars, Charlie Murray (as the drunk) and Lucien Littlefield (right) in a manner that suggested total inebriation. Loretta Young in her first film for Warner Bros. was also featured, and so was Larry Kent, but they made no impact at all. Harvey Thew and Howard Green wrote it (from a story by Harry Leon Wilson) and the director was Eddie Cline.

Audiences and critics both agreed that **Glorious Betsy** lived up to its title. A reworking of Rida Johnson Young's play about the romance between Napoleon's younger brother Jerome and a Baltimore girl called Elizabeth Patterson, it mixed sentimentality with action in nicely balanced proportions giving its two leading stars, Dolores Costello (left) and Conrad Nagel (right), lots of scope. Though Napoleon vetoes the romance, wishing his brother to marry Princess Fredericka of Wurttemberg instead, scenarist Anthony Coldeway defied the Emperor by coming up with the obligatory happy ending and produced a screenplay that positively billowed with romance. Alan Crosland directed and his cast included John Miljan, Marc McDermott, Betty Blythe, Paul Panzer, Michael Vavitch and Pasquale Amato (as Napoleon). It was a great success.

Director John G. Adolfi featured a stutterer in his part-talking melodrama **The Midnight Taxi,** not as a symbol of Vitaphone's teething trouble but, on the contrary, as a gesture of confidence in the new medium. Or possibly it was an industry 'in' joke. In either case it certainly pleased audiences who fell about laughing at the sight and sound of the afflicted man attempting to say his piece as quickly as possible. A story with a bootlegging background, it was full of action with carefully delineated goodies and baddies, and starred Helene Costello as the heroine who wastes a lot of time trying to get an unworthy sweetheart out of jail. Freddie Foy adapted it, and contributed the dialogue. The original story was by Darryl Zanuck, again using his Gregory Rogers alias. Also cast were Myrna Loy (illustrated) and Antonio Moreno.

Another typical Rin-Tin-Tin adventure, **Land of the Silver Fox** had Rinty showing his gratitude to a young fur trapper who rescues him from a brutal master. The dramatic highspot in this one was a blinding snow storm in which Rinty and his new owner are set upon by a pack of ferocious wolves. But the dog keeps the wolves at bay and is rewarded for his courage and loyalty by scenarist Charles Condon, who allows him to find a mate. Howard Smith wrote the story and the director was Ray Enright. Also cast were Carol Nye (as the trapper), John Miljan, Leila Hyams and Tom Santschi.

A good solid story (told in flashback), imaginative direction and high quality performances were the distinguishing features of **The Night Watch**. A First World War drama which begins in a courtroom where a court-martial is under way, then flashes back to events leading up to the trial (in which the captain of a war-ship is accused of shooting one of his own officers after finding his wife in another man's cabin aboard ship), it starred Paul Lukas (left) as the captain, and Billie Dove (centre) as his wife. It was directed by Alexander Korda and adapted by Lajos Biro from a play by M. Claude Farrere and Lucienne Nepoty. Others cast were Donald Reed, Nicholas Soussanin (right), Anita Garvine, Gustav Partos and Nicholas Bela. It was remade as *The Woman from Monte Carlo* in 1932. (First National.)

Emile Zola's *Therese Raquin* emerged as **Shadows of Fear**, a European import directed with extraordinary skill and insight by Jacques Feyder. The grim story of an unhappily married woman, who, aided by her artist lover, drowns her husband only to find living with the guilt of her sin intolerable – it featured Gina Manes (left) as the woman Therese, H.A. Schlettow as the lover Laurent, and Charles Barrois as the husband Marchaud. Wolfgang Zelzer (right) was also in it. The beautifully structured scenario was by F. Carlson and Willy Haas. Though not as technically accomplished as some American films of the same vintage, its power and impact were undeniable. (First National.)

◁ **Heart Trouble,** an impoverished vehicle for the rapidly diminishing talents of the once great Harry Langdon (illustrated), eschewed plot in favour of a series of unfunny sight gags (mainly concerned with comedian Langdon's endeavours to enlist in order to please his sweetheart) and should have finished up, in its entirety, on the cutting-room floor. It was written by Clarence Hennecke and Earle Rodney, featured Doris Dawson, Madge Hunt and Lionel Belmore and was directed by Langdon. In every respect it was a sad mistake. (First National.)

Charlie Murray (right) and Louise Fazenda (left) supplied most of the laughs in **Vamping Venus**, a farce directed by Eddie Cline, all about an Irish-American politician who, after receiving a bump on the head, wakes up in ancient Greece. Bernard McConville's story (later variations of which were Goldwyn's 1933 *Roman Scandals* and MGM's 1943 *Dubarry was a Lady*) was adapted by Howard J. Green, with parts in it for Russ Powell, Fred O'Beck, Gustav von Seyffertitz, Gus Partos and Thelma Todd.

Broad farce and lurid melodrama joined forces for **Do Your Duty**, a moderately successful film which starred Charlie Murray (left) as a police sergeant who is framed by a gang of crooks, is demoted in the force, but ultimately has his name cleared thanks to the intervention of Charles Delaney, a young patrolman in love with Murray's daughter. Intended to please uncritical audiences, it succeeded. Lucien Littlefield (right), Ed Brady, Washington Blue, Doris Dawson, Aggie Herring and George Pierce were also in it; William Beaudine was the director, Julien Josephson provided the story, and the screenplay was by Vernon Smith. (First National.)

Based on the play by George M. Cohan, **The Home Towners** was an all-talking feature that, technically, was a marked improvement on its predecessors. A cast capable of handling dialogue was assembled to tell the story of a man (Richard Bennett) who falls for a girl (Doris Kenyon) half his age much to the disapproval of an elderly friend (Robert McWade) who thinks the girl is only after his money and causes a great deal of trouble as he tries to prove his theory. The still shows (from left) Stanley Taylor, Doris Kenyon, Robert Edeson, Robert McWade (seated), Vera Lewis, Richard Bennett and Gladys Brockwell. Only Doris Kenyon seemed ill at ease negotiating the hazard of sound. Director Bryan Foy brought a fluency to Addison Burkhart's sensible adaptation, and his deployment of the Vitaphone process throughout was far more assured than was the case in his earlier *Lights of New York*, and not just a gimmicky appendage. The film was remade in 1936 as *Times Square Playboy* and in 1940 as *Ladies Must Live*.

Director Mack Sennett, temporarily abandoning his bathing beauties and Keystone Kops, ventured into World War One territory with **The Good-Bye Kiss** and effectively told the story of a doughboy whom everyone (including his girlfriend) assumes to be a coward, but who is of course really a hero. Some entertaining bits of comedy (supplied by Matty Kemp) offset the well-staged battle scenes and, in general, the company under Sennett's command acquitted themselves valiantly. They included Johnny Burke (as the hero, left), Sally Eilers (as his girlfriend, right), Wheeler Oakman, Irving Bacon, Lionel Belmore, Eugene Pallette and Andy Clyde. It was written by Mack Sennett and Jefferson Moffitt from a story by Moffitt, Phil Whitman and Carl Harbaugh. (First National.)

The second all-British screen version of ▷
George Pleydell Bancroft's play **The Ware
Case** featured a miscast Stewart Rome (left)
as Sir Hubert Ware, a man accused of
murdering his wife's brother. H. Manning
Haynes directed it from a screenplay by
Lydia Hayward, eliciting from a cast which
included Betty Carter (centre), Ian Fleming,
Wellington Briggs, Patrick Stewart, Cynthia
Murtagh and Cameron Carr, solid rather
than inspired performances. A moderate suc-
cess, it was a British production released by
First National in the US.

The Crash was a feeble effort which starred
Milton Sills (left) as a railway foreman who
unwisely marries Thelma Todd (centre),
an actress in a travelling show. The liaison
brought only unhappiness for the couple and
precious little comfort for audiences either. A
climactic train wreck in the last reel livened
up proceedings momentarily but by then it
was too late. Wade Boteler and William
Demarest (right) were also cast by director
Eddie Cline, and the screenplay, from a story
by Frank L. Packard, was by Charles Kenyon.
(First National.)
▽

◁ Director Benjamin Christensen succeeded in
creating suspense as well as mirth in **The
Haunted House,** a trifle which relied heavily
on the usual clichés associated with
hauntings. Owen Davis's plot, involving a
bunch of greedy relatives on the hunt for
some valuable securities left by the deceased
owner of the mansion, was translated to the
screen by Richard Bee and Lajos Biro, and
performed by Chester Conklin (left), Thelma
Todd (centre), Larry Kent, Edmund Breese,
Barbara Bedford (right), Flora Finch and
Montagu Love. (First National.)

△
Popular cowboy Ken Maynard (centre) and
his splendid white horse Tarzan were the
stars of **The Glorious Trail,** a Western in
which one man and his horse jointly
supervise the completion of a telegraph line,
bring to heel the bad guy responsible for
causing several tiresome Indian uprisings,
and hold their own against their attackers
until the troops arrive. Schoolchildren
everywhere found it riveting. It was written
by Marion Jackson, directed by Albert
Rogell and featured Gladys McConnell,
Frank Hagney, James Bradbury and Chief
Yowlache. (First National.)

◁ Based on the play by Hubert Henry Davies,
Outcast, adapted by Agnes Christine John-
stone, and directed by William A. Seiter,
was a tedious tale. It told the story of a
woman who jilts her lover for a wealthier
man, rues her decision, returns to boyfriend number one, is talked out of settling
down with him by his current lady friend
and finally returns to her husband and his
money. Corinne Griffith (centre right) starred
and Edmund Lowe (right), James Ford
(centre left), Huntly Gordon (left), Kathryn
Carver, Louise Fazenda and Patsy O'Byrne
were also cast. (First National.)

△
Pleasant, light entertainment was the
critic's verdict on **Beware of Bachelors,** a
well-acted but rather attenuated comedy in
which a young couple have to remain
married for a year in order to receive a
large monetary windfall from a kindly
relative. If they don't, the money goes to a
cousin. Enter the cousin whose only thought,
naturally, is to separate the couple in the
allotted time. Audrey Ferris (right) and
William Collier Jr (left) starred as the
young marrieds, with Tom Ricketts, André
Beranger, Clyde Cook, Dave Morris and
Margaret Livingston in support. It was
written by Robert Lord from a story by
Mark Canfield (Darryl F. Zanuck) and
adroitly directed by Roy Del Ruth.

△
A partial talkie, **My Man** (not to be confused
with the 1924 Vitagraph production starring
Patsy Ruth Miller) was a piece of bespoke
tailoring designed for its star Fanny Brice.
Fanny (left) played a West Side girl who,
after coping with a difficult sister (Edna
Murphy) and an unhappy love affair (with
Guinn Williams), finally becomes a Broad-
way star with the help of a solicitious
producer (André de Segurola). Darryl
Zanuck (as Mark Canfield) thought it all up,
Robert Lord provided a script and Joe Jackson
the dialogue while Archie Mayo directed.
Also cast were Richard Tucker, Ann Brody
(right) and Arthur Hoyt. Miss Brice's magical
way with a song made up for the lukewarm
plot. Songs included: I'd Rather Be Blue (by
Billy Rose and F. Fisher), My Man (by
Channing Pollock and Maurice Yvain),
Second Hand Rose (by Grant Clarke and
James Hanley).

There wasn't a dry eye after the premiere ▷ of **The Singing Fool**, the studio's part-talking successful follow-up to *The Jazz Singer*. The lugubrious story of a singing waiter cum songwriter (Al Jolson, right) who marries a singer (Josephine Dunn, left) has a baby boy called Sonny (Davey Lee), is two-timed by his wife and plummets to the depths of despair before being rescued by a kindly cigarette girl (Betty Bronson), it was a box-office sensation, grossing over four million dollars. Drenched in sentiment, the scenario by C. Graham Baker (from a story by Leslie S. Barrows) even included a saccharine death-bed scene involving little Master Lee (providing a cue for the De Sylva, Brown and Henderson song 'Sonny Boy', which was written as a joke, and which became the first song to sell over a million copies – the total number being a staggering three million). Yet the Jolson magic (for which he was paid $150,000) was all-pervasive in this part-talkie directed by Lloyd Bacon. Other songs included: It All Depends on You and I'm Sittin' on Top of the World (by de Sylva, Brown and Henderson), Keep Smiling at Trouble, Golden Gate and The Spaniard Who Blighted My Life.

△
Originally made as a silent, but with sound added after its completion, **The Barker** was good to look at, but not so good to listen to. It starred Milton Sills as a tent-show barker and its plot centred around the day-to-day activities of life in this colourful milieu. George Fitzmaurice's direction drew performances of quality from a cast that included Betty Compson, (illustrated), Dorothy Mackaill, Sylvia Ashton, George Cooper and Douglas Fairbanks Jr, but was powerless against the man at the sound controls who all but ruined it. The excellent photography was by Lee Garmes. Benjamin Glazer was responsible for the screenplay based on a play by John Kenyon Nicholson. (First National.)

Based on the book by Judge Ben Lindsay and Wainwright Evans (who also wrote the screenplay with Beatrice Van), **The Companionate Marriage** (released in Britain as **The Jazz Bride**) had Betty Bronson (right), Richard Walling (left), Alec B. Francis, June Nash, Edward Martindel, Arthur Rankin and Hedda Hopper demonstrating that the most successful marriages are usually based on trust and respect, rather than on sex alone. Erle C. Kenton's direction built steadily towards a strong, dramatic climax, with fine performances from an interesting cast contributing to the effectiveness of the film. (First National.) ▷

There were all sorts of interesting possibilities in the story of a group of aristocratic Russian refugees who accept menial positions in Paris in order to eke out a living, but in **Adoration**, director Frank Lloyd and his scenarist Winifred Dunn (working from a story by Lajos Biro) squandered them on a trite tale of suspected marital infidelity. Billie Dove was the star with Antonio Moreno (right), Lucy Doraine, Nicholas Soussanin, Nicholas Bela (left) and Lucien Prival in support. (First National.)
▽

◁ **On Trial**, adapted from the play by Elmer Rice, was another Vitaphone false start. The process, with its mechanical imperfections (the s's emerging as a sibilant hiss), the unvarying level of sound in both the long shots and the close-ups, plus the fright it seemed to induce in the players (dialogue punctuated by long, awesome pauses) did no more for Robert Lord and Max Pollock's screenplay than a few discreet subtitles could have accomplished. A court-room drama in which a man finds himself on trial for the murder of his friend, it featured Bert Lytell as the accused, with Pauline Frederick (left), Lois Wilson (right), Holmes Herbert, Richard Tucker, Jason Robards, Franklin Pangborn, Fred Kelsey and John Arthur in support. Archie Mayo directed.

△
Caught in the Fog, a part-talkie admirably directed by Howard Bretherton whose manipulation of sound was a marked improvement on Archie Mayo's *On Trial*, was occasionally hindered by certain members of the cast who, still struggling with the overhead microphone, slowed down the action with long pauses. For the rest, though, it was an entertaining thriller set on a fog-bound houseboat in Florida and involving a group of crooked guests and their search for a valuable necklace. It starred May McAvoy (still uneasy with sound) and Conrad Nagel, with Mack Swain (centre right), Charles Gerrard, Ruth Cherrington (left), Emil Chautard (centre left) and Hugh Herbert (right). It was written by Jerome Kingston and adapted by Charles Condon.

1929

In the autumn of 1929, Fox West Coast Theatres, who still owned a one-third interest in First National, had financially overextended itself and, in order to relieve the situation, sold this interest to Warner Bros. on November 4th for $10,000,000. Shortly after the purchase, all First National assets were conveyed to Warner Bros. who, before gaining complete control of First National, remained as a separate entity. From now on First National and Warner Bros. would be amalgamated. Where there was a duplication of facilities, the best one was retained. In the case of the studio, Warner Bros. moved all its production facilities to the First National plant at Burbank which, in 1929, officially became the home of all Warner Bros.–First National Pictures, the latter, however, becoming merely a trade name under which a certain portion of Warner Bros. product would, in future, be distributed.

In 1929, Warner Bros. produced 86 feature films, 45 of these under the First National banner. The company's net profit for the year was $14,514,628.

The important music publishing firm of Remick, Harms and Witmark was also purchased by Warner Bros. in 1929, and with it a catalogue of music worth over $10,000,000. Harry Warner's son Lewis was put in charge of it.

On May 16th, 1929, about 200 members of Hollywood's elite gathered at the Hollywood Roosevelt Hotel on Hollywood Boulevard to celebrate the second anniversary of the newly-formed Academy of Motion Picture Arts and Sciences, and to pay homage to the Academy's first ever award winners for the years 1927–1928. Paramount's **Wings** won the Best Film of the Year award with a special statuette going to Warner Bros. for producing **The Jazz Singer**, 'the pioneer outstanding talking picture which revolutionized the industry'. **The Jazz Singer** was nominated for two other awards: Best Writing (Alfred Cohn) and Best Engineering Effects (Nugent Slaughter) – the latter category being discontinued the following year. Ben Hecht won the writing award for **Underworld** (Paramount, 1927); and Roy Pomeroy the Engineering award for **Wings**. The only other Warner Bros. nomination, also in the writing category, was to Anthony Coldeway for **Glorious Betsy**. For 1928–9, MGM's **The Broadway Melody** won the Academy Award for Best Film. Warner Bros., however, won the Best Direction Oscar – it went to Frank Lloyd for **The Divine Lady**. Lloyd was also nominated for **Drag** and **Weary River**.

Although Rin-Tin-Tin was more subdued than usual in **The Million Dollar Collar**, when called on to help a couple of young lovers outwit a gang of crooks who are looking for a valuable necklace (hidden in Rinty's collar, in fact) he did his stuff admirably. An average adventure story, it was written by Robert Lord, directed by D. Ross Lederman and featured Evelyn Pierce (illustrated with Rinty), Matty Kemp, Tommy Dugan, Allan Cavin, Philo McCullough and Grover Liggon.

The Little Wildcat was a part-talkie that concentrated on the delineation of character through dialogue rather than on action. Central to the unexciting narrative was a Civil War veteran (George Fawcett) who spends his time reminiscing with his one-time captain and best friend. When the interest moves away from them, it focuses on the romantic activities of his two granddaughters, one of whom is involved with an aviator. The trouble is that grandfather hates aviators. a fact which salted E.T. Lowe Jr's screenplay (from a story by Fred E. Wright) with the only sense of drama or conflict it had. Ray Enright directed a cast that included Audrey Ferris (right), James Murray (left) and Doris Dawson.

The Lawless Legion was yet another in the ▷ long series of Ken Maynard Westerns, and was fairly conventional in its story (by Bennett Cohn and Fred Allen). This one had cattle rustlers fighting a resourceful rancher (Maynard, left) with the horse Tarzan rescuing his master on several breathless occasions. Lots of hard riding, hard fighting and hard stampeding kept the action going. Again Harry J. Brown was the director, with Nora Lane supplying what little love interest there was. Richard Talmadge, Paul Hurst (right), J.P. McGowan, Frank Rice and Howard Truesdell were also in the cast.

◁ Another Ken Maynard Western, **The Phantom City** was no better and no worse than his previous efforts or those yet to come. This one found him working together with a mysterious figure known as 'The Phantom Horseman'. In time the horseman's identity is revealed: it is none other than his very own father. Together they successfully prevent the bad guys from requisitioning a gold mine. Adele Buffington devised the story, Albert Rogell directed, and it featured Eugenia Gilbert, Maynard's faithful white horse Tarzan and James Mason (but not, unfortunately, the later and more famous James Mason). (First National.)

A crime melodrama with a plot-line that ▷ tied itself in knots, **In the Headlines** starred Grant Withers (right) and Marion Nixon (left) as a newspaper reporter and his assistant who, in the course of investigating a double murder, have a few close shaves themselves. At the final fade, however, their efforts to solve the crime are rewarded with a paid honeymoon. Joseph Jackson wrote it from a story by James A. Starr; it was directed by John Adolfi, and featured Clyde Cook, Edmund Breese (centre), Pauline Garon, Frank Campeau, Vivian Oakland, Hallam Cooley and Spec O'Donnell.

A silent Ken Maynard Western, **Cheyenne** had even less plot than usual and contented itself with a series of rodeo competitions, the clear winner inevitably being Maynard, much to the delight of his girlfriend (Gladys McDonnell) and the despair of his enemies who try in vain to stop him taking part. Basically a comedy, it also featured James Bradbury Jr, William Franey, Charles Whitaker, and the horse Tarzan. Marion Jackson wrote it from a story by Bennett Cohen and Albert Rogell was the director. (First National.)

Richard Barthelmess (right) sang the title song in **Weary River** several times before the end of this part-talkie, wearying everyone who saw it. One of the first of the studio's melodramas to feature a prison setting in the narrative, it centred around the star being sent to jail when a rival hood squeals on him. In prison, a talent for singing is revealed and, in no time at all, he is leading the local convicts' band and becoming quite famous for it especially for his maudlin rendering of that same title song. Love interest was supplied by Betty Compson (left), as a girl who featured heavily in his past and would do so again in his future. Flatly directed by Frank Lloyd, and written with a blunt pencil by Bradley King and Tom Geraghty, it was not one of the year's better efforts. Also cast were William Holden, Louis Natheaux, George E. Stone and Raymond Turner. (First National.) ▽

◁ **Scarlet Seas** was a pirate yarn replete with mutineers, men hanging from the yardarm and a treasure trove of priceless, sought-after pearls. It starred Richard Barthelmess (right) as a sea captain, and Betty Compson (left) as a cabaret star who catches his eye. Beautifully photographed by Sol Polito but directed without much flair by John Francis Dillon, it appealed mainly to youngsters. Bradley King wrote it from a story by W. Scott Darling. Also featured were Loretta Young, Knute Erickson and James Bradbury Jr. (First National.)

Harmless enough, too, was **Naughty Baby**, from a story by Charles Beahan and Garrett Fort (adapted by Tom Geraghty). It starred perky Alice White (centre) as a hat-check girl whose one desire in life is to better herself and marry into money. She is aided and abetted in this by three young admirers whose enthusiasm on Miss White's behalf leads to all sorts of crazy and unlikely adventures. Director Mervyn LeRoy, in his sound film debut, brought a fine surface sparkle to it, and assembled a cast featuring Jack Mulhall, Jay Eaton, Thelma Todd, Doris Dawson, Fred Kelsey, Rose Dione and Andy Devine. Ernest Haller was the cameraman. (First National.)

The lavish production **Dancing Vienna** opened with a visit by the Emperor Franz Josef to Heaven where he asks Mozart, Offenbach and Johann Strauss to use their influence to send back to earth the Spirit of the Waltz which, he fears, is being superseded by an intrusive new type of music called jazz. They oblige, turning Friederich Zelnick's stylishly directed film into an elaborate paean in praise of three-four time. The story — about a cabaret star who makes good and convinces her American lover's father that she is worthy of his son — was the work of F. Carlson and Willy Haas, and starred Lya Mara (right), as the singer, Ben Lyon (as her suitor) with Arnold Korff, Georg Burkhardt, Alfred Abel (left) and Olga Engel in support. (First National.)

A spoof melodrama with synchronized music and sound effects, **Seven Footsteps to Satan** starred Thelma Todd and Creighton Hale as the victims of a kidnapping. Spirited off to a mysterious house run by a man called Satan, they find that the whole thing has been an elaborate joke perpetrated by their uncle. There were plenty of grunts and groans on the accompanying Vitaphone disc — or were they coming from the audience? It was written by Richard Bee from a story by Abraham Merritt, directed by Benjamin Christensen and featured Ivan Christie, Sheldon Lewis, William V. Mong, Sojin, Laska Winters and Cissy Fitzgerald (illustrated). (First National.)

Director William A. Seiter's **Synthetic Sin** was a pretty mindless brew about an aspiring actress who decides that she is not really sophisticated or worldly enough to succeed in the big time. She remedies this by going to New York, hiring an apartment on Broadway, and learning all about life from her neighbours — a bunch of hoods. Colleen Moore (centre) was the girl, Antonio Moreno the nice guy she eventually marries, with Edythe Chapman, Kathryn McGuire, Gertrude Howard, Gertrude Astor (right) and Montagu Love also cast. It was written by Tom Geraghty from a play by Frederick and Fanny Hatton. Song: Betty (by H. Christy and Nat Shilkvet). (First National.)

Conquest raised improbability to an art form. The all-talking story of two pilots in love with the same girl (Lois Wilson), it starred Monte Blue as the more decent of the two chaps, who is left by his so-called buddy (H.B. Warner) to die when their plane spins out of control and collides with an Antarctic snow bank (illustrated). But Blue doesn't die at all and returns to civilization hell-bent on vengeance, particularly when he learns that Warner has married Miss Wilson. Mary Imlay Taylor's story was turned into a screenplay by C. Graham Baker and Eve Unsell. Tully Marshall and Edmund Breese were also cast, and the director was Roy Del Ruth. His tongue, one assumes, was well in his cheek.

His Captive Woman was a part-talkie that reserved its dialogue sequences for the trial scene, and its silence for the circumstances (shown in flashback) leading up to the trial. Stoically facing a murder charge was Dorothy Mackaill (left) who openly admits that she shot and killed a Broadway libertine. There were, however, reasons for her actions. Effectively photographed by Lee Garmes and well directed by George Fitzmaurice, the film's main faults were to be found in Carey Wilson's improbable screenplay (from a story by Donn Byrne). Others cast were Milton Sills (right), Gladden James, Jed Prouty, Sidney Bracey, George Fawcett and the earlier William Holden. (First National.)

A tissue-thin drama with dialogue that was barely audible, **Fancy Baggage** was an inept affair that starred Audrey Ferris, who, in order to retrieve some vital papers from her father's rival in business, pretends to be the rival's secretary. C. Graham Baker wrote it from a story by Jerome Kingston, John Adolfi directed it and it also featured Myrna Loy (right), Wallace MacDonald (left) and Edmund Breese.

Brave Ken Maynard again came to the rescue in **The California Mail** and succeeded, single-handedly, in overthrowing a gang of gold robbers. Action was the keynote in this one, with the climax of the story a ten mile stagecoach race. Marion Jackson wrote it, Albert Rogell directed it and it featured Dorothy Dwan, Lafe McKee, Paul Hurst, Fred Burns and the horse Tarzan. (First National.)

Ken Maynard (centre) surfaced yet again in **The Royal Rider** offering protection to a boy monarch (Philippe de Lacey) about to be overthrown in a revolution. Romance intruded in the shape of the royal governess (Olive Hasbrouck, right) but it was Maynard's horsemanship and his expertise with a lasso that the public came to see and they were not disappointed. Harry J. Brown directed from a screenplay by Sylvia Seid and Jacques Jaccard (story by Nate Gatzert). Also cast were Theodore Lorch (left) and Joseph Burke. (First National.)

Alexander Korda went on to do much better work than **Love and the Devil**, a drama which, like his earlier *Night Watch* (1928), concerned a married woman who is found in another man's bedroom. The ensuing complications formed the basis of the Leo Birinski-Joseph Laszlo story. Photographed by Lee Garmes and making use of a music score and appropriate sound effects, it featured Milton Sills (right), Maria Korda (left), Ben Bard (centre) and Nellie Bly Baker. (First National.)

There wasn't a great deal for highbrows in **Stark Mad**, a low-budget film about a group of people on a yachting expedition in Caracas who are searching for their host's missing son. What they don't know is that the vessel's captain is a dangerous criminal. Director Lloyd Bacon, realising that the plot was a faint carbon copy of some boys' paper serial, went all out for atmosphere and encouraged his cast to overplay as much as possible. The chief offender (as was so often the case) was Louise Fazenda whose familiar comic touches were by now causing boredom among audiences. Henry B. Walthall (illustrated) and Jacqueline Logan were also in it; so were Claude Gillingwater, Warner Richmond, John Miljan, André Beranger and Lionel Belmore. Harvey Gates scripted from a story by Jerome Kingston. ▷

Children of the Ritz was a feeble drama which starred Dorothy Mackaill (left) as a fashion-conscious socialite who marries the family chauffeur when daddy goes bankrupt. Why? Because the lucky man has just won $50,000. Miss Mackaill's penchant for good clothes, however, soon eats into her husband's fortune, forcing him to become a taxi driver. The entertainment value in Cornell Woolrich's story, which Adelaide Heilbron adapted, was just about nil, with interest concentrating solely on the star's elaborate wardrobe. John Francis Dillon directed a cast which included Jack Mulhall (as the chauffeur, right), James Ford, Richard Carlyle and Evelyn Hall. Song: Some Sweet Day (by Lew Pollack and Nat Shilkvet). (First National.)

In **Why Be Good?** Neil Hamilton (centre) played a rich young man called Winthrop Peabody Jr. and Colleen Moore (left) the clean-living but impecunious lass he falls for. Carey Wilson provided a very thin screenplay, a fact which William A. Seiter's direction was helpless to disguise. It was photographed by the admirable Sidney Hickox and featured a synchronized musical score. Also cast were Edward Martindel, Bodil Rosing, John St. Polis, Louis Natheaux, Lincoln Stedman and, playing an extra in her first film, Jean Harlow. Song: I'm Thirsty For Your Kisses. (First National.)

Texas Guinan played Texas Malone, a night-club entertainer, in **Queen of the Night Clubs**, a heavy-handed effort awash with skullduggery. Irked by Texas's popularity, her rivals set out to do the dirty on her and, in the process, gave employment to Eddie Foy Jr, the irrepressible Lila Lee, Jack Norworth, John Davidson, John Miljan and Charlotte Merriam. Never known for subtlety, Miss Guinan (centre) belted out her numbers with more brio than artistry and helped pep up an otherwise disappointing all-talking thriller. Bryan Foy directed from a screenplay by Addison Burkhard and Murray Roth.

Dyspeptic Claude Gillingwater playing an irascible old man indulged in histrionics in a comedy called **Stolen Kisses.** His problem was that he wanted grandchildren but his son and daughter-in-law were not giving him any. In a decidedly indelicate attempt to bring them closer together, he almost causes a divorce. In the end, however, he is rewarded for his efforts by becoming the proud grandfather of twins. May McAvoy (centre left) and Hallam Cooley (centre right) were the young couple with other roles going to Edna Murphy, Reed Howes, Arthur Hoyt, Agnes Franey and Phyllis Crane. Edward Lowe Jr wrote it with James A. Starr from a story by Franz Suppe and Ray Enright directed.

▽

Although Master Davey Lee (centre) could only be understood with difficulty and much straining of the ears, his charm and conspicuous lack of precocity (plus an ingratiating smile) saw him through **Sonny Boy,** a story about a youngster who is smuggled out of the house on the eve of his parents' divorce by his mother, (who fears she will lose custody of him) and her sister. Complications proliferate when the mother poses as the wife of her husband's bachelor lawyer (in whose vacant apartment she has ensconced herself as he is away for a month) especially when the lawyer's parents arrive unexpectedly. Somehow it all worked out right at the end. C. Graham Baker wrote the rather ludicrous screenplay from a story by Robert Lord and Archie Mayo directed. Others included in the cast were Gertrude Olmstead who played Davey's mother, Betty Bronson (left) as her sister, Edward Everett Horton as the lawyer, John T. Murray, Tommy Dugan (right), Jed Prouty and Edmund Breese.

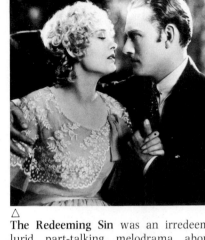

△

The Redeeming Sin was an irredeemably lurid part-talking melodrama about a Parisian dancer who, furious that a certain doctor was unable to save the life of her young brother, arranges for the unfortunate medic to be stabbed to death, then floated down the Paris sewers. Responsible for this gruesome tale were writers Harvey Gates (screenplay) and L.V. Jefferson (story), and director Howard Bretherton. Dolores Costello (left) was the vengeful dancer. Also cast were Conrad Nagel (right), Warner Richmond, Philippe de Lacey and Lionel Belmore. It was not a popular success.

A largely revamped remake of Vitagraph's 1923 production, **One Stolen Night** – from D.D. Calhoun's *The Arab* – starred William Collier Jr (left) as a member of a British cavalry regiment in the Sudan, who after nobly taking the blame when his brother steals the commissary funds, deserts his post and joins up with a vaudeville troop. Enter Betty Bronson (right, as a stooge in a whip act) who steals Collier Jr's heart, with plot complications in the shape of Harry Schultz as a sheikh with designs of his own on Miss Bronson. Stuff and nonsense, but entertaining in an exotic kind of way, it was directed by Scott R. Dunlap, written by Edward T. Lowe Jr and also featured Mitchell Lewes, Harry Todd, Charles Hill Mailes, Nina ◁ Quartero and Otto Lederer.

◁ **The Desert Song** was the first all-talking, all-singing operetta to come to the screen, and under Roy Del Ruth's direction, was a popular success. Sigmund Romberg's melodious score went some distance to disguise the basic weakness of the Otto Harbach, Laurence Schwab, Frank Mandel and Oscar Hammerstein II story, and John Boles (left) cut a dashing figure as the Riff's mysterious leader, The Red Shadow. Carlotta King (right) played Margot, the French girl who fails to realize, until all is revealed, that her rather weak boyfriend and the dashing Red Shadow are one and the same man. Louise Fazenda, John Miljan, Johnny Arthur, Edward Martindel, Jack Pratt, Otto Hoffmann and Myrna Loy were also featured but, like the principals, were victims of an unintentionally funny screenplay (by Harvey Gates) which elicited laughter where none was intended. Part of the film was photographed in Technicolor (by Barney McGill). Songs included: Riff Song, French Military Marching Song, Then You Will Know, Love's Yearning, Desert Song, Song Of The Brass Key, Sabre Song and Romance.

Bootleggers, crooks, hijackers and sundry other undesirables collided head on in **Kid Gloves**, a mind-boggling farrago in which a notorious bootlegger forces his lady-love to marry the titular hero (also known as Robin Hood of Machine Gun Alley) when he finds them together, even though they are total strangers whose paths just happened to cross. John Davidson was the bootlegger, Conrad Nagel (illustrated), Kid Gloves, and Lois Wilson the girl. Adapted by Robert Lord from a play by Fred Kennedy Myton, it featured Tommy Dugan, Maude Turner Gordon and Richard Cramer. Ray Enright directed.

▽

Two Weeks Off was a modest part-talkie comedy on the well-worn theme of mistaken identity. It starred Jack Mulhall (left) as a jobbing plumber whom everyone believes to be a famous film star, and Dorothy Mackaill (right) as a sales girl he meets on a two week vacation. The plumber goes along with the deception until he is exposed by a lifeguard who has his eye on Miss Mackaill as well. It was agreeably handled by director William Beaudine and his writers F. McGrew Willis and Joseph Poland, (from a story by Kenyon Nicholson and Thomas Barrows). Miss Mackaill coped admirably with her dialogue sequences and hers was the outstanding performance in a cast that also included Gertrude Astor, Jimmie Finlayson, Kate Price, Jed Prouty and Eddie Gribbon. Song: Love Thrills (by Al Bryan and George W. Meyer). (First National.)

▽

△

Director Gregory La Cava's handling of Maxwell Anderson's play **Saturday's Children** which came to the screen with its title as well as its essence intact, was full of good things, not least of which was the charming comedy touches with which the director imbued most of the action. A story of love and marriage, it featured Corinne Griffith (left) and Grant Withers (right) as the lovers, with Albert Conti, Alma Tell, Lucien Littlefield, Charles Lane and Ann Schaeffer in other roles. A part-talkie, it revealed Miss Griffith to be an actress better seen than heard. Forrest Halsey was responsible for the resourceful adaptation. The film was remade in 1940. Song: I Still Believe In You. (First National.)

▽

The Greyhound Limited, with its stencilled ▷ plot (by Albert Howson) cast Monte Blue (centre) as a do-gooding engine driver whose prevention of a marriage between his fireman pal (Grant Withers, top left) and an undesirable little flirt (Edna Murphy) results in the breakup of the two men's friendship. Withers goes completely to pieces, is arrested for a murder he did not commit, and sentenced to death. He is saved in the nick of time, however, by Blue, who apprehends the real murderer. Running no more than an hour, it used its time well, literally ending with a bang as an express train and a runaway wagon collide. The economical screenplay was the work of Anthony Coldeway, and the director was Howard Bretherton. Lucy Beaumont, Lew Harvey and Ernie Shields also appeared.

The story of Lord Nelson and Emma Hamilton came to the screen under Frank Lloyd's solid guidance in **The Divine Lady**, which starred the lovely Corinne Griffith as Emma and Victor Varconi (centre) as the admiral. Marie Dressler appeared as Emma's mother. Convincing approximations of the Bay of Naples and other geographical settings germane to the story added a touch of conviction to Agnes Christine Johnston and Forrest Halsey's otherwise fanciful screenplay from E. Barrington's novel. Also cast were H.B. Warner (Lord Hamilton), Ian Keith (Greville) with William Conklin, Michael Vavitch, Montagu Love (centre right) and Evelyn Hall. Basically a silent with sound-effects, it did however have a theme song, called Lady Divine (by Joseph Pasternak and Richard Kountz). (First National.)

Life at a co-ed State University was the subject of **Hot Stuff** which starred Louise Fazenda (left) as a kindly aunt who, on receiving a $10,000 accident claim, uses part of the money to send her niece (Alice White, right) to college. Aunty goes along as well, and a wild time was had by all — except audiences who found it fairly resistible. A part-talkie, it was written by Louis Stevens and Robert S. Carr and directed by Mervyn LeRoy. Also cast were William Bakewell, Doris Dawson, Ben Hall, Charles Sellon, Buddy Messinger and Andy Devine. (First National.)

▽

The Girl in the Glass Cage was a thoroughly ▷ implausible yarn about a movie house box-office cashier who not only has to contend with the advances of an underworld thug, but with an uncle who steals all her money. It starred Loretta Young (right) whose misfortunes, however, were insignificant compared with those suffered by the audience. Ralph Dawson was the director; James Gruen wrote it (from a story by George Kibbe Turner) and Carol Nye, Ralph Lewis, Matthew Betz, George E. Stone (left) and Lucien Littlefield (centre) played secondary roles. (First National.)

Everyone concerned with **The House of Horror** went over the top in an attempt to provide the predictable misadventures of Louise Fazenda (left) and Chester Conklin (right) in a crook-riddled antique shop with a patina of fun. Apparitions, sliding panels, trap doors etc., were all part of the furniture of a tepid plot, and added nothing but a sense of *déjà vu* to Richard Bee and William Irish's screenplay. It was directed by Benjamin Christensen and the cast included Thelma Todd, James Ford, William V. Mong and Dale Fuller. (First National.)

▽

◁The 50 per cent dialogue in **No Defense** was 50 per cent too much. Monte Blue starred as the foreman of a bridge construction gang who takes the blame when the bridge he is working on collapses. It wasn't his fault at all, the real culprit being the brother of the woman he happens to love. Blue (above) was too good to be true, but the film was anything but. There was no defence for Robert Lord's amorphous screenplay, nor Lloyd Bacon's direction. Also involved were May McAvoy, Kathryn Carver, William Desmond, Lee Moran (below) and William Tooker.

◁Love in high-society style was what **The Man and the Moment** was all about. Adapted by Agnes Christine Johnston from a story by 'It' girl Elinor Glyn, it was a typical Glyn-like brew in its ultra-sophisticated approach to love and marriage, with yachts and aeroplanes as part of life's every day bric-à-brac. The story involved a wealthy couple who, to disentangle themselves from a number of irksome problems, decide to entangle themselves and marry — only to separate immediately afterwards. They spend the first night on a yacht, but by morning the bride has disappeared out of a porthole. Billie Dove (illustrated) and current heart throb Rod La Rocque were the beautiful couple, the director was George Fitzmaurice, and the rest of the cast included Gwen Lee, Doris Dawson, Robert Schable, Charles Sellon and George Bunny.

Alexander Korda's first all-talking film **The Squall** failed to come to grips with the difficulties of sound. Set in Hungary (it was the last film Korda was to make using his native country as a background), it concerned the minx-like activities of a gypsy girl called Nubi (Myrna Loy, centre) who, while on the run from her husband, takes shelter in a farmhouse where she soon holds all the male members of the family in thrall. Just as things are getting out of hand, her husband arrives to take her back to the gypsy encampment and sanity is once again restored. The film failed on every level (direction, script, performances) and was the object of much derision on its release. Bradley King wrote the unspeakable dialogue from a play by Jean Bart, and suffering the consequences were Alice Joyce, Richard Tucker, Loretta Young and Nicholas Soussanin (left). Song: Gypsy Charmer (by Grant Clarke and Harry Akst). (First National.)

▽

Director Michael Curtiz was defeated by ▷
Vitaphone in **Glad Rag Doll** so that the
rather nondescript story of a rich man's
infatuation with a showgirl was made to
seem even more insubstantial than it was.
The few good ideas the film possessed – such
as the Pirandello-like opening – were soon
dissipated in a morass of bad dialogue,
badly spoken. C. Graham Baker was
responsible for the words, Harvey Gates
for the plot. Dolores Costello (left) was given
top billing as the show-girl, with Claude
Gillingwater, Ralph Graves (right) and
Audrey Ferris. Song: Glad Rag Doll (by Jack
Yellen, Dan Dougherty and Milton Ager).

△
Frozen River, a Rin-Tin-Tin vehicle with
the addition of about five per cent dialogue
as well as some poorly synchronized barking
sounds, was very much a formula effort
with Rinty preventing the proverbial gang
of crooks from stealing the proverbial
cache of gold from the proverbial kindly
old man. Little Davey Lee, fresh from his
triumph in *Sonny Boy*, made a token
appearance (to an orchestral accompaniment of 'Sonny Boy' in the background)
with other parts going to a self-conscious
Nina Quartero, Josef Swickard, Raymond
McKee (left), Duane Thompson and Frank
Campeau. John S. Fowler devised the story,
Anthony Coldeway wrote the scenario, and
F. Harmon Weight directed.

△
Director John Francis Dillon coped well
with the gremlins in the Vitaphone system
throughout **Careers** but was ultimately
defeated by an unconvincing screenplay (by
Forrest Halsey) which focused on the
unwillingness of a wife to make sacrifices
for the advancement of her husband's
career. Billie Dove was the wife and Antonio
Moreno the husband (a French attaché in the
colonies). The villain of the piece (apart from
the men who thought up the story) was
Noah Beery (left). Based on a play by Alfred
Schirokauer and Paul Rosenhayn, it also
featured Holmes Herbert, Carmel Myers,
Thelma Todd, Sojin, Kithnou, Robert Frazer
and Marte Faust (right). Song: I Love You, I
Hate You (by Al Bryan and George W.
Meyer). (First National.)

One of the studio's most ambitious films
to date, and also its longest (it ran 135
minutes), **Noah's Ark** was a retelling of the
biblical story paralleling, at the same time,
a First World War romance. A part-talkie,
(the first 35 minutes were silent), the
bizarre combination of narratives was
directed by Michael Curtiz with immense
panache and a thorough grasp of the epic
style. Particularly memorable were Anton
Grot's sets and the amazing and spectacular
scenes depicting the cataclysmic flood.
Cameraman Hal Mohr, however, had mis-
givings about these scenes when he learned
that one of Grot's massive temples was
expected to collapse, not only on the stuntmen but on the hundreds of extras supplied
by Central Casting as well. So he resigned,
and Barney McGill took his place. Mohr's
fears were not unfounded. In the shooting
of the flood scene no shots were faked, and
several extras did, in fact, drown. Adapted
by Anthony Coldeway from a treatment by
Darryl Zanuck the film starred Dolores
Costello (Miriam), Noah Beery (King Nephi-
lim), Louise Fazenda (as a tavern maid),
Guinn Williams (Ham), Paul McAllister
(Noah), Myrna Loy (as a slave girl) and
Malcolm Waite (Shem). Song: Heart O' Mine
(by Billy Rose and Louis Silvers).
▽

△
A part-talkie, **Prisoners** miscast Corinne
Griffith as an Austrian cabaret dancer not
averse to a spot of thievery every now and
then. She steals to attract the attention
of a young lawyer, is unsuccessfully
defended by him and sent to jail. But he's
there waiting for her on her release, as it
seems she stole his heart as well. Based on a
story by Ferenc Molnar, it was adapted by
Forrest Halsey, the essence of the original
being lost somewhere between Hungary and
Hollywood. William A. Seiter directed a
cast which included Miss Griffith (centre),
Ian Keith (as the lawyer, left), Otto Matiesen,
Julanne Johnston, Baron von Hesse and Bela
Lugosi. (First National.)

△

There was nothing good to be said about **From Headquarters**, a turgid drama in which Monte Blue (left) captains a squad of Marines in Central America in a search of a party of sightseers lost in the jungle. Adapted for the screen by Harvey Gates from a story by Samuel Hartridge and directed by Howard Bretherton, it squandered the varied talents of supporting players Guinn Williams (right), Gladys Brockwell, Lionel Belmore, Henry B. Walthall, Ethlyne Claire and Pat Hartigan.

△

Alice White (illustrated) played a virginal chorus girl in love with stage manager Charles Delaney in **Broadway Babies.** Then along comes Fred Kohler, a gin-and-grin guy from Detroit who almost steals her away from Delaney. But Alice's decision to remain with Delaney, coupled with the fact that Kohler gets flattened when a denizen of the underworld fires an air-gun at him, paves the way for a happy ending. Mervyn LeRoy directed it, Monte Katterjohn and Humphrey Pearson wrote it (from a story by Jay Gelzer) and the cast included Tom Dugan, Bodil Rosing, Sally Eilers and Marion Byron. Songs included: Wishing And Waiting For Love and Jig Jig Jigaloo (by Grant Clarke and Harry Akst) and Broadway Baby Doll (by Al Bryan and George W. Meyer). (First National.)

The show business setting of **Twin Beds**, a ▷ comedy-cum-farce, gave Vitaphone scope for a couple of interpolated musical items as well as a theme song called If You Were Mine. Based on a play by Margaret Mayo and Salisbury Field and opened out for the screen by F. McGrew Willis, it featured Patsy Ruth Miller (left), Jack Mulhall (right), Armand Kaliz, Edythe Chapman, ZaSu Pitts, Alice Lake and Bert Roach. Alfred Santell was the director. (First National.)

△

Although singing and dancing were not among Betty Compson's (right) talents, Darryl Zanuck had no qualms at all casting her as a musical comedy star in 'the first 100 per cent natural colour all singing production' **On With the Show,** substituting a professional dancer in the long shots, and hiring a professional singer to dub her vocals. A sort of trial run for the legendary **42nd Street** four years later, the film was restrictively shot through the claustrophobic camera-booths of the period and made few concessions to celluloid in the recounting of its by now hackneyed backstage intrigue. Irritating performances by Joe E. Brown (making his Warners debut) and Arthur Lake (left, as the light relief) and one of staggering incompetence by Sally O'Neil contributed to the overall gauche effect of the enterprise. Only Ethel Waters emerged with any credit singing 'Am I Blue?' and 'Birmingham Bertha'. Based on the play *Shoestring* by Humphrey Pearson, and written by Robert Lord, it was directed by Alan Crosland, with Larry Ceballos in charge of the musical numbers. Also featured were Louise Fazenda, Purnell P. Pratt, William Bakewell and the Fairbanks twins. Other songs included: In The Land Of Let's Pretend, Let Me Have My Dreams, Welcome Home, Don't It Mean A Thing To You? Lift The Juleps To Your Two Lips and On With The Show (by Grant Clarke and Harry Akst).

The Gamblers, in which several high-ranking company directors illegally borrow money from the Trust House to which they are attached, then gamble it on the stock market, was a well constructed drama that finally showed its director Michael Curtiz well on the way to mastering sound. Based on a play by Charles Klein, compellingly adapted by J. Grubb Alexander, it featured H.B. Warner, Lois Wilson, Jason Robards, Pauline Garon (centre right) and George Fawcett (centre), all of whom seemed thoroughly at home with the microphone. Certain plot implausibilities rankled, but not enough to scar a solid piece of film-making.

▽

△

In **The Careless Age,** a jealous young medical student strangles an actress with whom he is madly in love. She revives and all ends happily. However, in *Diversion*, the play (by John van Druten) on which it was based, the son, remorseful of his deed, asks his father for poison so he can take his own life, and the father complies. Harrison Macklyn's adaptation changed all that and removed the sting from the tail. John Griffith Wray directed a cast that included Douglas Fairbanks Jr (right), Carmel Myers (left), Loretta Young, Holmes Herbert, Kenneth Thomson, Wilfred Noy and Ilka Chase. As the play's setting was Mayfair, in London, most of them spoke with an upper-class accent which the microphones grossly exaggerated. Song: Melody Divine. (First National.)

◁ Vitaphone made good use of roaring football crowds in **The Time, the Place, and the Girl,** a musical comedy which charted the progress of a college football hero whose swollen head is deflated when, after graduating, he takes a job as a bond salesman. Though poor at selling bonds, he knows how to charm women, and his boss therefore has him concentrate his efforts on disposing of bad bonds to gullible females — one of whom turns out to be his employer's own wife. Howard Bretherton directed and Robert Lord wrote it from the play by W.M. Hough, Joseph E. Howard and Frank R. Adams. Grant Withers was the star, supported by (from left) Bert Roach, Betty Compson, John Davidson, Gertrude Olmstead, Vivian Oakland and Gretchen Hartman. Songs included: I Wonder Who's Kissing Her Now, Collegiate Doin' The Raccoon, Fashionette, Jack And Jill, How Many Times and If You Could Care.

There was a great deal of plot in **Madonna of Avenue 'A'**, a melodrama directed by Michael Curtiz whose chief asset was Dolores Costello's good looks. Miss Costello (right) played a schoolgirl who goes completely to pieces when she learns that her mother (Louise Dresser), whom she had always believed to be a fashionable woman of society, is a dance-hall hostess in a sleazy club. She marries a bootlegger, an act which causes Miss Dresser to have the man framed, which, in turn, results in Miss Dresser's remorseful suicide. The screenplay was the joint effort of Ray Doyle who adapted it from a story by Leslie S. Barrows and Bradley King who wrote the dialogue, and in the cast were Grant Withers (left), William Russell, Douglas Gerrard, Otto Hoffman and Lee Moran. Song: My Madonna (by Fred Fisher and Louis Silvers).

With movies having found a voice, the rise of the screen musical was imminent and inevitable – **Smiling Irish Eyes** was not however a particularly good example of the fast proliferating genre. A bit of blarney about a talented song-writing violinist who travels from Ireland to Broadway to seek fame and fortune, it starred James Hall (right) as the hopeful and Colleen Moore, in her first all-talking, all-singing, all-dancing picture as the lass he leaves behind – but with whom he once wrote the film's much played theme song, Smiling Irish Eyes. Miss Moore follows her man to America, where romantic complications disillusion her. But she survives them and lives happily ever after. A plodding and unimaginative effort, it was written by Tom Geraghty and directed by William A. Seiter, with Larry Ceballos providing the choreography. Claude Gillingwater, Robert Homans, Aggie Herring (left) and Betty Francisco were also cast. Other songs included: A Wee Bit Of Love and Old Killarney Fair (by Herman Ruby and Norman Spencer). (First National.)

Based on Zoë Akins' play *Declassée* (first made in 1925 by First National) **Her Private Life** took a sardonic view of modern society and concluded that most of its members were not particularly nice. Marriage and divorce featured prominently in Forrest Halsey's screenplay with Billie Dove (left) pilfering the acting honours from Roland Young (right) Montagu Love, Walter Pidgeon, Holmes Herbert, Thelma Todd and ZaSu Pitts. She played the indiscreet wife of a vulgar, self-made millionaire (Love) whose attraction to a young American (Pidgeon) results in an acrimonious divorce. Alexander Korda directed. Song: Love Is Like A Rose. (First National.)

Hard to Get was the tale of a working girl ▷ who deserts the chance of untold wealth with a millionaire philanderer (Edmund Burns) for one of workaday domesticity with a man she never feels she has to impress. (Charles Delaney in the role of an automobile mechanic). The film, based on a story by Edna Ferber and written by Richard Weil and James Gruen, was a modest success which starred Dorothy Mackaill (right), Jimmie Finlayson (below left), and Louise Fazenda, and featured Jackie Oakie (above left) and Clarissa Selwynne. The director was William Beaudine. Song: The Things We Want Most Are Hard To Get (by Al Bryan and George W. Meyer). (First National.)

Drag, directed by Frank Lloyd from a screenplay by Bradley King and Gene Towne and a story by William Dudley Pelley, had nothing whatsoever to do with men who dress up as women. The drag in the title referred to a couple who insist on moving in with their married daughter and son-in-law, cramping the hard working husband's style at every possible turn. Richard Barthelmess (right) starred as the put-upon husband, Alice Day (left) was his wife. Neither they, nor a cast which also included Lucien Littlefield (seated), Katherine Ward (centre left), Charlie Parker, Margaret Fielding (centre right), Tom Dugan (centre) and Lila Lee could do much with the stilted dialogue they had to turn into speech. Songs included: My Song Of The Nile and I'm Too Young To Be Careful (by Al Bryan and George W. Meyer). (First National.)

Edward Everett Horton's particular brand of comedy was unveiled to applause in **The Hottentot,** based on the Victor Mapes-Willie Collier stage success of 1920, and filmed by First National as a silent in 1923. Harvey Thew's refreshingly witty screenplay made a few changes and it emerged as a story about a simple horse lover who is mistaken for a champion steeplechase jockey and prevailed upon to take part in a forthcoming race. Roy Del Ruth directed it, and cast Patsy Ruth Miller (left) opposite Horton (right). Also in it were Douglas Gerrard, Edward Earle, Stanley Taylor, Gladys Brockwell and Otto Hoffman.
▽

△
William Holden (the earlier, who died in 1932), as the governor presiding over a murder case in **Fast Life,** summed it all up when he said 'This has been an awful ordeal for all of us'. He was referring to Douglas Fairbanks Jr's (centre) trial for a crime he did not commit, but could just as easily have been expressing his views on the over-heated, all-talking entertainment offered by scenarist John F. Goodrich (from a play by Samuel Shipman and John B. Hymer) which John Francis Dillon directed. Also cast were Loretta Young (right), Chester Morris, Frank Sheridan, Ray Hallor (left) and John St Polis. Song: Since I Found You (by Ray Perkins). (First National.)

△
Sophie Tucker (centre) squeezed every drop of pathos from **Honky Tonk,** and won cheers from enthusiastic audiences. The heartfelt story of a mother who sacrifices everything for her daughter's education, only to be reviled by the girl as soon as she realizes her mother is nothing more than a night-club entertainer, it featured Lila Lee as the daughter, with Audrey Ferris, George Duryea, Mahlon Hamilton and John T. Murray in support. The sort of entertainment with something for everyone, it was directed by Lloyd Bacon who showed off the assertive talent of the last of the red hot mommas to great effect. The dance director was Larry Ceballos. Songs (by Jack Yellen and Milton Ager) included: I'm The Last Of The Red Hot Mommas, I'm Doin' What I'm Doin' For Love, He's A Good Man To Have Around, I'm Feathering A Nest (For A Little Bluebird) and Some Of These Days.

◁ Adapted by Robert Lord (from Avery Hopwood's play *The Gold Diggers*, first filmed in 1923) **The Gold Diggers of Broadway**, the familiar story of three girls and their involvements with the usual wealthy suckers who seek out their company, starred Nancy Welford, Ann Pennington and Winnie Lightner as the golddiggers, with the other featured roles going to Conway Tearle, Lilyan Tashman, William Bakewell and Nick Lucas. Though the ads promised 'a profuse procession of revue spectacle scenes in amazing settings . . . superbly staged chorus dancing numbers . . . a story that had New York gasping and giggling for one solid year . . .' the film was mainly memorable for its use of two-colour Technicolor and for an Al Dubin-Joe Burke score that included 'Tiptoe Through The Tulips' and 'Painting The Clouds With Sunshine' (whose title was used in the 1951 remake of the same story starring Virginia Mayo). The director was Roy Del Ruth. Other songs included: In A Kitchenette, Go To Bed, And They Still Fall In Love, What Will I Do Without You?, Song of the Gold Diggers and Mechanical Man.

△ Myrna Loy (left) was top-billed at last in **Hardboiled Rose**, her chief contribution to Robert Lord's screenplay being to shield the reputation of her father by persuading her lover to take the blame and going to jail for dad's numerous misdeeds. The performances were better than the material, with Loy, Ralph Emerson, William Collier Jr, Gladys Brockwell (right) and Edward Martindel working overtime to salvage Darryl Zanuck's (Melville Crossman's) unconvincing story. F. Harmon Weight directed.

Leatrice Joy played the role Alice Brady created on stage in Townsend Martin's **A Most Immoral Lady** but brought nothing new to her interpretation of a lady who, together with her husband, operates a scheme to extort money from millionaires through blackmail and victimization. Sidney Blackmer (right) co-starred as the husband, with Walter Pidgeon as the man Miss Joy (left) really loves, but whom she mistakenly victimizes. John Griffith Wray's direction betrayed the piece's stage origins, a fault compounded by Forrest Halsey's screenplay. Also cast were Montagu Love, Josephine Dunn, Robert Edeson and Donald Reed. Songs included: Toujours and That's How Much I Need You. (First National.)
▽

◁ Although **Disraeli** marked the debut in a sound film of sixty-one year old George Arliss (whom the studio respectfully billed as Mr. George Arliss), the style of direction (by Alfred E. Green) and the histrionics of the performances were still squarely rooted in the silent era, with Arliss (illustrated) overacting as the distinguished British Prime Minister. Reduced to the level of a novelette, the film concentrated mainly on Disraeli's attempt to outwit the Russians in his attempts to purchase the Suez Canal and on his (highly fictionalized) endeavours at match-making. Those seeking a full assessment of the man and his work would have been better off in a library. Julien Josephson, working from the play by Louis N. Parker, wrote the screenplay with roles for Florence Arliss as Disraeli's wife, Lady Beaconsfield, Joan Bennett, Anthony Bushell, David Torrence and Ivan Simpson. Their efforts were received with critical approval. In 1921, Arliss and his wife had appeared in a silent version of the same subject.

◁ There was little the director Reginald Barker could do with **The Great Divide**, an antediluvian yarn about a wealthy miner who goes to the big city to find a girl, then tames her into a more wholesome way of life than the one she was used to. Ian Keith (right) was the bullish miner, Dorothy Mackaill the girl. Others involved were Lucien Littlefield (centre), George Fawcett, Ben Hendricks (left), Claude Gillingwater and, again playing a half-caste, Myrna Loy. Fred Myton wrote the screenplay from a story by William Vaughan Moody. Songs included: The End Of The Lonesome Trail and Si, Si, Senore. (First National.)

△
A remake of the 1923 silent version, **The Isle of Lost Ships,** with the addition of sound, was more interesting for what was seen and done than for what was said. Action in this instance very definitely spoke louder than words, and the bizarre story of a steamer which drifts into the Sargasso Sea, carrying a motley cargo of passengers, was always compelling. Irvin Willat's direction, full of eerie, atmospheric touches, did much to counteract some of the corny dialogue (by Fred Myton) which Noah Beery (as the captain), Virginia Valli (left), Jason Robards (right), Clarissa Selwynne and Robert E. O'Connor had to deliver. Song: Ship Of My Dreams. (First National.)

△
In **The Argyle Case**, director Howard Bretherton showed how effective talking pictures could be if the cast were allowed to forget the menacing overhead microphones and were given, instead, the freedom to deliver their lines as if they were something less than the Declaration of Independence. A first rate whodunnit, the question at the heart of Harvey Thew's ingenious screenplay (based on a play by Harriet Ford, Harvey J. O'Higgins and William J. Burns) was: who killed wealthy John Argyle and why? Enter a super-sleuth with all the answers. Thomas Meighan (right) was splendid as the shamus, with good work too, from H.B. Warner, Lila Lee (left), Gladys Brockwell, Bert Roach, Douglas Gerrard and ZaSu Pitts.

One of the more successful adaptations from stage to screen, **Evidence,** directed by John Adolfi with a solid command of cinematic technique and an awareness of both the limitations and the virtues of sound, was a sober drama graced by a workable screenplay and some fine performances. The story of a married woman who is compromised in the eyes of her husband by a man claiming to love her, it starred Pauline Frederick (illustrated), Conway Tearle (as the husband) and Lowell Sherman as the suitor. Miss Frederick's innocence is finally proven, but not before she is forced into social exile in England where she becomes a notorious woman. J. Du Rocher MacPherson wrote the play on which J. Grubb Alexander's screenplay was based. Also cast were William Courtenay, Alec B. Francis and a youngster with a tendency to cuteness called Freddie Burke Frederick. Song: Little Cavalier (by Al Dubin and M.K. Jerome).

Richard Barthelmess (left) was excellent in **Young Nowheres,** a simple, well-told drama about a hotel elevator operator who, together with one of the pretty chambermaids (Marion Nixon, right) on the premises, is accused of breaking and entering a suite belonging to one of the guests. They were, indeed, caught in the suite, but the unexpected circumstances that caused them to be there formed the basis of a well-made, cleverly scripted film. The screenplay was by Bradley King and the story by I.A.R. Wylie. The sympathetic direction was by Frank Lloyd, whose cast also included Anders Randolph, Raymond Turner, Jocelyn Lee and Bert Roach. (First National.)

78

The first all-talking drama to feature an actor in a dual role, **Dark Streets** was a superb showcase for Jack Mulhall (illustrated), who played twin brothers, one of whom is a policeman, the other a thief. The twin forces of good and evil were neatly, if somewhat simplistically, exploited in Bradley King's screenplay (from a story by Richard Connell) and the plot, which involved both men falling for Lila Lee, held the interest throughout. A better than average low-budget picture, it was crisply directed by Frank Lloyd. Also cast were Will Walling, Maurice Black and Earl Pingree.

An all-talking college caper enhanced by the personable Douglas Fairbanks Jr (left) and the attractive Loretta Young (right), **The Forward Pass** was a mild but quite diverting comedy in which (to cut a long story short) Fairbanks makes a forward pass at a crucial moment and helps win the big match as well as the girl. Howard Emmett Rogers wrote it, Eddie Cline directed it and his team of actors included Bert Rome, Lane Chandler, Guinn Williams, Allen Lane, Marion Byron and Floyd Shackleford. Songs included: One Minute Of Heaven, I Gotta Have You and H'lo Baby. (First National.)

Skin Deep, a melodrama to be taken with more than just a pinch of salt, was the story of an unfaithful wife who frames her racketeer husband so that he is sent to prison, moves in with one of his competitors, engineers her husband's escape, then tries to persuade him to murder the local District Attorney. The tale's plausibility was stretched even further when the husband, after being hurt in a car crash, has plastic surgery performed on his face and emerges not only with good looks but an upper class accent as well! Based on a story by Mark Edmund Jones, written by Gordon Rigby, and directed by Ray Enright, it starred Monte Blue (centre) and Betty Compson, with Davey Lee (left), Alice Day, Tully Marshall and John Bowers (right) in other roles. Song: I Came To You (by Sidney Mitchell, Archie Gottler and Con Conrad).

Billie Dove (illustrated), doing just the sort of thing she did when she was a Ziegfeld girl, gave **The Painted Angel** most of its zing, though the story, which charts her career from New Orleans singer to queen of the New York night clubs, was of secondary importance to the staging of the elaborate musical interpolations. Working from a routine screenplay by Forrest Halsey (story by Fannie Hurst), director Millard Webb brought a fair amount of visual excitement to the proceedings, particularly in the musical numbers, and was given sturdy support from Edmund Lowe as the man Miss Dove loves, and George MacFarlane as the man she doesn't. Also cast were Cissy Fitzgerald, J. Farrell MacDonald and Norman Selby. Songs (by Herman Ruby and M.K. Jerome) included: Help Yourself To Love, Bride Without A Groom, Only The Girl, Everybody's Darling and That Thing.

Clarinettist Ted Lewis's appearance in **Is Everybody Happy?**, a maudlin musical, was a decidedly unhappy one. In it, he underwent all manner of hardships as he was disowned by his parents, rejected by his girlfriend, etc, etc, only to emerge triumphant with the question 'Is Everybody Happy?' on his lips. The answer was a resounding No! The mawkish prose that passed for dialogue was written by Joseph Jackson and James A. Starr, Larry Ceballos staged the musical numbers and Archie Mayo directed. Apart from Lewis (centre) it also featured Alice Day (right), Ann Pennington, Lawrence Grant, Julia Swayne Gordon and Otto Hoffman. Songs (by Harry Akst and Grant Clarke) included: Wouldn't It Be Wonderful?, I'm The Medicine Man For The Blues, Samoa, New Orleans, In The Land Of Jazz, Start The Band, St. Louis Blues and Tiger Rag.

The Girl from Woolworth's was churned out as a show-case for a snappy, all-talking, all-singing Miss Alice White (left) who played a singing salesgirl in the music department of a large store. In time she is given her big break in show business but, in the end, opts for marriage rather than a career. Adele Commandini's screenplay (dialogue by Richard Weil and Edward Luddy) was a rag-bag of clichés to which director William Beaudine was unable to bring much freshness; and out of a cast that included Charles Delaney (as Miss White's amour, centre), Wheeler Oakman and Ben Hall, only Rita Flynn (right) made an impact. Song: Crying For Love (by Al Bryan and G.W. Meyer). (First National.)

After the phenomenal success Al Jolson had with *The Jazz Singer* and *The Singing Fool*, the studio used a similar formula and came up with **Say it With Songs**. The film, for which Jolson was paid half a million dollars, again featured Davey Lee, and again De Sylva, Brown and Henderson provided a mournful dirge ('Little Pal') with hopes of repeating their 'Sonny Boy' fluke. (They didn't.) The story, devised by Darryl Zanuck and Harvey Gates (with an adaptation and dialogue credit going to Joseph Jackson) had Jolson (centre) starring as a radio singer who accidentally kills a man for flirting with his wife and goes to jail for the crime. Marion Nixon played Jolson's wife with other roles being filled by Holmes Herbert, Fred Kohler, John Bowers and Kenneth Thomson. The director was Lloyd Bacon and the film was a monumental flop. Songs included: Why Can't You, Little Pal, Used To You and Seventh Heaven.

The remake of William Grew's play **The Sap** starred Edward Everett Horton (right) in the part played in the 1926 silent film by Kenneth Harlan. Basically the story of an impractical, much maligned dreamer who finally gets a chance to vindicate himself by coming to the aid of his brother-in-law, it was well performed by Horton (whose performance in the role bore very little resemblance to Harlan's), Patsy Ruth Miller (left) and Edna Murphy. Archie Mayo directed from a screenplay by Robert Lord, and his cast included Franklin Pangborn, Alan Hale, Russell Simpson and Jerry Mandy.

Paris, based on the stage musical by Cole Porter, Martin Brown and E. Ray Goetz, but without Porter's score to lend enchantment to it, came to the screen via First National and Vitaphone with Irene Bordoni recreating her stage role. Several sequences were photographed in colour and the accent was on spectacle rather than plot. Miss Bordoni and her co-star, the English song-and-dance man Jack Buchanan, both made their talkie debuts in this film, with Louise Closser Hale (centre left) featured as a mother who leaves Newton Centre, Massachusetts, for Paris, with the express purpose of preventing her son's marriage to Miss Bordoni. Jason Robards (right) was the son; Jack Buchanan (left) played Miss Bordoni's (centre right) stage partner. It was adapted by Hope Loring, choreographed by Larry Ceballos and directed by Clarence Badger. Songs (by Al Bryan and Ed Ward) included: Paris, I Wonder What Is Really On His Mind, I'm A Little Negative, Somebody Mighty Like You and My Lover.

The Show of Shows, blared the ads, was 'a ▷ connoisseur's collection of the supreme examples of almost every form of stage and screen entertainment.' To make good their boast, the studio engaged John Barrymore to do a soliloquy from *Henry VI Part III* while Beatrice Lillie, Louise Fazenda and Lloyd Hamilton joined compère Frank Fay for a series of sketches. Rin-Tin-Tin 'introduced' the elaborate 'Chinese Fantasy' (illustrated), Myrna Loy was featured as an Oriental princess (what else?) and was crooned to by Nick Lucas; Ted Lewis and his orchestra joined forces with Noah Beery, while the well-rounded Winnie Lightner broke into 'Singing In The Bathtub'. Also lending their talents were Richard Barthelmess, Alice White, Georges Carpentier, Irene Bordoni, Dolores Costello, Grant Withers, Loretta Young, Ann Sothern (here called Harriet Lake), Ben Turpin, Lupino Lane, Jack Mulhall, Chester Morris, Chester Conklin and The Williams Adagio Dancers. John Adolfi directed the part-Technicolor production, and the whole phantasmagoria was typical of the revue-type musical whose popularity was by now on the wane. Songs by numerous composers also included: Lady Luck, If I Could Learn To Love, Pingo Pongo, The Only Song I Know, Your Mother And Mine, Just An Hour Of Love, Li-Po-Li, Rock-A-Bye Your Baby With A Dixie Melody, If Your Best Friend Won't Tell You, Motion Picture Pirates and Your Love Is All I Crave.

△
A remake of the George M. Cohan musical play, but this time with the addition of songs (two of them by Cohan himself) **Little Johnny Jones** was the story of an American jockey who wins the Derby on a horse called Yankee Doodle. It starred Eddie Buzzell (centre) in the title role, with Alice Day, Edna Murphy, Robert Edeson, Wheeler Oakman and Donald Reed in support. It was written by Adelaide Heilbron and directed, without much conviction, by Mervyn LeRoy. Songs by a variety of composers included: Yankee Doodle Boy, Give My Regards To Broadway, Go Find Somebody To Love, My Paradise, Painting The Clouds With Sunshine and She Was Kicked On The Head By A Butterfly. (First National).

Director William Beaudine and his scenarist Ray Harris hardly did justice to Ernest Pascal's novel *The Dark Swan* (first made in 1924) which they called **Wedding Rings.** Recounting the romantic involvements of two totally different sisters, it took all sorts of liberties with the original, mainly in changing the plainer, more intelligent girl into pretty Lois Wilson. Olive Borden was the other sister. Also cast were H.B. Warner as the man Miss Borden steals from her sister, Kathlyn Williams, Aileen Manning, Hallam Cooley (illustrated) and James Ford. Song: Love Will Last Forever If It's True (by Al Bryan and Ed Ward). (First National.)
▽

In **Footlights and Fools,** Colleen Moore (left) was not wholly able to overcome a tendency towards cuteness but, for the most part, she tackled one of the best roles of her career like the trouper she was. Katherine Bush's story (which she adapted with Tom Geraghty and Carey Wilson) gave Miss Moore a chance to play two distinct characters: a musical comedy star called Fifi d'Auray, all temperament and fire; and, away from the footlights, plain Betty Murphy, in love with a boy unworthy of her. Audiences adored her in both guises. With interest focused so squarely and persistently on the star, there was little scope for the remaining players, but under William A. Seiter's direction, Raymond Hackett, Fredric March (right), Virginia Lee Corbin, Mickey Bennett and Edward Martindel did the best they could. Songs (by Al Bryan and George W. Meyer) included: If I Can't Have You, You Can't Believe My Eyes ◁ and Ophelia Will Fool You.

△
Conrad Nagel, Lila Lee, Pauline Frederick (centre), William Courtenay (right), Walter Byron, Alec B. Francis and Dale Fuller (left) were admirable in the all-talking film version of Somerset Maugham's play **The Sacred Flame.** The only trouble was that Harvey Thew's adaptation put words into their mouths whose resemblance to recognizable everyday speech was tenuous, to say the least. Nagel played the paralysed war hero, Lila Lee his wife. It was directed by Archie Mayo who kept it all rather stagebound. Song: The Sacred Flame.

△
The Love Racket, a trivial and cloying drama starred Dorothy Mackaill (centre) as a woman whose husband tells her they are not legally married, then walks out on her. Years later, she finds herself sitting on a jury trying a girl who murdered a man for doing the same thing. The deceased, it turns out, is none other than the very same man who deserted Miss Mackaill at the start of the film. William A. Seiter's direction was not inventive enough to rescue the far-fetched scenario, full of unbelievable coincidences, which John F. Goodrich wrote from a play by Bernard K. Burns. Also cast were Sidney Blackmer (right), Edmund Burns, Myrtle Stedman, Alice Day, Edith Yorke and Martha Mattox. (First National.)

Hearts in Exile, based on the play by John ▷ Oxenham, was written for the screen by Harvey Gates and directed (with two alternative endings) by Michael Curtiz. It starred Dolores Costello as the daughter of a Moscow fishmonger who marries a baron after her student lover tells her he is not yet ready to settle down. Some years pass and both the student (now a doctor) and the Baron find themselves exiled to Siberia – the former for two years, the latter for twenty. Because of the doctor's abiding love for Miss Costello, he exchanges places with the baron, who promises to arrange his escape as soon as he himself is out. This indeed happens, and in the process, the baron realises that the young couple are still deeply in love. So he shoots himself. The couple, meantime, are either recaptured, sent back to prison, and live unhappily ever after – or remain free and live happily, depending on which ending was screened. Production values were solid and strong performances came from a cast that also featured Grant Withers (as the medic, left), James Kirkwood (as the baron, right), Olive Tell, George Fawcett and William Irving. Song: Like A Breath Of Springtime.

Lupe Velez (illustrated with Rin-Tin-Tin) starred as **Tiger Rose**, a half-caste who weakened the knees of Canada's entire male population, including a sergeant (Monte Blue) in the North West Mounted Police. (Lenore Ulric had the same effect in the 1923 silent version.) Miss Velez, however, only had eyes for a railwayman called Bruce (Grant Withers) who, much to the chagrin of her numerous suitors, whisks her away to the big city, but not before killing a doctor who tries to stop him. The film gave Monte Blue a chance to deliver L.G. Rigby and Harvey Thew's dialogue (from a play by David Belasco and Willard Mack) in a thick Irish brogue, but served no other apparent purpose. George Fitzmaurice directed it, and the brilliant Tony Gaudio was the cameraman. Also in the cast were Rin-Tin-Tin (billed beneath Mr. Blue and Miss Velez), H.B. Warner, Gaston Glass, Bull Montana and Slim Summerville. Featured song: The Day You Fall In Love.

Wife-swapping was the subject of **So Long Letty**, a musical comedy by Elmer Harris in which Charlotte Greenwood (right) repeating the role she created on stage, played an eccentric wife whose place is temporarily taken by someone more conventional in aspect and behaviour when her husband's rich but irascible uncle drops in for a week (they're hoping to be left all his money). Bert Roach (centre left) was the husband, Claude Gillingwater the uncle and Patsy Ruth Miller (left) the replacement wife. Lloyd Bacon directed, and brought to Arthur Caesar and Robert Lloyd's screenplay a deft lightness of touch. Grant Withers (centre right) was also in the cast. Songs (again by Akst and Clarke) included: One Sweet Little Yes, Clowning, Beauty Shop, Am I Blue?, Let Me Have My Dreams, My Strongest Weakness Is You, So Long Letty, and Down Among The Sugar Cane.

▽

◁ Encouraged by the success of *The Hottentot*, Edward Everett Horton, starring in **The Aviator**, again found himself in the situation of being forced to pretend he was someone he wasn't. In this instance, Horton (centre) played a successful author who, to help out a friend, lends his name to a book on aeroplanes. As a result, he is considered an expert on the subject and finds himself having to prove it from the inside of a cockpit. Bursting with comic possibilities, most of them were fully explored in Arthur Caesar and Robert Lord's screenplay (based on a play by Otto Harbach and a story by James Montgomery) and in Horton's enjoyable performance. Roy Del Ruth directed the comedy, which also featured Patsy Ruth Miller, Johnny Arthur (left), Lee Moran (right), Bert Roach and Edward Martindel.

△

Warner Bros.' last film of the decade was the German-made drama **The Royal Box**, which featured Alexander Moissoi as the great English actor Edmund Kean, and which split the critics in their appraisal of its worth. Some declared that it was well acted and technically proficient; others that it was thoroughly inept. American audiences were equally divided, and the film, directed by Bryan Foy, emerged as little more than a curiosity. It was based on Dumas' play *Kean* with a scenario by E. Joseph, A. Hurley and Dr. H. Rundt; and featured Camilla Horn, Siegfried (Sig) Rumann, Egon Brecher and Leni Stengel.

The THIRTIES

For almost five years the arrival of sound managed to keep the Depression from affecting the film industry as drastically as it did the rest of the country, but as its novelty-value evaporated, so did audiences. The decade began with 80 million people going to the movies each week, compared with 110 million in 1929, and dropped to 50 million during 1932 and 1933. Having registered profits of $14 million in 1929, and $7 million in 1930, Warner Bros. lost nearly $8 million in 1931. In the same year Fox lost $3 million and RKO $5.6 million. The two major profit-makers that year were MGM with $12 million and Paramount with $6 million (compared with $18 million the previous year). By 1933, however, Paramount went into bankruptcy, MGM's profits had dropped to $1.3 million and RKO and Universal were thrown into receivership. Columbia and United Artists were also in difficulties, as was Warner Bros. who, in 1932 sustained a staggering $14 million loss, but pulled through on the quality and vitality of its product. Fortunately, by 1935 the studio was again in profit.

Darryl F. Zanuck, studio head Jack Warner's right hand man, was responsible for helping to mould the characteristic Warner Bros. look in the early part of the thirties. Eschewing the shimmery surface gloss of the films being made at MGM and the Continental sophistication that Paramount was peddling, Warner Bros. concentrated on realism. Its product echoed the headlines of the day, and its basic concern was for society's losers. For this crusading approach, it became known as the working man's studio, and its films, uncompromisingly shot in black and white to reflect the harshness of the Depression which spawned them, made few concessions to glamour.

During the early thirties, the Depression (and Prohibition) saw the rise of organized crime syndicates whose headline-making activities struck Zanuck (who called it 'spot news') as ideal film fodder. Who were the notorious underworld barons of the time? Where did they come from? What made them the way they were? Nothing could be more contemporary or compelling than finding out the answers, as **The Public Enemy** (1931), which brought James Cagney to stardom, and **Little Caesar** (1931), which did the same for Edward G. Robinson, proved. The studio reaped the considerable benefits of both films, and immediately put into production many more crime-orientated melodramas, most of which followed a similar pattern. They were violent, fast-moving, and tense. Though few ran more than 75 minutes (some even less), they each contained a tightly woven plot and were crammed with incident. They were brilliantly edited, with dissolves, wipes and quick cuts keeping the action constantly on the boil – or, at the very least, simmering. Every shot counted, every line of dialogue

advanced the narrative. Waste was not tolerated. The good guys as well as the bad spoke like machine-gun fire. James Stewart would have been left at the starting post.

Even the studio's musicals (after 1933) were more hard-hitting than was characteristic of the genre, thanks to the trend-setting **42nd Street** (1933) which successfully smashed Hollywood's unwritten moratorium on musicals, and ushered in a Golden Age of song and dance shows which lasted until the end of the decade when, once again, they fell into temporary disrepute. **42nd Street** was another backstage musical – but one with a difference. For director Lloyd Bacon's handling of the familiar material contained all the ingredients of the studio's popular crime melodramas, except that no one was killed. Though newcomer Ruby Keeler 'went out a youngster and came back a star', there was nothing particularly glamorous about the film's milieu, and Bacon's depiction of the Broadway theatre was uncompromisingly harsh. The only moments of sheer escapism were provided by Busby Berkeley's dazzling routines, a brilliant antidote to the sleazy backstage intrigues.

Throughout the decade, Berkeley, who was lured from Broadway to Hollywood by Samuel Goldwyn, and whose first film was **Whoopee** (1930) produced by Goldwyn and Florenz Ziegfeld, set a style and standard in dance direction that every other studio tried but failed to match.

Warner Bros.' gangster films and its musicals proved extremely lucrative throughout the thirties, as indeed did its series of 'women's films' which were economically made and were basically wish fulfilment dramas catering to the average girl's fantasies of the glamorous life. At the same time they had a sting in the tail. Life wasn't always roses, and Miss Average, at whom they were aimed, was deliberately made to feel, on leaving the cinema, that her ordinary humdrum existence was not so bad after all. These films were extremely popular, with Bette Davis, Barbara Stanwyck, Kay Francis and Loretta Young the chief exponents of the genre.

Another important part of Warner Bros.' activities during the thirties was its vast output of 'B-pictures' and 'programmers' (low-budget films). But the studio's greatest contribution to the movies throughout the decade was, apart from its ration of crime films and Busby Berkeley musicals, the prison dramas epitomized by **I am a Fugitive from a Chain Gang** (1932), **20,000 Years in Sing Sing** (1932), **Alcatraz Island** (1937), **Girls on Probation** (1938) and **Each Dawn I Die** (1939). These films were generally critical of the prevailing conditions in prisons and advocated, in the telling of a tautly constructed story, a change in the penal reform system. The studio also wore its social conscience on its sleeve in a diverse selection of films such as **Cabin in the Cotton** (1932),

Five Star Final (1931), Heroes for Sale (1933), Black Fury (1937), Black Legion (1939) and They Won't Forget (1939).

Also, throughout the thirties, the studio's commitment to the hardships of the blue-collar worker manifested itself (particularly during the Depression when the working man was at his most vulnerable) in such abrasive dramas and melodramas as Two Seconds (1932), Tiger Shark (1932), Boulder Dam (1936) and Draegerman Courage (1937).

In the latter half of the decade, with the studio again in the black, it began to relax its frenetic, assembly line approach to film-making, expanded its areas of activity, and, most conspicuously, increased the budgets for many of its films. The policy paid off handsomely, and resulted in pictures like Anthony Adverse (1936), The Adventures of Robin Hood (1938), Captain Blood (1935) and The Prince and the Pauper (1937). A great deal of money, too, was spent on prestige biographies such as The Life of Emile Zola (1937), The Story of Louis Pasteur (1936) and The Private Lives of Elizabeth and Essex (1939). In ten exciting years, the studio bought the rights of 1,518 stories, plays and novels, of which less than 500 were originals. And, of the originals, between 30 and 40 per cent were re-writes of earlier versions.

Naturally, not every film was a winner, but of the studio's 571 productions during the decade, a great many became classics, finding permanent niches in the industry's hall of fame.

Despite the Depression, or maybe because of it, the thirties was a decade of escapism, and with the exception of Warner Bros.' socially committed dramas and melodramas, cinema-goers, paying an average of 25 cents a ticket (10 cents for children) would never have known, from the content of most films on offer, that the country was in the doldrums.

By 1936 weekly cinema attendances had risen to 85 million from its 50 million low in 1932, with local theatres enhancing the appeal and pleasure of moviegoing by presenting double and even triple features or by giving lavish prizes to lucky ticket-holders. Then, as now, 'spin-off' merchandising was big business, with Shirley Temple dolls and rubber replicas of Disney cartoon characters (especially the seven dwarfs after the phenomenally successful release of Snow White and the Seven Dwarfs in 1937) heading the list.

Hedda Hopper and Louella Parsons were the arch priestesses of movie-gossip (and deadly enemies), with make-or-break powers; while Joseph I. Breen became the industry's voice of morality. Appointed in 1934 by Will Hays under pressure from the National Legion of Decency (a group comprising America's Roman Catholic Bishops) Breen had the authority to license films for screening, or, if they contravened what was known as the Production Code, to deny their exhibition in most American theatres. Long, tongue-involving kisses,

double beds, nudity (even in babies) and blasphemy were now strictly taboo. If a man kissed a woman while in bed, he had to have one foot firmly on the floor; crime must never, under any circumstances, be allowed to pay, and woe betide the film-maker who dared, even obliquely, to criticize any aspect of the US Government. Even film titles were changed, thus Infidelity became Fidelity and Good Girls go to Paris Too had the 'Too' dropped.

In the wake of the Production Code came the wholesome 'family' movie, and with it a plethora of new family-orientated stars in direct contrast to, say, Mae West, whose suggestive, sexually loaded films were partially responsible for Breen's appointment in the first place.

According to the trade paper Motion Picture Herald, between 1935 and 1938, Shirley Temple was America's top box-office star, her series of films – from Bright Eyes (Fox, 1934), in which she sang 'On The Good Ship Lollipop' to Little Miss Broadway (1938) – saving Twentieth Century-Fox from bankruptcy.

By 1939, however, she had slipped to fifth position, having been usurped by the talented and versatile Mickey Rooney who, in MGM's Andy Hardy series, became the country's most popular teenager. As the decade ended, Tyrone Power was America's second most popular box-office attraction, Spencer Tracy was rated third, and Clark Gable fourth.

Other successful series of the thirties included the Thin Man films at MGM, Philo Vance (Warner Bros.), Mr. Wong (Monogram), Torchy Blane (Warner Bros.), Nancy Drew (Warner Bros.), the Marx Brothers comedies made at Paramount and MGM, and, most notably, the James Whale-directed horror movies for Universal at the beginning of the decade.

In 1933 Mack Sennett, ruined by the stock market crash, filed a bankruptcy petition and his studio in the San Fernando Valley eventually became the Republic lot – a minor company concentrating on serials and low-budget Westerns. Twentieth Century Pictures merged with Fox and became Twentieth Century-Fox with Darryl F. Zanuck as head of production, a position he held until 1956; and Alfred Newman composed the rousing music over the studio's logo.

1935 saw David O. Selznick break from MGM to form Selznick International, and RKO filmed Becky Sharp, the first feature in three-colour Technicolor.

1936 saw a rise in the unions, with the studios now operating a 'closed shop'; in 1937 Loews Inc. revealed that Louis B. Mayer's salary was $1,296,503, and a monumental decade ended monumentally with the release of Selznick's Gone with the Wind, one of the top-grossing films in Hollywood's history – and one of the best.

1930

By the end of 1930 Warner Bros. owned 51 subsidiary companies, thus enabling the studio to handle all its operations from within its empire. Warner Bros. stock was valued at over $200 million and shareholders collected annual dividends of nearly $12 million. There were 18,500 people employed by the company whose annual salaries came to $36 million. Apart from the well equipped studios in Burbank and on Sunset Boulevard, Warner Bros. owned 93 film exchanges, as well as 525 theatres in 188 cities across America. In November 1930 Warner Bros.' executive offices and cutting rooms were moved to the First National Studios at Burbank. Darryl F. Zanuck was made head of production, and the year also, unfortunately, saw the murder of Motley Flint, one of the brothers' first benefactors. **Disraeli** received an Academy Award nomination for best picture of the year, but did not win (Universal's **All Quiet On The Western Front** did). George Arliss, however, won an Oscar for his work in **Disraeli** and was also nominated for **The Green Goddess**. Rowland Brown's original story for **Doorway To Hell** received an Oscar nomination, and the *New York Times* voted **Outward Bound** as one of the year's ten best films. The studio's net profit for the year was $7,074,621.

Not as effective as its silent predecessor, which also starred George Arliss (seated) as the Rajah of Rukh, **The Green Goddess,** directed by Alfred E. Green, gained little by the addition of sound. The sure-fire story (from the William Archer play) of a group of Britishers who escape death in a plane crash only to find themselves prisoners of an English-hating Rajah, had much of its initial impact dissipated by some inferior supporting performances as well as poor sound reproduction. Julien Josephson wrote the screenplay, and although all the basic ingredients of the story were there, the excitement of the earlier version was missing. Others in the cast were Alice Joyce, H.B. Warner, Ralph Forbes, David Tearle, Reginald Sheffield and Nigel de Brulier. It was remade in 1943 as *Adventure in Iraq*.

General Crack was John Barrymore's first full-length talkie and featured him (right) as Prince Christian Rudolph Augustus Ketlar (General Crack to his friends), a fictitious, early 18th century brigand-cum-lover who dethrones King Leopold III and abducts an archduchess. It was rather self-consciously directed by Alan Crosland, with J. Grubb Alexander and Walter Anthony supplying the scenario (from George Preddy's story dramatized by Thomas Broadhurst). Tony Gaudio's photography was splendid, and the cast included Marian Nixon (left), Armida, Hobart Bosworth, Douglas Gerard, Theodore Lorch and Otto Matiesen.

No expense was spared to bring Guy Bolton and Jerome Kern's 1920 stage musical **Sally** to the screen. Petite Marilyn Miller recreated the role she played on stage, looking enchanting. According to the publicity blurb, she was assisted in her endeavours to bring to life the story of a waitress who makes it to Broadway by '150 beauties in the largest indoor scene ever photographed in color . . . 36 Albertina Rasch girls who toe-dance more perfectly than other choruses can clog . . . and an orchestra of 110 to play the song hits that Sally made famous, and many new numbers added for the screen production'. It was adapted by Waldemar Young and directed by John Francis Dillon with Larry Ceballos responsible for the musical numbers. Others in the cast were Alexander Gray, Joe E. Brown (centre), T. Roy Barnes (right), Pert Kelton (left), Ford Sterling and Maude Turner Gordon. Songs included: Look For The Silver Lining, Wild Rose and Sally (by Jerome Kern and assorted lyricists) and Walking Off Those Balkan Blues, After Business Hours (That Certain Business Begins), All I Want To Do Do Do Is Dance, If I'm Dreaming Don't Wake Me Up Too Soon, and What Will I Do Without You? (by Al Dubin and Joe Burke). (First National.)

A pretty hackneyed vision of a South Sea Island — complete with hula girls, head hunters, unscrupulous traders, weird ceremonial rites, etc. — was to be seen in **Isle of Escape,** a five-and-ten-cent story whose hero arrives not a second too soon to save the heroine from a cruel fate at the hands of the resident savages. The natives were restless; so were audiences. It was written by Lucien Hubbard (whose cupboard of ideas was bare on this occasion) from a story by Jack McLaran and a play by G.C. Dixon, directed by Howard Bretherton and featured Monte Blue, Betty Compson, Noah Beery, Nina Quartero (left), Duke Kahanamoku (right) and Myrna Loy. Song: My Kalua Rose (by Ed Ward and Al Bryan).

Corinne Griffith (illustrated) recreated her 1924 role as Mildred Harker, the victim of a messy divorce, in **Lilies of the Field.** In this instance, though, practice did not make perfect, and Miss Griffith's decline into the jazzy world of nightclubs, where she takes a job, turns into a gold-digger and is finally arrested for vagrancy, was a lugubrious business indeed. A couple of well-mounted production numbers staged (by Roy Mack) in the night-club momentarily relieved the all-pervading gloom. Audiences stayed away and director Alexander Korda ended his association with Warner Bros.-First National. It was written by John F. Goodrich from William Hurlbut's play and also featured Ralph Forbes, May Boley, John Loder, Freeman Wood and Patsy Page. Song: I'd Like To Be A Gypsy. (First National.)

Melodrama ran riot in **Playing Around,** a sober little tale which put Alice White through a compendium of emotions as a poor tenement girl who throws over her clean-living young suitor (William Bakewell) in favour of a shady, smooth-talking type called Nick (Chester Morris). Nick, however, blots his copy book with her when he wounds her shop-assistant father in a hold-up, an act which sends Miss White straight back to Mr Bakewell, in whose welcoming embrace she lives happily ever after. Adele Commandini and Frances Nordstrom adapted from the story by Vina Delmar, and the director was Mervyn LeRoy. Also cast were Marion Byron, Maurice Black, Lionel Belmore, Helen Werle (centre), Shep Camp and Ann Brody. Songs included: That's The Lowdown On The Lowdown, We Learn About Love Every Day, You're My Captain Kidd and Playing Around (by Sam Stept and Bud Green). (First National.)

A frolicsome comedy, well directed by Ted ▷ Wilde, **Loose Ankles** starred Loretta Young as a giddy young thing who defies the terms of her grandmother's will (which stipulates that she will inherit only if the man she marries is approved of by her two maiden aunts, and if no scandal is attached to her name) by advertising for a young man to compromise her. The man who answers the ad is a bashful Douglas Fairbanks Jr and, predictably, a love affair which starts in jest ends as the real thing. Louise Fazenda (left) and Ethel Wales (centre right) played the aunts, with other parts going to Eddie Nugent (right), Inez Courtney, Daphne Pollard (centre left) and Otis Harlan. It was written by Gene Towne from a play by Sam Janney, and choreographed by Roy Mack. Songs included: Loose Ankles and Whoopin' It Up.

A film with a strong feminine appeal, **The** ▷ **Other Tomorrow,** written by Fred Myton and James A. Starr from a story by Octavus Roy Cohen, starred Billie Dove (left) as the wife of a jealous man, and Grant Withers as her childhood sweetheart who is forced to appear as a coward in order to protect Miss Dove from slander. In the end Withers gets Miss Dove, but not before a dramatic climax in which the husband is conveniently killed. Unashamedly romantic, it was well directed by Lloyd Bacon whose cast also included Kenneth Thompson (right), Frank Sheridan, Otto Hoffman and William Grainger. (First National.)

Second Choice turned out to be second best for its two stars, Dolores Costello (centre left) and Jack Mulhall (centre right), both at sea in a script (by Joseph Jackson from a story by Elizabeth Alexander) which required them to be jilted by their respective partners. Though director Howard Bretherton gave it a glossy sheen, he could not disguise its basic vacuity; nor could a cast which also included Chester Morris, Edna Murphy, Charlotte Merriam, Edward Martindel and Ethlyne Clair.

◁The successful Broadway musical **No, No, Nanette** made a felicitous transfer to the screen under the guidance of director Clarence Badger, and although its plot was not particularly original (it tells of the complications that befall a married bible-manufacturer who innocently helps three girls from three different cities only to find them simultaneously arriving at his cottage in Atlantic City), its infectious good spirits (and tunes) turned it into an instant hit. Howard Emmett Rogers' screenplay (from the play by Otto Harbach and Frank Mandel) didn't stint on the laughs, the Technicolor sequences were dazzling, and the cast, though not exceptional, were adequate for the demands of the lightweight material. They included Bernice Claire (left), Lucien Littlefield (right), Alexander Gray, Lilyan Tashman, Bert Roach and ZaSu Pitts. The dance director was Larry Ceballos. Songs included: As Long As I'm With You, King Of The Air, No, No, Nanette, Dancing On Mars, I Want To Be Happy and Tea For Two. (First National.)

Written especially for Winnie Lightner (centre), **She Couldn't Say No** told the tedious story of a nightclub entertainer who is elevated to stardom through the efforts of a reformed gangster (Chester Morris). Unfortunately Chester loves a woman with more breeding than Winnie (Sally Eilers) but his romance with her comes to an end when he stops a bullet and dies. Miss Lightner was fine in the film's jokier moments, but wasn't up to the dramatics. The Arthur Caesar-Robert Lord dialogue (from a play by Benjamin M. Kaye, adaptation by Harvey Thew) hardly stretched the rest of the cast (Tully Marshall, Johnny Arthur and Louise Beavers) any more than did Lloyd Bacon's sloppy direction. It was remade in 1940. Songs included: Darn Fool Woman Like Me, Watching My Dreams Go By and Bouncing The Baby Around (by Al Dubin and Joe Burke).

Oscar Hammerstein II and Laurence Stallings' stage musical *Rainbow* came in for some rough treatment in its screen incarnation **Song of the West.** Starring John Boles (left) and Vivienne Segal (right), neither in particularly good voice on this occasion and both the victims of poor sound recording, this romantic operetta with its Wild West background had little to recommend it except Dev Jennings' Technicolor photography which, at least, pleased the eye. For the rest, Harvey Thew's screenplay and Ray Enright's direction gave scant support to the other members of the cast which included Joe E. Brown, who dies in the course of the story, Edward Martindel, Harry Gribbon, Marie Wells and Sam Hardy. Songs (by Oscar Hammerstein II and Youmans) included: Come Back To Me, The Bride Was Dressed In White and Hay Straw.

Mexico and Texas provided the twin settings for **Under a Texas Moon,** a Technicolor adventure directed with a nice sense of the romantic by Michael Curtiz and starring Frank Fay (right) as desperado Don Carlos, with Raquel Torres (left), Armida, and Myrna Loy as the combined feminine interest. Fay found working with Curtiz an imposition, and vice versa. It was written by Gordon Rigby from a story by Stewart Edward White, and, also featured Noah Beery, Georgie Stone, Fred Kohler, Betty Boyd, Tully Marshall and Inez Gomez. Song: Under A Texas Moon (by Roy Perkins).

△ In **Strictly Modern,** Dorothy Mackaill (illustrated) starred as a novelist eluded by true love until she meets and falls for a man who once left her cousin stranded at the church on her wedding day. A moderately entertaining bon-bon of a film, it was written and adapted by Ray Harris, Gene Towne and J. Morris from the play by Hubert Henry Davis, and featured Sidney Blackmer, Julianne Johnston, Warner Richmond, Mickey Bennett and Katherine Clare Ward. William A. Seiter directed. (First National.)

△

A fair amount of witty dialogue plus a few good songs (by Rodgers and Hart) gave **Spring is Here** its two main selling points. The story of a martinet father who, against his daughter's wishes, thrusts a bashful suitor onto her, it starred Lawrence Gray, Alexander Gray (centre), Bernice Claire (centre right), Wilbur Mack (right), Louise Fazenda (left) and Ford Sterling (far left). John Francis Dillon directed (from a screenplay by James A. Starr which was based on a Broadway musical with a book by Owen Davis). Songs included: Have A Little Faith In Me, Cryin' For The Carolines, What's The Big Idea? and Bad Baby. (First National.)

In **Son of the Gods**, Richard Barthelmess (left) had the misfortune of being cast as a man who has gone through life believing he is Chinese, when, in fact, it turns out that he is indisputably Caucasian. An inordinately silly screenplay by Bradley King from a Rex Beach novel, with direction by Frank Lloyd that failed to help either, also featured Constance Bennett, Dorothy Matthews (centre), Barbara Leonard, Jimmy Eagles and Frank Albertson. It was photographed by Ernest Haller in black and white and Technicolor. Song (by Ben Ryan and Sol Vidinsky): Pretty Little You.

▽

△

The Furies (based on Zoë Akins' play) reached the screen as a programmer starring H.B. Warner (left), Jane Winton (second right), Montagu Love and Lois Wilson. The story of a son who accuses his mother and her lover of murdering his father, its similarity to *Hamlet* began and ended right there. Forrest Halsey wrote the screenplay, Alan Crosland directed and apart from its leading players, who were not at their best, the cast included Carl Stockdale (centre left), Natalie Moorhead (centre right), Theodore von Eltz (second left) and Tyler Brooke (right). (First National.)

Showgirl in Hollywood plotted the up-and-down course of a New York musical comedy performer who is spotted in a nightclub by a film producer and earmarked for Hollywood stardom. A behind-the-scenes look (in Technicolor and black-and-white) at the inner workings of the movie business, the film starred Alice White (left) as the showgirl, with Jack Mulhall (centre), Blanche Sweet (who was excellent), John Miljan, Ford Sterling (right), Virginia Sale and Herman Bing in support. It was based on J.P. McEvoy's novel *Hollywood Girl* and adapted by Harvey Thew and James A. Starr, whose attempted satirization of the movie industry was completely off target, though it did provide the uninitiated with an accurate idea of how early sound films were made. The dance director was Jack Haskell and the supervisor Robert Lord. Songs (by Bud Green and Sammy Stept) included: Hang On To The Rainbow, I've Got My Eye On You (not the Cole Porter standard which was written later) and There's A Tear For Every Smile In Hollywood. (First National.)

▽

Rin-Tin-Tin's first all-talkie was a lame ▷ adventure called **On the Border.** The chief activity was smuggling and the only surprise was a tramp who turns out to be a government official. It was written by Lillie Hayward who, unlike its star, had no new tricks up her sleeve; and featured Mexican singer-and-dancer Armida, as well as John Litel, Philo McCullough, Bruce Covington and Walter Miller. The director was William McGann.

Billie Dove (right) was somewhat upstaged by Kay Francis (loaned to Warner Bros. from Paramount Pictures) and Basil Rathbone (another newcomer to the studio) in **A Notorious Affair.** She played a socialite who sacrifices her position in society by marrying a violinist (Rathbone, centre left) only to discover that he is having an affair with a countess (Francis). Content to remain in the wings, she returns to him when he is struck down by illness and nurses him back to health. The quintessential 'woman's picture', it was based on a play by Audrey and Waverley Carter called *Fame*, and adapted for the screen by J. Grubb Alexander. Lloyd Bacon directed efficiently, and his supporting cast featured Montagu Love and Kenneth Thompson. (First National.) ▽

Dumbbells in Ermine won no awards for cinematic excellence, but was a moderately entertaining comedy about a young girl who falls in love with a prizefighter. There was plenty of plot in Harvey Thew's adaptation of Lynn Starling's play *Weak Sisters*, and director John Adolfi, aided by a cast that included Barbara Kent (left) as the heroine, Beryl Mercer as her scheming grandmother, Robert Armstrong (right) as the prizefighter and James Gleason (centre, who also wrote the dialogue) as a trainer, kept it simmering along nicely. ▽

In **Hold Everything,** Joe E. Brown (centre) this time found himself pretending to be a champion prizefighter, with the usual hilarious results. The more lyrical sections, involving a romance between real-life boxer George Carpentier and Sally O'Neill, were less entertaining and slowed down the snappy pace set by director Roy Del Ruth. Based on a musical play by B.G. De Sylva and John McGowan, and scripted by Robert Lord, the film (in Technicolor) also featured Winnie Lightner, Bert Roach, Dorothy Revier and Edmund Breese. Songs (by Al Dubin and Joe Burke) included: Take It On The Chin, When Little Red Roses Get The Blues For You, Sing A Little Theme Song, Physically Fit, Girls We Remember, All Alone Together, Isn't This A Cockeyed World and You're The Cream In My Coffee. ▽

Rin-Tin-Tin starred in **The Man Hunter,** a tale about a business woman (Nora Lane) who takes a trip to Africa to investigate why an ivory concern she has out there is yielding such poor returns. The reason, she discovers, is that her chief employee has been selling the stuff and pocketing the profits. Rinty comes to the rescue, and in the process saves the film from tedium. Charles Delaney (illustrated with Rinty), Pat Hartigan, Christiane Yves and Floyd Shackleford were also in the substandard adventure (written by Lillian Hayward and James A. Starr) and the director was Ross Lederman. ▷

Those Who Dance was a pedestrian remake of the 1924 First National melodrama whose workaday plot rested on the attempts of a girl (Lila Lee, left), with the help of a policeman (Monte Blue, right), to clear her innocent brother of a murder rap. It was unashamed hokum and its cast, clearly brighter than Joseph Jackson's script (from a story by George Kibbe Turner) played it as such. William Beaudine's direction, however, was unoriginal throughout. Also cast were Betty Compson, Bill Boyd, William Janney. Wilfred Lucas and De Witt Jennings.

An Oriental cloak-and-dagger adventure drenched in Fu Manchu movie platitudes, **Murder Will Out** blamed the Chinese for all the foul play perpetrated in J. Grubb Alexander's screenplay (from Murray Leinster and Will Jenkins' story). In the end, though, when the real culprits are unmasked, none of them turn out to have funny voices or slit eyes. Jack Mulhall (left), Lila Lee (centre left), Malcolm McGregor, Hedda Hopper (centre right), Alec B. Francis (right) and Claude Allister appeared under the run-of-the-mill direction of Clarence Badger. (First National.)

△
Another Corinne Griffith vehicle, **Back Pay** was the hearts-and-flowers story of a small-town girl who jilts her sweetheart for a war profiteer. When, however, her home-town lad returns from the war blinded and near death, she relinquishes her profiteer and goes back to boyfriend number one. And although he dies, she remains faithful to his memory. Miss Griffith (left) was not particularly compelling as the heroine and brought little light and shade to Francis Edward Faragoh's screen adaptation of the Fannie Hurst novel on which it was based. William A. Seiter directed, and the cast also included Grant Withers (right) as the blinded young man, Montagu Love as the war profiteer as well as Vivian Oakland, Geneva Mitchell, Bill Bailey and Hallam Cooley. (First National.)

The Russian Revolution provided the back- ▷ ground to **Song of the Flame**, an elaborately produced, all-Technicolor operetta which, despite its no-expense-spared approach remained a bore. Based on a play by Oscar Hammerstein II, Otto Harbach, Herbert Stothart and George Gershwin, it was flatly adapted to the screen by Gordon Rigby, and came alive only in the musical interludes staged by Jack Haskell. It starred Alexander Gray (right), Bernice Claire (left, as The Flame), Alice Gentle, and Noah Beery. Alan Crosland directed. Songs (by Gershwin, Stothart, Harry Akst, Grant Clark and Ed Ward) included: Cossack Love Song, One Little Drink, Song Of The Flame, Petrograd, Liberty Song, The Goose Hangs High, Passing Fancy and When Love Calls. (First National.)

John Barrymore wearing modern dress was something of a novelty on the screen and therefore all the more welcome in **The Man from Blankley's**, a comedy based on S. Anstey's play and directed, most entertainingly, by Alfred E. Green. Barrymore (left) played a drunken, hiccupping Scottish peer who, in his inebriated state, walks into the wrong house one evening where he is mistaken by the hostess for the man she has hired from Blankley's department store to serve as the 14th guest at her dinner party – 13, of course, being an unlucky number. In the course of the evening, the misunderstandings inherent in the basic situation multiply with great comic effect, giving Barrymore a rare chance to show off another facet of his talent. Harvey Thew and Joseph Jackson's screenplay wasn't as sparkling as it could have been, but Barrymore's central performance was – which was all that mattered. Loretta Young (centre), Louise Carver, Emily Fitzroy (as the hostess), May Milloy, Dale Fuller and Edgar Norton were also cast. ▷

The Flirting Widow, set in England, was a depressing little remake of *Slightly Used* (1927) in which Dorothy Mackaill (left) invents a lover for herself by writing to an imaginary colonel in Arabia so that her younger sister, whose father has forbidden her to marry before she (Miss Mackaill) does, can get on with her own romance. Basil Rathbone (centre) played the 'imagi-▽

nary' colonel who actually exists, and brought to an otherwise lamentable effort its only point of interest. William Austin, Wilfred Noy (right), Leila Hyams, Claude Gillingwater and Emily Fitzroy were also in it but made nothing of John F. Goodrich's improbable screenplay (from the story *Green Stockings* by A.E.W. Mason). The director was William A. Seiter. (First National.)

The Warner Bros. backlot did very well as the Bay of Naples, the setting of Ole Olsen and Chic Johnson's first film for the studio, **Oh! Sailor Behave!** Adapted from Elmer Rice's successful Broadway comedy by Joseph Jackson (dialogue by Jackson and Sid Silvers), it starred the famous comedy team as a pair of American sailors on the lookout for a man with a wooden leg who has robbed a Navy storehouse. One of their methods of detection is to aim a pea-shooter at the legs of possible suspects, and all those who jump are deemed innocent of the crime. In tandem with this was the love interest involving Charles King (centre) and Irene Delroy (left). A moderate box-office success, it was directed by Archie Mayo, with Lotti Loder, Noah Beery, Lowell Sherman, Vivian Oakland and Lawrence Grant (right) in support. Because of the studio's increasing distrust of musicals the film's release was delayed. Songs included: Love Comes In The Moonlight, Leave A Little Smile, Tell Us Which One Do You Love, Highway To Heaven (by Al Dubin and Joe Burke) and The Laughing Song (by Olsen and Johnson).

◁ In **Sweet Mama**, (released in Britain as **Conflict**) Alice White succeeded almost single-handedly in bringing to justice a gang of hoods while at the same time managing to steer her crooked lover back to the straight and narrow. She certainly worked hard, but to no avail. The territory traversed by Earl Baldwin's screenplay (from a story he wrote with Frederick Hazlitt Brennan) was too well-worn for surprises and failed to generate interest. Richard Cramer (left), David Manners (second right), Rita Flynn, Kenneth Thomson (centre left), Lee Shumway (centre right), Lew Harvey (second left) and Lee Moran (right) also appeared for director Eddie Cline. (First National.)

As in all Rin-Tin-Tin adventures, virtue triumphed over vice, and **Rough Waters**, the nineteenth and last Rinty offering from the studio, was no exception. The pulse-quickening story of three murderous gangsters who hide out with a fortune of stolen loot in a house occupied by an elderly sea-captain and his daughter, it gave Rinty, in his swansong, yet another opportunity to help his police officer master to bring the bad guy to justice. Lane Chandler, Jobyna Ralston, Edmund Breese, Walter Miller and Richard Alexander were the human factors in James A. Starr's screenplay, and the director was John Daumery.

The combination of Al Jolson (illustrated) as an 'endman' in a travelling minstrel show and a musical score by Irving Berlin was a winning one and **Mammy**, photographed in black-and-white with sequences in Technicolor, was a smash. Based on Berlin's play *Mr. Bones*, which he wrote with James Gleason, it was adapted by Gordon Rigby with more than a touch of the melodramatics about it, especially when Jolson is shot in a scene during the show after a rival has substituted real bullets for blanks. With Jolson around for most of the film's running time, the supporting players had a hard time making their presences felt. They included Lois Moran, Louise Dresser, Lowell Sherman, Hobart Bosworth and Tully Marshall. It was supervised by Walter Morosco and directed by Michael Curtiz. Songs included: To My Mammy, Across The Breakfast Table, Looking At You, Let Me Sing And I'm Happy, Knights Of The Road and Yes, We Have No Bananas (sung to Verdi's *Miserere* from *Il Trovatore*).

Based on a play by Tom Barry and brought to the screen by Walter Anthony with its plot more or less intact, **Courage** charted the tribulations that befall a widow whose sorry lot it is to bring up seven children, six of whom are set against her. The basic material deserved better performances than it was accorded, though Belle Bennett (centre) as the long-suffering mother did well enough in the role created on stage by Janet Beecher. Archie Mayo was the director, and his cast also included Marian Nixon, Don Marion (left), Byron Sage (centre left), Rex Bell, Richard Tucker, Leon Janney (right), Carter de Haven Jr (centre right) and Blanche Frederici. It was remade in 1938 as *My Bill*.

△
Recaptured Love starred John Halliday (left) as a happily married middle-aged man who falls for a young cabaret dancer (Dorothy Burgess). He divorces his wife (Belle Bennett, right), marries the entertainer, but soon discovers the error of his ways. His former wife takes him back but not before she exacts a revenge of her own. Inconsequential and unconvincing, it was written by Charles Kenyon from a play by Basil Woon, directed by John Adolfi, and the cast also featured Richard Tucker, George Bickel, Brooks Benedict, Sister 'G' and a precocious youngster called Junior Durkin (centre).

◁ A Technicolored, operetta-like romp, **Sweet Kitty Bellairs** was set in Merrie England when men wore powdered wigs and fought duels, and starred Claudia Dell (left) as the flirtatious heroine who spends a summer in Bath, and steals the heart of a notorious highwayman. Hardly a story to mull over, its chief virtues lay in the pretty way it looked, and the charming manner in which director Alfred E. Green handled J. Grubb Alexander's screenplay (from a novel by Agnes and Egerton Castle and the play by David Belasco). Also lending their talents to the innocuous but entertaining enterprise were Ernest Torrence (right), Walter Pidgeon, Perry Askan, June Collyer, Lionel Belmore and Arthur Edmund Carewe. Songs: You-u-u and I Love You.

△
Amnesia was the subject of **The Matrimonial Bed** (released in Britain as **A Matrimonial Problem**), a moderately amusing comedy adapted by Seymour Hicks and Harvey Thew from a play by Yves Mirande and André Mouëzy-Eon. The victim was Frank Fay (centre), who, after an accident, loses his memory for five years, during which time his wife (Florence Eldridge), believing him to be dead, remarries. Complications arise when, by chance, Miss Eldridge bumps into her husband who has sought employment as a barber. Lilyan Tashman (right), James Gleason, Beryl Mercer, Vivian Oakland, Arthur Edmund Carewe and Marion Byron (left) were also featured, and the director was Michael Curtiz. It was remade in 1941 as *Kisses For Breakfast*.

◁ **Bride of the Regiment** (released in Britain as **Lady of the Rose**) was based on the stage play *Lady in Ermine* by Rudolph Schnazer and Ernst Welisch (which had been filmed before, with Corinne Griffith as the star, in 1927). Yet another cinema operetta, it was a tedious business which not even Technicolor and a certain amount of spectacle could alleviate. Vivienne Segal played a countess who, to save her husband (Allan Prior) from a firing squad, flirts with an Austrian colonel (Walter Pidgeon) who wishes to seduce her. Drunk with champagne the colonel falls asleep, dreams that she has willingly submitted to him, and consequently frees her husband the count. The contrivances of the plot (screenplay by Ray Harris and Humphrey Pearson) hardly added up to adult entertainment. John Francis Dillon directed (with Jack Haskell staging the musical numbers), and his cast included Louise Fazenda (left), Ford Sterling (right), Lupino Lane and Myrna Loy. Songs (by Al Bryan, Ed Ward and Al Dubin) included: Broken-hearted Lover, Dream Away, Heart Of Heaven, I'd Like To Be A Happy Bride, One Kiss, Sweetheart and Then Goodbye. (First National.)

Shot on location in San Quentin, **Numbered Men** was the kind of behind bars melodrama that would soon become synonymous with the studio, Directed by Mervyn LeRoy, and based on the play *Jailbreak* by Dwight Taylor, the Al Cohn-Henry McCarthy screenplay focused on a chain of incidents that occurred after an inmate, serving a ten-year sentence for counterfeiting, hears that a fellow convict has been messing around with his girl. Conrad Nagel and Raymond Hackett starred, with Bernice Claire (right), Tully Marshall, Ralph Ince (left), Fred Howard and the earlier William Holden in support. (First National.)

◁ Erich von Stroheim's appearance in **Three Faces East** raised it above the level of routine espionage melodrama and gave Oliver H.P. Garrett and Arthur Caesar's screenplay (from a play by Anthony Paul Kelly) a conviction it did not deserve. Von Stroheim (centre) played a German spy who is engaged as a butler by the First Lord of the Admiralty. It was a compelling performance which director Roy Del Ruth exploited most effectively. Other good performances, too, came from Constance Bennett (also a spy, left) and William Courtenay (centre left) as a British secret service official. Anthony Bushell (centre right), Charlotte Walker and William Holden (right) were also cast.

△ Murder most foul in an old house was the subject of **In the Next Room**, a poorly made thriller that literally took Vitaphone back to scratch in its sound reproduction and took the art of acting back to before the flood. Basically a who-dunnit, it was directed by Eddie Cline from a screenplay by Harvey Gates and James A. Starr (and the play by Eleanor Robson Belmont and Harriet Ford) and starred Alice Day (right) and Jack Mulhall (left) with Robert O'Connor (centre), John St Polis, Claude Allister and DeWitt Jennings in support. (First National.)

Credulity was stretched to breaking point in **Road to Paradise**, a piece of hogwash about a couple of men and a girl who rob a house belonging to the girl's double (who turns out to be the twin sister she hasn't seen since childhood). Loretta Young (centre) played both sisters, with Jack Mulhall (left), Raymond Hatton, Kathlyn Williams (right), Dot Farley and George Barraud in support. Based on a play by Mitchell Dodson and Zelda Sears, it was written for the screen by F. Hugh Herbert. William Beaudine directed. (First National.)

△ Director Bryan Foy went all out for slapstick in **The Gorilla** (first made by First National, 1927), a predictable mystery melodrama in which a couple of sleuths (one of them made up to look like a gorilla himself) are employed by the owner of a mansion to track down the hairy beast who has taken up residence there and is causing no end of bother. Based on a play by Ralph Spence and brought to the screen by Spence, Herman Ruby and W. Harrison Orkow, it involved the talents of Joe Frisco, Harry Gribbon, Edwin Maxwell, Lila Lee (left), Walter Pidgeon and Roscoe Karns. (First National.)

◁ The operetta **Golden Dawn** by Otto Harbach, Oscar Hammerstein II, Emmerich Kalman and Herbert Stothart (seen on the stage in 1927), with its East African setting, retained its title in the Technicolor movie version. Unfortunately, colour wasn't what was needed to give this story, of a native uprising against the British and the Germans in the First World War, credence. The acting ranged from the inoffensive (Vivienne Segal, Walter Woolf, centre right) to the thoroughly offensive (a blacked-up Noah Beery, left) with Alice Gentle, Lupino Lane, Dick Henderson, Sojin, Otto Matieson (centre left) and Marion Byron somewhere in between. Director Ray Enright unfortunately allowed the improbabilities of Walter Anthony's screenplay to affect his judgment. Today it's merely camp, especially the staging of the musical numbers by Larry Ceballos. Songs included: (by Harbach, Hammerstein II and Kalman) Whip Song, Dawn, My Bwana, We Too; and (by Grant Clarke and Harry Akst) My Heart's Love Call, Africa Smiles No More, Mooda's Song and In A Jungle Bungalow.

What attracted Howard Hawks to **The** ▷ **Dawn Patrol** (whose story he devised with John Monk Saunders) was the challenge it provided in the aerial sequences, as well as the message at the heart of the heroics: that war is a synonym for waste. Richard Barthelmess, Douglas Fairbanks Jr, Neil Hamilton, William Janney, James Finlayson and Clyde Cook were among the actors assembled to tell the story of a squadron leader who is hated by his officers because of the tragically high death toll in his unit. And although many of the scenes on terra firma were grounded by stilted dialogue as writers Hawks, Dan Totheroh and Seton I. Miller attempted – somewhat uneasily – to come to grips with characterization through the spoken word, the aerial photography was (and remains) superb, boasting some of the finest dogfights ever put onto film. After completion, **The Dawn Patrol** came in for legal trouble. Howard Hughes claimed that whole sections of his movie *Hell's Angels* were used in the film; and writer R.C. Sheriff sued Warner Bros. for lifting 'substantial portions' of his celebrated play *Journey's End* and putting them into the screenplay. Both lost their cases, and the film, benefiting from the resultant publicity, went on release with great success. It was supervised by Robert North and remade in 1938. (First National.)

Pure fantasy, **The Second Floor Mystery** was a modest comedy based on a story by Earl Derr Biggers in which a young man communicates with the girl of his dreams through the personal columns of the London *Times*. The correspondence leads to a series of dramatic adventures involving the talents of H.B. Warner as an Inspector-cum- ▷ murderer, Claude King, John Loder, Claire McDowell, Judith Vosselli, Crauford Kent and Sidney Bracy. Heading the cast were Loretta Young and Grant Withers (both centre right). Roy Del Ruth directed from a screenplay by Joseph Jackson.

◁ **Top Speed**, a musical comedy that was funnier than it was musical, starred Joe E. Brown (right) as a humble order clerk who pretends to be a millionaire. He wins a boat race in a vessel owned by his sweetheart's father and even sees to it that the villain of the piece gets his come-uppance in the end. A treat for Brown fans and a pleasant surprise for his detractors, it featured several songs (staged by Larry Ceballos) and a cast that included Bernice Claire (left), Jack Whiting, Frank McHugh (in the first of many films he made for Warner Bros.), Laura Lee, Rita Flynn and Edmund Breese. Mervyn LeRoy directed, and his handling of the big boat race was first-rate. It was based on a play by Harry Ruby, Bert Kalmar and Guy Bolton and written for the screen by Humphrey Pearson and Henry McCarty. Songs (by Kalmar and Ruby) included: Goodness Gracious, I'll Know And She'll Know, Keep Your Undershirt On, What Would I Care, Sweeter Than You and (by Al Dubin and Joe Burke) As Long As I Have You And You Have Me. (First National.)

The plot of **Dancing Sweeties**, a musical in which a young couple meet in a dance contest, marry, divorce when the ambitious husband realizes that his wife is unable to learn new, more intricate dance steps, but are reunited at the end, was more original than many current screen romances but failed to realize its potential in Gordon Rigby and Joseph Jackson's under-developed screenplay. Showing little confidence in the material, director Ray Enright resorted to clichés. Grant Withers (second left) was passable as the husband, though Sue Carol (left) as his wife made little impact. Also cast were Edna Murphy (second right), Tully Marshall, Eddie Phillips (right), Kate Price and Ada·Mae Brougham. Songs included: Wishing And Waiting For Love (by Grant Clarke and Harry Akst), Hullabaloo (by Bobby Dolan and Walter O'Keefe), I Love You, I Hate You (by Al Bryan and Joseph Meyer) and The Kiss Waltz (by Al Dubin and Joe Burke). Another song, Dancing With Tears In My Eyes, was removed from the final print, but nonetheless went on to become a big hit.

A singularly childish drama, **Divorce Among Friends** was basically a triangle situation (husband, wife and other woman) with a bibulous fourth character waiting in the wings to help resolve the situation by marrying the other woman so that everyone can live happily ever after. It was written by Arthur Caesar and Harvey Thew from a story by Jack Townley, and directed by Roy Del Ruth with less assurance than usual. James Hall and Irene Delroy (right) were the bickering married couple, Natalie Moorhead the third point of the triangle and Lew Cody (left) the inebriated friend. Edward Martindel and Margaret Seddon also appeared.

Edward Everett Horton (right) came to the ▷ rescue of **Wide Open** playing a timid employee who has an idea how to improve his boss's business but lacks the courage to do anything about it. However, the boss's daughter (Patsy Ruth Miller), who is far from timid, arrives and knows exactly how to go about it. Complications break out like a rash but are resolved by the final fade with Horton and Miller altar-bound. Based on a story by Edward Bateman Morris and adapted by James A. Starr and Arthur Caesar, it was directed by Archie Mayo with a cast that included T. Roy Barnes, Louise Beavers (left), Louise Fazenda, Edna Murphy and Vera Lewis.

Dorothy Mackaill gave a good account of ▷ herself doing the Hula in **Bright Lights**, a Technicolor musical with a backstage setting, but there was little else to admire in Humphrey Pearson's screenplay, which also gave employment to Noah Beery (as a villain). The story of an actress who forsakes the footlights for marital respectability, but finds all sorts of obstacles in the way of her happiness, it featured Frank Fay, Inez Courtney, Eddie Nugent, Edmund Breese, Daphne Pollard and Frank McHugh (irritating as a drunken reporter). The film was directed by Michael Curtiz with Robert North supervising, and the musical numbers were staged by Larry Ceballos. Songs included: Nobody Cares If I'm Blue, I'm Crazy For Cannibal Love, Chinatown, Song Of The Congo and You're An Eyeful Of Heaven. (First National.)

◁ What distinguished **The Office Wife** from other romantic offerings of the sort was the fact that the pretty heroine (Dorothy Mackaill, right), set her sights on an older, more mature man instead of the conventional good-looking younger one. Lewis Stone (left), her married employer, was the victim of her seductive wiles and together they made an attractive couple. Natalie Moorhead also appeared as Stone's overthrown but independent wife, with strong support from Joan Blondell (in her second film for Warner Bros. – her first, Sinners Holiday, was released shortly afterwards), Hobart Bosworth, Blanche Frederici, Brooks Benedict and Dale Fuller. The film was directed by Lloyd Bacon from Charles Kenyon's screenplay and a story by Faith Baldwin.

In **Big Boy**, the film of his 1925 stage success, ▷
Al Jolson (left) played a negro jockey (in
blackface) who triumphs over adversity and
wins the Kentucky Derby. Jolson's singing
was the main attraction in this routine
musical, though some of the wisecracks in
the William K. Wells-Perry Vekroff screen-
play were spot on. Alan Crosland directed
Jolson much more lightheartedly than he
had done in *The Jazz Singer*, inspired prob-
ably by the energy of the original play (by
Harold Atteridge, Buddy De Sylva, James P.
Hanley and Joseph Meyer). The rest of the
cast included Louise Closser Hale, Lloyd
Hughes, Eddie Phillips and Noah Beery.
Songs included: What Will I Do Without
You? (by Al Dubin and Joe Burke), Tomorrow
Is Another Day, Liza Lee (by Bud Green and
Sammy Stept), Down South (by Sigmund
Spaeth and George Middleton) and The
Handicap March (by Dave Reed Jr and
George Rosey).

◁ As an outlaw called Pancho Lopez in **The
Bad Man** (which had been made by First
National in 1923), Walter Huston dominated Clarence Badger's mediocre film. Looking and sounding just like the name of the
character he played, Huston (left) made
as much of a meal out of the undernourished
vehicle as was humanly possible. But by
the time he stopped a ranger's bullet,
audiences hardly cared whether he lived or
died. Howard Estabrook wrote it from a
story by Porter Emerson Browne and it
also featured Dorothy Revier (right), James
Rennie, Sidney Blackmer and O.P. Heggie.
It was remade in 1937 as *West of Shanghai*.
(First National.)

George Arliss' superb character study of
the managing director of a bankrupt firm
of shipowners was the chief reason for
seeing **Old English**, Walter Anthony and
Maude Howell's adaptation of John Gals-
worthy's celebrated Victorian drama. In an
attempt to make provision for his two
grandchildren, Arliss (right) as Sylvanus
Heythrop indulges in some financial hanky-
panky, knowing that the only honourable
way out of his fraudulent dealings is
death. So he enjoys one last luxurious meal
and expires peacefully, and conveniently, in
his favourite armchair after finishing a
liqueur. It was not what he did but the way
he did it that gave the film its fascination,
and although the supporting performances
(by Leon Janney, Doris Lloyd, Betty Lawford (left), Ivan Simpson and Harrington
Reynolds) were not of the best, it hardly
mattered with Arliss in such splendid form.
Alfred E. Green directed.
▽

Audiences could not be blamed for failing to support **Scarlet Pages**, an old-fashioned tear-jerker in which a woman attorney, while defending a cabaret dancer charged with murdering her sadistic foster father, discovers that the girl in the dock is none other than her own daughter who, twenty years ago, she had abandoned in an orphanage. Elsie Ferguson (repeating the role she created on stage) played the attorney, Marion Nixon (centre front) was her daughter. John Halliday, Grant Withers, Helen Ferguson, De Witt Jennings and Charlotte Walker were also in the cast. Ray Enright directed with his tongue not nearly far enough in his cheek; and it was written (from the play by Samuel Shipman and John B. Hymer) by Walter Anthony and Maude Fulton. (First National.)

Joining Joan Bennett, Joe E. Brown, James Hall, Anders Randolph and Laura Lee in **Maybe It's Love** were the 1929 All-American football team in an attempt to add a touch of male glamour as well as authenticity to the screenplay by Joseph Jackson and Mark Canfield (Darryl Zanuck) of a campus flirt's attempts to lure away from various colleges around the country the eleven best footballers in America in order to ensure a resounding victory for her own college. It generated much laughter (intentional) and was a fair success. Joan Bennett was the flirt, Joe E. Brown (centre) a football star who loses his glory when he is replaced on the team by one of the new arrivals. William Wellman directed. Songs included: Maybe It's Love and All American.

College Lovers was another typical campus comedy with romance and football featuring as the chief ingredients. Earl Baldwin's story (scenario by Douglas Doty) also involved a college flirt, this time in the shape of Marion Nixon (left). She causes havoc by winning the hearts of the two best players (Russell Hopton, centre and Guinn Williams, right) in the football team, though the man she really loves (Jack Whiting) is not at all athletic. There is disruption in the big game, of course – the final outcome of which is a tie. In director John Adolfi's battle of style over content, the outcome was also a tie. Others in the cast were Frank McHugh, Wade Boteler, Phyllis Crane and Richard Tucker. Songs included: Up And At 'Em and One Minute Of Heaven. (First National.)

Based on H.V. Esmond's play *When We Were Twenty-one*, **The Truth About Youth** was a competent, thoroughly entertaining little film in which, after much deliberation compounded by misunderstandings and complications, Loretta Young (centre left) decides to settle down with a middle-aged Conway Tearle (centre right) instead of youthful David Manners (left). The film also featured Myrna Loy as a cabaret dancer with whom Manners is smitten, as well as J. Farrell MacDonald, Harry Stubbs and Myrtle Stedman (right). It was written for the screen by W. Harrison Orkow and directed by William A. Seiter. (First National.)

A young actor from Broadway called James Cagney made his film debut in **Sinner's Holiday** playing the same role he had created on stage. Basically a romance between a carnival barker and a young girl whose mother runs a penny arcade, it also involved murder and rum-running, a heady combination which the intelligent performances of Cagney and Grant Withers (right) miraculously managed to rescue from out-and-out melodrama. It was written by Harvey Thew from an unsuccessful play by Marie Baumer and directed by John Adolfi. Also cast were Joan Blondell (her debut at the studio), Evalyn Knapp (left), Otto Hoffman, Purnell Pratt, Lucille La Verne and Warren Hymer.

A remake of the 1923 silent version, **The Girl of the Golden West** starred Ann Harding (left) as Minnie and James Rennie (right) as the handsome highwayman Johnson. Waldemar Young's adaptation, labouring under the creaking melodrama of the original, was workable enough, though some of the dialogue was unbelievable. Unfortunately John Francis Dillon's direction tended, at times, to minimize some of the story's high points, such as the vital card-game between Jack Rance (Harry Bannister, centre) and Minnie, the outcome of which determines whether she and Johnson retain their freedom. Also in the cast were Ben Hendricks Jr, J. Farrell MacDonald and George Cooper. (First National.)

'30

Old fashioned even by 1930s standards, **One Night at Susie's** was a gangster melodrama which featured Helen Ware as a good Samaritan who shares a Broadway rooming house with a gang of hoods, and who ministers to their every need. Douglas Fairbanks Jr (right) appeared as a man serving a prison sentence for a crime he did not commit, with Billie Dove (left) prominently featured as his chorus-girl sweetheart, guilty of the crime. Also cast were Tully Marshall, James Crane, John Loder and Claude Fleming. It was written by Forrest Halsey and Kathryn Scola from a story by Frederick Hazlitt Brennan and directed by John Francis Dillon. (First National.)

John Barrymore got a second crack at playing Captain Ahab in the sound version of **Moby Dick**, an altogether more impressive attempt than the earlier silent film, *The Sea Beast* (1926). Relishing every moment of Melville's brilliantly cinematic tale, Barrymore (centre) gave as thrilling a performance as any his screen audiences had seen from him, with Joan Bennett as Faith (Dolores Costello, whom Barrymore had originally wanted, was pregnant at the time), Lloyd Hughes as the evil Derek, and Walter Long as Starbuck offering excellent support. Directed for maximum impact by Lloyd Bacon (scenario by J. Grubb Alexander), it was both a popular and prestigious success. Also cast were May Boley, Tom O'Brien, Nigel de Brulier, Noble Johnson (left, as Queequeg), Jack Curtis and John Ince.

The adventures of two gold-digging shopgirls out to ensnare a rich old man, was the subject of **The Life of the Party**. Cleverly written by Arthur Caesar from a story by Melville Crossman (Darryl Zanuck), and snappily directed by Roy Del Ruth, it starred Winnie Lightner as gold-digger Flo, with Irene Delroy as her chum. Charles Judels was effectively cast as a hot-tempered couturier. Other amusing performances came from Charles Butterworth (centre), Jack Whiting (left) and Arthur Hoyt. It was shot in Technicolor and originally conceived as a full-scale musical. But as musicals were now more unpopular than ever, most of the film's numbers were cut. The songs that remained included Can It Be Possible?, One Robin Doesn't Make A Spring and Somehow.

The story of a one-time bootlegging baron ▷ whose attempts to go straight are thwarted when his wife deserts him and his kid brother is killed by some of his erstwhile rivals, **Doorway to Hell** (released in Britain as **A Handful of Clouds**) was directed by Archie Mayo from a screenplay by George Rosener. It was slick, if unmemorable entertainment. The film starred Lew Ayres as the bootlegger and also featured James Cagney (right) as the man to whom Ayres turns over his interests when he first quits the racket. Had the roles been reversed, it might have been more convincing. Still, Mayo's direction was tireless. Also cast were Robert Elliott (left), Charles Judels, Dorothy Matthews, Leon Janney and Kenneth Thompson.

97

Outward Bound, based on Sutton Vane's ▷ play and written for the screen by J. Grubb Alexander, was a deeply moving drama. Basically revolving round a young man's semi-conscious thoughts following his and his girl-friend's unsuccessful suicide attempt, it takes place on board a phantom ship *en route* to nowhere, and involves a group of ill-assorted people, all of whom turn out to be dead. In the role created on stage by Alfred Lunt, Leslie Howard (left, making his talking picture debut) played one of the doomed passengers, with Douglas Fairbanks Jr (second left) and Helen Chandler (third left) as the young pair of would-be suicides. Repeating their stage performances were Lyonel Watts and Beryl Mercer (second right), with other roles going to Alec B. Francis, Alison Skipworth (third right), Montagu Love (right) and Dudley Digges. Robert Milton, who directed it on stage, did so on this occasion as well, and managed to retain the essence of the original, while at the same time using to good advantage the greater freedom of movement afforded by the camera. It was remade in 1944 as *Between Two Worlds*.

A miscast Richard Barthelmess (right), wearing a girdle to alleviate the visible evidence of a paunch, showed discomfort both with the girdle and his role in The Lash, in which he played a nobleman turned desperado. As a result, he was hardly convincing in this routine romantic adventure (circa, 1848) which also starred Mary Astor (left) as his *amour*. Others caught up in Bradley King's screenplay (story by Lanier and Virginia Stivers Bartlett) were Fred Kohler, Marion Nixon, James Rennie and Robert Edeson. The director was Frank Lloyd, whose heart, clearly, was not in it. (First National.)
▽

Charles Bickford's performance in **River's End,** in which he played a dual role – that of a Royal Canadian Mounted Policeman and the man he is out to get – was first rate, and so was director Michael Curtiz's handling of the double exposure photography which convincingly had the two men conversing with each other. Otherwise, the story contrived by James Oliver Curwood and written for the screen by Charles Kenyon, was a *Boy's Own* affair whose main plot point pivoted on the wanted man (who turns out to be innocent) posing as the Mountie after the latter's death. Evalyn Knapp starred with Bickford (right) as the heroine who falls for the impostor believing him to be the policeman, with other roles going to J. Farrell MacDonald, ZaSu Pitts, Walter McGrail, David Torrence and Junior Coughlan (left). First filmed in 1922, it was remade for a third time in 1940.

Man to Man was a well directed (by Allan Dwan) melodrama in which an 18-year-old boy is forced to leave college when it becomes known that his barber father is serving a prison sentence for murder. When the father is pardoned, he and his son are awkwardly reunited in a small Kentucky town, and it takes a misunderstanding to bring them together again. It was based on a story by Ben Ames Williams, scripted by Joseph Jackson with the excellent Phillips Holmes (right) as the son and Grant Mitchell as the father. Also cast were Lucille Powers (left), Barbara Weeks, Charles Sellon, Dwight Frye, Robert Emmett O'Connor, Russell Simpson, Paul Nicholson and Otis Harlan.

◁ **Captain Thunder** was a comic melodrama clumsily directed by Alan Crosland which starred Victor Varconi (right) as a desperado (albeit a lightweight one) who, in spite of doing some really dreadful things, was not to be taken seriously. Just as well, for Varconi's accent (supposedly that of a Mexican outlaw) was so thick that most of what he said was unintelligible. The same applied to co-star Fay Wray (left), whose idea of a Spanish accent must have amused any Spaniard. Also cast were Charles Judels, Robert Elliott, Natalie Moorehead, Bert Roach and Frank Campeau. Gordon Rigby and William K. Wells wrote the screenplay from a story by Pierre Coudere and Hal Devitt.

Marilyn Miller's stage success **Sunny** transferred to the screen with its star (centre) repeating her Broadway success in the role of the English circus horseback performer who, dressed as a boy, stows away on board a New York-bound ocean liner. She is, of course, discovered, but made to feel more than at home by a group of kindly passengers, and marries one of them to avoid immigration problems at Ellis Island. Utter nonsense, of course, but Miss Miller's singing and dancing had an infectious sparkle that kept cinemas full wherever it was shown. Adapted by Humphrey Pearson and Henry McCarthy from the musical play by Otto Harbach, Oscar Hammerstein II and Jerome Kern, it also featured Joe Donahue (as the man Sunny marries), Lawrence Gray (second left), O.P. Heggie (in hat), Inez Courtney, Barbara Bedford and Clyde Cook. It was well directed by William A. Seiter, with Theodore Kosloff as the dance director in charge of the ballet sequences. Songs (all written by Harbach, Hammerstein II and Kern) included: Sunny, Who?, D'ya Love Me?, Two Little Love Birds and I Was Alone. (First National.)
▷

Edward G. Robinson's first film for Warner Bros., **The Widow from Chicago**, was one of his least memorable. He played a notorious prohibition baron involved in the beer racket, with Alice White (left) as a young woman whose brother (a policeman) Robinson (centre) has killed, and whose death she is determined to revenge. Relying heavily on coincidence and with a performance by Miss White that left much to be desired, there was little to admire in Earl Baldwin's improbable screenplay, and even less in Edward Cline's cumbersome direction. But Robinson's performance was not without the authority that was soon to make him a star. Also cast were Neil Hamilton (right), Frank McHugh and Lee Shumway. (First National.)

▽

△

A remake of the 1921 silent version, **The Way of All Men**, (released in Britain as **Sin Flood**) with Douglas Fairbanks Jr (right), Dorothy Revier (left), Noah Beery, Anders Randolph, Robert Edeson, William Courtenay and Ivan Simpson, asked audiences to suspend belief above the expected level for such nonsense, and they refused. The film told the story of a motley group of people trapped in an underground cafe when a Mississippi levée gives way and causes flood havoc, and was feverishly directed by Frank Lloyd. It was written for the screen by Bradley King, with its back to reality. Henning Berger wrote the play on which the screenplay was based. (First National.)

Nothing was what it appeared to be in **Sweethearts and Wives**, a comedy thriller set in a derelict inn in France and involving a phoney detective, a maid and a wife in search of a missing necklace. Written by Forrest Halsey from the play *Other Men's Wives* by Walter Hackett, it starred suave Clive Brook (left, as a divorce detective) and Billie Dove (centre), with Sidney Blackmer (right), Crauford Kent, Leila Hyams, and John Loder in support. Clarence Badger directed. (First National.)

1931

The Depression forced a general economy drive on the studio and in the first half of the year 900 employees were dismissed and salaries were cut by between 20 and 30 per cent. In February the Warner family suffered a tragic blow: Lewis Warner, Harry's 22-year-old son, and a director of the music publishing outfit bought by the company in 1929, died when an infected wisdom tooth, aggravated by an unpressurized aeroplane trip to Havana, poisoned the rest of his system.

Though receiving no screen credit for their efforts, Robert Lord, Raymond Griffith and Henry Blanke became the studio's official supervisors, and such players as Bette Davis, James Cagney, Barbara Stanwyck, Edward G. Robinson, Joan Blondell, Loretta Young, Mary Astor and Douglas Fairbanks Jr, became the cream of the Warner Bros. stock company.

John Monk Saunders won an Academy Award in the Best Original Story category for **The Dawn Patrol.** John Bright and Kubec Glasmon were nominated in the same category for **The Public Enemy**, as were Lucien Hubbard and Joseph Jackson for **Smart Money. Five Star Final** was nominated for Best Film (though the eventual winner was **Grand Hotel**). The year unfortunately ended with a net loss of $7,918,604.

1931 was also the year in which Warner Bros. leased the Teddington studios in England, where throughout the remainder of the decade and into the Forties, they produced a series of low-budget features (quota quickies) which were generally distributed in Great Britain only (see page 445).

△
What little plot there was in **Sit Tight** involved Winnie Lightner (not at her best) training Paul Gregory to become a champion wrestler. Propping up the slender edifice was Joe E. Brown (right) whose duties as supervisor of a health clinic provided some incidental humour to a rather dreary comedy. Also, the sight of Brown wrestling with a burly masked opponent in the ring lifted the laugh-level somewhat, but not enough to salvage Rex Taylor and William K. Wells' basically unfunny script. Lloyd Bacon directed a cast that also included Claudia Dell, Don George, Lotti Loder and Hobart Bosworth. Song: Face It With A Smile.

△
The Naughty Flirt starred Alice White as the girl of the title, who jilts one boyfriend (Paul Page) for another (Douglas Gilmore) only to leave the latter stranded at the altar as she undergoes a change of heart and decides on sweetheart number one after all. Richard Weil and Earl Baldwin wrote the trite screenplay (story by Frederick Bowen), Edward Cline directed it, and also featured were Myrna Loy (illustrated), Robert Agnew and George Irving. (First National.)

In **Going Wild**, Joe E. Brown (centre) again ▷ found himself impersonating someone, this time an ace aviator. Inevitably, Brown is made to prove his worth, with the usual madcap consequences. It was directed by William A. Seiter and featured Lawrence Gray (left), Laura Lee, Walter Pidgeon, Ona Munson, Frank McHugh (right) and May Boley. Humphrey Pearson and Henry McCarthy wrote it, from a story by Humphrey Pearson.

The time spanned was 30 years in **Mother's Cry**, a moving account of a widow's abortive attempts to raise her four children as respectable members of the community. One of her sons becomes a thug and kills his sister; a second girl settles for a life of dreary domesticity with a man old enough to be her father, while the second son, a gifted architect and the apple of his mother's eye, is forced to leave town to avoid a scandal and the ruin of his career. It could have been unbearably maudlin, but was given distinction by the central performance of Dorothy Peterson (right) as the mother and by a script by Lenore J. Coffee (from a novel by Helen Grace Carlisle) that was sensitively characterized. Hobart Henley's direction was first rate. The producer was Robert North. Also cast were Helen Chandler, David Manners, Evalyn Knapp, Edward Woods, Pat O'Malley, Reginald Pasch and Sidney Blackmer. (First National.)

▽

△
The least successful element in William A. Wellman's railroad drama **Other Men's Women** (originally titled **The Steel Highway**) was a triangle romance that developed when a railroad fireman realizes he is in love with his best friend's wife. One of the studio's 'working man' films, it starred Grant Withers (on ground), Mary Astor, Regis Toomey, James Cagney and Joan Blondell. It was written by William K. Wells from a story by Maude Fulton.

'No buzzard like you will ever put the cuffs on Rico,' snarled Edward G. Robinson (right) in **Little Caesar**, the first of the studio's great 'social conscience' crime offerings. And he was right. After almost fifty years, unmanacled by time and changing attitudes, the film remains a masterpiece. Though Francis Edward Faragoh's screenplay, adapted from the novel by W.R. Burnett, was restricted by the rigid economy measures which characterized much of the studio's activities in the early part of the thirties ▷ (particularly in the area of crime films) forcing much of the action to take place in sleazy, low-budget settings, it managed to make a virtue of its limitations and was largely responsible for convincing Jack Warner that quality and quantity were not synonymous. Clearly based on the character of Al Capone, **Little Caesar** chronicled with such impact the rise and fall of an Italian gangster that, to the end of his life, and despite the many other parts he played, Robinson was still closely associated with the role of Rico. Against all odds, Robinson – who was, after all, not physically attractive in the traditional Hollywood sense and had a voice to match his looks – became a star. If anything, his slight, unglamorous appearance enhanced his popularity during the Depression era of the underdog, and if **Little Caesar** made a star of its hero (who in reality was afraid of guns and had to have eyelids taped to prevent him from blinking every time he pulled the trigger), it also bestowed on Warner Bros. a quality status it had hitherto rarely managed to achieve, established Darryl Zanuck (in charge of production) and Hal Wallis as producer as major talents in the industry and gave Mervyn Le Roy ('a great director, with a small g', according to Jack Warner) the kind of recognition he was waiting for. The enormous success of **Little Caesar**, (budgeted at $700,000) which also starred Douglas Fairbanks Jr, William Collier Jr, Ralph Ince and Glenda Farrell, led to a tidal wave of socially committed crime-orientated films during the next few years that enhanced Warner Bros.' reputation throughout the cinema-going world. (First National.)

△
The songs written by Richard Rodgers and Lorenz Hart for **The Hot Heiress**, an 'original' screen musical by Herbert Fields, made little impact on the public and, as a result of their negative reactions to a generally indifferent effort, the composers withdrew from their next two assignments for the studio. The simple story of a riveter (Ben Lyon, right) who is taken up by a Port Chester society woman (Ona Munson, left) and who is passed off as an architect, it did nothing to revive the dying Hollywood musical or enhance the careers of any of its participants. Clarence Badger, more at home with melodramas than musicals, directed it with a limited understanding of the genre and was unable to breathe any life into a cast whose members also included Walter Pidgeon, Thelma Todd, Tom Dugan, Inez Courtney and Holmes Herbert. Songs included: You're The Cats, Riveter's Song, Like Common People Do and Too Good To Be True. (First National.)

A rather flaccid comedy momentarily enlivened by the energetic carryings-on of comedians Olsen (left) and Johnson (right), **Fifty Million Frenchmen** came to the screen via the stage in mediocre Technicolor and, as a result of audiences' dwindling interest in musicals, without its original Cole Porter score, though some of the show's tunes surfaced as background to the action. Adapted by Joseph Jackson from the musical comedy by Herbert Fields, and with dialogue by Al Boasberg and Eddie Walsh, the plot had William Gaxton (repeating the role he played on Broadway) accepting a $50,000 bet that, without spending a franc (it takes place in Paris), he can woo and win pretty Claudia Dell in the space of two weeks. Olsen and Johnson are employed to see that he loses. The climactic chase was the best thing in an otherwise lacklustre curiosity. Lloyd Bacon directed a cast that also included Helen Broderick (also from the Broadway original), Lester Crawford, John Halliday, Charles Judels, Carmelita Geraghty and, in the small part of a fakir, Bela Lugosi.
▽

Lewis Stone appeared in **My Past**, vying ▷ with Ben Lyon for the affections of Bebe Daniels (right). There was little more to Charles Kenyon's screenplay than that (it was based on a novel by Dora Macy), so director Roy Del Ruth padded it out with romantic settings and gave it a smooth, MGM-type gloss. Stone was top-notch and the rest of the cast (Joan Blondell, left, Natalie Moorhead, Virginia Sale and Daisy Belmore) were adequate.

△
Always on the lookout for a new star to add to his roster of contract players, Jack Warner signed Barbara Stanwyck (whose box-office lure was reinforced after her starring role in Columbia's *Ladies of Leisure*) to a non-exclusive contract, her first film for the studio being an undistinguished weepie called **Illicit** in which she was billed as 'Miss Barbara Stanwyck'. Directed by Archie Mayo and with a screenplay by Harvey Thew, it was the story of a love affair that turns sour after marriage. Miss Stanwyck (left) finds, to her cost, that married life is not particularly glamorous, and when her husband, James Rennie (right), looks elsewhere for romance, she walks out on him – but returns for the final clinch. Joan Blondell, Ricardo Cortez (centre) and Charles Butterworth provided the light relief. The critics were not keen, but it prospered all the same, thanks to its leading lady.

Running for just under an hour, **The Lady Who Dared** was an efficient programmer which starred Conway Tearle (right) as a diamond smuggler in South America who finds himself involved in a plot to compromise the wife (Billie Dove) of the US Viceconsul (Sidney Blackmer). When it comes to the crunch, Tearle cannot go through with it, and Miss Dove's reputation (which rests on a tell-tale photo) remains unsullied. Forrest Halsey and Kathryn Scola wrote the screenplay from a story by Kenneth J. Saunders and William Beaudine directed it. Also cast were Judith Vosselli (centre right), Cosmo Kyrle Bellew (centre left), and Ivan Simpson (left).
▽

Too Young to Marry (from the play *Broken Dishes* by Martin Flavin, in which Bette Davis appeared on Broadway) was a modest reworking of the familiar theme of the henpecked husband who suddenly asserts himself to the complete surprise and astonishment of his nearest and dearest. In this instance, the mouse who becomes a lion was overplayed by O.P. Heggie (right), with Emma Dunn as his wife, Loretta Young (left) as the only one of his three daughters who sides with him, and Grant Withers as her boyfriend. Heggie's other two daughters were played by Virginia Sale and Aileen Carlisle, with further roles filled by J. Farrell MacDonald, Lloyd Neal and Richard Tucker. It was written by Francis E. Faragoh and directed by Mervyn LeRoy. It was re-made in 1936 as *Love Begins at Twenty* and in 1940 as *Calling All Husbands.*
▽

◁ Based on William Vaughan Moody's 1906 play *The Great Divide* (first filmed in 1929) but with its title changed and its characters given different names, **Woman Hungry** (released in Britain as **The Challenge**) bore little resemblance to the original stage drama about the moral gulf between Puritan New England and the Wild West. Pared down (in Howard Estabrook's adaptation) to a melodramatic narrative in which a desperado forces a young woman to become his wife against her will, it emerged as routine film fare whose poor use of Technicolor, except in the depiction of some background scenery, further underlined the artificiality of the whole thing. Wooden performances from the protagonists Lila Lee (right) and Sidney Blackmer also failed to help matters. Clarence Badger was the director, and had as little success with this as he had had with *The Hot Heiress*. Also among the hopelessly inadequate cast were Raymond Hatton, Fred Kohler, Kenneth Thomson, Olive Tell (left), David Newell, J. Farrell MacDonald, Tom Dugan and Blanche Frederici. (First National.) It was not a commercial success.

Although Roy Del Ruth's **The Maltese** ▷ **Falcon**, a slick, effective screen transfer of Dashiell Hammett's celebrated story, was later eclipsed by John Huston's classic 1941 remake, it was all the same a nice blend of humour, intelligence and suspense. Ricardo Cortez played detective Sam Spade with a suavity absent from Bogart's more flinty performance in the same role, but Bebe Daniels (left) was merely serviceable as Brigid, and Dudley Digges (centre) as Gutman was altogether less menacing than Sydney Greenstreet. Compared with the sophisticated Huston version, there was a certain melodramatic air about Del Ruth's treatment of the story, even though his settings were far more chic than the seedy environment in which Huston placed his detective. Still, both films called Spade Spade, and if Huston's version comes closer in spirit to the original, Del Ruth's admirable sense of style cannot be overlooked in the comparison. Maude Fulton, Lucien Hubbard and Brown Holmes wrote the screenplay, which differs in certain details from the 1941 version, but retains most of the novel's essential plot points. Otto Matieson (right), Oscar Apfel, J. Farrell MacDonald and Una Merkel were also included in the cast.

◁ A few amusing moments delivered by comedian Charles Butterworth and the reliable Guy Kibbee provided the sum total of pleasure –to be gained from a rather desperate comedy called **Side Show**, which starred Winnie Lightner (left) as a girl ready for anything – such as standing in for the side show's truant high diver. There was nothing director Roy Del Ruth could do with William K. Wells and Arthur Caesar's material: the star was far from her best, and Donald Cook (right), Evalyn Knapp, Louise Carver and Luis Alberni gave only indifferent support.

Adapted from the novel by Dora Macy, ▷ Barbara Stanwyck's second effort for the studio, **Night Nurse**, under the capable direction of William A. Wellman, whose favourite leading lady she was to become, was a lurid melodrama. In it the night nurse of the title, (Miss Stanwyck) finds herself assigned to a case in which a drug addict and a brutal fist-flinging chauffeur plot to starve two young children in a murderous attempt to extort their inheritance money from the children's dipsomaniac mother. Clark Gable played the sadistic chauffeur (James Cagney was originally cast, but after his success in *The Public Enemy* was replaced in order to appear in *Smart Money*) and although, at one point, he attempts to show the nurse who's boss with a sharp right to her jaw, she gets her revenge by putting one of her bootlegger friends onto him. This side of Miss Stanwyck (right) was the reverse of her 'weepie' image, and audiences loved her for her versatility. So did the critics, who also recognized in Gable a promising new talent. It was written by Oliver H.P. Garrett and Charles Kenyon and also featured Joan Blondell (centre), Ben Lyon (left), Charles Winninger, Vera Lewis and Blanche Frederici in the cast.

◁ Douglas Fairbanks Jr gave one of his best performances ever in **Chances**, a wartime romance in which two brothers. Fairbanks (centre) and Anthony Bushell, fall in love with the same girl (Rose Hobart) while on a three-day furlough in London. Based on a story by A. Hamilton Gibbs, it was adapted with admirable fidelity to the original by Waldemar Young, and directed with great sensitivity by Allan Dwan. The acting was excellent, with sturdy support supplied by Mary Forbestein, Florence Britton and Robert Bennett. (First National.)

The hero of **Star Witness**, a gangster melodrama directed by William A. Wellman from a screenplay by Lucien Hubbard, was Charles (Chic) Sale as an ageing war veteran who refuses to be intimidated by a gang of crooks and whose evidence and canny behaviour facilitate the conviction of the head man. Certain coincidences in the narrative stretched credulity to its limits, but in the main, it was well written, well directed and well performed entertainment with Sale in fine form as the old man. Good work, too, came from Walter Huston (centre) as a District Attorney. Also in it were Grant Mitchell, Ralph Ince (left), Frances Starr, Sally Blane and Edward Nugent (right).
▽

Marriage *à la mode* was the theme of **Party Husband** in which a liberated husband (James Rennie) and wife (Dorothy Mackaill, illustrated), by following separate life styles, find the foundation of their relationship beginning to crumble. The husband's mother (Mary Doran) comes to the rescue just in time, indulges in a spot of marital underpinning, and reunites the couple. Charles Kenyon's over-talkative screenplay (from a story by Geoffrey Barnes) rammed home its point about the sanctity of the marriage vow, and Clarence Badger directed competently. Dorothy Peterson, Paul Porcasi, Don Cook, Joe Donahue and Barbara Weeks supported. (First National.)

▽

△

The Public Enemy (released in Britain as **Enemies of the Public**) took a clinical look at the criminal mind, made a super-star out of James Cagney (right) and a minor star of Mae Clarke (left) who, in one of the film's most celebrated scenes, has a grapefruit twisted into her face. The shock registered on Miss Clarke's face was completely genuine, for she had been assured by Cagney that the grapefruit would not actually touch her, although the scene would be shot in such a way as to give the impression that it did. The story of Tom Powers (Cagney), a Chicago slum kid whose childhood dabbling in petty thievery was to find full expression during Prohibition, it etched an accurate picture of the ferocious criminal underworld of the late twenties, and by starting its story in 1909 when Powers was still a boy, gave audiences a documentary-like look at the environmental influences that helped turn him into the fully-fledged hood he eventually became. Though typical of the studio's many society-versus-the-criminal melodramas, **The Public Enemy**, together with *Little Caesar*, remains a classic of the genre. Directed by William A. Wellman with a toughness that never resorts to sensationalism (most of the killings are done off camera) and with a focal performance from Cagney

that is compulsively watchable (and which, despite the 'come-uppance' ending, glamourizes violence through the sheer forcefulness of the star's personality), it remains as strong today as it was nearly 50 years ago. Kubec Glasmon, John Bright and Harvey Thew wrote it from Bright's original story *Beer and Blood* (whose title did not find favour with the Hays office). Jean Harlow, Joan Blondell, Beryl Mercer, Donald Cook and Leslie Fenton were also cast.

The most durable feature about John Barrymore's **Svengali** was the make-up man's ability, every time Barrymore (left) as Svengali mesmerised Trilby, to obliterate his irises – substituting, instead, gaping cavernous white holes. It was a superbly eerie trick and it did wonders for director Archie Mayo's rather lack-lustre version of the famous George du Maurier story. Nothing, however, animated Marian Marsh's insipid Trilby (centre), or Bramwell Fletcher's suitor. It was written for the screen by J. Grubb Alexander and also featured Luis Alberni, Lumsden Hare, Paul Porcasi (right) and Carmel Myers.
▽

After a break of two years, Dolores Costello (left) returned to the screen in **Expensive Women**, a gesture which benefited neither the film nor her career. She played an amorous young thing who flits from man to man, finally and arbitrarily choosing one for keeps. Adapted by Harvey Thew from a story by Wilson Collison, and performed in a variety of extraordinary accents by a cast that included (right) Warren William (not nearly as happy here as he was dashing about in *Honor of the Family*), Anthony Bushell, Joe Donahue, H.B. Warner and Allan Lane, it was directed by Hobart Henley in a manner no better than it deserved. (First National.)
▽

Gold Dust Gertie, (released in Britain as **Why Change your Husband?**) a farce in search of a few good musical numbers, allowed the team of Olsen (right) and Johnson (left) – the former sporting a moustache for the first and last time on the screen – to shoulder the burden of the plot entirely on their own. They played two bathing-suit salesmen who, at different times, were both married to Winnie Lightner (centre). Unfortunately for them, their ex-spouse is hell-bent on fleecing them for as much alimony as she can, and the plot pivots on their frantic attempts to give her the slip. Lloyd Bacon directed (repeating the flying motor-boat gag used by Mervyn LeRoy in *Top Speed*); it was written by William K. Wells and Ray Enright from a story by Len Hollister and featured Dorothy Christy, Claude Gillingwater, Arthur Hoyt, George Byron and
◁ Charley Grapewin in support.

An indifferent screenplay by Byron Morgan from a potentially good story by Donald and Rowland V. Lee, adapted by Robert Lord, did little to lend credence to the events that befell Walter Huston (centre) as a ruthless racketeer in **The Ruling Voice**. Loretta Young (left) also starred (as Huston's daughter). Others involved were Doris Kenyon, David Manners (right), John Halliday, Dudley Digges and Gilbert Emory. Rowland V. Lee also directed and managed, despite the film's flaws, to keep audiences interested. (First National.)

After the runaway successes of *Little Caesar* and *The Public Enemy*, the smart way to earn money, figured Jack Warner, was to put the stars of those two hits – Edward G. Robinson (left) and James Cagney (right) – into one movie. The result was **Smart Money**, a routine (as it turned out) but financially successful underworld picture in which Robinson dominated as a barber who prefers illegal gambling to hair-cutting. Alfred E. Green directed; Kubec Glasmon and John Bright wrote the screenplay (with additional dialogue by Lucien Hubbard and Joseph Jackson). Boris Karloff also appeared, as did Evalyn Knapp, Morgan Wallace and Noel Francis.
▽

A World War I musical story, **Men of the Sky** starred Irene Delroy as a French spy whose activities, encouraged by her father (John St. Polis), end tragically when she, her American aviator lover (Jack Whiting, centre left) and her father are discovered and shot by the enemy. It was written by Jerome Kern and Otto Harbach, and directed by Alfred E. Green. Also cast were Frank McHugh, Edwin Maxwell, Otto Matieson and Lotti Loder. Songs (by Kern and Harbach) included: Every Little While, Boys March, Stolen Dreams and You Ought To See Sweet Marguerite. (First National.)
▽

◁**Children of Dreams** did little to revitalize the screen musical which, by mid-1931, had become box-office cyanide, thanks to the mindlessness of the plots churned out by every studio in Hollywood. A particularly silly example was this one, which was set in an apple orchard in California and involved a romance between a couple of poor, itinerant pickers – Paul Gregory (centre left) and Margaret Schilling – the latter who, to save her father from going to jail, embarks on a career as an opera singer. Written by Oscar Hammerstein II and Sigmund Romberg, it contained the usual quantities of tedious sentimentality germane to such occasions, though the two young leading players were pleasant and personable, making it more palatable than it might have been. Alan Crosland directed. Also in it were Tom Patricola (centre right), Charles Winninger, Bruce Winston and Marion Byron. Songs (by Romberg and Hammerstein II) included: Fruit Picker's Song, Oh, Couldn't I Love That Girl, Her Professor, Children Of Dreams, Sleeping Beauty, If I Had A Girl Like You, Seek Love and Yes Sir.

Anticipating CinemaScope, VistaVision and ▷ other wide screen processes by more than 20 years, the all-talking **Kismet**, photographed in 65 mm Vitascope, was a great popular success and a triumph for its star Otis Skinner who, at 72, impersonated Hajj the beggar, a character half his age, with an energy that would have been remarkable in any actor but was a miracle in a septuagenarian. (Skinner had played the role twice before: first in Edward Knoblock's 1911 play, then as a silent in 1920.) Also cast in this sumptuous, well directed (by John Francis Dillon) production were Loretta Young (right) one of Warner Bros.' great screen beauties, as Hajj's daughter, Sidney Blackmer (left) as the Wazir, David Manners as the Caliph, Mary Duncan as Zeleeha, Montagu Love as a jailer and Edmund Breese as Jawan. Howard Estabrook did the adaptation, and John Seitz was the cameraman. (First National.)

△ **Captain Applejack** was a remake of the popular play written by Walter Hackett which first came to the screen in 1923. John Halliday (centre) starred as the timid hero who finds the courage to prevent a gang of crooks from filching a horde of hidden treasure from his home, with other parts going to Mary Brian, Kay Strozzi (left), Louise Closser Hale, Alec B. Francis and Arthur Edmund Carewe (right). Maude Fulton provided the screenplay and Hobart Henley the direction.

△ Based on Philip Barry's play *You and I*, **The Bargain** told of a father's disappointment when his artist son decides to give up his studies and enter business as a soap manufacturer. The father (Lewis Stone, right), who is also in soap, is particularly upset as he had hoped his son (John Darrow) would become the artist he himself had always wanted to be. Wittily written by Robert Presnell, and with a fine supporting performance from Una Merkel as a servant turned artist's model, the film was not without its moments. But it was hurt by poor sound reproduction, trite direction (by Robert Milton) and inferior acting from both Darrow and Evalyn Knapp (as his sweetheart). Lewis Stone and Doris Kenyon (left), however, were fine. (First National.)

Bought told the story of a woman of dubious antecedents (her parents were never married) and the various relationships she has before finally settling down. Constance Bennett (left, then earning $30,000 per week) was the star, with Richard Bennett (right), her real-life father, playing her father in the film. Also featured were Ben Lyon, relative newcomer Ray Milland, Dorothy Peterson and Doris Lloyd. It was written by Charles Kenyon and Raymond Griffith from the novel by Harriet Henry and directed in such a way (by Archie Mayo) as to appeal mainly to the ladies in the audience. ▽

A sorry little programmer, **Compromised** (released in Britain as **We Three**) was the story of a boarding-house servant (Rose Hobart, top) who befriends a wealthy but dissolute young man (Ben Lyon), saves him from drowning in alcohol, marries him and after ten years together almost loses him to a society woman. Waldemar Young adapted from Edith Fitzgerald's play, and John Adolfi directed a cast which included Juliette Compton, Claude Gillingwater, Bert Roach and Emma Dunn. (First National.) ▽

◁ Leon Janney (left), happily indulged in a neat bit of upstaging throughout **Father's Son**, stealing all the acting honours from Lewis Stone (right) and Irene Rich (centre) as the young misunderstood son whose banker father (Stone) simply does not understand young boys in general and his own son in particular. Little more than a series of adventures indulged in by Master Janney, it boasted a fine performance, too, from John Halliday as the family doctor who brings the youngster back home after he has run away. Mickey Bennett, Robert Dandridge, George Reed and Gertrude Howard were also in the cast; the script (from a Booth Tarkington story) was by Hope Loring, and the sensitive, well observed direction was the work of William Beaudine. There were lots of satisfied customers for this one, which was remade in 1941. (First National.)

An exceptionally dismal musical, **Her Majesty, Love**, directed by William Dieterle in a heavy, Germanic manner, starred Marilyn Miller (right) as a poor barmaid, W.C. Fields as her uncouth father, Leon Errol as her much married suitor and Ben Lyon (left) as the man she really loves. Apart from a memorable sequence in which Fields somehow manages to introduce his renowned juggling act into a formal dinner party, the pleasures were strictly rationed. R. Bernauer and R. Oesterreicher wrote the story which, in turn, was adapted by Robert Lord and Arthur Caesar, with Henry Blanke (who became one of the studio's major producers over the next couple of decades) and Joseph Jackson responsible for the dialogue. Also cast were Chester Conklin, Virginia Sale, Ford Sterling and Harry Stubbs. Songs included: You're Baby Minded Now, Because Of You, Don't Ever Be Blue and Though You're Not The First Wine. (First National.)

△ Director William Dieterle, working from the novel by John Monk Saunders (who also wrote the adaptation and dialogue) turned **The Last Flight** into a moving and often remarkable drama involving four injured World War I ex-airmen who, realizing they can never return home to their parents or their parents' conventional values, take to a reckless life of wine and women in Paris after the armistice. Very Scott Fitzgerald in atmosphere, the psychological insights revealed by Saunders and Dieterle gave this 'lost generation' drama a complexity and a richness of texture which made it especially compelling. In a uniformly fine cast, which included (from left) Richard Barthelmess, Helen Chandler, Elliott Nugent, David Manners, Walter Byron and Johnny Mack Brown, Helen Chandler, as a typical twenties flapper who latches onto the men, was particularly striking. An almost forgotten and neglected example of genuinely creative film-making, **The Last Flight** has only recently been rescued from the oblivion that followed its first release. (First National.)

Apart from the light relief supplied by Joan Blondell, Ivan Simpson and Joe Donahue, **The Reckless Hour** was an ineptly made melodrama about a hapless, unworldly girl who falls for a lying cad whose promises of happiness are as false as he is, and who, ultimately, is rescued from total ruin by a kindly artist in a happy-ever-after ending. Written by Florence Ryerson and Robert Lord from a story by Arthur Richman, and directed by John Francis Dillon, its cast was headed by Dorothy Mackaill (right), Conrad Nagel (left, as the artist) and Walter Byron (as the cad). H.B. Warner was the heroine's father. (First National.)

Blonde Crazy (released in Britain as **Larceny Lane**), offered James Cagney (left) a marvellous opportunity to consolidate the impact he made in *The Public Enemy*, this time playing a quick-witted bellhop turned con-man. Under Roy Del Ruth's energetic direction, it gave him every opportunity to sparkle, which he did. So did Joan Blondell (right) as his chambermaid sidekick in petty crime. They made a perfect team and audiences flocked, so much so that Cagney, in an act as pugnacious as any he had perpetrated in his films, walked out from his $450 a week contract on the grounds that he was underpaid. His point, reluctantly taken by Jack Warner, resulted in a new five-year contract at $1,000 a week. Louis Calhern, Noel Francis and Ray Milland were also featured and the engagingly written script was by Kubec Glasmon and John Bright. Songs included: When Your Lover Has Gone, I Can't Write The Words, I'm Just A Fool In Love With You and Ain't That The Way It Goes?

◁ The cliff-hanging situation posed in **I Like your Nerve** is whether or not pretty Loretta Young will be sold off for $200,000 to an Englishman in lieu of gambling debts incurred by her guardian. As Miss Young's co-star (illustrated) is Douglas Fairbanks Jr (looking and behaving uncannily like his father), audiences did not require Nostradamus' special skills to know that the unpleasant transaction would never take place. A comedy that broke no new ground, it was written by Houston Branch from a story by Roland Pertwee, directed by William McGann, and in secondary roles featured Claude Allister, Henry Kolker, Boris Karloff and Ivan Simpson. (First National.)

In **Local Boy Makes Good**, Joe E. Brown (left), as a bookish botanist, makes the mistake of writing a note to a girl he fancies from a rival college in which he describes himself as the best athlete on the campus. He has no intention of sending the note, but as a prank, one of his mates does. The inevitable occurs, with Brown again having to pretend to be someone or something he isn't. By now the returns on the well-worn gag were diminishing fast; so were the laughs. It was written by Robert Lord from a story by J.C. and Elliott Nugent, and directed by Mervyn LeRoy. Also cast were Dorothy Lee (right), Ruth Hall, Edward Woods and Wade Boteler.

Looking for another Svengali-type role for John Barrymore, scenarists J. Grubb Alexander and Harvey Thew, working from Martin Brown's story *The Idol*, came up with **The Mad Genius.** In it, Barrymore (left) played a club-footed puppeteer with an improbable yearning to be a ballet dancer; a yearning he satisfies through a young lad (Donald Cook) whom he encourages to become the dancer he himself could never be. He succeeds, but when the lad falls in love with a pretty ballerina, turns against him. It was brilliantly designed by Anton Grot,

whose sets included ceilings (made of muslin) making nonsense of the claim that Orson Welles' *Citizen Kane* (RKO 1941) was the first film to do so. Directed with more than the occasional dollop of *Grand Guignol* by Michael Curtiz, whose strict working methods were anathema to Barrymore, and with a splendidly dominating central performance by the star, the film was an effective excursion into horror which, however, found the public indifferent. As a result, Warner Bros. refused to renew Barrymore's contract on the same lucrative terms as he had hitherto enjoyed. **The Mad Genius** was, in fact, the star's last film for the studio. Also among the cast were Marian Marsh, Carmel Myers (right), Charles Butterworth, Boris Karloff and Frankie Darro.

George Arliss' play **Alexander Hamilton**, which he wrote with Mary Hamlin, was adapted for the screen by Julien Josephson and Maude Howell, with Arliss (centre) successfully repeating his stage role. The production's period detail lent additional interest to a plot that had Hamilton's political career threatened as a result of a scandalous affair with a married woman. Fine supporting performances rounded it all off nicely. Alan Mowbray played George Washington, Charles Middleton was Justice John Jay, with Lionel Belmore as General Philip Schuyler, Montagu Love as Thomas Jefferson, John T. Murray as Count Talleyrand, Gwendolin Logan as Martha Washington and Doris Kenyon as Betsy Hamilton. John Adolfi directed.

One of the more successful operettas of the period, written as a screen original by Oscar Hammerstein II and Sigmund Romberg, **Viennese Nights** was an entertaining, if at times schmaltzy, saga that spanned 40 years telling the story of a young composer (Alexander Gray, right), a philanderer (Walter Pidgeon) and a pretty woman (Vivienne Segal, centre) who marries the latter when she should have settled for the former. A plethora of plot was punctuated by some glorious Romberg waltzes and enhanced by Technicolor. The cast also included Bert Roach (left), Milton Douglas, Jean Hersholt, June Purcell and Louise Fazenda. Alan Crosland was the director. Songs included: I Bring A Love Song, I'm Lonely, You Will Remember Vienna, Here We Are, Regimental March, Yes, Yes, Yes, and Viennese Nights.

A Soldier's Plaything brought no credit to its director Michael Curtiz – nor to anyone else involved with it. The comic exploits of a couple of soldiers after armistice has been declared, it starred Ben Lyon and Harry Langdon (centre), who becomes involved with a blind girl, with Lotti Loder, Fred Kohler, Noah Beery, Jean Hersholt and Otto Matieson in support. Vina Delmar wrote the story from which Perry Vekroff fashioned the limp screenplay, and Arthur Caesar the dialogue. Songs included: Forever, Oui, Oui, Honey Boy, Ja, Ja, Ja and Side By Side.

The melodramatic ring in the title **Honor of the Family** was reflected in the film's content, with subtlety being an ingredient nowhere in evidence. Credited to a story by Balzac, but really the work of scenarists James Ashmore Creelman and Roland Pertwee, it told the outmoded tale of a wealthy but senile old man's love for a calculating seductress and how, just in time, catastrophe is averted with the fortuitous arrival of the old man's dashing nephew who takes matters into his own hands and saves the day, but not, alas, the film. Warren William (far left) played the part of hero with all the dash and bravado he could muster, Bebe Daniels (centre) was the wily temptress and Alan Mowbray her swordsman lover. Others in director Lloyd Bacon's cast were Frederick Kerr (as the old man), Dita Parlo, Allan Lane and Harry Cording. (First National.)

Aimed at family audiences, **Misbehaving** ▷ **Ladies,** whose title was more titillating than its subject merited, starred Lila Lee as a small-town girl from the mid-West who, as a child, left America for Europe, grew up, and married a prince. With the death of her husband, she returns to her home town, where, initially, she is mistaken for a seamstress. Enjoying the deception, she continues to play at being a menial with humorous, and almost scandalous, results. Louise Fazenda and Lucien Littlefield were on tap to supply the laughs (or groans, depending on audiences' particular predilections), and Ben Lyon (centre) the romance. William Beaudine directed from a screenplay by Julien Josephson (story by Juliet Wilbur Tompkins) and his cast included Julia Swayne Gordon, Emily Fitzroy, Martha Mattox, Virginia Grey and Oscar Apfel.

Five Star Final exposed the iniquities of a muck-raking, New York tabloid and the ruthless way it exploited people for its own circulation-building ends. Edward G. Robinson (centre) as a hard-bitten editor (but with a streak of humanity) is asked by newspaper magnate Oscar Apfel to resuscitate a 20-year-old unsolved murder case in an attempt to attract readers regardless of the pain the exercise will cause to the family involved. Unevenly directed by Mervyn LeRoy from Byron Morgan's screenplay (based on the play by Louis Weitzenkorn) the

film's undeniable impact was mainly to be felt in the hard-hitting scenes that take place in the newspaper offices themselves. They compensated, in part, for the mawkish and banal moments between the victimized mother (Frances Starr) and her equally distraught husband (H.B. Warner). Completing the cast for producer Hal B. Wallis were Anthony Bushell, Ona Munson, Aline MacMahon (her debut at the studio), Boris Karloff, Evelyn Hall and George E. Stone. It was remade in 1936 as *Two Against the World.*

Joe E. Brown (right) played chaperon to William Collier Jr (left) in **Broad-Minded**, a comedy with more of Brown's particular brand of humour than plot to jolly things along. The reason for Brown's acting as chaperon is simply that Collier's father is against his son's liaison with a young woman who has set her sights on him. So, Brown, being an older and wiser cousin, is chosen to do something about the situation. Complications bred like rabbits, providing more groans than laughter. Director Mervyn LeRoy was hamstrung by Bert Kalmar and Harry Ruby's screenplay, which had a bad effect on all the actors concerned including Ona Munson, Marjorie White, Holmes Herbert, Thelma Todd and Bela Lugosi. (First National.)

Frank Fay (centre) did an impressive salvage job on **God's Gift to Women**, a farce based on the play *The Devil was Sick* by Jane Hinton and adapted for the screen by Joseph Jackson and Raymond Griffith. He played an ardent Gallic womanizer who stops at nothing to win the affection of an American millionairess (Laura La Plante), and brought a lot of fun to the flimsy story. Also on hand to bask in Fay's reflected glory were Joan Blondell (right), Charles Winninger, Arthur Edmund Carewe, Alan Mowbray, Yola d'Avril (left), Charles Judels and Louise Brooks (above centre). Michael Curtiz directed with the full realization that without Fay there would have been no film.

Technicolor did wonders for **Kiss Me Again** (released in Britain as **Toast of the Legion**) based on Victor Herbert's operetta *Mademoiselle Modiste* which charted the bumpy course of love for Paul de St Cyr (Walter Pidgeon), a French Lieutenant, and Mademoiselle Fifi (Bernice Claire), a cabaret singer. Frank McHugh (right) made heavy weather of the comedy bits, but there were acceptable performances from Albert Gran (left), June Collyer (centre) Edward Everett Horton (second left), Judith Vosselli (second right) and crusty old Claude Gillingwater. Julien Josephson and Paul Perez adapted it from Henry Blossom and Victor Herbert's play. Again directing was William A. Seiter. Songs included: Kiss Me Again, The Mascot Of The Troop and The Time, The Place And The Girl. (First National.)

Dorothy Mackaill (left) starred in **Safe in Hell**, a strange drama set in a tropical rogues' sanctuary where extradition orders do not apply. It was released in Britain as **The Lost Lady**. One of the island's inhabitants is Gilda (Miss Mackaill), taken there by a sailor lover after she burns down a hotel in New Orleans. Her adventures in the sanctuary, which end in death when she is throttled by the island's executioner for murdering a man, formed the basis of Houston Branch's story which William A. Wellman directed and Maude Fulton scripted. Also cast were Donald Cook (right), John Wray and Ralf Harolde. (First National.)

The first of William Powell's nine films for the studio, **Road to Singapore** was a sultry melodrama in which Doris Kenyon (front row, second left) commits adultery with Powell (front row, centre left) and is caught by her boorish doctor husband (Louis Calhern). Based on a play by Roland Pertwee and a story by Denise Robins, J. Grubb Alexander's screenplay was awash with platitudes, most of them echoed in Alfred E. Green's direction. The uneven cast included Marian Marsh, Alison Skipworth, Lumsden Hare, Ethel Griffies and Douglas Gerrard. Songs included: African Lament, Hand In Hand, Yes Or No, Singapore Tango and I'm Just A Fool In Love With You.

There was an air of contrivance about the ▷ remake of **Penrod and Sam** that robbed Booth Tarkington's story of most of its charm and all of its truth. An adult's view of children, it put its two leading youngsters – Leon Janney (right) and Junior Coghlan – into various situations, all of them calculated, as if by computer, for emotional effect. Unfortunately, the machinery at the heart of William Beaudine's direction showed, and the emotions experienced were synthetic. Waldemar Young wrote the screenplay, which included parts for Matt Moore, Dorothy Peterson (playing Penrod's mother, centre), Johnny Arthur, ZaSu Pitts, Charles Sellon, Wade Boteler and Helen Beaudine. It was remade for a third time in 1937. (First National.)

The Millionaire, starring George Arliss, from the story by Earl Derr Biggers and with an excellent screenplay by Julien Josephson and Booth Tarkington (the latter supplying the dialogue), was a diverting comedy all of whose elements knitted together adroitly and entertainingly. Finding retirement a bore, the millionaire (Arliss) seeks diversion by buying himself a half interest in a gas station. He changes his name, pretends to be impoverished, finds he has been swindled in the transaction, and sets out to exact a light-hearted revenge – all these activities being kept a secret from his family. John Adolfi's direction beautifully matched the spirit of the piece and brought out the best, not only in Arliss (left), but in a cast which also included Mrs Arliss, Evalyn Knapp, David Manners, Noah Beery, J. Farrell Mac-Donald (right) and James Cagney. It was remade in 1947 as *That Way With Women.*

Conrad Nagel (right) sporting a monocle, was miscast in **Right of Way** as a well-dressed Quebec lawyer who, in the course of a misconceived drama, loses his memory, becomes a tailor and falls in love with a woman other than his wife, only to discover.

on regaining his memory, that his wife, believing him dead, has remarried. Lots of plot but little drama characterized the effort, and audiences were not impressed. It was written by Francis E. Faragoh from the novel by Sir Gilbert Parker and also starred Loretta Young and Fred Kohler, with William Janney (left), Snitz Edwards, George Pierce and Halliwell Hobbes in support. (First National.)

Avoiding satire by a hair's breadth, Robert ▷ Lord's screenplay for **Big Business Girl,** based on a story by Patricia Reilly and Harold N. Swanson, kept tabs on a girl in New York who works her way up from stenographer to advertising copy writer, while at the same time promoting her jealous boyfriend's singing career. Loretta Young (right), Ricardo Cortez and Jack Albertson (centre) starred, with Joan Blondell, Frank Darien, Dorothy Christy and Bobby Jordan in support. Better by far than the majority of films on the career-girl subject, it was directed with skill by William A. Seiter. Song: Constantly. (First National.)

A crime thriller in the *Little Caesar* mould but with a newspaper background, **The Finger Points,** written by John Monk Saunders, W.R. Burnett and Robert Lord, had the characteristic Warner look. The story of a newspaper reporter who supplements his meagre income by accepting hush money from underworld chiefs, it starred Richard Barthelmess (right) as the reporter, and Fay Wray (left) as a colleague who tries, unsuccessfully, to get him to change his ◁ allegiance from the hoods to the editor. Regis Toomey, Robert Elliott and relative newcomer Clark Gable (as a gangster) were featured in support. It was directed by John Francis Dillon who did his best to cover up the holes in an uneven screenplay. (First National.)

1932

Fed up with the bickering of his stars about matters of studio policy, and still feeling the yoke of the Depression, Jack Warner, together with Darryl Zanuck, issued a statement on July 25th which made it clear that, in future, no artist currently under contract to the studio would be given any say whatsoever in any aspect of a film's production. The statement was followed by further cuts in salary as a result of which James Cagney, now dissatisfied with his $1,000 a week, again quit. (Joan Blondell was earning a mere $250 a week.) Cagney's act of defiance involved the Academy of Arts and Sciences in an arbitration case which resulted in the star's return to the studio at a salary of $1,750 a week.

Rin Tin Tin died at the age of sixteen. The films he had made from 1923 to 1930 earned over $5,000,000 for his owner, Leland Duncan. The *New York Times* voted **The Mouthpiece** as one of the year's Ten Best films. Joe E. Brown, who made several very successful films, was voted one of the top ten box-office stars of the year. Despite the studio's economy measures, the net loss recorded for the year was $14,095,054.

△
The glamorous Lil Dagover (illustrated) was recruited from Germany (with much accompanying ballyhoo) to make her American debut in **The Woman from Monte Carlo,** a remake of Alexander Korda's 1928 *The Night Watch*. Though Harvey Thew's screenplay differed quite radically from the silent version (and from Claude Ferrer and Lucien Nepoty's play on which it was based), it still involved the wife of a Lieutenant Commander Corlax being found in the cabin of another Lieutenant on board the *Lafayette*. Not one of director Michael Curtiz's more memorable efforts, it failed to make an American star of Miss Dagover and sank, taking with it Walter Huston (as the Captain), Warren William, John Wray and Robert Warwick. (First National.)

John Wayne's first Western for Warner ▷ Bros. was **Haunted Gold**, a remake of the 1929 horse opera *The Phantom City* which starred Ken Maynard. Together Wayne (left) and heroine Sheila Terry outwit a gang of bandits who, like themselves are searching for an abandoned gold mine. Erville Alderson, Harry Woods, Otto Hoffman, Martha Mattox and Blue Washington (right) were in it too, it was written by Adele Buffington, and the director was Mack V. Wright.

△
Manhattan Parade featured the team of Joe Smith and Charles Dale as a couple of Broadway producers harassed by the unreasonable demands made on them by the Russian director (Luis Alberni) of their latest spectacle. Robert Lord and Houston Branch's screenplay had every opportunity to satirize certain aspects of the New York theatre, but the humour employed was of the sledgehammer variety and, though the joint presences of Messrs Smith and Dale guaranteed laughs, they came mainly from slapstick comedy. Based on a play by Samuel Shipman, it was directed by Lloyd Bacon and also starred Winnie Lightner, Charles Butterworth and Walter Miller, with Greta Grandstedt, Bobby Watson (left), Dickie Moore, Charles Middleton and Claire McDowell (right) in support. It was photographed in Technicolor. Songs included: I Love A Parade, Temporarily Blue and I'm Happy When You're Jealous.

Some nicely turned dialogue (by Maurine Watkins) and the sympathetic playing of Loretta Young (right) made **Playgirl** the sort of 'woman's picture' that men enjoyed as well. The story of a working girl (Young) who has the misfortune to meet and marry a young man (Norman Foster, left) with a passion for gambling, the film focused on the difficulties of ekeing out an existence in a city like New York, and painted a convincing picture of the pressures of life during the Depression. Ray Enright directed it and his cast included Winnie Lightner, Guy Kibbee, Noel Madison, Polly Walters and Dorothy Burgess.

▽

William Powell (left) starred in **High Pressure**, a consistently entertaining comedy which benefited greatly from Powell's disarming presence as a tycoon manqué who sees a fortune to be made in artificial rubber and forms the Golden Gate Artificial Rubber Company. Unfortunately, the inventor of the process (Harry Beresford) cannot be found . . . Based on Aben Kandel's play *Hot Money*, it was written in an amusing, light-hearted manner by Joseph Jackson whose screenplay gave work to Evelyn Brent as Powell's girlfriend, George Sidney, Frank McHugh, Guy Kibbee, Evalyn Knapp (right), Ben Alexander, John Wray, Charles Judels, Luis Alberni and Lucien Littlefield. The director was Mervyn LeRoy.

▽

◁ Edward G. Robinson's best role since *Little Caesar* was that of silver-miner Yates Martin (based on the legendary H.A.W. Tabor) in **Silver Dollar**. The rags-to-riches story of a man who squanders away the wealth and power he has earned and is ruined when silver is demonetized, it gave Robinson (left) a glorious opportunity to explore the ramifications of a complex personality, which he did with gusto. Alfred E. Green directed from Carl Erickson and Harvey Thew's screenplay (based on a story by David Karsner), and cast Aline MacMahon as Robinson's wife and Bebe Daniels (right) as the beauty he leaves her for. Also cast were Jobyna Howland, De Witt Jennings and Robert Warwick. (First National.)

The Man Who Played God (from the play *The Silent Voice* by Jules Eckert Goodman, and in fact released as **The Silent Voice** in Britain) starred George Arliss who, in 1922, appeared in the silent version in the same role: that of Montgomery Royale, a concert pianist whose career is wrecked when an anarchist's bomb explodes and deafens him. He is befriended in his affliction by an attractive young woman called Grace with whom he falls deeply in love, but whom he sacrifices to another man when he realizes that although his love is not requited, she is unselfishly prepared to give up her own happiness to live with him. A blonde Bette Davis (left), making her first appearance at the studio, was personally chosen by Arliss (right) to play the role of Grace, although it was Violet Heming, playing a close friend of the stricken pianist who, together with Arliss, took all the acting honours. The film was tastefully directed by John Adolfi whose device of eliminating the sound whenever the deaf Arliss was, for whatever reason, unable to read the lips of whoever was sharing the scene with him, was most effective. The screenplay was by Julien Josephson and Maude Howell and the producer was Jack L. Warner. It was remade in 1955 as *Sincerely Yours*.

▽

A slightly updated version of Clare Kummer's 1917 play, **A Successful Calamity** was another marvellous vehicle for George Arliss (centre right). He played a millionaire who, after returning from a lengthy business trip to Europe, finds the numerous changes in both his house and his family disorientating. So, in the hope of changing things still further, he feigns poverty — with amusing results. Writers Maude Howell, Julien Josephson and Austin Parker presented their star with a bespoke screenplay which also contained good parts for Mary Astor (as Arliss' wife), Evalyn Knapp (centre left), Grant Mitchell, David Torrence, Randolph Scott (left) and William Janney (right). John Adolfi's direction was spot on.

▽

△ **Under Eighteen** was under nourished and under done. It starred Marian Marsh (left) as a wistful slum girl about to be compromised by a leering Warren William (as a seductive theatrical producer) but who is saved by the intervention of a local grocery boy (Regis Toomey). It was written by Maude Fulton and Charles Kenyon from a story by Frank M. Dazey, directed by Archie Mayo, with Anita Page, Emma Dunn, Joyce Compton, J. Farrell MacDonald, Paul Porcasi (right) and Judith Vosselli in support.

The central force of **Blessed Event**, adapted from Manuel Seff and Forrest Wilson's play by Howard Green, was its star Lee Tracy (left) who, as an unscrupulous circulation-building gossip columnist gave the most outstanding performance of his career. There was solid support too, from Mary Brian, Allen Jenkins (right), Ruth Donnelly, Ned Sparks and, making his debut with the studio, Dick Powell. Roy Del Ruth directed. Songs included: How Can You Say No When All The World Is Saying Yes? and I'm Making Hay In The Moonlight.

▽

Another film set in the newspaper world, and an exposé of the 'yellow press' not unlike the previous year's hard-hitting *Five Star Final*, **The Famous Ferguson Case** was more concerned with the methods in which a murder is reported in the gutter press (and its tragic consequences) than the actual solving of the crime itself. The film featured Joan Blondell as a sob-sister columnist, Tom Brown (right), Adrienne Dore, Vivienne Osborne (left), Walter Miller, Leslie Fenton and J. Carrol Naish. It was written by Courteney Terrett and Harvey Thew from the story *Circulation* by Granville Moore. Lloyd Bacon directed. (First National.)

The celebrated Lubitsch touch might have helped to give **Jewel Robbery** the insouciance absent from William Dieterle's direction, as would a stronger, more stylish performance from Kay Francis (left) as the baroness who falls for the roguish charms of master robber William Powell (right). Still, Erwin Gelsey's screenplay was not without sparkle, Powell was excellent and the supporting players pretty good too. They included Hardie Albright, Andre Luguet, Henry Kolker, Lee Kohlmar and Spencer Charters. It was based on a play by Ladislaus Fodor.

Proving that **It's Tough to be Famous** was Douglas Fairbanks Jr (centre) as a naval officer who risks his life to save the crew of a damaged submarine only to find his heroics rewarded with instant celebrity. How he copes with the ticker-tape parade and other such manifestations of fame formed the basis of this engaging comedy which Alfred E. Green directed with wit and skill. Also in it were Mary Brian, Ivan Linow, Lillian Bond, Terrence Ray, Walter Catlett (right front), J. Carrol Naish and Oscar Apfel. Robert Lord wrote the screenplay from a story by Mary McCall. (First National.)

A formula comedy, **Beauty and the Boss** based on a Hungarian play by Ladislaus Fodor and Paul Frank was all about a Viennese businessman who finds that his plethora of pretty secretaries are having a distracting effect on him. So, when plain Marian Marsh (left) applies for a job, he hires her on the spot. Except, of course, she isn't plain at all and soon blossoms into the prettiest girl in the office. Warren William (right) was the smooth-talking boss, with other parts going to Charles Butterworth, David Manners, Mary Doran and Lillian Bond. The screenplay was by Joseph Jackson and the assured direction the work of Roy Del Ruth.

Director William Dieterle, working with familiar material, brought his considerable talents to bear on **Man Wanted**, and emerged with an entertaining romantic comedy with no pretensions other than to entertain. The story of a sophisticated couple who tire of each other, the wife falling for her suave secretary, it was breezily written by Charles Kenyon and Robert Lord and starred Kay Francis (right, as the wife) and David Manners (left) as the secretary, with Andy Devine, Una Merkel, Kenneth Thomson and Claire Dodd in support.

A conventional murder mystery, **Miss Pinkerton**, adapted by Niven Busch and Lillie Hayward from a magazine serial by Mary Roberts Rinehart, was short on thrills but kept the audience guessing as to who killed Herbert Wynne (Allan Lane). The butler? The housekeeper? The demonic doctor? And what part did nurse Pinkerton (Joan Blondell, illustrated) play in it all? It was directed by Lloyd Bacon and featured enjoyable performances from George Brent (as Inspector Patten), Mae Madison, John Wray, Ruth Hall, Henry Gordon, Blanche Frederici, Holmes Herbert and Mary Doran. (First National.)

⊲ Ruth Chatterton (centre), of whom even Bette Davis (left) admits having been in awe, starred in **The Rich Are Always With Us**, a tale of New York society in which La Chatterton, reverentially billed as 'Miss Ruth Chatterton' files for divorce, meets George Brent (second left), but remains loyal to her husband (John Miljan, second right) after he is badly smashed up in a car accident. Advertised as 'witty, naughty and gay . . . a spectacular story of how the other half lives – and loves – and lies', it had a patina of chic imposed on it by Ernest Haller's glossy photography and Alfred E. Green's well-paced direction. But although it was lovely to look at, most of the pleasures, such as Orry-Kelly's stunning gowns and Bette Davis' performance as a flapper infatuated with Brent, were incidental. Rather than the 'sumptuous portrayal of sensuous society in the perfumed fragrance of Park Avenue and Paris boudoirs' which the ads went on to proclaim, the film was a moderately diverting trifle, of special significance only to Miss Chatterton and Brent who fell in love in the course of its filming and married. Austin Parker wrote it.

The Crowd Roars starred James Cagney (foreground) as a racing-driver whose obsessive determination to keep his younger brother (Eric Linden) out of motor racing results in the accidental death on the track of a buddy who tries to bring the alienated brothers together. Cagney's charisma gave a basically unsympathetic role a compulsive watchability it would otherwise not have had, and director Howard Hawks, by concentrating on action rather than on anything resembling plausible character motivation, ensured that the film riveted attention. The less than scintillating screenplay was by Niven Busch, Kubec Glasmon and John Bright. Also cast were Joan Blondell, making the most of a small part, Ann Dvorak, Guy Kibbee and Frank McHugh. It was remade in 1939 as *Indianapolis Speedway*.

Charles (Chic) Sale (centre) appeared as the usual benevolent old father in **The Expert**, a gentle but somewhat diffuse comedy based on the novel by Edna Ferber. The story of an elderly man and the adventures that befall him when he comes to Chicago to take up residence with his son, it relied heavily on its star's personality rather than on Julien Josephson and Maude Howell's workaday script. Complementing Sale was six-year-old Dickie Moore (centre right) as the orphaned kid next door. The relationship between the old man and the boy was the best thing in Archie Mayo's film. Also cast were Earle Foxe (as the son), Lois Wilson, Ralfe Harolde, May Boley and Noel Francis. It was remade in 1939 as *No Place to Go*.

David Freedman's play *Mendel Inc.* was translated to the screen as **The Heart of New York**, the title referring to the Jewish population of the city in general and Hester Street in particular. It starred George Sidney as a poor plumber who invents the washing machine and turns himself into a millionaire. But it's not all plain sailing for the plumber as Arthur Caesar and Houston Branch's screenplay demonstrated. Also on hand to milk the situation for most of its laughs were Smith and Dale, Hester Street's matchmakers and general factotums known as Schnapps and Shtrudel. The screenplay and direction (by Mervyn LeRoy) were on roughly the same level of subtlety, but who cared? Also cast were Anna Apfel (left) Aline MacMahon, Marion Byron (right), Oscar Apfel, Donald Cook and Ann Brody.

Lester Elliott's **Two Seconds** concerns the last two seconds of a man's life before his execution in the electric chair. The film relives the bleakness and despair of his pathetic existence in which he is forced to murder his wife. Edward G. Robinson starred as the self-loathing murderer in Harvey Thew's adaptation. Mervyn LeRoy's uncompromising direction underlined the utter hopelessness which permeated so many lives in the Depression, and drew fine performances from Robinson as well as Vivienne Osborne (centre) as the dance-hall prostitute who shanghaies Robinson (right) into marriage. Preston Foster, J. Carrol Naish (left), Guy Kibbee and Adrienne Dore were also cast. (First National.)

Edna Ferber's **So Big,** first filmed in 1925 with Colleen Moore for First National, was the story of Selina Peake (Barbara Stanwyck) a woman of great strength who, after the death of her father, becomes a schoolteacher in a farming district in Illinois. Life is hard, but she copes and finds strength in her friendship with a young sculptor played by George Brent. In time she meets and marries a farmer who dies a few years afterwards, leaving her to care for his land as well as a small son (Dickie Moore, left). When the boy grows up, (Hardie Albright) he is something of a disappointment and it is Brent, now a successful sculptor, to whom

◁ In an unashamed attempt to cash in on the *Grand Hotel* bandwagon, the studio quickly assembled a modest but adroit melodrama called **Union Depot** (released in Britain as **Gentleman for a Day**) which substituted a large railway terminal for a hotel lobby and followed the fortunes of a variegated collection of people. Those under scrutiny included Douglas Fairbanks Jr. (second left) as a sophisticated thief, Joan Blondell (second right) as a chorus girl, Alan Hale as a counterfeit baron carrying a violin-case stashed with currency, Frank McHugh as a genial drunk, and, best of all, George Rosener as a 1932-style sex maniac hotly in pursuit of Miss Blondell. Others passing through the terminal included Guy Kibbee (left), Ruth Hall, Dickie Moore, David Landau (right) and Mae Madison. It was tautly directed by Alfred E. Green and written for the screen by Kenyon Nicholson and Walter DeLeon from the play by Gene Fowler, Douglas Durkin and Joe Laurie.

Miss Stanwyck (right) turns for support and affection. Although epic in its time span, this version ran a mere 82 minutes, hardly enough to do justice to its convoluted plot. The novel won a Pulitzer prize, but there were no awards for this version of it, though Miss Stanwyck's performance and the solid dramatic qualities it contained were praised. Guy Kibbee was featured; so were Bette Davis, Mae Madison, Alan Hale and Robert Warwick. The screenplay was by J. Grubb Alexander and Robert Lord. Lucien Hubbard produced and the director was William A. Wellman. It was again remade in 1953.

Bearing hardly any resemblance to the George S. Kaufman play *The Butter and Egg Man* on which it was based, **The Tenderfoot** featured Joe E. Brown as a hare-brained cowboy who inadvertently finds himself involved with a group of gangsters and becomes the backer of a Broadway show which features leading lady Ginger Rogers (illustrated). With a workmanlike screenplay by Earl Baldwin, Monty Banks and Arthur Caesar, and direction by the reliable Ray Enright, its mediocre subject obviously appealed to someone in the studio's story department for it was remade five years later as *Dance Charlie Dance*, and three years after that as *Angel from Texas*. Also cast were Lew Cody, Vivienne Oakland and Robert Greig.
▽

Another John Wayne western, **The Big Stampede,** cast Wayne (left) as a deputy sheriff who brings a cattle-rustling baron to heel. Kurt Kempler wrote it from a story by Marion Jackson, and Tenny Wright directed a cast that included Noah Beery, Mae Madison (right), Luis Alberni, Berton Chur-
◁ chill, Paul Hurst and Sherwood Bailey.

△
When invention in a Joe E. Brown vehicle flagged, directors invariably turned their cameras on the comedian's cavernous mouth for a quick laugh, and so it was with **Fireman Save My Child,** a moderate comedy which had Brown (illustrated) as a fireman whose hobby is playing baseball. Female interest was supplied by Evalyn Knapp as the girl back home with Lillian Bond as the more sophisticated city type. Guy Kibbee, George Meeker, George Ernest, George MacFarlane and Virginia Sale also managed to find their way into the Ray Enright-Robert Lord-Arthur Caesar screenplay which Lloyd Bacon, who co-authored the story, directed. (First National.)

After an affair with a wealthy young man, Ann Dvorak (left) finds herself abandoned and with a baby to care for. But not for long. Her talent for attracting men is boundless and in **The Strange Love of Molly Louvain** she is wanted by no fewer than three of them. Directed by Michael Curtiz, it was relentless in its portrayal of gangsterdom and was a not particularly edifying or entertaining experience. One of Miss Dvorak's lovers was a ruthless murderer (Leslie Fenton, centre), another a newspaper reporter (Lee Tracy), while the third was a youngster called Jimmy (Richard Cromwell, right). It was based on a play by Maurine Watkins and adapted for the screen by Erwin Gelsey and Brown Holmes. Others in it were Guy Kibbee, Evalyn Knapp, Frank McHugh, Charles Middleton and Mary Doran. (First National.)

In **Street of Women**, from a novel by Polan Banks, Alan Dinehart (left) wants a divorce from his wife, Marjorie Gateson. Roland Young, on the other hand, wants to marry Kay Francis (centre). Miss Francis, however, only has eyes for Alan Dinehart. Mr. Dinehart loves his daughter Gloria Stuart, while Miss Francis is devoted to her brother, Allen Vincent (right). And just for good measure, Miss Stuart and Mr. Vincent happen to be in love with each other. Work it all out and you have the gist of the Mary McCall screenplay which director Archie Mayo managed to turn into a most acceptable entertainment.

The sheer professionalism in the foreground ▷ of William A. Wellman's direction turned **Love is a Racket** (released in Britain as **Such Things Happen**), a routine newspaper story, into a first-rate melodrama and painted an engrossing picture of the Broadway scene at its sleaziest. Douglas Fairbanks Jr (centre) starred as a gossipmonger in love with an actress (Frances Dee), but unfortunately for him, didn't get the girl. Courteney Terrett wrote the screenplay from a story by Rian James, with parts for Ann Dvorak (right), Lee Tracy (left), Lyle Talbot, Warren Hymer and William Burress. (First National.)

Guy Kibbee (centre left), 'so dumb that every time he opens his mouth he subtracts from the total sum of human knowledge', starred in **The Dark Horse**, a political send-up in which nitwit Kibbee runs for governor. A typical 'B' picture (the lack of close-ups indicating a lack of time), it bore all the hallmarks of the studio's efficient production-line approach to their less prestigious efforts. Alfred E. Green's direction, enhanced by Sol Polito's sharp photography and the not-a-second-wasted editing (by Owen Marks) ripped through the plot (an original by Darryl Zanuck alias Melville Crossman, Joseph Jackson and Courteney Terrett, which was scripted by Jackson and Wilson Mizner), drawing from it a great deal of fun and some good performances from Kibbee, Warren William (right) and Frank McHugh (left). Bette Davis and Vivienne Osborne (centre right) provided the feminine interest.

The Purchase Price, directed by William A. ▷ Wellman, starred Barbara Stanwyck (right) as a torch singer who, to get away from her racketeer lover (Lyle Talbot), travels to Elk's Crossing in North Dakota where she becomes the mail-order bride of farmer George Brent (left). The couple are married within hours of meeting and you know it's not going to work out, or not to begin with, at any rate. By concentrating on the wilder aspects of Robert Lord's screenplay (from a story by Arthur Stringer), Wellman managed to make a moderately successful job of it.

Having played a gangster, a cabbie, a con-man, a racing-car driver and a gambler, James Cagney (right) turned to prize-fighting in **Winner Takes All**. He went into training for the assignment and the results were splendid. His role as an egotistical but not too bright boxer who jilts a good woman (Marian Nixon) for a no-good society dame (Virginia Bruce, centre) only to discover he's made an error of judgement, gave him every opportunity to flex his dramatic muscles, which he did to good effect. The performance was a triumph of talent over mediocre material, and the film was a huge success. Also helping to give the commonplace a touch of class was Roy Del Ruth's no-nonsense direction and first rate supporting performances by Guy Kibbee, Clarence Muse, John Roche (left) and Allan Lane. Wilson Mizner and Robert Lord wrote the screenplay.

Two Against the World had most of the world against the film. A shoddy melodrama about a society woman who gamely takes the rap for a murder committed by her no-good brother, only to find herself being defended by the young lawyer with whom she happens to be in love, its computerized dialogue was punched out by Sheridan Gibney (from a play by Marion Dix and Jerry Horwin) and its equally mechanical direction was by Archie Mayo. Constance Bennett (left) starred as the self-sacrificing lady, with Neil Hamilton, Gavin Gordon, Helen Vinson, Allen Vincent (right), Alan Mowbray and Oscar Apfel in support.

Another vehicle for Charles (Chic) Sale, Stranger in Town starred him as the founder of a small town called Boilsville, Arkansas where he once officiated as both its postmaster and general groceryman. Ann Dvorak (right) was his granddaughter and David Manners (left) the rival store owner with whom she falls in love. Noah Beery, Maude Eburne, Lyle Talbot and John Larkin were also in the cast. It was written without sparkle by Carl Erickson and Harvey Thew, and directed by Erle C. Kenton in similar fashion.

A Joe E. Brown comedy with the word 'mouth' in the title was inevitable and it finally happened with You Said a Mouthful. Not one of the comedian's better efforts, it was all about an inventor (Brown, right) who hopes to make his fortune with something he calls 'non-sinkable bathing suit material'. He is mistaken for a champion swimmer (mistaken identity being obligatory in a Brown scenario) and, as a result, indulges in a round of mirth-provoking aquatics. Ginger Rogers (left) co-starred as Brown's inamorata, with other roles going to Preston Foster, Sheila Terry, Guinn Williams, Harry Gribbon and Oscar Apfel. It was written by Robert Lord and Bolton Mallory (from a story by William B. Dover) and directed by Lloyd Bacon (First National.)

Doctor X was a scary melange of cannibalism, necrophilia, dismemberment and rape. Lionel Atwill was the sinister eponymous hero, with Preston Foster as the lab assistant who, at full moon, coats his body in a kind of synthetic skin, then slips away to strangle the odd victim or two. Lee Tracy (left) played a newspaper reporter who suffers a fate almost worse than death when he is shut in a closet full of skeletons, is exposed to poisonous fumes, hides under a sheet in a morgue, and, most terrifying of all, fights off a monster with superhuman strength in a narrow, Dr. Caligari-like corridor. Photographed in Technicolor and directed with a characteristically Germanic sense of the baroque by the versatile Michael Curtiz, Doctor X was that rare specimen: a horror film that was genuinely horrific (partly thanks to the Max Factor Company for supplying the mask effects). It was written by Robert Tasker and Earl Baldwin (from a play by Howard W. Comstock and Allen C. Miller) and, apart from Messrs Atwill, Foster and Tracy, featured Fay Wray, John Wray, Harry Beresford, George Rosener (right) and Robert Warwick. (First National.)

Weekend Marriage (released in Britain as Weekend Lives) propounded the thesis that a woman's place is in the home and that chaos results when she swaps roles with her husband and becomes the breadwinner. Loretta Young (left) found herself in just such a situation when her husband (Norman Foster, right) loses his job and his self-respect at the same time. He gains a mistress, however, and the only way his wife can win him back is by relinquishing the pants she is wearing. Sheridan Gibney's screenplay (from a story by Faith Baldwin) accurately reflected the problems faced by many married couples, and the various emotions experienced by the protagonists, as the emphasis of their roles was reversed, had a ring of truth about them. but the story could have been more original and the insights more profound. Thornton Freeland directed and his cast included George Brent, Aline MacMahon, Vivienne Osborne and Sheila Terry. (First National.)

In **Ride Him Cowboy** (released in Britain as **The Hawk**), John Wayne (illustrated) saves a horse called Duke from being shot (the horse, it transpires, was charged with the murder of a rancher) and tames the animal who then assists him in bringing to justice the real murderer. Basically an equine variation of a Rin-Tin-Tin adventure, it was written by Scott Mason from a story by Kenneth Perkins, directed by Fred Allen and featured Ruth Hall, Otis Harlan, Henry B. Walthall and Harry Gribbon.

Donning a moustache, and a hook for a left hand, Edward G. Robinson (centre) in **Tiger Shark** brought passion and power to his role of a Portuguese tuna fisherman on whom Lady Luck resolutely refuses to smile. Having lost his wife (Zita Johann) to his best friend (Richard Arlen, top left), he lands up in the jaws of a man-eating shark, who, not content with just a hand this time, finishes off the job. Apart from the excellent performances, director Howard Hawks' depiction of the small fishing community was rich in documentary-like detail, and did not sentimentalize Wells Root's touching screenplay from Houston Branch's novel *Tuna*. Also cast were Leila Bennett, J. Carrol Naish and Vince Barnett. (First National.)

All manner of adventures befell Loretta Young (centre) in **They Call it Sin** (released in Britain as **The Way of Life**), a quickie about a young, musically gifted lass from Kansas who arrives in New York in order to marry a flashy playboy (David Manners, right) but finds herself in the clutches of a suave theatrical roué (Louis Calhern) instead. In the end she drops both for an ordinary doctor, ordinarily played by George Brent (left). Alberta Stedman Eagan wrote the novel on which it was based, and Lillie Hayward and Howard J. Green the screenplay. Thornton Freeland directed a cast which also included Una Merkel, Helen Vinson and Nella Walker. No fireworks, but not quite a damp squib either. (First National.)

Set in a maternity ward, **Life Begins** focused on a cross-section of women about to become mothers and paid particular attention to the sad plight of Grace Sutton (Loretta Young), a mother-to-be serving a prison sentence for murder. Dominating the ward was Aline MacMahon (right) whose characterization of an authoritative but compassionate head nurse gave Earl Baldwin's rather rambling screenplay (from a play by Mary McDouglas Axelson) the little cohesion it had. Strong performances from Gloria Shea (left), Eric Linden, Glenda Farrell, Dorothy Peterson, Vivienne Osborne, Frank McHugh (centre) and Gilbert Roland also helped. But it was too harrowing (Grace dies in childbirth) for popular success. The director was James Flood. (First National.)

Class conflict in a Deep South plantation was the steamy theme of Michael Curtiz's **Cabin in the Cotton**, adapted from Harrison Kroll's novel. It showed Richard Barthelmess on his way out, and the fast rising Bette Davis on her way in. Davis (right) as a wealthy bitch of a Southern belle who gives Barthelmess (left, as an indignant sharecropper's son) the run-around, demonstrated she could be sexy as well as nasty and her handling of Paul Green's screenplay (which contains one of her favourite lines: 'Ah'd love to kiss yuh, but ah jes' washed mah hay-uh') was immensely effective. Despite Curtiz's opposition to her presence in the film ('Goddamned, nothing, no-good sexless son of a bitch,' he once muttered within earshot of her), she gave audiences the first indication of the type of role she would soon make uniquely her own. Others in the cast were Dorothy Jordan, David Landau, Tully Marshall, Henry B. Walthall and Berton Churchill.

A very limited budget and a running time of only 63 minutes resulted in director Mervyn LeRoy's **Three on a Match** becoming something of a masterpiece of compression. It is the story of three slum girls who meet for the first time after a twelve-year separation. One is now a secretary (Bette Davis, left), another a wealthy socialite (Ann Dvorak, right), while the third is a showgirl (Joan Blondell, centre). Defying the superstition that the last person to light a cigarette from the same match will die, they do just that, and it is Ann Dvorak who lights up last. With pace substituting for style, Lucien Hubbard's tough, witty screenplay, like LeRoy's direction, managed to develop the characters as well as the plot in a convincing no-nonsense manner, which was neatly echoed in Sol Polito's photography (the montages conveying the passing of time were particularly effective) and the snappy editing by Ray Curtis. Others among the very capable cast were Lyle Talbot, Glenda Farrell and Humphrey Bogart. It was remade in 1938 as *Broadway Musketeers*.

Richard Barthelmess starred in an improbable tale of two doctors in **Alias the Doctor.** He played Karl, an orphan living with a Bavarian farming family who, together with Stephen (Norman Foster), the son of the family, studies medicine and succeeds where Stephen does not. But he ruins his career when he takes the blame for an operation Stephen performs while still a student, and is sent to jail for three years. The saint-like quality Barthelmess brought to it all was as hard to accept as the content of Houston Branch's screenplay (from a play by Emric Foldes). Lloyd Bacon was the floundering director. Others in the cast were Lucille La Verne, Adrienne Dore, Oscar Apfel, Marian Marsh (illustrated) and John St Polis. (First National.)

▽

Unhampered by Hays Office restrictions, **Scarlet Dawn,** a drama set in the Russian revolution about an exiled aristocrat (Douglas Fairbanks Jr, left) and his love for a serving girl (Nancy Carroll, right) had two things going for it: Anton Grot's remarkable settings (from ornate villas rich in icons and draperies to a squalid kitchen in Turkey) and director William Dieterle's explicit approach to all matters sexual, nowhere better illustrated than in an encounter Fairbanks has with his mistress (Lilyan Tashman) and the orgy scene that follows. Critics and audiences, however, found it slow-moving and ponderous and refused to become involved in the Niven Busch-Erwin Gelsey-Douglas Fairbanks Jr screenplay, based on Mary McCall's novel *Revolt.*

▽

△

It seems that New York's Central Park was unsafe even in 1932 — at least according to Ward Morehouse's story **Central Park,** adapted by Morehouse and Earl Baldwin. Set entirely in the park's precincts, it involved several incidents within its boundaries, the most dramatic being the escape of a lion from the park's zoo, and the consequent havoc caused when the beast runs amok in a Casino during a dinner-dance. John Adolfi's fast-moving direction went a long way to disguise that fact that it was a load of nonsense, so did the performances of Joan Blondell (left), Wallace Ford, Guy Kibbee (right), Henry B. Walthall and Patricia Ellis. Songs included: Young Love and Central Park. (First National.)

△

George Brent (left) was a victim of Wall Street's worst hour in **The Crash,** mainly as a result of certain incorrect information given to him by his sybaritic wife — Ruth Chatterton (right). Spurning the idea of poverty, Miss Chatterton takes herself to Bermuda with a $5,000 letter of credit, where she meets a wealthy Australian sheep-farmer whom she thinks it might be fun to marry. Now read on . . . Based on a novel by Larry Barretto and with a facile screenplay by Barretto and Earl Baldwin, it was more notable for the stylishness of its leading lady's wardrobe than for its very ordinary content. Brent seemed ill at ease, though there was fair support from Paul Cavanagh, Henry Kolker, Lois Wilson and Barbara Leonard. The director was William Dieterle. (First National.)

Edward G. Robinson (illustrated) failed to convince audiences and critics that he was a Chinese hatchet man in **The Hatchet Man** (released in Britain as **The Honourable Mr Wong**), a bloody drama set in San Francisco and involving Robinson (as a powerful member of the Chinese community), in a series of Tong wars. Loretta Young was cast as Robinson's unfaithful wife, with Leslie Fenton (as the object of Miss Young's affections), Edmund Breese, Tully Marshall, Noel N. Madison, J. Carrol Naish and Blanche Frederici also pretending to be Orientals. It was written by J. Grubb Alexander from a play by Achmed Abdullah and David Belasco, and directed by William Wellman. (First National.)

▽

Crooner took some satirical swipes at the machinery of fame. It starred David Manners (centre) as a college saxophonist who, in six months, is built up into a major singing star by agent Ken Murray, only to stumble into oblivion when success goes to his head. Predating *A Face in the Crowd* by a quarter of a century, its writer Rian James was as savage about the catastrophe of success as Budd Schulberg would be, except that **Crooner**'s milieu was radio not TV. It was expertly directed by Lloyd Bacon from a screenplay by Charles Kenyon. Also cast were Ann Dvorak as the crooner's girlfriend, Sheila Terry, William Janney, Eddie Nugent, J. Carrol Naish and Guy Kibbee. Songs included: I Send My Love With The Roses (by Al Dubin and Joe Burke), Three's A Crowd (by Al Dubin and Harry Warren), Sweethearts Forever (by Irving Caesar and Cliff Friend) and Now You've Got Me Worrying For You and Banking On The Weather (by Irving Kahal and Sammy Fain).

A powerful drama based on certain biographical incidents concerning a celebrated New York lawyer, **The Mouthpiece** starred a stylish Warren William (centre right) who, in the film's opening scenes, is shown persuading a jury to convict an innocent man. Swayed by his rhetoric, the jury return a verdict of guilty and the prisoner is sent to the chair. As a result of his actions, William suffers a total moral collapse and becomes a 'front man' for a group of mobsters, in the process of which directors James Flood and Elliott Nugent exposed the slimy, desperately corrupt legal system as it operated in the underworld. It was written by Joseph Jackson and Earl Baldwin and featured Sidney Fox, J. Carrol Naish (centre left), Aline MacMahon, Noel Francis (right) and Guy Kibbee.

One of the most vehement, eloquent and far-reaching of all social protest films, **I am a Fugitive from a Chain Gang** shattered audiences with its harrowing depiction of the brutalities perpetrated by guards attached to a prison chain-gang. It starred Paul Muni (centre) as James Allen, an out-of-work war veteran who is framed in a lunch-wagon holdup and finds himself serving a prison sentence in a Georgia chain-gang for a crime he did not commit. He escapes, makes his way to Chicago, gets a job with a construction firm and marries. But he is betrayed by his wife, and returns to prison on the understanding that he will be paroled in ninety days. His parole is refused and he escapes once again – this time as a desperate, broken man, destined to spend the rest of his life as a fugitive. Based on Robert E. Burns' autobiographical account of his own experiences in a chain-gang, the film, apart from the gripping narrative fashioned by Sheridan Gibney and Brown Holmes, was an explosive indictment and condemnation of the type of brutality and sadism that resulted in convicts being indiscriminately beaten, incarcerated in sweat boxes and bound together with dehumanizing chains. Apart from Muni's magnificent performance, which won him an Oscar nomination, there was outstanding support from a large cast that included Glenda Farrell (as his Judas-like wife), Helen Vinson, Preston Foster, David Landau, Hale Hamilton, Edward J. McNamara, Allen Jenkins, Berton Churchill and Edward Ellis. The committed direction was by Mervyn LeRoy. Although by no means a commercial subject, audiences gave this classic social drama overwhelming support, making it one of the studio's most successful productions of the year. Whether or not conditions in Georgia chain-gangs improved as a result of the film was difficult to asses, but it certainly made the public aware of the shocking conditions that prevailed in such colonies and brought shame and disgrace on many of the penal authorities in the South.

Kay Francis (right) with her limited acting talent and conspicuous lisp did nothing better during her years at Warner Bros. than **One Way Passage,** a high quality weepie about two doomed lovers. He (William Powell, left) is wanted for murder; she (Miss Francis) is dying of an incurable disease. They indulge in a brief shipboard romance under the cupid-playing surveillance of con-tricksters Frank McHugh and Aline MacMahon. Economically directed by Tay Garnett (the entire film runs only 69 minutes) and movingly scripted by Wilson Mizner and Joseph Jackson from Robert Lord's Oscar-winning original story, the film was a great popular success with suave William Powell in the guise of a lawbreaker scoring a notable personal success. It was remade in 1940 as *Till We Meet Again.*

Very reminiscent of *School Days* (1922), **Big City Blues** pursued a favourite theme of the studio's: the innocent at large in the corrupt metropolis. Eric Linden (right) played a bumpkin from Indiana who, thanks to the nefarious activities of his city-slicker cousin (Walter Catlett), becomes involved in a murder. The film also starred Joan Blondell (centre) as the understanding woman who manages to set him straight. Based on a story by Ward Morehouse who wrote the screenplay with Lillie Hayward, it was little more than a programmer, but, under Mervyn LeRoy's direction, a good one. Also cast were Jobyna Howland, Evalyn Knapp, Ned Sparks, Guy Kibbee, Inez Courtney (left) and Humphrey Bogart. Songs included: Big City Blues, New York Town and My Baby Just Cares For Me.

In **Lawyer Man**, William Powell's suave gift of the gab takes him on a one-way ticket to success, from mouthpiece of the lower classes to assistant prosecutor. *En route* he finds himself facing a blackmail charge levelled by attractive Claire Dodd. But the jury fails to agree on a verdict, and the charge is dropped. Based on Max Trell's novel, Rian James' and James Seymour's screenplay was ordinary, but Powell (right) and Joan Blondell (centre, as his secretary) were more than adequate compensation. Helen Vinson, Alan Dinehart, Allen Jenkins, David Landau and Sheila Terry were also among the cast, and the director was William Dieterle.

James Cagney (left) had to learn to drive for his role in **Taxi!** in which he played the leader of a group of independent taxi drivers who fearlessly fight for cabbie's rights against a powerful union. Lovely Loretta Young (right, who replaced Nancy Carroll, who replaced Joan Blondell, who replaced Dorothy Mackaill) played his wife and had little to do but show concern over her husband's belligerent behaviour. Also featured in a large cast were George E. Stone, Guy Kibbee, Ray Cooke, Dorothy Burgess, Leila Bennett, Nat Pendleton, Berton Churchill and, in a small role, George Raft. It was vigorously directed by Roy Del Ruth, snappily scripted by Kubec Glasmon and John Bright, and well supported by the public, who made it one of the studio's most successful films of the year.

Fancifully based on the career of Ivar Kreuger, **The Match King** starred Warren William (illustrated) as the titular hero, known in Houston Branch and Sidney Sutherland's screenplay (and in Einar Thorvaldson's novel on which it was based) as Paul Kroll. Kroll's belief in the supremacy of the ordinary match as a powerful artefact was entertainingly conveyed under Howard Bretherton's direction (and in William's immaculate performance), as was his unscrupulous belief that the best way to get money is to borrow it, then borrow more to pay back the first lot, and even more to pay back the second, etc. Kroll's business ventures – which involved murder, forgery, blackmail and every other crooked ruse in the book – lent a touch of melodrama to the proceedings, but William gave Kroll's numerous activities just the right sort of dramatic perspective. The outcome was highly enjoyable. Strong support came from Lili Damita (as a film star who attracts Kroll's attention), Glenda Farrell, Harold Huber, Spencer Charters and John Wray. (First National.)

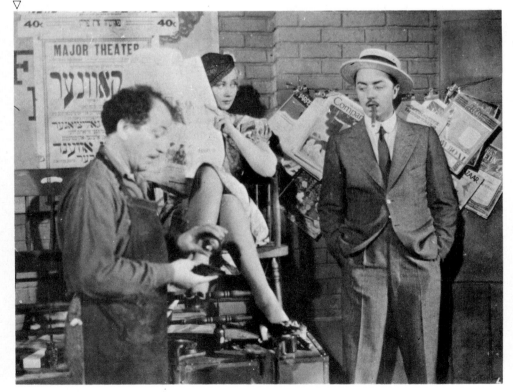

1933

The Depression continued to take its toll on the studio's fortunes in 1933 and, in March, all Warner Bros. personnel took a 50 per cent salary cut for an eight week duration. When the Academy of Motion Picture Arts and Sciences stipulated that the studio rescind the cuts, the brothers refused. The Academy advised Warner Bros. personnel to seek back pay, dated from 6 March, but still Jack Warner and his brothers said no. In the midst of all this Darryl Zanuck (by then earning $5,000 a week) decided to accept an offer from Joe Schenck to head production for a new company, Twentieth Century, which was to merge with Fox the following year. Shortly after Zanuck's resignation, Jack Warner restored all salaries to their pre-March status. **42nd Street** made its appearance during the March brouhaha. Though it made a profit and assured the film musical a healthy future for the next few years, the studio's losses for the year totalled $6,291,748.

Both **42nd Street** and **I Am A Fugitive From A Chain Gang** received Oscar nominations, but the Best Film award went to Fox's **Cavalcade** from the play by Noel Coward. Paul Muni was nominated as Best Actor for **I Am A Fugitive From A Chain Gang**, but lost to Charles Laughton in Alexander Korda's **The Private Lives Of Henry VIII**. Robert Lord won an Oscar in the Best Original Story category for **One Way Passage**. Nathan Levinson was nominated in the Best Sound Recording category for three films: **42nd Street**, **Golddiggers of 1933** and **I Am A Fugitive From A Chain Gang** but lost to Harold C. Lewis from Paramount for **A Farewell To Arms**.

△
The real picture snatcher in **Picture Snatcher** was Alice White who walked off with almost all the acting honours in this Lloyd Bacon actioner, though it was James Cagney who was top cast as Danny Kean, a racketeer turned smear-photographer. Cagney (right) played Cagney with his usual tough, pugnacious, straight-from-the-shoulder manner and imbued the role with the sheer force of his personality. Ralph Bellamy, Patricia Ellis and Ralf Harolde (left) co-starred; and Allen Rivkin and P.J. Wolfson wrote the so-so screenplay from a story by Danny Ahearn. The production was supervised by Ray Griffith.

'Don't come if you're afraid to see what's ▷ on the other side of **The Keyhole**' tantalized the ads for this Michael Curtiz-directed programmer in which elegant Kay Francis (centre) and bland George Brent were teamed for the first time. The banal story of a wealthy woman (Francis) who discovers she is not legally married and takes advantage of the fact by ditching her husband (Monroe Owsley) in favour of a private detective (Brent), its only excuse seemed to be to provide some mild diversion for Depression-weary cinemagoers. Framed in sets by the remarkable Anton Grot, and with costumes by Orry-Kelly, it all looked classier than anything in Robert Presnell's vapid screenplay sounded. Light relief between the bouts of Brent/Francis romanticising were provided by Glenda Farrell and Allen Jenkins, and Ferdinand Gottschalk (left) and Henry Kolker (right) were in it too. Alice D. G. Miller wrote the story on which it was based; and the production was supervised by Hal Wallis.

△
First called **A Bad Boy**, then **The Inside**, and finally **Hard to Handle**, this comedy about a frenetic press agent whose wheeler-dealing involved him in everything from promoting grapefruit to marathon dances, was, as far as the plot was concerned, a shambles. But James Cagney's dynamic central performance blasted its way through the Wilson Mizner-Robert Lord screenplay (from a story by Houston Branch) leaving audiences dazed. There was a marvellous performance, too, from Ruth Donnelly as the heroine's mother, which delighted the crowds and made sure, for once, that Cagney (left) did not have it all his own way. Mary Brian (right), Allen Jenkins and Claire Dodd provided stalwart support; while Mervyn LeRoy, taking his cue from his leading man, directed it all as though he were about to run out of film. Ray Griffith supervised.

Girl Missing was a thriller of sorts in ▷ which a pretty young thing called Daisy (Peggy Shannon) suddenly disappears from her Palm Beach Hotel on the night of her wedding. Where could she be? And who is the dead body propped up in a chair on the hotel lawn? Unfortunately, a lot more was missing from this effort than the girl. Where, for example, was the script (allegedly by Carl Erickson, Don Mullaly and Ben Markson)? Or the direction (by Robert Florey)? There wasn't much evidence, either, of talent in the performances of Ben Lyon (centre) as Daisy's husband, Lyle Talbot as her former lover, or Mary Brian (left) and Glenda Farrell (right) as chorus girls. No wonder audiences were missing too. Henry Blanke supervised the shenanigans and, in small parts, cast Guy Kibbee, Harold Huber, Edward Ellis, Ferdinand Gottschalk and Helen Ware.

Having spent time peddling bottled medicines across the country, Warren William (centre) decides to continue conning the gullible by becoming a clairvoyant, which he did with marked success in **The Mind Reader,** a moderately diverting trifle which gave its star his second showy role in just four months. Constance Cummings co-starred as his pretty but stupid wife, with Allen Jenkins (left) on hand as a pickpocket. Natalie Moorhead, Clara Blandick, Mayo Methot, Clarence Muse (right) and Harry Beresford were also featured in the Wilson Mizner-Robert Lord screenplay (from a play by Vivian Cosby) and the director was Roy Del Ruth. Hal Wallis supervised. (First National.)

Pure escapism, **The Working Man** (based on a novel by Edgar Franklin) was the simple story of a wealthy shoe manufacturer (George Arliss, right) who puts his business in the hands of his nephew and takes himself off to Maine for a fishing vacation. While casting his line, he meets a high-living man (Theodore Newton) and his directionless sister (Bette Davis) who turn out to be the children of his biggest business rival. Posing as an out-of-work victim of the Depression, he is given a job by the brother and sister in the rival factory where he not only re-organizes the lives of his aimless young employers, but, for fun, goes into competition with his very own nephew. J. Farrell MacDonald (left) was also in the cast. Directed with the right tongue-in-cheek approach by John Adolfi, engagingly scripted by Maude T. Howell and Charles Kenyon, it added up to 73 minutes of wholesome fun, supervised by Lucien Hubbard.
▽

One of the studio's more successful horror films, **The Mystery of the Wax Museum,** directed by Michael Curtiz, and starring Lionel Atwill as the mentally and physically scarred owner of a wax museum, was genuinely horrific. The scenes showing the destruction by fire of the museum, with the slowly melting wax figures distorting the grotesque forms, as well as the gruesome climax in which an agonized Fay Wray literally crumbles Atwill's face to reveal how hideously disfigured it is, were as terrifying as anything conceived by that arch-deacon of terror, James Whale, down the road at Universal. Written by Don Mullaly and Carl Erickson from a story by Charles Belden and filmed in eerie Technicolor by Ray Rennahan, the film also featured Glenda Farrell as the fearless viper-tongued reporter who helps put paid to Atwill's terrifyingly murderous antics, with Frank McHugh, Allen Vincent and Gavin Gordon in supporting roles. Henry Blanke supervised the production.

Lilly Turner, written by Gene Markey and Kathryn Scola from the play by Philip Dunning and George Abbott, miscast Ruth Chatterton (left) as Lilly, the wife of a carnival-show magician. Not only is Lilly deserted when her husband learns she is going to have a baby, but he turns out to be a bigamist as well. Miss Chatterton was too sophisticated an actress for this sort of role, and, as a result, the finished product lacked conviction. The two other men in ▷ her life were Frank McHugh (right) as a drink-sodden barker who offers to make a respectable woman of her, and George Brent as an engineer. No prizes for guessing whom she chooses. William A. Wellman directed a cast that also included Ruth Donnelly, Guy Kibbee, Gordon Westcott, Marjorie Gateson, Arthur Vinton and Robert Barrat, and the production was supervised by Hal Wallis. (First National.)

As programmers go, **The Parachute Jumper** went. A far-fetched yarn in which Douglas Fairbanks Jr (right), lately discharged from service, finds employment with Leo Carrillo, first as a bodyguard, then as a pilot engaged to smuggle narcotics out of Canada and into the States, it was a makeshift effort which made rather better use of stock aerial and newsreel footage than it did of the script. It also starred Bette Davis (left) who hated every second of it (and was doubtless instrumental in having an extract of it appear in *Whatever Happened to Baby Jane*, 1962, to illustrate the poor quality of the scripts that were thrust on her at the start of her career) and featured Frank McHugh, Claire Dodd, Sheila Terry and Harold Huber. Alfred E. Green directed it without enthusiasm, and it was written by John Francis Larkin from Rian James' story *Some Call It Love*. Ray Griffith supervised the production.
▽

Director Michael Curtiz employed a harsh, ▷
semi-documentary style in his approach to
20,000 Years in Sing Sing. He relished
the idea of the hero (Spencer Tracy)
admitting to a crime he did not commit and
burning in the electric chair for it, and
brought his formidable talents to bear on
this hard-hitting prison drama in which
tough-guy Tracy (right), through the influence of an enlightened warden (Arthur
Byron) reveals an uncharacteristic streak
of sensitivity. The film eloquently reflected
the studio's social conscience in matters of
prison reform, managing at the same time
to be first-class entertainment. Tracy, on
loan from Fox (Jack Warner originally
wanted Cagney for the role, but Cagney,
in the throes of demanding a rise in weekly
salary from $1,750 to $3,000, said no),
brought his usual blend of tough-guy cynicism and human decency to the part of mobster Tom Connors; Bette Davis as his moll
emoted with a quite frightening intensity.
The screenplay by Wilson Mizner and Brown
Holmes was based on Warden Lewis E.
Lawe's book – adapted by Courteney Terrett
and Robert Lord. It ended in ironic fashion
with the song 'Happy Days Are Here Again'
following the announcement of Connors'
death sentence – a juxtaposition which sent
audiences home with something to think
about. Also cast were Lyle Talbot (left),
Grant Mitchell, Warren Hymer and Louis
Calhern. Ray Griffith supervised. (First
National.) It was remade in 1940 as *Castle on
the Hudson.*

△
In **Frisco Jenny**, Ruth Chatterton played a
cashier in her father's Barbary Coast saloon
who annoys the old man (Robert Emmet
O'Connor) by announcing her desire to
marry piano-player James Murray. Dad
slaps her face and the reverberations (or
so it appears) bring on the San Francisco
earthquake. For in no time at all, the
walls come tumbling down. As the plot
(by Gerald Beaumont, Lillie Hayward and
John Francis Larkin) thickens, Jenny has
a son whom she keeps hidden until she
can do so no longer, then hands him over
to wealthy foster parents. Time passes,
the son grows up, becomes a lawyer and,
in the best *Madame X* tradition, unknowingly
finds himself facing his mother on the
witness stand. Unlike *Madame X*, however,
he is there to prosecute, rather than to
defend her. It all ended in tears with
audiences remaining indifferent to Miss
Chatterton's (centre left) sorry plight. Donald
Cook (right) played the son, with other parts
going to Louis Calhern, Hallam Cooley,
Helen Jerome Eddy, Pat O'Malley and
Harold Huber. Wilson Mizner and Robert
Lord wrote the screenplay, Ray Griffith
supervised the production, and William A.
Wellman directed. (First National.)

Though **From Headquarters** set out to
anatomize the process by which murders are
solved (hence the involvement of autopsy
surgeons, ballistics experts, toxicologists,
etc.) it was pretty routine entertainment
which starred George Brent (right) as a
police lieutenant assigned to finding out who
killed Kenneth Thomson. As to *why* Thomson
was killed, no mystery was involved at all:
he was an unsavoury, crooked, double-
crossing playboy, heavily into drugs. Margaret Lindsay (left), Eugene Pallette, Hugh
Herbert, Dorothy Burgess, Theodore Newton, Hobart Cavanaugh and Henry O'Neill
also featured in Robert N. Lee and Peter
Milne's screenplay; Sam Bischoff supervised the production and William Dieterle
directed.
▽

△
Richard Barthelmess (illustrated) took to
the air again in **Central Airport**, but that's
where the similarity to *Dawn Patrol* (1930)
ended. He played an ace pilot who teams up
with parachutist Sally Eilers, and together
they made an excellent duo, both on the
ground and in the air. When, however, he
refuses to marry her, believing that pilots
should remain single because of the high risk
factor involved in aeronautics, she ups and
marries his brother (Tom Brown) instead.
Barthelmess seemed ill at ease with Rian
James and James Seymour's screenplay (from
a story by Jack Moffitt) and director William
A. Wellman equally ill at ease with Barthelmess. Also cast were Glenda Farrell, Harold
Huber, Grant Mitchell and Claire McDowell.
Hal Wallis supervised the production. (First
National.)

Joan Blondell (centre) a welcome addition ▷ to any cast list, and hitherto operating mainly from the sidelines, was the centre of attraction in **Blondie Johnson**, an underworld melodrama predicated on the premise that crime certainly *does* pay. At least it does for Blondie Johnson, whose rise from petty con-artist to kingpin in a lucrative insurance racket, is little short of spectacular. She gets caught in the end (it was, after all, 1933) but not before a good time was had by all. Chester Morris (left), Allen Jenkins, Claire Dodd, Earle Foxe, Arthur Vinton (right) and Sterling Holloway were in it too; Earl Baldwin wrote it, the slick direction was by Ray Enright, and the production was supervised by Lucien Hubbard. (First National.)

Typical of the studio's 'quickies', **Bureau of Missing Persons**, with its shoestring budget, its sleazy interiors and no-time-to-catch-your-breath storyline, involved a group of people (including Bette Davis) all on the lookout for someone or other. Miss Davis, for example, happens to be looking for her husband. In vain, as it turns out, for he has been murdered. The catch, however, is that Bette is wanted for murder herself. The best moment comes with the arrival of a ransom note to the Bureau instructing that a certain amount of money be attached to a carrier pigeon. Unperturbed by the request, and in all seriousness, police chief Lewis Stone hires a plane and follows the bird to the kidnappers! Whether intended or not, the film emerged as a comedy, and the critics treated it as the potboiler it was. Although Davis starred, she did not appear for the first half hour, and even then had only a mere half-dozen scenes. The production was supervised by Henry Blanke and directed by Roy Del Ruth from Robert Presnell's far-fetched screenplay. Also cast were Pat O'Brien (right), Glenda Farrell, Allen Jenkins (left), Ruth Donnelly, Hugh Herbert, Alan Dinehart, Marjorie Gateson and Tad Alexander. (First National.)
▽

The question posed in **Grand Slam** was: should husbands and wives be allowed to play in the same bridge game? And the answer was: yes, but only if they are insanely in love, though, at the same time, temporarily separated. It also helped, of course, if the wife was Loretta Young. In director William Dieterle's entertaining satire on bridge tournaments, Miss Young (left) graduated from hat-check girl to being the glamorous wife of bridge champion Paul Lukas, and, in the process got to wear a lot of Orry-Kelly's stunning clothes. So did co-star Helen Vinson. It was written by David Boehm and Erwin Gelsey (from a novel by B. Russell Herts) and offered employment to Glenda Farrell, Frank McHugh (right), Walter Byron, Roscoe Karns and De Witt Jennings. Hal Wallis supervised ◁ its production.

△

George Arliss (centre) was the distinguished star of **The King's Vacation**, a comedy set in a mythical kingdom involving Philip, a monarch of eighteen years standing, who suddenly decides he would like to abdicate in favour of the simple life. Eighteen years prior to the film's start he was married, morganatically, to a pretty young woman whom he was forced to divorce if he wished to be king. Now, with the permission of his second wife, Wilhelmina (Florence Arliss), who hints that she, too, has a lover to whom she can return, Philip journeys to France where he meets up with his former spouse (Marjorie Gateson) only to discover that, although he has not remarried, she lives in the very kind of opulent splendour he is trying to avoid. He returns to Wilhelmina, who has taken a small house without servants, and, as her boast of a former liaison was not true, it is clear that the couple will see out the rest of their days together. Charmingly written by Ernest Pascal and Maude T. Howell, and well directed by John Adolfi, the film also featured Dudley Digges, Dick Powell, Patricia Ellis, O. P. Heggie and Douglas Gerrard. The production supervisor was Lucien Hubbard.

By late 1932, Barbara Stanwyck was under sole contract to the studio and in **Ladies They Talk About** she played a tough, wise-cracking cookie who knew how to take care of herself. In 69 minutes the movie told the story of a bank-robber, played by Stanwyck (centre right), who, after being sentenced by evangelist Preston Foster (whom she goes on to marry!), finds herself in the women's division of San Quentin, which, naturally she commandeers as soon as she arrives. The plot turned unconsciously melodramatic, but the screenplay (by Brown Holmes from a play by Dorothy Mackaye and Carlton Miles) had some crackling exchanges between the inmates, and genuinely attempted, albeit without much success, to make a few pertinent points about prison reform and the plight of women without men. The critics carped; so did the Hays Office. Ray Griffith supervised the production, Howard Bretherton directed, and the cast included Lyle Talbot, Dorothy Burgess, Lillian Roth, Maude Eburne, Ruth Donnelly, Helen Ware and Robert McWade.
▽

Paul Muni (right) aged three generations in **The World Changes**, a well-structured drama written by Edward Chodorov from a Sheridan Gibney story and competently directed by Mervyn LeRoy. The saga of an ambitious Dakota farm boy who moves to Chicago and into the meat-packing business where he makes a fortune by inventing the refrigerated freight-car ('ice-boxes on wheels, ice-boxes on wheels' is his Eureka-like shout of ecstasy), it was too similar in content to the Edward G. Robinson vehicle I Loved A Woman, and made little impression on the box-office. Mary Astor co-starred as Muni's snobbish wife who could accept her husband's money but not his method of making it, with other roles going to Aline MacMahon (centre right), Douglass Dumbrille (centre, as Buffalo Bill), Donald Cook, Patricia Ellis, Jean Muir (left), Guy Kibbee, Anna Q. Nilsson and Henry O'Neill. Robert Lord supervised. (First National.)
▽

△
Apart from his outsized mouth and an ability to make some people laugh, Joe E. Brown (centre) was, in his salad days, a professional baseball player. This made him the natural choice for **Elmer the Great**, the film version of the Ring Lardner-George M. Cohan play. That Lardner and Cohan intended their hero to be a pitcher rather than the home-run hitter he turns out to be in Tom Geraghty's screenplay, was of little consequence. All that mattered in this remake of Paramount's 1929 *First Company*, was that Elmer, after nearly missing the big game because of his involvement with a gang of crooks, wins the day for the Cubs against the Yankees. As was the case with most Brown performances, the hero emerged as a caricature, but under Mervyn LeRoy's assured direction both he and the film were amiable enough. Love interest was supplied by Patricia Ellis, with Frank McHugh adding to the quota of predictable laughs. Others involved were Claire Dodd, Sterling Holloway (left), Emma Dunn (right), Douglass Dumbrille, Charles Delaney, Jessie Ralph (standing right) and J. Carrol Naish. Ray Griffith supervised.

It was no accident that the studio which championed the rights of the underdog, the persecuted and the suppressed, should be drawn to **Voltaire** as a subject. And in George Arliss (illustrated) they found just the man to portray the great eighteenth century wit and activist. Not as faithful to the facts as it could have been, but far more entertaining than it might have been, it also starred Doris Kenyon and Margaret Lindsay with Theodore Newton, Reginald Owen, Alan Mowbray and Gordon Westcott in support. The screenplay, which abounded in such lines as 'You can burn my body, but never my soul; that is in the keeping of the people of France!' was by Paul Green and Maude T. Howell (from the novel by George Gibbs and E. Lawrence Dudley). John Adolfi directed with Ray Griffith supervising.
▽

△
A computerized comedy, **Havana Widows** was formula film making at its manufactured worst. A tired caper about a couple of chorus girls (Joan Blondell, left, and Glenda Farrell) who, for a change, do their gold-digging in Cuba rather than on Broadway, its predictable cast included Guy Kibbee as a business man with a thirst for adventure, Frank McHugh as the obligatory inebriate, Allen Jenkins as the po-faced thug, and Ruth Donnelly as his prudish wife. Also cast were Lyle Talbot, Hobart Cavanaugh and Ralph Ince. Earl Baldwin wrote it, Ray Enright was the director and Robert Lord supervised. (First National.)

Hollywood's look at the medical profession in **Mary Stevens M.D.** was unedifying, to say the least. The story – of a woman physician's (Kay Francis) passion for fellow physician Lyle Talbot, an unmitigated scoundrel who, while paralytically drunk, thinks nothing of operating on children – had about as much integrity as a lie. Miss Francis (right) flees to Paris to have Talbot's (centre) illegitimate baby, but the child dies of infantile paralysis on the way back to the States. The star did her best with this lurid material (story by Virginia Kellogg; screenplay by Rian James and Robert Lord) but was not helped by Lloyd Bacon's insensitive direction. Hal Wallis supervised the production, but failed to curb its excesses. Also cast were Glenda Farrell (left), Una O'Connor, who was excellent and Hobart Cavanaugh.
▽

△
A remake of Ken Maynard's 1927 Western for First National, **Somewhere in Sonora**, written by Joe Roach from a story by Will L. Comfort, was refurbished for John Wayne (centre) with Henry B. Walthall also cast as the father of a son shanghaied in Sonora by a gang of crooks. Wayne reciprocates Walthall's friendship by agreeing to find the boy and bring the villains to justice. It was directed by Mack V. Wright and featured Shirley Palmer, Paul Fix, Ann Faye, Billy Franey, Ralph Lewis, Frank Rice and J. P. McGowan.

Detective roles fitted William Powell like a piece of bespoke tailoring, as his work in **Private Detective 62** demonstrated. Cast as an undercover man who falls for attractive Margaret Lindsay, a gambler he is investigating in Paris, Powell's performance was as smooth and as glossy as polished glass. Rian James' screenplay (from a story by Raoul Whitfield) offered scope for character delineation which both its star (right) and director, Michael Curtiz, explored most effectively. Arthur Hohl (left) played the heavy, with other parts going to Ruth Donnelly (centre), Gordon Westcott, James Bell, Arthur Byron, Sheila Terry, Natalie Moorhead and Hobart Cavanaugh. Hal Wallis supervised.

▽

The story of a beer baron who, at the end of Prohibition enrols in California's high society, **The Little Giant** was Edward G. Robinson's first comedy success. Audiences enjoyed the sight of the little tough guy committing one social *faux pas* after another ('Why doncha fill it up?' he asks when offered a measure of brandy in a balloon glass) and were pleased, in the end, when Robinson (illustrated) got the girl (Mary Astor). Roy Del Ruth directed; Robert Lord wrote it with Wilson Mizner, and the cast included Helen Vinson, Kenneth Thomson, Russell Hopton, Berton Churchill and Donald Dillaway. Ray Griffith supervised. (First National.)

▽

△

Satiated with a steady diet of screen musicals (usually in a revue format) that were little more than a collection of flatly staged production numbers enhancing a scenario of mind-boggling stupidity, Depression audiences showed their discontent with the genre by staying away. The studio more or less declared a moratorium on musicals because of this — until production head Darryl Zanuck signed Rian James and James Seymour to write a musical that had more than just a soupçon of plot and which wasn't simply a series of song cues. Also available to the studio was dance director Busby Berkeley whose talent Zanuck recognized as being exceptional, and who needed to be put to work. The result was **42nd Street** — the definitive backstage musical, and a breakthrough in the genre. Mervyn LeRoy was going to direct, but withdrew as a result of illness. Lloyd Bacon stepped in, and together with Berkeley (who was actually engaged by LeRoy, and whose first film was Eddie Cantor's *Whoopee* for Sam Goldwyn in 1931), created a *nouvelle vague* in musicals. Before the production was completed (it was budgeted at a mammoth $400,000) Zanuck, to make quite sure that no other studio would benefit from Berkeley's unparalleled visual flair, signed him to a seven year contract. It was a shrewd move which paid off handsomely. **42nd Street's** plot was no more substantial than previous efforts (harassed producer has problems with temperamental leading lady who also happens to be mistress of show's backer) but the quality of its screenplay and the atmosphere it created gave it a distinction and a freshness to which audiences responded with gratitude. It also contained the now famous cliché of the understudy stepping into the star's shoes and tearing the place apart ('You're going out a youngster,' the director tells his terrified ingenue, 'but you've got to come back a *star*!'). Warner Baxter was the director, Ruby Keeler (centre) his great white hope. Other roles went to Bebe Daniels, George Brent, Una Merkel, Guy Kibbee, Dick Powell and Ned Sparks, with Ginger Rogers, Allen Jenkins, Henry B. Walthall and Edward G. Nugent in support. The score which gave Berkeley an opportunity to create cinema history with no fewer than three sensational production numbers, was by Al Dubin and Harry Warren. Hal Wallis supervised the production. Songs included: 42nd Street, You're Getting To Be A Habit With Me, Young and Healthy and Shuffle Off To Buffalo.

In **The Man from Monterey,** U.S. Captain John Wayne (left) is sent to Monterey to encourage local Mexican landowners to register their property under Spanish land grants if they do not wish it to become public domain. Inevitably he encounters some shady goings-on, sees that justice prevails and saves the heroine from marrying the heavy. Ruth Hall (centre left), Nina Quartero, Lillian Leighton (centre right), Luis Alberni, Francis Ford and Donald Reed (right) were in it, Lesley Mason wrote the screenplay and the director was Mack V. Wright. Leon Schlesinger produced.

▽

Significant social comment or sentimental ▷ melodrama? Director Archie Mayo and writer Edward Chodorov (working from a story by Islin Auster) couldn't make up their minds. Consequently, **The Mayor of Hell,** in which warden James Cagney turns his attentions to the sorry plight of boys in a reform school and the conditions under which they live, was something of a muddle. There were two good reasons for seeing it, though: the high-octane performances of both Cagney and Frankie Darro. Though Darro's role as one of the hapless inmates was really the predominant one, the studio's insistence on building up the Cagney character's importance toppled the film's structure with unsatisfying results. The leading lady was Madge Evans (she played the resident nurse) who replaced Glenda Farrell, herself a replacement for Joan Blondell. As the loathsome school superintendent, Dudley Digges was first-rate. Lucien Hubbard supervised the production. The film was remade in 1938 as *Crime School.*

◁ In an attempt to glamourize Barbara Stanwyck whom the studio felt needed an extra dose of feminine charm after her role in *Ladies They Talk About,* costume designer Orry-Kelly was engaged to outfit her in a series of stunning gowns. The marvellous creations he came up with, however, hardly compensated for the rather hackneyed plot of **Baby Face** in which a young girl, by lavishly spreading her favours (mainly smiles), works her way up from a sleazy speakeasy existence to become a New York society dame living in a swanky apartment, with the vice-president of a bank for a playmate. But was the lady happy? Of course she wasn't. Gene Markey and Kathryn Scola's screenplay from a story by Mark Canfield (Zanuck), was slick, but the ending phoney. Apart from Stanwyck (left) whose performance managed to overcome the triteness of the plot, the cast included George Brent, Donald Cook, Douglass Dumbrille and a young John Wayne (right). It was directed by Alfred E. Green and supervised by Ray Griffith.

One of the studio's most successful series of thrillers were the Philo Vance offerings, and in **The Kennel Murder Case,** they surfaced with a real winner. Less remarkable for its rather mundane plot (a collector of *chinoiserie* is bumped off and Vance, with the help of an enthusiastic Doberman Pinscher, finds out whodunnit) than the directorial skills director Michael Curtiz employed in the unfurling of it, it was stylistically a little gem. William Powell (left) returned to the role of Vance (he had played it three times before at Paramount in 1929 and 1930) with his characteristic insouciance, and there were enjoyable performances too, from Eugene Pallette (centre) as a slow-witted police sergeant, and Mary Astor as the murdered man's niece. Also on hand were Ralph Morgan, Robert McWade (right), Helen Vinson, Paul Cavanagh, Jack La Rue, Robert Barrat, Arthur Hohl and Henry O'Neill. Based on *The Return of Philo Vance* by S.S. Van Dine, it was adapted by Robert Presnell and written for the screen by Robert N. Lee and Peter Milne. Presnell also supervised. ▷

△

One of the last innovations made by Darryl Zanuck before leaving Warner Bros. to form Twentieth Century, was to put Bette Davis's name above the title, which he did for **Ex-Lady,** a remake of the Barbara Stanwyck vehicle *Illicit* (1931). The emancipated story of a girl who does not necessarily believe that love and marriage are inseparable, it was notable only in that, by appearing a year before the introduction of the Catholic League of Decency's strict censorship code, it allowed its star to appear *en deshabille* in a variety of 'daring' boudoir scenes. 'So frank . . . so outspoken . . . so true . . .' said the ads. 'So what?' said the public. Also starring with Davis (left) were Gene Raymond, Frank McHugh, Monroe Owsley (right) and Claire Dodd, with Kay Strozzi, Ferdinand Gottschalk and Alphonse Ethier in support. It was written by David Boehm from a story by Edith Fitzgerald and Robert Riskin, and directed by Robert Florey. Lucien Hubbard supervised.

The success of *42nd Street* left the studio in no doubt as to the kind of musical escapism Depression-torn audiences wanted. Its follow up, **Gold Diggers of 1933**, loosely based on Avery Hopwood's play, was an even more elaborate piece of escapism which consolidated the reputation of its dance director Busby Berkeley who, in the film's three major production numbers, revealed himself to be the enviable possessor of the most fertile imagination in his particular field. Boasting no fewer than three love stories for the price of one (Warren William and Joan Blondell, Guy Kibbee and Aline MacMahon – a teaming the studio would return to on several more occasions – and Dick Powell and Ruby Keeler – ditto) the Erwin Gelsey-James Seymour screenplay (with dialogue by David Boehm and Ben Markson) traversed familiar backstage territory, this time focusing on the efforts of songwriter Powell to raise $15,000 to stage a show he has written. Directed by Mervyn LeRoy with a pace and attack rare in musicals, and with a top-notch score by Al Dubin and Harry Warren, **Gold Diggers of 1933** opened with the prophetic 'We're In The Money' (sung by Ginger Rogers). Though the film's production costs were twenty times the amount songwriter Powell needed for *his* show, it grossed a fortune. Robert Lord supervised the production. Other songs included: I've Got To Sing A Torch Song, Pettin' In The Park, The Shadow Waltz and My Forgotten Man.

Leslie Howard (left), Douglas Fairbanks Jr and Paul Lukas, an impressive triumvirate of performers on any occasion, weren't able to do much for **Captured!** a heavy-going prisoner-of-war drama which Edward Chodorov adapted from a novel by Sir Philip Gibbs. Set in a German prison camp, and involving a motley collection of British, American and French captives, the film concentrated on the individual problems of its protagonists without ever involving the audience's sympathies. Director Roy Del Ruth, though succeeding in showing that war is hell, also succeeded, on this occasion, in making cinema-going a painful experience. Margaret Lindsay as Howard's unfaithful wife supplied feminine interest, with other roles in the hands of Arthur Hohl (centre), Robert Barrat, J. Carrol Naish (right), John Bleifer and Philip Faversham (centre right). The production was supervised by Hal Wallis.

The attractive cast assembled for **Goodbye Again**, the film version of Allan Scott and George Haight's play, was largely responsible for keeping this Michael Curtiz-directed comedy bouyant. About a famous novelist (Warren William, left) who re-kindles an erstwhile affair with a former flame (Genevieve Tobin, right) while his smitten secretary (Joan Blondell) views the proceedings with jealous disapproval, it was entertaining in a lightweight, undemanding way, and offered good performances from Hugh Herbert (as Miss Tobin's husband), Helen Chandler, Ruth Donnelly, Wallace Ford and Hobart Cavanaugh. Ben Markson wrote it and the production, which ran 65 minutes, was supervised by Henry Blanke. It was remade in 1941 as *Honeymoon for Three*. (First National.)

◁ **The Telegraph Trail,** with Marceline Day (left) and Frank McHugh, featured John Wayne (right) as a government security scout whose responsibility it is to see that a supply train safely reaches the men who are constructing the first telegraph line across the Western plains. Otis Harlan, Yakima Canutt, Albert J. Smith and Clarence Geldert also appeared in it for director Tenny Wright, and it was written by Kurt Kempler.

A romance with a boxing background, **The Life of Jimmy Dolan** (released in Britain as **The Kid's Last Fight**) broke no records and set no new standards. It told the story of a boxer who accidentally kills a newspaperman at a party but redeems himself when his abilities as a prizefighter help to finance a health farm for invalid children. The film starred Douglas Fairbanks Jr (centre) as the fighter and Aline MacMahon as the health farm's local Florence Nightingale. It was based on a play by Bertram Millhauser and Beulah Marie Dix, written for the screen by David Boehm and Erwin Gelsey, and directed, with the kind of fluid efficiency that characterized the studio's bread-and-butter efforts throughout the decade – one review called it neat and sure-footed – by Archie Mayo. Also cast were Loretta Young, Guy Kibbee, Lyle Talbot, Shirley Grey (right), Fifi D'Orsay (left), Harold Huber, George Meeker and a young Mickey Rooney. Hal Wallis supervised.

▽

▷

An overdose of feminine interest alien to Maugham's novel tended, on the whole, to draw attention away from the quartet of males who formed the basis of **The Narrow Corner,** especially as the interplay between Douglas Fairbanks Jr, Ralph Bellamy, Dudley Digges and Arthur Hohl was the film's most successful aspect. Still, the story of a young Englishman (Fairbanks, right) on the run for killing a man in Australia, and the people he meets in his wanderings, was effectively handled by director Alfred E. Green, who, working from a screenplay by Robert Presnell captured the novel's sultry atmosphere very well indeed. Patricia Ellis (left) was the girl to whom Bellamy was formerly engaged, and with whom Fairbanks Jr falls in love. Also cast were Reginald Owen, Henry Kolker, William V. Mong and Willie Fung. Hal Wallis was in charge of production.

▽

The enormous success of *42nd Street* and *Golddiggers of 1933* encouraged the studio to continue its series of backstage musicals, and **Footlight Parade,** with its excellent screenplay by Manuel Seff and James Seymour, plus Lloyd Bacon's sure-footed direction, as well as songs by Al Dubin and Harry Warren and Sammy Fain and Irving Kahal — and, of course, the incomparable Busby Berkeley-directed production numbers, was another massive achievement for all concerned. James Cagney, a Broadway producer, finds himself out of work because the two men who back his shows (Guy Kibbee and Arthur Hohl) believe that, with the arrival of talking pictures, the live theatre is doomed. Undaunted, Cagney decides to stage a series of prologues i.e. stage presentations that precede the screening of the feature film. The first hour or so of **Footlight Parade,** which was given its impetus by the dynamic Cagney, dealt with the preparation of the prologues, and the plot, such as it was, involved a conflict between the management and the creative talent employed in the show. The picture that director Lloyd Bacon painted of Broadway was of a hard, even brutal world where only the most talented survived. Fantasy impinged only in the last forty minutes, when Berkeley unleashed three of the greatest examples of screen choreography audiences had ever seen. Apart from Cagney, the film also starred Joan Blondell, Dick Powell and Ruby Keeler, with Ruth Donnelly, Claire Dodd, Hugh Herbert and Frank McHugh in support. The production was supervised by Robert Lord. Songs included: Honeymoon Hotel and Shanghai Lil (by Al Dubin and Harry Warren) and By A Waterfall and Ah, The Moon Is Here (by Sammy Fain and Irving Kahal).

Poor Richard Barthelmess (left) suffered the ▷ troubles of Job in **Heroes for Sale.** The story of a war veteran who, after being socially ostracized for drug addiction, becomes a millionaire only to find himself deeply involved in a worker's strike, it was directed by William A. Wellman and written by Robert Lord and Wilson Mizner. Another of the studio's 'social conscience' dramas, it also starred Aline MacMahon and Loretta Young, with Gordon Westcott, Berton Churchhill, Robert Barrat, Charles Grapewin and Grant Mitchell in support. The worthy but downbeat production was supervised by Hal Wallis. (First National.)

△ Director William A. Wellman tended to over-sentimentalize the theme of **Wild Boys of the Road** (released in Britain as **Dangerous Age**), another in the studio's series of socially committed dramas. This one dealt with a trio of young people who decide to take to the road in Depression-scarred America rather than remain at home burdening their families. Unable to find work, they travel from city to city on freight trains, dodging railroad detectives and generally trying to eke out an existence in the most wretched of conditions. A happy ending robbed the narrative of the power it strived for (and only occasionally achieved) but the performances throughout were consistently good, with Frankie Darro (centre), Dorothy Coonan (left), soon to become Mrs Wellman, and Edwin Phillips, especially so. Earl Baldwin wrote it from a story by Daniel Ahearn. Robert Presnell supervised the production and, in supporting roles, cast Rochelle Hudson, Ann Hovey (right), Arthur Hohl, Grant Mitchell, Sterling Holloway, Claire McDowell and Robert Barrat. (First National.)

◁ Kay Francis (centre) served a twenty year prison sentence for a crime she did not commit in **The House on 56th Street.** Based on a novel by Joseph Santley, and rather patchily directed by Robert Florey, the film's basic concern was with the house of the title and what happened to it and its inhabitants over a period of 25 years. Miss Francis responded better to Orry-Kelly's attractive 'gay nineties' costumes than she did to Austin Parker and Sheridan Gibney's sentimental screenplay, though Margaret Lindsay as her daughter was splendid. The production was supervised by James Seymour, and featured Ricardo Cortez, Gene Raymond (centre left) as Miss Francis' husband, Frank McHugh, Sheila Terry, William Boyd, Phillip Reed and Henry O'Neill.

Murder and mayhem aboard a train from Seattle to New York, with a valuable cargo of silk as the prize, formed the basis of **The Silk Express,** a racy melodrama which Ray Enright directed from a screenplay by Houston Branch and Ben Markson. Neil Hamilton (front centre, as an enterprising young silk importer), Guy Kibbee (centre left, as a railway detective), Dudley Digges (as a desperately ill professor *en route* to the Rockefeller Institute) and Sheila Terry (third right, as his daughter) starred, with reliable support from Allen Jenkins (far right), Arthur Byron, Harold Huber (centre right) and Arthur Hohl (as the villain determined to corner the raw silk market for himself). A modest but effective brew of thrills, humour and romance. Henry Blanke supervised.

◁Ruth Chatterton and directors Michael Curtiz and William Dieterle invested Donald Henderson Clark's routine story **Female** (screenplay by Gene Markey and Kathryn Scola) with a style and sense of humour it might otherwise not have had. A high-powered president of a motor-company by day, but an amorous filly by night, Miss Chatterton (left) combined these two distinct facets of her personality most adroitly, leaving little room for George Brent, as the engineer she falls for, to make much of an impression. Also cast were Johnny Mack Brown, Ruth Donnelly, Lois Wilson, Ferdinand Gottschalk (right), Phillip Reed, Rafaela Ottiano and Douglass Dumbrille. The production was supervised by Henry Blanke. (First National.)

In **She Had To Say Yes,** a modest comedy, Busby Berkeley got sole directorial credit for the first time. He was assisted by George Amy whom Jack Warner assigned to the film to help out with some of the more technical aspects. Loretta Young (right) was the star. She played a secretary in the garment business whose after-hour activities involved her in entertaining out-of-town buyers. Miss Young was only twenty at the time, but had appeared in forty films (her first being *Naughty but Nice* for First National at the age of 14). Her chores on this one were her last for the studio. Regis Toomey played her fiancé, Lyle Talbot (left) the man she finally settled for. Others cast were Winnie Lightner, Hugh Herbert and Ferdinand Gottschalk. Rian James and Don Mullaly wrote it from a story by John Francis Larkin. The public said no, and it flopped. The supervisor was Henry Blanke. (First National.)

Employees' Entrance, directed by Roy Del Ruth from a screenplay by Robert Presnell (based on a play by David Boehm) starred Warren William (centre), as a dictatorial department-store manager, whose utter ruthlessness in his public as well as his private life elicited both admiration and contempt from his colleagues. Stopping at nothing to get what he wants, be it promotion at double the salary, or another man's wife, he eventually gets his much-deserved come-uppance and the spectacle was joyful to behold. Equally joyful was William's *vivace* performance, with good work too from Loretta Young as the married woman he falls for, and Alice White as a blonde flirt. Also cast were Wallace Ford, Albert Gran, Allen Jenkins, Marjorie Gateson, Hale Hamilton and Ruth Donnelly. Lucien Hubbard supervised. (First National.)

The woman Edward G. Robinson loved in **I Loved A Woman** was Kay Francis. But his social-climbing wife (Genevieve Tobin, centre) refuses to give him a divorce forcing the lovers to meet in secret. In time, however, Miss Francis' success in her chosen career as a singer inspires Robinson (left) to reach new heights in his own career (meat-packing) and in no time at all he becomes Chicago's most powerful beef baron. But disaster was just around the corner. . . . The performances of Robinson and Kay Francis brought a touch of class to the soap-opera histrionics of Charles Kenyon and Sidney Sutherland's screenplay (from the novel by David Karsner), and under Alfred E. Green's workmanlike direction, the comedy found an appreciative audience. J. Farrell MacDonald, Henry Kolker and Robert Barrat were in it too. Henry Blanke supervised. (First National.) ▷

In **Lady Killer** James Cagney, once again partnered with Mae Clarke (centre) played a cinema usher who, after being fired, turns to crime. By chance he finds himself appearing in a movie while hiding from the police. He becomes a star and at once plot complications follow. Cagney (foreground left) didn't grind a grapefruit in poor Miss Clarke's face this time; he simply pulled her out of bed by the hair. Everything audiences expected from him – the aggression, the vitality, the fast-talking bully-boy tactics – was on hand, and, as usual, he made a meal of them all. Russell Hopton (right), Margaret Lindsay, Henry O'Neill, Leslie Fenton (kneeling right), and Douglass Dumbrille (behind left) also appeared, and under Roy Del Ruth's fast-paced direction the comedy, which also took a few satiric swipes at Hollywood, sparkled. The screenplay was by Ben Markson and Lillie Hayward from a story by Rosalind Keating Shaffer, and Henry Blanke supervised production.

A 40 carat weepie, **Ever in my Heart**, directed by Archie Mayo, gave Barbara Stanwyck her first crack at tragedy. The story began in New England in 1909 with Stanwyck (left) meeting and falling in love with Otto Kruger (right). They marry against the wishes of her parents, and all goes well until the outbreak of war, in the course of which Kruger becomes a German spy, thus sorely trying Stanwyck's loyalty. It ends unhappily ever after when, to save Kruger from the firing squad, Stanwyck poisons him and he dies in her arms. Labelled as a woman's picture, it gave its star a chance to pull out all her emotional stops, which she did most compellingly. Bertram Millhauser wrote the screenplay from his and Beulah Marie Dix's story, with other roles going to Ralph Bellamy, Ruth Donnelly, Laura Hope Crews, Frank Albertson, Donald Meek, Clara Blandick, Harry Beresford and Wallis Clark. The production was supervised by Robert Presnell.

Broad humour cohabited with satire a trifle uneasily in **Convention City**, a comedy devoted to the antics of salesmen and their annual anything-goes conventions. Though lacking a really razor-edged script to slice through the over-exuberant, over-playing high-jinks of the protagonists, the film was nevertheless extremely funny in parts and predictably cast Joan Blondell (right) as a gold-digger, Guy Kibbee (left) as a wife-avoiding businessman, Ruth Donnelly as the wife he avoids, and Frank McHugh and Hugh Herbert as the statutory drunks. Also on hand, and obviously enjoying themselves here, were several members of the regular Warner Bros. stock company, including Dick Powell, Mary Astor, Patricia Ellis, Hobart Cavanaugh, Grant Mitchell and Gordon Westcott. Allen Jenkins and Glenda Farrell were, however, unaccountably missing. The best performance came from Adolphe Menjou as an experienced salesman just as adept at selling himself as his product. Working from a story by Peter Milne, it was written by Robert Lord and directed by Archie Mayo, under the supervision of Henry Blanke. (First National.)

Niven Busch (working in conjunction with Manuel Seff) wrote the screenplay for **College Coach** (released in Britain as **Football Coach**), a cynical, mildly satirical tale about professional football coaches and the milieu in which they operate. Towards the end of the film, their vision blurred and the story's contours went awry. Still, Pat O'Brien as the aggressive coach gave a very convincing account of himself; so did Arthur Byron ▷ as the college president and Ann Dvorak as the coach's wife. Pulling their weight, too, were Lyle Talbot, Hugh Herbert, Arthur Hohl, Guinn Williams, Nat Pendleton and Donald Meek. Top-cast as a concession to the box-office, but miscast as a football player, was Dick Powell (bottom centre), whose singing was more convincing than his acting. William A. Wellman was the director, with Robert Lord in charge of production. Songs included: Lonely Lane, Men of Calvert (by Sammy Fain and Irving Kahal), Just One More Chance (by Sam Coslow and Arthur Johnston), Meet Me In The Gloaming (by Arthur Freed, Al Hoffman and Al Goodhart) and What Will I Do Without You (by Johnny Mercer and Hilda Gottlieb).

Joe E. Brown (centre) starred in **Son of a Sailor**, a mélange of would-be humorous situations which pleased only his most ardent admirers. He played Handsome Callahan, a fight-shy clown who, much to his surprise, is promoted for conspicuous acts of courage when he inadvertently finds himself involved in espionage and recovers some vitally important Navy documents. Flinging themselves headlong into the spirit of Al Cohn and Paul Gerard Smith's unrestrained screenplay (with additional dialogue by Ernest Pagano and H.M. Walker) were Thelma Todd, Sheila Terry, Jean Muir, Johnny Mack Brown and Frank McHugh. James Seymour supervised and Lloyd Bacon directed this rather disappointing comedy. (First National.)

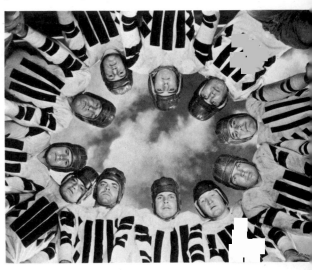

1934

Poland banned all Warner Bros.-First National Films because its Minister of the Interior felt that they represented a strong bias against his countrymen, many of whom, he claimed, were portrayed as vicious Polack hoodlums in the studio's series of crime dramas. Two films, **The Life Of Jimmy Dolan** and **The Match King**, were cited as examples. In August, Mrs Benjamin Warner, the mother of the Warner brothers, died of a cerebral haemorrhage at the age of 76. The year ended badly with a massive studio fire which caused the death of the studio's fire chief, Albert Rounder, as well as hundreds of thousands of dollars worth of damage. Also, irreplaceable early Vitagraph, Warner Bros. and First National prints were destroyed in the blaze, together with their production records. The studio's net loss for the year was $2,530,513.

Two films, **Flirtation Walk** and **Here Comes The Navy**, were nominated for Best Picture Oscars. They were pipped by Columbia's **It Happened One Night**.

Cosmopolitan Productions, William Randolph Hearst's company, which had hitherto been associated with MGM, moved to Burbank to become part of Warner Bros. The studios at Teddington, England, which had been leased by Warner Bros. since 1931, were bought by the company during the year.

△

Charles Farrell (left) and Bette Davis (right) were below par in **The Big Shakedown**. A trite, unconvincing story of a dishonest druggist (Farrell) who becomes involved with a racketeer (Ricardo Cortez) shortly after the repeal of prohibition, it was a 64-minute potboiler out of which only Glenda Farrell (no relation to Charles), playing a gutsy girl called Lil, emerged if not with distinction, at least with her self-respect intact. It was directed by John Francis Dillon from a screenplay by Niven Busch and Rian James (story by Sam Engel and Niven Busch) and supervised by Sam Bischoff. (First National.)

△

Originally made by First National in 1928 under the direction of Mervyn LeRoy, and with Arthur Lake, Mary Brian and Alice White, the second version of **Harold Teen** (released in Britain as **Dancing Fool**) – about a nit-witted small-town journalist whose social blunders temporarily spoil his chances of romance with a High School graduate called Lillums – starred Hal LeRoy (left, as Harold) and Rochelle Hudson as the girl he loves. Paul Gerard Smith and Al Cohn's practically invisible screenplay (from the comic strip by Carl Ed) made no demands on the intellect, and whatever plot complications they devised were resolved in the finale of a musical show organized by Patricia Ellis (right), the leader of the town's 'younger set'. Guy Kibbee, Hobart Cavanaugh, Chick Chandler, Eddie Tamblyn, Douglass Dumbrille and Mayo Methot were also in the cast, under the direction of Murray Roth and Robert Lord supervised the production. Songs included: How Do You Know It's Sunday?, Simple And Sweet, Two Little Flies On A Lump Of Sugar and Collegiate Wedding (by Irving Kahal and Sammy Fain).

The subject of compulsive gambling was given a superficial but entertaining treatment in **Dark Hazard**, which starred Edward G. Robinson as a man who is only happy at the race track, the dog track or around a roulette wheel. It ended unhappily with Robinson (right) losing his wife as well as all his money. Based on a novel by W.R. Burnett (who wrote *Little Caesar*) it gave its star a chance to tackle a role that relied on his being dominated by others rather than vice versa; and, as usual, he brought his formidable intelligence to it. Genevieve Tobin (left) played his wife, Glenda Farrell an old flame. Also cast were Robert Barrat, Gordon Westcott, Hobart Cavanaugh and George Meeker. Ralph Block and Brown Holmes wrote it, Alfred E. Green directed and the production was supervised by Robert Lord. It was remade as *Wine, Women and Horses* in 1937. (First National.) ▷

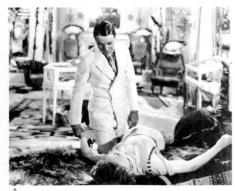

Obviously inspired by *I am a Fugitive from a Chain Gang*, **Massacre** had the distinction of being one of the few films of the thirties that took as its subject the plight of the contemporary Red Indian in America. But the sort of exploration the same subject was given 35 years later in Abraham Polonsky's *Tell them Willie Boy is Here* (Universal, 1969) was not encouraged by Jack Warner who saw the film more as an action melodrama than as a balanced piece of social comment. Nonetheless, the film, though depicting all government agents as humanity's scum, had moments of sincerity and conviction and, under Alan Crosland's direction Richard Barthelmess (left), Ann Dvorak, Dudley Digges, Claire Dodd (right), Henry O'Neill and Robert Barrat turned in fine performances. It was written by Ralph Block and Sheridan Gibney from a story by Robert Gessner. The production was supervised by Robert Presnell. Also cast were Arthur Hohl, Sidney Toler, Douglass Dumbrille and William V. Mong. (First National.)

The hardships of life on a farm in Maine was the subject of **As the Earth Turns**, an adaptation (by Ernest Pascal) of Gladys Hasty Carroll's novel. It told, with poignancy and sincerity, of the attempts of one Stan Janowski to make a go of farming, and his relationship with Jen Shaw, an upstanding young woman who shares his outlook on life. Donald Woods was Stan; Jean Muir (centre) played Jen, with other roles going to Russell Hardie (centre left), Emily Lowry, Arthur Hohl, Dorothy Appleby (left), Clara Blandick (centre right), David Landau (right) and George A. Billings. The director was Alfred E. Green, and the production was supervised by Robert Lord.

Kay Francis at her conspicuously world-weary best indulged in all manner of unsavoury activities in **Mandalay**, a torrid melodrama which was set in the tropics. Tired of a lover who pops up all over the place like an irrepressible cork, she poisons him, then flings him out of a porthole. Director Michael Curtiz, whose ability to make cinematic bricks out of straw was nowhere better demonstrated than in the climax of this routine programmer, made his star look good throughout. Ricardo Cortez played a charming cad, with Warner Oland, Lyle Talbot (centre), Ruth Donnelly (left), Lucien Littlefield (right), Shirley Temple, Etienne Girardot, Herman Bing and Reginald Owen in support. Austin Parker and Charles Kenyon wrote the screenplay from a story by Paul Hervey Fox. Robert Presnell supervised. Song: When Tomorrow Comes (by Irving Kahal and Sammy Fain). (First National.)

In **Bedside** Warren William (left) played a medical charlatan with such calculating conviction that it was difficult to feel anything but contempt for him. More interested in gambling than in the Hippocratic oath, he inherits a medical diploma from a drug-addicted doctor whom he befriends, sets up a practice, hires a press agent (Allen Jenkins) to let the world know of his existence, then engages a qualified doctor (Donald Meek) as his assistant, but who, in fact, does all the work. William's day of reckoning comes when the girl he loves (Jean Muir, right) is run over by a car and he finds himself unable to help her. A wildly improbable tale, it was written by Lillie Hayward and James Wharton from a story by Manuel Seff and Harvey Thew (with additional dialogue by Rian James), directed by Robert Florey and also featured David Landau, Kathryn Sergava, Henry O'Neill, Renee Whitney and Walter Walker. Sam Bischoff supervised the production. (First National.)

A marital comedy in which Adolphe Menjou and Genevieve Tobin were less than blissfully married, **Easy to Love** was easy to digest in the presence of its two stars who made the most of a rather attenuated plot (wife catches husband with brunette and claims that she, too, is having an affair – which, of course, she isn't). Style triumphed over content and the film's seventy minutes passed with audiences feeling no pain. Mary Astor (illustrated), Edward Everett Horton, Patricia Ellis, Hugh Herbert, Hobart Cavanaugh and the ever-reliable Guy Kibbee were in it too; it was written by Carl Erickson and Manuel Seff (and adapted by David Boehm) from a play by Thompson Buchanan, and directed by William Keighley who, four years later, married the film's leading lady. Henry Blanke supervised. Song: Easy To Love (by Irving Kahal and Sammy Fain – not to be confused with the later Cole Porter number of that name).

Though not really a musical, **Fashions of 1934** gave choreographer Busby Berkeley ample opportunity to display his vivid choreographic imagination once again. He staged a finale in which fifty beautiful girls, clad in ostrich plumes, formed themselves into human harps, and then into a sixty-foot long feathered galleon with fans taking the place of oars. Berkeley's work crowned a story of a New York couturier (William Powell) who, with the assistance of his secretary-cum-model, plunders the latest Parisian *haute monde* designs and calls them his own. Powell (right) lent a sure touch of sophistication to the proceedings, while Bette Davis (centre), her face made up by Perc Westmore in such a way as to neutralize the very features which were to carry her to stardom, was his co-star. The glamorous, fashion-plate image which director William Dieterle sought for her was further enhanced by Orry-Kelly's riotous gowns. Verree Teasdale co-starred as a phoney Russian duchess. Frank McHugh was a photographer's assistant who always kept a miniature camera in the top of his cane, and Reginald Owen played a talented Parisian couturier on whose designs Powell had designs. F. Hugh Herbert and Carl Erickson wrote the extremely entertaining screenplay from a story by Harry Collins and Warren Duff. Songs included: Spin A Little Web Of Dreams and Broken Melody (by Irving Kahal and Sammy Fain). (First National.)

Hi, Nellie!, a comedy thriller, gave Paul Muni a chance to try his hand at something lighter than the roles hitherto associated with him. He played a rebellious managing editor of a newspaper who finds himself demoted to heart-throb columnist – a position previously held by an attractive blonde. Muni (right) returns to his former glory, however, by successfully indulging in a spot of detective work concerning a murdered banker. One of the star's few flops (the title may have had something to do with its failure to attract the public), the film was nonetheless well made and well acted with fine performances from Glenda Farrell (left), Douglass Dumbrille, Robert Barrat, Ned Sparks and Hobart Cavanaugh. It was written by Abem Finkel and Sidney Sutherland (from a story by Roy Chanslor) and directed by Mervyn LeRoy whose eye for a cliché (where newspaper offices were concerned) was not to be underestimated. The production was supervised by Robert Presnell. It was remade in 1937 as *Love is on the Air*, in 1942 as *You Can't Escape Forever* and in 1949 as *House Across the Street*. ▷

Heat Lightning, adapted by Brown Holmes and Warren Duff from the play by Leon Abrams and George Abbott and sluggishly directed by Mervyn LeRoy, gave Aline MacMahon her first starring role. She played Olga, a filling station attendant in the South-west, who has the misfortune to become involved with a couple of murderers (Preston Foster and Lyle Talbot), one of whom (Foster) she once loved. Making the best of a role for which she was basically miscast, Miss MacMahon gave the film what minimal interest it had, receiving little support from her co-stars or from Ann Dvorak (front centre), Glenda Farrell (right), Ruth Donnelly (back centre), Frank McHugh (left) and Theodore Newton. The production was supervised by Sam Bischoff. It was remade in 1941 as *Highway West*. ▽

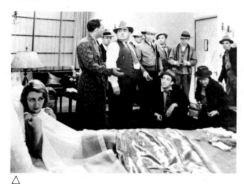

△
Speed was all-important in **I've Got Your Number**, a racy comedy about the inner workings of the telephone service in general, and the adventures of two of its service engineers (Pat O'Brien, standing left, and Allen Jenkins, kneeling centre) in particular. Joan Blondell (left) co-starred as a girl accused of taking part in a bond burglary but, thanks to the efforts of the engineers (who seem to repair reputations as well as phones), proved innocent of the crime. The dialogue (written by Warren Duff and Sidney Sutherland) from a story by William Rankin, was fast and furious; so was Ray Enright's direction. Also cast were Glenda Farrell, Eugene Pallette (centre left), Gordon Westcott, Henry O'Neill, Hobart Cavanaugh, Renee Whitney and Robert Ellis. Sam Bischoff supervised.

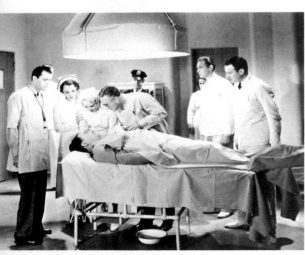

◁ Though the everyday workings of a large hospital were generally conveyed in a manner now familiar from any TV scalpel opera, **Registered Nurse** departed even further from reality in its highly improbable plot about a nurse who finds herself pursued by two doctors after her husband goes insane. Robert Florey directed the nonsensical tale (from a screenplay by Lillie Hayward and Peter Milne, and from the play by Florence Johns and Wilton Lackaye, Jr), casting Bebe Daniels (second left), Lyle Talbot (left) and John Halliday (centre) in key roles with Irene Franklin, Sidney Toler, Gordon Westcott, Minna Gombell, Mayo Methot and Beulah Bondi in support. The production was supervised by Sam Bischoff. (First National.)

◁ Momentarily deserting his characteristic guise as every gold-digger's ideal sugar-daddy, Guy Kibbee (left) starred in **Big Hearted Herbert** as a crusty old self-made grouch whose endless catalogue of dislikes finally wears down his long-suffering family. The time has come, they decide, to do something that will give the old boy a different, more sanguine outlook on life. And, of course, they succeed. So did director William Keighley in making a pleasing screen comedy from the play by Sophie Kerr and Anna Steese Richardson (screenplay by Lillie Hayward and Ben Markson). Aline MacMahon played Kibbee's wife, with other roles going to Patricia Ellis, Helen Lowell, Philip Reed, George Chandler (right), Robert Barrat, Henry O'Neill, and Marjorie Gateson. James Seymour supervised.

△
The best thing about **Gambling Lady** was its pairing of Barbara Stanwyck (left) with Joel McCrea (centre) for the first of several movies in which they were to co-star. Stanwyck played the daughter of a gambler who committed suicide because he was unable to pay his debts. This does not prevent Stanwyck from following her father's footsteps to the gaming tables, where she meets and falls in love with McCrea. In no time at all (66 minutes to be precise) the plot is thickened by murder and blackmail. A game of 21 in which Claire Dodd, as an ex-girlfriend of McCrea's, is forced to part with every jewel she is wearing, was particularly effective. But then the entire film was a pretty slick affair, which also featured C. Aubrey Smith, Pat O'Brien (right) and Arthur Treacher. Archie Mayo directed the fast-paced screenplay by Ralph Block and Doris Malloy, and Henry Blanke supervised production.

The cinema continued its love affair with trains and the devious people who travel on them in **I am a Thief,** a par-for-the-track thriller starring Ricardo Cortez (centre right) as a passenger on the Paris to Istanbul Express, who is carrying the fabulous Karenina diamonds. Mary Astor (right) wants them; so do Irving Pichel (left) and Robert Barrat (centre). Also in it were Dudley Digges, Arthur Aylesworth and Ferdinand Gottschalk (centre left). Ralph Block and Doris Malloy wrote the story and screenplay. Robert Florey was the director. Henry Blanke supervised.

▽

◁ Working from a story by Ben Hecht, Ben Markson's screenplay for **Upperworld** managed to imbue the tale of a likeable millionaire (Warren William, centre) accused of a double murder he did not commit, with a freshness not immediately apparent in the narrative. Energetically directed by Roy Del Ruth and with top notch performances from Mary Astor and Ginger Rogers (right) as the women in the accused's life, the results were most enjoyable. Robert Lord supervised, and his cast included Andy Devine, Dickie Moore, Henry O'Neill, J. Carrol Naish (left), Sidney Toler, Theodore Newton, Robert Barrat and Ferdinand Gottschalk.

The trials and tribulations of the working man were a staple part of the studio's output in the thirties and forties. The celebrated German director, G.W. Pabst, with his only American film, offered a fine example of the subject in **A Modern Hero.** It starred Richard Barthelmess (centre) giving one of his best performances as a callously ambitious circus rider who betters himself in business, only to find his dreams of continued success turning into nightmares when the stock-market crashes. Pabst's views on capitalism and industrialization, as they affected his hero, were given full expression in Gene Markey and Kathryn Scola's screenplay (from the novel by Louis Bromfield). Jean Muir, Marjorie Rambeau (right), Verree Teasdale, Florence Eldridge, Dorothy Burgess and Hobart Cavanaugh (left) also featured in the cast and the production was under the supervision of James Seymour.

▽

△
A sort of *Grand Hotel* of the nightclub circuit, **Wonder Bar** – set in a Paris nightspot – revolved around the activities of its staff and paying customers. Al Jolson (centre) was the owner of the club, Dolores Del Rio (centre left) the main cabaret attraction. Jolson and band-singer Dick Powell (right) were both in love with Miss Del Rio, though she only had eyes for her dance partner Ricardo Cortez (left). He, in turn, was being pursued by wealthy socialite Kay Francis (centre right). Add to this a sub-plot involving Guy Kibbee and Hugh Herbert who, despite the presence of Fifi D'Orsay and Merna Kennedy (Mrs Busby Berkeley) as their respective wives, were flirting with a couple of the club's hostesses – plus a score by Harry Warren and Al Dubin to help take your mind off the plot, and gowns by Orry-Kelly, and you had the quintessential Warner Bros. thirties musical. Berkeley outdid himself with a production number involving an octagon of mirrors which multiplied his chorus line into infinity; but this triumph was later spoilt by the cloying bad taste of 'Going To Heaven On A Mule' which Jolson sang in black-face surrounded by 200 black children playing angels. Earl Baldwin wrote it from a play by Geza Herczeg, Karl Farkas and Robert Katscher. The film was efficiently directed by Lloyd Bacon and supervised by Robert Lord. The cast also featured Louise Fazenda, Henry O'Neill, Robert Barrat, Ruth Donnelly, Hal LeRoy and Henry Kolker. Songs included: Wonder Bar, Why Do I Dream Those Dreams, Don't Say Goodnight, Vive La France and Tango Del Rio. (First National.)

Working from a story by Paul Finder Moss and Jerry Wald, Warren Duff and Harry Sauber wrote **Twenty Million Sweethearts**, a modest musical and an engaging little satire on the air waves. It starred Dick Powell (left) as a singing waiter and Pat O'Brien (standing right) as the man who discovers and introduces him to radio. (The following year in *Stars over Broadway* Mr O'Brien would do the same for hotel porter James Melton.) Ginger Rogers (centre) appeared in her first starring role in this movie which also featured the Four Mills Brothers, Ted Fiorito and his Band, Allen Jenkins, Henry O'Neill and Joseph Cawthorne. But it was Powell's film, and it helped to consolidate his clean-cut image. Ray Enright directed, Sam Bischoff supervised. Songs included: Fair And Warmer, What Are Your Intentions and I'll String Along With You (by Al Dubin and Harry Warren). (First National.) It was remade as a vehicle for Doris Day in 1949, called *My Dream Is Yours*.

▽

Journal of a Crime asked audiences to swallow whole a story in which heroine Ruth Chatterton goes backstage to shoot her husband's actress mistress and escapes without being seen. However, hiding in that very theatre is a fugitive from an altogether different shooting who, hapless man, is blamed for Miss Chatterton's crime. Stricken with guilt, Miss C. decides to confess but, before she can do so, is knocked over by a car while trying to save the life of a child, and loses her memory. Based on a play by Jacques Deval, it was written by F. Hugh Herbert and Charles Kenyon and hammily directed by William Keighley. Apart from a floundering Miss Chatterton (centre), the film starred Adolphe Menjou (left) as her unfaithful husband (whose love is restored to her in the end) and Claire Dodd as the other woman, with Georges Barbier, Douglass Dumbrille, Noel Madison, Henry O'Neill and Walter Pidgeon in support. The production was supervised by Henry Blanke. (First National.)

▽

A Very Honourable Guy found Joe E. Brown (centre) as an honest gambler in a quandary. Either he pays off a gambling debt to an unscrupulous crook, or he suffers the consequences. As a way out of his problems he sells his body to a demented scientist, makes a fortune, and, in the process, forgets the day when his debt is due to be called in. Brown fans found its 62 minutes too short by half; others groaned at its length. The heroine was Alice White. Robert Barrat played the mad scientist and Alan Dinehart (foreground right) a gangster. It was written by Earl Baldwin from a story by Damon Runyon, and directed by Lloyd Bacon. Also cast were Irene Franklin, Hobart Cavanaugh (centre right), Harold Huber, Joe Cawthorne with appearances, too, by composers Harry Warren and Al Dubin. Robert Lord was the supervisor. (First National.)

▽

A fanciful comedy that made a few wry ▷ comments on the divorce facilities offered in Reno, **The Merry Wives of Reno** was written by Robert Lord with additional dialogue by Joe Traub. It relied mightily on coincidence to tell its lightweight story of three families who find themselves involved in divorce proceedings when the respective heads of two of the families happen to leave their overcoats in the home of the third. Margaret Lindsay (centre), Donald Woods, Guy Kibbee, Glenda Farrell, Hugh Herbert (left) and Ruth Donnelly (right) were prominently featured, with other roles going to Frank McHugh, Hobart Cavanaugh and Roscoe Ates. H. Bruce Humberstone directed, and Robert Lord supervised.

◁ **Side Streets** (released in Britain as **A Woman in her Thirties**), in spite of hard effort from the cast, was to be side stepped. The woebegone tale of a San Franciscan business woman and the destitute sailor she marries, it starred Aline MacMahon (right) and Paul Kelly (left) with Ann Dvorak, Helen Lowell, Dorothy Tree, Henry O'Neill and Mayo Methot in support. Alfred E. Green turgidly directed the screenplay by Manuel Seff from a story by Ann Garrick and Ethel Rill, and Sam Bischoff supervised the production. (First National.)

Although Bette Davis (left) was billed second only to James Cagney (right) in **Jimmy the Gent**, there was not much in it for her. Apart from Cagney himself, his hair closely cropped to facilitate his performance as a con man, the showier female role went to Alice White, who also co-starred together with Allen Jenkins and Alan Dinehart. In telling the story of a racketeer who sets out to find the missing heirs to large, unclaimed estates, and invents them if they don't exist, director Michael Curtiz concentrated more on the humour of the situation than on its criminal implications. Bertram Millhauser wrote the flip, Runyonesque screenplay (from a story by Laird Doyle and Ray Nazarro) and Robert Lord supervised production. Also cast were Arthur Hohl, Phillip Reed, Hobart Cavanaugh, Mayo Methot, Ralf Harolde, Philip Faversham and Nora Lane. ▷

In **Smarty** (released in Britain as **Hit Me Again**) Warren William (right) and Joan Blondell indulged in a neat bit of marital sparring as a squabbling couple who find their irrational behaviour leading them in and out of the divorce courts. In the end they realize that, despite their quarrels, they only have eyes for each other, and all ends happily. A programmer with no other purpose than to provide mild diversion (which it did), it also featured Edward Everett Horton, Frank McHugh, Claire Dodd (left), Joan Wheeler, Virginia Sale and Leonard Carey. F. Hugh Herbert and Carl Erickson wrote the screenplay (from the former's play) and Robert Florey directed. The supervisor was Robert Presnell.
▽

△
Based on a Polish play by Marja Morozowicz Szczepkowska and written for the screen by Charles Kenyon, **Dr. Monica** had Kay Francis (right) sacrificing her love for her husband when she learns that his affections veer in the direction of Jean Muir. Warren William played the husband and, considering how unmitigated a cad he turns out to be, hardly suffered at all for his selfish behaviour. The ladies did their best in such lugubrious circumstances, and were given adequate support by Verree Teasdale (left), Phillip Reed, Emma Dunn, Herbert Bunston and Ann Shoemaker. William Keighley directed for supervisor Henry Blanke.

Although show business was well served, ▷ history came something of a cropper in **Madame Dubarry**, an entertaining if grossly inaccurate account of the life and times of the legendary courtesan. The story began with her unofficial appointment as mistress to the King and continued through to the accession of Louis XVI and her banishment from court. Dolores Del Rio (left) played La Dubarry and while no one disputed the star's beauty, that inner 'something' that made Madame the most talked about woman in France was simply not there. Still, it wasn't that sort of film anyway, and there was plenty of fine acting on hand from Reginald Owen as Louis XV, Victor Jory as d'Aiguillon and Osgood Perkins as Richelieu. The large cast also included Verree Teasdale, Ferdinand Gottschalk, (right), Anita Louise (as Marie Antoinette), Henry O'Neill and Hobart Cavanaugh. Edward Chodorov wrote it, William Dieterle directed, and the production was supervised by Henry Blanke.

Something of a curiosity, **He Was Her Man** starred James Cagney as a safe-cracker, who, on being released from prison, becomes involved with a former prostitute (Joan Blondell). Although Cagney (centre right) ◁ again proved himself superior to his material and capable of rising above mediocrity, the film, unadventurously scripted by Tom Buckingham and Niven Busch, and directed by Lloyd Bacon, was pretty pallid stuff. It was the seventh and last time the two stars were to appear together. Also cast were Victor Jory (centre), Frank Craven, Gino Corrado (centre left), Harold Huber, Russell Hopton, and Ralf Harolde. Robert Lord, who provided the original story, also supervised.

The actual plot of **Fog over Frisco** in which Margaret Lindsay (centre), as a society girl, sets out to defend the reputation of her step-sister (Bette Davis) after reading a newspaper item claiming her to be a regular frequenter of a notorious underworld hangout, was of secondary importance to the breathtaking manner in which William Dieterle directed it. Rarely has 67 minutes of screen-time been more resourcefully used. Also cast were Donald Woods (left), Lyle Talbot, Arthur Byron (right), Hugh Herbert and Douglass Dumbrille (in doorway). It was written by Robert N. Lee and Eugene Solow from a story by George Dyer, and supervised by Henry Blanke. It was remade as *Spy Ship* in 1942. (First National.)
▽

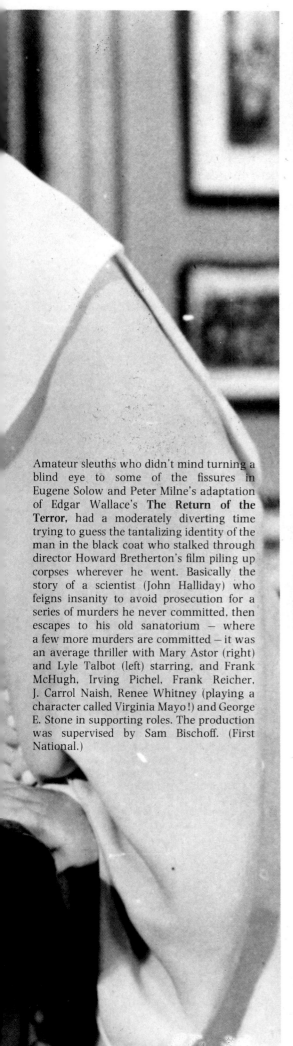

Playing the role of an egotistical actor in **The Man With Two Faces**, Edward G. Robinson (centre) hid behind whiskers, false eyebrows, a nose constructed of putty and a Gallic accent as thick as onion soup as he set out to murder his brother-in-law (Louis Calhern) who, in turn, was driving his sister (Mary Astor, right) insane. The Hays Office, for some unknown reason, allowed Robinson, quite literally, to get away with murder, and a good time was had by all. Ricardo Cortez, Mae Clarke and John Eldredge had featured roles, Archie Mayo directed and the screenplay (based on the George Kaufman-Alexander Woollcott stage play which starred Basil Sydney in the Robinson role) was by Tom Reed and Niven Busch. Robert Lord supervised. (First National.)

An excellent script (by Warren Duff and Sidney Sutherland with additional dialogue by F. Hugh Herbert and Erwin Gelsey) turned **The Friends of Mr. Sweeney** into a delightful comedy. It starred the talented Charles Ruggles (centre) as a timid writer of a conservative weekly whose meek personality undergoes a radical change when the mendacity at the core of his life is exposed by an erstwhile college chum (Eugene Pallette). Contributing to the film's success were the performances of Berton Churchill as Ruggles' hypocritical boss, Robert Barrat, Harry Tyler (right), Ann Dvorak (left) as Ruggles' secretary, William Davidson and Dorothy Tree. Based on the novel by Elmer Davis, it was directed by Edward Ludwig for supervisor Sam Bischoff.

Amateur sleuths who didn't mind turning a blind eye to some of the fissures in Eugene Solow and Peter Milne's adaptation of Edgar Wallace's **The Return of the Terror**, had a moderately diverting time trying to guess the tantalizing identity of the man in the black coat who stalked through director Howard Bretherton's film piling up corpses wherever he went. Basically the story of a scientist (John Halliday) who feigns insanity to avoid prosecution for a series of murders he never committed, then escapes to his old sanatorium — where a few more murders are committed — it was an average thriller with Mary Astor (right) and Lyle Talbot (left) starring, and Frank McHugh, Irving Pichel, Frank Reicher, J. Carrol Naish, Renee Whitney (playing a character called Virginia Mayo!) and George E. Stone in supporting roles. The production was supervised by Sam Bischoff. (First National.)

◁ In **The Circus Clown**, Joe E. Brown (centre) as the circus-struck son of an ex-circus performer, not only had to contend with knife-throwers, aerialists, and other such human attractions to which the big top is prone, but all the animals as well. Not one of the comedian's vintage efforts, it elicited smiles rather than guffaws, and did disappointing business. Burt Kalmar and Harry Ruby wrote it (with additional dialogue by Paul Gerard Smith); Ray Enright directed, and the cast included Patricia Ellis (right), Dorothy Burgess, Donald Dillaway and Gordon Westcott. James Seymour supervised. (First National.)

It was the same formula as before: ambitious young songwriter needs backer for a show, falls for sympathetic young girl, finds backer, gets girl. The songwriter in this instance was Dick Powell (centre), Ruby Keeler (right) was his girl, and Hugh Herbert (who else?) the fortuitous 'angel' and President of the Ezra Ounce Foundation for the Elevation of American Morals. What really mattered in **Dames**, however, was not its snowflake of a plot, but the genuinely creative production numbers devised by master dance director Busby Berkeley — who again surpassed himself, both in the visual realization of some of his most ambitious flights of fancy and in sheer inventiveness and flair. Ranging from the simple but effective 'The Girl At The Ironing Board' (by Al Dubin and Harry Warren) sung by a spunky Joan Blondell (left), to the title number 'Dames' (also by Dubin and Warren), in which literally hundreds of girls clad in white blouses and black tights, twist themselves into a panoply of abstract patterns and mosaics — Berkeley's eye for a pleasing cinematic image (as well as a pretty girl) had never been surer. Ray Enright directed Delmer Daves' screenplay from a plot line devised by Daves and Robert Lord, who also supervised production. Also cast were Guy Kibbee, ZaSu Pitts, Arthur Vinton and songwriter Sammy Fain who made a brief appearance as — a songwriter. Other songs included: I Only Have Eyes For You (by Dubin and Warren) When You Were A Smile On Your Mother's Lips and A Twinkle In Your Daddy's Eye (by Irving Kahal and Sammy Fain) and Try To See It My Way (by Mort Dixon and Allie Wrubel).

The first of eight films James Cagney was to make with Pat O'Brien, **Here Comes the Navy** (originally called **Hey Sailor**) was also the first film Cagney made after the formation of The Catholic League of Decency. This meant toning down the rough stuff, especially when a woman was on the receiving end. More interesting for its depiction of life in the navy than its routine plot in which cocky Cagney (left) redeems himself in the eyes of his fellow sailors after an act of heroism which nearly costs him his life, it was nonetheless popular with audiences. Female interest was supplied by Gloria Stuart (right) and Dorothy Tree, with Frank McHugh, Guinn Williams, Robert Barrat and Willard Robertson in support. Lloyd Bacon directed, and Ben Markson and Earl Baldwin provided the screenplay for supervisor Lou Edelman. Song: Hey Sailor (by Irving Kahal and Sammy Fain).

A formula boxing drama, but not without merit, **The Personality Kid** traced the rise and fall of a prizefighter who allows success to get the better of him, and in so doing, ruins his marriage – almost. After being down and out, he is saved at last when his estranged wife announces she's going to have a baby. With something really worthwhile to fight for now, the champ pulls himself together in preparation for fatherhood. Pat O'Brien (right) was suitably cast as the boxer, and although in real life, he had been a champion fighter in his University days, was coached, on this occasion by Jackie Fields – with former champions Mushy Callahan and Marvin Shechter his opponents in the ring. Though the fight scenes themselves were somewhat tame, F. Hugh Herbert and Erwin Gelsey's screenplay (adaptation by David Boehm, from a story by Gene Towne and C. Graham Baker) pulled fewer punches and the results were agreeably entertaining. The production was supervised by Robert Presnell, directed by Alan Crosland, and featured Glenda Farrell and Claire Dodd (left) as the women in O'Brien's life, with other parts going to Henry O'Neill, Robert Gleckler, Thomas Jackson and Arthur Vinton.

The story of a basically selfish family whose one unselfish member is compassionate, understanding mum (Aline MacMahon, centre). **The Merry Frinks** (released in Britain as **The Happy Family**), a felicitous combination of humour and pathos, emerged as a light-hearted and entertaining comedy which broke no records but pleased those who bothered to see it. Hugh Herbert (far right), Allen Jenkins, Helen Lowell (right), Joan Wheeler, Guy Kibbee (centre right), Frankie Darro (3rd left), Ivan Lebedeff, James Burke (2nd left) and Harold Huber were in it too; it was written by Gene Markey and Kathryn Scola and directed by Alfred E. Green. Robert Lord supervised the production. (First National.)

Supervisor Robert Lord cast Bette Davis (left) as a sexy home-breaker in **Housewife**. She played an advertising copywriter who, after composing a successful commercial for a cosmetic firm, allows fellow copywriter and one-time lover George Brent (right) to claim it as his own. She then moves in on him in an unsuccessful attempt to lure him away from his wife (Claire Dodd). Ruth Donnelly, Hobart Cavanaugh and Robert Barrat also appeared, and Alfred E. Green directed, rather leadenly, from a rather heavy script by Manuel Seff and Lillie Hayward (story by Miss Hayward and Robert Lord). More effective as a critic than as an artist on this occasion, Davis summed it up in five little words: 'Dear God! What a horror!' Song: Cosmetics By Dupree (by Mort Dixon and Allie Wrubel).

Considering the flimsiness of plot in **Midnight Alibi** (old lady living in seclusion for forty years befriends a gambler on the run for a murder he did not commit), screenwriter Warren Duff, working from a story by Damon Runyon, fleshed out the tale most adroitly. He was greatly helped by Alan Crosland whose direction captured the colourful atmosphere of the original, and by a cast that included Richard Barthelmess (centre) as the fleeing gambler, Ann Dvorak as the woman he loved, Helen Lowell as the old woman plus Harry Tyler (centre right), Henry O'Neill, Robert Barrat, Paul Hurst (left) and Vincent Sherman, who would soon become one of the studio's top directors. (First National.)

Joe E. Brown's rise from station agent to bike-riding champion, with dashes of villainy and romance en route, formed the mediocre content of **6 Day Bike Rider**. Audiences did not have to be blessed with a sixth sense to keep two laps ahead of Brown (illustrated) and his antics; nor did writer Earl Baldwin to realize that for Brown addicts the situation was fool-proof. Lloyd Bacon directed, Sam Bischoff supervised, and the cast included Maxine Doyle, Frank McHugh and Arthur Aylesworth. (First National.)

Based on an autobiographical novel by ▷
H. Bruce Lockhart, and set in the Russia
of 1917, **British Agent** was a somewhat
curious spy melodrama in which Leslie
Howard (right) as an unofficial British
emissary hiding out in Moscow, and the
elegant Kay Francis (left) as a Cheka spy,
become romantically involved. J. Carrol
Naish impersonated Trotsky; Irving Pichel
was Stalin. Directed by Michael Curtiz with
uncharacteristic sluggishness, it was of
interest more for its performances than
for the unconvincing content of Laird
Doyle's screenplay. Also cast were William
Gargan, Phillip Reed, Walter Byron, Ivan
Simpson, Cesar Romero, and Halliwell
Hobbes. The production was supervised by
Henry Blanke. (First National.)

Gentlemen are Born, a well-intentioned
drama about the difficulties encountered by
college graduates in finding jobs after
leaving the cloistered protection of the
university, dissipated its theme by dragging
its quartet of hapless graduates through
situations of crushing banality. This was a
pity, since the idea behind it all was valid
enough, and the performances by Franchot
Tone (second left), Ross Alexander (centre),
Dick Foran (left) and Robert Light, first
class. Adding glamour to Eugene Solow and
Robert Lee Johnson's screenplay were Jean
Muir (right), Margaret Lindsay (centre left)
and Ann Dvorak, with Charles Starrett,
Russell Hicks, Arthur Aylesworth and Henry
O'Neill also cast. The film was directed by
Alfred E. Green, and the production was
supervised by Edward Chodorov. Songs:
When You Call The Roll and Alma Mater
(by Irving Kahal and Sammy Fain). (First
National.)
▽

Director Michael Curtiz was on top form
with **The Key**, an atmospheric drama
involving the Black and Tans in the Ireland
of the twenties. William Powell played a
Captain of the British Army whose proud
boast was that he was decorated three
times: once for bravery, twice for indiscretions. The tone of his performance was
derived from the latter boast; so was the
main narrative thread for, in no time at all,
Powell was having an affair with the wife
(Edna Best) of a captain in British Intelligence (Colin Clive, left). How he redeemed
his caddish behaviour made for excellent
cinema. Hobart Cavanaugh, Halliwell
Hobbes, Henry O'Neill, Phil Regan, Donald
Crisp and Arthur Treacher were also
featured in Laird Doyle's excellent screenplay (from the play by R. Gore-Brown and
J.L. Hardy). The production supervisor was
Robert Presnell. Song: There's A Cottage In
Killarney (by Mort Dixon and Allie Wrubel). ▷

In **The St. Louis Kid** (released in Britain as
A Perfect Weekend), James Cagney (right)
played a truck-driver involved in a milk-war
between dairy farmers and truck-drivers.
Patricia Ellis (centre right) was his leading
lady, and had the rare opportunity of taking a
swipe at her leading man rather than the
other way round. Ray Enright directed from
a screenplay by Seton I. Miller and Warren
Duff (story by Frederick Hazlitt Brennan) kept
it constantly on the move, with Allen Jenkins
(left) supplying the humour. Also cast were
Hobart Cavanaugh, Spencer Charters and
Addison Richards (centre left). Sam Bischoff
supervised.
▽

Josephine Hutchinson (right) made a rather
inauspicious screen debut in **Happiness
Ahead**, a musical with a window-cleaning
background in which she played a bored
heiress who pretends to join the proletariat.
But it hardly mattered, for the consummate
skill with which Mervyn LeRoy directed it
guaranteed a good time. A catchy score also
helped, as did the sunshine presence of Dick
Powell as the manager of a window cleaning
company. Also cast were John Halliday
(left) Frank McHugh, Allen Jenkins, Ruth
Donnelly, Dorothy Dare, Marjorie Gateson,
and Jane Darwell. The screenplay was by
Harry Sauber and Brian Marlow, and the
production was under the supervision of
Sam Bischoff. Songs included: Beauty Must
Be Loved (by Irving Kahal and Sammy Fain),
There Must Be Happiness Ahead, Pop Goes
Your Heart and All On Account Of A
Strawberry Sundae (by Mort Dixon and
Allie Wrubel) and Massaging Window Panes
(by Bert Kalmar and Harry Ruby). (First
National.)
▽

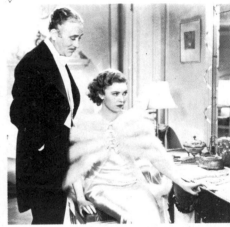

△ Made in Spanish, **The Singer of Naples (El Cantate de Napoles)** starred Enrico Caruso Jr (centre) as a blacksmith's son who sings his way up from cafe crooner to a star of La Scala in Milan. Carmen Rio (right) was featured as his Neapolitan sweetheart, Mona Maris as her rival. Elizabeth Reinhardt wrote it from a novel by Armon Chelieu, and Howard Bretherton directed. The Spanish cast included Alfonso Pedroza, Francesco Maran, Antonio Vidal and Emilia Leovalli.

△ Moving at a supersonic pace **Murder in the Clouds,** set in a West Coast airport, was breathlessly directed by D. Ross Lederman from a story and screenplay by Roy Chanslor and Dore Schary. Ace pilot Lyle Talbot (left) is assigned the job of transporting a high-powered scientist, complete with plans for a revolutionary type of explosive, to Washington. Enter the villains, who sabotage the assignment by taking Talbot's place at the controls. Contributing to the high altitude thrills were Ann Dvorak (far left), Gordon Westcott, Robert Light, George Cooper, Charles Wilson, Wheeler Oakman (right) and Henry O'Neill. Sam Bischoff supervised the production. (First National.)

I Sell Anything was the one about the guy who, getting ideas above his station, deserts his humble origins for a crack at the big-time, only to return to his roots with his tail between his legs. Pat O'Brien was the guy, the origins he deserted were Second Avenue (where he was an auctioneer known as Spot Cash Cutler), and the big time he tried to crack was Park Avenue (where he had a go at selling fake antiques). His Park Avenue lady was Claire Dodd; his Second Avenue rose Ann Dvorak (centre). Roscoe Karns (right), Hobart Cavanaugh, Russell Hopton (left) and Robert Barrat were in it too; it was written by Brown Holmes and Sidney Sutherland from a story by Albert J. Cohen and Robert T. Shannon, the director was Robert Florey, and the supervisor Sam Bischoff. (First National.)

▽

△ Critics deplored what screenwriters Gene Markey and Kathryn Scola did to Willa Cather's Pulitzer-prizewinning novel, **A Lost Lady** (released in Britain as **Courageous**), and audiences didn't approve either. Barbara Stanwyck (second left) played the heroine – a young girl who, out of gratitude, marries an elderly lawyer (Frank Morgan, left) only to discover, when she falls in love with Ricardo Cortez, that she has made a great mistake, and that her loyalty to Morgan causes her nothing but misery. Although a happy ending was superimposed on the authoress' original intentions, there was nothing happy about the movie in general or Alfred E. Green's direction in particular. Also cast were Lyle Talbot, Philip Reed, Hobart Cavanaugh and Rafaela Ottiano. James Seymour supervised. (First National.)

△ Warren William (illustrated) having successfully played Philo Vance, was again cast as a sleuth – this time in the guise of Erle Stanley Gardner's Perry Mason in **The Case of the Howling Dog.** Eschewing the usual touches of melodramatic hokum so germane to the genre, the film, which kept audiences wondering whether co-star Mary Astor was guilty of murder or not – was underpinned by an intelligent, if somewhat wordy screenplay (by Ben Markson) which Alan Crosland's direction did wonders to keep fluid. The film was also characterized by the complete absence of background music save on one isolated occasion when the title number from *Dames* blared forth from a radio. Sam Bischoff was in charge of production, and the supporting players included newcomer Helen Trenholme, Alan Jenkins, Grant Mitchell, Dorothy Tree, Helen Lowell, Gordon Westcott and Harry Tyler.

There was patriotic flag-waving a-plenty in **Flirtation Walk**, a military musical whose most saleable ingredients were Dick Powell and Ruby Keeler (centre). Set largely in West Point Academy (to whom the film is dedicated) it focussed on life in such institutions in general, and on the innocent, oh-so-shy romance between Powell and Keeler in particular. In the words of one reviewer, it was 'a splendid laboratory specimen of the adolescent cinema'! Tunefully assisted by a pleasing and professional Mort Dixon-Allie Wrubel score, plus some rousing dance routines staged by Bobby Connolly, it looked and sounded better than it really was, and was a big hit at the box-office. The film was written by Delmer Daves (from his and Lou Edelman's story), supervised by Robert Lord, and directed by Frank Borzage, whose cast also included Pat O'Brien, Ross Alexander, Glen Boles, John Eldredge, Henry O'Neill, Guinn Williams, John Darrow and Frederick Burton. Songs included: Flirtation Walk, I See Two Lovers, Mr And Mrs Is The Name and When Do We Eat? (First National.) ▷

◁ Jean Muir followed *As the Earth Turns* with **Desirable.** In it she portrayed (excellently) a girl whose selfish, vain, actress mother (Verree Teasdale, centre) has kept her in school rather than have to admit to the world at large that she has a nineteen-year-old daughter. But she cannot keep the girl hidden for ever, as Miss Muir's sudden arrival in New York proves. George Brent (centre left) was co-starred as one of Miss Teasdale's suitors, with other roles going to Arthur Aylesworth, Joan Wheeler, Barbara Leonard, Charles Starrett and John Halliday (right). It was written by Mary McCall Jr, and directed by Archie Mayo. The production was supervised by Edward Chodorov.

◁ A well-worn farce on the by now tired gold-diggers theme, **Kansas City Princess** starred Joan Blondell (left) and Glenda Farrell (right) as a pair of money-crazy broads who, to escape a couple of their victims (and to further Manuel Seff and Sy Bartlett's so-what screenplay), disguise themselves as girl scouts(!) and make for New York where, on arrival, they fleece a couple of aldermen. After that they set their sights on a dim-witted millionaire. Though the screenplay offered little to laugh about, William Keighley's direction at least kept it moving. Robert Armstrong, Hugh Herbert, Osgood Perkins, Hobart Cavanaugh and Gordon Westcott were in it too, and the production was supervised by Lou Edelman.

△
The question at the core of **The Firebird** – which Charles Kenyon adapted from a play by Lajos Zilhazy, and which William Dieterle directed, was: who killed a rather unendearing mime artist called Herman Brandt? Set in Vienna, and with a cast including Ricardo Cortez (as Brandt), Verree Teasdale (centre), Lionel Atwill (right), Anita Louise (left), C. Aubrey Smith, Dorothy Tree, Helen Trenholme, Hobart Cavanaugh and Robert Barrat, the whole concoction, when stripped of its romantic setting, was a routine whodunnit with no startling surprises – a case of schnitzel dressed as lamb.

Despite the success of **The Kennel Murder Case,** Jack Warner felt that its star William Powell wasn't worth the money he was asking so, for the studio's second Philo Vance mystery **The Dragon Murder Case,** Warren William (2nd right) was brought in. A strange tale involving a swimming pool and the bizarre drowning (or was it murder?) of a young man, it clicked at the box-office, justifying Jack Warner's faith in it. The script was originally offered to Michael Curtiz, who turned it down, as did Archie Mayo, Mervyn LeRoy and Alfred Green in quick succession. It was finally directed by H. Bruce Humberstone. F. Hugh Herbert and Robert N. Lee wrote it from the novel by S.S. Van Dine with Rian James taking an adaptor's credit. The production was supervised by Henry Blanke and featured Lyle Talbot, Margaret Lindsay, Robert McWade, Helen Lowell, Dorothy Tree, Robert Barrat, George E. Stone, George Meeker, and Eugene Pallette (second left) as Sergeant Heath. (First National.) ▽

△
As portrayed by Guy Kibbee (left) Sinclair Lewis' most enduring creation (first filmed in 1924) **Babbitt** emerged, warts and all, as a rather lovable old boy. Though scenarists Mary McCall Jr (who wrote the screenplay) and Tom Reed and Niven Busch (who did the adaptation) showed the novelist's quintessential mid-Western businessman in a variety of guises – the main storyline devised for this remake involved the hero in a crooked real-estate deal, as well as in a blackmail situation with another woman. The splendid Aline MacMahon (right) played Mrs Babbitt, with other parts going to Claire Dodd, Maxine Doyle, Glen Boles, Minna Gombell, Alan Hale and Berton Churchill. Because the irony and cynicism at the core of Lewis' novel was at no point integrated into William Keighley's direction, the film, supervised by Sam Bischoff, emerged as little more than lightweight, amiable entertainment. (First National.)

1935

In September, the Warner brothers were sued by restaurant owner Edward Hutchinson who claimed that the disreputable character portrayed by Al Jolson in **Go Into Your Dance** was a blatant representation of himself. The case was settled out of court. In November, Benjamin Warner died in Youngstown, Ohio, while on a visit to one of his daughters.

The Warner Bros. stock company continued to expand, with names such as Margaret Lindsay, Glenda Farrell, Hugh Herbert, Guy Kibbee, George Brent, Claire Dodd, Hobart Cavanaugh and Barton MacLane featuring prominently in film after film. The economic crisis was almost over and the studio showed a profit of $674,158.

Two of the studio's films were nominated for Best Film of the Year. They were **A Midsummer Night's Dream** and **Captain Blood**. The winner was **Mutiny on The Bounty** (MGM). Bette Davis, however, won her first Oscar for **Dangerous**, with other Oscars going to cameraman Hal Mohr and editor Ralph Dawson for **A Midsummer Night's Dream**, and to songwriters Harry Warren and Al Dubin for 'Lullaby of Broadway' from **Gold Diggers Of 1935**. Nathan Levinson was nominated for Best Sound Recording for **Captain Blood**, and, in a new category, Best Dance Direction, Busby Berkeley was nominated for his staging of 'Lullaby of Broadway' and 'The Words Are In My Heart' from **Gold Diggers Of 1935**, and Bobby Connolly for 'A Latin From Manhattan' from **Go Into Your Dance** and 'Playboy From Paree' from **Broadway Hostess**. The winner was Dave Gould for 'I've Got A Feelin' You're Foolin'' from MGM's **Broadway Melody Of 1936**. The award for Best Dance Direction was in fact only given for three years, being discontinued in 1937.

△

In **Bordertown** Paul Muni (right), appropriately nicknamed 'Savage' by a society debutante (Margaret Lindsay), with whom he becomes infatuated, gave a smoulderingly intense and highly praised performance as a Mexican lawyer relentlessly pursued by Bette Davis (left), the wife of his casino-owning employer (Eugene Pallette). Miss Davis consolidated the personal success she had scored in *Of Human Bondage* (RKO 1934), keeping the part just this side of hysteria, and showing the studio just what she could do when given the chance. Tony Gaudio's superb photography, characteristic of the Warner Bros. 'house style', gave the Mexican ghetto sequences a harsh, drab realism which was sharply contrasted with the superficial glitter of Pallette's casino. It was written by Laird Doyle and Wallace Smith from a novel by Carroll Graham, and capably directed by Archie Mayo. Robert Lord did the adaptation and supervised, and his production also included Robert Barrat, Henry O'Neill, Hobart Cavanaugh, Gavin Gordon and William B. Davidson.

△

It was love at first sight for George Brent (left) and Kay Francis (right) in **Living on Velvet** — a soap-sud of a melodrama directed by Frank Borzage — whose screenplay by Jerry Wald and Julius Epstein showed off its two stars to better advantage than usual. Brent played a pilot responsible for the deaths of his parents and sister in a plane crash; Miss Francis was the ultra-sophisticated woman he meets at a party, and who instantly gives his guilt-ridden life new meaning. Marriage complications and personality changes follow — but it all ends happily. Warren William was originally meant to get the girl, but his contract with the studio was in its last stages, and Jack Warner saw no reason why, in the circumstances, he should emerge a winner. Also cast were Helen Lowell, Henry O'Neill, Samuel S. Hinds and Russell Hicks. The production was supervised by Edward Chodorov. Song: Living On Velvet (by Al Dubin and Harry Warren). (First National.)

Of the many films directed by William Dieterle, **The Secret Bride** (released in Britain as **Concealment**) was his least favourite. He made it only because he could not extricate himself from his contractual commitments, and it turned out to be a verbose bore, as well as a monumental waste of Barbara Stanwyck's talent. Miss Stanwyck (centre back) played a woman whose marriage to district attorney Warren William (centre), had to be kept a dark secret so that he could continue, without prejudice, his attempts to clear his wife's father of certain political accusations. Tom Buckingham, F. Hugh Herbert and Mary McCall Jr scripted, Henry Blanke supervised, and Glenda Farrell and Grant Mitchell co-starred with Arthur Byron, Henry O'Neill, Douglass Dumbrille and Arthur Aylesworth in support.

▽

△

The real villains of **The White Cockatoo**, a lukewarm mystery melodrama, were its writers Ben Markson and Lillie Hayward, who failed to animate Mignon G. Eberhart's novel on which it was based. The film starred Jean Muir (left) as the young claimant to a vast fortune whose only legitimate proof of entitlement was a small piece of paper. Naturally, there were others after the fortune as well, and thereby hung the tenuous thread of the plot. There was, of course, skulduggery, but to little cinematic effect. Alan Crosland directed, and his cast included John Eldredge (right), Ruth Donnelly, Minna Gombell, Walter Kingsford, Ricardo Cortez and Gordon Westcott. Henry Blanke supervised.

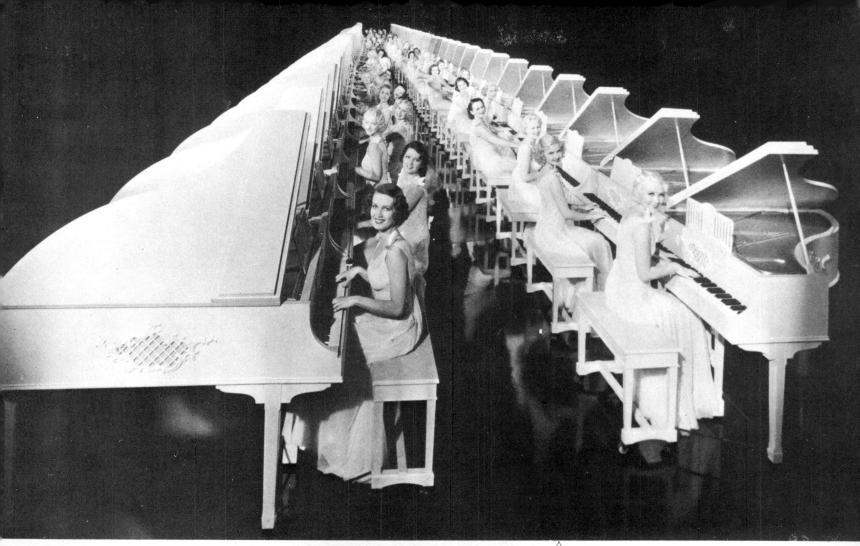

Ann Dvorak, who couldn't actually sing, and ▷
Rudy Vallee (centre) who couldn't really act,
were teamed for **Sweet Music**, a slight but
nevertheless diverting farrago whose meagre
storyline involved them in a Beatrice and
Benedick type of romance. Of more consequence than the plot were the songs, and, as
they were supplied by those teams of resident
tunesmiths Irving Kahal and Sammy Fain,
Mort Dixon and Allie Wrubel, (and the title
song by Al Dubin and Harry Warren), the
customers left the cinema satisfied. A strong
supporting cast that included Ned Sparks,
Helen Morgan, Alice White, Allen Jenkins,
Joseph Cawthorn and Robert Armstrong
helped to buttress the Jerry Wald-Carl Erick-
son-Warren B. Duff screenplay (from a story
by Jerry Wald); the beautifully arranged
dances were staged by Bobby Connolly, with
the overall direction the responsibility of
Alfred E. Green. Sam Bischoff supervised the
very successful production. Songs included:
Sweet Music, Good Green Acres Of Home,
Ev'ry Day, Fare Thee Well, Annabelle, I
See Two Lovers and There's A Different
You.

Maxwell Anderson's 1926 play *Saturday's
Children* surfaced yet again as **Maybe it's** ▷
Love, a lifeless remake (it first appeared
on the screen in 1929) which starred Gloria
Stuart (second left) and Ross Alexander
(left) as the young married couple with in-
law trouble. In a futile attempt to inject
laughter into Jerry Wald and Harry Sauber's
screenplay (adaptation by Lawrence Hazard),
director William McGann also cast Frank
McHugh (centre). Others in this unfortunate
effort were Ruth Donnelly (far right), Henry
Travers (right), Helen Lowell (centre right),
Joseph Cawthorn, Maude Eburne and J.
Farrell MacDonald. The production was
supervised by Harry Joe Brown. (First
National.)

△
Although **Golddiggers of 1935** contained
the extraordinary 'Lullaby of Broadway'
number, which is probably Busby Berkeley's
finest achievement and the most mature
expression of his art, the film itself (directed
in its entirety by Berkeley), lacked the bite
of its 1933 predecessor. A silly story, which
starred Dick Powell as a medical student-
cum-hotel-clerk who falls for pretty guest
Gloria Stuart, its interest began and ended
with Berkeley's three production numbers.
Manuel Seff and Peter Milne's tiresome
screenplay had little to offer, but some
incidental pleasures were supplied by
Adolphe Menjou (as a Russian impresario),
Alice Brady, Glenda Farrell, Frank McHugh,
and Hugh Herbert. Songs included: Lullaby
Of Broadway, I'm Going Shopping With
You and The Words Are In My Heart (by
Al Dubin and Harry Warren). (First
National.)

James Cagney and Pat O'Brien starred in **Devil Dogs of the Air**, as much a salute to the Air Force as *Here Comes The Navy* (1934) was to the Marines. The story, which had Cagney (right) and O'Brien (left) fighting for the favours of Margaret Lindsay, was hardly epoch-making, but the special effects were super. There was action in plenty, and the glimpses the film offered of air force life were authentic and educative. Lloyd Bacon directed the $350,000 production with his customary zeal, and was the perfect catalyst for his two male stars, whose chemistry was explosive. Also cast were Frank McHugh, Helen Lowell, Robert Barrat, John Arledge, Russell Hicks and Ward Bond. The screenplay was by Malcolm Stuart Boylan and Earl Baldwin. Lou Edelman produced the film for Cosmopolitan Productions, the company Marion Davies and William Randolph Hearst shifted from MGM to Warner Bros.

An undistinguished version of Somerset Maugham's *The Sacred Flame*, **The Right to Live** (released in Britain as **The Sacred Flame**) starred Josephine Hutchinson (centre) and George Brent as the adulterous lovers, with Colin Clive (right) outacting them both as the invalid husband who, it is dramatically revealed by nurse Peggy Wood, did not die of natural causes. Ralph Block wrote the screenplay, William Keighley directed with competence rather than flair, and the cast included Henrietta Crosman, C. Aubrey Smith, Leo G. Carroll and Halliwell Hobbes. James Seymour supervised.

Always one jump ahead of the other major studios when it came to turning topical news headlines into screen fodder, it was characteristic of Warner Bros. to recognize the dramatic potential of the real-life Shemanski case. Mike Shemanski was a Pennsylvania coal miner who was murdered by three company policemen. Judge M.A. Mussmano wrote an account of the case which, together with Harry R. Irving's play *Bohunk*, formed the basis for Abem Finkel and Carl Erickson's screenplay **Black Fury**. Paul Muni starred as Joe Radek, a miner whose popularity among the men is exploited by a group of unscrupulous racketeers determined to gain a stranglehold on the Mineworkers' Union. Canvassing for the abolition of extremism as practised by both managements and the unions, and preaching enlightened co-operation between them, the film was considered an important contribution to the cinema of commitment. Make-up man Perc Westmore did an excellent job on Muni (centre), who gave another convincing portrayal of one of society's victims; Karen Morley was the girl who walked out on him, and John Qualen played his best friend who gets murdered by a thug (Barton MacLane). **Black Fury** also featured William Gargan, J. Carrol Naish, Tully Marshall, Mae Marsh, Henry O'Neill, Akim Tamiroff, Ward Bond and Effie Ellsler. It was directed by Michael Curtiz whose generous budget provided for the construction of a mine, complete with shafts, tunnels, and drills, on the Warner Ranch. But the production, supervised by Robert Lord, was not a success at the box-office, and failed to pass several state censorship bodies, being banned outright in Pennsylvania. (First National.)

Predicated on the belief that Cinderella stories rarely fail to find favour with the public, **The Church Mouse** told of a superefficient but strait-laced secretary, (Laura La Plante, left) who, after gaining employment with a prominent banker (Ian Hunter, right), changes her dowdy image and blossoms into an irresistible beauty. On this occasion, familiarity bred content. It was written by W. Scott Darling (from a play by Paul Frank and Ladislaus Fodor), directed by Monty Banks and featured Edward Chapman, Jane Carr, Clifford Heatherley and John Batten. The film was made in England at Warner Bros.' Teddington Studios. (First National.)

◁ The liberties taken by scenarists Tom Reed and Brown Holmes with Ben Hecht's novel **The Florentine Dagger,** brought results that were pretty dire, and reduced an ingenious whodunnit to something less than routine. At the final fade, it hardly mattered who had killed art dealer Victor Ballau (Henry O'Neill, centre right). Far more pressing was how soon it would all be over. Margaret Lindsay, C. Aubrey Smith (right), Robert Barrat, Donald Woods (left), Henry Kolker, Florence Fair and Herman Bing were also in it and Robert Florey directed.

△

A paper-thin vehicle which nonetheless gave Irene Dunne a crack at some glorious Jerome Kern-Oscar Hammerstein II songs, **Sweet Adeline** – set in the gay nineties, and all about a Hoboken lass who happens to be the chief attraction at her father's *biergarten* – was, on the whole, pretty dull. Donald Woods co-starred as the songwriter with whom Miss Dunne (illustrated) becomes romantically involved, with Hugh Herbert, Ned Sparks, Joseph Cawthorn, Louis Calhern and Winifred Shaw in support. Erwin S. Gelsey wrote it, Bobby Connolly staged the dance numbers, Edward Chodorov supervised the production, and Mervyn LeRoy directed. Songs included: Here Am I, Why Was I Born?, Don't Ever Leave Me, 'Twas Not So Long Ago, We Were So Very Young, and Out Of The Blue.

△
Red Hot Tires (released in Britain as **Racing Luck**) was a tepid racing drama in which Lyle Talbot had the misfortune to be found guilty of murder after a collision during a big race. The audience, and co-star Mary Astor, knew he was innocent, but the remainder of the film, in which Talbot (right) escapes from jail and becomes a racing star under an assumed name in South America, concerned itself with proving this fact. Tristram Tupper's screenplay (additional dialogue by Dore Schary), made no new inroads into originality; ditto the direction by D. Ross Lederman. Also cast were Roscoe Karns, Frankie Darro (left), Mary Treen and Henry Kolker. Sam Bischoff supervised the production. (First National.)

Marginally better than *The Secret Bride*, Barbara Stanwyck's last movie for the studio under her present contract was **The Woman in Red.** Working from a screenplay by Mary McCall Jr and Peter Milne (and the novel *North Shore* by Wallace Irwin), Robert Florey directed this tale of a professional horsewoman (Stanwyck, centre) who marries a socialite (Gene Raymond, left) only to find herself the butt of his snobbish uppercrust family. The film relied solely on its star's presence for its *raison d'etre*. and in that respect was well served. There were good performances too, from Genevieve Tobin (centre left), John Eldredge, Phillip Reed and Dorothy Tree. But with so indifferent a script, it didn't really matter. The production was supervised by Harry Joe Brown. Song: So Close To The Forest (by J. Young and L. Reginald). (First National.)

△
While the Patient Slept so did the audience. An inferior thriller set in an old house and involving the odd murder or two, it starred Aline MacMahon (right), Guy Kibbee (second right) and Lyle Talbot (centre left) with Patricia Ellis, Allen Jenkins, Hobart Cavanaugh, Dorothy Tree and Henry O'Neill in support. Written without much ingenuity by Robert N. Lee and Gene Solow (from the novel by Mignon G. Eberhart, with additional dialogue by Brown Holmes), and ponderously directed by Ray Enright for supervisor Harry Joe Brown, it was not one of the studio's more memorable efforts. (First National.)

In 1933 the Production Code Authority insisted that gangsterism should in no way be glorified. This, coupled with the Catholic Legion of Decency's demands on the film industry, resulted in crime movies taking on a slightly different complexion. Stars such as James Cagney and Edward G. Robinson were, in the immediate future, to be seen squarely on the side of Uncle Sam. Cagney (right), whose salary was now $4,500 a week, was cast in **G-Men** (which cost $450,000 to make) as a lawyer who ▷ joins the Justice Department and becomes a G-Man for the sole purpose of avenging the murder of a friend. His tough, staccato delivery complimented William Keighley's well paced, action-filled direction and he gave his most celebrated performance since *Public Enemy* (1931). Feminine interest, as supplied by Ann Dvorak (left) and Margaret Lindsay. took a backseat in this exciting roller-coaster ride of a movie, though supporting players Barton MacLane, Robert Armstrong, Lloyd Nolan and William Harrigan each managed to make his presence felt. Seton I. Miller wrote the screenplay and the production was supervised by Lou Edelman. Song: You Bother Me An Awful Lot (by Irving Kahal and Sammy Fain). (First National.)

△
Guy Kibbee and Aline MacMahon starred in **Mary Jane's Pa** (released in Britain as **Wanderlust**), a pleasant home-spun story of a middle-aged journalist who deserts his one-man newspaper and his family to satisfy his wanderlust. Years later he returns, believing his wife to be in difficulties, but finds that, in fact, she is doing pretty well on her own. How he wins back her love and respect formed the basis of Tom Reed and Peter Milne's screenplay (from a play by Edith Ellis Furness, and the novel of the play by Norman Way). William Keighley, directing for supervisor Robert Presnell, employed a cast that included Tom Brown (right), Robert McWade, Minor Watson and Nan Gray (left). (First National.)

A **Night at the Ritz** was a one-joke farce that succeeded in keeping audiences amused thanks to the eccentric performance of Erik Rhodes (centre) as the world's finest chef. The joke was that Rhodes couldn't cook at all – a drawback unknown to William Gargan, who took it upon himself to publicize Rhodes' supposed culinary excellence. Written by A.J. Cohen, R.T. Shannon and Manuel Seff, the film was snappily directed by William H. McGann. Agreeable performances from its principals, and a supporting cast that included Patricia Ellis, Allen Jenkins (centre left), Dorothy Tree, Paul Porcasi, Berton Churchill, Bodil Rosing, Gordon Westcott and Arthur Hoyt – it made the most of the least and was an easily digestible entertainment.

The second of four Perry Mason thrillers which Warner Bros. filmed with Warren William (centre right) as Erle Stanley Gardner's internationally renowned lawyer, **The Case of the Curious Bride** found Margaret Lindsay in a pickle when she discovered that her first husband, whom she believed to be dead, was, in fact, alive and kicking. Making his American debut as the husband was an Australian actor called Errol Flynn (as a corpse!). Donald Woods, Claire Dodd and Allen Jenkins (left) co-starred, with Barton MacLane, Winifred Shaw and Warren Hymer (centre left) in support. Tom Reed wrote the screenplay, Michael Curtiz directed and Harry Joe Brown supervised production. (First National.)

The sort of romantic yarn women read under the hairdryer, **The Girl from Tenth Avenue** (released in Britain as **Men on her Mind**) told how Ian Hunter (seated) after being jilted by fiancée Katherine Alexander, goes on a sorrow-drowning spree with Bette Davis (left) whom he has never met before, and wakes up the next morning married to her. Also in it were Colin Clive, Alison Skipworth, John Eldredge (centre) and Phillip Reed (right). It was written by Charles Kenyon (from a play by Hubert Henry Davies) and directed by Alfred E. Green. The best that could be said of it was that it only ran 69 minutes. Henry Blanke supervised production. (First National.)

Joan Blondell (right) was given top billing in **The Travelling Saleslady**, and found herself selling, (apart from her own sparkling personality), a commodity known as 'The Cocktail Toothpaste' which comprised whisky flavour in the morning, martini flavour just before dinner, and champagne flavour before bed. As refreshing as a mouthwash, the film corralled the additional talents of Glenda Farrell, William Gargan, Hugh Herbert (left), Grant Mitchell, Al Shean and Ruth Donnelly – all of whom did their particular thing most agreeably for director Ray Enright, writers F. Hugh Herbert and Manuel Seff (story by Frank Howard Clark), and supervisor Sam Bischoff. (First National.)

Child star Jackie Cooper starred with Mary Astor in a sentimental weepie called **Dinky** all about a mother whose main fear, after being framed and accused of fraud, was that her young son at military school would hear about it. Cooper (right) had done better and more important work than this, Astor (left) would do so in the future. Written by Harry Sauber from a story by John Fante, Frank Fenton and Samuel Gilson Brown, and directed by D. Ross Lederman and Howard Bretherton (proving conclusively that two heads are not better than one) the film was nothing to enthuse over. Others in it were Roger Pryor, Henry Armetta, Bette Jean Haney, Henry O'Neill and Jimmy Butler. The production was supervised by Sam Bischoff.

What was noteworthy about **The Goose and the Gander** was just how much plot writer Charles Kenyon managed to pack into a mere 65 minutes of screenplay time. A farce, in which Kay Francis (centre left) attempts to sabotage an adulterous rendez-vous between Genevieve Tobin (right, who is married to her former husband) and George Brent (left), it developed all kinds of complications which happily, director Alfred E. Green managed to keep in comical check. Brent had little to do but give his usual impersonation of a rather wooden debonair, leaving the acting to a cast which included Claire Dodd (centre right) as a jewel thief and John Eldredge (centre) as her accomplice. The production was supervised by James Seymour.

Based on the best-seller by Alice Hobart, Laird Doyle's screenplay for **Oil for the Lamps of China** did a fine job of dramatizing the conflict experienced by an American oil representative (Pat O'Brien, left) in China. What comes first? Loyalty to oneself? Or loyalty to the company one represents? Though director Mervyn LeRoy was unable to impart to the film the authenticity of setting so vividly captured in MGM's *The Good Earth* (1937), certain traces of the Chinese life-style did occasionally penetrate the Hollywood backlot haze through which most foreign countries were depicted. Josephine Hutchinson (right) played O'Brien's wife, (and had an excellent scene pleading, on behalf of her husband, for his job), with other roles going to Jean Muir, Lyle Talbot, Arthur Byron, John Eldredge, Henry O'Neill, Willie Fung and Donald Crisp. A box-office disappointment, the film was nonetheless a bold tackling of an important theme. The production was under the supervision of Robert Lord. (Cosmopolitan – First National.)

One of the more substantial Joe E. Brown comedies, **Alibi Ike** told the amiable tale (by Ring Lardner) of an eccentric baseball player who finds himself involved in a number of wild situations. A scrt of funny-thing - happened - on - the - way - to - the - ballgame, it also featured a mis-used Olivia de Havilland as his demure leading lady, with Ruth Donnelly, Roscoe Karns, William Frawley and Eddie Shubert pitching for director Ray Enright and screen writer William Wister Haines. Even non-admirers of Brown (illustrated) liked this one. Edward Chodorov supervised.

Farce and comedy vied for pride of place in **Going Highbrow**, with neither reaching the finishing post. Concocted by Edward Kaufman and Sy Bartlett from a play by Ralph Spence, and indecisively directed by Robert Florey, it told the story of a *nouveau riche* and his wife (Guy Kibbee and ZaSu Pitts) who seek the advice of an incompetent business consultant (Edward Everett Horton) as to the best methods of breaking into society. The suggestion they are given is to throw a lavish party for their daughter. The trouble is that they don't have a daughter, so they quickly set out to acquire one in the shape of pretty June Martell (right). The cast, none of whom shone here, included Ross Alexander (left), Judy Canova, Nella Walker, Gordon Westcott and Arthur Treacher. Sam Bischoff supervised. Songs included: One In A Million and Moon Crazy (by Louis Alter and Jack Scholl).

Go into your Dance (released in Britain as **Casino de Paris**) was the only film Al Jolson made with his wife, Ruby Keeler. Its success indicated that a sequel was in order but Jolson, fearing comparison with his missus, and not wishing to become part of a husband and wife team, refused. Not that he needed to worry – **Go into your Dance** was his film all the way, with Miss Keeler at her most ineffectual. Another backstage story, but this time with the added attraction of a murder, it featured Jolson (centre) as an entertainer whose irresponsible attitude towards his profession brings down the wrath of Actor's Equity who suspend him.

Undaunted, he spends all his spare time (and money) on the racetrack, only changing his delinquent ways after a shoot-out in which a colleague is killed and his sweetheart (Ruby Keeler) wounded. The film had the authentic Warner Bros. look about it plus a crackling score by ace songwriters Al Dubin and Harry Warren. Helen Morgan made one of her last film appearances, playing a nightclub singer. She returned shortly afterwards to New York and an unhappy personal life. Also cast were Glenda Farrell (as Jolson's sister), Benny Rubin, Phil Regan, Barton MacLane, Sharon Lynne, Patsy Kelly, Akim Tamiroff and Joseph Cawthorn, with

fleeting appearances by Dubin and Warren. The movie was written by Earl Baldwin (from a story by Bradford Ropes) and energetically directed by Archie Mayo, who kept the whole thing going successfully. Bobby Connolly provided the dance routines which were certainly pleasant enough, although they lacked Busby Berkeley's flair, and Sam Bischoff was the supervisor. Songs included: About A Quarter To Nine, Mammy, I'll Sing About You, A Good Old Fashioned Cocktail With A Good Old Fashioned Girl, Go Into Your Dance, Little Things You Used To Do, Casino De Paree and She's A Latin From Manhattan. (First National.)

◁ Max Reinhardt's screen version of **A Midsummer Night's Dream** was the studio's burnt offering to culture in general and to Shakespeare in particular. It combined the sublime with the ridiculous, and was nothing if not a heated talking point for years after its release. The production was dogged by problems. William Dieterle, an erstwhile student of the great Reinhardt, was recruited to assist the maestro when it became evident that Reinhardt's lack of film experience was about to jeopardize the entire, expensive undertaking; and photographer Ernest Haller was replaced after Jack Warner complained that the majority of the forest scenes were barely visible – a literal case of not seeing the wood for the trees. Hal Mohr, Haller's replacement, hacked his way through the studio-built foliage (each tree had real leaves which were glued on separately then sprayed with silver paint), and thinned Anton Grot's sets to allow for the installation of additional lighting equipment. As a result, much of the film, particularly the ending, was visually sublime, as indeed were the special effects, which turned the dawn retreat of the fairies into something quite magical. Less than magical, however, were many of the performances – most notably James Cagney as Bottom (left), the Hermia of Olivia de Havilland and the Lysander of Dick Powell. Mickey Rooney was a nimble Puck until he broke a leg during shooting and had to be wheeled around by unseen stage-hands behind the bushes on a bicycle. Victor Jory offered a suitably sinister Oberon and Anita Louise (right) a beautiful, though pallid Titania. Surprisingly, the best performance of all came from Joe E. Brown as Flute the bellows mender. Others cast were Jean Muir as Helena, Ian Hunter as Theseus, and Frank McHugh as Quince. Reinhardt also engaged the noted Viennese composer Erich Wolfgang Korngold to arrange the Mendelssohn music and, happily for the brothers Warner, Korngold remained at the studio, where, over the next few years, he was to compose some of the greatest film scores of all time. The ambitious production was under the supervision of Henry Blanke.

The trouble with **Stranded** was that it couldn't make up its mind whether it wanted to editorialize or entertain. In the event it did a bit of both and finished up as an unsatisfactory hybrid. Kay Francis (centre) starred as a do-gooding member of the San Franciscan-based Traveller's Aid Society; George Brent was a construction worker on the Golden Gate Bridge. How – after a romance which began nine years prior to the film's start – they finally made it to the altar, formed the basis of Delmer Daves' unconvincing screenplay (from a story by Frank Wead and Ferdinand Reyher). The efficient direction was by Frank Borzage. Also cast were Patricia Ellis, Donald Woods, Barton MacLane, Robert Barrat and June Travis. The production was supervised by Sam Bischoff.

In **Front Page Woman**, two rival newspaper reporters – Bette Davis (centre left) and George Brent (centre) – set out to prove which one is the better journalist when their respective editors send them to cover a massive fire. The fact that they happen to be romantically involved with each other gave the Roy Chanslor, Lillie Hayward, Laird Doyle screenplay (from a Richard Macauley story) added spice. Breezily directed by Michael Curtiz, and with Winifred Shaw, Roscoe Karns (right) and J. Carrol Naish also cast, it added up to pretty good entertainment and, at the same time, struck an early blow for Women's Lib. Sam Bischoff supervised.

◁ In **Shipmates Forever**, the fourth of Dick Powell's six releases in 1935, Powell (left) played the son of an admiral (Lewis Stone). He prefers singing to sailoring but, in the end, succumbs to family pressure and the good counsel of girl-friend Ruby Keeler (right). Delmer Daves' story and screenplay was helped by Frank Borzage's direction; so was a cast that included Ross Alexander, Eddie Acuff, Dick Foran, John Arledge and Robert Light. Lou Edelman supervised the production. Songs included: Don't Give Up The Ship, I'd Rather Listen To Your Eyes, All Aboard The Navy, I'd Love To Take Orders From You and Do I Love My Teacher (by Al Dubin and Harry Warren). (Cosmopolitan – First National.)

Busby Berkeley's staging of the musical numbers came to the rescue of **In Caliente**, a fairly ordinary musical, whose paper-thin plot had magazine editor Pat O'Brien (left) falling in love with tempestuous Mexican dancer Dolores Del Rio (centre) after reviewing her act unfavourably. Ralph Block and Warren Duff thought it up; Jerry Wald and Julius Epstein wrote it down. The cast included Leo Carillo (as Miss Del Rio's father), Edward Everett Horton (centre right), Glenda Farrell, the elegant de Marcos, the Canova Family (including Judy), Phil Regan, Winifred Shaw and Herman Bing. Lloyd Bacon directed. Songs included: The Lady In Red, In Caliente and To Call You My Own (by Mort Dixon and Allie Wrubel) and Muchacha (by Al Dubin and Harry Warren). (First National.)
▽

Page Miss Glory was the first of four films which Marion Davies was to make for Warner Bros. in a deal which involved William Randolph Hearst shifting his Cosmopolitan Pictures from MGM to Burbank. Though Miss Davies (centre) was an attractive light comedienne with more talent than she has been credited with, the Joseph Schrank-Phillip Dunning play which the team of Delmer Daves and Robert Lord adapted to the screen, was not a particularly good vehicle for her. Its slender story of a promoter (Pat O'Brien, right) who sends a composite photograph of a girl to a beauty contest, then has to find the real thing when he discovers his entry has won, was a cute idea – but it did nothing to justify the expense and upkeep of Miss Davies' celebrated bungalow which accompanied her from MGM. Also accompanying the star in her first Warner Bros. effort were several members of the Warner Bros. stock company, including Dick Powell, Mary Astor (left), Frank McHugh, Lyle Talbot, Patsy Kelly, Allen Jenkins, Barton MacLane, Hobart Cavanaugh and Joseph Cawthorn. The direction was by Mervyn LeRoy and cowriter Robert Lord supervised. Song: Page Miss Glory (by Al Dubin and Harry Warren).

Broadway Gondolier, directed by Lloyd Bacon from a Warren Duff and Sig Herzig screenplay (story by Herzig, E.Y. Harburg and Hans Kraly), was little more than a showcase for Dick Powell (centre left). The star played a taxi driver with an all-consuming ambition to succeed as a radio singer. Thanks to the efforts of Joan Blondell (left) and Louise Fazenda (right) who contrive an elaborate scheme that takes him to Venice, he finally makes it. It was pretty mediocre stuff, sporadically enlivened by Al Dubin and Harry Warren's pleasing score, and by a cast which included Adolphe Menjou (centre right), The Mills Brothers, the Canova Family and Ted Fiorito and his band. Songs included: The Rose In Her Hair, Lonely Gondolier, Outside Of You, You Can Be Kissed, Sweet And Low, The Pig And The Cow and Lulu's Back In Town.

Every trick in comedian Joe E. Brown's comic lexicon was taken out and dusted off for Bright Lights (released in Britain as Funny Face). A Busby Berkeley-directed musical, it was about a vaudevillian (Brown, right) who after making it big on Broadway, allows success to go to his head, losing his values and his wife in the process. Brown's own vaudeville background clearly imparted a sense of authenticity to his antics: the Berkeley chorines looked good and the musical numbers were staged with his customary panache. Nothing, however, could disguise the fact that Bert Kalmar and Harry Ruby's screenplay (from a story by Lois Leeson) was a compendium of clichés, and that the characters played by Ann Dvorak, Patricia Ellis, William Gargan, Joseph Cawthorn, Henry O'Neill, Arthur Treacher, Gordon Westcott, Joseph Crehan and William Demarest breathed as if by artificial respiration. Songs included: She Was An Acrobat's Daughter (by Bert Kalmar and Harry Ruby), Toddling Along With You, You're An Eyeful Of Heaven (by Mort Dixon and Allie Wrubel), and Nobody Cares If I'm Blue (by Grant Clark and Harry Akst). (First National.)

Isabel Dawn and Boyce de Gaw concocted a pathetic programmer called Don't Bet on Blondes. About an opportunist who insures a Kentucky colonel against the likelihood of his actress daughter abandoning the stage (and with it the source of his income) should she ever be tempted to marry, it starred Guy Kibbee as the colonel, Claire Dodd (right) as his daughter and Warren William as the insurer. William (left) was unable, however, to insure against the film's failure. As a society boy who falls for Kibbee's daughter, Errol Flynn, in his second American film, had two scenes, on a golf course and in a night-club, on the evidence of which, only Nostradamus could possibly have tipped him for stardom. Robert Florey directed, Sam Bischoff supervised, and the cast included William Gargan, Vince Barnett, Hobart Cavanaugh and Spencer Charters.

A really under-nourished variation on the by now tedious golddiggers theme, We're in the Money again starred Joan Blondell (illustrated) and Glenda Farrell, this time with their wily feminine sights set on a potential defendant in a breach of promise action. Though the two stars were their usual diverting selves, the film failed to hold audiences' attention. F. Hugh Herbert and Brown Holmes wrote it from a story by George R. Bilson, and Ray Enright directed for supervisor Harry Joe Brown. Hugh Herbert, Ross Alexander, Hobart Cavanaugh, Phil Regan, Anita Kerry, Lionel Stander and Henry O'Neill were in it too. Up to their necks. Song: So Nice Seeing You Again (by Mort Dixon and Allie Wrubel).

A shameless piece of sentimental blarney, The Irish in Us starred James Cagney (centre), Pat O'Brien (left) and Frank McHugh (right) as three tough brothers all overseered by a quintessentially Irish mother (Mary Gordon), whose love for her boys is as thickly spread as her brogue. The film offered little plot: work-shy Cagney feuds with brother over the love of a girl (Olivia de Havilland), becomes a fight promoter, steps into the ring when his boxer takes an overdose of gin, and wins both the girl and the fight. Spirited performances from Frank McHugh, Allen Jenkins and J. Farrell MacDonald kept the comedy largely buoyant. Earl Baldwin wrote it from a Frank Orsatti story; Lloyd Bacon directed; Sam Bischoff supervised. (First National.)

South African child star Sybil Jason (centre), with an accent not altogether accessible to American audiences, was top-billed in a Shirley Temple-like vehicle called **Little Big Shot**. A sentimental gangland melodrama, it was a makeshift story about a racketeer's daughter (Jason) who, shortly before her father's assassination, is entrusted to the care of a couple of sidewalk drifters. A sort of underworld Little Orphan Annie, it had Miss Jason experiencing all manner of adventures, and involved the services of Glenda Farrell, Robert Armstrong (left), Edward Everett Horton (right), Jack La Rue, Arthur Vinton, J. Carrol Naish, Edgar Kennedy and Addison Richards. It was written by Jerry Wald, Julius J. Epstein and Robert Andrews from a story by Harrison Jacobs, and directed, with his customary flair, by Michael Curtiz. Sam Bischoff supervised the production. Songs included: I'm A Little Big Shot Now, Rolling In Money and My Kid's A Crooner (by Mort Dixon and Allie Wrubel).

The Payoff took another fanciful look at ▷ the world of newspapers and the men who write them. The story of a once-acid sports columnist who goes soft after becoming the pawn of a crooked wrestling promoter, it starred James Dunn (right), and Claire Dodd (left), at her bitchiest best as the nagging wife who sets off the charge on his downfall. Also cast were Alan Dinehart, as the owner of a gambling casino, and the man for whom Miss Dodd deserts her husband, Patricia Ellis, Joseph Crehan and Frankie Darro. Robert Florey directed from a screenplay by George Bricker and Joel Sayre and Bryan Foy supervised. Unauthentic, but entertaining. (First National.)

◁ A forerunner, almost, of the popular TV series *Upstairs, Downstairs*, **Personal Maid's Secret** turned out to be a pleasant filler which dealt primarily with life 'below stairs'. The heroine was a maid called Lizzie (Ruth Donnelly), and the film followed her fortunes from head maid of a fashionable household to her employment in a similar capacity with an altogether less grand family, but one whose social position was steadily rising. Margaret Lindsay and Warren Hull co-starred, with other roles to Anita Louise (right), Arthur Treacher, Gordon Elliot (left) and Henry O'Neill. Lillie Hayward and F. Hugh Herbert wrote it from a story by Lillian Day; Arthur Greville Collins directed and the production supervisor was Bryan Foy.

Typical of the studio's crime-doesn't-pay melodramas, **Special Agent** starred George Brent (right) as a newspaperman-cum-undercover agent assigned to penetrate a crooked syndicate masterminded by Ricardo Cortez. With a little help from Cortez's bookkeeper (Bette Davis, centre right), Brent successfully nails Cortez for evasion of income tax. He also asks the bookkeeper to marry him. She says yes and they live happily ever after. If you watch the film closely, you'll notice a scene in which at one point Cortez's lips move, but no sounds emerge from his mouth. This is because the Hays Office demanded a cut which supervisor Sam Bischoff felt couldn't be accommodated without throwing the story line into utter confusion. So a compromise was reached by blotting out the offensive line while at the same time keeping the scene intact. It was written by Laird Doyle and Abem Finkel from a story by Martin Mooney. Jack La Rue, Henry O'Neill (seated left), Joe King (left), Paul Guilfoyle (centre), Joseph Crehan and J. Carrol Naish co-starred and William Keighley was the director.

About as substantial as a hole in the air, **I Live for Love** (released in Britain as **I Live for You**), directed by Busby Berkeley from a screenplay by Jerry Wald, Julius J. Epstein and Robert Andrews, was a small-scale musical programmer (it ran a mere 64 minutes) about a tempestuous and temperamental leading lady (Dolores Del Rio, right) and her romance with heart-throb street-singer Everett Marshall (left). Unfortunately, Marshall failed to throb, thus rendering the whole exercise meaningless. Still, Berkeley kept it moving, and its box office returns were everything supervisor Bryan Foy hoped they'd be. Also cast were Guy Kibbee, Allen Jenkins, Berton Churchill and Don Alvarado. Songs included: Mine Alone, Silver Wings, I Wanna Play House, I Live For Love and A Man Must Shave (by Mort Dixon and Allie Wrubel).
▽

◁ The third of the studio's Perry Mason thrillers, **The Case of the Lucky Legs** kept audiences chuckling at the antics of the leading man, Warren William. Playing a somewhat hungover Mason, William (left) sets out to discover who embedded a surgeon's scalpel in a chest belonging to a 'lucky legs' contest promoter. Genevieve Tobin was delightful as Mason's spunky secretary Della Street, with very strong support from Patricia Ellis, Lyle Talbot, Allen Jenkins, Barton MacLane, Peggy Shannon and Porter Hall. Adapted by Edward Chodorov from the story by Erle Stanley Gardner, and written by Brown Holmes and Ben Markson with plenty of humour, it was directed by Archie Mayo and supervised by Henry Blanke. (First National.)

△ A shoddily made, uninterestingly performed drama, about a factory foreman with delusions of grandeur (he gate-crashes high society much against the sober wishes of his wife), **Man of Iron** starred Barton MacLane (centre) as the foreman, Dorothy Peterson as his wife, and Mary Astor as a stenographer; with Joseph Crehan, Craig Reynolds, Joseph King and John Qualen in support. William Wister Haines wrote it from a story by Dawn Powell, and the direction was by William McGann. Bryan Foy supervised. (First National.)

△

Turning to radio for its stars as well as for its subject matter, **Stars over Broadway** marked the screen debuts of operatic tenor James Melton and popular singer Jane Froman (left) and told the story (by Mildred Cram) of a fast-talking agent (Pat O'Brien), who turned a hotel porter (Melton) into a radio personality, only to see his fifty percent commission disappear when Melton decides he'd rather sing opera than pop. O'Brien says no way. Melton takes to drink, O'Brien (right), relents, Melton goes to Italy for proper operatic training. And Miss Froman? She sings her heart out – which was just as well as spoken dialogue all but defeated her. Busby Berkeley and Bobby Connolly were engaged to stage the musical numbers but, doubtful as to the pulling power of the stars, supervisor Sam Bischoff kept a low profile on the budget, and the film's one major production number, which was to have employed a forest of movable silver trees, (to the tune of 'September In The Rain') was cancelled. William Keighley directed a cast which also included Jean Muir, Frank McHugh, Phil Regan, Frank Fay and E.E. Clive. The screenplay was by Jerry Wald and Julius J. Epstein. Songs included: Broadway Cinderella, Where Am I?, At Your Service Madam, You Let Me Down, Over Yonder Moon, September In The Rain (by Al Dubin and Harry Warren – background music only) and Carry Me Back To The Lone Prairie (by Carson J. Robison). There were also operatic extracts from *Aida* and *Martha*.

They could have sold tissues by the boxful at every performance of **I Found Stella Parish**, a 40-carat weepie devised by John Monk Saunders, and written as a vehicle for Kay Francis (centre) by the prolific Casey Robinson. The saga of an actress who stops at nothing to prevent her little daughter (Sybil Jason) from learning the truth about her shady past, it was one of Miss Francis' more successful efforts and kept America's womanhood in tears for months. Mervyn LeRoy at his soppiest directed it, with Orry-Kelly again dressing its star in such a way as to draw attention to her glamorous appearance rather than to her limited talents as an actress. Supervised by Harry Joe Brown, the production also starred the suave Ian Hunter, with Paul Lukas, Jessie Ralph and Barton MacLane in support. (First National.)

◁ The doctor Paul Muni really wanted to play was Dr. Pasteur, not **Dr. Socrates**, and a scene in a bookshop in the latter film even showed him reading a copy of *The Life of Louis Pasteur*. Muni (centre) didn't have more than a few months to wait to realize his ambition, and he accepted his role in **Dr. Socrates** with as good a grace as W.R. Burnett's melodrama (about a small-town doctor who puts a team of gangsters out of business by injecting morphine into their veins) would allow. His performance, enhanced by excellent work from his favourite cameraman, Tony Gaudio, saved the film from utter banality. Robert Lord who supervised, also provided the screenplay (from a story by W.R. Burnett, adapted by Mary McCall Jr), and doing their best for director William Dieterle were Ann Dvorak (left), Barton MacLane (right), John Eldredge, Hobart Cavanaugh, Robert Barrat, Mayo Methot and Henry O'Neill.

Even without recourse to witty one-liners or throwaway colloquialisms—James Cagney (centre), for once genteelly garbed in brocaded waistcoats and stiff wing-collars – was the undoubted hero of **Frisco Kid**, a melodramatic and not particularly notable action film set along San Francisco's notorious Barbary Coast. The raffishness of the period was well contained in Lloyd Bacon's assured direction, but the material was pretty routine. Making the most of the two-dimensional characters bestowed on them by writers Warren Duff and Seton I. Miller, were Margaret Lindsay, Ricardo Cortez, Lili Damita, Donald Woods and Barton MacLane (left). Film buffs quick off the mark will also notice the appearances of several personalities from the silents: Bill Dale, Helene Chadwick, Alice Lake and Vera Stedman. Sam Bischoff supervised.

▽

After two decidedly forgettable appearances (total running time about seven minutes) in low budget programmers, Errol Flynn (left) got his chance when Jack Warner decided to cast him in **Captain Blood.** (Robert Donat was the studio's initial choice but withdrew from the film due to a contractual misunderstanding). Flynn played Peter Blood, an English surgeon who becomes a pirate fighting the tyranny of James II, and the French on the side of William of Orange. Somewhat tentative and self-conscious in his quieter moments, Flynn was clearly more at ease in the action sequences. Olivia de Havilland, also still a relative newcomer, starred opposite Flynn as Arabella Bishop, the niece of a plantation owner. Michael Curtiz directed with the brand of panache that made him one of the studio's most valuable craftsmen and demonstrated, particularly in the brilliantly choreographed duel between Flynn and Basil Rathbone, what a master of action sequences he was becoming. Apart from a handful of scenarist Casey Robinson's melodramatic caption titles (Blood! Blood! BLOOD! reads one of them), some blatantly obvious model work, and some footage from the 1923 Vitagraph silent version of *Captain Blood* which Warner's had acquired in 1928, Hal B. Wallis' production (supervised by Harry Joe Brown) was, for the most part, handsomely mounted. The film found favour with audiences and critics, and made stars of both Flynn and de Havilland, who were to appear together seven times in all. Erich Wolfgang Korngold contributed the stirring score. Also cast were Lionel Atwill, Ross Alexander, Guy Kibbee (right) and Henry Stephenson. (First National.)

▽

△

Relying on the particular appeal of the Misses Blondell (sitting) and Farrell (right) – this time as a couple of show girls whose only means of finding the fare back to New York is to win a popularity contest by enlisting the votes of the US Pacific Fleet – **Miss Pacific Fleet,** as the so-called comedy was christened, was a squib of a show. It also employed (and squandered) the talents of Hugh Herbert, Allen Jenkins, Warren Hull, Guinn Williams and Eddie Acuff. Directed by Ray Enright from a screenplay by Lucille Newmark, Peter Milne and Patsy Flick (story by Frederick Hazlitt Brennan), and supervised by Earl Baldwin, it had nothing whatsoever to recommend it.

△

Moonlight on the Prairie starred Dick Foran (right) as an out-of-work rodeo star. Against impossible odds, he brings a cattle rustler to justice after the blackguard appropriates a ranch belonging to a woman he has recently widowed. Light relief was supplied by George E. Stone, with other roles in the D. Ross Lederman-directed horse opera going to Robert Barrat (centre), Sheila Manners (centre left) and Dickie Jones (left). It was written by William Jacobs for supervisor Bryan Foy. Songs included: Covered Wagon Days and Moonlight On The Prairie (by M.K. Jerome, Joan Jasmyn, Vernon Spencer and Bob Nolan).

△

A thoroughly undistinguished musical, **Broadway Hostess,** designed as a show case for Winifred Shaw (right) charted the over-familiar progress of a show-girl's rise to stardom. Genevieve Tobin, Lyle Talbot (left), Allen Jenkins, Phil Regan, Marie Wilson and Spring Byington were other victims of George Bricker's lustreless screenplay (and direction to match by Frank McDonald); the dance director was Bobby Connolly, and the production supervisor Bryan Foy. Songs included: He Was Her Man, Let It Be Me, Weary, Who But You and Playboy of Paree (by Mort Dixon and Allie Wrubel) and Only The Girl (by Herman Ruby and M.K. Jerome). (First National.)

1936

On 14 October 1936, the studio's most promising female star, Bette Davis, who was earning $3,000 a week, told a court of law that Jack Warner had forced her into inferior roles and was working her over 14 hours a day. Warner brought the case to trial in England, claiming that Davis had broken her contract by walking out of the studio and signing with producer Ludovic Toeplitz. Davis was found guilty and returned to Hollywood, but not without winning a victory of sorts. Not only did Jack Warner pay her costs, but offered her a better selection of scripts.

Anthony Adverse, one of Warner Bros.' most expensive films to date, was nominated for an Academy Award as Best Picture; so was the prestigious Story of Louis Pasteur, but MGM's The Great Ziegfeld won. Paul Muni, however, received the Best Actor Award for Louis Pasteur, with other Oscars going to Gale Sondergaard (Best Supporting Actress) for Anthony Adverse, Jack Sullivan (Assistant Director) for The Charge of the Light Brigade and Tony Gaudio (Cinematography) for Anthony Adverse. Pierre Collings and Sheridan Gibney both won two Oscars (Best Original Story and Best Screenplay) for The Story of Louis Pasteur. 1936 was also the year in which the studio decided to increase their output of low-budget 'programmers' (few of which would run much more than an hour) and Bryan Foy was made head of the 'B' picture division at the studio, supervising no fewer than 29 productions during the year. The year ended with the studio showing a net profit of $3,177,312.

A remake of George Ade's *The College Widow* ▷ (1927), **Freshman Love** (released in Britain as **Rhythm on the River**) was a minor effort which starred Frank McHugh (left) as a college coach whose attempts to turn his team into winners were doomed to failure. Enter Patricia Ellis (right) who, effortlessly, woos two rival oarsmen, Warren Hull (centre) and Walter Johnson, over to McHugh's team and saves the day. Earl Felton and George Bricker wrote it, William McGann directed, Bryan Foy supervised, and the cast included Joe Cawthorn, George E. Stone, Mary Treen and Henry O'Neill. Songs included: Collegiana, That's What I Mean, Freshman Love and Romance After Dark (by M.K. Jerome and Jack Scholl).

◁ Paul Muni's portrayal of the passionate struggle against prejudice and hostility in **The Story of Louis Pasteur** kindled the studio's faith in prestige biopics, an area of film-making hitherto held in disregard by the Warner hierarchy. In fact, so certain was Jack Warner that the Pasteur film would fail, he allocated a budget of no more than $330,000 to supervisor Henry Blanke – a pitifully small amount for an important production. Even the sets were doctored leftovers, including the Academy of Science amphitheatre which was a redressed nightclub from a Busby Berkeley production number. But Muni's (illustrated) dedicated, awesomely intelligent performance as the scientist pursuing a cure for anthrax and hydrophobia, aligned to Sheridan Gibney and Pierre Collings' dignified screenplay resulted in triumph for all concerned – on both sides of the camera. The superb photography was by Tony Gaudio and the purposeful direction by William Dieterle. Josephine Hutchinson co-starred as Madame Pasteur, Anita Louise was his daughter Annette, with other roles going to Donald Woods, Fritz Leiber, Henry O'Neill, Porter Hall, Akim Tamiroff and six-year-old Dickie Moore.

After a series of indifferent roles in indifferent films, Humphrey Bogart (left) was given his big break in **The Petrified Forest**. As 'Duke' Mantee, ('the last great apostle of rugged individualism'), a relentless killer on the run from prison, he repeated the role he had created on Broadway in Robert E. Sherwood's highly acclaimed drama, and became an important acquisition to the studio's roster of male leads. Also recruited from the stage production was Leslie Howard (centre) as Alan Squier, an itinerant poet. Howard meets and falls in love with Gabby Maple (Bette Davis, right), an artist-cum-waitress who works in a gas-station in Arizona but yearns to study art in Paris. Archie Mayo's leisured, lyrical direction, deceptively slow at first but moving unerringly towards the film's tense and affecting climax, retained the essence of the stage-play without loss of cinematic fluidity. The same could be said of Charles Kenyon and Delmer Daves' skilfully fashioned screenplay. When shooting was almost completed, the studio wanted the ending to be changed to something less downbeat but Leslie Howard was adamant that the movie version, like the play, should end with his death. He got his way. Also cast were Genevieve Tobin, Dick Foran and Charley Grapewin. The production was under the supervision of Henry Blanke.

Song of the Saddle in which The Singing Kid, Dick Foran (front centre), brings the murderers of his father to justice ten years after the killing took place, gets an 'A' for action. William Jacobs wrote it, Louis King directed (for supervisor Bryan Foy), and the cast included Alma Lloyd (far left), Charles Middleton, Addison Richards, Eddie Shubert, Jim Farley (centre left), Monte Montagu, Myrtle Stedman (centre), Victor Potel and Kenneth Harlan (right). Songs: Underneath A Western Sky and Vengeance (by M.K. Jerome, Jack Scholl and Ted Fiorito). (First National.)
▽

When director Mervyn LeRoy submitted the screenplay (by Sheridan Gibney from the Hervey Allen best-seller) of **Anthony Adverse** to the Breen office for approval, he was shocked when it was returned with a cut involving forty pages of script. The reason for the cut was one scene in which the hero, as a little boy, was depicted naked. LeRoy refused to comply, and after meetings with Breen, an arrangement was reached whereby the film would be shot as written, submitted for approval afterwards, and only then would cuts be made if Breen still thought it necessary. Breen didn't, though if he *really* had had the film's interest at heart he would have, if only to reduce the running time (136 minutes) to something resembling more of a movie and less of an endurance test. Its picaresque plot, about the adventures of a young man (Fredric
▽

Based on Barry Connor's 1925 play *Applesauce*, **Brides Are Like That**, directed by William McGann from a screenplay by Ben Markson, told the amiable story of a pleasant young man (Ross Alexander, centre) who goes through life believing he can get whatever he wants by flattery. He proves this by convincing his rival in love (Dick Purcell, right), that he, (Purcell), is too lofty a specimen to allow marriage to ruin his life – thus leaving the way open for his own pursuit of Anita Louise (left). Joseph Cawthorn, Mary Treen, Joseph Crehan and husband-and-wife Kathleen and Gene Lockhart were in it too, and the modest but enjoyable production was under the supervision of Bryan Foy. (First National.)
▽

March) in 19th century America and Mexico, and how his experiences matured him, was punctuated with the sort of contrivances and coincidences better suited to 19th century swashbuckling literature than 20th century film-making. Even an interesting cast, including Olivia de Havilland, Edmund Gwenn, Claude Rains (left), Anita Louise (centre), Louis Hayward (right), and Donald Woods was unable to lubricate its creaking joints. The supporting cast included Gale Sondergaard, Billy Mauch, Akim Tamiroff, Ralph Morgan, Henry O'Neill, Scotty Beckett and Luis Alberni. **Anthony Adverse**, supervised by Henry Blanke, was one of the studio's most ambitious projects to date (and LeRoy's last major production for the studio) and added to the ever-growing prestige of the company. It was also a huge financial success.

Dick Powell and Ruby Keeler were teamed for the sixth and last time in **Colleen** (it was also Miss Keeler's penultimate film for the studio), an impoverished musical which featured Hugh Herbert as an eccentric millionaire who, against his family's wishes, entrusts a gold-digging floozie (Joan Blondell, left) with his dress shop. His nephew, Dick Powell, however, has other ideas. He hires Ruby Keeler for the job. It was a pretty mindless brew, directed by Alfred E. Green and performed without much spirit by Miss Keeler who was here even less animated than usual. Jack Oakie (right), Louise Fazenda, Paul Draper, Marie Wilson, Luis Alberni and Hobart Cavanaugh were also featured in the Peter Milne-F. Hugh Herbert screenplay (story by Robert Lord). The dance numbers were created and staged by Bobby Connolly. Songs included: I Don't Have To Dream Again, You've Gotta Know How To Dance, An Evening With You and A Boulevardier From The Bronx (by Al Dubin and Harry Warren).
▽

Dangerous starred Bette Davis (left) as a jinxed alcoholic actress. Just when her total ruin seems imminent, she is taken up by an architect (Franchot Tone, right, on loan from MGM), through whose kindness and understanding she is ultimately saved from herself. Though the story was one prolonged melodramatic cliché, Davis' dogged determination not to allow Laird Doyle's over-heated screenplay to sink her, paid off handsomely. Miss Davis insisted, for example, on looking as unglamorous as possible in the first half of the film so as to lend her appearance the kind of authenticity which the author's efforts so lacked. This gave the story a patina of credibility (no mean feat ▷ under the circumstances), and won the actress her first Oscar. Director Alfred E. Green could not be blamed for the cop-out ending which was imposed on the production by the Hays Office. Also starred were Alison Skipworth, John Eldredge, Dick Foran and, playing 'the other woman' yet again, Margaret Lindsay. Harry Joe Brown supervised the film which was remade in 1941 as *Singapore Woman*.

The joint talents of director Michael Curtiz and the screen's number one zombie, Boris Karloff, united to make **The Walking Dead** a superior foray into horrorland. Having been executed for a murder he did not commit, Karloff is brought back from the dead, and immediately sets about taking revenge on the men who sent him to the chair. The odyssey, as scripted by Ewart Adamson, Peter Milne, Robert Andrews and Lillie Hayward (from a story by Ewart Adamson and Joseph Fields) was genuinely hair-raising, with Messrs Curtiz and Karloff (centre) conjuring up just the right atmosphere for this kind of hokum. Lou Edelman supervised the production, casting Ricardo Cortez, Edmund Gwenn, Marguerite Churchill (right), Warren Hull, Barton MacLane, Henry O'Neill, Joseph King, Paul Harvey and Joseph Sawyer in other roles.

A remake of George M. Cohan's 1928 *The Home Towners*, **Times Square Playboy** (released in Britain as **His Best Man**) – about a interfering out-of-towner who comes to New York as best man for a wedding and promptly makes mischief between the families concerned – starred Gene Lockhart (on floor) as the troublemaker, Kathleen Lockhart (right) as his wife, and Warren William (left) and June Travis as the couple he places at loggerheads. Also cast were Barton MacLane, Dick Purcell and Craig Reynolds. The talky screenplay (it bickered more than it talked) was by Roy Chanslor, William McGann directed, and Bryan Foy supervised production. It was not an improvement on the earlier version or even on the stage play, despite its fidelity to the latter. Song: Lookin' For Trouble (by M.K. Jerome and Joan Jasmyn).

Director Howard Hawks was very much at home with his material in **Ceiling Zero**, a melodrama of civil aviation based on Frank Wead's Broadway success of the same name and with a screenplay by Wead himself. It starred an irrepressible James Cagney (centre) as Dizzy Davis who, to spend some time with his girlfriend (June Travis, right), shirks his duties by pretending to have a heart attack. His behaviour inadvertently causes the death, in a plane crash, of the pilot who stood in for him. In a somewhat mawkish finale, Cagney redeems himself by courageously setting off in bad weather to test a de-icing invention, and meets a violent end in the process. Hawks redeemed himself too, not at the end but in the middle, with a series of brilliantly directed action sequences. Also cast in this Cosmopolitan production were Pat O'Brien (left), Stuart Erwin, Henry Wadsworth, Barton MacLane, Martha Tibbetts and Isabel Jewell. Harry Joe Brown supervised.

Ricardo Cortez (centre right) solved a double murder in **The Murder of Dr. Harrigan**. Set in a hospital bearing no resemblance to reality, Peter Milne and Sy Bartlett's screenplay (from a story by Mignon G. Eberhart with dialogue by Charles Belden) centred its attention on uncovering the culprit, though the film was too routine to generate any real sense of involvement. Kay Linaker (right), Mary Astor, Joseph Crehan (left), Frank Reicher (centre right), Anita Kerry and Phillip Reed were in it, direction was by Frank McDonald and supervision by Bryan Foy. (First National.)

Al Jolson's least successful or entertaining film for Warner Bros. was **The Singing Kid** in which he played a musical comedy star who, after losing his voice, goes to the country for a rest. In time, Jolson (centre) finds his voice as well as a girl-friend and, after a few minor complications, returns to Broadway with both. Also cast were Sybil Jason, Edward Everett Horton, Lyle Talbot, Allen Jenkins, Beverly Roberts, Claire Dodd, The Yacht Club Boys, Cab Calloway and his Band and Winifred Shaw. Robert Lord, who also supervised, provided the musty story from which Warren Duff and Pat C. Flick wrote the screenplay; Bobby Connolly staged the musical numbers and the director was William Keighley. Songs included: My How This Country Has Changed, You're The Cure For All That Ails Me, Here's Looking At You and Save Me Sister (by E.Y. Harburg and Harold Arlen), and You Gotta Have That Hi-Di-Ho In Your Soul (by Irving Mills and Cab Calloway). (First National.)

Snowed Under, a witless comedy of little consequence, was bogged down by an awful screenplay by F. Hugh Herbert and Brown Holmes, from a story by Lawrence Saunders. All about a playwright who retreats to the country in search of a third act and finds, to his dismay, that he has been followed there by his first two wives, plus a woman whose intention it is to become wife number three, it totally sabotaged the efforts of George Brent (as the playwright), Genevieve Tobin, Glenda Farrell and Patricia Ellis (foreground), as the women in and out of his life, Frank McHugh (centre), Porter Hall and Helen Lowell. Ray Enright directed in a manner which suggested that his mind was elsewhere and, in the circumstances, it probably was. Harry Joe Brown supervised. (First National.)

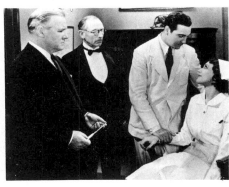

A joyless effort, **The Widow from Monte Carlo** wasted Dolores Del Rio's (left) good looks on the soggy story of a widowed noblewoman who is successfully pursued to the altar by a persistent Warren William. Louise Fazenda was in it too, as were Colin Clive (right), Mary Forbes, Viva Mundon, Olin Howland, Warren Hymer and E.E. Clive. Based on a play by Ian Hay and A.E.W. Mason, it was written by F. Hugh Herbert with Charles Belden and George Bricker supplying the less than sparkling dialogue. Arthur Greville Collins directed and the supervisor was Bryan Foy.

Using the construction of the massive Boulder Dam as their background, Sy Bartlett and Ralph Block, working from a story by Dan M. Templin, fashioned a rather predictable screenplay called, predictably, **Boulder Dam**. It was about a mechanic (Ross Alexander, centre, in his first starring role), who, after an accidental killing in Detroit, attempts to evade arrest by changing his name and seeking employment on the Dam. The overworked Patricia Ellis co-starred as a nightclub singer whom he befriended, with other parts going to Lyle Talbot (centre left), Eddie Acuff, Henry O'Neill, Egon Brecher, Eleanor Wesselhoeft and Joseph Crehan. Sam Bischoff supervised the production, and his director was Frank McDonald.

The Golden Arrow saw the beginning of Bette Davis' long and bitter battle with the studio for better scripts. After her success in *Of Human Bondage* (1934) for RKO, *Dangerous* and *The Petrified Forest*, Miss Davis (centre) regarded as an insult this trivial tale of a phoney cosmetic heiress who tricks a newspaper reporter (George Brent, left) into a marriage of convenience in order to rid herself of fortune hunters. Eugene Pallette, Dick Foran, Ivan Lebedeff, Earle Foxe (right) and Hobart Cavanaugh were also cast, Charles Kenyon wrote the screenplay from Michael Arlen's stage play, and Alfred E. Green directed. Sam Bischoff supervised. (First National.)

The happy ending attached to **I Married A Doctor**, a remake of Sinclair Lewis' rather sour *Main Street* (1923) robbed the story of the impact the author clearly intended, despite Josephine Hutchinson's (right) strong portrayal of the outsider who has to suffer the slings and arrows of outrageous gossips and scandalmongers. A generally excellent cast that included Pat O'Brien (left), Ross Alexander, Guy Kibbee, Louise Fazenda, Olin Howland, Robert Barrat and Margaret Irving, plus a strong, workable script by Casey Robinson, Harriet Ford and Harvey O'Higgin served merely to underline the disappointment caused by the film's misconceived last reel. Archie Mayo directed for production supervisor Harry Joe Brown. (First National.)

In **Sons O'Guns** Joe E. Brown (centre) was again forced to become something he wasn't: this time a doughboy. A peace-loving Broadway song-and-dance man for whose latest show he is required to wear a soldier's uniform, he finds himself involved in a war parade while still in costume. Before he knows it, he is a fully-fledged soldier in Brest, where, after a stint in jail for releasing a flock of carrier-pigeons, he escapes, takes Hill 23 and is awarded the Croix de Guerre. Written by Jerry Wald and Julius J. Epstein from a play by Fred Thompson and Jack Donahue, and directed without any concessions to subtlety by Lloyd Bacon, it also featured Joan Blondell (wildly parodying a French accent), Eric Blore, Winifred Shaw, Robert Barrat, Beverly Roberts, G.P. Huntley Jr and Craig Reynolds. The production was under the supervision of Harry Joe Brown. Songs included: In The Arms Of An Army Man and For A Brick And A Quarter A Day (by Al Dubin and Harry Warren).

Dick Purcell, doing a passable imitation of James Cagney (whether intended or not), was prominently featured in **Jailbreak** (released in Britain as **Murder in the Big House**), another of the studio's prison melodramas but this time one without a message. He played a convict who, once inside, is accused of the murder of Joseph King (centre) another convict and his sworn enemy. Enter Craig Reynolds as an intrepid newspaper reporter temporarily turned prisoner who, with a bit of help from Detective Captain Barton MacLane (left) solves the crime. Also using the prison as a main thoroughfare was June Travis (right) who, in the end, gets to marry Reynolds thus insuring that romance was not entirely overlooked. Addison Richards, George E. Stone, Eddie Acuff, Joseph Crehan and Mary Treen were in it too, it was written by Robert D. Andrews and Joseph Hoffman (from a story by Jonathan Finn) and directed by Nick Grinde for supervisor Bryan Foy.

The best thing about **Road Gang** (released in Britain as **Injustice**) was its illustrious antecedent, *I am a Fugitive from a Chain Gang* (1932). A grim depiction of brutality in a prison camp in the South, its attempt to cash in on the Mervyn LeRoy classic failed conspicuously, leaving director Louis King with little more than a routine programmer on his hands. Dalton Trumbo (who would later turn his talents to more impressive projects) wrote the screenplay (from an original story by Abem Finkel and Harold Buckley) and the film starred Donald Woods, Kay Linaker and Carlyle Moore Jr, with Henry O'Neill, Joseph King and Addison Richards in secondary roles. Bryan Foy supervised. (First National.)

The Big Noise (released in Britain as **Modern Madness**) starred Guy Kibbee (left) as a wool manufacturer who, after his retirement, buys a half interest in a dry-cleaning concern. All goes well until he is forced to pay protection money, at which point the star turns hero and single-handedly dry-cleans the town of its underworld element. To call the enterprise feeble is to praise it. George Bricker and William Jacobs wrote it from a story by Edmund Hartmann; the director was Frank McDonald, and the production supervisor Bryan Foy. Also cast were Warren Hull as Kibbee's partner, Alma Lloyd, Dick Foran, Marie Wilson, Henry O'Neill, Olin Howland, Virginia Brissac and André Beranger.

Painting an alarming picture of the extent to which organized crime had infiltrated the fabric of American life in the mid-thirties, **Bullets or Ballots** was a tough, hard-hitting, well-scripted (by Seton I. Miller from his and Martin Mooney's story), well acted, tautly directed (by William Keighley) melodrama that certainly made the most of its 81 action-packed minutes. It told the all-involving story of a New York strong-arm squad detective Edward G. Robinson (right) who ostensibly goes to work for an underworld racketeer (Barton MacLane) after he is demoted from the force. In reality, however, he has not been demoted but only made to look as though he has been in order to help uncover the racket-game's top man. It was typical of the type of economical first-rate crime melodrama so closely associated with the studio, especially its 'March of Time'-like opening. Also featured were Joan Blondell, Humphrey Bogart (left), Frank McHugh, Joseph King, Richard Purcell, George E. Stone, Joseph Crehan, Henry O'Neill and Henry Kolker. The production was supervised by Lou Edelman. (First National.)

◁ The injustices suffered by the Cheyenne tribe at the treacherous hands of white buffalo traders was the subject of **Treachery Rides the Range**. A better-than-average Western, Dick Foran and co-star Paula Stone featured as the traditional hero and heroine. William Jacobs wrote it, Frank McDonald directed, and the cast, under Bryan Foy's supervision, included Monte Blue as a colonel and Jim Thorpe as an Indian chief, with other parts going to Craig Reynolds, Carlyle Moore Jr, Monte Montague, Henry Otho and Don Barclay. Songs included: Ridin' Home and Leather And Steel (by M.K. Jerome and Jack Scholl).

Chic Sale fans had a good time watching the old boy (right) apprehend a criminal in **Man Hunt**. For the rest of the audience, it was a rag-bag of tired old leftovers indifferently warmed up by director William Clemens and his writer Roy Chanslor (from a story by Earl Felton). Ricardo Cortez was in it too; so were Marguerite Churchill (left), William Gargan, Richard Purcell, Maude Eburne, Olin Howland and Addison Richards. Bryan Foy supervised.

The **Public Enemy's Wife** (released in ▷ Britain as **G-Man's Wife**) was Margaret Lindsay (centre) who had the misfortune to spend three years in prison for a crime of which she was completely innocent. When, finally, she is released, her husband (Cesar Romero), a jewel thief and a 'lifer', warns her that if she ever hitches up with another man, he will kill the guy. Ignoring her husband's threat, she divorces him, and having wasted three years behind bars, wastes not a second more in becoming engaged to playboy Dick Foran (right). The pressing question now is: will Romero carry out his threat? Abem Finkel and Harold Buckley (working from a story by P.J. Wolfson and David O. Selznick) supplied the answer in a far-fetched but moderately entertaining script to which director Nick Grinde brought nothing that was not already there. Pat O'Brien (left) played a G-man, with Joseph King, Dick Purcell, Addison Richards and Hal K. Dawson giving worthy support to the stars. The production was supervised by Sam Bischoff.

◁ Ross Alexander's (right) efforts to drive the oil companies of the world out of business by inventing a gasoline substitute of his own, were as abortive as William Jacobs' screenplay for **Hot Money**, and director William McGann's attempts to make something of it. The sort of film that gave programmers a bad name, it also starred Beverly Roberts, with Joseph Cawthorn, Paul Graetz (left), Andrew Tombes, Harry Burns and Anne Nagel in support. The production was supervised by Bryan Foy. Song: What Can I Do? I Love Him (by Ruth and Louis Herscher).

△
Kay Francis (centre) did her best to bring a touch of verisimilitude to her portrayal of Florence Nightingale in **White Angel** and, although fundamentally miscast, almost pulled it off. Allowing for the usual quota of historical inaccuracies, director William Dieterle did a commendable job, and the scenes at Scutari Hospital in the Crimea had considerable impact. Taken from Lytton Strachey's account of the life of Florence Nightingale and written for the screen by Mordaunt Shairp from a story by Michel Jacoby, the film also featured Ian Hunter, Donald Woods, Nigel Bruce, Donald Crisp, Henry O'Neill and Billy Mauch. The production was supervised by Henry Blanke (First National.)

◁ In **Hearts Divided**, a remake of *Glorious Betsy* (1928), Dick Powell (right), complete with curls and pantaloons, looked ridiculous. But it was thoroughly in keeping with the equally ridiculous things done to Rida Johnson Young's play about Napoleon's younger brother's romance with a Baltimore beauty called Betsy. Powell wasn't quite up to the challenge nor, unfortunately, was his co-star Marion Davies (left) on whose insistence Powell was cast. The excellent Frank Borzage battled in vain with Laird Doyle and Casey Robinson's screenplay which even defeated such talented performers as Claude Rains, Charlie Ruggles, Edward Everett Horton, Arthur Treacher and Henry Stephenson. The production was supervised by Harry Joe Brown. Songs included: My Kingdom For A Kiss and Two Hearts Divided (by Al Dubin and Harry Warren), and the Negro spirituals Nobody Knows The Trouble I Seen and Rise Up Children And Shine, sung by the Hall Johnson Choir. (Cosmopolitan-First National.)

Martin Flavin's play *Broken Dishes* had been memorable only in that it featured a newcomer by the name of Bette Davis. The screen version of it, retitled **Love Begins at Twenty** (released in Britain as **All One Night**) did not, alas, have even that particular distinction. The tedious story of a henpecked husband who finally finds the courage (in booze) to start wearing the pants in his family, it was a pretty ineffectual entertainment. Hugh Herbert played the husband (Donald Meek did it on the stage) with Dorothy Vaughan (centre right) as his wife, and Patricia Ellis (centre) as his daughter. Warren Hull (right), Hobart Cavanaugh, Clarence Wilson, Robert Gleckler, Anne Nagel, Arthur Aylesworth and Mary Treen were in it too; it was written by Dalton Trumbo and Tom Reed, directed by Frank McDonald and supervised by Bryan Foy. (First National.)

Full of good things, though by today's standards somewhat racist in its description of blacks as shuffling, simple-minded innocents, Marc Connelly's **The Green Pastures**, directed by William Keighley, found the studio courageously attempting to break new ground. Basically a retelling of the Bible as seen through the eyes of black children in an out-of-the-way Southern Sunday school, its folksy, homespun approach to religion was typified by the memorable line 'Gangway for de Lawd God Jehovah!' prior to Rex Ingram's impressive and dignified entrance as 'De Lawd'. Considered by Connelly to be a fable whose objective was to illustrate 'certain aspects of a living religion in the terms of its believers', it was greatly enhanced by the emotive music supplied by the Hall Johnson Choir, and by Rex Ingram's (left) towering performance in the central role. There were good performances from Eddie 'Rochester' Anderson (as Noah), Oscar Polk (right), Frank Wilson, George Reed, Abraham Gleaves and Myrtle Anderson. Though a prestigious success for the studio, the box office pastures were unfortunately anything but green. Henry Blanke supervised. Songs included: Joshua Fit De Battle Of Jericho And De Walls Came Tumblin' Down, De Old Ark's A-Moverin', Let My People Go, Run, Sinner, Run, Death's Gwinter Lay His Cold Hands On Me and When The Saints Come Marchin' In (arranged and conducted by Hall Johnson). ▷

△
Margaret Lindsay (centre) was deserving of better things than **The Law in her Hands**, in which she played an underworld lawyer who decides that a career is all very well but marriage (to District Attorney Warren Hull) is even better. Written with seemingly little sense of purpose by George Bricker and Luci Ward and directed by William Clemens, it also featured Glenda Farrell, Lyle Talbot, Eddie Acuff, Addison Richards, Dick Purcell, Al Shean and Joseph Crehan. The production was supervised by Bryan Foy. (First National).

A melodrama with a circus background, **The Bengal Tiger**, apart from starring Barton MacLane, featured a scene-stealing tiger called Satan. MacLane (left) played a drunken lion-tamer who, to make up for causing the death of his elderly assistant, offers to marry the old man's daughter (June Travis, right). She, however, only has eyes for trapeze artist Warren Hull – a liaison of which MacLane does not approve. Audiences, frankly, couldn't care one way or the other and could hardly be blamed for their indifference to the Roy Chanslor-Earl Felton screenplay which director Louis King directed with a conspicuous lack of enthusiasm. Paul Graetz, Joseph King, Don Barclay and Gordon Hart were also in it under the supervision of Bryan Foy.
▽

△
Earthworm Tractors starred Joe E. Brown (illustrated) as a salesman whose line is tractors simply because his fiancée wants him to think big. Whatever laughs could be squeezed, cajoled, wheedled or milked from a tractor, Brown managed to squeeze, cajole, wheedle and milk. One of the comedian's better efforts, it contained an extremely funny sequence in which Brown, in order to save prospective client Guy Kibbee a vast removal fee, attaches the tractor to Kibbee's house (which is on

rollers ready to be transported to another part of town) and moves the edifice himself while Kibbee and family – unaware of what is about to happen – are having dinner. Written by Richard Macaulay, Joe Traub and Hugh Cummings (story by William Hazlett Upson) and directed by Ray Enright, it featured June Travis, Dick Foran, Carol Hughes, Gene Lockhart, Olin Howland, Joseph Crehan, Sarah Edwards and Charles Wilson. Sam Bischoff supervised. (First National.)

Two Against the World (released in Britain as The Case of Mrs. Pembrook), while set in the world of radio, not newspapers as was Mervyn LeRoy's *Five Star Final* (1931), was nonetheless a remake of the LeRoy film. This tedious version starred Humphrey Bogart (left) in the role of a compassionate radio station manager bitterly opposed to the raking up of a twenty-year-old murder case. He fears the damage that might be done to the interested parties, particularly the woman originally charged with the crime but exonerated in a court of law. With a lacklustre screenplay by Michel Jacoby and direction and performances that were equally dull, there were many more than two against this one, and it died an early death. Directed by William McGann and supervised by Bryan Foy, the film also featured Beverly Roberts, Helen McKellar and Henry O'Neill. (First National.)

The anti-feminist undertones in Erle Stanley ▷ Gardner's novel The Case of the Velvet Claws were totally eliminated for the film version in which Perry Mason (Warren William, centre) actually finds himself married to his secretary Della (Claire Dodd). Before the honeymoon can take place, however, Mason is shanghaied at gun point by Winifred Shaw. and forced to investigate a case involving blackmail and, inevitably, murder. Tom Reed's adaptation kept audiences reasonably involved in the sinister goings-on, and director William Clemens brought it all to a satisfactory conclusion. Gordon Elliott, Joseph King, Addison Richards, Eddie Acuff (centre right), Olin Howland, Kenneth Harlan and Dick Purcell were featured, and the production supervisor was Bryan Foy. (First National.)

Kay Francis, by now earning $227,000 a year, was given the key role in a plot-laden tear-jerker called Give Me Your Heart (released in Britain as Sweet Aloes). Scripted by Casey Robinson from the play *Sweet Aloes* by Jay Mallory (alias Joyce Carey), the stage version had starred Diana Wynyard in the West End and Evelyn Laye in its more successful Broadway run. Now Miss Francis (centre) played the woman whose indiscreet affair with a married man results in much suffering and a child she is unable to keep. The general consensus of critical opinion was that the star looked as chic as ever, but was decidedly deficient in the emoting department. Patric Knowles (right) played the man she loved, and George Brent (left) the attorney she marries and with whom she finds eventual happiness. The well-groomed production, supervised by Robert Lord, also featured Roland Young, Henry Stephenson and Frieda Inescort, and was directed by Archie Mayo.

A remake of Dashiell Hammett's *The Maltese Falcon*, William Dieterle's version called Satan Met A Lady changed the bejewelled falcon of the original to a gem-filled ram's horn and played it for laughs. The villainous Gutman became Madame Barrabas (Alison Skipworth) and Sam Spade's secretary (Marie Wilson) an irritating little scatterbrain in place of the author's intended model of high-toned seriousness. Bette Davis (left), who considers the film to be one of the low spots of her entire career, co-starred with Warren William (right) as Sam Spade, here christened Ted Shayne. Both stars, together with Arthur Treacher, Winifred Shaw, Porter Hall and Maynard Holmes who supported them, had little idea of what was happening in Brown Holmes' messy screenplay. The production was supervised by Henry Blanke. ▽

Strikingly similar to Paramount's *Thirteen Hours by Air* (1936), Fugitive in the Sky concentrated on the efforts of a wanted killer to hi-jack a passenger airliner, and provided all the *déjà vu* thrills the operation entailed. A competent screenplay (by George Bricker) and adequate direction by Nick Grinde made it all quite acceptable; so did the performances of Jean Muir (as an air hostess), Warren Hull, John Litel, Howard Phillips, Carlyle Moore Jr, Winifred Shaw and Gordon Oliver. The production supervisor was Bryan Foy. ▽

Singing cowboy Dick Foran (centre), assisted by his horse Smoky, were the heroes of The California Mail. Against some crooked opposition, Foran, who played a pony-express rider, wins a contract to carry the mail by stage-coach and in the end gets the girl as well. Harold Buckley and Roy Chanslor wrote it, Noel Smith directed. The production was supervised by Bryan Foy and also featured Linda Perry, James Farley and Gene Alsace. Songs included: Ridin' The Mail and Love Begins At Evening (by M.K. Jerome and Jack Scholl).

One of the studio's more modest Busby Berkeley-directed musicals, **Stage Struck** was another backstage story. This time the plot featured Joan Blondell as a no-talent stage performer who finances a Broadway show for herself and engages Dick Powell (left) to direct it. A clash of temperament between the two of them is suave Warren William's cue to intercept and effect a reconciliation. No one was able to do much with the material (written by Tom Buckingham and Pat C. Flick from a story by supervisor Robert Lord), and it took Blondell's real-life marriage to Powell prior to the film's release to generate interest in the finished product. Frank McHugh, Jeanne Madden, Carol Hughes, Hobart Cavanaugh and Spring Byington were also cast. Songs included: In Your Own Quiet Way, Fancy Meeting You, You're Kinda Grandish and The New Parade (by E.Y. Harburg and Harold Arlen). (First National.)

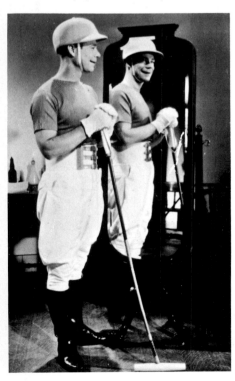

Joe E. Brown's swansong for Warner Bros., **Polo Joe** was another gigantic cliché from which no-one emerged with credit. Again pursuing a vocation for which he was never intended, Brown (illustrated) attempts to become a polo player when he learns that the girl he is trying to impress (Carol Hughes) won't contemplate a romantic liaison with anyone not adept at that particular sport. Those who were amused by the sight of the wide-mouthed comedian trying to come to grips with a foul-tempered pony might have enjoyed themselves; for others it was slim pickings. Richard (Skeets) Gallagher, Joseph King, Gordon Elliott, Fay Holden and George E. Stone were also in it; it was written by Peter Milne and Hugh Cummings, and directed by William McGann with the ferocity of a chukka in progress. The production was supervised by Bryan Foy.

In order to boost his mistress's flagging career, William Randolph Hearst persuaded Jack Warner to hire the services of Clark Gable (left) from MGM for **Cain and Mabel,** a musical comedy in which Marion Davies (right) starred as a waitress turned musical comedy star, and Gable as a boxer. After going along with a romance engineered by newspaper man Roscoe Karns, the couple decide they really *do* love each other — and reject their public images to become private love-birds. Miss Davies was better at bringing life to Laird Doyle's screenplay (story by H.C. Witwer) than she was at interpreting the songs, and although she did her best to look convincing, the strain showed. Allen Jenkins, Walter Catlett, David Carlyle, Hobart Cavanaugh, Ruth Donnelly and Pert Kelton performed gamely for director Lloyd Bacon and production supervisor Sam Bischoff, and William Collier, E.E. Clive and Joseph Crehan were in it too. The musical numbers, by Al Dubin and Harry Warren, were staged by Bobby Connolly but, in spite of the collective effort, the film was not a success. Songs included: Coney Island, Here Comes Chiquita, I'll Sing You A Thousand Love Songs (which interpolated L'Amour Toujours L'Amour), Those Endearing Young Charms, The Shadow Waltz and The Rose In Her Hair.

Blackmail, a couple of murders, an attempted suicide, and a poisoning were the attention-getters which writers Luci Ward and Roy Chanslor (working from a story by Mignon G. Eberhart) laid on in **Murder by an Aristocrat.** But as directed by Frank McDonald, they could have doubled the number of deaths, trebled the methods, and quadrupled the list of suspects and it would not have made much difference. All about a blackmailing rogue who, after demanding $25,000 from his family, is quite understandably murdered by one of them, it was dead to begin with, rendering resuscitation in the guise of every whodunnit cliché known to the cinema useless. William Davidson played the blackmailer with other featured parts going to Lyle Talbot (right), Marguerite Churchill (left), Claire Dodd, Virginia Brissac (centre) and John Eldredge. Stuart Holmes, Gordon Elliot, Joseph Crehan, Florence Fair, Mary Treen and Milton Kibbee were there too. Bryan Foy supervised production. (First National.)

A racy screenplay (by Roy Chanslor from a story by Michel Jacoby) all about a press agent who blows the gaff on Hollywood in a radio programme (his motive being to revenge himself on a film-star enemy), **Here Comes Carter** (released in Britain as **The Voice of Scandal**) was a pleasing trifle and one of the year's better efforts from the Bryan Foy stable. Ross Alexander (right, as the news commentator), Glenda Farrell (as a secretary) and Anne Nagel (as a singer) starred, with Hobart Cavanaugh, Craig Reynolds, George E. Stone, John Sheehan and Wayne Morris (left) in support. The director was William Clemens. Songs included: You On My Mind and Through The Courtesy Of Love (by M.K. Jerome and Jack Scholl). (First National.)

Dick Foran (left) took to the trail again in **Trailin' West** (released in Britain as **On Secret Service**) as a secret serviceman sent by President Lincoln to track down a gang of renegade guerrillas. The film was written by Anthony Coldeway, directed by Noel Smith, and featured Paula Stone (right), Gordon Elliott, Addison Richards (centre), Robert Barrat and Joseph Crehan. Bryan Foy supervised. Songs included: Moonlight Valley and Drums of Glory (by M.K. Jerome and Jack Scholl). (First National.)

▽

Humphrey Bogart (left) denied ever having made **Isle of Fury**. It is not difficult to understand his reticence, but the evidence alas, is against him. The wildly improbable story of a fugitive from justice seeking the safety of a South Sea Island – and the love of a good woman (Margaret Lindsay, second left) – it meandered aimlessly through its 60 minute running time, making its single hour seem like three. Scripted by Robert Andrews and William Jacobs (from Somerset Maugham's novel *Narrow Corner*) and directed by Frank McDonald with his eyes shut, it hardly consolidated the reputation Bogart was gaining for himself after his forceful appearance in *The Petrified Forest*. Bryan Foy supervised.   ▷

Three Men on a Horse, adapted by Laird Doyle from the John Cecil Holm-George Abbott stage success, was a likeable farce about a writer of greeting card verses who discovers that he has an additional string to his bow: he can pick race-horse winners. Mervyn LeRoy directed this amiable non-sense amiably, and recruited the original star from the Broadway stage show, Sam Levene. For support, he cast several members of the studio's regular stock company including Frank McHugh (seated left), Joan Blondell (right), Guy Kibbee and Allen Jenkins, utilizing the additional talents of Carol Hughes, Teddy Hart, Eddie 'Rochester' Anderson, Edgar Kennedy (left) and Paul Harvey. There were lots of funny scenes, which produced lots of action at the box-office. The production was supervised by Sam Bischoff. (First National.)

▽

△

Pat O'Brien, nursing a magnificent obses-sion, (the establishment of a trans-Pacific airline), starred in director Ray Enright and writer Frank 'Spig' Wead's aviation drama **China Clipper.** The plot had O'Brien (centre right) navigating the usual clichés to which such yarns are prone (blinding ambition taking its toll on marriage and everyday friendships, etc.) with everything tying itself into a neat little bow at the fade. Beverly Roberts, Ross Alexander and Hum-phrey Bogart (left) co-starred, with Marie Wilson, Henry B. Walthall (right), Joseph Crehan and Joseph King in featured roles. The associate producer was Louis F. Edelman and the production supervisor Sam Bischoff. (First National.)

Though there was nothing in **Gold Diggers of 1937** to match the incomparable 'Lullaby Of Broadway' sequence in its 1935 prede-cessor, its storyline was marginally stronger. Dick Powell (at the height of his popularity) played an insurance agent who, after being forced by a couple of con-men (Osgood Perkins and Charles D. Brown) to sell a million-dollar policy to theatrical producer Victor Moore, discovers that Moore could ex-pire at any moment. How Powell (left) with the aid of secretary-cum-showgirl Joan Blon-dell (right) keeps Moore alive and kicking, was the red meat of Warren Duff's screenplay (based on a Broadway play of the previous year by Richard Maibaum, Michael Wallach and George Haight). Directed by Lloyd Bacon and glossily produced by Hal B.   ▷ Wallis, it had Busby Berkeley again staging the dance numbers; the score was by E.Y. Harburg and Harold Arlen, supplemented at Berkeley's request (he felt the Harburg-Arlen numbers did not give him enough to work on) by the always reliable team of Al Dubin and Harry Warren. Also cast were Lee Dixon, Rosalind Marquis, Irene Ware, William Davidson and Olin Howland. Earl Baldwin supervised. Songs included: Speaking Of The Weather and Let's Get Our Heads Together (by E.Y. Harburg and Harold Arlen) and With Plenty Of Money And You (The Gold Digger's Song) and All's Fair In Love And War (by Al Dubin and Harry Warren). (First National.)

△

The Captain's Kid starred Guy Kibbee as an old sea captain in a New England village, and Sybil Jason (centre) as the little girl whom he delights with his salty tales of murder and piracy. Melodrama entered the picture in the shape of a murder committed by Kibbee (right) in self-defence when a gangster attacks him during a search for hidden treasure. Another of supervisor Bryan Foy's programmers, it was ground out by director Nick Grinde, written by Tom Reed from a story by Earl Felton, and featured May Robson (centre), Jane Bryan, Fred Law-rence, Dick Purcell and Mary Treen. Songs included: Drifting Along and I'm The Captain's Kid (by M.K. Jerome and Jack Scholl). (First National.)

△

A well-made programmer with a racing background, **Down the Stretch** starred Mickey Rooney (left) as the son of a dis-graced jockey who finds himself suffering for his father's bad reputation. Patricia Ellis (right), however, sees good in the lad and gives him a chance to prove himself. But Rooney is framed by a crooked syndicate, thus making it even more difficult to live down his father's reputation, especially as it is now a case of like-father-like-son. William Jacobs wrote it and William Clemens directed. Also in it were Dennis Moore, William Best, Gordon Elliott and Virginia Brissac, and the production was supervised by Bryan Foy. (First National.)

Michael Curtiz may have fractured the English language everytime he opened his mouth to direct a scene ('Bring on the empty horses!' he demanded across a crowded set; 'Stop standing in bundles' was how he once admonished a group of extras). But when working with such action-packed material as **The Charge of the Light Brigade**, there was nothing fractured about the results. And although, ironically, the actual 'charge' itself — which must rank among the great action sequences on film — was directed not by Curtiz but by a second unit director called B. Reeves Eason, his overall grip on the film was unmistakeable. So was the attention to detail. Actual postage stamps of the period were used (regardless of whether they would be noticed or not), and the uniforms were the authentic ones worn by the 27th Dragoons. This made it all the stranger that Curtiz allowed his writers, Michel Jacoby and Rowland Leigh, to manufacture a romantic triangle involving Errol Flynn (centre), his brother (Patric Knowles), and Olivia de Havilland, at the expense of historical accuracy. Still, only historians complained (the action was partly transferred from the Crimean War of 1853–1856 to India of 1850) and the film, which had the largest, most exacting schedule of Flynn's career, established him as a major star. It cost $1,200,000 to make, was photographed in Sonora, the High Sierras, and Chatsworth near Los Angeles, by Sol Polito, had a score by Max Steiner, and also starred Henry Stephenson, Nigel Bruce, Donald Crisp and David Niven with C. Henry Gordon, G.P. Huntley Jr, Robert Barrat, Spring Byington, E.E. Clive and J. Carrol Naish in support. The production was supervised by Sam Bischoff.

Who killed bed-ridden millionaire Harry Davenport? The question was asked, and answered, in **The Case of the Black Cat**, a further instalment in the studio's Perry Mason series, with Ricardo Cortez (right) inheriting the mantle of predecessor Warren William. Not quite author Erle Stanley Gardner's ideal conception of his attorney-sleuth, Cortez's performance was, all the same, not without merit, and aided by a workable screenplay by F. Hugh Herbert, he responded well to William McGann's competent, though uninspired direction. (The film was started by Alan Crosland who died six days after he was involved in a car smash along Sunset Boulevard on July 16th, 1936. He was 41 years old). The plot boasted no fewer than three murders and utilized the talents of June Travis (left) as Della Street, Jane Bryan, Craig Reynolds, Carlyle Moore Jr, and Gordon Elliott. Bryan Foy supervised. (First National.)

A drama with an ice hockey background, **King of Hockey** (released in Britain as **King of the Ice Rink**) suffered in that its central character, played by Dick Purcell (centre) was too unsympathetic to win audience concern. Having been socked in the eye by team-mate Wayne Morris (right), Purcell's optic nerves were injured, thus keeping him out of the team. There followed a quick descent to the gutter, with girl-friend (Anne Nagel) and her hero-worshipping sister (Ann Gilles) somehow scraping enough money together to pay for the operation that would restore Purcell's sight to him. Supervisor Bryan Foy's production was better than average for such programmer material (it ran a mere 57 minutes), but in the absence of a central character to root for, had little going for it except a series of ice-hockey sequences and even they weren't particularly exciting. It was written by George Bricker, directed by Noel Smith, and also featured Marie Wilson, George E. Stone, Joseph Crehan (centre right) and Gordon Hart.

171

1937

With **The Life of Emile Zola**, the studio won its first Academy Award for Best Film of the Year. In addition, **Zola** won Oscars for Joseph Schildkraut (Best Supporting Actor) and Norman Reilly Raine, Heinz Herald and Geza Herczeg (Best Screenplay). Paul Muni was nominated for his performance in the title role, but lost to Spencer Tracy in **Captains Courageous** (MGM). **Zola** was nominated for several other Oscars: Heinz Herald and Geza Herczeg for Best Original Story, Anton Grot for Best Art Direction, Nathan Levinson for Best Sound Recording and Max Steiner and the Warner Bros. Studio Music Department for Best Score. **Zola** was voted as one of the year's Ten Best by the *New York Times*, as well as the Best Film of the Year by the New York film critics, who voted Muni as Best Actor. Also among the *New York Times* Ten Best was **They Won't Forget.**

In the Best Dance Direction Oscar category, Busby Berkeley's Finale to **The Varsity Show**, as well as Bobby Connolly's 'Too Marvellous for Words' from **Ready Willing and Able** were nominated, but the winner was Hermes Pan for the 'Fun House' number in RKO's **Damsel in Distress**. And from **Mr Dodd Takes the Air**, Al Dubin and Harry Warren's 'Remember Me?' received an Oscar nomination for Best Song. The winner was 'Sweet Leilani' from **Waikiki Wedding** by Harry Owens. The studio chalked up a net profit for the year of $5,876,182.

Despite a plethora of action, **Smart Blonde**, the first of the Torchy Blane series, never got off the ground. Basically concerned with finding out who killed night-club owner Joseph Crehan, it starred Glenda Farrell (right, as ace-reporter Torchy), Barton MacLane (left, as Steve McBride of the homicide department), and Winifred Shaw to give it some sort of box-office appeal and entertainment value. Not being miracle workers, however, they were unable to effect anything remotely resembling a salvage operation. Frank McDonald directed from a screenplay by Don Ryan and Kenneth Gamet (story by Frederick Nebel) and the production was supervised by Bryan Foy. Song: Why Do I Have To Sing A Torch Song (by M.K. Jerome and Jack Scholl).

◁**Guns of the Pecos** was a Western about old time Texas rangers and their efforts to rid the Pecos of troublesome cattle thieves. It featured Dick Foran whose singing, on this occasion, added nothing to Harold Buckley's screenplay (from a story by Anthony Coldeway) except 10 minutes to the running time, which even with songs, came to only 57 minutes. Noel Smith directed, Bryan Foy supervised, and the cast included Anne Nagel (centre), Fay Holden (right), Gordon Hart, Joseph Crehan, Eddie Acuff and Robert Middlemass (left). Songs included: When A Cowboy Takes A Wife and The Prairie Is My Home (by M.K. Jerome and Jack Scholl). (First National.)

The contrived plot of **Once a Doctor** involved the foster son (Donald Woods, left) and real son (Gordon Oliver, centre) of an eminent doctor (Joseph King, right). Oliver brings about his foster brother's expulsion from the medical profession by blaming him for the death of a patient – ethical dereliction being the cause. In the end, Oliver admits his misdemeanour, leaving the way open for Woods to win the girl they were both after (Jean Muir), and, of course, to be reinstated into the medical profession. Written by Robertson White and Ben Grauman Kohn from a story by Frank Dougherty and Paul Perez, it was another Bryan Foy-supervised quickie, which William Clemens directed without much style. Also cast were Henry Kolker, Gordon Hart, Ed Stanley (far right), Louise Stanley and David Carlyle. (First National.)

Not the least convincing element in **God's Country and the Woman** was the sight of a Technicolored George Brent (right) – at times his hair looks quite purple – as a Paris-trained ladykiller who, on arrival in America finds himself working a lumber plantation in competition with tough but pretty Beverly Roberts (left). William Keighley directing from a screenplay by Norman Reilly Raine and a story by James Oliver Curwood, turned it into passable but undistinguished melodrama, with colour undoubtedly adding visual interest to the backgrounds of sky and trees. The Warner Bros. stock company, represented by Barton MacLane, Robert Barrat, Alan Hale and Joseph Crehan were on hand doing their usual thing for producer Hal B. Wallis and associate producer Lou Edelman. Bette Davis, its original star, fled to England rather than make the film.
▽

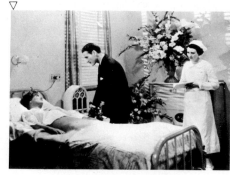

Riding high on *Captain Blood* (1935) and *The Charge of the Light Brigade* (1936), Hal Wallis and Henry Blanke cast Errol Flynn in **The Green Light**. The story of a dedicated young surgeon (Flynn, centre) who jettisons his own promising career rather than allow an elderly physician responsible for a fatal surgical mishap to take the blame, it was idealistic nonsense, old-fashioned even by 1937 standards. Anita Louise, Margaret Lindsay and Sir Cedric Hardwicke co-starred, with Bess Flowers (right) and Spring Byington in support. Milton Krims wrote the screenplay from Lloyd C. Douglas' novel, and director Frank Borzage strained to give it credibility. Critics gave it the red light, audiences the green, and it made money. (Cosmopolitan-First National.)
▽

Sing Me A Love Song (released in Britain as ▷
Come up Smiling), James Melton's second
musical, was a programmer whose lack of
solid production values reflected the studio's
lack of faith in his ability to attract
audiences. Sig Herzig and Jerry Wald's
screenplay (from a story by Harry Sauber)
turned Melton (right) into a playboy who
becomes an incognito clerk in his own store,
and falls in love with fellow worker Patricia
Ellis (centre left). Directed by Ray Enright
and supervised by Sam Bischoff, it featured
Hugh Herbert (as a comic kleptomaniac) as
well as Allen Jenkins (centre right), ZaSu
Pitts (left), Dennis Moore, Nat Pendleton
and Ann Sheridan. The musical numbers
were staged by Bobby Connolly. Songs
included: Summer Night, The Little House
That Love Built, That's The Least You Can
Do For A Lady (by Al Dubin and Harry
Warren) and Your Eyes Have Told Me So
(by Gus Kahn, Walter Blaufuss and Albert
von Tilzer). (First National.)

In the third and worst version of Booth
Tarkington's Penrod and Sam, scenarists
Lillie Hayward and Hugh Cummings turned
Tarkington's boys into miniature G-men
whose adventures were straight out of
Baron von Munchhausen. Directed by
William McGann for supervisor Bryan Foy,
it featured Billy Mauch (illustrated), Frank
Craven, Spring Byington, Craig Reynolds,
Harry Watson, Jackie Morrow and Philip
Hurlic. (First National.)
▽

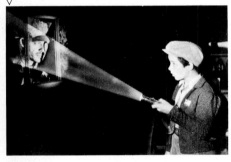

△
A variation on the theme of the district
attorney who finds himself profitably employed by the underworld then, at the
request of some decent girl, reforms,
Midnight Court was a strong contender for
the studio's dreariest film of 1937. Written
by Don Ryan and Ken Gamet, and directed
by Frank McDonald with very little evidence
of adequacy, it starred John Litel as the
D.A. and Ann Dvorak as his girl, with
Carlyle Moore, Joseph Crehan, Walter
Miller, William B. Davidson and John J.
Sheehan in support. Bryan Foy supervised
the production.

△
Humphrey Bogart suffered the woes of Job in
The Great O'Malley, a soap opera about a
feud between Bogart (right) and a tough cop
(Pat O'Brien, left), and the numerous catastrophes which befall Bogart and his family
as a result, but it all came right in the end if
you bothered to wait that long. Ann Sheridan played Bogart's long-suffering sister,
Sybil Jason his crippled daughter; with other
roles going to Frieda Inescort, Donald Crisp
and Henry O'Neill. William Dieterle directed
a screenplay written in molasses by Milton
Krims and Tom Reed (story by Gerald
Beaumont). Harry Joe Brown was associate
producer.

Insidious secret societies in general and
the Ku Klux Klan in particular were under
attack in Black Legion. Humphrey Bogart
(left) starred as a disillusioned factory worker
who joins the 'pro-American' Klan when he
loses the factory foremanship to a foreigner,
only to discover – after it is too late – just
how evil and corrupt the organization he
has sided with really is. Directed by Archie
Mayo with frightening realism, the film's
thesis that bigotry, mob terrorism and
violence were 100% un-American activities
was forcefully conveyed in Abem Finkel
and William Wister Haines' often chilling
screenplay (from an original story by
Robert Lord, who was also associate
producer). This was especially notable in a
lengthy courtroom oration delivered by a
judge before passing sentence on the
Legionnaires. Hitting audiences with tremendous force, Black Legion also won
praise and respect from most of the major
critics and became a subject of controversy
for months after its release. The uniformly
well-drilled cast included Dick Foran, Helen
Flint (right), Erin O'Brien-Moore, Ann Sheridan, Robert Barrat, Paul Harvey, John Litel
and Eddie Acuff.
▽

Claude Rains' impeccable performance as a Russian fortune hunter – the model of which was clearly the real-life Alexandre Stavisky – was the prime reason for seeing **Stolen Holiday** (story by Virginia Kellogg and Warren Duff; screenplay by Casey Robinson), which was not all that dissimilar in content to the Bayonne pawnshop scandal that took place in France. Kay Francis (right) was also in it, and the collection of gowns she was obliged to wear throughout Hal Wallis' sumptuous production (supervised by Harry Joe Brown) was another reason for seeing the movie. For the rest, this story of a Parisienne model (Francis) who marries swindler Rains to protect him from the long arm of the law, was really rather ordinary. Michael Curtiz was the director, and his cast included Ian Hunter (left) as the man to whom Kay turns after husband Rains is murdered, Alison Skipworth, Alex d'Arcy, Charles Halton, Frank Reicher, Frank Conroy and Egon Brecher. (First National.)

A clash between the dictator of a non-extradition island called Caribo and gun smugglers ensconced there formed the workaday plot of **Men in Exile,** which John Farrow directed for supervisor Bryan Foy. Written by Roy Chanslor, from a story by Marie Baumer and Houston Branch, it featured Dick Purcell (right), June Travis (left), Alan Baxter, Margaret Irving, Victor Varconi, Olin Howland and Veda Ann Borg and was all over in less than an hour. (First National.)

A production number towards the end of **Ready Willing and Able** featured a giant-sized typewriter on whose keys Ruby Keeler (centre) and Lee Dixon danced. Could they have been writing the script at the same time? A really puerile musical, in which stage-struck Ruby pretends to be a famous London star, it boasted one good song: 'Too Marvellous For Words' by Johnny Mercer and Richard Whiting, which production supervisor Sam Bischoff, in the absence of anything else resembling quality, had the good sense to reprise about 4,765 times. Allen Jenkins, Louise Fazenda, Carol Hughes, Ross Alexander, Winifred Shaw, Teddy Hart, Jane Wyman and Hugh O'Connell were also featured; it was written by Jerry Wald, Sig Herzig and Warren Duff (story by Richard Macaulay) and directed by Ray Enright. Songs apart from 'Too Marvellous For Words' included: Just A Quiet Evening, Sentimental And Melancholy, Gasoline Gypsies, The World Is My Apple, Handy With Your Feet, There's A Little Old House and Ready, Willing And Able.

An assembly-line comedy, with proficiency substituting for inspiration, **The King and the Chorus Girl** (released in Britain as **Romance is Sacred**) found aristocratic Fernand Gravet (left) falling head over heels for Folies Bergère chorus girl Joan Blondell (right) – with a little help from Jane Wyman and Edward Everett Horton. Adapted by Norman Krasna and Groucho Marx from their story *Grand Passion*, it was produced and directed by Mervyn LeRoy, and also featured Alan Mowbray, Mary Nash, Luis Alberni and Kenny Baker. Songs included: For You and On The Rue De La Paix (by Ted Koehler and Werner Heymann).

In **Land Beyond the Law,** Dick Foran (centre) as a young ranch-hand becomes unwittingly involved with a gang of killers and rustlers. A formula Western, it featured Linda Perry, Cy Kendall, Glenn Strange, Jim Corey (left), and Harry Woods (right), it was written by Luci Ward and Joseph K. Watson (from a story by Marion Jackson) and directed for supervisor Bryan Foy by B. Reeves Eason. Songs included : Whisper While You're Waiting and Song Of The Circle Bar (by M.K. Jerome and Jack Scholl).

A classic triangle situation, but a long way from being classically told, **Her Husband's Secretary** didn't so much scrape the bottom of the barrel as excavate it. Jean Muir (left), Beverly Roberts (centre), and Warren Hull (right) paid the price for being in the studio's resident company by having to star in the film. Lillie Hayward wrote it on rubber, stretching Crane Wilbur's story out of all proportion to its intrinsic worth. Joseph Crehan, Clara Blandick, Addison Richards and Harry Davenport were also in it for director Frank McDonald and supervisor Bryan Foy. (First National.)

Hal B. Wallis, the producer of **Call it a Day**, should have done just that when he read Casey Robinson's adaptation of Dodie Smith's breezy play of the same name. A chronicle of the events that befall a prosperous English family in the course of an ordinary spring day, its cosiness bordered on the coy even though, at one point, the accountant husband (Ian Hunter) of the family in question is seduced by a *femme fatale* client (Marcia Ralston) of his. ('Do you mind if I slip into something more comfortable?' she asks, with mind-boggling originality!). Olivia de Havilland played the daughter (who is also tempted to try infidelity, but resists), with Anita Louise, Alice Brady (left), Roland Young (right), Frieda Inescort (centre), and Bonita Granville appearing for director Archie Mayo. Henry Blanke was the production's supervisor.

The first film Bette Davis made for the ▷ studio after her much-publicized court-case in England was **Marked Woman**, whose screenplay (by Robert Rossen and Abem Finkel) was the best she had had since *Of Human Bondage* (1934) and *The Petrified Forest* (1936). Grateful that Jack Warner was not vindictively withholding good quality material from her because of the trouble she had recently caused him, Miss Davis (right) tore into the role of night-club hostess (a euphemism for prostitute) with all the passion at her considerable command. Based on the trial of New York racketeer Lucky Luciano who was sent to prison on the evidence of prostitutes, it was ably directed by Lloyd Bacon, with a cast that included Humphrey Bogart (left), Eduardo Ciannelli, Lola Lane, Isabel Jewell. Rosalind Marquis and Mayo Methot, and featured songs by Busby Berkeley's favourite composers, Harry Warren and Al Dubin. Hal B. Wallis produced and Louis F. Edelman was the associate producer. (First National.) Songs: My Silver Dollar Man and Mr And Mrs Doakes.

Set in the 1880's, **Prairie Thunder** starred cowboy Dick Foran (left) who, while on an assignment to repair breaks in the telegraph lines perpetrated by hostile Red Indians, discovers that it is really a white man who is responsible for these acts of vandalism. Earl Repp wrote it, B. Reeves Eason directed, Bryan Foy supervised and Ellen Clancy (right), Al Smith, Yakima Canutt and Frank Orth (foreground left) were in it. (First National.)
▽

Melody for Two completed James Melton's three-picture contract with the studio, and was his last major screen role. Stardom simply eluded him, and this one hardly helped. Melton (centre) played an unsympathetic bandleader, forever bitching about the arrangements he is given to play. His co-star, Patricia Ellis (left), eventually kindles the sweet light of reason in him, but by then it was too late – audiences didn't give a damn. Louis King directed for supervisor Bryan Foy, working from a screenplay by George Bricker, Luci Ward and Joe K. Watson, and a story by Richard Macaulay. The musical numbers were staged by Bobby Connolly and Richard Vreeland. Also cast were Marie Wilson, Fred Keating, Dick Purcell, Winifred Shaw (right), Eddie (Rochester) Anderson and Donald O'Connor. One good thing did emerge from it: the Al Dubin-Harry Warren classic, 'September In The Rain', which was first heard as background music in *Stars over Broadway* (1935). Other songs included: A Flat In Manhattan, An Excuse For Dancing, Jose O'Neill The Cuban Heel (by M.K. Jerome and Jack Scholl) and Melody For Two (by Al Dubin and Harry Warren).

There was a limited amount of pleasure to be derived from Robert Barrat's performance in **Mountain Justice**. He played a thoroughly objectionable 'mountain man' whose 'ornery' behaviour towards his medically-minded daughter (Josephine Hutchinson, illustrated) results in his death (by his daughter's hand). Considering that he was also planning to marry off his youngest girl, who was little more than a child, it was clear to all that he got what he deserved. George Brent was in it too, so were Guy Kibbee and Margaret Hamilton, Mona Barrie and Robert McWade. It was written by Norman Reilly Raine and Luci Ward, and directed by Michael Curtiz for supervisor Lou Edelman. (First National.)

Brought into existence for no reason other than to give an inebriated Hugh Herbert (right) a chance to indulge in a spot of amiable blackmail as he engineers a romance between an elevator operator and a chambermaid (Tom Brown and Mary Maguire), **That Man's Here Again** came and went in a very short time. A remake of Ida Wylie's 1929 *Young Nowheres* (though you'd barely know it), it featured Joseph King, Teddy Hart, Arthur Aylesworth, Al Herman (left) and Tetsu Komai. Louis King directed it; Bryan Foy supervised. (First National.)
▽

◁ The historic Oklahoma landrush was the setting for **The Cherokee Strip** (released in Britain as **Strange Laws**), a Dick Foran (left) Western, in which his horse Smokey is lamed by the bad guys in their crooked attempts to get there first. Jane Bryan (centre right), Tommy Bupp (centre left), Edmund Cobb (right) and Joseph Crehan were also in it. Joseph K. Watson and Luci Ward wrote it from a story by Earl Repp, and Noel Smith directed for supervisor Bryan Foy. Song: My Little Buckaroo (by M.K. Jerome and Jack Scholl). (First National.)

Elaborately produced by Hal Wallis, **The Prince and the Pauper**, based on Mark Twain's novel, was basically for the young 'uns. Although Errol Flynn received top billing and indulged in some routine swordplay, grand larceny was committed by the Mauch twins, Billy and Bobby (centre) playing the Prince and the Pauper who exchange identities much to the confusion of everyone around them. The film ended with an elaborate, no-expense-spared coronation ceremony, nicely timed, no doubt, to coincide with the coronation of George VI a week after its release. William Keighley directed with a pleasing sense of period (16th century London), Erich Wolfgang Korngold's score was appropriately rousing, while Laird Doyle's screenplay was certainly workmanlike, though it could have had more excitement in it. Claude Rains played the unpleasant Earl of Hertford, Henry Stephenson was the Duke of Norfolk and Alan Hale the Captain of the Guard. Also cast were Barton MacLane, Eric Portman, Leonard Willey, Murray Kinnell, Halliwell Hobbes and Phyllis Barry. Robert Lord supervised the production. (First National.) The film was remade as *Crossed Swords* (released in Britain as *The Prince and the Pauper*) in 1978.

Donald Woods (third left), who had a featured role in *The Case of the Curious Bride*, was upgraded to play Perry Mason himself in **The Case of the Stuttering Bishop**. This was a routine thriller which found Mason investigating whether the grand-daughter of a millionaire was an impostor or the real McCoy. Written by Don Ryan and Kenneth Gamet from a story by Erle Stanley Gardner, and capably directed by William Clemens, it also starred Ann Dvorak, with other roles going to Anne Nagel, Linda Perry, Craig Reynolds, Gordon Oliver, Joseph Crehan, Helen MacKellar and Edward McWade. Bryan Foy supervised. (First National.)

◁ Supervisor Bryan Foy's ability occasionally to turn out programmers of very good quality was well demonstrated in his factual drama **Draegerman Courage**. A re-creation of the Nova Scotia mine disaster in which one man died and two were subsequently rescued after an heroic ten-day search by a mine crew, it managed, in its 60-minute running time, to chart the workings of a crew with a certain accuracy, as well as to incorporate a touch of romance into the narrative. It starred Jean Muir, Barton MacLane (centre) and Henry O'Neill (as a country doctor and the film's central character), with Robert Barrat, Addison Richards, Helen MacKellar, Gordon Oliver and Joseph Crehan in support. It was written by Anthony Coldeway and directed by Louis King. (First National.)

△
A re-make of the 1923 version, **The Go-Getter** had George Brent (foreground) proving his worth to his tough but lovable father-in-law (Charles Winninger) after he loses his leg in a U.S. Navy dirigible crash. Winninger owns a lumber and navigation company and Brent, one of his employees, gets his chance to demonstrate that a fellow with one leg is just as good as a fellow with two when he courageously steps in and saves the day after a strike cripples Winninger's company. Anita Louise provided the female interest, with members of the much-worked Warner Bros. stock company (John Eldredge, Henry O'Neill, Joseph Crehan, Willard Robertson) in supporting roles. Winninger made sure it was his film though, and director Busby Berkeley (this was his first non-musical venture) encouraged him all the way. Delmer Daves wrote the screenplay for producer Hal B. Wallis with Sam Bischoff as associate producer. Song: It Shall Be Done (by M.K. Jerome and Jack Scholl).

The second Torchy Blane mystery **Fly-Away** ▷
Baby, written by Don Ryan and Kenneth
Gamet from a story by Dorothy Kilgallen,
proved once again that ace reporter Torchy
(Glenda Farrell, right) didn't need a hound
to help her sniff out the whereabouts of a
murderer, even if she had to go half-way
across the world to find him. Which, in
this instance, she did. Barton MacLane
(left) was her police lieutenant friend, with
other parts going to Gordon Oliver, Hugh
O'Connell, Marcia Ralston and Tom Kennedy. Frank McDonald directed for supervisor Bryan Foy.

△
Having already been a West Point cadet in
Flirtation Walk (1934), Dick Powell (left)
joined the marines for **The Singing Marine**,
a musical whose title tells it all. The slender
plot had Powell entering a radio talent
contest, winning it and becoming famous
overnight. But fame goes to his head, he
becomes insufferable and loses his girl
(Doris Weston, centre), as well as the friendship of his buddies. Predictably, though, he
realizes what a fool he's been and returns to
being the nice, shy guy he always was. Ray
Enright directed, with Busby Berkeley contributing two of the musical sequences.
The screenplay was by Delmer Daves. Also
cast were Lee Dixon, Hugh Herbert, Jane
Darwell, Allen Jenkins, Larry Adler (as
himself, right), Guinn Williams, Veda Ann
Borg and Jane Wyman. Songs (by Al Dubin
and Harry Warren) included: I Know Now,
'Cause My Baby Says It's So, Night Over
Shanghai (lyrics by Johnny Mercer), The
Lady Who Couldn't Be Kissed, You Can't Run
Away From Love Tonight and The Song Of
The Marines (which, soon after the film's
release, became the Marine Corps official
song).

As the perennial champions of the labouring
man and his problems, the brothers Warner
considered all types of work worthy of
glorification. In **Slim** (a re-working of the
1932 **Tiger Shark**), efficiently directed by
Ray Enright, tribute was paid to the fearless
men who risk their lives repairing high-
◁ tension cables on the top of electrical towers.
The young Henry Fonda (left) played Slim,
Pat O'Brien (right) was his buddy and co-
worker, and Margaret Lindsay the girl in
the middle. As much a documentary-style
examination of linesmanship as a romance,
it was written by William Wister Haines,
and featured Stuart Erwin, J. Farrel Mac-
Donald, Dick Purcell, Jane Wyman, John
Litel and Craig Reynolds. Produced by Hal
B. Wallis, the production supervisor was
Sam Bischoff.

Illicit love in a far-flung British desert
outpost was the red meat of **Another Dawn**.
Unfortunately, it all turned rather rancid in
William Dieterle's soap-opera treatment
of a triangle situation in which a well-
spoken, stiff-upper-lipped Englishman (Errol
Flynn, illustrated), despite his infatuation for
the wife (Kay Francis) of his commanding
officer (Ian Hunter), behaves impeccably,
only giving way to his passions when the
C.O. flies off on what is clearly a suicide
mission. The original screenplay was by
Laird Doyle who clearly believed that
words spoke louder than actions. Erich
Wolfgang Korngold, believing, on the other
hand, that a good theme spoke louder than
both, came up with a real pippin – so much
so that he incorporated it into the violin
concerto he composed for Jascha Heifetz
some time later. Harry Joe Brown supervised,
and his cast included Frieda Inescort, Herbert
Mundin, G.P. Huntley, Jr, Clyde Cook and
Mary Forbes.

▽

The bad guys in **Blazing Sixes**, another
Dick Foran Western, were a group of
meanies who went about robbing US gold
shipments. Posing as a thief in order to
catch one, government agent Foran (centre)
infiltrates the gang and brings the crooks
to justice. Helen Valkis, Gordon Hart, Tom
Foran, John Merton and Glenn Strange were
also featured in John T. Neville's screenplay
(from a story by Anthony Coldeway) which
Noel Smith directed for supervisor Bryan
Foy. Songs: In A Little County Town and
Ridin' On To Monterey (by M.K. Jerome and
Jack Scholl).
▽

Of the several boxing films made by Warner
Bros. (most of which contained the word 'kid'
in the title), **Kid Galahad** was by far the best.
The story of a querulous fight manager
(mesmerically played by Edward G. Robinson, left) who turns a bellhop (Wayne Morris,
centre) into a prize-fighter, it showed its
director, Michael Curtiz, brilliantly supervising some effective fight scenes with a
gentle, almost mellow approach to the
personal relationships explored in the scenario. Bette Davis as Robinson's mistress
didn't have much to do in Seton I. Miller's
screenplay (from a story by Francis Wallace), and apart from Robinson, the acting
honours were shared by Humphrey Bogart
(right) as a crooked promoter, Harry Carey,
Jane Bryan and Wayne Morris. Like several
previous Robinson vehicles, the actor died
in the last reel. The film, which Hal Wallis
produced and Sam Bischoff supervised, suffered no such fate, and though its title has
since been changed to **The Battling Bellhop**
to avoid confusion with a later Presley remake also called *Kid Galahad* (United Artists
1962), it is still a classic of the genre, and
was remade in 1941 as *The Wagons Roll
at Night*. Song: The Moon Is In Tears
Tonight (by M.K. Jerome and Jack Scholl).
(First National.)
▽

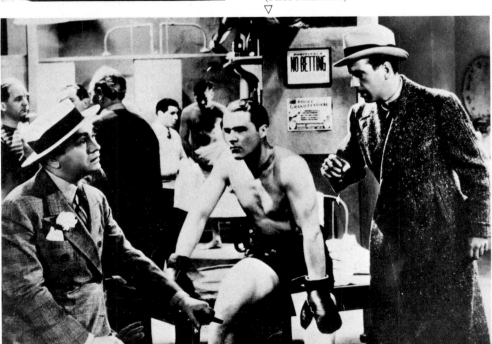

A fair deal for share-croppers was writer Anthony Coldeway's concern in **White Bondage**, yet another Bryan Foy quickie whose basic plot involved a newspaper reporter's determination to prove that the share-cropper's dissatisfaction stemmed from short-weight scales. His investigations almost lead to his being lynched, but he is saved, just in time, by a farm girl. Nothing, however, could save director Nick Grinde's film from being a well-intentioned bore. The cast included Jean Muir (left), Gordon Oliver, Howard Phillips, Joseph King and Virginia Brissac (right).

A remake of *The Butter and Egg Man* (First National, 1928) – but bereft of George S. Kaufman's gift for satire, **Dance, Charlie, Dance**, about a gullible 'angel' who is conned into sinking money into a doomed play, starred Stuart Erwin as the young innocent, with Jean Muir, Glenda Farrell (centre), Allen Jenkins (right), Addison Richards, Charles Foy (left) and Chester Clute in other roles. Crane Wilbur and William Jacobs were responsible for the lifeless screenplay (from the play by George S. Kaufman), and Frank McDonald for the equally moribund direction. Bryan Foy supervised. (First National.) Songs: Dance, Charlie, Dance and Ballet De Bunk (by M.K. Jerome and Jack Scholl). (First National.)

Running 120 minutes, **Varsity Show** was the longest of the studio's series of thirties musicals in time but one of the shortest in plot. The undergraduates of Winfield College are in a quandary: their annual stage show is imminent, but it lacks a producer. Enter Dick Powell, successful Broadway impresario and a Winfield alumnus. Busby Berkeley was engaged to stage the finale which he designed as a tribute to schools, colleges, universities and academies everywhere – one of its highlights being a series of overhead shots in which the boys and girls of the chorus spelled out the initials of several noted places of learning. Fred Waring, Priscilla Lane, Walter Catlett, Ted Healy, Rosemary Lane, Lee Dixon and Sterling Holloway were featured in the Jerry Wald-Richard Macaulay-Sig Herzig-Warren Duff screenplay, and William Keighley directed. The production supervisor was Lou Edelman. Songs included: Love Is On The Air Tonight, Moonlight On The Campus, Old King Cole, Have You Got Any Castles Baby?, We're Working Our Way Through College, On With The Dance, You've Got Something There and When Your College Days Are Gone (by Johnny Mercer and Richard Whiting).

Kay Francis, playing a singer, endured almost as much as her audiences in **Confession**. An unashamedly melodramatic film, it had its heroine performing in sidewalk cafés when, at the very least, she should have been gracing the opera houses of Europe! Not only that, but when she finds evil Basil Rathbone (left), who was once responsible for separating her from her husband and little girl, making advances to the same little girl who isn't so little any more, she kills him. All too silly for words, especially Julius J. Epstein and Margaret Levino's words, (story by Hans Rameau) and for Joe May's limited directorial talents. Hal Wallis produced, Henry Blanke supervised, and the cast included Ian Hunter, Donald Crisp, Jane Bryan (right), Mary Maguire, Dorothy Peterson, Laura Hope Crews and Veda Ann Borg. Song: One Hour Of Romance (by Jack Scholl and Peter Kleuder). (First National.)

In **Empty Holsters**, Dick Foran (centre) is sent to jail for five years when the heavy who is after his girl as well as the bank her father owns, arranges for a stage coach to be held up, then testifies that the man responsible was Foran. John Thomas Neville wrote it from a story by Earl Repp; B. Reeves Eason directed it, Bryan Foy was the supervisor, and the cast included Pat Walthall, Emmett Vogan, Wilfrid Lucas, Earl Dwire and Charles Lemoyne. Songs: Old Corral and I Gotta Get Back To My Gal (by M.K. Jerome and Jack Scholl). (First National.)

Ever Since Eve starred Marion Davies (right) as a stenographer whose good looks get her into amorous scrapes with her various male employers. To avoid their unwanted advances, she deglamorizes herself by donning a pair of horn-rimmed spectacles and slipping into some mannish tweeds. All sorts of tedious complications ensue as a result of the deception, which scriptwriters ▷ Lawrence Riley, Earl Baldwin and Lillie Hayward (story by Gene Baker and Margaret Lee) were unable to turn to cinematic advantage. Lloyd Bacon directed; Hal Wallis produced and Earl Baldwin supervised. Their cast included Robert Montgomery (centre), Frank McHugh, Marcia Ralston (left), Louise Fazenda and Barton MacLane. Songs included: Wreaths Of Flowers (by Hoopii Haaia), Ever Since Eve (by M.K. Jerome and Jack Scholl), and Shine On Harvest Moon (by Jack Norworth and Nora Bayes). (Cosmopolitan-First National.)

Having failed to turn James Melton into a star, the studio had a second try at ransacking radio for new talent and came up with singer Kenny Baker (centre) whom they starred in **Mr. Dodd takes the Air.** Clarence Budington Kelland's mildly satirical story (adapted by William Wister Haines and Elaine Ryan) was about a small town electrician who so impresses some radio executives with his singing that they take him to New York. But Baker develops bronchitis and undergoes a change of range from baritone to tenor. Audiences didn't buy it, and who could blame them? Jane Wyman was co-starred (her first big role after years of service in the background), with Gertrude Michael, Alice Brady, Harry Davenport (left), Frank McHugh (right) and Henry O'Neill in support. The production, under the supervision of Mervyn LeRoy, was directed by Alfred Green. Songs included: Am I In Love?, If I Were A Little Pond Lily, The Girl You Used To Be, Here Comes The Sandman and Remember Me? (by Al Dubin and Harry Warren.)

Inspired by their own promotional campaign for Gold Diggers of 1937 in which a bevy of chorus girls crossed the continent by plane, the studio came up with **Talent Scout** (released in Britain as **Studio Romance**), the basic idea of which was to glorify the people who spot new talent across the length and breadth of the country. What actually emerged from the George Bilson-William Jacobs screenplay was a rather tired story about an unknown young girl singer (Jeanne Madden, centre) who finds overnight fame when she is discovered, not by a talent scout, but by a popular Hollywood matinée idol who happens to fall in love with her. Donald Woods (right) was the heart-throb film star, with other roles assigned to Fred Lawrence, Rosalind Marquis, Joseph Crehan and Charles Halton (left). William Clemens directed for supervisor Bryan Foy. Songs included: In The Silent Picture Days, I Am The Singer, You Are My Song, Born To Love and I Was Wrong (by M.K. Jerome and Jack Scholl). (First National.)

All about a group of itinerant, down-on- ▷ their-luck show folk who stage a fake public wedding inside the mouth of a stuffed whale to stimulate trade at one of their side-shows, **Public Wedding** starred Jane Wyman (right) and William Hopper (centre) as the bride and groom who find to their dismay that, when the stunt is over, they are legally married. Not one of supervisor Bryan Foy's best efforts, it featured Dick Purcell, Berton Churchill, James Robbins, Marie Wilson and Veda Ann Borg. Ray Chanslor and Houston Branch wrote it, and the director was Nick Grinde.

◁ A routine prison melodrama, **San Quentin** starred Pat O'Brien as a humane ex-army officer who becomes yard captain of San Quentin, and Humphrey Bogart (centre) as a con jailed for robbery. Interest attached to the relationship only in that Bogart's sister, a night-club singer played by Ann Sheridan (left), happens, through the long arm of coincidence, to be in love with O'Brien (right). In fact, the Peter Milne-Humphrey Cobb screenplay relied too heavily on coincidence, making it difficult to accept the film on any but the most superficial level. A speeded up car chase towards the end added a touch of excitement to an otherwise undistinguished effort. Harry Warren and Al Dubin provided a catchy number called 'How Could You' for a nightclub sequence, and Barton MacLane, Joseph Sawyer and Veda Ann Borg appeared in featured roles. Lloyd Bacon directed for supervisor Sam Bischoff. (First National.)

There could be no reason for the existence of **Marry the Girl** other than that the studio abhorred a vacuum almost as much as nature does. Rather than have some employable actors remaining idle for a couple of weeks, producer Hal Wallis put them to work in an attenuated comedy whose only issue was whether Hugh Herbert (right) and Mary Boland, as a brother and sister team who run a news syndicate, are able to prevent their niece (Carol Hughes) from marrying Mischa Auer. It won't be giving too much away to say that they succeed. Harry Joe Brown supervised the production, which was written by no fewer than four people: Sid Herzig, Pat C. Flick, Tom Reed and Edward Hope (who supplied the story). The director was William McGann and the cast included Allen Jenkins, Frank McHugh (left) and Alan Mowbray.

When Dick Foran (right) returns to find his father killed and his ranch stolen, his troubles are further compounded by the local sheriff who lays a murder rap on him and sends him to jail. Foran, however, manages to smuggle a few guns into the prison, and after escaping with some of the inmates, forms **The Devil's Saddle Legion.** Their aim? Justice, of course. Directed by Bobby Connolly (whose terrain was usually dance direction in musicals) and written by Earl Repp, it featured Anne Nagel (left), Gordon Hart, George Chesebro and Max Hoffman. Gordon Hollingshead supervised. Songs included: Ridin' To My Home In Texas, Dog's Country and When Moonlight Is Riding The Range (by M.K. Jerome and Jack Scholl).

A remake of *The Trespasser* (United Artists, 1929), which starred Gloria Swanson, **That Certain Woman** was a Peg's Paper story of a gangster's widow and her attempts to make a fresh start in life by working as a secretary to an attorney (Ian Hunter). Melodramatic even to the point of including a tug-of-war over a child, Edmund Goulding's screenplay (he also directed it) had Bette Davis (centre right) treading syrup for most of its 91 minutes. Still, Goulding justified his reputation for being both a starmaker and a woman's director by making Davis look more glamorous than she had ever looked before (particularly in the film's final scene), as a consequence of which he quickly became one of her favourite directors. Also cast were Henry Fonda (right), Anita Louise, Katharine Alexander, Sidney Toler (left), Minor Watson and Donald Crisp (centre left). Robert Lord supervised the production, with Hal B. Wallis as executive producer. (First National.)

A remake of *Dark Hazard*, which starred Edward G. Robinson, **Wine Women and Horses** – with Barton MacLane (centre left) in the Robinson role – was the story of a reformed gambler whose wife leaves him in disgust when he is unable to resist the lure of betting any longer and returns to the scene of his former losses. Written by Roy Chanslor from the novel by W.R. Burnett, directed by Louis King, and supervised by Bryan Foy, it was no improvement on the original, but not bad either. Also cast were Ann Sheridan (as MacLane's wife), Dick Purcell, Peggy Bates, Stuart Holmes (left), Walter Cassell, James Robbins (right), Lottie Williams and Kenneth Harlan (centre right).

Love was barely featured at all in **Love is on the Air** (released in Britain as **The Radio Murder Mystery**), but Ronald Reagan was, as a radio announcer who gets the chop for bringing crooked local politics into one of his broadcasts. But Reagan (right) gets his job back in the end by being on the spot when the villains of the piece are finally apprehended, and by broadcasting the news live. A remake of Paul Muni's *Hi Nellie*, it was written by Morton Grant and George Bricker from a story by Roy Chanslor, and directed by Nick Grinde for supervisor Bryan Foy. Also featured were June Travis, Eddie Acuff (left), Bill Welden, Robert Barrat and Addison Richards. (First National.)

A melodrama with a newspaper background, **Back in Circulation** was not to be taken seriously. As a city editor and an ace news reporter respectively, Pat O'Brien and Joan Blondell gave performances that verged on the libellous in their futile attempt to give Warren Duff's screenplay (from a story by Adela Rogers St. Johns) a much needed fillip. But nothing could redeem this tale of a widow (Margaret Lindsay) on whom Miss Blondell manages to pin a murder rap. Hal Wallis' production, supervised by Sam Bischoff and directed by Ray Enright, went the way of all flesh – taking with it John Litel (centre left), Eddie Acuff (centre right), Craig Reynolds (left), and Regis Toomey (centre). (First National.)

A footballer filler whose central and only issue was whether Carlton could snatch a victory for themselves with the score standing at 0–13 against them, **Over the Goal** featured members of the University of Southern California football team, as well as June Travis, William Hopper, Mabel Todd, William Harrigan (centre left), Gordon Oliver, Willard Parker (centre) and newcomer Johnny Davis. William Jacobs and Anthony Coldeway wrote it; and it was directed by Noel Smith for supervisor Bryan Foy. Songs included: Scattin With Mr Bear and As Easy As Rollin' Off A Log (by M.K. Jerome and Jack Scholl). (First National.)

The Great Garrick, adapted by Ernst Vajda ▷ from his story *Ladies and Gentlemen*, had the members of the Comedie Francaise taking a light-hearted revenge on the famous English actor of the title after he announces that the reason for his trip to Paris is to give them all a lesson or two in dramatic art. It was an entertaining curiosity, handsomely produced by Mervyn LeRoy, stylishly directed by James Whale; and with a cast that included Brian Aherne (right), Olivia de Havilland (left), Edward Everett Horton, Melville Cooper, Marie Wilson and Lionel Atwill.

To his female audiences, Erroll Flynn's combination of brawn, charm and uncommon good looks made him the masculine equivalent of Mae West. Little wonder, then, that he should star in a film demanding a combination of all these qualities called **The Perfect Specimen**. Written by Norman Reilly Raine, Lawrence Riley, Brewster Morse and Fritz Falkenstein (from a story by Samuel Hopkins Adams), it was designed to give Flynn (left) a crack at comedy, replacing his sword (in one scene) with boxing gloves. If Flynn proved as adroit in the ring as he was on a parapet, he wasn't experienced enough to provide the required comic timing, and was not entirely at home in this corny story of a wealthy, upper-class young man whose hot-house existence is shattered when he meets and falls in love with a vivacious and beguiling newspaper reporter (Joan Blondell, right). Also involved in it were Hugh Herbert, Edward Everett Horton, Dick Foran, Beverly Roberts, Allen Jenkins and May Robson. Michael Curtiz directed, Hal B. Wallis produced.

Hal B. Wallis' superb production of **The Life of Emile Zola**, in which Paul Muni (right) gave a towering performance as Zola under William Dieterle's intensely-felt direction, emerged as that *rara avis*: a prestigious as well as a financially successful film. No expense was spared in the recreation of period detail, and the film was the first ever to win an Academy Award as Best Film of the Year for Warner Bros. If only for its powerful recreation of the 'I accuse' courtroom scene, it deserved the soubriquet 'classic'. It was written by Norman Reilly Raine, Geza Herczeg and Heinz Herald whose screenplay elicited flawless performances from Joseph Schildkraut (as Dreyfus), Gale Sondergaard, Gloria Holden, Donald Crisp (left), Erin O'Brien Moore, John Litel, Henry O'Neill, Morris Carnovsky, Louis Calhern and Ralph Morgan. Henry Blanke supervised. An interesting sideline is that not once, throughout the Dreyfus ◁ affair, was the word 'Jew' mentioned.

In a pretty dire programmer called **The Footloose Heiress**, Ann Sheridan (illustrated) played a society heiress who elopes with someone not at all worthy of her (Craig Reynolds), in order to win a $5,000 bet that she will be married by midnight on her eighteenth birthday. Written by Robertson White and dispiritingly directed by William Clemens, it also featured Anne Nagel, Hugh O'Connell, William Hopper and Teddy Hart. Bryan Foy supervised.

Inspired by the real-life Leo M. Frank case in 1913, and based on Ward Greene's novel *Death In The Deep South*, Mervyn LeRoy's abrasive **They Won't Forget** was an outspoken condemnation of prejudice and bigotry in the Deep South and an eloquent protest against lynching. The story of a teacher who is accused and convicted of raping one of his 15-year-old pupils, then lynched when the governor commutes the death sentence, the film featured Claude Rains (illustrated) as a ruthlessly ambitious prosecuting attorney who, with the aid of an equally unscrupulous press, uses the murder to catapult him into the governor's seat by fanning the flames of Southern prejudice. The atmosphere created by LeRoy of a small town waiting for an excuse to alleviate the boredom of its day-to-day existence, was quite remarkable, and his handling of the black janitor who discovers the murdered girl's body, brought a rare and refreshing dignity to the treatment of the negro in the cinema of the thirties. Robert Rossen and Aben Kandel contributed a screenplay of extraordinary boldness, the intensity of which was reflected in the performances of Rains, Gloria Dickson, Edward Norris, Otto Kruger, Allyn Joslyn, Elisha Cook and Clinton Rosmond (as the black janitor). The film also marked the debut of fifteen-year-old Lana Turner (as the murdered victim) whose famous 'sweater' scene instantly singled her out for stardom. **They Won't Forget** was LeRoy's last film for Warner Bros. under his current contract. He succumbed to an offer from MGM, and, the following year, so did Miss Turner. (First National.)

The third Torchy Blane mystery, **The Adventurous Blonde,** was a somewhat confused tale in which a group of reporters, envious of Torchy's success, plan a fake murder so that she will get 'exclusive' information about it to her discredit. Trouble is, the fake murder becomes a reality, and the inevitable question now is, whodunnit? It came as no surprise that the least likely suspect was the culprit. Glenda Farrell (centre) and Barton MacLane (left) played Torchy and her heavy-going policeman fiancé – with Anne Nagel, Tom Kennedy, George E. Stone, Natalie Moorhead, William Hopper, Charles Foy and Virginia Brissac (right) in support. It was written by Robertson White and David Diamond, directed by Frank McDonald, and supervised by Bryan Foy. (First National.)

A third re-make of Porter Emerson Browne and C.H. Towne's play *The Bad Man* (first seen as a film from First National in 1923, then from Warner Bros. in 1930), **West of Shanghai** changed its setting from Latin America to North China. Boris Karloff (centre right) was cast as an endearing Chinese war lord who, before stepping in front of a Nanking firing squad, does away with the heavy, a role which anticipated Karloff's Mr Wong series at Monogram Studios the following year. Crane Wilbur wrote it, the director was John Farrow, and the cast, working for supervisor Bryan Foy, included Beverly Roberts (right), Ricardo Cortez, Gordon Oliver (centre left), Sheila Bromley and Vladimir Sokoloff. (First National.)

◁ **Alcatraz Island,** directed by William McGann for supervisor Bryan Foy, eschewed some of the more fanciful elements that had a way of creeping into prison dramas. It told the straightforward tale of Gat Brady (John Litel, left) who, after being sent to Alcatraz on a tax-evasion charge, is framed for the murder of an inmate who once tried to kidnap his daughter. It was written by Crane Wilbur, and its cast included Ann Sheridan, Mary Maguire, Gordon Oliver, Addison Richards, George E. Stone (centre), Ben Welden, Dick Purcell (right) and Vladimir Sokoloff. (First National.)

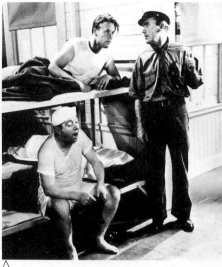

Fact and fiction merged unobtrusively in **Submarine D-1,** a documentary-like look at life under water. Though it starred Pat O'Brien (right), George Brent, Wayne Morris (top left), Frank McHugh (bottom left) and Doris Weston, they were all upstaged by the submarine itself, whose own story proved to be far more interesting than the one fashioned by Frank Wead, Warren Duff and Lawrence Kimble in which O'Brien and Morris vied for the love of Miss Weston. Lloyd Bacon directed, Lou Edelman supervised, and the cast also included Henry O'Neill, Dennis Moore, Veda Ann Borg, and Broderick Crawford. Ronald Reagan was initially in it too, but finished up on the cutting room floor. (First National.)

Verree Teasdale stole the thunder from Kay Francis in **First Lady,** a faithful adaptation (by Rowland Leigh) of George S. Kaufman and Katherine Dayton's 1935 stage play. Basically an extended cat-fight between the two women (Miss Francis is the wife of the Secretary of State, while Miss Teasdale's spouse is a singularly ineffectual member of the Supreme Court), their series of clashes take on war-like proportions when the former learns that the latter is about to present America with a new Presidential candidate. Because Miss Francis (right) wasn't up to the bitchiness the part demanded, her altercations with her nemesis had about as much effect as applauding with one hand – though the lines, in themselves, were fine. So, too, were Preston Foster, Anita Louise (left), Walter Connolly, Victor Jory, Marjorie Rambeau, Marjorie Gateson and Louise Fazenda. Harry Joe Brown supervised for producer Hal Wallis, and the director was Stanley Logan who never allowed his camera to get in the way of the talk.

Expensive Husbands was a Bobby Connolly-directed morsel about a film-star (Beverly Roberts, centre) who marries an Austrian prince (Patric Knowles, left) in Europe to impress her friends and public back home. Jean Negulesco, Lillie Hayward and Jay Brennan wrote it from a story by Kyrill de Shishmareff, Bryan Foy supervised production, and the cast included Allyn Joslyn (right), Gordon Oliver, Eula Guy, Robert Fisher and Fritz Feld.

▽

△

Dick Foran, trading his horse for a fire-engine, was the star and hero of **She Loved A Fireman**, in which the more he doused the flames in burning warehouses, the more he kindled them in the heart of co-star Ann Sheridan (left). Written by Morton Grant and Carlton Sand and directed by John Farrow, it was a best-forgotten effort which also involved Robert Armstrong (right), Hugh O'Connell, Veda Ann Borg, Eddy Chandler and Eddie Acuff. Bryan Foy supervised. (First National.)

Originally called **Gentlemen after Midnight**, the title of this film was changed to **It's Love I'm After** prior to its release. A delightful and wholly successful comedy, it starred a vibrant Bette Davis (left) and a beguilingly urbane Leslie Howard (right) as an actor-actress team whose impending marriage has been postponed eleven times. Their relationship is personified in the opening scenes of the film when, during a performance of *Romeo and Juliet*, they hiss and snarl at each other out of the corners of their mouths. With the appearance of Olivia de Havilland as an ardent admirer of Mr Howard, Davis pushed the comedy into top gear and sent it roaring along to its satisfactory conclusion. Casey Robinson's witty screenplay (from a story by Maurice Hanline) was immeasurably enhanced by excellent, larger than life performances from a variety of established supporting players parodying themselves, viz: Patric Knowles, Eric Blore, Bonita Granville, Spring Byington, E.E. Clive and George Barbier, while Archie Mayo's light, sure-footed direction endowed the whole pleasing concoction with an air of madcappery which both audiences and critics adored. Harry Joe Brown supervised. (First National.)

▽

△

Tovarich, based on the stage success by Jacques Deval and Robert Sherwood, told the amusing story of a couple of aristocratic Russian emigrés in Paris who, finding themselves impoverished, are forced to enter domestic service. Charles Boyer (right) becomes a butler, Claudette Colbert (left) a housemaid. What transpires when they are recognized by friends of their employer, gave the film its satirical and highly entertaining pivot, and its stars a delicious opportunity to sparkle. Anton Grot's settings, Charles Lang's photography, and Max Steiner's score were all suitably top-notch for this Hal B. Wallis production. Anatole Litvak directed, and assembled a cast which included Anita Louise, Basil Rathbone, Melville Cooper, Isabel Jeans and Morris Carnovsky. Robert Lord supervised. Songs included: Raposchal, Shto Mnie Joie and The Volga Boatman.

Hugh Herbert fluttered to little effect in **Sh! the Octopus** in which he played a blithering detective who, together with side-kick Allen Jenkins, is engaged in investigating the strange goings-on in a lighthouse. Not all the ghosts in Shakespeare could have imparted to director William McGann's feeble effort the chills it so desperately sought – and the whole sorry enterprise, which also featured Marcia Ralston, John Eldredge and George Rosener (illustrated) – came and went in a trice. George Bricker adapted from a play by Ralph Murphy and Donald Gallagher, and Bryan Foy supervised. (First National.)

▽

◁ Protection rackets and what to do about them were the twin subjects of **Missing Witness**, another quickie from the Bryan Foy stable. John Litel was appointed to investigate the whole matter and, while he was doing so, newcomer Jean Dale (centre, as a secretary who passes on vital information to Litel, left), was having a romance with detective Dick Purcell (right). As written by Kenneth Gamet and Don Ryan, and directed by William Clemens, the whole venture didn't really add up to very much. Also in the cast were Raymond Hatton, Sheila Bromley, William Haade, Harland Tucker and Ben Welden. (First National.)

The true story of a cavalry horse which was smuggled into England and became a Grand National winner, **Sergeant Murphy** was originally conceived as an 'A' picture and offered to James Cagney, who turned it down. It finished up with associate producer Bryan Foy, who cast Ronald Reagan (right) in the Cagney role, with other parts going to Mary Maguire (left), Donald Crisp, Ben Hendricks, William Davidson and Max Hoffman. William Jacobs wrote it from a story by Sy Bartlett, and the director was B. Reeves Eason. It was an efficient programmer.

Boris Karloff (centre) was predictably creepy in **The Invisible Menace**, a mystery tale set in a fog-bound army base with murder as the first item on its agenda. John Farrow's direction had several good moments, but the thrills in Crane Wilbur's screenplay (from a play by Ralph S. Zink) were for the most part computerized. So were the performances of Regis Toomey, Marie Wilson, Henry Kolker, Eddie Craven and Eddie Acuff. The associate producer was Bryan Foy. The film was remade in 1943 as *Murder on the Waterfront*.

Hollywood in general and broadcasting in particular were the twin targets at which Jerry Wald, Maurice Leo and Richard Macaulay took swipes in their lightweight screenplay for **Hollywood Hotel**. A Busby Berkeley-directed musical, it was one of the last of the studio's more opulent examples of the (by now) dying genre. Based on the popular radio programme of the same name, the film's story was of little consequence compared with the engaging talents of its stars Dick Powell (right), Rosemary Lane (left), Lola Lane, Ted Healy, Johnny Davis, Alan Mowbray, Frances Langford, Hugh Herbert, Glenda Farrell, Allyn Joslyn, Benny Goodman and his orchestra, Harry James and (playing herself) Louella Parsons; or the clutch of delightful Johnny Mercer-Richard Whiting songs. These included: Can't Teach My Heart New Tricks, I'm Like A Fish Out Of Water, I've Hitched My Wagon To A Star, Let That Be A Lesson To You, Silhouetted In The Moonlight, Sing You Son Of A Gun, and what has since become the industry's unofficial theme song. Hooray For Hollywood.

◁ **The Patient in Room 18**, a competent hour-long thriller about the murder of a hospital patient and the theft of $100,000 worth of radium, starred Patric Knowles (centre) as the detective who solves the mystery (he just happens to be a patient at that very hospital when the crimes are being committed). Ann Sheridan (right) was his leading lady. It was neatly written by Eugene Solow and Robertson White from a story by Mignon G. Eberhart. Capably directed by Bobby Connolly and Crane Wilbur for associate producer Bryan Foy, it also featured Eric Stanley, John Ridgely, Rosella Towne, Harland Tucker, Cliff Clark and Jean Benedict. (First National.)

A romance with a dirt-track auto-racing background, **The Daredevil Drivers** paired Dick Purcell (centre) and Beverly Roberts for romance, with indifferent results. Written by Sherman Lowe from a story by Charles Condon, and directed by B. Reeves Eason who was more at home in the action sequences than with the love scenes, it also featured Joan Blondell's sister Gloria, Gordon Oliver and Charles Foy, with Al Herman (left) and Ferris Taylor (right) in support. The associate producer was Bryan Foy. (First National.)

There was one joke at the heart of a semi-musical called **Swing Your Lady**, and not a very good one at that. In a desperate attempt to remain solvent, an unsuccessful wrestling promoter hits on the idea of matching a dim-witted giant with an Amazonian lady blacksmith. An unhappy Humphrey Bogart starred as the promoter; Nat Pendleton (left) was the hunk of beef on which Bogart's hopes rested, and Louise Fazenda played the unfortunate lady wrestler. Also cast were Penny Singleton, Frank McHugh (right), Allen Jenkins, Ronald Reagan and Leon Frank. Joseph Schrank and Maurice Leo were responsible for the screenplay (from the play by Kenyon Nicholson and Charles Robinson) and Ray Enright was the director. He was given assistance on the musical numbers from Bobby Connolly. Songs included: Mountain Swingaroo, Hillbilly From Tenth Avenue, The Old Apple Tree, Swing Your Lady and Dig Me A Grave In Missouri (by M.K. Jerome and Jack Scholl).

Is it better to lose gracefully than to fight for ▷ what one wants? Or is life one long struggle in which only the fittest survive? In **Love, Honour and Behave**, Wayne Morris and Priscilla Lane (foreground) have to come up with the right answer if their marriage is to be saved, and they opt for the battleground. Veering uneasily between comedy and farce, the film was a rather unsatisfactory hybrid which did, however, benefit from the two engaging central performances. It was written by Clements Ripley, Robert Buckner and Michel Jacoby from a story by Stephen Vincent Benet, and directed by Stanley Logan for producer Hal B. Wallis and his associate Lou Edelman. Also cast were John Litel (right), Mona Barrie (centre right), Thomas Mitchell (centre left), Dick Foran, Dickie Moore, Barbara O'Neill (left) and Margaret Irving. Song: Bei Mir Bist du Schoen (by Sammy Cahn, Saul Chaplin and Sholom Secunda).

In **Blondes at Work**, ace reporter Torchy Blane (Glenda Farrell, right) was sent to jail for contempt of court. She still got her scoop, however, by solving the mystery surrounding the murder of a department store owner and emerged with her reputation ruffled but untarnished. The writer was Albert DeMond who relied heavily on coincidence to see his story through to its inevitable climax. The director was Frank McDonald, and the cast included Barton MacLane as Torchy's boring detective fiancé, Tom Kennedy, Betty Compson (left), Rosella Towne and John Ridgely. The associate producer was Bryan Foy.

Barton MacLane (centre) had a win on points in **The Kid Comes Back**, a boxing melodrama which featured him as a long-standing fighter who has never quite made it, but still hopes for a crack at the title. With little help from George Bricker's tired screenplay (story by E.J. Flanagan), MacLane's performance energized Bryan Foy's production, turning the routine into the worthwhile. B. Reeves Eason directed, with a cast that included Wayne Morris (left), Dickie Jones (centre left), June Travis (right), Maxie Rosenbloom and Joseph Crehan.
▽

◁ Two Penrods for the price of one was the main selling point of **Penrod and His Twin Brother**, an amiable adolescent-orientated adventure, and a vehicle for the Mauch twins (centre). Based on characters created by Booth Tarkington, but with a story line and screenplay by William Jacobs and Hugh Cummings that was light years away from what Tarkington might have devised (Penrod's double materializes from Chicago and becomes involved in some junior G-men antics), it also featured Jackie Morrow, Frank Craven, Spring Byington, Charles Halton, Claudia Coleman and Phillip Hurlic. William McGann directed and the associate producer was Bryan Foy.

Not renowned for quality Westerns, the studio made a stab at putting matters to rights with **Gold is Where You Find It**, a largish scale, Technicolored adventure, respectably directed by Michael Curtiz from a screenplay by Warren Duff and Robert Buckner (original story by Clements Ripley). All about California gold-rush miners and their clash with local ranchers, it starred George Brent (right), Claude Rains, Olivia de Havilland, and Margaret Lindsay (centre left), with John Litel, Marcia Ralston (left), Barton MacLane, Tim Holt (centre right), Sidney Toler and Henry O'Neill in support. It looked impressive and had its fair share of action, including a well-staged landslide. But gold it wasn't, as producer Hal Wallis found out from the disappointing box-office returns. (First National.)
▽

△

Kay Francis' (left) attempts to rescue her husband Pat O'Brien's (right) failing advertising agency was construed by him as meddling, and led to all sorts of marital complications in **Women Are Like That**. Horace Jackson's screenplay (story by Albert Carr) attempted but failed to come to grips with the perennial battle of the sexes, and not even the happy ending salvaged the exercise. Stanley Logan directed it for associate producer Robert Lord, with a cast which included Ralph Forbes, Melville Cooper, Thurston Hall, Grant Mitchell, Gordon Oliver and John Eldredge. (First National.)

△

Over the Wall was a lightweight prison film with a happy ending. It starred Dick Foran (right), framed for a murder he did not commit, John Litel as the prison chaplain who helps him to prove his innocence, and June Travis as the girl he settles for. In Sing-Sing Foran – like Richard Barthelmess before him in *Weary River* (1929) – discovers he has a talent for singing and, on his release, determines to become a crooner. It was written by Crane Wilbur and George Bricker (from a story by Lewis E. Lawes) and directed by Frank McDonald for associate producer Bryan Foy. Also cast were Dick Purcell, Tommy Bupp (centre), Veda Ann Borg, George E. Stone and Ward Bond (left). Songs included: One More Tomorrow, Have You Met My Lulu and Little White House On The Hill (by M.K. Jerome and Jack Scholl).

△

Based on an unsuccessful play by Damon Runyon and Howard Lindsay, **A Slight Case of Murder** starred Edward G. Robinson (right), Jane Bryan, Willard Parker and Ruth Donnelly (centre right). The story of a beer baron (Robinson) who, with the repeal of Prohibition, goes straight, only to find his considerable fortune dwindling because his beer – which he has never tasted – is undrinkable, it was a pleasant farce which successfully burlesqued the underworld. Wittily scripted by Earl Baldwin and Joseph Schrank and directed by Lloyd Bacon with an infectious sense of fun, it also featured Allen Jenkins, Margaret Hamilton (left), Bobby Jordan (centre left), Eric Stanley and Harold Huber. Hal B. Wallis produced; Sam Bischoff was his associate. (First National.)

He Couldn't Say No starred Frank McHugh (right front) as a timid advertising clerk who, after a series of unlikely events involving a statue called 'Courage', finally gets the girl of his dreams rather than the one thrust on him by a domineering Cora Witherspoon. Robertson White, Joseph Schrank and Ben Grauman Kohn wrote the nonsense from a story by Norman Matson; the director was Lewis Seiler, and the cast included Jane Wyman, Berton Churchill, Diana Lewis and Ferris Taylor. The associate producer was Bryan Foy.

▽

Convinced that she has a father, little Janet Chapman (centre), an orphan brought up by nuns in an orphanage, and the heroine of **Little Miss Thoroughbred**, sets out, one day, to find him. What she finds, instead, is a gambler called Nails Morgan (John Litel, left) who, through a series of singularly implausible events, decides to adopt her. Written by George Bricker and Albert DeMond with a sugar-coated pen, and sentimentally directed by John Farrow, it also featured Ann Sheridan (right), Frank McHugh, Eric Stanley and Robert Homans. The associate producer was Bryan Foy.

▽

In **Accidents Will Happen**, Ronald Reagan (right) played an incorruptible young insurance claims adjuster, who, after his wife (Sheila Bromley) does the dirty on him, decides to eschew his honest life for one of crime. Partnered by Gloria Blondell (left), he enters the fake-accident racket, and becomes a master of fraud until the law catches up with him. Written by George Bricker and Anthony Coldeway and directed by William Clemens for associate producer Bryan Foy, it was a moderately entertaining programmer which a little more conviction in all departments would have improved considerably. Also in it were Dick Purcell, Addison Richards, Hugh O'Connell, Janet Shaw, Andy Lawlor and Kenneth Harlan.

▽

In **Fools For Scandal**, an impoverished ▷ French Marquis (Fernand Gravet, left), in a rather elaborate prank, instals himself as cook and butler to a film star (Carole Lombard in order to compromise her into acquiescence. The material totally deflated Allen Jenkins, Isabel Jeans, Marie Wilson and Marcia Ralston (right) – not to mention its two stars and producer-director Mervyn Le Roy. Only Ralph Bellamy, as an insurance agent in love with Miss Lombard, brought an air of competence to this forlorn comedy. The screenplay, by Herbert and Joseph Fields, was adapted from *Return Engagement*, a play by Nancy Hamilton, Rosemary Casey and James Shute. Rodgers and Hart were commissioned to provide the film with several songs, most of which were removed from the final release print, or relegated to background music. Those that did survive included 'There's A Boy In Harlem' and 'How Can You Forget?' A sequence called 'Le Petit Harlem', directed by Bobby Connolly, also remained.

'Half-angel, half-siren, all woman!' pro-
claimed the ads for **Jezebel**, the highly
successful award-winning drama which the
studio fashioned for their often ill-used star
Bette Davis (right). The film was the
actress's compensation for Jack Warner's
refusal to loan her to David O. Selznick for
Gone With the Wind. Determined to out-
Scarlett Scarlett, Davis totally committed
herself to the role of Julie Marston, a wilful
Southern belle who does everything in her
considerable power to goad her fiancé
(Henry Fonda) into jealousy, but who
reforms when he is stricken with the plague.
Fortunately, director William Wyler, aware
of his leading lady's tendency to chew the
scenery if given half a chance, restrained her
mannerisms and toned down the energy
quotient of her performance, while at the
same time allowing none of the essential
Davis magnetism to disappear in the
process. The result was her finest performance to date and a second Oscar. In less
talented hands, there can be little doubt that

the rather trite story, based on a stage flop
by Owen Davis and scripted by Clements
Ripley, Abem Finkel and John Huston, with
assistance from Robert Buckner, would
have been faintly ludicrous. Apart from
Wyler's painstaking attention to atmosphere
and detail reflected in the overall quality of
the film, and Miss Davis' towering central
performance, the soggy plot was kept this
side of credibility by Fay Bainter's (left)
sterling, Oscar-winning performance as
Aunt Belle, George Brent was miscast as the
rejected Buck Cantrell (but then, when
wasn't he!). Margaret Lindsay once again
played the 'other woman', without much
impact, while Spring Byington, Henry
O'Neill, Gordon Oliver and John Litel
contributed their usual solid performances.
Max Steiner wrapped it all up in one of
his most memorable scores. Hal B. Wallis
was the executive producer, Henry Blanke
his associate. The film cost the studio
$1,073,000 to make, but its success justified
the expense.

Dick Powell (left) undoubtedly welcomed the change of pace that **Cowboy from Brooklyn** offered, for it gave him an opportunity to indulge in a spot of light comedy. But the finished results were pitiful. The story of a singing drifter who takes a ranch job, is discovered by a talent scout (Pat O'Brien in the kind of role that by now seemed glued to him), and elevated into radio stardom, it did nothing for its star and even less for his fans. The screenplay, by Earl Baldwin, was based on a play by Louis Peletier and Robert Sloane, and featured Priscilla Lane (centre), Dick Foran (right), Ann Sheridan and Ronald Reagan. Hal B. Wallis produced and the associate was Lou Edelman. Lloyd Bacon directed. Songs included: I've Got A Heartful of Music, I'll Dream Tonight, Ride, Tenderfoot, Ride (by Johnny Mercer and Richard Whiting) and Cowboy From Brooklyn (by Johnny Mercer and Harry Warren).

The three corpses in residence in **Mystery House** weren't the only dead things in director Noel Smith's chiller. Sherman Lowe and Robertson White's screenplay (from a story by Mignon G. Eberhart) was pretty lifeless too; so were the performances of Dick Purcell, Ann Sheridan (right), Anne Nagel (left), Anthony Averill (centre left) and William Hopper (centre). All about a house full of killers and a detective determined to find out who's who and what's what, it offered no surprises and even fewer thrills. The associate producer was Bryan Foy. (First National.)

Busby Berkeley directed **Men Are Such Fools**, which starred Humphrey Bogart (left), Priscilla Lane (centre) and Wayne Morris (right), none of whom emerged with credit. The title certainly told the truth in the case of Bogart, who might have done better to invite suspension rather than appear in such lack-lustre material. The screenplay (by Norman Reilly Raine and Horace Jackson from a magazine story by Faith Baldwin), told of an ambitious secretary who plays off her footballer husband against Bogart in the hope of furthering her career via the air waves. Also sabotaged by the poor screenplay were Hugh Herbert, Penny Singleton, Johnnie Davis and Mona Barrie. The associate producer was David Lewis.

In **Torchy Blane in Panama,** Lola Lane (right) and Paul Kelly, as Torchy and her dreary assistant Steve, took over the roles created by Glenda Farrell and Barton MacLane, but apart from that it was the formula as before. All about a bank robbery in which a teller is slain, it involved miracle reporter Torchy in a trip to Panama to apprehend the culprit. Written by Anthony Coldeway (from characters created by Fred Nebel) and directed for associate producer Bryan Foy by William Clemens, it also featured Tom Kennedy, Anthony Averill, Betty Compson and Hugh O'Connell. (First National.)

As **The Amazing Dr. Clitterhouse**, Edward G. Robinson (left), in the role created on stage by Cedric Hardwicke, was slightly miscast as a psychiatrist, who, in order to study the criminal mentality, becomes a criminal himself and eventually resorts to cold-blooded murder. Robinson could not quite eliminate his *Little Caesar* (1931) origins from his performance, with the result that there was no element of surprise in his transformation from good guy to killer. Still, the John Wexley-John Huston screenplay (adapted from Barré Lyndon's play) was as deft as Anatole Litvak's direction, and the excellent cast included Claire Trevor, Humphrey Bogart (right), Gale Page, Donald Crisp, Allen Jenkins, Thurston Hall, John Litel, Henry O'Neill and Maxie Rosenbloom (centre). The associate producer was Robert Lord. (First National.)

Mr. Chump, an ineffectual comedy, featured Johnnie Davis (left) as a trumpet-playing dreamer who infects Lola Lane (centre) Penny Singleton (right), Donald Briggs, and Chester Clute with a desire to speculate on various business deals. Unfortunately, the speculations go awry and his colleagues all land up in jail. George Bricker wrote it, director William Clemens was unable to do much with it, and the associate producer was Bryan Foy.

Warner Bros. gave radio-star Rudy Vallee ▷ (right) another crack at movie stardom in **Gold Diggers in Paris**. But, as was the case with Kenny Baker, it was not to be, and the hit of the show, as had so often happened before, was Busby Berkeley, whose staging of the musical numbers, though less elaborate than on some previous occasions (budgets for musicals were being drastically reduced at this point in the studio's history), were just as inventive. Earl Baldwin and Warren Duff's screenplay – which had Vallee and his troupe of nightclub dancers inadvertently taking part in an international dance festival in Paris under the guise of the American Ballet Company – gave Berkeley ample opportunity to bring on the dancing girls, and Curt Bois plenty of scope for his particular brand of comedy. Also cast were Hugh Herbert, Allen Jenkins, Gloria Dickson, Rosemary Lane (left), Melville Cooper, Ed Brophy and Eddie Anderson. Sam Bischoff was the associate producer and Ray Enright the director. Songs included: The Latin Quarter, I Wanna Go Back To Bali, Put That Down In Writing, A Stranger In Paree (by Al Dubin and Harry Warren) and Day Dreaming All Night Long, Waltz Of The Flowers and My Adventure (by Johnny Mercer and Harry Warren).

△ Bonita Granville (right) starred as the **Beloved Brat** (released in Britain as **A Dangerous Age**) – an adolescent with parent problems. Mom and Dad have too much money, don't know how to handle her, and bring about a minor revolution in the household which the compassionate understanding of Dolores Costello (as a teacher) is able to quash. Donald Crisp was the child's father, Natalie Moorhead her mother, with other parts going to Lucille Gleason, Emmett Vogan, Donald Briggs, Loia Cheaney and Stymie Beard (left). It was directed by Arthur Lubin, who couldn't decide whether he was making a treatise on child psychology or a movie; and the associate producer was Bryan Foy. Lawrence Kimble wrote it from the story *Too Much of Everything* by Jean Negulesco. (First National.)

A remake of *Courage* (1930) from the play by Tom Barry, **My Bill** starred Kay Francis (left) as a widow with four children, three of whom give her a rough time (in the original film, the mother had seven children, one of whom was illegitimate). The film had little to recommend it except the performances of John Litel and Helena Evans in a cast that also included Dickie Moore (back to camera) as the son who remains on his mother's side, Bonita Granville (centre right), Anita Louise (centre) and Bobby Jordan (right). Vincent Sherman and Robertson White's screenplay was as pedestrian as John Farrow's direction. Bryan Foy was associate producer. (First National.)

When Were You Born? was an astrological thriller which starred Anna May Wong (centre) as a zodiac freak. She volunteers to help the police track down a murderer by sifting through several suspects' birth signs, as well as any other astrological data associated with them. More Horoscope than Horror-scope, the script was written by Anthony Coldeway (story by Manly P. Hall), directed by William McGann, and also featured Margaret Lindsay (right), Lola Lane, Anthony Averill (left) and Charles Wilson. The associate producer was Bryan Foy. (First National.)
▽

The message behind **White Banners**, which Lenore Coffee, Cameron Rogers and Abem Finkel adapted from a story by Lloyd C. Douglas, was simple: turn the other cheek in adversity. And that is exactly what small town professor Claude Rains (left) does when he finds he has been cheated out of the patent of the iceless ice-box he has been working on. Undaunted, he returns to the drawing board and comes up trumps with an even more sophisticated ice-box. The film's message was competently conveyed by director Edmund Goulding, and the sheer goodness inherent in Douglas' Christian doctrine was echoed in the performances of Rains and Fay Bainter as his wife. Others in the cast were youngsters Jackie Cooper (right) and Bonita Granville, Henry O'Neill, Kay Johnson and James Stephenson. Hal B. Wallis was the producer, Henry Blanke his associate.
▽

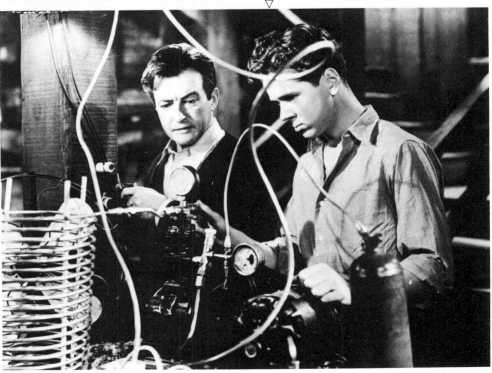

△

Strictly for juveniles, **Penrod's Double Trouble** was a likeable melodrama in which young Penrod is kidnapped, then rescued when his pet dog leads his friends to the deserted old house in which he is being held captive. Based on characters created by Booth Tarkington, it was written by Ernest Booth and Crane Wilbur, and directed by Lewis Seiler. Billy and Bobby Mauch (centre) starred, with Dick Purcell, Gene and Kathleen Lockhart, Hugh O'Connell and Phillip Hurlic also in it. The associate producer was Bryan Foy. (First National.)

While audiences could not get enough of Errol Flynn the swashbuckler, a little of Flynn (right) the light, urbane comedian was quite sufficient to ensure their loyalty to Cary Grant! Although **Four's A Crowd** was a decided improvement on Flynn's first fumbling attempt at comedy (in *The Perfect Specimen*, 1937) it was, nonetheless, forgettable nonsense. But it *did* feature Walter Connolly, Hugh Herbert, Franklin Pangborn, Herman Bing and Margaret Hamilton, as well as Olivia de Havilland (left), Rosalind Russell and Patric Knowles in more stellar roles. The screwball story of a public relations man whose wealthiest client also happens to be his most difficult, it was written by Casey Robinson and Sig Herzig and directed by Michael Curtiz for associate producer David Lewis.

▽

△

Bonita Granville (right) starred as Nancy Drew in **Nancy Drew, Detective**, a mystery yarn about an old lady who bequeathes a quarter of a million dollars to a school, is thought to be eccentric, and is kidnapped by a gang of crooks who want the money for themselves. Enter Nancy Drew who proves that there is nothing eccentric about the woman, and sees to it that the money goes to the school for which it was intended. Contrived by Kenneth Gamet from a story by Carolyn Keene, and directed with a deficiency of thrills by William Clemens, it also featured John Litel, James Stephenson, Frankie Thomas (left) and Frank Orth. The associate producer was Bryan Foy.

△

Sob sister Torchy Blane's adventures continued with **Torchy Gets Her Man**, which reinstated Glenda Farrell (right) and Barton MacLane as the intrepid reporter and her man, detective Steve McBride. Together they bring a notorious counterfeiter (Willard Robertson) to justice. Other parts went to Tom Kennedy (left), George Guhl, John Ridgely and Tommy Jackson. It was written by Albert DeMond and directed by William Beaudine for associate producer Bryan Foy.

◁ Milton Krims wrote the intelligent screenplay (from the novel by Myron Brinig) for **The Sisters**, in which Bette Davis starred as the eldest of three sisters who, each in her own particular way, discovers that life is made up of more or less equal portions of pain and joy. The film covered a period of four years – from Theodore Roosevelt's inauguration to the election of William Howard Taft – and featured the San Francisco earthquake of 1906 as its climax. As potboilers go, it was above average entertainment, whose most interesting aspect was the casting of Errol Flynn (as a newspaper reporter) opposite Davis (centre). Others included were Anita Louise (right), Ian Hunter, Beulah Bondi, Alan Hale, Jane Bryan (left), Dick Foran, Henry Travers, Patric Knowles, Lee Patrick, Laura Hope Crews, Harry Davenport and Mayo Methot. It was directed by Anatole Litvak and produced by Hal B. Wallis with David Lewis as his associate.

Comedians Olsen and Johnson were the ▷
original choice for the roles of two daffy
screenwriters in the Sam and Bella Spewack
adaptation of their Broadway hit **Boy
Meets Girl**. George Abbott was the intended
director, and Marion Davies slated for the
female lead. But with the unavailability of
Messrs Olsen and Johnson and the carping
of Miss Davies at certain aspects of the
script, the studio decided to give James Cagney (left), now earning $150,000 per film
plus 10% of the profits, and Pat O'Brien
(centre right) a crack at it, with Marie
Wilson (centre) standing in for Miss Davies,
and director Lloyd Bacon in place of Abbott.
The result, despite the fact that none of the
leads was ideally cast, was another solid
smash for Warner Bros. Audiences loved
the preposterous yarn about a couple of
prank-prone writers who, just for fun, con-
coct a Western, which, to the chagrin of its
egotistical star (Dick Foran) features a scene-
stealing infant. Ralph Bellamy (right), Frank
McHugh, Ronald Reagan, Penny Singleton,
Bruce Lester, Paul Clark and Dennis Moore
were also in it. Bacon directed it all at
the speed of light for producer Hal B. Wallis and associate Sam Bischoff. Song: With A
Pain In My Heart (by M.K. Jerome and
Jack Scholl).

The Busby Berkeley-directed **Comet Over
Broadway** revealed its origins all too clearly.
Based on a short story by Faith Baldwin
which appeared in *Cosmopolitan*, it was a
soap-opera *par excellence*, with sentimentality and melodrama constantly at loggerheads. The story of a married woman's
devouring ambition to become an actress, it
starred Kay Francis as the actress, John
Litel as a husband driven to murder, and
Ian Hunter as the sophisticated impresario
who helps the actress to realize her dream
by offering her the star role in a Broadway
play. Berkeley's genius was sadly compromised in his attempts to breathe life into
Mark Hellinger and Robert Buckner's still-
born screenplay and the result was decidedly
forgettable; a comet that was burned out
before it even began. Also cast were
Donald Crisp, Minna Gombell, Sybil Jason,
Melville Cooper (right) and Ian Keith (left).
The associate producer was Bryan Foy.
(First National.)

Kay Francis' disenchantment with the
studio (losing *Tovarich* to Claudette Colbert
was a particularly bitter pill to swallow),
and the paucity of good roles coming her
way, resulted in a threatened law suit and a
fall from grace with the studio's executives.
Jack Warner's displeasure manifested itself
in giving her films like **Secrets of an
Actress,** a banal story in which she was
cast (right) as an actress torn between
architect Ian Hunter, who has promised to
finance a play for her, and his urbane but
married partner George Brent (left). It took
three writers (Milton Krims, Rowland Leigh
and Julius J. Epstein) to devise a screenplay
that director William Keighley was unable
to rescue. The best performance came from
Isabel Jeans as Francis' inebriated room-
mate. Also cast were Gloria Dickson, Penny
Singleton and Dennis Moore. David Lewis
was the associate producer.

An efficiently made, moderately entertaining crime melodrama, **Racket Busters**
top-cast Humphrey Bogart (left) as a no-
nonsense gangleader who works a protection racket on New York's truckers. His
activities are opposed by George Brent
(right), a popular trucker whose resistance
Bogart interprets as an invitation to war.
Also cast were Gloria Dickson, Allen
Jenkins, Walter Abel, Henry O'Neill and
Penny Singleton. Lloyd Bacon directed from
a screenplay by Robert Rossen and Leonardo
Bercovici and made the most of the film's 71
minute running time. The associate producer was Sam Bischoff for Cosmopolitan
Productions.
▽

Crime School was a piece of social comment
dressed up as entertainment. Its message
– that brutalizing youngsters in institutions
only made their delinquent conditions worse
– was wrapped up in a palatable yarn which
◁ found Humphrey Bogart (right) as a Deputy
Commissioner of Correction. He takes over
the running of a reformatory, and through
the consideration he shows the lads, wins
their co-operation. The Dead End Kids
featured prominently, so did Gale Page as
the woman in Bogart's life; Cy Kendall
(left), Weldon Heyburn (centre) and Billy
Halop were also included in the cast. The
tough, sardonic and wise-cracking screenplay was by Crane Wilbur and Vincent
Sherman, and the director was Lewis
Seiler for associate producer Bryan Foy.
(First National.)

The attractive Technicolor photography (by Allen M. Davey) guaranteed that at least **Valley of the Giants**, a routine melodrama involving lumbermen and their brawls, would always be pleasing to the eye. For the rest, it was back to the assembly line as Wayne Morris (illustrated), Claire Trevor, Frank McHugh, Alan Hale, Donald Crisp, Charles Bickford and John Litel helped to convey an unmistakable feeling of *déjà vu* to the proceedings. Peter B. Kyne wrote the novel on which it was based, Seton I. Miller and Michael Fessier adapted it for the screen, and William Keighley directed it in the same way he might have directed traffic. The associate producer was Lou Edelman.

Every cliché known to mankind and then some surfaced in **Heart of the North**, a Northwest Mounted Police epic in Technicolor. Among the chief ingredients were a fur-trapper's daughter (Gloria Dickson), the fur-trapper himself (Russell Simpson), hero Dick Foran (illustrated), a clifftop skirmish, a canoe overturned by rapids, and a race against time to save an innocent man from a lynch mob. It was assembled, rather than written by Lee Katz and Vincent Sherman (story by William Byron Mowery) directed by Lewis Seiler, and featured Allen Jenkins, Patric Knowles, Janet Chapman, James Stephenson and Anthony Averill. The associate producer was Bryan Foy. (First National.)

◁ All about a pleasant but witless young woman who, because of the bad company she keeps, finds herself serving a prison sentence before finally being rehabilitated, **Girls on Probation**, written by Crane Wilbur, was a melodrama ponderously directed by William McGann. Jane Bryan (right) and Ronald Reagan starred, with other roles going to Anthony Averill, Sheila Bromley (left), Henry O'Neill, Elisabeth Risdon and Sig Rumann. The associate producer was Bryan Foy. (First National.)

Dick Powell only sang one song ('You Must Have Been A Beautiful Baby') and hummed another ('There's A Sunny Side To Every Situation') in **Hard to Get**, an improbable romance which found audiences hard to please. About an impoverished but go-getting young architect who is reduced to working as a filling-station attendant, the movie co-starred Olivia de Havilland (left) as a spoiled young heiress who seeks revenge on Powell (right) after he refuses to give her credit when she runs out of both gas and cash. In this instance, getting her revenge took the form, after a few false starts, of falling in love with the object of her anger. Charles Winninger played her millionaire dad who eventually puts up the money to finance one of Powell's architectural schemes, with other roles going to Thurston Hall (as an all purpose butler), Isabel Jeans (as Winninger's wife), Bonita Granville (as his younger daughter), Penny Singleton (as his maid) and Allen Jenkins (as Powell's filling-station assistant.) It was written by Jerry Wald, Maurice Leo, and Richard Macaulay (from a story by Wally Klein, Joseph Schrank and Stephen Morehouse Avery), and directed for producer Hal B. Wallis and associate producer Sam Bischoff by Ray Enright.

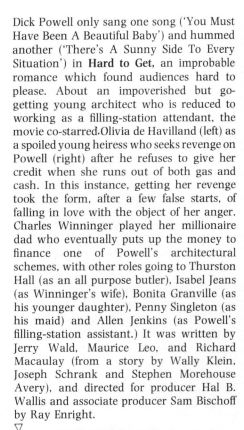

◁ After their comedy success in *Boy Meets Girl*, James Cagney and Pat O'Brien teamed up for **Angels With Dirty Faces**, a tough drama masquerading as social comment, and typical of the studio's belief that people are all victims of society; the more corrupt the society the more corrupt the victims. Cagney (right, with the Dead End Kids) played Rocky Sullivan, a well-known criminal who, on returning to his old slum-infested neighbourhood finds himself something of a hero, a fact which pleases him as much as it disturbs the local parish priest (O'Brien) who worries that Rocky's presence will have an adverse influence on the lads, and undermine his own authority over them. In the film's memorable final scene, with Cagney about to meet his maker via the electric chair, O'Brien begs him to become a coward and turn yellow, thus destroying the hero-worshipping boys' illusions about him. Vigorously directed by Michael Curtiz from an intensely earnest screenplay by John Wexley and Warren Duff (story by Rowland Brown), it showed off Cagney at his histrionic best. Also cast were Humphrey Bogart, Ann Sheridan, George Bancroft and Marilyn Knowlden. The associate producer was Sam Bischoff. (First National.)

Enthusiasm was the key-note of **Brother Rat**, a comedy about three cadets at Virginia Military School, and the three girls who occupy their love-lives. Ronald Reagan, Wayne Morris (right) and Eddie Albert were the guys; Priscilla Lane (left), Jane Wyman and Jane Bryan the dolls. Between them they injected a lot of fun into the Richard Macaulay – Jerry Wald screenplay (based on a play by John Monks Jr and Fred Finkelhoffe), and with able assistance from director William Keighley, helped keep the caper buoyant. The best touch was expectant father Eddie Albert sneaking off parade duty to practice baby-talk on a total stranger's uncomprehending offspring. Joining in the merriment were Johnnie Davis, Henry O'Neill and Gordon Oliver. Hal B. Wallis and Robert Lord were producer and associate producer respectively. It was remade in 1952 as *About Face*. (First National.)

▽

◁ **Garden of the Moon** was an amiable, small-scale musical set, for most of the time, in a night club called Garden of the Moon. The club's dyspeptic owner (Pat O'Brien, left) is at loggerheads with band-leader John Payne (a role originally intended for Dick Powell) over the affections of Margaret Lindsay (right), in a role originally offered to Bette Davis. Miss Davis decided that suspension was preferable to the part. The film was directed by Busby Berkeley (his last musical for the studio) without the kind of panache his admirers had come to expect of him, from a screenplay by Jerry Wald and Richard Macaulay. Also featured were Johnnie Davis, Melville Cooper, Isabel Jeans and Penny Singleton. The score (pleasant but unmemorable), was by Al Dubin and Harry Warren with assistance from Johnny Mercer. The associate producer was Lou Edelman. Songs included: Garden Of The Moon, The Girl Friend Of The Whirling Dervish, Love Is Where You Find It (not to be confused with the more celebrated song sung by Kathryn Grayson in MGM's *The Kissing Bandit*, 1948), The Lady On The Two Cent Stamp and Confidentially. (First National.)

John Garfield caused something of a ▷ sensation as Mickey Borden in **Four Daughters**, a beguiling account of how romance affects the lives of four girls in a small-town American family. Garfield's characteristically shabby presence, his indolent manner and his caustic sense of humour, imparted a sense of reality to what would certainly otherwise have been a highly sentimental piece of pulp fiction, and made him an overnight star. The personality created by Garfield (right, with Priscilla Lane) in **Four Daughters** (and exploited so brilliantly by director Michael Curtiz) was to feature, with only slight variations, in many future movies. Lenore Coffee and Julius Epstein wrote the screenplay from Fannie Hurst's story *Sister Act*, and the associate producer was Henry Blanke. Others in the cast were Rosemary and Lola Lane, Claude Rains, Jeffrey Lynn, Frank McHugh, Dick Foran, May Robson and Gale Page.

◁ Edmund Goulding's **The Dawn Patrol** followed the earlier (1930) Howard Hawks version and even included some aerial footage from the first film. Hawks' theme – the tragedy of sending men to almost certain death in the service of their country – was also the theme of the remake, but while Errol Flynn (centre right) as brave officer Courtney and David Niven (left) as his best friend were more convincing than Richard Barthelmess and Douglas Fairbanks Jr, their counterparts in the 1930 version, there was no question that, while airborne, the Hawks film was superior. Seton I. Miller and Dan Totheroh wrote the screenplay (from the John Monk Saunders story), and Max Steiner the stirring score. Also cast were Basil Rathbone (centre left), Donald Crisp (right), Melville Cooper, Barry Fitzgerald and Carl Esmond. The producer was Hal B. Wallis.

△

There was little cohesion, and even less conviction, in **Broadway Musketeers**, the story of three women, Margaret Lindsay (right), Ann Sheridan (centre) and Marie Wilson (left), who were once orphans in the same home and whose lives in adulthood continue to impinge on one another. Based on a story by Don Ryan and Ken Gamet, who also wrote the screenplay, it was directed by John Farrow for associate producer Bryan Foy, and featured John Litel, little Janet Chapman (who never grew any taller or older despite the several years spanned by the film), Dick Purcell, Richard Bond and Anthony Averill. Songs: Has It Ever Occurred To You? and Who Said That This Isn't Love (by M.K. Jerome and Jack Scholl).

1939

Apart from the controversial **Confessions of a Nazi Spy**, the last year of the decade was a pretty routine one for Warner Bros. despite three fine performances in three above average films: from Bette Davis (**Dark Victory**), Paul Muni (**Juarez**) and James Cagney (**The Roaring Twenties**). **Dark Victory**, one of the studio's biggest moneymakers, was nominated for a Best Picture Academy Award, and its star for Best Actress. Neither, in the event, stood a chance against **Gone with the Wind** and Vivien Leigh, though the *New York Times* voted **Dark Victory** and **Juarez** as two of the year's Ten Best films. The only Oscar won by Warner Bros. in 1939 was for a short subject film called **Sons of Liberty**, directed by Michael Curtiz with Claude Rains. Brian Aherne was nominated as Best Supporting Actor for his performance in **Juarez** but lost to Thomas Mitchell in **Stagecoach** (United Artists). Anton Grot was nominated for Best Art Direction for **The Private Lives of Elizabeth and Essex** but lost to Lyle Wheeler for **Gone With The Wind**.

By the end of 1939, James Cagney was earning $12,500 a week, Paul Muni $11,500, Edward G. Robinson $8,000, Claude Rains $6,000, George Raft $5,000, Errol Flynn $5,000, Bette Davis $4,000, Pat O'Brien $4,000, Frank McHugh $1,600, John Garfield $1,500, Olivia de Havilland $1,250, Priscilla Lane $750, Ann Sheridan $500 and Jane Wyman $200. The net profit was $1,740,907, for the year. The studio's other top box-office hits were: **Angels with Dirty Faces** (released November, 1938) and **Dodge City**.

After *Cowboy from Brooklyn* and *Hard to Get*, Dick Powell became a three-time loser with **Going Places** in which he didn't even get to sing its hit song, 'Jeepers Creepers'. That honour went to Louis Armstrong. The fourth screen version of Victor Mapes and William Collier's play *The Hottentot*, it cast Powell (centre) as a sports-goods salesman who, in order to stimulate trade, poses as a famous jockey, mixes with a set of horse-loving socialites and falls in love with Anita Louise. The jape misfires, however, when he finds himself having to ride Miss Louise's horse in a forthcoming race. Believe it or not, he wins. Ray Enright directed the Hal B. Wallis production (associate producer Benjamin Glazer), and Jerry Wald, Sig Herzig and Maurice Leo wrote it. Also cast were Allen Jenkins, Ronald Reagan (centre left), Walter Catlett, Thurston Hall and Harold Huber. **Going Places** unfortunately went nowhere. Songs included: Say It With A Kiss and Oh, What A Horse Was Charley (by Harry Warren and Johnny Mercer). (First National.)

◁ **Off the Record** starred Joan Blondell as a newspaper reporter whose investigative piece on the slot-machine rackets sends young Bobby Jordan (right) to reform school. To make amends, Blondell (left), assisted by boyfriend and colleague Pat O'Brien (centre) more or less adopts the youth and points him along the straight-and-narrow path of domesticity. Attractively performed, but hardly informative about the problems of juvenile delinquency, or, for that matter, the workings of a major newspaper, the film was nonetheless a moderately entertaining affair whose social pretensions never got in the way of the plot. It was written by Niven Busch, Lawrence Kimble and Earl Baldwin from a story by Saul Elkins and Sally Sandlin, and directed by James Flood with a cast that included Alan Baxter, William Davidson, Morgan Conway and Clay Clement. The associate producer was Sam Bischoff.

Though the plot of **Torchy Blane in Chinatown** (about a series of murders connected with the smuggling of Chinese jade curios) pivoted on Oriental skul-duggery, Chinatown itself did not feature in the adventure at all. Again Glenda Farrell (right) was the insatiable reporter, with Barton MacLane (left) as her dim-witted detective friend. George Bricker wrote it from a story by Will F. Jenkins, William Beaudine directed, and the cast included Henry O'Neill, Tom Kennedy, Patric Knowles and James Stephenson. The associate producer was Bryan Foy. (First National.)
▽

The studio's only comedy to reach the screen via Broadway in 1939 was **Yes, My Darling Daughter**. The story of a young girl (Priscilla Lane, centre right) who announces to her family that she intends to spend a weekend with her fiancé (Jeffrey Lynn, centre), it brought upon itself the wrath of the New York State Board of Censors who forbade its release unless certain 'suggestive' lines and scenes were removed. With a snip-snip here and a snip-snip there, the producer Hal B. Wallis finally managed to satisfy the omnipotent powers that be and, thanks to the resultant publicity, found himself with a box-office winner on his hands, so much so that the film opened simultaneously in two Broadway cinemas. A totally innocent comedy with impeccable morals, the film also featured Ian Hunter and Fay Bainter (centre left) as Miss Lane's parents, Roland Young (left), May Robson (right), Genevieve Tobin and Robert Homans. It was directed by William Keighley who kept it light, breezy and inoffensive, and was adapted from Mark Reed's play by Casey Robinson. The associate producer was Benjamin Glazer. (First National.)
▽

Looking as though he were *en route* to a fancy dress ball, and sounding like an expatriate from Manhattan, James Cagney, his tongue very firmly in his cheek, took the law into his own hands in **The Oklahoma Kid** in order to avenge his family's honour and the lynching of his old man (Hugh Sothern). The customers enjoyed it all (there was a lot to enjoy, especially Humphrey Bogart's blacker-than-black heavy), and the sheer pleasure of hearing Cagney (centre left) sing 'Rockabye Baby' in Spanish and 'I Don't Want To Play In Your Yard', was alone worth the price of admission. Working from a script by Warren Duff, Robert Buckner and Edward E. Paramore, director Lloyd Bacon directed with his customary zing. Rosemary Lane (left, insipid next to the Cagney flamboyance) provided the feminine interest. Also in it were Donald Crisp (right), Joe Devlin (centre right), Harvey Stephens, Ward Bond, John Miljan and Arthur Aylesworth. The associate producer was Sam Bischoff.

▽

△

A remake of W.R. Burnett's *Doctor Socrates* (1935), with Kay Francis (right) in the Paul Muni role, **King of the Underworld** had its moments but lost its balance towards the end and toppled into absurdity. Humphrey Bogart (left) once again essayed his familiar interpretation of a gang-lord-cum-Napoleon, with Kay Francis as a surgeon who, though innocent, finds herself implicated when her husband is murdered by Bogart. All that was really required to go along with the implausibilities in the George Bricker–Vincent Sherman screenplay was suspension of disbelief. Lewis Seiler directed and his cast included James Stephenson, John Eldredge and Jessie Busley. The associate producer was Bryan Foy.

◁ The rather half-hearted story-line devised by Michael Fessier for **Wings of the Navy** – Olivia de Havilland (left) switching romantic allegiance from older brother George Brent (centre left) to younger brother John Payne (right) – was an unnecessary garnish to the red meat of the film. Basically, the film was a documentary about the Pensacola Naval Air Training Station's process to turn new recruits into skilled pilots. It was made with the co-operation of the US Government, and was full of interesting information concerning flying dreadnoughts, the launching and landing of seaplanes, and combat flying. There was no room, however, for romance to rear its head, and consequently when it did, was about as useful to the proceedings as a third wing. Frank McHugh, John Litel, Victor Jory, Henry O'Neill, John Ridgely and John Gallaudet were also among the cast; it was efficiently directed by Lloyd Bacon, and produced by Hal B. Wallis with Lou Edelman as associate producer.

△

John Garfield's second starring role, in the moderately profitable **They Made Me A Criminal**, didn't have quite the impact of *Four Daughters*, though it did consolidate his position as a major Hollywood talent. A remake of *The Life of Jimmy Dolan* (1933), it was about a boxer who, falsely accused of murder after a drunken brawl, is forced to travel West. He fetches up at a desert ranch run by two women and the six New York ruffians (the Dead End Kids) they are trying to reform. Garfield (right) falls in love with one of the women (Gloria Dickson), and complicates his life still further when he agrees to enter a prize-fight contest in order to raise money for the ranch. Surprisingly, it was directed by Busby Berkeley (resisting overhead shots and the temptation to turn the Dead End Kids into chorus-boys), in a sober, workmanlike way; the screenplay was by Sig Herzig (based on a novel by Bertram Millhauser and Beulah Marie Dix), and the photography by James Wong Howe. The movie also starred Claude Rains (somewhat miscast as a detective on Garfield's trail), Ann Sheridan and May Robson, with John Ridgely, Barbara Pepper and Ward Bond in support. Hal Wallis produced with Benjamin Glazer as associate.

Altogether more successful (in its modest way) than *Nancy Drew, Detective*, **Nancy Drew, Reporter** again featured Bonita Granville (right) as the sleuthing reporter who, on this occasion, sets out to help a woman accused of murder prove her innocence. Needless to say, Nancy, (with assistance from her boyfriend Ted, played by Frankie Thomas), traces the real murderer, and justice is seen to be done. Kenneth Gamet wrote the script from his own story which, in turn, was based on characters created by Carolyn Keene. It was directed by William Clemens for associate producer Bryan Foy, and also featured John Litel, Frank Orth, Renie Riano, Vera Lewis, Louise Carter, Dickie Jones (left) and Mary Lee (centre). (First National.)

▽

A quickie, but with considerably more interest than most, **On Trial** was a murder drama in which a young lawyer (Edward Norris) takes over the defence of prisoner John Litel (centre) and, with no co-operation at all from his client (who refuses to defend himself against the murder charge), proves his innocence, finds the man's lost wife (Margaret Lindsay, right) and restores him to her and his young daughter (Janet Chapman, left). Don Ryan wrote the screenplay (from a play by Elmer Rice) whose surprise ending added to its entertainment value. Terry Morse directed, the associate producer was Bryan Foy, and the cast included James Stephenson, Larry Williams, William Davidson and Gordon Hart.

▽

Not surprisingly, the subject of **Secret Service of the Air** was secret service investigators. It was a luke-warm drama with a tired plot line (by Raymond Schrock), about the smuggling of aliens across the border, and with the hero (Ronald Reagan, left) posing as a counterfeit money agent in order to apprehend the villains. Noel Smith directed for associate producer Bryan Foy, and the cast included John Litel, John Ridgely (right), Ila Rhodes, James Stephenson, Eddie Foy Jr, Rosella Towne (centre) and Larry Williams.

△
At the premiere of **Confessions of a Nazi Spy**, there were almost as many policemen and special agents in attendance as there were customers. Based on the revelations of former FBI agent Leon G. Turrou, and closely adhering to the facts of an actual spy trial involving high-ranking officials in the Reich and their American counterparts, it was the first major motion picture to deal with the incipient threat of Nazism and to warn the world of the peril in which democracy was being placed. If its message came through loud and clear at the time, its narrative line – involving the uncovering of a network of Nazi agents by a team of G-men led by Edward G. Robinson, (centre) who, together with Jack Warner and everyone else involved with the production, received threatening letters – was less compelling than the blatant anti-Nazi propaganda which was its *raison d'être*. Directed in a semi-documentary style by Anatole Litvak, and written (in secret), by Milton Krims and John Wexley, it also starred Francis Lederer, George Sanders, Paul Lukas, Henry O'Neill (left), Lya Lys and Sig Rumann. A moderate success in the US, it was banned in many countries in Europe. The associate producer was Robert Lord. (First National.)

John Garfield (left) commenced work on **Blackwell's Island** before the release of *Four Daughters*. When, in the middle of shooting, *Four Daughters* turned him into a star, the studio, uncharacteristically concerned that a major new talent was being wasted on a product unworthy of it, assigned Michael Curtiz to build up Garfield's role as a hard-hitting reporter – not that the stretching process added much to Crane Wilbur's screenplay. Still, the story, based by Wilbur and Lee Katz on an actual raid on Welfare Island prison in 1934, was very much in the studio's exposé tradition, and had reporter Garfield sentencing himself to prison then escaping in order to tell the world exactly what was going on inside. William McGann directed, and his handling of a cast that included Rosemary Lane (right), Dick Purcell and Victor Jory was nothing special. The associate producer was Bryan Foy. (First National.)

▽

△
The annual transcontinental race for women pilots was the subject of **Women in the Wind**, a tepid drama in which Kay Francis (right) simply *had* to win in order to get the money for her brother's operation. Based on a novel by Francis Walton and written for the screen by Lee Katz and Albert DeMond, it was directed by John Farrow, and featured William Gargan, Victor Jory, Maxie Rosenbloom, Eddie Foy Jr, and Eve Arden (left). The associate producer was Bryan Foy. It would be three years before Miss Francis filmed at Warner Bros. again.

Aimed at the youngsters, **Code of the Secret Service** was a 58 minute quickie in which a US Secret Service agent is sent to the Mexican border to apprehend a gang of counterfeiters. Ronald Reagan (left), Rosella Towne (right), Eddie Foy Jr and Moroni Olsen were in it; Lee Katz and Dean Franklin wrote it, the director was Noel Smith, and the associate producer Bryan Foy. (First National.)
▽

The adventures of ace-reporter Torchy Blane (Glenda Farrell, centre), and her slow-witted fiancé Steve (Barton MacLane, centre right) continued in **Torchy Runs for Mayor**. Here, our heroine unearths some damaging evidence against an underworld baron who is controlling the city by graft. The evidence leads to murder, and all sorts of other excitements, which Earle Snell's screenplay (from an idea by Irving Rubine based on Frederick Nebel's characters) and Ray McCarey's direction explored with dogged predictability. Tom Kennedy (centre left), Frank Shannon, Irving Bacon, Jack Mower, John Miljan, and Joe Cunningham were also featured, and the associate producer was Bryan Foy.
▽

◁ Considering that the studio allowed Humphrey Bogart to wear the same clothes in film after film and kept casting him in the same old roles, the title of his latest excursion into *déjà vu* – **You Can't Get Away With Murder** – was ironical. For the studio were doing just that and, in the process, were in danger of sabotaging a promising career. The story of a petty hood's pernicious influence on Dead End Kid Billy Halop, the Robert Buckner-Don Ryan-Kenneth Gamet screenplay was full of solid production values, with direction to match by Lewis Seiler. But there was nothing fresh about the material and, although well-performed by Bogart (centre), Halop (right), and a cast including Gale Page, John Litel, Henry Travers and Harvey Stephens (left), it was the product of a factory rather than of the human imagination. Sam Bischoff was associate producer. (First National.)

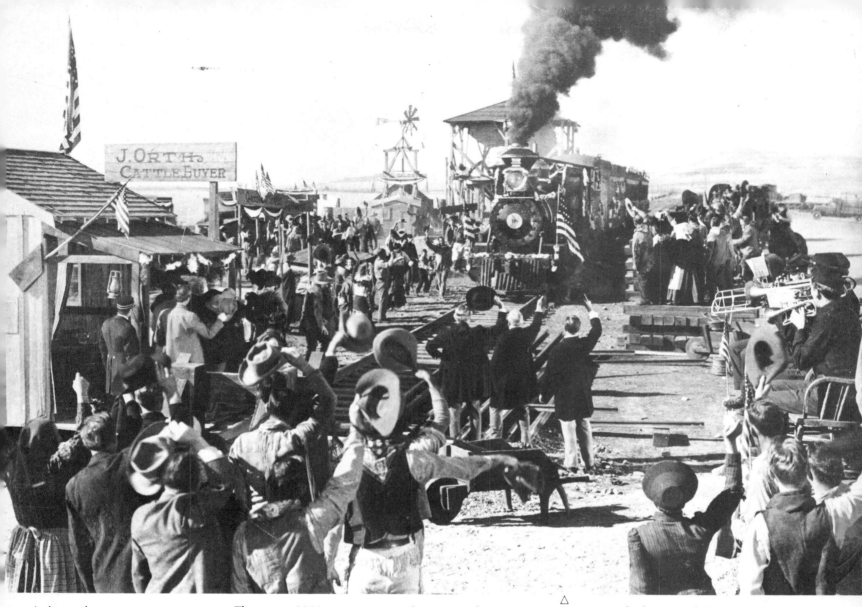

A better-than-average programmer, **The Adventures of Jane Arden**, very much in the Torchy Blane mould, featured Rosella Towne as a reporter who unmasks a jewel smuggling syndicate by posing as a smuggler herself and becoming a carrier for the gang. Dangerous work for a girl, but writers Lawrence Kimble, Charles Curran and Vincent Sherman, working with characters created by Monte Barrett and Russell E. Ross, made sure she came up trumps. The associate producer was Mark Hellinger, his director was Terry Morse, and the cast included William Gargan, James Stephenson (right), Benny Rubin, Peggy Shannon (left), and Dennie Moore.

1939 was an extraordinary year for Bette Davis, whose three money-making hits, **Dark Victory**, *The Old Maid* and *The Private Lives of Elizabeth and Essex* firmly established her as the country's number one female star and the studio's most bankable asset. On the profits of **Dark Victory** alone, Jack Warner was able to build three new sound stages on the lot. 'Who wants to see a dame go blind?' Warner asked soon after filming on **Dark Victory** commenced. Half the world, it seemed, for, of all Davis' pictures to date, this weepie based on a 1934 stage play by George Brewer Jr and Bertram Bloch, was the most successful. The sad, sad story of Judith Traherne (Davis, right), a flighty heiress who suffers from brain tumours, it was elevated beyond belief by the star's poignant, absolutely controlled performance. The scene towards the end of the film, in which she and her best friend Ann – touchingly played by Geraldine Fitzgerald (centre) in her first American film – plant hyacinth bulbs just as she begins to go blind, was superb. So was her heartrending death scene which climaxed the film. If handkerchiefs rustled, the sound-track would certainly have been obliterated by the noise. Max Steiner's lushly romantic score also made quite sure that no possible tear was left unshed. Director Edmund Goulding, bringing a sensitivity of touch rare to the most masculine of all studios, tastefully milked Casey Robinson's screenplay for every drop of pathos, and drew convincing performances from Ronald Reagan, Humphrey Bogart, Henry Travers, Cora Witherspoon, Virginia Brissac and even George Brent (left) as Davis' doctor husband. David Lewis was the associate producer.

Action was the keynote of director Michael Curtiz's **Dodge City** (filmed in Technicolor) in which Errol Flynn, in his first Western, played an Irish soldier of fortune who finds himself responsible for the safety and well-being of a small frontier town in the mid-West. It was the classic confrontation between hard-working cattlemen and the corrupt dude who has the town sewn up to his own political advantage, with the film's style and pace compensating for Robert Buckner's indifferent screenplay. Audiences were kept on the edge of their saddles with cattle stampedes, attempted lynchings, shoot-outs, and a saloon brawl as destructive to the surrounding merchandise as anything ever filmed. Romantic interest was supplied by Olivia de Havilland (wasted) and Ann Sheridan (even more wasted), but as kisses were secondary to punches, it hardly mattered. Flynn emerged the undoubted hero, his English accent (initially a source of concern to Jack Warner) in no way diminishing his credibility, or his popularity with cinemagoers. Also cast were Bruce Cabot, Frank McHugh, Alan Hale, John Litel, Henry Travers, Henry O'Neill, Victor Jory and William Lundigan. Robert Lord was the associate producer.

In **Sweepstakes Winner**, Marie Wilson (right) entrusts a thousand dollars to racing tout Allen Jenkins (centre left) who loses it. She is compensated when, in exchange for a meal, he gives her a winning ticket in the Irish Sweepstake, and sells her an old horse who miraculously regains his form. A moderately amusing screenplay by John Kraft and Albert DeMond (from a story by DeMond and Hugh Cummings) helped while away the film's 59 minutes without much pain, and the performances were slightly above par for the course. William McGann directed for associate producer Bryan Foy, and the cast included Johnnie Davis (centre), Charles Foy (left), Jerry Colonna and Vera Lewis. (First National.)

A nasty and deep-rooted feud between two aggressive longshoremen formed the paltry, difficult-to-like substance of **Waterfront**. Written by Lee Katz and Arthur Ripley from a play by Kenyon Nicholson, and directed by Terry Morse for associate producer Bryan Foy, it featured Gloria Dickson (right), Denis Morgan (centre), Marie Wilson, Larry Williams, Sheila Bromley, Ward Bond and Aldrich Bowker. It could have pleased punch-drunk customers only.

The Nancy Drew series continued well with **Nancy Drew, Trouble Shooter** in which Nancy tracks down the murderer of one Henry Clarke through clues provided by the plants growing across the victim's grave. Unlikely but fun, with Bonita Granville (left) and Frankie Thomas (centre) in good form as Nancy and Ted. Also cast were John Litel, Aldrich Bowker, Charlotte Wynters, Edgar Edwards, Willie Best (right) and Renie Riano. Kenneth Gamet wrote it from original characters created by Carolyn Keene, William Clemens directed, and Bryan Foy was the associate producer.

Juarez's three interlinked plots revolved around the intrigue surrounding Napoleon III's efforts to bring Mexico under French rule, the sad romance between Maximilian, Napoleon's appointed Emperor of Mexico, and Carlotta, and the political efforts of Benito Juarez to liberate Mexico from foreign rule and establish a democracy. It was a mighty canvas, and producer Hal Wallis, in association with Henry Blanke, was determined to make something quite memorable of it. They only partially succeeded, despite fine performances from Bette Davis as Carlotta, Paul Muni as Juarez (illustrated), Claude Rains as Napoleon III, Brian Aherne as Maximilian and a supporting cast of 1,186 – including Donald Crisp, Joseph Calleia, Gale Sondergaard, Gilbert Roland and Henry O'Neill. Less happily, the film featured John Garfield as Porfirio Diaz, Juarez's revolutionary general. Garfield's accent was against him, and director William Dieterle was unable to use it to advantage. In all other aspects of the movie, however, great pains were taken to ensure accuracy and authenticity. The screenplay (by John Huston with Aeneas MacKenzie and Wolfgang Reinhardt), though basically fashioned from Bertita Harding's *The Phantom Crown* and Franz Werfel's play *Juarez and Maximilian*, called on 357 other sources of information. Care was lavished on every aspect of the production and designer Orry-Kelly, using what he called 'visual psychology', created several dresses for Davis whose tones, as the film progressed, changed from white in the first scenes, to grey in the middle ones, and finally, after she goes mad, to black. Anton Grot, the art director, drew some 3,643 sketches from which the film's 34 sets were built, the largest being a recreation of Mexico City, and Erich Wolfgang Korngold composed over 3,000 bars of music. All the same, **Juarez** was not the money maker the studio had hoped for; nor was it a complete critical success, the general consensus being that it was too didactic and not quite entertaining enough.

In **The Man Who Dared**, a re-make of *Star Witness* (1931), the murder of a detective by a hired thug is witnessed by the Carter family whose lives, as a result, become endangered. Though given police protection, young Billy Carter is kidnapped and threatened with death should his family testify. It is grandfather Carter, who, taking matters into his own hands, rescues young Billy and alerts the police as to the kidnappers' whereabouts. Written by Lee Katz from a story by Lucien Hubbard, and directed by Crane Wilbur for associate producer Bryan Foy, it was just another time-filler. The cast included Charles Grapewin (centre, as grandfather), Henry O'Neill, Dickie Jones, Jane Bryan, Elisabeth Risdon, and James McCallion. (First National.)

Hell's Kitchen, a melodrama, was another vehicle for the Dead End Kids. The film had a social conscience inasmuch as it showed how, after leaving reform school, the kids become the victims of brutal superintendent (Grant Mitchell) of the Hell's Kitchen Shelter. Help is just around the corner, however, in the guise of ex-racketeer Ronald Reagan who assists in the running of the shelter – not entirely for philanthropic purposes, but to facilitate his parole. Entertaining enough but negligible as social comment, it was written by Crane Wilbur and Fred Niblo Jr, directed by Lewis Seiler and E.A. Dupont, and in addition to the Dead End Kids (including Billy Halop, left, and Leo Gorcey, right), featured Margaret Lindsay, Stanley Fields, Vera Lewis and Robert Homans. The associate producers were Bryan Foy and Mark Hellinger.

As the decade approached its end, so did Dick Powell's contract with the studio. His last film for Warner Bros. was a pretty mediocre musical called **Naughty But Nice** in which, as an indication of his falling stock, he was given second billing to Ann Sheridan (in the midst of the studio's 'oomph girl' campaign) and fewer songs than her to sing. Powell (left) played a serious musicologist who, *en route* to getting his symphony published, finds himself involved with the *hoi-polloi* of Tin Pan Alley, one of whom happens to be Miss Sheridan (centre). Richard Macaulay and Jerry Wald's screenplay attempted to inject satire into the proceedings, the main target being Tin Pan Alley's perpetual 'borrowings' from the classics, but it misfired to the point of tedium. The film featured the music of Wagner, Liszt, Mozart and Bach not to mention Johnny Mercer and Harry Warren. The routine direction was by Ray Enright, and the associate producer was Sam Bischoff. Among others in the cast were Gale Page (right), Helen Broderick, Ronald Reagan, Allen Jenkins and ZaSu Pitts. Songs included: Corn Pickin', Hooray For Spinach, I'm Happy About The Whole Thing, In A Moment Of Weakness and I Don't Believe In Signs.

John Garfield (right) was understandably unhappy about his role in **Dust Be My Destiny**, for it was yet another in the studio's seemingly inexhaustible supply of social melodramas concerning the sorry plight of the under-privileged. In this instance Garfield, after being released from prison for a crime he did not commit, is arrested for vagrancy and sent to work on a farm. But even here fate is against him and, after falling in love with the step-daughter of the farm's drunken foreman, he is accused of killing the man in a fight. At his trial, Garfield's attorney uses his client as a sociological symbol to demonstrate the sad circumstances which force a life of vagrancy on men and women from the other side of the tracks. Though excessively predictable, Robert Rossen's screenplay (from a story by Jerome Odlum) was full of quality, and the performances of Billy Halop, Bobby Jordan, Priscilla Lane (left), Frank McHugh and Charles Grapewin, were first class. It was directed by Lewis Seiler for associate producer Lou Edelman. (First National.)

Each Dawn I Die was a hard-hitting melodrama whose plot centred on the plight of an innocent newspaper reporter who is sent to prison as a result of a frame-up. (*Strange Alibi* and *I Was Framed* were to follow the same course in 1941 and 1942 respectively). The film starred James Cagney (left) and George Raft (right), a combination that proved explosive. Resisting all temptation to overdo his role of reporter-turned-criminal, Cagney played with admirable restraint, and in the process brought to the Norman Reilly Raine-Warren Duff-Charles Perry screenplay (from a novel by Jerome Odlum) a unity it might otherwise have lacked. Aware of the fissures in the script, director William Keighley, while giving the action sequences their due, realized that the screenplay's strength lay in the Cagney-Raft relationship and developed this aspect of it most effectively. Jane Bryan provided the obligatory female interest, with George Bancroft, Maxie Rosenbloom, Stanley Ridges, Alan Baxter and Victor Jory offering strong support. The associate producer was David Lewis. (First National.)

After the success of *Four Daughters*, the studio, aware that they were onto a good thing, refashioned the earlier movie, and, using more or less the same cast as the one they had previously assembled, hired the Epstein brothers (Julius J. and Philip G.) to write **Daughters Courageous**. In it, a peripatetic Claude Rains (left) returns home just in time to intercept a marriage between his ex-wife (Fay Bainter) and a local businessman (Donald Crisp). At the same time, his daughter (Priscilla Lane) settles for John Garfield as a prospective spouse, but both men disappear before their presence in the small town becomes too disruptive. Again, director Michael Curtiz drew the very best from Garfield who, as the sequel's chief *raison d'être*, ensured its success. May Robson (right) was also featured. Hal Wallis produced with Henry Blanke as associate. (First National.)

With the word 'kid' in the title, **The Kid from Kokomo** (released in Britain as **Orphan of the Ring**) had to be a boxing film. And, indeed it was, though a pretty wretched one as it turned out. The farcical tale of a fighter who believes that he and Whistler had the same mother, and that her living counterpart is a booze-sodden kleptomaniac in the shape of May Robson, it starred Pat O'Brien (centre left), as the brainless fighter with Wayne Morris (right), Joan Blondell (left), Jane Wyman, Stanley Fields and Sidney Toler on hand to share the punishment meted out by writers Jerry Wald and Richard Macaulay (story by Dalton Trumbo). Also going down for the count was director Lewis Seiler. The referee was Sam Bischoff, who should have stopped it before it began. (First National.)

All about a Western hick who is signed by a talent scout to play for a professional football team and finds himself involved with a bunch of gamblers, **The Cowboy Quarterback**, a feeble remake of *Elmer the Great* (1933), starred Bert Wheeler (centre) as the hick with Gloria Dickson, Marie Wilson (left), DeWolf Hopper, William Demarest (right), Eddie Foy Jr, and William Gould in support. Fred Niblo Jr wrote the screenplay from a story by Ring Lardner and a play by Lardner and George M. Cohan. Noel Smith directed for associate producer Bryan Foy. (First National.)

A remake of *The Crowd Roars* (1932), **Indianapolis Speedway**, written by Sig Herzig and Wally Klein from a story by Howard and William Hawks, was a racing-car melodrama about an older driver, his kid brother rival, and the fatal crash on the track that changes their lives. Pat O'Brien (in car, right) and John Payne (in car, left) were the brothers, with Ann Sheridan and Gale Page supplying feminine interest. Also cast were Frank McHugh, Grace Stafford, Granville Bates, John Ridgely, Regis Toomey, John Harron, Ed McWade and William Davidson. It was directed by Lloyd Bacon, whose handling of the action sequences was more convincing than the scenes away from the track, and the associate producer was Max Siegel.

△

Jane Wyman (right) taking over from Glenda Farrell, played the heroine in **Torchy Plays With Dynamite**. The last (and one of the least) of the series, it had Torchy foiling an escaped bandit by deliberately getting sent to prison in order to make contact with the heavy's girl-friend. Earle Snell and Charles Belden wrote it from a story by Scott Littleton (based on characters originally created by Frederick Nebel), it was directed by Noel Smith, and featured Allen Jenkins, Tom Kennedy, Sheila Bromley (left), and Joe Cunningham. The associate producer was Bryan Foy.

△

Centring on a hobby-mad family whose hobbies come in handy when the son is able to call for help on his short-wave radio-set during a forest fire, and the father can use his telephoto camera to take a snapshot of the man who started it, **Everybody's Hobby** was a good idea that went awry in the writing (screenplay by Kenneth Gamet and William Brockway). The performances of Irene Rich (centre), Henry O'Neill, Aldrich Bowker (left), Jane Sharon (right), Jackie Moran and John Ridgely, under the makeshift direction of William McGann, didn't help much either. The associate producer was Bryan Foy. (First National.)

△

Not really a sequel to *Angels With Dirty Faces* (1938), but more a box-office follow-up, **Angels Wash Their Faces** again featured the Dead End Kids (illustrated), this time in an attempt to clear the name of a kid thrown into jail for an insurance fire he did not start, and in which one of their number lost his life. The gang not only apprehends the arsonists, but makes quite sure that Ann Sheridan and Ronald Reagan (as the District Attorney's personable son) get together for a happy ending. Miss Sheridan exhibited more 'oomph' than talent, but ultimately the film suffered from a deficiency of both. Michael Fessier, Niven Busch and Robert Buckner wrote it from a story by Jonathan Finn; Ray Enright directed and the associate producer was Max Siegel. With the Dead End Kids were Bonita Granville, Frankie Thomas, Henry O'Neill and Margaret Hamilton. (First National.)

The same creative team responsible for *Dark* ▷
Victory (writer Casey Robinson and director
Edmund Goulding), brought the studio
another solid winner with **The Old Maid**. In
this one, from the play by Zoë Akins and the
novel by Edith Wharton, a 31-year-old
Bette Davis aged in the course of the film,
ending up as a severe, tight-lipped old
maid of 60, who has allowed her illegitimate
daughter to be raised by her cousin (Miriam
Hopkins). Although Davis (left) and Hopkins were temperamentally ill-suited, the
latter upstaging the former at every con-
ceivable opportunity, thanks to Goulding's
careful and tactful work at the helm, both
women shone in two nicely contrasted
performances. The cast also included George
Brent (right), Donald Crisp, Cecilia Loftus,
Jane Bryan (as the daughter), William Lundigan, James Stephenson and, in her last
screen appearance, Louise Fazenda. The
musical score was again by Max Steiner and
the cameraman was Tony Gaudio. Hal B.
Wallis was the producer. Henry Blanke his
associate. (First National.)

A remake of *The Expert* (1932), **No Place
To Go** charted the havoc caused in the
Plummer household when son Joe (Dennis
Morgan, left) takes his father (Fred Stone,
centre right) out of an old soldier's home
and allows him to move in with him and his
socially ambitious wife (Gloria Dickson,
centre left). Also featured was young
Sonny Bupp as a bootblack whom the old
man befriends. It was based on a play by
Edna Ferber and George S. Kaufman,
written for the screen by Lee Katz, Lawrence
Kimble and Fred Niblo Jr, and directed by
Terry Morse. The associate producer was
Bryan Foy, and the cast included Aldrich
Bowker, Charles Halton (centre) and Georgia
Caine (right). (First National.)

▽

◁ Brought back to life after being executed and
buried, the mysterious Doctor X alias
Marshall Quesne (Humphrey Bogart) spends
most of his spare time in **The Return of
Doctor X** committing murder in a never-
ending search for a life-enhancing Type
One blood, without which he might just as
well go back to his coffin. Bogart (left),
sporting a two-toned crew-cut and an
expression of decided biliousness, was the
only reason for seeing this Vincent Sherman-
directed piece of ghouliana which, judging
by the box office returns, wasn't reason
enough. Lee Katz wrote the screenplay,
entrapping, in the process, Wayne Morris,
Rosemary Lane, Dennis Morgan, Lya Lys
(right) and John Litel. The associate producer was Bryan Foy. (First National.)

Smashing the Money Ring was a straightforward melodrama which again cast Ronald
Reagan (left) as a secret service agent. This
time, in order to get to the bottom of a
counterfeit racket, he resorts to the old ploy
of managing to get himself committed to
prison where, in due course, and by becoming one of the mob, he learns that
the source of the counterfeit notes he is
looking for is under his very nose in the
prison print shop. Too familiar for anything but counterfeit thrills, it was average
programmer fare, directed by Terry Morse
and written by Anthony Coldeway and Raymond L. Schrock from a story by Jonathan
Finn. The associate producer was Bryan Foy,
and the cast, who managed fairly well with
mediocre material, included Eddie Foy Jr,
Margot Stevenson, Joe Downing (right),
Charles Brown, Elliott Sullivan, Joe King and
Charles Wilson. (First National.)

▽

△

The best of the series so far, **Nancy Drew
and the Hidden Staircase** crammed in as
much humour, action and suspense as its
60 minute running time could comfortably
contain. Nancy and her boy-friend Ted find
themselves tracking down a murderer
through an underground passage and, at
the same time, foil a plot to prevent the
building of a new children's hospital.
Kenneth Gamet scripted from a story by the
series' creator, Carolyn Keene; it was
directed by William Clemens, and once
again featured Bonita Granville (left) as
Nancy and Frankie Thomas (right) as Ted,
with other parts going to John Litel, Frank
Orth, Renie Riano, Vera Lewis and Louise
Carter. The associate producer was Bryan
Foy.

A sequel to the popular and critically acclaimed *Four Daughters* (1938), **Four Wives** (left to right: Priscilla, Rosemary and Lola Lane, Gale Page), was directed by Michael Curtiz from Julius J. and Philip G. Epstein and Maurice Hanline's warm-hearted screenplay, suggested by Fannie Hurst's story *Sister Act*. It takes up the story of the Lemp family by finding a husband (Jeffrey Lynn) for the previously widowed Priscilla Lane whose tormented husband (John Garfield in the earlier film), drove his car over a cliff; and by providing the rest of the sisters with offspring. Possibly a touch too sentimental in approach, it was rescued from mawkishness by the splendid performances of Claude Rains, Eddie Albert (as a young doctor suitably impressed with Ehrlich and Pasteur, two gentlemen close to the studio's heart), May Robson, Frank McHugh, Gale Page, and Rosemary and Lola Lane. Also cast were Dick Foran, Vera Lewis and John Qualen. John Garfield made a brief appearance as the ghost of his former self. It was produced by Hal B. Wallis with Henry Blanke as associate producer. (First National.)
▽

Bette Davis wanted Laurence Olivier to ▷ portray the Earl of Essex in the studio's Technicolor production of **The Private Lives of Elizabeth and Essex**. But she was given Errol Flynn, whom she considered too inexperienced to cope with Maxwell Anderson's blank verse, chunks of which were lifted from his play *Elizabeth The Queen*, and placed in the Norman Reilly Raine-Aeneas MacKenzie screenplay. Obviously self-conscious at being co-starred with the first lady of the lot, and perfectly aware of his own inadequacies as a serious actor, Flynn (right) tried to bluff his way through the role with much bravado but little conviction. At his insistence the film's title was changed from *Elizabeth the Queen* to include the character he played (*The Knight and the Lady* was his first choice, but Davis baulked) though neither he, nor anyone else in a cast which included Olivia de Havilland, Donald Crisp, Alan Hale, Nanette Fabares (later Fabray) and Henry Daniell, managed to make an impression as long as director Michael Curtiz gave Davis (left) her inimitable way with corny 'historical' utterances which, with her usual brilliance, she made convincing. It all looked splendid, and Erich Wolfgang Korngold's score was outstanding. Hal B. Wallis and Robert Lord were, respectively, producer and associate producer.

Having neither the impact nor the entertainment value of *Confessions of a Nazi Spy*, **Espionage Agent** was directed with little sense of involvement and even less sense of dramatic cogency by Lloyd Bacon. The warning it gave audiences about the potential infiltration of spy rings into the American way of life was certainly sobering, but not reason enough to fill cinema seats. Nor was the casting of Joel McCrea (left), Brenda Marshall (centre), Jeffrey Lynn, George Bancroft and Stanley Ridges (right). Based on a story by Robert Buckner, the screenplay was by Warren Duff, Michael Fessier and Frank Donaghue. The associate producer was Lou Edelman. (First National.)

A Bryan Foy-produced programmer with a ▷ racing background, **Pride of the Blue Grass** featured Edith Fellows (centre right), James McCallion (centre left), Granville Bates (right), Sam McDaniels (left), Arthur Loft (centre) and a horse called Gantry the Great. The predictable story told of a temperamental stallion who, although blind, manages to win the Grand National for the only jockey who has ever been able to ride him successfully. Gantry may have won, but the film was a loser all the way. Vincent Sherman wrote it, and the director was William McGann.

The first of two films teaming Humphrey Bogart (centre) with George Raft (left), **Invisible Stripes**, well directed by Lloyd Bacon from an uneven screenplay by Warren Duff, underwent a process of emasculation as a result of Hays Office demands. Still, the familiar story of an ex-con's attempts to go straight against overwhelming odds, was given a necessary fillip by its two stars as well as a cast which included William Holden (as Raft's younger brother), Jane Bryan, Flora Robson, Lee Patrick, Henry O'Neill, Joseph Downing (centre left), Marc Lawrence (standing right) and Paul Kelly (right). It was, however, unsuccessful at the box office. The producer was Hal B. Wallis and his associate was Lou Edelman.

We Are Not Alone was a sombre, well- ▷ acted drama set in England at the time of the First World War. The story involved a gentle, violin-playing country doctor who is accused of murdering his wife and having an affair with a young Austrian governess. Paul Muni (right) played the doctor (it was, he claimed, his favourite film role), Jane Bryan was the governess and Flora Robson (left) the wife. All three central performances were superb. Based on the novel by James Hilton, and written for the screen by the author himself and Milton Krims, it was directed by Edmund Goulding who successfully conveyed the story's essential Englishness by way of the Burbank backlot. A strong supporting cast included Raymond Severn (as Muni's seven year-old son), Una O'Connor, Henry Daniell, Montagu Love, James Stephenson, Cecil Kellaway and Alan Napier. The film was not a success, and its failure was attributed to the unwillingness of audiences to show sympathy to an Austrian on the eve of World War II. Hal B. Wallis was the producer with Henry Blanke his associate. (First National.)

Kid Nightingale was yet another boxing film with the word 'kid' in the title but, this time, one that was intended strictly for laughs. It told the far-fetched story of an operatic tenor ▷ (John Payne, right) with pugilistic tendencies, who falls in with a crooked promoter and has to be rescued by Jane Wyman (left). It had few virtues, but chief among them were the comic performances of Walter Catlett, Harry Burns and Ed Brophy, who mined the screenplay – written by Charles Belden and Raymond Schrock from a story by Lee Katz – for the few nuggets they could get. Charles Brown and John Ridgely were also in the cast, and it was directed by George Amy. The associate producer was Bryan Foy.

A melodrama set in a military college, ▷ **Dead End Kids On Dress Parade**, written by Tom Reed and Charles Belden, told the familiar story of a rebellious young kid who, after getting into one fight after another, saves the life of one of the cadets in a fire, and wins the respect of his colleagues. Cloyingly directed by William Clemens, the film featured The Dead End Kids (left to right: Bobby Jordan, Huntz Hall, Leo Gorcey, Gabriel Dell), John Litel, Cissie Loftus, Aldrich Bowker and Frankie Thomas. The associate producer was Bryan Foy.

Vouchsafing its authenticity, author, reporter and columnist Mark Hellinger assured audiences, in the opening credits for his story **The Roaring Twenties**, that all the characters depicted in this 'memory of the past' were composites of criminals he knew, and that the prohibition incidents were based on fact. The story of a returning First World War veteran who thumbs his nose at society and turns bootlegger after a brief fling as a cab driver, it starred James Cagney (right) as Eddie Bartlett, a mobster, who when finally on the skids, redeems his tawdry life by sacrificing himself to save the husband of the woman he loves (Priscilla Lane, centre). Less violent and more sentimental than some of the studio's earlier ration of crime films, it was tautly directed in a documentary-like fashion by Raoul Walsh (replacing Anatole Litvak), whose evocation of the era was masterly. Jerry Wald, Richard Macaulay and Robert Rossen wrote the screenplay with effective roles for Humphrey Bogart, Jeffrey Lynn, Frank McHugh, and, as the nightclub hostess, Gladys George (who replaced Ann Sheridan who replaced Lee Patrick who replaced Glenda Farrell!). Hal B. Wallis produced with Sam Bischoff as associate.

◁ **On Your Toes** was a musical that could have danced all night, and should have, for when the plot intruded into the musical numbers, it was dreadful. The story of an American composer-hoofer who is mistaken for a traitor by a visiting Russian ballet company, it starred Eddie Albert in the role created for the stage by Ray Bolger) and dancer Vera Zorina. Apart from the notable 'Slaughter On Tenth Avenue' ballet choreographed by Balanchine, it was exceptionally dull. Also cast were James Gleason (right), Alan Hale, Frank McHugh, Leonid Kinskey, Donald O'Connor (centre) and Queenie Smith (left). Ray Enright directed Jerry Wald and Richard Macaulay's flabby screenplay (from the stage play by George Abbott, Richard Rodgers and Lorenz Hart) and the associate producer was Robert Lord. Songs included: There's A Small Hotel, Quiet Night and On Your Toes (by Rodgers and Hart). (First National.)

Made prior to the release of *Juarez* and ▷ bought by the studio to avoid a plagiarism suit, **The Mad Empress**, a Mexican production produced and directed by Miguel C. Torres, again recounted the story of Maximilian and Carlotta, eschewing the political implications entirely and concentrating on the couple's doomed occupancy of an alien country. Conrad Nagel (left) and the beautiful Austrian actress Medea Novara (centre) made little impact as the protagonists, leaving the acting honours to Lionel Atwill (right) as Bazaine. Also cast were Guy Bates Post as Napoleon, Evelyn Brent as the Empress Eugenie and Jason Robards Sr as Juarez. It was written by Jean Bart, Jerome Chodorov and Miguel C. Torres.

Jane Wyman (illustrated) starred in **Private Detective**, an inconsequential quickie in which she played a private detective whose closest rival is Dick Foran in the homicide squad. Forced to work together on a case, they find they quite like each other after all, and, just as you knew they would, decide to get married. Earl Snell and Raymond Schrock wrote it from a story by Kay Krausse: it was directed by Noel Smith, the associate producer was Bryan Foy and the cast included Gloria Dickson, Maxie Rosenbloom, John Ridgely and Morgan Conway. (First National.)

One of the most turbulent decades in the history of the American cinema, the forties brought out both the best and worst in Hollywood. It was a period of drastic change as well as immense creativity and, by the end of it, the values and foundations on which the industry had been built were unrecognizable. The old Hollywood was in the throes of giving way to the new, and nothing would be quite the same again.

After the spectacular culmination of the golden thirties with the unprecedented success of **Gone with the Wind** (MGM, 1939) the forties began badly with the outbreak of war. European and British markets no longer yielded the limitless profits of the previous decades, and when the Japanese attacked Pearl Harbour in 1941, revenue from the Far East disappeared as well. As a result the studios panicked and imposed a period of austerity upon themselves which, after the money-no-object extravagance of the thirties, came as something of a shock to the system. The number of studio personnel was halved and many stars were forced to take salary cuts. To aggravate matters, the forties also saw the abolition of the 'block booking' system thus giving exhibitors the right to choose what products they wished to show without being forced to take the bad with the good.

The decade was also characterized by labour disputes, the most serious being an eight month union strike at the studios in 1945. With the war over, and the pressure on money relaxed, the majority of studio employees felt that they were underpaid, and held out for better working conditions and a better deal.

Riots broke out on October 7th, 1945 and Warner Bros. in Burbank was the focal point of disturbances. The strike officially ended on October 25th, but flared up again the following year, on September 28th, with skirmishes between police and pickets occurring at both Warner Bros. and MGM.

Believing these strikes to have been Communist inspired, a vigorous Communist purge, led by J. Parnell Thomas, chairman of the House Un-American Activities Committee, devastated Hollywood and affected the lives and careers of nineteen 'unfriendly' witnesses and over three hundred actors, directors and writers whom the Committee deemed to

The FORTIES

be Communists or Communist sympathizers. It was the bleakest period in Hollywood's history.

After the high profits reaped by Warner Bros. during the war years, when the need for escapist entertainment was at its most pressing, the industry suffered a mighty body blow in 1947 with the news that Britain was imposing a 75% tax on all foreign earnings, thus reducing Hollywood's major annual source of outside revenue from $68 million to $17 million (although this tax was to be short-lived). As a result, further studio economies and lay-offs were necessary, and despite the previous year's record gross of $1,750 million (the most profitable year in Hollywood's chequered history), money was not quite as plentiful as it had been during and just after the war. By 1948, regardless of the economies being made, employment fell by 25%. Yet, although Warner Bros. was as hard hit as anyone else by the various economic changes that were taking place in the industry, its tight production operation under the brilliant supervision of Jack Warner and production chief Steve Trilling (who replaced Hal B. Wallis in 1944) resulted in a net profit in 1948 of $11,837,253.

Having had to contend with strikes, cut-backs, the war and Communist witch-hunts, the end of the decade brought the industry two more crises: television, which, in the United States, reduced the weekly audience attendances from 80,000,000 to 70,000,000; and the Consent Decree, a law which finally prevented the major studios from making as well as exhibiting their films in their own cinema chains across the country. It was, in fact, the beginning of the end for the old Hollywood system.

Warner Bros. however, sometimes jokingly known as the 'San Quentin of studios', continued the rigid production policy it had begun in the thirties. Jack Warner abhorred waste, whether of manpower, time or money. In the early part of the forties, long-term stars and directors, often working a 14 hour day, were shunted from script to script, without the power of veto. Failure to report to work resulted in suspension and only Bette Davis, the undisputed queen of the lot and one of the studio's top money-makers, had any say in the choice of roles offered her.

Because of the war and the cut-backs in spending it necessitated, the annual number of productions declined dramatically. Jack Warner imposed a moratorium on musicals, the public having grown weary of the genre by the end of the thirties, and in 1940 and 1941, only two Warner Bros. musicals – the melodramatic **Blues in the Night** and the raucous **Navy Blues** – were made.

Technically though, the studio's product improved immeasurably during the forties. Thanks to the development of celluloid lacquers, black-and-white prints had a gloss and brilliance to them in striking contrast to some of the more grainy efforts of the thirties; and with the purchase of a new fog machine (seen to marvellous effect in **Out of the Fog**) plus sundry other 'special effect' equipment there was nothing the studio could not now achieve or simulate.

There were fewer 'B' features than there had been in the previous decade and, apart from the numerous war films which were such a staple part of the Warner Bros. output in the first half of the forties, and which included **Sergeant York** (1941), **Captains of the Clouds** (1942), **Across the Pacific** (1942), **Destination Tokyo** (1943), **Air Force** (1943), **Mission to Moscow** (1943), **Action in the North Atlantic** (1943), **Watch on the Rhine** (1943), **Hollywood Canteen** (1944), **In our Time** (1944), **Pride of the Marines** (1945), and **Objective Burma** (1945), there were several important propaganda short subjects such as **Service with the Colors, Meet the Fleet, March on the Marines, Wings of Steel, Soldiers in White, The Tanks are Coming, Here comes the Cavalry, Beyond the Line of Duty, Rear Gunner, Winning your Wings, Commandos of the Skies, Take-Offs and Landings** and **Thirteen Aces.**

The studio's quality products included such films as **Dr. Ehrlich's Magic Bullet** (1940), **Saturday's Children** (1940), **The Sea Hawk** (1940), **High Sierra** (1941), **The Strawberry Blonde** (1941), **Out of the Fog** (1941), **The Maltese Falcon** (1941), **The Man who came to Dinner** (1941), **The Treasure of the Sierra Madre** (1948), **Kings Row** (1941), **Now Voyager** (1942), **Yankee Doodle Dandy** (1942), **Mr. Skeffington** (1945), **Mildred Pierce** (1945), **The Big Sleep** (1946), **Life with Father** (1947), **White Heat** (1949), **Johnny Belinda** (1948), **The Fountainhead** (1949) and the incomparable **Casablanca** (1943).

Throughout the decade, Warner Bros. made or released a total of 275 feature films, many of them among the most memorable in Hollywood's history.

1940

The studio made 45 feature films in 1940, two of which, **All This And Heaven Too** and **The Letter**, were nominated for Academy Awards for Best Picture. (The winner was David O. Selznick's **Rebecca**.) Also nominated for various Oscars were Norman Burnside, Heinz Herald and John Huston (Best Original Story) for **Dr. Ehrlich's Magic Bullet**, Ernest Haller (Best Cinematographer) for **The Letter**, Barbara O'Neill (Best Supporting Actress) for **The Letter** and Bette Davis (Best Actress) for **The Letter**. (Ginger Rogers won it for RKO's **Kitty Foyle**.) The only Oscar won by the studio in 1940 was for a two-reel short-subject called **Teddy, The Rough Rider**.

In July, 1940, Paul Muni's contract was dissolved (both **Juarez** and **We Are Not Alone** were box-office failures); so was William Dieterle's, whose **Dr. Ehrlich's Magic Bullet** and **A Despatch From Reuters** were among the last of the studio's prestige biopics. The net profit for the year was $2,747,472.

Calling Philo Vance, a remake of *The Kennel Murder Case* (1933), was a case of familiarity breeding boredom. The one in which a consortium of foreign agents endeavour to lay their hands on the top secret plans of a new fighter plane, it starred James Stephenson (right) as Philo Vance, whose main business in Tom Reed's convoluted screenplay (from a story by S.S. Van Dine) was to find out who murdered the plane's designer, which he finally does – with some canine assistance. William Clemens directed for associate producer Bryan Foy, and his cast included Margot Stevenson (centre), Henry O'Neill, Ed Brophy, Ralph Forbes (left) and Martin Kosleck.
▽

△
A remake of the 1932 melodrama *Life Begins*, **A Child is Born** was a slick, often moving account of life in a maternity ward, one of whose main characters included a gangster's moll who dies in childbirth. Written by Robert Rossen (from the play by Mary M. Axelson) and adroitly directed by Lloyd Bacon it starred Geraldine Fitzgerald (right), with Jeffrey Lynn (left), Gladys George, Gale Page, Spring Byington, Henry O'Neill, Johnnie Davis, John Litel, Gloria Holden, Eve Arden, Nanette Fabares (later Fabray) and Hobart Cavanaugh in support. The associate producer was Sam Bischoff.

Double agent Margaret Lindsay more than met her match in master spy-cum-butler Boris Karloff (right), whose presence gave **British Intelligence** (a remake of *Three Faces East*, first made in 1926 then again in 1930), an interest out of all proportion to Lee Katz's screenplay (from the play by Anthony Paul Kelly). Directed by Terry Morse for associate producer Bryan Foy, its topicality in no way compensated for the inferior nature of the material. Also cast were Maris Wrixon, Holmes Herbert, Bruce Lester, Clarence Derwent (left) and Leonard Mudie.
▽

A vehicle for May Robson (centre), **Granny Get Your Gun** featured her as a wealthy gun-toting widow who, believing her granddaughter (Margot Stevenson) to be guilty of the murder of her husband, takes the blame herself, only to discover that the girl is innocent. In no time at all (the film barely runs an hour) Granny becomes deputy sheriff and, of course, brings in the real culprit. Robson's winning performance bulldozed its way through Kenneth Gamet's screenplay (from a story by Erle Stanley Gardner), making the mindless farrago just about palatable. Bryan Foy was the associate producer, George Amy the director, and the cast included Harry Davenport (right), Hardie Albright, Arthur Aylesworth (left), Clem Bevans and William Davidson.
▽

△
Not nearly as successful as *Brother Rat* (1938), the encore, **Brother Rat and a Baby** (released in Britain as **Baby Be Good**), with its mindless screenplay by Fred Finkelhoffe and John Monks Jr, involved its star Wayne Morris in such inflammatory escapades as arson as well as stealing a Stradivarius which he pawns for petty cash. A cast including Priscilla Lane (right, as a Southern belle), Eddie Albert, Jane Bryan, Ronald Reagan (left), Jane Wyman (centre), Arthur Treacher (as the butler), Jesse Busley and Moroni Olsen brought a degree of effervescence to Ray Enright's flat direction. Hal B. Wallis was the producer and Robert Lord his associate.

A formula war drama glorifying World War I in general and **The Fighting 69th** in particular, William Keighley's patriotic depiction of the famous regiment was not to be taken seriously for a moment. However, the battle scenes achieved a genuinely terrifying quality, and also of interest was the footage which gave audiences an idea of the regiment's training routine. But the story, in which James Cagney (centre) played an obnoxiously cocky Irishman whose cowardice results in the deaths of several of his comrades, was straight from the bottom drawer. Norman Reilly Raine, Fred Niblo Jr and Dean Franklin were responsible for the all-male screenplay (Priscilla Lane was originally cast as the only woman but her role was eliminated from the final script) in which Pat O'Brien (again cast as a man of the cloth), George Brent, Jeffrey Lynn, Alan Hale, Frank McHugh, Dennis Morgan, Dick Foran, William Lundigan, Guinn Williams, John Litel and Henry O'Neill portrayed a wide spectrum of characters. The public responded enthusiastically, making **The Fighting 69th** a box-office hit.

Castle on the Hudson (released in Britain as **Years Without Days**) was almost a scene for scene remake of Michael Curtiz's *20,000 Years in Sing Sing* (1933) in which Spencer Tracy had scored such a success. No doubt hoping that the same story would establish John Garfield (right) as another of the studio's indomitable tough guys, he was cast in this hard-hitting drama of a gangster who refuses to take part in a prison break because the day the break is planned has never been his lucky day. The role did little to stretch his capabilities, nor did the movie itself enhance his reputation. Written by Seton I. Miller, Brown Holmes and Courteney Terrett from Lewis E. Lawes' original story, it was directed without distinction by Anatole Litvak, and also featured Ann Sheridan, Pat O'Brien, Burgess Meredith (left) and Henry O'Neill. The associate producer was Sam Bischoff.

One of the most successful and moving screen biographies of the forties, **Dr. Ehrlich's Magic Bullet** starred a restrained Edward G. Robinson (illustrated) as Dr. Paul Ehrlich, the man responsible for finding, in salvarsan, a cure for syphilis. Directed with impeccable taste by William Dieterle, (screenplay by John Huston, Heinz Herald, and Norman Burnside from the letters and notes in the possession of Ehrlich's widow), it was a personal triumph for Robinson, whose performance as the dedicated scientist was certainly his finest since *Little Caesar* (1931). The impressive supporting cast included Ruth Gordon as Frau Ehrlich, Otto Kruger as his opponent Dr. Emil von Behring, Donald Crisp, Sig Rumann, Henry O'Neill, Edward Norris and Maria Ouspenskaya as a moneyed dowager whose dinner guests go into a state of shock when Ehrlich begins a frank discussion on syphilis. The associate producer was Wolfgang Reinhardt. (First National.)

Three Cheers for the Irish was a warm-hearted domestic comedy and, at the same time, a warming over of a well-worn domestic theme — the enmity (largely ethnic) that exists between a father and his son-in-law. In this instance the father (Thomas Mitchell, right) is a retired Irish cop; the son-in-law (Dennis Morgan) a young Scotsman who has not only taken the cop's daughter's hand in marriage, but also his place in the force. Priscilla Lane was cast as the daughter, with other roles going to Alan Hale (centre) as an over-exuberant Irish practical joker, Virginia Grey, Irene Hervey, William Lundigan, Joe King, Frank Jenks (left) and Morgan Conway. Richard Macaulay and Jerry Wald wrote the screenplay, Lloyd Bacon directed (just about keeping the sentimentality palatable) and the producer was Sam Bischoff. Two cheers were all they deserved. (First National.) Song: Dear Old Donegal.

A stream of sentimentality flowed through **It All Came True**, but under Lewis Seiler's competent direction, the Michael Fessier-Lawrence Kimble adaptation of Louis Bromfield's novel *Better Than Life* was not without virtue. The whimsical and far fetched tale of a gangster's attempts to turn the run-down boarding house in which he is hiding into a successful night-club, it starred Ann Sheridan (right) as a singer, Jeffrey Lynn as a struggling songwriter and Humphrey Bogart (left) as the fugitive, with ZaSu Pitts, Una O'Connor, Jessie Busley and John Litel in secondary roles. Fanciful but likeable, it was produced by Hal B. Wallis, with Mark Hellinger as associate. Songs included: Angel In Disguise (by Kim Gannon, Stephen Weiss and Paul Mann), The Gaucho Serenade (by James Cavanaugh, John Redmond and Nat Simon), Pretty Baby and Memories (by Gus Kahn and Egbert van Alstyne), Ain't We Got Fun (by Richard A. Whiting), Put On Your Old Grey Bonnet (by Stanley Murphy and Percy Wenrich) and When Irish Eyes Are Smiling (by Chauncey Olcott and George Graff Jr).

Having single-handedly saved *Dodge City* from corruption, Errol Flynn (right) was despatched, the following year, to **Virginia City** to save a few wagon-loads of gold from the clutches of Southerner Randolph Scott during the Civil War. Labouring under Robert Buckner's script (as wooden as a Wells Fargo wagon and just as shaky) Flynn and director Michael Curtiz were unable to rescue the film from banality. Apart from Humphrey Bogart (centre) sporting a moustache and a wavering accent as a Spanish renegade, an ill-used Miriam Hopkins appeared as a saloon singer, and other roles went to Frank McHugh, Alan Hale, Guinn Williams (left), John Litel, Douglass Dumbrille and Moroni Olsen. Hal B. Wallis produced with Robert Fellows as associate.

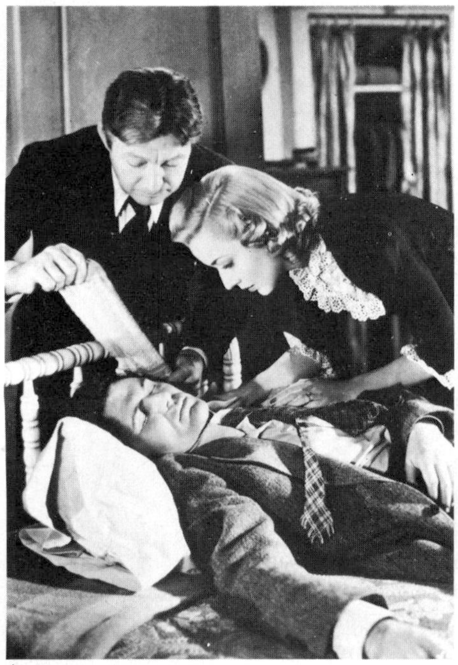

△
After complaining to Jack Warner that he was becoming too much of a fixture in the studio's roster of crime movies, John Garfield (foreground) was given a chance to prove his versatility in **Saturday's Children**, a Depression drama about a reticent young inventor called Rimes Rosson, whose dream of a life in the Philippines is thwarted when he is tricked into marriage by his boss's daughter (Anne Shirley, right). The studio's overriding concern for the average middle-class American's battle to overcome hard times and to slice a piece of the cake for himself, was very much in evidence in this Julius J. and Philip G. Epstein screenplay (based on Maxwell Anderson's successful play) remade from Gregory La Cava's 1929 version. Also cast were Claude Rains (left), Lee Patrick, Roscoe Karns and George Tobias. It was directed by Vincent Sherman and produced by Hal B. Wallis. The associate producer was Henry Blanke. Despite Garfield's affecting performance, and the deep and genuine concern the movie expressed for men like Rimes Rosson, it was a box office flop.

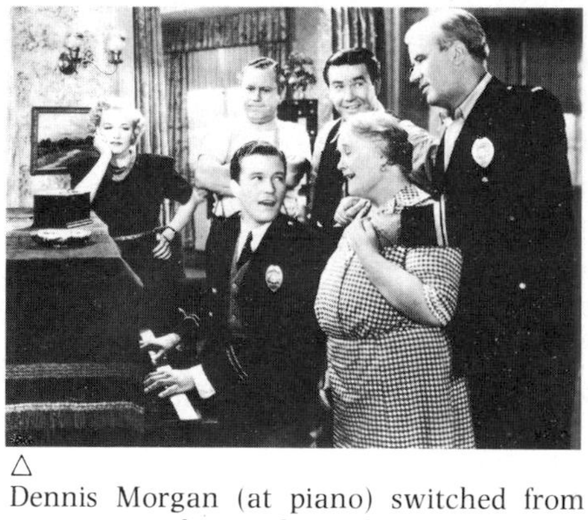

△
Dennis Morgan (at piano) switched from crooning to law enforcement in **Tear Gas Squad**, and singlehandedly routed a formidable gang of hoods. Charles Belden, Kenneth Gamet and Don Ryan's screenplay boggled the imagination, and so did Terry Morse's direction. John Payne, Gloria Dickson (left), George Reeves, Frank Wilcox, Mary Gordon (second right) and Harry Shannon (right) were also in it, and the associated producer was Bryan Foy. Song: I'm An Officer Of The Law (by M.K. Jerome and Jack Scholl).

King of the Lumberjacks was a hoary old chestnut, set in a northwoods lumber camp, all about a fellow who quite unknowingly marries his best friend's sweetheart. Crane Wilbur's screenplay, from a story by Robert E. Kent, abounded in such incidental excitements as bar-room brawls and runaway trains, and if you didn't mind the triteness of it all, it was a harmless enough time-killer. It starred John Payne (left), and Gloria Dickson (right) with Stanley Fields, Joe Sawyer, Victor Kilian and Earl Dwire also cast. William Clemens directed and the associate producer was Bryan Foy.
▽

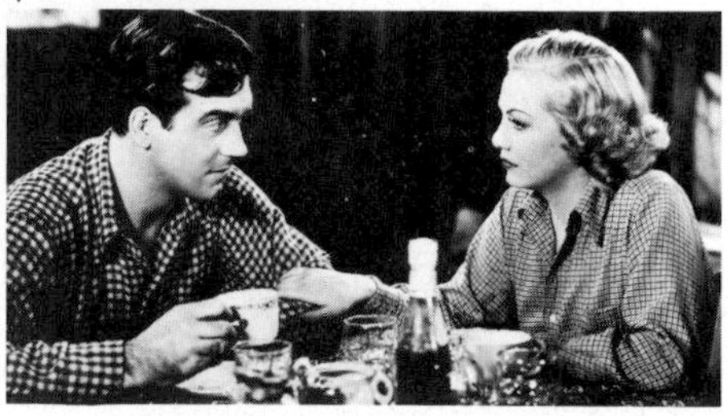

A remake of *One Way Passage* (1932), with Merle Oberon (centre right) and George Brent (right) subbing for Kay Francis and William Powell, **'Til We Meet Again** re-told the hearts-and-flowers story of two doomed passengers aboard a Transatlantic ocean liner. She (Miss Oberon) is suffering from an incurable cardiac disease; he (Mr Brent) is on his way to San Quentin prison. Frank McHugh, who appeared in the original version, was in this one too, so was Pat O'Brien (centre) as a detective, Binnie Barnes, Geraldine Fitzgerald (left), Eric Blore, George Reeves, Frank Wilcox, Marjorie Gateson and Henry O'Neill. Warren Duff wrote it from a story by Robert Lord, and it was produced and directed by Edmund Goulding. The associate producer was David Lewis. (First National.)
▽

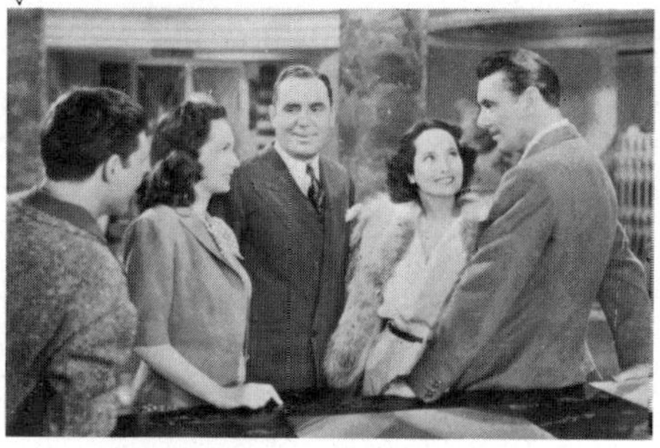

The transformation of tough-guy Edward G. Robinson (centre) from hard-boiled racketeer to endearing orchid-cultivating monk in **Brother Orchid** was one of the most joyful screen sights of the year, and one of the best spoofs on gangsterism to emerge from Hollywood. What initially started as an obligation to the studio on Robinson's behalf (he was ▷ given the role of Dr Ehrlich in *Dr Ehrlich's Magic Bullet* on condition that he agreed to star in one last crime film) turned into a triumph for him and his most successful film since *A Slight Case of Murder* (1938). Vigorously directed by Lloyd Bacon from an Earl Baldwin screenplay (story by Richard Connell), Hal Wallis' production also featured Ann Sothern, Humphrey Bogart, Ralph Bellamy, Donald Crisp, Allen Jenkins and Cecil Kellaway. The producer was Hal B. Wallis, and the associate producer was Mark Hellinger.

A breezy farce whose theme was one-upmanship, and whose plot revolved around the adventures of a pair of Texas yokels who get the better of a couple of Broadway theatrical sharps, **An Angel From Texas** was another remake of George S. Kaufman's 1925 play *The Butter And Egg Man*. First filmed under its original title by First National in 1928, it was re-made by Warner Bros. in 1932 as *The Tenderfoot*, and again, by Warner's Teddington Studios in England, as *Hello Sweetheart* in 1935. In 1937 it re-appeared as *Dance Charlie Dance*. The studio filmed it one more time, in 1953, as *Three Sailors and a Girl*. Eddie Albert (centre), Rosemary Lane, Jane Wyman (2nd left), Wayne Morris (2nd right) and Ronald Reagan (right) were in this particular version with Ruth Terry, John Litel, Hobart Cavanaugh (left) and Ann Shoemaker in support. It was written by Fred Niblo Jr and Bertram Millhauser; Ray Enright directed, and the associate producer was Robert Fellows. (First National.)
▽

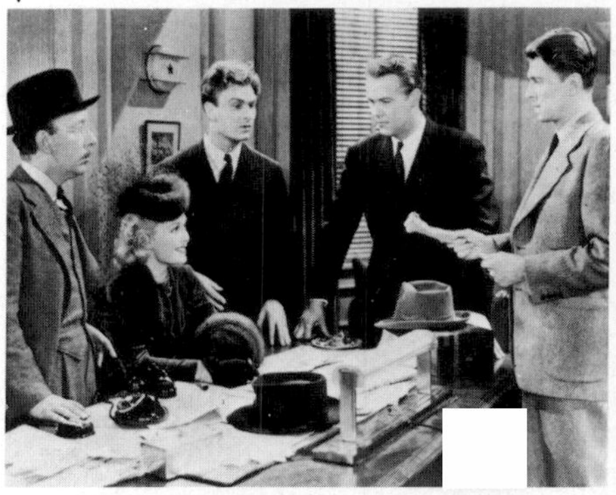

A melodramatic spy-thriller, tautly directed by Lewis Seiler from a serviceable screenplay by Raymond L. Schrock, **Murder in the Air** involved a bunch of saboteurs in an attempt to lay their hands on a deadly piece of government hardware called an 'inertia projector', supposedly a sophisticated instrument capable of depriving all electrical objects of their power. Ronald Reagan (right) of the FBI (again!) was suitably bold in his successful attempts to bring the villains to bay; Eddie Foy Jr supplied the laughs and Lya Lys (left) the intrigue. The associate producer was Bryan Foy. (First National.)
▽

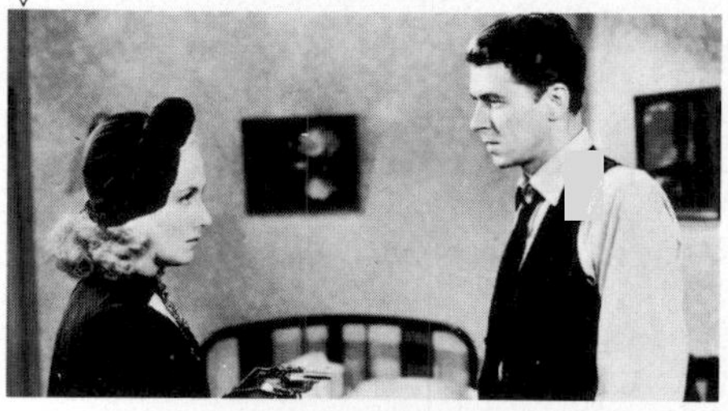

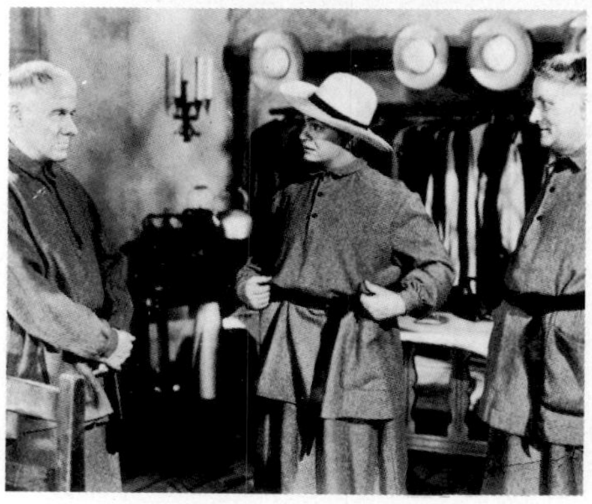

Familiar but slick, **A Fugitive From Justice** was yet another crime melodrama. It starred Roger Pryor (3rd left) as an insurance investigator who, together with the underworld and the law, goes a-hunting for a criminal lawyer (Don Douglas) who is carrying a policy worth a million dollars. The gangsters want him dead; Pryor and the police, for reasons of their own, want him alive. Alex Gottlieb, who wrote the screenplay, did well by Leonard Neubauer, who wrote the story. Terry Morse directed it, and the associate producer was Bryan Foy. Also cast were Lucille Fairbanks, Eddie Foy Jr, Sheila Bromley, Morgan Conway and John Galaudet. (First National.)
▽

A perfect antidote to the war raging across Europe, **Torrid Zone** was a little gem of escapist entertainment. With its faint echoes of MGM's *Red Dust* (1932) and the Hecht-MacArthur-Howard Hughes comedy *The Front Page* (United Artists, 1931), it wisecracked its way through a plot involving gutsy nightclub singer Ann Sheridan's stormy romance with ex-plantation foreman James Cagney (centre) somewhere in the tropics of Central America. 'Oomph girl' Miss Sheridan (left) did the impossible in this, her second starring role: she pilfered the acting honours from under Cagney's hitherto-unassailable nose. Pat O'Brien played the plantation owner (it was the eighth and last time he and Cagney were to appear together) with falsetto-voiced Andy Devine. Helen Vinson (right), Jerome Cowan, George Tobias, George Reeves and John Ridgely in support. The original screenplay was by Richard Macaulay and Jerry Wald, and the direction by William Keighley. The producer was Hal B. Wallis, with Mark Hellinger as the associate producer. (First National.) Song: Caballero (by M.K. Jerome and Jack Scholl).
▽

△

George Brent (right) played a gangster's lawyer in **The Man Who Talked Too Much**, with William Lundigan as his idealistic younger brother. Their involvement with the criminal set was of little consequence, providing neither insight nor entertainment. Tom Reed and Walter DeLeon's screenplay was deficient in suspense as well as in characterization, and the direction by Vincent Sherman equally unpromising. Also cast were Virginia Bruce (left), Brenda Marshall, Richard Barthelmess, and George Tobias as a muscle man called Slug McNutt. The associate producer was Edmund Grainger. (First National.)
▽

The corn was as high as an elephant's eye ▷ (8,000 feet, to be precise) in **Flight Angels**, a soap-opera of the air which zeroed in on the private lives and public duties of air stewardesses and the men who pilot the planes in which they serve. Romance, drama and excitement co-habited shamelessly in Maurice Leo's familiar screenplay (from a story by Richard Macaulay and Jerry Wald) but with undoubtedly entertaining results. Lewis Seiler directed a cast that included Virginia Bruce (left), Dennis Morgan, Wayne Morris, Ralph Bellamy, Jane Wyman (centre), Nell O'Day (centre right), Margot Stevenson (right) and John Litel. The associate producer was Edmund Grainger. (First National.)

Adapted for the screen by Casey Robinson from Rachel Field's best-seller, **All This and Heaven Too** took its time (140 minutes) to recount, in flashback, the true story of Henriette Deluzy Désportes, a governess accused of having had an affair with her employer, the Duc de Praslin, and participating in the murder of his wife. A subdued Bette Davis (right) played the governess, Charles Boyer returned from France especially to appear as the Duc, and the supporting roles were filled by Virginia Weidler (on loan from MGM), Helen Westley, Walter Hampden, Henry Daniell, Harry Davenport, George Coulouris, June Lockhart (left) and Ann Todd (the American child actress, not the British star). Budgeted at $1,370,000 (the rights alone cost $100,000) producer Hal B. Wallis and his associate David Lewis had every confidence in director Anatole Litvak's ability to deliver them a hit. He did. (First National.) Song: All This And Heaven Too (by M.K. Jerome and Jack Scholl).

A re-working in part of *Bordertown* (1935), **They Drive by Night** was a robust melodrama (from A.I. Bezzerides' novel *The Long Haul*) about a couple of brothers (George Raft and Humphrey Bogart) in the road haulage business and the events that overtake their lives: Bogart (left) loses an arm in a motor accident, and Raft (right) becomes romantically involved with the wife (Ida Lupino) of a powerful trucking baron. Plot and characterization in the Richard Macaulay-Jerry Wald screenplay didn't really add up to much, but its cast, augmented by Ann Sheridan (seated right) as a waitress and Alan Hale as Lupino's husband, made it all seem better than it really was. Under Raoul Walsh's taut direction, Raft gave one of the best performances of his career. Hal B. Wallis' production (associate producer was Mark Hellinger) also featured Gale Page (seated left), Roscoe Karns (centre), John Litel, Henry O'Neill, Joyce Compton (standing left) and George Tobias. (First National.) *Note*: The film is not to be confused with the Warner Bros. (Teddington) production of the same name, a suspense drama directed in England by Arthur Woods and starring Emlyn Williams and Ernest Thesiger, which necessitated a change of title for the studio's American picture in Britain where it became **The Road to Frisco.**

Gambling on the High Seas mixed romance with melodrama in a routine story starring Wayne Morris. He played a reporter attempting to find the sort of conclusive evidence that will send the gangster-owner of a gambling ship (and a murderer to boot) to the electric chair. How he finds that evidence, as well as the love of his life (Jane Wyman, right) formed the gist of Robert E. Kent's screenplay (from a story by Martin Mooney). George Amy directed for associate producer Bryan Foy, and the cast included Gilbert Roland (left) as the murderer, William Pawley, Murray Alper, Frank Wilcox, Robert Strange and John Litel.

A remake of *The Hometowners* which George M. Cohan wrote in 1926 and which was first filmed in 1928, **Ladies Must Live** was about a bigoted 'Main Streeter' who sees New York through jaundiced eyes. He puts a spoke in the wheel of his millionaire pal's marriage because he believes the man's fiancée and her family are gold-diggers. It starred Wayne Morris (centre right) and Rosemary Lane (right), with Roscoe Karns (left), Lee Patrick (centre left), George Reeves and Ferris Taylor in support. It was written by Robert E. Kent, who brought nothing fresh to the story, and directed without enthusiasm by Noel Smith. The associate producer was William Jacobs. (First National.)

Several ever-familiar ingredients germane to cops-and-robbers melodrama, such as suspect bank-tellers, stolen funds, robberies, and the climactic chase, were in evidence in **Money and the Woman.** A routine programmer based on a story by James M. Cain (script by Robert Presnell Sr) it featured Jeffrey Lynn (right), Brenda Marshall (centre), John Litel (left), Lee Patrick, Henry O'Neill, Roger Pryor, Guinn Williams, William Gould and Ed Keane. William K. Howard directed, and the associate producer was William Jacobs.

'Delightful nonsense,' was the verdict reached by critics and audiences alike for **My Love Came Back,** a frothy comedy concocted by Walter Reisch and scripted by Ivan Goff, Robert H. Buckner and Earl Baldwin. It starred Olivia de Havilland (left) as a violin student studying on a scholarship at an academy, and Charles Winninger as the elderly owner of a phonograph factory who is secretly sponsoring her, and whose wicked urge to rejuvenate himself was the comedy's highpoint. The plot was of secondary importance to the frolicsome mood created by director Kurt Bernhardt, who drew winning performances from a cast that also included Jeffrey Lynn, Eddie Albert, Spring Byington, (as Winninger's understanding wife), Jane Wyman (right), S.Z. Sakall, Grant Mitchell and Ann Gillis. The producer was Hal B. Wallis and Wolfgang Reinhardt was his associate.

This third remake of **River's End** (the first was in 1922, the second in 1930) starred Dennis Morgan (right) as John Keith, a man falsely accused of murder. Keith's resemblance to a certain Sergeant Conniston is so marked that on the sergeant's death, Keith becomes his double and tracks down the real murderer. The film's Saskatchewan setting was sufficiently romantic to woo a new generation of moviegoers, and James Oliver Curwood's story (scripted by Barry Trivers and Bertram Millhauser) again proved gripping. Ray Enright directed a cast including Elizabeth Earl (centre), George Tobias (left) and James Stephenson for associate producer William Jacobs.

New York was the **City for Conquest** in this James Cagney-Ann Sheridan drama, and rarely has the personality of a major metropolis been so accurately, lovingly, and lyrically recorded. Responsible was director Anatole Litvak, whose efficient handling of his cast enabled Cagney (right), as a truck-driver turned prizefighter, and Sheridan (centre) as his girlfriend, to give performances as fine as anything they had done to date. John Wexley's screenplay (from the novel by Aben Kandel) also offered meaty roles to Arthur Kennedy (making his debut in the role of Cagney's sensitive musician brother), Frank Craven, Donald Crisp, Frank McHugh, George Tobias, Jerome Cowan, Anthony Quinn (left), Lee Patrick and Blanche Yurka. Elia Kazan appeared, briefly, as a hood. Litvak also produced, with William Cagney as associate producer.

An insipid remake of *Too Young to Marry* (1931) and *Love Begins at Twenty* (1936), **Calling All Husbands** (from Martin Flavin's play *Broken Dishes*) starred Ernest Truex (left) as the henpecked Homer Trippe, Florence Bates as his bullying wife, and George Tobias (right) as Oscar Armstrong, the man she regrets not having married. Written by Robert E. Kent, and directed by Noel Smith, it also featured Lucille Fairbanks, George Reeves, Charles Halton and Virginia Sale. The associate producer was William Jacobs.

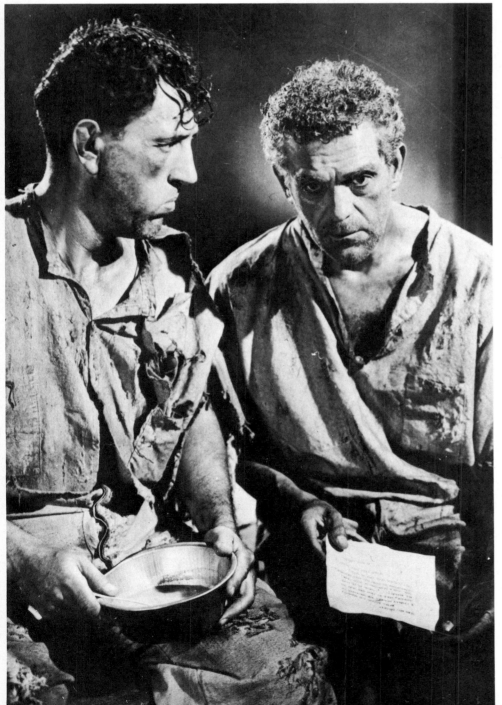

Based on private papers belonging to Mrs Rockne and reports by intimate friends and associates, and written for the screen by Robert Buckner, **Knute Rockne-All American** (released in Britain as **A Modern Hero**) was more of a patriotic flag-wave for football than a biography of Notre Dame coach Knute Rockne. Still, football enthusiasts from coast to coast were inspired by its reverential sentiments and supported it to box-office success. Pat O'Brien (centre) starred as the legendary coach, Gale Page was his wife. Hal B. Wallis produced with Robert Fellows as his associate producer. It was directed by Lloyd Bacon with a cast that included Ronald Reagan, Donald Crisp, Albert Basserman, John Qualen and Dorothy Tree.

Originally due for release in February of 1939, but held up because of the protests of French consular attachés in America, **Devil's Island** was a savage exposé of the appalling conditions that prevailed in the notorious French penal colony. Boris Karloff (right) starred as a surgeon who finds himself facing a treason charge for treating the wounds of an escaped convict; James Stephenson appeared as the prison's sadistic prison commandant (who uses a miniature guillotine as a cigar clipper) and Nedda Harrigan was the wife who finally betrays her husband by helping Karloff to expose him for the brute he is. A clichéd ending, in which a group of convicts escape in an open boat across the Atlantic, tended to halt an otherwise worthy piece of cinematic realism firmly in its tracks, but there was enough that was powerful and provocative in the earlier sequences to make it worthwhile. It was written by Kenneth Gamet and Don Ryan (from a story by Anthony Coldeway and Raymond L. Schrock) and directed for associate producer Bryan Foy by William Clemens. Also cast were Adia Kuznetzoff (left), Rolla Gourvitch, Will Stanton, Robert Warwick and Pedro de Cordoba.

△
John Garfield remained bitterly resentful of the roles the studio was offering him, and **Flowing Gold** was precisely the sort of movie with which he no longer wished to be associated. The story of an aimless drifter on the run from the law for killing a man in self-defence, it was pretty routine stuff which only served to reinforce the moody, introverted, untrusting Garfield persona. Its setting was a Western oil-field (where Garfield hopes to be safe from the law), and what little interest there was in Kenneth Gamet's screenplay (story by Rex Beach) concerned a triangle relationship between Garfield (right), Pat O'Brien (left, as an oil-field foreman) and Frances Farmer (centre), a tough Stanwyck-type girl perfectly capable of looking after herself. Though the movie ends with an avalanche, **Flowing Gold**, directed by Alfred E. Green, caused no landslide at the box-office. But it was successful enough to convince studio executives (though not Garfield) that they were right in the use they were making of their star. Also cast were Raymond Walburn (centre right), Tom Kennedy and Granville Bates for associate producer William Jacobs.

◁ Errol Flynn's success as *Captain Blood* (1935) encouraged Jack Warner to give audiences an encore in the shape of another Rafael Sabatini adventure, **The Sea Hawk**, even though the screenplay by Howard Koch and Seton I. Miller bore little relation to the Sabatini original. The film was first produced in 1924 by First National and directed by Frank Lloyd with Milton Sills in the Flynn role. The story of Captain Geoffrey Thorpe (Flynn) and his reckless acts of piracy against the Spanish, it was another top-notch, Michael Curtiz-directed action film which showed off Flynn (left) to impressive advantage as he contrasted his gentlemanly good manners in the court scenes with his athletic prowess when provoked into swordplay. **The Sea Hawk** also showed off the studio's enormous new sound stage, and the two full-scale ships that were built especially for the $1,700,000 production. Flora Robson, who had scored such a personal success in the 1937 British film *Fire Over England* (released by United Artists) was engaged to repeat her interpretation of Elizabeth I (less histrionic in every way than Bette Davis' interpretation in the 1939 *The Private Lives of Elizabeth and Essex*), while Brenda Marshall provided the romance amidst the derring-do. The villains were Claude Rains and Henry Daniell, with Alan Hale, Una O'Connor, James Stephenson, Gilbert Roland and William Lundigan in other key roles. Erich Wolfgang Korngold's score, his last for an historical adventure, was also one of his finest. Sol Polito was the cameraman, and the brilliant art direction was by Anton Grot. The producers were Jack Warner and Hal B. Wallis, with Henry Blanke as associate.

The sort of plot on which the silent cinema flourished, **Father is a Prince** (a remake of the 1934 film *Big Hearted Herbert*), was a programmer from associate producer William Jacobs. It told an old-fashioned story of a carpet-sweeper manufacturer who is more concerned about hoarding his money than about the happiness of his family. His selfishness leads to a major domestic crisis in which his wife has a breakdown and almost dies. But disaster is averted when father sees the error of his ways and buries his parsimony and thoughtlessness just in time for a happy ending. Grant Mitchell and Nana Bryant (right) were Mr and Mrs, with other parts going to John Litel (left), George Reeves, Jan Clayton, Lee Patrick, Billy Dawson, Richard Clayton, John Ridgely and Vera Lewis. It was written by Robert E. Kent (from the play by Sophie Kerr Underwood and Anna S. Richardson) and directed by Noel Smith. (First National.)
▽

△
From its justly celebrated opening scene, in which Bette Davis empties a barrel-load of bullets into the man she loves, to its eerie climax in which (courtesy of the Hays Office but unfaithful to Somerset Maugham) she is stabbed, William Wyler's assured handling of **The Letter** made compulsive viewing. In a multi-textured part (previously played on stage by Gladys Cooper, Katharine Cornell, and, in 1929, on the screen by Jeanne Eagels), Davis (right) again turned melodrama into art with a portrayal as finely honed as such steamy material (screenplay by Howard Koch) allowed. She received brilliant support from James Stephenson (left) as her attorney, Herbert Marshall (centre) as her husband (he had appeared briefly as the lover in the earlier screen version) and Gale Sondergaard as the sinister Eurasian widow of the murdered man. Cecil Kellaway was in it, too, but only fleetingly in a party scene. Contributing to the effectiveness of Robert Lord's production were Max Steiner's dramatic musical score, and Tony Gaudio's moody black-and-white photography. Also cast were Frieda Inescort, Bruce Lester and Willie Fung. (First National.) It was loosely remade in 1947 as *The Unfaithful*.

△
A top-notch translation from stage to screen, S.N. Behrman's **No Time for Comedy** was a winner. James Stewart (left) starred as a sort of Neil Simon-type playwright who comes to the conclusion that his comedies are too lightweight to be important. This leads him to write a serious play that also happens to be irredeemably lousy. The film achieved a deliciously wistful quality under William Keighley's seasoned direction, with Rosalind Russell (right) as Stewart's actress wife and Genevieve Tobin and Charlie Ruggles offering marvellous support. Also cast were Allyn Joslyn, Clarence Kolb and Louise Beavers. The ubiquitous Epstein brothers were responsible for the intelligent, entertaining screenplay. Hal B. Wallis was the producer with Robert Lord as his associate. The movie was re-released in the U.S.A. in 1954 under the anything-but-compulsive title of **Guy With a Grin**. (First National.)

A remake of *Brides Are Like That* (1936). ▷
Always A Bride, from the play by Barry
Conners, dealt with the subject of flattery,
and showed how a young man flattered his
way to the top to become the town's mayor
while, at the same time, winning the girl of
his choice (Rosemary Lane, left). George
Reeves (centre) was the flatterer, with other
parts going to John Eldredge (right),
Virginia Brissac, Francis Pierlot and Oscar
O'Shea. Robert E. Kent wrote the take-it-or-
leave-it screenplay, and the equally indifferent direction was by Noel Smith. The
associate producer was William Jacobs.
(First National.)

△

In an attempt to unshackle himself from the
broody, introverted character he was so
often called on to play, John Garfield (centre
right) went to the other extreme in **East of
the River**. The film was a really wretched
piece of conveyor-belt movie-making in
which he took to a life of crime on the
streets of a studio-fabricated New York. His
adopted brother (William Lundigan, left), on
the other hand, was a respectable college
graduate with only one thing in common
with Garfield: they both loved the same girl
(Brenda Marshall, right). The heightened
sense of bravado Garfield brought to the
role only made Fred Niblo Jr's screenplay
appear shallower than it was (story by John
Fante and Ross B. Wills). Other victims
trapped in Harlan Thompson's production
were Marjorie Rambeau (centre left), George
Tobias, Moroni Olsen and Douglas Fowley.
It was directed by Alfred E. Green.

Majorie Rambeau (centre right) was unable
to obliterate the impact made by Marie
Dressler's *Tugboat Annie* (MGM, 1933) in a
sequel called **Tugboat Annie Sails Again**.
Walter De Leon's screenplay (based on
characters created by Norman Reilly Raine)
takes up the story some years after the
death of Annie's husband, and is all about
the waterfront queen's efforts to stay afloat
despite heavy opposition from rival captains. She does. So did the movie – but
only just. It was buoyed along by a romance
between Ronald Reagan (right) and Jane
Wyman (left) with other hands on deck
comprising Alan Hale, Granville Bates,
Clarence Kolb (centre left), Paul Hurst, and
Chill Wills. Lewis Seiler directed, and the
associate producer was Edmund Grainger.
(First National.)
▽

In **South of Suez**, an efficient piece of 'B'
picture making, George Brent (centre) fell in
love with Brenda Marshall, the beautiful
daughter of a man he has (erroneously) been
accused of murdering. Barry Trivers' screenplay, (from a story by Sheridan Gibney), also
involved the South African diamond mining
industry and, for atmosphere, London in
thick fog. The film was directed by Lewis
Seiler for associate producer William Jacobs,
and featured George Tobias, James Stephenson, Lee Patrick (right), Eric Blore and Cecil
Kellaway.
▽

Another of the studio's prestige biographical
dramas, **A Dispatch from Reuters** (released
in Britain as **This Man Reuter**) was a
respectable and compelling account of the
tribulations that befell the German founder
of the celebrated news-gathering service
that still bears his name. The climax of the
film, in which Reuter scooped the world
with the news of Lincoln's assassination,
was particularly effective. So, too, was
Edward G. Robinson's (right) gentle portrayal of the title role. Milton Krims provided the screenplay (from a story by
Valentine Williams and Wolfgang Wilhelm)
and William Dieterle directed (somewhat
over earnestly at times), with Edna Best,
Eddie Albert (left), Albert Basserman, Nigel
Bruce, Gene Lockhart, Montagu Love and
Otto Kruger offering sturdy support. It was
produced by Hal B. Wallis with Henry
Blanke as associate.
▽

1941

Thirty-seven feature films were released by Warner Bros. in 1941, including **Target For Tonight**, a propaganda film made by the RAF in Britain. Steve Trilling, a casting director, became Jack Warner's assistant and would soon replace Hal B. Wallis as head of production. In June of 1941, despite the fact that musicals were, temporarily, box-office poison, Jack Warner decided to take a risk and bought the rights to Irving Berlin's **This Is The Army**, a Broadway revue which he felt was ideally suited to the current mood of the nation. The war effort was being served equally well with the preparation of several instructional documentaries at the old Vitagraph Studios which had fallen into disuse. Because of the war and the inevitable cutbacks resulting from it, the studio's latest contracts were negotiated in months and weeks rather than years. **The Maltese Falcon**, **One Foot In Heaven** and **Sergeant York** were all nominated for Best Picture in the year's Oscar stakes, but the winner was **How Green Was My Valley** (20th Century-Fox). Gary Cooper, however, won a Best Actor Oscar for his performance in **Sergeant York**, and Mary Astor an Oscar for Best Supporting Actress in **The Great Lie**. William Holmes won the studio's only other Oscar in 1941 for his editing of **Sergeant York**. Sydney Greenstreet was nominated as Best Supporting Actor for **The Maltese Falcon** but lost to Donald Crisp in **How Green Was My Valley**. **Sergeant York** and **One Foot In Heaven** appeared on the *New York Times* Ten Best list, while the New York film critics voted Gary Cooper the best actor of the year for **Sergeant York**. The studio announced a net profit of $5,429,302. Top Warner Bros. money-makers of the year were **Dive Bomber**, **Meet John Doe**, **The Sea Wolf**, **The Strawberry Blonde**, **The Bride Came C.O.D.** and **Sergeant York**.

Though Roger Pryor (centre right), Eve Arden (right) and Cliff Edwards were billed above Clem Bevans (centre left) in **She Couldn't Say No**, it was Bevans, as an eighty year old involved in a breach of promise suit with a spinster he'd been courting for fifteen years, who was the sole reason for staying the course. A tired programmer which also featured Vera Lewis (left), it was written by Earl Baldwin and Charles Grayson from a play by Benjamin M. Kaye, and directed by William Clemens for associate producer William Jacobs. (First National.)

Though **The Case of the Black Parrot** was bereft of a parrot of any colour, it was full of clichés, including the one in which a couple of mysterious figures are seen silhouetted in front of a window as the clock chimes midnight. All about a reporter (William Lundigan, left) who solves a case involving a Buhl cabinet and its contents of hidden diamonds, it looked very much as though the butler was responsible for the two murders committed during the course of it, until, finally, all was revealed. It was written by Robert E. Kent from a play by Burton E. Stevenson, the director was Noel Smith and the cast included Maris Wrixon (right), Eddie Foy Jr, Charles Waldron and Paul Cavanagh. The associate producer was William Jacobs. (First National.)

Based on the life of the forgotten actress, Mrs Leslie Carter, and her association with theatrical impresario David Belasco, **Lady With Red Hair** was a companion piece of sorts to *The Great Garrick* (1937) but not as entertaining. With Miriam Hopkins (illustrated) doing her professional best to overcome a slight case of miscasting (Mrs Carter was one of the great beauties of her time), interest settled mainly on the impeccable Claude Rains, who played the

flamboyant impresario with consummate skill. He managed this despite the stodgy screenplay by Milton Krims and Charles Kenyon (from the story *Portrait of a Lady With Red Hair* by Norbert Faulkner and N. Brewster Morse, based on the memoirs of Mrs Leslie Carter), and the equally stodgy direction by Curtis (formerly Kurt) Bernhardt. The period detail throughout, as in *The Great Garrick*, was exemplary. Also cast were Richard Ainley, Laura Hope Crews, Helen Westley, John Litel, Mona Barrie, Cecil Kellaway and Victor Jory. Jack Warner produced; Edmund Grainger was the associate producer.

There was practically no attempt on writer Robert Buckner's part to convey any historical accuracy to the events of **Santa Fe Trail**. He simply recorded the fact (Hollywood fashion) that cavalry commander Jeb Stuart (Errol Flynn, centre) and his militia effected the final capture at the Harper's Ferry massacre of abolitionist John Brown (Raymond Massey, left). Using history as a mere frame for director Michael Curtiz's largely successful portrait of Flynn as the archetypal hero — unswervingly loyal to his army, regardless of whether the cause to which he has devoted himself was a worthy one or not — the film equivocated when it came to taking sides and was only comfortable in the 'Boys' Own' action sequences. For the rest, Curtiz's handling of the romantic interest (supplied by Olivia de Havilland) and the comic elements (supplied by Alan Hale and Guinn Williams) was decidedly perfunctory. Also on the trail were Ronald Reagan (as George Armstrong Custer), William Lundigan, Van Heflin (centre left), Gene Reynolds, Ward Bond (right) and Henry O'Neill. It was produced by Jack Warner and Hal B. Wallis with Robert Fellows as associate.

A remake of *Goodbye Again* (1933), **Honeymoon for Three** had the temerity to cast George Brent (centre right) as a literary Don Juan at whose feet a profusion of ladies unconvincingly throw themselves. All about Brent's romance with a former sweetheart while on a lecture tour in Cleveland, it starred Osa Massen (left) as the girl who comes back for a second helping, and Ann Sheridan as Brent's adoring secretary, through whose intervention a disastrous situation is averted. The Epstein brothers' and Earl Baldwin's screenplay (from a play by Allan Scott and George Haight) was powerless against the miscasting of Brent; so was Lloyd Bacon's direction. Charlie Ruggles played Miss Massen's put-upon husband, with other parts going to Jane Wyman (right), William T. Orr (centre left), Lee Patrick, and Walter Catlett as a waiter whose confusion during a restaurant scene – in which Brent is simultaneously entertaining two parties, neither being aware of the other's presence – was the brightest spot in an otherwise pallid comedy. The associate producer was Henry Blanke.

The third film to chronicle the events that befell the Lemp family, **Four Mothers**, written in molasses by Stephen Morehouse Avery, eschewed romantic problems (all four sisters were quite happily married at this point in the saga) in favour of financial ones. It starts when brother-in-law Frank McHugh goes bankrupt in a Florida land scheme, the repercussions of which affect the entire family. At a stroke they lose their life savings as well as their credibility in the community. But not for long. Honest endeavour and family solidarity win through in the end, and the Lemps emerge from their catastrophe in triumph. The familiar cast – Priscilla (far left), Rosemary (right), and Lola (centre right) Lane, Claude Rains (centre), Jeffrey Lynn, Eddie Albert, Vera Lewis, Gale Page (centre left) and Dick Foran – brought a certain conviction to the unconvincing material, notwithstanding William Keighley's over-emphatic direction, which made it uphill all the way. The associate producer was Henry Blanke. Song: Moonlight And Tears (by Jack Scholl and Heinz Roemheld).

Father's Son, based on a Booth Tarkington story, was first seen as a film in 1931. The remake had little of the first version's appeal and none of its charm. As the selfish father with a scant understanding of young boys in general and his own son in particular, John Litel (left) was no match for Lewis Stone, but then neither Frieda Inescort (as gentle, understanding mum, centre) nor Billy Dawson (as the irritant son, right) were as good as Irene Rich and Leon Janney in the original. Fred Niblo Jr's screenplay had little going for it, and D. Ross Lederman's direction was all but invisible. Christian Rub, Bernice Pilot, Phillip Hurlic, Sammy McKimm and Sonny Bupp were also in it for associate producer William Jacobs.

Eddie Albert (centre) starred as **The Great Mr. Nobody**, playing an accident-prone reporter whose life is comprised of a series of catastrophes. Albert's deft performance did wonders for Ben Markson and Kenneth Gamet's screenplay (story by Harold Titus), turning a basically trite little tale into an enjoyable romantic comedy, with Joan Leslie dispensing the romance. It was directed by Ben Stoloff and the cast included Alan Hale (right), John Litel, William Lundigan, Dickie Moore, Paul Hurst (left) and Billy Benedict. The associate producer was William Jacobs.

Both Paul Muni and George Raft turned down the role of 'Mad Dog' Roy Earle (of the Dillinger gang) in director Raoul Walsh's **High Sierra**. It went, instead, to Humphrey Bogart (centre right), whose tough but sympathetic portrayal of a hunted criminal fleeing into the Sierra Madre mountains gave him his first chance to project a fully rounded, three-dimensional character. Scripted by John Huston and W.R. Burnett from the latter's novel (Burnett wrote *Little Caesar*), dramatically photographed by Tony Gaudio, and with a cast including Ida Lupino (right), Arthur Kennedy (centre left), Alan Curtis (in background), Cornel Wilde (left), a dog named Pard, Joan Leslie as the clubfooted girl with whom Bogart falls in love, Henry Hull and Henry Travers, it was melodrama of the highest order. The producers were Jack Warner and Hal B. Wallis, with Mark Hellinger as associate. (First National.) The film was later re-made twice: as *Colorado Territory* (1949) and *I Died A Thousand Times* (1955).

Gary Cooper's 55th film, **Meet John Doe**, ▷
was also one of his very best. Brilliantly
written by Robert Riskin, from a story by
Richard Connell and Robert Presnell, its
timely appearance in 1941 warned, in the
most entertaining way, of the dangers of
Fascism. Cooper (right) played a hungry,
down-and-out bush-leaguer suffering from
an arm injury who is picked up by columnist
Barbara Stanwyck (left) and promoted into
a massive newspaper publicity stunt. Under
Stanwyck's guidance, he becomes 'John
Doe', the people's mouthpiece, championing
the cause of decency and fair play in a
country pickled in misery, corruption and
hypocrisy. What starts out as a jape snow-
balls out of all proportion and, before long,
John Doe clubs are surfacing across the
length and breadth of the country. It is only
when the paper's power-crazed editor
(Edward Arnold) decides to ask Stanwyck's
'creation' to nominate him as a third party
candidate for the presidency, that Cooper,
alias John Doe, refuses. Arnold vindictively
exposes him as a fraud and the John Doe
industry collapses overnight. Again Cooper
finds himself destitute but, as he is about to
take his own life, is saved by Stanwyck who
professes her love for him. Produced and
directed by Frank Capra and with Cooper,
Stanwyck, and Arnold all superb in their
respective roles, **Meet John Doe**, despite its
unsatisfactory ending, was as eloquent a
statement on the privilege of democracy
and the sheer necessity of the 'little man' for
whom democracy was created, as the
cinema had ever offered. And as pleasur-
able. Fine performances were also given by
James Gleason (as the paper's tough
managing director), Walter Brennan, Regis
Toomey, Harry Holman, Gene Lockhart and
Spring Byington.

△
A traditional but passable whodunnit, **The
Nurse's Secret** starred Lee Patrick as the
nurse assigned to an ailing dowager, and
Regis Toomey (left) as a police inspector
assigned to solving a murder committed in
the dowager's residence. Several suspects
stood to benefit from the crime, including
Ann Edmonds, George Campeau, Clara
Blandick, and Leonard Mudie. Also cast
were Julie Bishop, Charles D. Waldron
(right) and Charles Trowbridge. It was
written by Anthony Coldeway from a story
by Mary Roberts Rinehart, and directed
with the requisite amount of suspense by
Noel Smith. The associate producer was
William Jacobs.

The Great Lie was the improbable story of a wealthy woman (Bette Davis, left), whose passion for George Brent (centre), whom she believes to have been killed in a plane crash, drives her to an act of desperation. She offers to make a cash settlement on her rival in love (Mary Astor, as a concert pianist) if she will allow her to adopt the baby she (Mary) is carrying, and which she knows to be Brent's. Based on Polan Banks' novel *January Heights*, Lenore Coffee's screenplay, a made-to-measure job for its two stars, indulged in a riot of wish-fulfilment fantasies depicting the protagonists as the epitome of elegance, and in Astor's case, talented enough to play the Tchaikovsky Piano Concerto. In complete contrast to the studio's social dramas of the thirties, soap operas like **The Great Lie** bore as much resemblance to real life as Flash Gordon did to the science of astronomy. But they scored heavily at the box-office and this one was no exception. Davis and Astor (right) in combat were riveting. In fact it was Davis who, in order to improve the ludicrous story-line, insisted that Astor's part be built up. As a result, Astor won an Oscar for best supporting performance and thanked Davis – and Tchaikovsky – in her acceptance speech. Max Steiner's score pounded away soupily, and Edmund Goulding, directing a cast that also included Lucile Watson, Hattie McDaniel and Virginia Brissac, brought a patina of sophistication to the proceedings which, considering the plot, was something of a miracle. The producers were Jack Warner and Hal B. Wallis, with Henry Blanke as associate.

Million Dollar Baby was a comedy which starred Priscilla Lane (left) as a young woman who inherits a million dollars from crotchety May Robson (centre). And is she happy? Of course not. The message, writ large, was that money does not necessarily bring contentment. On inheriting her fortune, Miss Lane loses her boyfriend (Jeffrey Lynn) and is prepared to sacrifice her windfall to get him back. Which is exactly what she does. It took four extremely talented writers – Casey Robinson, Richard Macaulay and Jerry Wald (story by Leonard Spigelgass) – to think it all up, and although some of the dialogue was undeniably witty, the overall effort lacked sparkle. It was directed without much style by Curtis Bernhardt, and featured Ronald Reagan (right) as a concert pianist, Lee Patrick, Helen Westley, George Barbier, Nan Wynn, John Qualen and Walter Catlett. It was produced by Hal B. Wallis with David Lewis as his associate.

Kisses For Breakfast (a remake of *The Matrimonial Bed*, 1930) was a pleasant, undemanding farce about a newly married husband who, after an amnesia attack, finds himself a second 'wife'. Inevitably, the two women meet with amusing, if predictable, results. Lewis Seiler directed from a screenplay by Kenneth Gamet (from the play by Seymour Hicks based on the French play by Yves Mirande and André Mouezy Eon), and the cast included Dennis Morgan (centre), Jane Wyatt (right), Lee Patrick, Shirley Ross (left), Jerome Cowan, Una O'Connor and Barnett Parker. The associate producer was Harlan Thompson.

Set in Hong Kong on the eve of the Japanese invasion, **Passage From Hong Kong**, a feeble romantic comedy with undercurrents of crime, concerned a writer of thrillers (Keith Douglas, right) who attempts to woo a reluctant Lucille Fairbanks by inventing a murder story in which he claims to be implicated. Based on the same material as *The Second Floor Mystery* (1930), (screenplay by Fred Niblo Jr from a story by Earl Derr Biggers), it was directed by D. Ross Lederman for associate producer William Jacobs and featured Paul Cavanagh (left), Richard Ainley, Marjorie Gateson, Gloria Holden and Lumsden Hare.

In **Thieves Fall Out**, Jane Darwell (centre) played a conniving grandmother who outwits a gangster to ensure her shy grandson's happiness and future prosperity. Eddie Albert (left) was the grandson, and the Charles Grayson-Ben Markson screenplay (from a play by Irving Gaumont and Jack Sobel) involved him in selling a legacy in order to obtain enough money to marry his sweetheart, Joan Leslie (right). A mixture of domestic comedy and melodrama, it moved smoothly from one to the other under Ray Enright's direction, but the chief virtue of the enterprise was Jane Darwell's energetic central performance. Also cast were Alan Hale, William T. Orr, John Litel, Anthony Quinn, Edward Brophy and Minna Gombell. Edmund Grainger was associate producer.

Having spent his last film aboard the fog-bound vessel *Ghost*, in *The Sea Wolf*, it was appropriate that John Garfield's next film be called **Out of the Fog**. Based on Irwin Shaw's play *The Gentle People*, it was the sinister story of a petty hoodlum (Garfield, centre, back in one of his more familiar guises) who terrorizes and robs two elderly men (Thomas Mitchell and John Qualen) of the money they have saved for a fishing boat. The victims decide to avenge themselves by murdering Garfield but are spared the effort when he falls overboard from their boat leaving behind his wallet containing the stolen cash. Toning down the cocky characterization he had used in *East of the River* the previous year to a more acceptable level of brashness, Garfield's performance was outstanding. The film – another in the studio's conscience-stricken series of the underdog's right to overcome the overwhelming disadvantage of an unpromising environment – was excellently made with a script by Robert Rossen, Jerry Wald and Richard Macaulay, and taut direction by Anatole Litvak. As in *The Sea Wolf*, Ida Lupino (right) provided the romantic interest, and others in the cast were Eddie Albert (left), George Tobias and Aline MacMahon.

An undernourished melodrama based on a play by Leon Abrams and George Abbott, **Highway West** was a remake of *Heat Lightning* (1934). It was about a wife (Brenda Marshall) who discovers that her respectable businessman-husband (Arthur Kennedy) isn't respectable, and isn't a businessman, but a gunman, who goes to jail for his activities. Also cast were William Lundigan, Olympe Bradna, Slim Summerville (left), Willie Best (centre), John Ridgely (right) and Noel Madison. It was scripted by Allen Rivkin, Charles Kenyon and Kenneth Gamet and directed by William McGann for associate producer Edmund Grainger. (First National.)

A fictional account of the notorious Younger brothers' disgust with Southern carpet-baggers, and their gun-slinging, fist-flying descent into lawlessness as a protest, **Bad Men of Missouri** was an action-packed Western which turned the brothers into Robin Hoods who robbed and plundered in the service of down-trodden settlers. Fisti-cuffs atop a moving stagecoach, jailbreaks and cattle stampedes were prominent features of Charles Grayson's pacey screenplay (story by Robert E. Kent) and Ray Enright's fast direction. Dennis Morgan (centre), Wayne Morris (right), and Arthur Kennedy (left) gave spirited performances as the brothers, Jane Wyman supplied romance and Walter Catlett humour, with other roles going to Victor Jory, Alan Baxter and Faye Emerson for associate producer Harlan Thompson. (First National.)

A fifty minute remake of *Public Enemy's Wife* (1936), **Bullets For O'Hara** was a cops-n'-robbers melodrama about a detective (Roger Pryor) who, with the help of gangster Anthony Quinn's wife (Joan Perry, centre right), brings about Quinn's downfall. The chief of its many implausibilities was having mobster Quinn (centre left) successfully posing as a man of society. Raymond L. Schrock's screenplay added up to rather less than met the eye (the story was by David O. Selznick and P.J. Wolfson), and despite William K. Howard's efficient direction, failed to generate interest. Also in the large cast were Maris Wrixon, Dick Purcell (left), Hobart Bosworth, Richard Ainley, Roland Drew (right), De Wolfe Hopper, Joan Winfield, Joseph King, Victor Zimmerman, Hank Mann and Frank Mayo. The associate producer was William Jacobs.

A cadaverous remake of *Dangerous* (1936), **Singapore Woman** gained nothing by switching locales (the earlier film, which starred Bette Davis, was set in New York and Connecticut), and M. Coates Webster's screenplay (from the story by Laird Doyle) about a jinxed woman and the men who show her that life *is* worth living after all, was a ponderous affair indeed. Brenda Marshall (illustrated), was the leading lady with problems (an oriental curse being one of them), with David Bruce and Jerome Cowan as the men in her life. Also cast were Virginia Field, Rose Hobart, Heather Angel, Richard Ainley and Dorothy Tree. It was directed in a straightforward, matter-of-fact manner by Jean Negulesco, and the associate producer was Harlan Thompson. (First National.)

Largely reminiscent of the studio's 1937 ▷
offering *Slim*, itself a remake of *Tiger Shark*,
Manpower — in which two tough power
linemen fight for the attentions of a sexy
cafe hostess, with tragic results — was little
more than an excuse to bring together three
dynamic stars: Edward G. Robinson, George
Raft (left) and Marlene Dietrich (right). The
chemistry between them was fine, but the
plot was routine, and despite the energetic
performances of the famous trio, there was
not enough manpower on hand to dispose
of the clichés in the Richard Macaulay-
Jerry Wald screenplay (story by Fred Niblo
Jr). Raoul Walsh directed it all in his best
tough-guy manner only to come a cropper
with his painful attempts at humour. Also
featured were Alan Hale, Frank McHugh,
Eve Arden, Barton MacLane, Ward Bond and
Walter Catlett. Hal B. Wallis produced and
his associate was Mark Hellinger. Songs: I'm
In No Mood For Music and He Lied And I
Listened (by Frederick Hollander and Frank
Loesser).

With war the main item on everybody's
agenda, there was a desperate need for
escapist entertainment – desperate being
the appropriate word in the case of **Navy
Blues** – a musical that alternated frenzy
with boredom as its crew charted a noisy
course for Honolulu. Expiring *en route*
were Ann Sheridan, Jack Oakie (centre),
Martha Raye, Jack Haley (left), Herbert
Anderson, Jack Carson (right) and Jackie
Gleason. It took four men to commit the
drivel to paper (Sam Perrin, Jerry Wald,
Richard Macaulay and Arthur T. Horman)
and two producers (Hal B. Wallis and Jerry
Wald) to capture it forever on celluloid. The
director was Lloyd Bacon. Songs included:
In Waikiki, You're A Natural, Navy Blues,
and When Are We Going To Land Abroad?
(by Arthur Schwartz and Johnny Mercer).

▽

◁ Ronald Reagan (front left) starred as a
newspaper reporter in **Nine Lives Are Not
Enough**, with Howard da Silva (left) as a
perennially frantic city editor, and James
Gleason and Ed Brophy as two witless cops.
Fred Niblo Jr's screenplay (story by Jerome
Odlum) about a boarding-house murder
was an amalgam of practically every
second-rate thriller that springs to mind,
but under A. Edward Sutherland's direction
it was, mercifully, all over in 63 swift
minutes. One body more, and it would most
certainly have outstayed its welcome. Also
cast were Faye Emerson, Peter Whitney,
Charles Drake, Joan Perry (right), Vera
Lewis, Ben Welden, Cliff Clark, Howard Hickman and Joseph Crehan. The associate producer was William Jacobs.

△

More than vaguely reminiscent of Paramount's *The Cat and the Canary* (1939), **The
Smiling Ghost** was a facile, haunted-
mansion comedy, replete with hidden
sliding panels, footsteps that go creak in the
night, lights that dim on cue and black-
faced servants in fear of their own
shadows. Wayne Morris (left), Brenda
Marshall and Alexis Smith (centre left)
starred, with Alan Hale, Lee Patrick, David
Bruce, Helen Westley, Willie Best, Roland
Drew (centre) and Richard Ainley (right) in
support. Kenneth Gamet wrote it from a
story by Stuart Palmer, the director was
Lewis Seiler, and the associate producer
Edmund Grainger.

△

One of the numerous war films glorifying the
services, **Dive Bomber** — made with the full
co-operation of the Naval Air Corps — was,
on a documentary level, the story of a group
of medical men and their experiments in the
field. It showed, for example, how to solve
the problem of 'blacking out' after a pilot
extricates himself from a power dive. On a
Hollywood level, it involved Errol Flynn
(left) in a novelettish yarn about a surgeon
who devotes his life to aviation medicine
after the death of a pilot on whom he
happened to be performing an operation.
Romance intruded in the shape of Alexis
Smith, but the film's love-affair, clearly, was
up in the air with the planes, and at that
altitude **Dive Bomber** was an unequivocal
success. Frank Wead and Robert Buckner
wrote the mundane screenplay, Michael
Curtiz was at the controls and Max Steiner's
score added more than a dollop of patriotism
to the proceedings. Although Flynn, Fred
MacMurray (centre), Ralph Bellamy and
Alexis Smith were top-starred, it was the
superb Technicolor photography (by Bert
Glennon, Winton C. Hoch, Elmer Dyer and
Charles Marshall) that made the most
impact. Hal B. Wallis was the producer with
Robert Lord as his associate. (First National.)

◁ When, in 1941, Americans were still undecided about their involvement in the European war, along came an enormous commercial hit, whose hero, a Tennessee hillbilly, was something of an inspiration to enlisting men. The story of Alvin York, who in 1918, in Argonne, singlehandedly captured 132 Germans, **Sergeant York** chronicled, with exemplary fidelity to the facts, the inner conflicts that beset York when, after a boisterous youth, he became a religious pacifist and waged a private war with himself as to whether he should remain a pacifist or enlist. For years, the real-life York refused to allow his story to be dramatized (Cecil B. DeMille considered it a suitable subject, but was turned down), and only agreed when Jesse L. Lasky personally approached him, on condition that he (York) supervised every phase of the production, and that Gary Cooper (illustrated) impersonated him in the film. There was no doubting the patriotic element coursing through the screenplay by Abem Finkel, Harry Chandler, Howard Koch and John Huston, but in 1941 why not? Director Howard Hawks, with a fair amount of money to spend on the action sequences, kept it moving briskly without letting us forget that the studio back-lot doubled as a rather idealized Tennessee. Others in the cast were Walter Brennan, Joan Leslie (her Southern drawl as phony as some of the back-drops), Stanley Ridges, George Tobias, Ward Bond, Margaret Wycherley and Noah Beery Jr. Hal B. Wallis produced.

△

In **The Body Disappears**, a farce which relied more on trick photography for its effects than on Scott Darling and Erna Lazarus' screenplay, leading man Jeffrey Lynn turned invisible after being injected with a serum invented by Edward Everett Horton (left). Horton followed suit; so did leading lady Jane Wyman. The only thing not injected with the stuff was the film itself — which, in the circumstances, was an oversight not easily forgiven. Herbert Anderson, Marguerite Chapman, Craig Stevens and Willie Best (right) were in it too; it was directed by D. Ross Lederman and the associate producer was Ben Stoloff.

◁ A winning combination of talent and money was lavished on **One Foot in Heaven**, an engaging adaptation by Casey Robinson of Hartzell Spence's best-selling biography of his Methodist Minister father William Spence who, at the turn of the century, followed a peripatetic existence wandering from one parish church to another. The film provided a series of episodes rather than a continuous story line, with Fredric March (centre) as Spence striking just the right note of piety. Irving Rapper's direction, on the other hand, often toppled into sentimentality. But it did have the appropriate turn of the century atmosphere, and the clash between Spence's religious beliefs and the fast changing quality of life he encountered on his travels was nicely articulated. Also cast were Martha Scott (centre right), Beulah Bondi, Gene Lockhart (right), Elisabeth Fraser, Laura Hope Crews, Grant Mitchell and Moroni Olsen (left). It was produced by Jack Warner and Hal B. Wallis with Robert Lord as associate.

A shallow and redundant re-make of *Oil for the Lamps of China* (1935), **Law of the Tropics** – about a young rubber planter (Jeffrey Lynn, left) who incurs the disapproval of his employers by marrying torch-singer Constance Bennett (right) – painfully demonstrated the one adage the studio stubbornly refused to acknowledge: if at first you succeed, why try again? Regis Toomey, Mona Maris, Hobart Bosworth, and Frank Puglia were in it too; it was written by Charles Grayson from a novel by Alice Tisdale Hobart and directed by Ray Enright for associate producer Ben Stoloff.

International Squadron was a remake of the James Cagney-Pat O'Brien vehicle, *Ceiling Zero* (1936) but, unlike most of the studio's retreads, emerged as solid entertainment in its own right. It starred Ronald Reagan (right) as an irresponsible flier who, after ferrying Lockheed bombers to London, joins the Royal Air Force and ultimately pays for his cocky behaviour (his irresponsibility having resulted in the deaths of two of his colleagues) by going on a suicide mission. Based on a story by Frank Wead and scripted by Barry Trivers, it was directed by Lothar Mendes, who kept the proceedings excitingly airborne, and also featured James Stephenson (centre), Julie Bishop, Cliff Edwards, Reginald Denny, Olympe Bradna, William Lundigan (left), John Ridgely and Joan Perry. The associate producer was Edmund Grainger.

Robert Rossen's screenplay for **Blues in the Night** (from a play by Edwin Gilbert) tended, at times, towards melodrama but, by and large, this serious little musical gave audiences a fairly accurate picture of itinerant jazz musicians as they frittered away their lives on a series of one-night stands, and on a sundry collection of good and not-so-good women. With a generally strong cast including Priscilla Lane (2nd right), Betty Field, Lloyd Nolan, Jack Carson, Richard Whorf, Wallace Ford, Billy Halop and Elia Kazan (as a clarinettist), plus the bands of Jimmy Lunceford and Will Osborne, it was above average entertainment, directed with a keen appreciation of the film's particular milieu by Anatole Litvak. The associate producer was Henry Blanke. Songs included: Hang On To Your Lids Kids, Blues In The Night, This Time The Dream's On Me and Says Who? Says You Says I (by Johnny Mercer and Harold Arlen).

◁ **Target For Tonight**, a documentary made by the Royal Air Force, put audiences in the cockpit of a bomber called *F For Freddie* as it set off on a bombing raid over Germany. Both informative and compulsively entertaining, it was as much a human document as a factual anatomy of how such raids were planned. Credit for this was due entirely to the keenly observed direction of Harry Watt, who also wrote the compelling screenplay. Made in Britain by the Crown Film Unit with a cast comprised entirely of R.A.F. personnel, it was undoubtedly one of the most impressive and stirring war films to be released by Warner Bros. during the decade.

Lloyd Nolan and Craig Stevens played brothers in **Steel Against the Sky**, a melodrama with a bridge-building background in which they both fall for boss' daughter Alexis Smith (centre). Stevens (right), who gets to save Nolan's (left) life twice in Paul Gerard Smith's screenplay (story by Jesse Lasky Jr and Maurice Hanline), also gets the girl (as, indeed, he did in real life). It was directed by A. Edward Sutherland, and the cast included Gene Lockhart, Edward Ellis, Walter Catlett, Howard da Silva, Julie Bishop and Edward Brophy. The associate producer was Edmund Grainger.

▽

Through the good offices of producer Henry Blanke, John Huston, hitherto a scriptwriter at the studio, finally got to direct a film: **The Maltese Falcon**. The fact that Dashiell Hammett's novel had already been filmed twice (in 1931, and again in 1936 as *Satan Met A Lady*), was of little consequence to Jack Warner who firmly believed you couldn't keep a good yarn down; and when he read Huston's scene by scene breakdown of Hammett's novel, which he mistook as the final draft screenplay, Warner was so delighted that the flavour of the book had been retained that he immediately set a production date. George Raft was asked to play the role of Sam Spade, but turned it down on the grounds that he did not want to work with an inexperienced director. So, as had been the case with *High Sierra*, Humphrey Bogart (left) inherited it. Other roles went to Mary Astor (right), Peter Lorre (centre), Gladys George, Barton MacLane, Lee Patrick, Ward Bond, Jerome Cowan, Elisha Cook Jr, and, making his film debut at the age of 61, the 280 lb. 'Fat Man' from Britain, Sydney Greenstreet (seated). Without having the foggiest notion that a masterpiece was to emerge, Warner gave Huston the usual 'gangster flick' budget of $300,000, plus a shooting schedule of six weeks, while associate producer Henry Blanke just gave advice: 'Make every shot count,' he told Huston, 'No detail can be overlooked.' After completion, a written foreword describing the history of the Falcon was added at Warner's request (he felt that the story was confusing without it) and in October 1941, the film was released. It set new standards in crime thrillers and turned Bogart into a major star.

In **Three Sons O' Guns**, Wayne Morris (right), Tom Brown (centre) and William T. Orr (left) played ne'er-do-wells who, after dodging the draft and giving their mother (Irene Rich, centre left) a bad time, are finally forced to enlist. Though they baulk at the idea of active service, the army makes men of them all, transforming them from spoilt slobs to decent, worthwhile citizens. Fred Niblo Jr wrote it, the director was Ben Stoloff, and the cast included Marjorie Rambeau, Moroni Olsen, Susan Peters and Barbara Pepper. The associate producer was William Jacobs. (First National.)
▽

Philip Dorn convincingly played an underground leader in **Underground** – a war drama dedicated to exposing the savagery of the Nazi regime – with Jeffrey Lynn (right) cast as the brother who betrays him. Indifferent performances from Lynn, Karen Verne (left) and Mona Maris weakened the impact of Charles Grayson's compelling screenplay (story by Oliver H.P. Garrett and Edwin Justus Mayer), though Vincent Sherman's direction eliminated as much flak as was possible in the circumstances. Others in the cast were Frank Reicher, Martin Kosleck, Erwin Kalser and Egon Brecher. Jack Warner and Hal B. Wallis produced, and the associate producer was William Jacobs. (First National.)
▽

◁ **Affectionately Yours** was a dismal and dispiriting comedy about an ace newspaper reporter's efforts to woo back his ex-wife. Based on a story by Fanya Foss and Aleen Leslie, and scripted by Edward Kaufman, it was a screwball comedy that misfired, leaving Dennis Morgan (as the reporter, right), Merle Oberon (as his ex-wife, left), and Rita Hayworth (as 'the other woman') with soot on their attractive faces. Ralph Bellamy played a hapless rival suitor, with other roles going to George Tobias, James Gleason, Jerome Cowan, Renie Riano, Frank Wilcox, Grace Stafford, Carmen Morales and, from *Gone With the The Wind* (Selznick, 1939), Hattie McDaniel and Butterfly McQueen. The sluggish direction was by Lloyd Bacon. Hal B. Wallis was responsible for the production, with Mark Hellinger as his associate. (First National.)

△

The clichés positively somersaulted over each other in **Shining Victory**, a romantic drama based on the play *Jupiter Laughs* by A.J. Cronin. The story of a psychiatrist whose research programme in a Scottish sanatorium is interrupted when he falls in love with his assistant and brings about a crisis of conscience in himself, was saved from banality by an accomplished cast and a convincing screenplay by Howard Koch and Ann Froelich. Irving Rapper directed for producers Jack Warner and Hal B. Wallis, and failed to notice, in one scene, that Bette Davis, disguised as a nurse, had sneaked onto the set and into the shot pretending to be an extra. James Stephenson (centre) was the doctor, Geraldine Fitzgerald (right) his assistant, with other roles going to Donald Crisp, Barbara O'Neill, Montagu Love (left) and Sig Rumann. Production-wise it was a shining victory over its pedestrian content. (First National.)
▽

Bette Davis and James Cagney, together for the first time since *Jimmy The Gent* (1934), slummed it in **The Bride Came C.O.D.**, a Julius J. and Philip G. Epstein-scripted comedy which strained desperately for guffaws, but succeeded only in raising the occasional smile. A piece of nonsense about a temperamental oil heiress (Davis, illustrated) whose elopement with a Hollywood bandleader (Jack Carson) is curtailed when her father (Eugene Pallette) hires a charter pilot (James Cagney) to bring his daughter back to him unwed, it was a routine potboiler whose best ingredient was Max Steiner's score. Stuart Erwin, George Tobias, Harry Davenport and William Frawley co-starred, and William Keighley directed. Hal B. Wallis produced, William Cagney was his associate. Despite its indifferent quality, the public bought it and it made a fortune – perhaps because of the unassailable drawing power of its two stars.

◁ The studio's last release of the year, **You're In The Army Now**, was also one of its most embarrassing. All about a couple of vacuum cleaner salesmen – Jimmy Durante (right) and Phil Silvers (centre) who find themselves drafted into the army, it sunk under the weight of its stars' top-heavy attempts at slapstick and the raucous, knockabout antics perpetrated both in the screenplay (by Paul Gerard Smith and George Beatty), and in Lewis Seiler's direction. Also involved were Jane Wyman (left), Regis Toomey, Donald MacBride, George Meeker and Joseph Sawyer. The associate producer was Ben Stoloff.

1942

By mid-1942 Jack Warner's production supervisors, known as associate producers since 1938, finally had the title 'producer' conferred on them, and henceforth would be credited as such on the screen. **Kings Row** and **Yankee Doodle Dandy** were nominated for Oscars for Best Picture of the Year, but MGM's **Mrs. Miniver** received the Academy Award. **Yankee Doodle Dandy** did, however, receive three other Oscars: for Best Actor (James Cagney); Best Music Scoring in a Musical Picture (Ray Heindorf and Heinz Roemheld); and Best Sound Recording (Nathan Levinson and the Warner Bros. Sound Department). Max Steiner won the Oscar for Best Music Scoring in a non-musical film for **Now, Voyager**, and a two-reeler called **Beyond The Line Of Duty** won an Oscar for Best Short Subject. Bette Davis was nominated for **Now, Voyager** but lost to Greer Garson in **Mrs. Miniver**. James Cagney won the New York Film Critics award as Best Actor for **Yankee Doodle Dandy**. The *New York Times* voted **Yankee Doodle Dandy** one of its Ten Best for the year, and also **Casablanca**, which it reviewed in November, 1942 although the film was not officially released until 1943. The net profit for the year was $8,554,512. Top money-makers were **In This Our Life, Yankee Doodle Dandy** and **Now, Voyager**.

The attack on Pearl Harbour understandably minimized the impact of **All Through The Night**, an adroit comedy-thriller about Nazi saboteurs who plan to blow up a battleship in New York harbour. In the wartime circumstances, such behaviour was no laughing matter. Still, judged on its own merits, it was a perfectly acceptable gangster spoof, with its sub-text, directed at Fascism, helping to freeze the smile on our faces. Apart from the fun offered by the film's knockabout plot, the sight of Humphrey Bogart (right) as a Broadway racketeer, and Barton MacLane as his former rival, caricaturing themselves without restraint, was an incidental pleasure, skilfully exploited in the Leonard Spigelgass-Edwin Gilbert screenplay, and underlined in Vincent Sherman's direction. Also involved in this entertaining hodge-podge of a film were Conrad Veidt, Karen Verne, Jane Darwell, Frank McHugh (left), Peter Lorre, Judith Anderson, William Demarest, Jackie Gleason, Phil Silvers and Wallace Ford. Hal B. Wallis produced; Jerry Wald was his associate. Song: All Through The Night (by Arthur Schwartz and Johnny Mercer — not to be confused with the Cole Porter standard).

◁ Until **They Died With Their Boots On**, no film had attempted to tell the full story of George Armstrong Custer and his famous last stand. The part of Custer was a natural for Errol Flynn, whose salary in 1941 totalled $240,000, and whose ability to combine roguish spoilt-boy pranks with manly acts of heroism and valour, perfectly equipped him to fill the shoes of Custer, at least as seen by writers Wally Kline and Aeneas MacKenzie in their highly romanticized version of one of the most stirring (and futile) incidents in American history. Though Michael Curtiz was originally offered the directorial chores, Flynn's continuing vendetta with the fiery director ('the work horse of Warners' as he was known) resulted in Raoul Walsh being signed instead. Like Curtiz, Walsh was very much an action director; the climactic charge at the film's end more than justified its build-up and was most effectively stage-managed. Appearing with Flynn (right) for the last time was Olivia de Havilland (left) as his loving wife. Their scenes together had a poignancy matched only by their work together in *The Adventures of Robin Hood* (1938). Others in the cast included Arthur Kennedy, Charles Grapewin, Gene Lockhart, Anthony Quinn, Sydney Greenstreet, Regis Toomey, Hattie McDaniel and, in a small part, a newcomer called Byron Barr who soon changed his name to Gig Young. Hal B. Wallis produced; the associate producer was Robert Fellows.

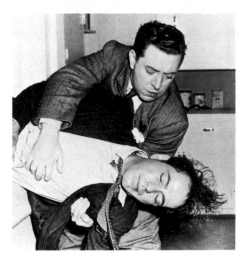

A drama about the first steamship to sail regularly between England and America, and the people responsible for her creation, **Sons of the Sea** (released in Britain as **Atlantic Ferry**) starred Michael Redgrave (right) and Valerie Hobson (left). A well-mounted propaganda piece, it was splendidly directed by Walter Forde from a screenplay by Gordon Wellesley, Edward Dryhurst and Emeric Pressburger (story by Derek and Wynne MacIver), and in secondary roles featured Griffith Jones, Margaretta Scott, Hartley Power and Bessie Love. The film was made in England at the Warner Bros. Teddington Studios.
▽

△

The George S. Kaufman-Moss Hart Broadway success, **The Man Who Came To Dinner**, was purchased at Bette Davis' request (she saw it as a vehicle for herself and John Barrymore) at a cost of a quarter of a million dollars, and handed to the industrious Epstein brothers to 'open out' for the screen. Barrymore couldn't remember his lines, so the part of Sheridan Whiteside — actually a thinly disguised Alexander Woollcott, as indeed several other characters were disguised versions of well-known people — went to Monty Woolley (right), who had created him on Broadway. The simple story of an overbearing dinner guest who remains on in the Ohio household to which he has been invited after a leg injury puts him in a wheelchair, it was laced with witty lines and witty performances — most notably from Woolley himself, Ann Sheridan (centre) as Lorraine Sheldon (Gertrude Lawrence), Jimmy Durante as Banjo (Harpo Marx), Reginald Gardiner as Beverly Carlton (Noel Coward), and Bette Davis (left), making the most of her rather colourless role as Woolley's patient secretary. Also cast were Grant Mitchell as the dyspeptic head of the household, Billie Burke as his wife, Mary Wickes as the put-upon Nurse Preen, and Richard Travis as the would-be playwright who is finally hooked by Davis. William Keighley directed with a crowd-pleasing touch. Hal B. Wallis produced, with Jack Saper and Jerry Wald as his associates.

James Cagney's first Technicolor film for the ▷ studio was a PR job for the Royal Canadian Air Force called **Captains of the Clouds**. A semi-documentary look at how members of that distinguished service were trained, the slender story devised by screenwriters Arthur T. Horman, Richard Macaulay and Norman Reilly Raine was familiar to the point of *déjà vu*, and had a cocky and rebellious Cagney (illustrated) once again redeeming his bad behaviour by sacrificing his life in a glorious act of heroism, a narrative ploy of which the studio never seemed to tire. Max Steiner's appropriately patriotic score and the breathtaking aerial photography were good points in an otherwise uninspired effort. Completing the cast were a host of the studio's stock players including Dennis Morgan, Brenda Marshall, Alan Hale, George Tobias and Paul Cavanagh, as well as the Reginalds Gardiner and Denny. Michael Curtiz directed, and the title song was by Harold Arlen and Johnny Mercer. Hal Wallis was the producer; William Cagney his associate.

Made in Britain at Warner Bros.' Teddington studios in 1941, and released in the US the following year, **The Prime Minister** starred John Gielgud as Disraeli (right), Diana Wynyard as Mary-Anne Wyndham Lewis, Stephen Murray as Gladstone, Owen Nares as Lord Derby, Fay Compton as Queen Victoria and Lyn Harding as Bismark. Little more than a series of incidents culled from the great PM's life (his first fumbling speech in the House of Commons, his visits to Queen ▷ Victoria, his relationship with Mrs Wyndham Lewis etc.) the film failed to make an impact on American audiences and received only a limited release. Gielgud's performance was unfavourably compared with George Arliss' in the same role (1929), part of the blame being levelled at Brock Williams and Michael Hogan's musty screenplay. Thorold Dickinson directed it, Max Milder produced and the cast also included Glynis Johns (left), Will Fyffe, Kynaston Reeves, Margaret Johnston and Leslie Perrins.

△ What Constance Bennett (right) was doing in a run-of-the-mill Western called **Wild Bill Hickok Rides**, was anybody's guess. She played a dance-hall hostess and was as out of place as the film's star, Bruce Cabot (left), would have been in a Restoration comedy. Still, Charles Grayson, Paul Gerard Smith and Raymond Schrock's story of a law-abiding homesteader who gets to keep his land thanks to the efforts of Mr Hickok (against whom the acquisitive villains are really no match at all), had its fair share of excitement within its pre-defined boundaries. Warren William, Ward Bond, Betty Brewer, Russell Simpson, Frank Wilcox and Howard da Silva were also in it; it was directed by Ray Enright, and Edmund Grainger was the associate producer.

◁ Nancy Coleman (centre) played an Allied agent in **Dangerously They Live**, a World War II melodrama about espionage. As the possessor of some secret information the Nazis badly want, she is captured, escapes, is involved in an accident, and loses her memory. Enter John Garfield (centre right), in the unlikely guise of a hospital intern, who facilitates her recovery and ensures that the vital information stays where it belongs — with the Allies. The film, released in the same month as Pearl Harbour, found a ready audience in the prevailing anti-Nazi climate of the country, despite its incredible plot. Almost as unbelievable was Garfield's performance. He had no wish to make the film at all, but having been suspended for a considerable period, agreed to do so because he needed the money. After his relentless bitching about his stereotyped criminal roles, on this occasion he only had himself to blame. Robert Florey's direction didn't help much; neither did Marion Parsonnet's confused screenplay. Also in the cast were Moroni Olsen (left), Raymond Massey (centre left), and Esther Dale (right). Ben Stoloff was the associate producer.

Amiable was the word for **The Male Animal**, a comedy based on the Elliott Nugent-James Thurber Broadway success about a stuffy college professor (engagingly played by Henry Fonda, left) who is forced to face two crises in his life at the same time: the defection of his wife (Olivia de Havilland, centre) in favour of a one time campus hero and former flame (Jack Carson, right); and his superior's interference with his teaching methods. How the professor coped formed the basis of an entertaining, well-written (by the Epstein brothers and Stephen Morehouse Avery) comedy which delved deeper for its laughs than its surface situation might indicate. Elliott Nugent directed a strong cast which included Joan Leslie, Eugene Pallette, Don DeFore and Herbert Anderson. Hal B. Wallis produced with associate Wolfgang Reinhardt. It was remade in 1952 as a musical called *She's Working Her Way Through College*.

◁ There were yawns all round for **Murder in the Big House**, a remake of *Jailbreak* (1936) in which a couple of fearless reporters successfully uncover a murder ring inside a state penitentiary. Van Johnson (until then an unknown chorus boy) and George Meeker (right) were the reporters; Faye Emerson the female lead. (The earlier version had Craig Reynolds in the Johnson role and June Travis as his co-star. By 1942 Reynolds was doing active service with the marines; Miss Travis had retired.) Raymond Schrock wrote the screenplay from a story by Jerome Chodorov, and the director was B. Reeves Eason. William Jacobs was the associate producer and the large cast included Frank Wilcox, Michael Ames, Roland Drew, Joseph Crehan, William Gould, Douglas Wood, John Maxwell and Ruth Ford. Because Van Johnson (centre) soon became a major star at MGM, and Faye Emerson (left) married into the Roosevelt family, the studio decided to re-issue the film in 1945 in a first-release house under the title **Born For Trouble**. On this occasion, curiosity value resulted in a brisker box-office trade than the first time round. Either way, though, the film was a failure.

Fifth Column activists in Paris before the German invasion of the Low Countries was the theme of **So This Was Paris** (released in Britain as **This Was Paris**), an entertaining adventure into espionage which starred Griffith Jones (left) as a British Intelligence officer and Ann Dvorak (centre) as the French dress designer (and Fifth Columnist) he falls for. Also cast were Ben Lyon, Mary Maguire, Robert Morley, Harold Huth, Vera Bogetti and Harry Welchman. It was written by Brock Williams and Edward Dryhurst from a story by Gordon Wellesley and Basil Woon and directed by John Harlow at Warner's Teddington Studios in England.

◁ The bullet scars suffered in **Bullet Scars** were as a result of a bank-robbery, its attendant shoot-out, and a skirmish between cops and robbers in a mountain hideout. There was a bit of kidnapping in it as well, the victims being a doctor (Regis Toomey, right) and a nurse (Adele Longmire, left) whose services are needed to patch up a bullet-scarred gunman. They fall in love, proving that good can come of evil. No good, however, came from the movie, which was just another programmer relegated to the second half of a double-bill. Robert E. Kent wrote it from a story by Charles Belden and Sy Bartlett for director D. Ross Lederman and associate producer William Jacobs. Also cast were Howard da Silva, Ben Welden, John Ridgely, Frank Wilcox and Hobart Bosworth.

△ Reminiscent of *Each Dawn I Die* (1939), **I Was Framed** told the all-too-familiar story of a newspaper reporter (Michael Ames, right) whose meddling in politics results in his being framed and sent to jail. He escapes, determined to revenge himself on the men who framed him. It was written by Robert E. Kent from a story by Jerome Odlum and directed by D. Ross Lederman. Also cast were Julie Bishop, Regis Toomey (left), Aldrich Bowker, Sam McDaniel and Joan Winfield. The associate producer was William Jacobs.

All about war planes and the men who make them, **Wings for the Eagle** was a competent drama whose informative approach to its subject made for intelligent, agreeable entertainment. Though the real star was the hardware, human interest was supplied by Dennis Morgan (foreground right) and Jack Carson, both of whom were seeking the attention of wise-cracking Ann Sheridan (right), and by George Tobias (left) and Russell Arms as a father and son team prematurely broken up by the death of Arms in the air. It was written by Byron Morgan and Harrison Orkow, directed by Lloyd Bacon and produced by Robert Lord. Also cast were Don DeFore, Tom Fadden, John Ridgely and George Meeker.

▽

Kings Row, based on the best-seller by Henry Bellamann, took a look at life in small-town America but, unlike the cosy meanderings of, say, Thornton Wilder's *Our Town*, portrayed a community touched by murder, madness and sadism. Central to the story was Parris Mitchell (Robert Cummings, right), a young medical student who, as a result of tragedies befalling his best friend and best girl, as well as the doctor who had encouraged him in his studies, soon discovers that Kings Row is not the 'good place to live in' he once supposed it to be. Drawing on the cream of the studio's talent – both in front of and behind the cameras – producer Hal B. Wallis provided director Sam Wood with a team of thoroughbreds that carried the entire project to triumph. Casey Robinson was assigned the task of telescoping the novel's sprawl into 127 minutes, James Wong Howe photographed it brilliantly and, in the process, seemed to probe the very soul (if it had one) of Kings Row and its inhabitants; William Cameron Menzies designed the film, and, together with director Wood, contributed to its powerful structure; Erich Wolfgang Korngold produced a massive, dark-toned score that strikingly encompassed the vast compendium of emotions on display. The acting was also splendid and confounded the cynics, who had assumed that Ronald Reagan (centre) as Cummings' best friend, and Ann Sheridan (left), as the girl from the 'other side of the tracks' whom ▷ he marries, were too lightweight for their roles. The same cynics, however, were right about Robert Cummings who, as Parris, lacked the authority the role demanded. Other fine performances were given by Betty Field, Charles Coburn, Judith Anderson, Claude Rains, Nancy Coleman and Maria Ouspenskaya. Worried by the sombre nature of the film, at a time of war, the studio sat on it for a year after its completion. The war was still on when it was released, and their fears were not entirely unfounded as it was only moderately successful.

Bette Davis (who earned $252,333 in 1941) had a career that was nothing if not varied. After playing Monty Woolley's secretary in *The Man Who Came to Dinner*, she flung herself back into the limelight with **In This Our Life**, scripted by Howard Koch from Ellen Glasgow's Pulitzer prize-winning story of a woman who ruins her sister's life by stealing her husband. In the end Davis (right) gets her come-uppance when she is killed in a car smash. The sister was played by Olivia de Havilland, the husband by Dennis Morgan. Charles Coburn, George Brent (left), Frank Craven, Billie Burke, Hattie McDaniel, Lee Patrick and Ernest Anderson (centre) co-starred in this improbable mixture (incest and racial discrimination lurk in the background) with John Huston (misguidedly allowing Davis to have it all her own way) in the director's chair. Interesting sideline: in the roadhouse sequence several members of Huston's cast from *The Maltese Falcon* made unbilled appearances. Look hard enough and you'll spot Humphrey Bogart, Mary Astor, Sydney Greenstreet, Peter Lorre, Ward Bond, Elisha Cook Jr, Barton MacLane and, as the bartender, Huston's father, Walter. The associate producer was David Lewis.

▽

Edward G. Robinson's contract with the ▷ studio came to an end with the third and least successful of his gangster-spoof series, **Larceny Inc.**, about a small-time hood who, on being paroled from prison, comes to the conclusion that crime really does pay. He buys a shop adjoining a bank and drills a tunnel from his premises into the vault. The seen-it-all-before script was written by Everett Freeman and Edwin Gilbert (from a play by Laura and S.J. Perelman). Director Lloyd Bacon wisely concentrated on the performances rather than the plot, and was fortunate to have, as well as Robinson (left), Jane Wyman, Broderick Crawford (centre left), Jack Carson, Ed Brophy (centre right) and Anthony Quinn (right) in his cast. Hal B. Wallis produced; the associate producers were Jack Saper and Jerry Wald.

△

Singer Gloria Warren's career was launched (and promptly sunk) in **Always In My Heart**, an uneasy mixture of music and domestic melodrama about a mother (Kay Francis, returning to the studio after making eight films away from it since her departure in 1939) who is just about to take a second husband for herself when husband number one (Walter Huston) returns to the bosom of his family, having served a 13-year prison sentence for a crime he did not commit. Too silly for words, especially scenarist Adele Commandini's words (from a play by Dorothy Bennett and Irving White), it was partially redeemed by Huston's stalwart presence but not by Miss Francis whose talents were insufficient to rise above inferior material, nor by Gloria Warren as her teenage daughter. Borah Minnevitch (centre left) and his Rascals (illustrated) were on hand to play the harmonica, with other parts going to Patti Hale, Frankie Thomas, Una O'Connor, Anthony Caruso (centre right), Armida (centre) and Frank Puglia. It was directed by Joe Graham for producers Walter MacEwen and William Jacobs.

Though a great deal of **Yankee Doodle ▷ Dandy** was unadulterated corn, its heart was in the right place, and its timely appearance assured it enormous success. A routine biopic of the great showman George M. Cohan, its strongest selling point (apart from the perennial Cohan songs themselves) was James Cagney's mesmeric portrayal (foreground) of the versatile pint-sized entertainer. Director Michael Curtiz, working from a screenplay by Robert Buckner and Edmund Joseph, realized exactly what was needed to make flag-waving material of this kind of work, and directed it all with a patriotic zeal which would have warmed its subject's heart. All the other creative contributions were top-notch too, from James Wong Howe's photography to Milo Anderson's costumes. Nor were there any blemishes in a cast that included Joan Leslie (as Mrs Cohan), Walter Huston, Richard Whorf, George Tobias, Irene Manning, Rosemary De Camp, Jeanne Cagney, S.Z. Sakall, Frances Langford and Eddie Foy Jr, (playing Eddie Foy Sr) who appeared with Cagney in a memorable scene where the two of them rib each other most endearingly. Songs included: Give My Regards To Broadway, I Was Born In Virginia, Mary's A Grand Old Name, So Long Mary, and Yankee Doodle Boy. The producers were Jack Warner and Hal B. Wallis, with William Cagney as associate producer. The box-office gross was $4,800,000.

△

One of the worst films of 1942, **Lady Gangster** starred Faye Emerson (right) as a moll who is shown the error of her ways by district attorney Frank Wilcox, through whose love virtue comes to triumph over vice. It was scripted by Anthony Coldeway from a play by Dorothy MacKaye and Carlton Miles, and directed by Robert Florey who, understandably, on this occasion called himself Florian Roberts. The cast also included Roland Drew, Jackie Gleason, Ruth Ford, Julie Bishop (left), Virginia Brissac and Dorothy Vaughan. The associate producer was William Jacobs.

Resembling little more than a series of out-takes from previous Humphrey Bogart (who, at this point in his career, was earning a yearly $114,000) vehicles, **The Big Shot** was a dull variation on the theme of a thrice arrested hood trying to keep on the right side of the law, but unable to stay the course. In this instance, though prevented at gun-point from taking part in an armoured car robbery by former lover Irene Manning, Bogart (left) is mistakenly picked out by a witness in an identity parade, and, ironically, put on trial for a crime he did not commit. Assembly-line entertainment at best, it was written by Bertram Millhauser, Abem Finkel and Daniel Fuchs, and directed by Lewis Seiler as if it were just one more chore. Which, of course, it was. Richard Travis (right), Susan Peters and Stanley Ridges co-starred and the producer was Walter MacEwen.

▽

◁ **Busses Roar** was a melodrama that squeaked. All about a saboteur's abortive attempt to plant a bomb on a San Francisco-bound bus, timed to explode at the precise moment that the bus passes through an oil field, it had no sense of urgency or excitement in George Bilson and Anthony Coldeway's screenplay. The direction by D. Ross Lederman failed to engender any, and in a cast that included Richard Travis, Julie Bishop, Charles Drake (left), Elisabeth Fraser, Richard Fraser, Frank Wilcox and Willie Best, only newcomer Eleanor Parker (right) acted with anything amounting to conviction. The associate producer was William Jacobs.

△

A sorry remake of *Fog Over Frisco* (1934), **Spy Ship** starred Irene Manning (centre) in the role (originally created by Bette Davis) of an unsavoury American fifth columnist whose nefarious trade is selling secrets to the enemy. She dies halfway through, but the film, alas, lingered fitfully on to its bitter end. Written by Robert E. Kent from the story by George Dyer, and directed with action in mind by B. Reeves Eason, it also starred Craig Stevens (right), and featured Maris Wrixon (left), Michael Ames, Peter Whitney, John Maxwell and William Forrest. The associate producer was William Jacobs.

△

Escape From Crime demonstrated that there was no escape from the one about the ex-con who, for the sake of his family, attempts to go straight (as a newspaper photographer), but is bucked by his past. A remake of James Cagney's 1933 *Picture Snatcher*, it starred Richard Travis in the Cagney role with Julie Bishop as his wife. Jackie Gleason, Frank Wilcox, Rex Williams and Wade Boteler were in it too; it was written by Raymond Schrock from a story by Danny Ahearn, and directed by D. Ross Lederman with William Jacobs as the associate producer.

A willing suspension of disbelief and the proverbial pinch of salt was all that was necessary to accept **Desperate Journey** for the entertaining nonsense it was. The wildly improbable story of five men who are shot down in Nazi Germany and who attempt, through a plethora of adventures and mis-adventures, to return to England, it starred Errol Flynn (centre left) as an Australian, Ronald Reagan (right) as an American, Arthur Kennedy (left) as a Canadian, Alan Hale (centre right) as a World War I Scottish veteran, and Ronald Sinclair as an Englishman. Also on hand were Nancy Coleman, Raymond Massey and the irre-pressible Sig Rumann. Arthur T. Horman wrote the screenplay, and Raoul Walsh directed. It was released at the same time as Flynn's rape scandal hit the headlines – and did excellent business despite lines like Flynn's 'Now for Australia and a crack at the Japs!' Hal B. Wallis produced.

Ann Sheridan (centre) should have been given an award for the remarkable salvage job she almost managed on **Juke Girl**, a tedious melodrama about itinerant Florida crop-pickers involved in a deadly marketing war. An endurance test for audiences, the film tested the mettle of its stars as well. Shot, for the most part, at night in freezing weather, glycerine had to be sprayed on the actors' faces to simulate the sweat caused by Florida's humidity. In several scenes, extras in the background were asked to smoke cigarettes to help disguise the vapour steaming from the breath of the leading players. Though A.I. Bezzerides' screenplay (from the story *Jook Girl* by Theodore Pratt) was hardly deficient in action, the territory it covered was too well-worn for renewed excitement. And although director Curtis Bernhardt did his best to give the impression that he and his cast were labouring to good advantage, the thrills, such as they were, were synthetic. Not much better could be said for the performances of Ronald Reagan (left), Richard Whorf, Gene Lockhart, Faye Emerson, George Tobias (right) and Alan Hale. Without Miss Sheridan's witty way with the occasional line, it simply would not have played. The associate producers were Jack Saper and Jerry Wald.

If the Japanese had bombed the Panama canal during the shooting of **Across The Pacific**, there would have been no film – for this was the action-packed story of a successful attempt to thwart Japanese agents south of the border. Intrigue and counter-intrigue were the film's chief char-acteristics. This was no accident since, in many ways, it was an attempt on behalf of director John Huston to repeat his *Maltese Falcon* success, even to its casting: Hum-phrey Bogart (left), Mary Astor (right) and Sydney Greenstreet. During the production, however, Huston was called up for active service and was forced to quit before the end of shooting – but not before writing Bogart into a cliff-hanging situation from which it was almost impossible to extricate him. It was left to director Vincent Sherman to step in and save the day. All the same, **Across The Pacific**, with its powerful screen-play by Richard Macaulay (from a story by Robert Carson), its trio of excellent star per-formances, and its subtle and compelling direction was first-rate. The producers were Jerry Wald and Jack Saper.

There was nothing new about **You Can't Escape Forever**, a third remake of *Hi Nellie!* (1934) whose subject audiences couldn't escape at all. This time George Brent (right) was the star, playing a managing editor of a newspaper who finds himself demoted to agony columnist after refusing to buy a document from eccentric Erville Alderson which purports to expose the details of a powerful crime syndicate. After Alderson's sudden demise, Brent and his girl-friend colleague, Brenda Marshall (centre) spring into action and penetrate the syndicate themselves. There was nothing penetrating about Fred Niblo Jr and Hector Chevigny's screenplay (from the familiar story by Roy Chanslor), nor in the direction by Jo Graham. The producer was Mark Hel-linger, and the cast included Paul Harvey, Roscoe Karns (left), Charles Halton, Edward (Eduardo) Cianelli, George Meeker, Joseph Downing and Gene Lockhart.

Barbara Stanwyck (right, now earning $100,000 a year) returned to the studio after an absence of seven years to play the heroine of Stephen Longstreet's **The Gay Sisters**. Geraldine Fitzgerald and Nancy Coleman (left) completed the sorority, and the plot had them reluctantly selling their Fifth Avenue mansion in the name of progress. Stanwyck was particularly peeved at the sale, as the man involved was her despised husband (George Brent) whom she had tricked into marriage in order to lay her hands on a much-needed inheritance. At one point in Lenore Coffee's unexciting screenplay, Stanwyck observed that 'love is something you cut out of yourself, or it moves in and cuts you apart'. Her entire characterization was pickled in cynical observations of that ilk; and while she certainly made a meal of the role, the film was noteworthy only in that Byron Barr who appeared in it changed his name to that of the character he played – Gig Young. Irving Rapper directed, Henry Blanke pro-duced and the lush score was by Max Steiner.

It is a moot point whether or not **The Hidden Hand** was meant to be taken serious-ly, or regarded simply as a send-up of every haunted house thriller ever made. Certainly Milton Parsons' (left) performance as a mental asylum escapee could not have been for real. The plot involved no fewer than six murders, excluding the death of a pet raven called Poe, and centred on a family fortune and who would inherit it after the owner's death. Craig Stevens, Elisabeth Fraser and Julie Bishop starred, with other parts going to Willie Best (right), Frank Wilcox, Cecil Cunningham and Ruth Ford. It was written by Anthony Coldeway from a play by Rufus King, and directed by Ben Stoloff. The associate producer was William Jacobs.

△

As snugly as Errol Flynn (right) fitted into the role of George Armstrong Custer in *They Died With Their Boots On*, he was even better cast as James J. Corbett in **Gentleman Jim**. Remarkably similar in temperament and background to the man who became the first heavyweight champion of the world under the Marquis of Queensberry rules, Flynn's performance was not only his favourite but his most endearing, and the one on which he worked hardest, impressively emulating Corbett's revolutionary boxing style. The film (written with an authentic period flavour by Vincent Lawrence and Horace McCoy) was marred only by its tacked-on love interest (with Alexis Smith, left) and some heavy-handed humour made even heavier by Raoul Walsh whose direction of the action set-pieces were splendid, but whose moments of 'light relief' were not nearly light enough. The cast included Jack Carson, Alan Hale (as Flynn's father), John Loder, William Frawley, Minor Watson, Greg McClure and Ward Bond. It was produced by Robert Buckner.

△

The George S. Kaufman-Moss Hart comedy, **George Washington Slept Here** underwent major surgery in its transfer from the Broadway stage to the silver screen: its comedy was amputated. The story of an unwilling husband (Jack Benny, right) who is persuaded by his wife (Ann Sheridan, centre) to buy a converted farmhouse in Pennsylvania (in the play it was the wife who was unwilling), it flatly refused to amuse, and nothing director William Keighley attempted, could inject life into Everett Freeman's screenplay. Not even a cast which included Percy Kilbride (centre back), Charles Coburn (centre right), Hattie McDaniel (left), Franklin Pangborn, and Charles Dingle (centre left) were able to keep Jerry Wald's misbegotten production buoyant.

△

Flying Fortress was an unsuccessful effort which starred Richard Greene (right) as an American playboy. First refusing to take the war seriously, he later joins the R.A.F. and, during a bombing raid over Germany, proves that underneath that irresponsible mien beats a truly heroic heart. The film also featured Carla Lehman (left), Betty Stockfield, Donald Stewart, Charles Heslop and Sidney King, who were worth their weight in air. It was directed (in England at the Warner Bros. Teddington Studios) by Walter Forde and written by Brock Williams, Gordon Wellesley and Edward Dryhurst. The war effort deserved better than this.

▽

A passable programmer, with echoes of *G-Men* (1938), **Secret Enemies**, written by Raymond Schrock (story by Seton I. Miller) and breathlessly directed by Ben Stoloff, was about the routing of a group of Nazi agents in a luxury hotel by the sharp witted F.B.I. It starred Craig Stevens (centre right) and Faye Emerson, with other roles going to John Ridgely, Charles Lang, George Meeker (centre left), Robert Warwick (right), Frank Reicher (left) and, in a very minor role, Monte Blue. The producer was William Jacobs.

The quintessential wish-fulfilment weepie, **Now, Voyager**, from the best-seller by Olive Higgins Prouty, offered Bette Davis (left) one of the best roles of her career. She played a New England spinster who blossoms into a fashionable woman of poise and charm after her domineering mother (Gladys Cooper) causes her to have a breakdown – and she was superb. Producer Hal B. Wallis originally wanted Irene Dunne for the role, but Davis changed his mind for him and proved, irrefutably, that no characterization was beyond her formidable range. Paul Henreid (right) was cast as the romantic architect with whom Davis has a doomed affair; ('Let's not ask for the moon,' she tells him in the film's celebrated final line, 'when we have the stars') and, by lighting two cigarettes at the same time before handing one of them to her, he set a new trend in lovers' smoking habits. Claude Rains was impeccable as a compassionate psychiatrist, with other parts going to Bonita Granville, Ilka Chase, John Loder and Franklin Pangborn. Max Steiner wrote one of the best scores of the decade, and Casey Robinson's screenplay was a model of solid storytelling, compellingly directed by Irving Rapper.

▷

1943

In 1943, Humphrey Bogart renegotiated a new seven-year contract at $3,500 a week (for 40 weeks a year); and Olivia de Havilland, chagrined by the fact that the months in which she had been on suspension were being added on to the end of her contract, decided to take Jack Warner to court – and won her case. Henceforth contracts would run for as long as they were originally negotiated and not a day more, unless prematurely terminated or extended by mutual consent. **Casablanca** won the Academy Award for Best Film of the Year, and **Watch On The Rhine** was nominated in the same category. Paul Lukas was voted by the Academy as Best Actor of the Year, beating Humphrey Bogart who was also nominated for **Casablanca**. Michael Curtiz won the Oscar for Best Director (**Casablanca**), George Amy for Best Editing (**Air Force**), Ray Heindorf for Music Scoring in a Musical Picture (**This Is The Army**), Norman Krasna for Best Original Screenplay (**Princess O'Rourke**) and Julius J. and Philip G. Epstein and Howard Koch for Best Screenplay (**Casablanca**). The *New York Times* considered **Air Force** and **Watch On The Rhine** among the year's Ten Best; while the New York Film Critics voted **Watch On The Rhine** the best film of the year and Paul Lukas best actor for his work in it. They voted Ida Lupino best actress of the year for **The Hard Way**. The company made a net profit of $8,238,483, and their biggest moneyspinners were **Air Force**, **Casablanca** and **This Is The Army**.

Writing in his autobiography about **Casablanca**, arguably the studio's most enduring achievement, Jack Warner recalled a conversation with the film's director Michael Curtiz, in which Curtiz remarked to him: 'Well, Jock, the scenario isn't the exact truth, but ve haff the facts to prove it.' Regardless of what was, or wasn't the truth, **Casablanca** captured the mood and the immediacy of a war-time situation involving political refugees from Nazi-occupied Europe and their desperate attempts to attain exit visas to Lisbon – and freedom. Set in Rick's Café-Americain, owned by Richard Blaine (Humphrey Bogart, left), a man who once fought with Spanish loyalists and smuggled arms to Ethiopia but now refuses to stick his neck out for anyone, its plot centred on the unexpected arrival at the café of Victor Laszlo (Paul Henreid) and his wife Ilsa (Ingrid Bergman, right), the only woman Rick has ever loved. Their affair, which began and ended in Paris shortly before the Nazi occupation, starts all over again, shines through the film's numerous and somewhat far-fetched sub-plots, and ends – as it did once before – unhappily, when Ilsa and her husband, having obtained the necessary exit visas for which they came to Casablanca in the first place, board the plane leaving Rick to resolve his inner conflicts by again sticking his neck out and working on the side of peace. Based on an unproduced play called *Everybody Goes to Rick's* (by Murray Burnett and Joan Alison) which the studio purchased because of its exotic locale, the material, as originally worked over by Julius J. and Philip G. Epstein, amounted to little more than a heady concoction of melodramatic incidents with no discernible narrative thrust, and whose excitement relied on stock situations and two-dimensional characters. Howard Koch was called in to give the Epstein treatment its centre of gravity, and although he succeeded, it was Michael Curtiz, bulldozing his way through the clichés, who was responsible for turning second-rate material into sublime screen entertainment. Nor can one underestimate Curtiz's superb cast (apart from the principals, there were fine performances from Claude Rains, S.Z. Sakall, Sydney Greenstreet, Conrad Veidt, and Peter Lorre) and the way in which their personalities melded together to turn, by some miraculous alchemy, lines such as 'Was that cannon fire, or is my heart pounding?' into cinematic gold. Musically, apart from the incomparable Dooley Wilson's 'As Time Goes By' (by Herman Hupfeld), Max Steiner's score contributed immeasurably to the film's overall success; so did the brilliant chiaroscuro of Arthur Edeson's black-and-white photography. **Casablanca** went on general release during the timely Casablanca Conference of Anglo-American leaders at the beginning of 1943, and benefited greatly from the resultant publicity. The three Academy Awards it won a few months later further helped to establish it as one of the year's biggest grossing films. Today its popularity has not diminished, and it remains one of the greatest films of its decade. And to think the studio originally wanted Ann Sheridan, Ronald Reagan and Dennis Morgan . . . The producer was Hal B. Wallis.

△

Audiences didn't know whether to giggle, gulp, or groan at **The Mysterious Doctor**, a mindless thriller about a headless ghost that stalks a small mining village, and sabotages the British war effort in the process. By the time the logical explanations were trotted out it seemed as though the American film industry itself had been sabotaged. Director Ben Stoloff took it much more seriously than was healthy; it was written by Richard Weil, and the cast included Eleanor Parker (who certainly deserved a better fate), John Loder (right), Bruce Lester, Lester Matthews (left), Forrester Harvey (centre right), Matt Willis, Clyde Cook and Creighton Hale. The associate producer was William Jacobs.

◁ No real-life Nazi agents could have been as devious as the ones in **The Gorilla Man**, especially as portrayed by Paul Cavanagh (centre) and John Abbott. Posing as English doctors, they set out to discredit British Commando John Loder (right front) who has some vital enemy information, by entering a sanatorium, and proclaiming him to be clinically insane. They then go about murdering a few women, the blame for which falls on Loder, after whose insane behaviour, they argue, the important information he has to impart will not be taken seriously. Anthony Coldeway wrote the improbable screenplay, D. Ross Lederman directed, the associate producer was William Jacobs, and the cast included Ruth Ford (right), Marian Hall, Richard Fraser (standing right), Lumsden Hare (left), Mary Field (standing left) and Rex Williams.

△

A poor man's *They Drive by Night*, **Truck Busters** pitted an independent trucker (Richard Travis, right) against a large transport combine with less than riveting results. It was written by Robert Kent and Raymond Schrock, directed by B. Reeves Eason for associate producer William Jacobs, and featured Don Costello (as the heavy), Virginia Christine (left), Ruth Ford (centre), Charles Lang, Richard Fraser, Michael Ames and Monte Blue.

The Hard Way opened with Ida Lupino about to commit suicide on the set the studio had used for *Out of the Fog* (1941). Stopped just in time and asked the reason why by a solicitous policeman, the answer given (in a lengthy flashback) was that, in attempting to carve out a successful show-business career for her young sister (Joan Leslie), she played too many wrong cards and alienated too many people, including Miss Leslie herself. Originally offered to Bette Davis, who rejected the role, Lupino (right) tore into the bitchy melodramatics of the Daniel Fuchs-Peter Viertel screenplay with all the determination of an actress out to win her first Oscar. Director Vincent Sherman succeeded in giving the rambling, somewhat disjointed plot a semblance of cohesion and, working with a cast that included Dennis Morgan, Jack Carson, Gladys George (left) and Faye Emerson came up with an entertaining piece of women's magazine fiction. Jerry Wald produced.

The heroic, yet unsentimental war-time story of men at sea, Action in the North Atlantic starred Humphrey Bogart (centre) as Joe Rossi, executive officer of the *Sea Witch*, and Raymond Massey (right) as its captain. The action promised in the title happened when the *Sea Witch*, one of a convoy *en route* to Murmansk, was separated from the rest of the ships during a German submarine attack, and continued non-stop for most of the film's 127 minute running time. Authoritative performances from a cast which also included Alan Hale, Julie Bishop, Ruth Gordon, Sam Levene, Dane Clark and Kane Richmond (left), plus a crackling screenplay by John Howard Lawson (with additional dialogue by W.R. Burnett and A.I. Bezzerides) and confident, muscular direction by Lloyd Bacon made this Jerry Wald production (shot entirely on the backlot, and owing an immeasurable debt of gratitude to the special effects department) one of the most rousing propaganda films of the forties.

The external problems surrounding the shooting of Edge of Darkness were hardly a help to the okay-but-only-just product. Errol Flynn (illustrated), the film's star, was in the midst of his rape scandal; Ann Sheridan, his co-star, had just parted from her husband George Brent, and a heavy fog halted location shooting in the Californian town of Monterey causing an uneasy delay during which co-stars Judith Anderson and Ruth Gordon had to be restrained from leaving the film and returning to New York where a stage production of *The Three Sisters* awaited them. But the fog and all the attendant problems lifted, and director Lewis Milestone was eventually able to complete the melodrama – which paid homage to the courage of a Norwegian fishing village and the brave men and women who brought about an anti-Nazi revolt (leader Errol Flynn) during the occupation. More timely than artistic, and coming at the end of a cycle of war films with a similar theme, Edge of Darkness was received with respect from the critics, most of whom acknowledged its good intentions, and praised director Milestone's fresh handling of familiar material. Robert Rossen wrote the screenplay from the story by William Woods. Also cast were Walter Huston, Nancy Coleman, Helmut Dantine, John Beal and Morris Carnovsky. The producer was Henry Blanke.

'Fried Jap coming down,' quipped George Tobias in Air Force, one of the best aviation films of the period. By following the flight of the Mary Ann, a Boeing B-17 (Flying Fortress) bomber from its San Francisco take-off on December 6th, 1941 to Hickham Field, Hawaii, the Philippines, the South Pacific, and finally, after being attacked and severely damaged in the battle of the Coral Sea, to Australia, director Howard Hawks created a convincing and informative picture of an airman's life off the ground. Most of the film was shot in Tampa, Florida, where Hawks was given the use of an actual Flying Fortress (the film was, after all, made at the suggestion and with the co-operation of the Army Air Corps) and, for the interiors, art director John Hughes designed a replica of the B-17 costing $40,000, which cinematographer James Wong Howe photographed to good effect. Contributing to the realism was the studio's special effects department, whose main problem was to create the illusion of a 350 mph gale hitting the plane's Plexiglass nose. They solved it by aiming air hoses against wind machines until the required velocity was reached. Enhancing the sense of realism still further was the inclusion of actual newsreel footage – especially of the Coral Sea Battle – expertly integrated into the narrative by editor George Amy. A cast including John Ridgely, Harry Carey Sr (centre), Gig Young, Charles Drake (left), Arthur Kennedy (right) and headed by John Garfield, giving his stereotyped portrayal of the authority-defying tough guy who in the end comes up trumps, contributed substantially to the film's overall impact. Air Force was written by Dudley Nichols with the aid of William Faulkner (who contributed a moving death-bed scene for the plane's commander), and was produced by Hal B. Wallis.

One of the few films Jack Warner wished he had never made, Mission to Moscow – based on the book by former Ambassador to Russia, Joseph E. Davies – was a blatant attempt to bully Americans into thinking that the Russians were trustworthy allies. Walter Huston (left front) played Davies (a brief prologue featured the real-life Davies vouchsafing the film's content as 'the truth

as I saw it') who, during his two year stay in Moscow, befriended numerous Russian leaders, all of whom (he, and the film claimed) were aware of the scourge of Nazism before anybody else saw it. The film's pro-Russian sentiments were re-inforced by the Ambassador's belief that Soviets and Americans were basically similar beings. The result was the most controversial film in the studio's history, attacked by its detractors for supporting the Russian regime, and praised by others as a brave and necessary gesture in the fostering of a common understanding between the two great powers. As a piece of film-making – regardless of its political stance – it was, for the most part, well-made and absorbing, directed by Michael Curtiz whose unfailing cinematic eye was most notable in the big dramatic courtroom scenes during the purge trials. An inordinately large cast included Ann Harding as Davies' wife and Eleanor Parker as his daughter, with resident 'foreigners' Vladimir Sokoloff as the Soviet President, Oscar Homolka as Litvinov, and Manart Kippen as Stalin. Dudley Field Malone appeared as Churchill. Also helping to infuse life into Howard Koch's screenplay were George Tobias, Richard Travis, Helmut Dantine, Victor Francen, Jerome Cowan (extreme right), Minor Watson (centre), Moroni Olsen (right) and Henry Daniell. The associate producer of this contentious offering was Robert Buckner.

One of the shortest of the studio's pro-grammers (it ran a mere 48 minutes), and also one of its worst, was **Murder on the Waterfront** (a remake of *Invisible Menace*, 1938). Set in a Navy Yard, it concerned the murder of an inventor of a device to protect guns against high temperatures, and featur-ed Warren Douglas (left), Joan Winfield (right), John Loder and Ruth Ford. It was written by Robert E. Kent from a play by Ralph Spencer and the associate producer was William Jacobs. B. Reeves Eason direc-ted. Brief but interminable.

There was more World War II cloak-and-dagger stuff in **Background to Danger**. Set in neutral Turkey, it was an unsuccessful attempt to capture *Casablanca's* ambience of war-time intrigue, and starred George Raft (right) who, ironically, had turned down the Bogart role in the Curtiz classic. Despite a well-handled car chase towards the end, the cumbersome screenplay by W.R. Burnett (from a novel by Eric Ambler) failed to generate any real tension. Raoul Walsh directed a cast which also included Brenda Marshall (left), Sydney Greenstreet, Peter Lorre (centre), Osa Massen and Turhan Bey.
▽

Films like **Thank Your Lucky Stars** brought to the troops at the front, as well as to their families back home, the kind of entertainment only a major Hollywood studio could finance. They usually had a story, albeit a flimsy one (in this instance a bit of fluff about two producers — S.Z. Sakall and Edward Everett Horton — who become involved with an unknown songwriter, Joan Leslie, and a singer, Dennis Morgan) but it hardly mattered with the roster of talent on hand. Apart from Leslie and Morgan, the charity show which climaxed the movie featured Dinah Shore, Alexis Smith, Hattie McDaniel, Willie Best, Jack Carson, Alan Hale, Eddie Cantor, Errol Flynn and, singing that heart-felt war-time lament, 'They're Either Too Young Or Too Old' (written by Arthur Schwartz and Frank Loesser) Bette Davis. John Garfield was in it too, near the start of the film giving a quite excruciating rendering of 'Blues In The Night' by Harold Arlen and E.Y. Harburg. David Butler directed; Mark Hellinger produced. Songs included: How Sweet You Are, I'm Riding For A Fall, Good Night Good Neighbour, Love Isn't Born, It's Made, Thank Your Lucky Stars and We're Staying Home Tonight (by Arthur Schwartz and Frank Loesser).

Lillian Hellman's distinguished and doggedly anti-Fascist Broadway hit, **Watch on the Rhine**, brought the studio a great deal of prestige, but not much money; Dashiell Hammett's adaptation of the play had Paul Lukas (right) repeating the role of anti-Nazi resistance leader Kurt Muller which he had created on the stage. Also repeating their stage roles were George Coulouris (left) as the blackmailing Rumanian count, Donald Woods (centre left), Donald Buka and Eric Roberts as Lukas' sons, and Lucile Watson (centre right) as the naive Fanny Farrelley. Bette Davis (centre) agreed to accept the secondary role of Sara Muller (which she played without distinction), while Geraldine Fitzgerald was cast as the Rumanian's wife. Though director Herman Shumlin (who had been responsible for the Broadway production) made no attempt to underplay the didacticism of Miss Hellman's tone (appropriate at the time, but heavy-handed now), his stirring film extolled the virtues of goodness, human courage and dignity. The producer was Hal B. Wallis.

Adventure in Iraq starred John Loder (left), Ruth Ford (right), Warren Douglas (centre left) and Paul Cavanagh (centre right), and a rather indifferent adventure it turned out to be. All about a couple of men and a woman who fall into Nazi-Arab hands, and their attempts to escape, it was a remake of William Archer's *The Green Goddess* (1930), scripted by George Bilson and Robert E. Kent, and directed by D. Ross Lederman. The associate producer was William Jacobs, and his cast also included Barry Bernard, Peggy Carson and Bill Crago.

The first film Errol Flynn (right) made after his rape case, **Northern Pursuit**, was a silly war drama in which he starred as a Canadian Mountie who pretends to defect in order to apprehend a group of Nazi saboteurs. The best moment was the sight of Flynn assuring his bride (Julie Bishop, left) that she is the only woman who ever meant anything to him, then staring into the camera and retracting with 'What am I saying?' During filming Flynn collapsed, and although the studio officially announced the problem to be respiratory, it was in fact tuberculosis. After a week in hospital, Flynn returned to the set and, together with co-stars Helmut Dantine, John Ridgely and Gene Lockhart completed the film. Frank Gruber and Alvah Bessie wrote the far-fetched screenplay and Raoul Walsh, making heavy weather of the lighter moments, directed. Jack Chertok produced.

The stage version of **This is the Army**, ▷
Irving Berlin's rousingly patriotic paean to
the American soldier, earned $1,951,045.11
for Army Emergency Relief, and the
supremely entertaining, equally flag-waving
screen version directed by Michael Curtiz
made much, much more – though the
brothers Warner took back only enough to
cover the film's initial cost. Featuring the
350 fighting men who appeared in the
Broadway presentation, as well as a
plethora of stars and personalities including
Joan Leslie, George Murphy, Ronald Reagan,
George Tobias, Alan Hale, Charles Butterworth, Dolores Costello, Frances Langford,
Gertrude Niesen, Kate Smith and Sergeant
Joe Louis, it was grand entertainment from
start to finish. Most of the principals gave
their services free, while the military men
worked for their regular soldier's pay.
Irving Berlin wrote the show's music and
lyrics and appeared in one number ('Oh
How I Hate To Get Up In The Morning'), and
the screenplay was by Casey Robinson and
Captain Claude Binyon. Hal B. Wallis pro-
duced. Songs included: This Is The Army Mr.
Jones, The Army's Made A Man Out Of Me,
God Bless America (sung by Kate Smith), I'm
Getting Tired So I Can Sleep, What The Well
Dressed Man In Harlem Will Wear, I Left My
Heart At The Stage-Door Canteen, Give A
Cheer For The Navy, American Eagles and
Poor Little Me I'm On K.P.

Olivia de Havilland (as a princess, left) fell
for pilot Robert Cummings (centre left) in
Princess O'Rourke and as a result, caused
quite a diplomatic furore. It was written as
well as directed by Norman Krasna, and
certainly had its fair share of good moments,
though the somewhat coy finale involving
the services of Franklin D. Roosevelt
wasn't one of them. The President contributed far less to the proceedings than the
supporting cast which included Charles
Coburn, Jack Carson (right), Jane Wyman
(centre right), Harry Davenport and Gladys
Cooper. Hal B. Wallis produced. Song:
Honourable Man (by Ira Gershwin, E.Y.
Harburg and Arthur Schwartz).
▽

◁ **Find the Blackmailer** was a programmer,
uninterestingly directed by D. Ross Lederman, but buoyed up by a neat performance
from Jerome Cowan (centre) as a cynical
private eye involved in a plot to track down a
talking blackbird before it turned stool
pigeon. Inspired (if that's the right word) by
a story by G.T. Fleming Roberts and written
by Robert E. Kent, it also featured Faye
Emerson, Gene Lockhart (right), Marjorie
Hoshelle (left), Robert Kent and Wade Boteler. It ran a mere 55 minutes – which was
quite enough. William Jacobs produced.

△

When Bette Davis, as a long-suffering
novelist in John Van Druten's **Old Ac-
quaintance,** had had about as much as she
could take of her childhood friend (Miriam
Hopkins, left) and almost throttled her,
audiences cheered. So did most of the crew
members on the production who were as
fed up with Miss Hopkins' off-stage histrionics as was Miss Davis. All the same, the
electricity generated by the two women
transcended the trashy situations which
Van Druten and Lenore Coffee's screenplay
put them through, and the result was
compulsively entertaining. Gig Young, John
Loder (right), Anne Revere, Roscoe Karns
and Phillip Reed were in it too; it was directed by Vincent Sherman and the producer
was Henry Blanke.

△

First written as a novel in 1924 by Margaret
Kennedy and later adapted as a play by Miss
Kennedy and Basil Dean, **The Constant
Nymph** told the slender story of an un-
fulfilled composer (Charles Boyer, left) who
takes a post as tutor to a musically orien-
tated British family in their Alpine retreat.
Directed by Edmund Goulding, whose
sympathy with the subject was lovingly
apparent throughout, it was given more
dramatic weight than it deserved. No
expense was spared in Henry Blanke's
handsome production and, with a cast that
included Joan Fontaine (centre left), Alexis
Smith (right), Charles Coburn, Dame May
Whitty, Peter Lorre (centre right), Joyce
Reynolds and Jean Muir. Kathryn Scola's
screenplay was brought touchingly to life.
The film's impressive score was by Erich
Wolfgang Korngold, who was also heard on
the sound track playing the piano for Boyer.

1944

Though the company made a net profit of $6,953,462 in 1944, it was not a particularly distinguished year, with the total output of feature films dropping to 19. For the first time in twelve years not a single Warner Bros. release was even nominated for an Academy Award for Best Picture. (The Oscar went to Paramount's **Going My Way**.) Bette Davis was nominated for Best Actress for her performance in **Mr. Skeffington** but lost to Ingrid Bergman in MGM's **Gaslight**. The only Oscar won by the studio was for a two-reeler called **I Won't Play. Destination Tokyo**, however, appeared on the *New York Times* Ten Best List. The top moneyspinners were **Arsenic And Old Lace, Mr. Skeffington** and **Thank Your Lucky Stars**.

In Our Time teamed Ida Lupino (left) and ▷ Paul Henreid (right) in a well-meaning but unsuccessful romance set in pre-war Poland. With Henreid cast as a nobleman who, to the chagrin of his snobbish, blue-blooded family, marries an English tourist (Lupino), it was as much an acknowledgment of Polish courage and heroism during the early years of the war, as it was a love story. Vincent Sherman's pedestrian direction, however, failed to underpin the drama in the situation, and blame must also be placed on Howard Koch and Ellis St. Joseph's turgid screenplay. Also involved were Nancy Coleman, Mary Boland, Victor Francen, Nazimova, and Michael Chekhov. The producer was Jerry Wald.

As was the case with *Air Force*, complete ▷ War Department co-operation was provided for **Destination Tokyo**, another flag-waving, but ultimately exciting, account of life aboard *Copperfin*, a wartime submarine. Its plot involved audiences in a journey from San Francisco, through the Aleutian Islands to a climactic attack on Tokyo harbour, where the delivery of a sealed note results in James A. Doolittle's famous raid. As in *Air Force*, newsreel footage was interspersed with the fictional lives of the characters, adding to the authentic 'feel' of the overall product. Cary Grant (centre, who had earned over $350,000 in 1941) and John Garfield starred, both almost caricaturing their screen personas. Garfield was the rough-and-ready, cocky girl-chaser; Grant the suave, respectable, smooth-talking officer. Less happily cast though, was Dane Clark whose lurid over playing of many of his scenes showed just what a good actor Garfield (whose style Clark seemed to be emulating) really was. The supporting cast included John Ridgely (left), Robert Hutton, Warner Anderson (centre right) and Warren Douglas (right). Clocking in at 135 minutes, **Destination Tokyo** outstayed its welcome by about a quarter of an hour, yet thanks to Delmer Daves' sure-footed direction (the entry into Tokyo Harbour was especially well handled), and Franz Waxman's appropriately patriotic score, Jerry Wald's production (screenplay by Delmer Daves and Albert Maltz) was a box-office winner.

◁ A remake of *Outward Bound* (1930) by Sutton Vane, **Between Two Worlds,** for which producer Mark Hellinger assembled an impressive cast including John Garfield (left), Paul Henreid, Sydney Greenstreet, Eleanor Parker, Edmund Gwenn, George Coulouris, Faye Emerson (right), Sara Allgood, Dennis King and Isobel Elsom, was an out-and-out clash between style and content. The combatants were director Edward A. Blatt and writer Daniel Fuchs whose differing approaches to the piece failed to mesh. A fantasy, in which a group of 'dead' passengers find themselves on a fog-bound vessel *en-route* to the other world, it was directed as hard-core realism, which consequently robbed the piece of the fragility and atmosphere inherent in the screenplay. Another minus factor was the miscasting of Garfield in the role of a breezy newspaper reporter. Lacking directorial control (and confidence in the whole project), he overacted badly – as he was apt to do on such occasions.

Despite his notorious rape scandal, Errol Flynn remained a major star at Warner Bros. In 1944, a contract was drawn up which gave him not only a choice of scripts and a say in production, but also a percentage of the profits – should there be any. His first film under the new arrangement was **Uncertain Glory**, an uncertain, thoroughly inconsistent contribution to the war effort, which starred Flynn (left) as a Frenchman condemned to the guillotine. He escapes, and with the help of a detective (Paul Lukas, right) and a young woman (Jean Sullivan, centre), becomes a Resistance hero. Sabotaged by Laszlo Vadnay and Max Brand's poorly conceived screenplay (story by Vadnay and Joe May), director Raoul Walsh understandably lost interest in the material, and it showed. The producer was Robert Buckner.

In **Crime by Night** Jerome Cowan made his last starring appearance before being relegated to character roles below the title. A programmer with a little more quality than most, it featured Cowan (right) as a private-eye who, while on holiday with his secretary (Jane Wyman, centre right), becomes involved in a murder case. William Clemens directed efficiently, making the most of Richard Weil and Joel Malone's often witty screenplay (story by Geoffrey Homes). Also cast were Faye Emerson, Charles Lang, Eleanor Parker and Stuart Crawford. William Jacobs produced.

Purporting to be a musical biopic of Nora Bayes and her husband Jack Norworth, **Shine On, Harvest Moon** was, in fact, little more than a platitudinous backstage musical circa 1905 with Ann Sheridan (as Nora) and Dennis Morgan (as Jack) agreeing to become partners both domestically and professionally. He's a song-writer, she's a honky-tonk girl in vaudeville and we follow them through the thick and thin of their careers. The film's chief handicap was that Miss Sheridan was no Nora Bayes, but the songs were pleasant enough, especially the title song (shot in Technicolor, although the rest of the film was in black-and-white); so was the singing of Irene Manning, who co-starred with Jack Carson, S.Z. Sakall and Marie Wilson. Four writers piled the clichés into the screenplay (Sam Hellman, Richard Weil, Francis Swann and James Kern), David Butler directed, LeRoy Prinz staged the musical numbers and the producer was William Jacobs. Songs included: Shine On Harvest Moon (by Jack Norworth and Nora Bayes), Time Waits For No One (by Cliff Friend and Charles Tobias), I Go For You and So Dumb But So Beautiful (by M.K. Jerome and Kim Gannon), When It's Apple Blossom Time In Normandy (by Mellor, Gifford and Trevor), and Take Me Out To The Ball Game (by Albert von Tilzer and Jack Norworth).

Working from Harold M. Sherman's play, *Mark Twain*, scenarist Alan Le May delivered a top-heavy screenplay that reduced its subject to a massive cinematic platitude. The attempt to tell the life story of Samuel Clemens (alias Twain), and to cram as much incident as possible into the 130 minutes running time, resulted in a case of too much plot and insufficient insight. **The Adventures of Mark Twain** encapsulated Twain's youth, his life as a Mississippi riverboat man, his Wild West and gold-mining affiliations, his fame as a well-travelled writer, his publishing mishaps (and the ensuing bankruptcy), his love-affair with Olivia Langdon (Alexis Smith), and his honourable and exhausting attempts to clear his debts. Unfortunately, little was gleaned about the inner man, and even less about the country which inspired his greatest works. But director Irving Rapper did have Fredric March (illustrated) making the most of the least and, especially in the second half of the film, looking remarkably like Twain in his latter years. The large supporting cast assembled by producer Jesse L. Lasky included Donald Crisp, Alan Hale, C. Aubrey Smith, John Carradine, William Henry and Robert Barrat.

Based on Joseph A. Fields' Broadway success, **The Doughgirls** reached the screen in a decidedly dehydrated version so as to appease the Hays Office. Set in a wartime Washington hotel, and involving a group of husband-seeking girls, the fun wasn't quite as fast and furious as it should have been. Blame it on the James V. Kern-Sam Hellman screenplay (additional material by Wilkie Mahoney), on Mr Hays, or on James V. Kern's direction, but not on the nicely judged performances of Alexis Smith (centre left), who had little to do but did it well, Jack Carson, Irene Manning, Charlie Ruggles, Alan Mowbray, John Alexander, Craig Stevens, and, most especially, Eve Arden (right). Only the star Ann Sheridan (centre right) and Jane Wyman (left) seemed slightly ill at ease with their material. Mark Hellinger produced.

246

Hardly the ones to turn a blind eye or a deaf ear to a contemporary situation, whether political or sociological, the Warner Bros. hierarchy pulled **The Desert Song** out of their trunk of old scripts, dusted it off, and refurbished it as a timely operetta all about Nazis and anti-Nazis in the French Morocco of 1939. A cloak-and-dagger tale, it told of the Nazi attempt, through the agency of a local chieftain, to lay a railway track between Dakar and the North African coast – the labourers being the poor, oppressed Riffs. What the Nazis don't know, however, is that the real leader of the Riffs is an American who fought in the Spanish Civil War; and that it is he who makes quite sure that the track is never completed. Dennis Morgan (right) was the hero; Irene Manning (left) his leading lady. Together they made beautiful music (courtesy of Sigmund Romberg) and helped the amiable nonsense along considerably. Also cast were Bruce Cabot (as Colonel Fontaine), Gene Lockhart, Lynne Overman, Faye Emerson, Victor Francen, Curt Bois and Jack La Rue. It was written by Robert Buckner from the play by Laurence Schwab, Otto Harbach, Frank Mandel, Oscar Hammerstein II and Sigmund Romberg, and the director was Robert Florey. It was photographed in Technicolor. Songs included: The Riff Song, Desert Song, One Alone, Romance (by Otto Harbach, Oscar Hammerstein II and Sigmund Romberg), Fifi's Song (by Jack Scholl and Romberg), Gay Parisienne (by Scholl and Serge Walters), and Long Live The Night (by Scholl, Mario Silva and Romberg).

Joseph Kesselring's successful stage play, **Arsenic and Old Lace**, was transferred to the screen in an adaptation by Julius J. and Philip G. Epstein, with Frank Capra directing at a jolly pace, and with an exuberant disregard for good taste. The celebrated yarn about a couple of 'harmless' old biddies who lure lonely men to their Brooklyn home, then poison them with elderberry wine, it starred Josephine Hull (centre) and Jean Adair (right) as the sisters in crime, with Cary Grant over-acting outrageously as an urbane theatre critic, Priscilla Lane as his girl-friend and Raymond Massey (in the role played on stage by Boris Karloff) as a homicidal nephew with a few cadavers of his own. Also cast were Peter Lorre as Massey's splendidly eccentric sidekick, Jack Carson, Edward Everett Horton (left), James Gleason, John Alexander and Grant Mitchell. Despite its comically indifferent attitude to death, the film found war-time audiences willing to accept the light-hearted mayhem in place of the grimmer realities at the front. Capra also produced.

There were long faces all round for **Make Your Own Bed**, which purported to be a comedy, with Jane Wyman (right) and Jack Carson (left) appearing as a romantically involved pair of private detectives. They are pressed into domestic service by Alan Hale (centre left) whose excuse is that he requires protection against a group of Nazis. How the couple coped, or failed to cope, was the basis of Francis Swann and Edmund Joseph's mirthless screenplay, which director Peter Godfrey did nothing to jolly along. It was produced by Alex Gottlieb with a cast that included Irene Manning (centre right), George Tobias, Robert Shayne, Tala Birell, Ricardo Cortez, Marjorie Hoshelle, Kurt Katch and Harry Bradley.

A slender little comedy based on a Broadway play by Josephine Bentham and Herschel Williams, **Janie** told how a 16-year-old girl (Joyce Reynolds, centre), much to the displeasure of her parents, commandeers their home to entertain what appears to be an entire squadron of soldier admirers. More interesting today for what it reveals about adolescent mentality during the forties than it was when it first appeared, it was written for the screen by Agnes Christine Johnston and Charles Hoffman and frenetically directed by Michael Curtiz, who was clearly more at home in exotic Casablanca than he was in suburbia. Alex Gottlieb produced, and the cast included Edward Arnold and Ann Harding (as the parents), Robert Hutton (left), Robert Benchley, Alan Hale, Clare Foley, Hattie McDaniel and Dick Erdman (right). Songs included: Keep Your Powder Dry (by Jule Styne and Sammy Cahn) and Janie (by Lee David).

Recruiting Humphrey Bogart (centre), Claude Rains, Sydney Greenstreet, Peter Lorre (left), and Helmut Dantine (centre left) from *Casablanca*, then lumbering himself with a complex series of flashbacks within flashbacks, director Michael Curtiz, in this tribute to the Free French, failed to make **Passage to Marseilles** a smooth crossing. About a Devil's Island convict (Bogart) who escapes to Britain and joins the Bomber Command in order to fight the Germans, it refused to generate excitement, either on screen or at the box-office, and squandered the talents of its capable cast. Only the bleak scenes depicting life on Devil's Island had any impact. The stodgy screenplay was by Casey Robinson and Jack Moffitt (from the story by Charles Nordhoff and James Norman Hall), and the cast included Michele Morgan, George Tobias (right), Victor Francen, John Loder and Vladimir Sokoloff. Hal B. Wallis produced.

Two of the many pleasures in the film version of Eric Ambler's novel *A Coffin for Dimitrios*, filmed as **The Mask of Dimitrios**, were the presences of Sydney Greenstreet and Peter Lorre (right), the Laurel and Hardy of international intrigue, who this time found themselves pursuing Zachary Scott (making his screen debut) halfway across the world. It was directed by Jean Negulesco whose cast included Steven Geray, Victor Francen, John Abbott and, less happily, Faye Emerson. Frank Gruber's heavily fissured screenplay, with its numerous flashbacks, ultimately worked against the proceedings, but for most of the performances alone, the film was worth a visit. The producer was Henry Blanke.

△
Another quintessential 'weepie', **Mr Skeffington**, from the novel by 'Elizabeth', covered a period of twenty-six years – from 1914 to 1940 – and was the story of a vain, irresponsible society woman (Bette Davis) who marries Job Skeffington (Claude Rains) simply because he loaned her adored brother $25,000, and who honestly believes that, because she is not in love with him, she can philander to her heart's content. Diptheria robs her of her looks, and only in the last scenes when Job, a victim of a Nazi concentration camp, returns home blind and therefore unable to see how physically grotesque his wife has become, does her icy heart thaw and she welcomes him back. Out of such vintage trash often comes marvellous entertainment and, in the capable hands of director Vincent Sherman

(working from a rambling, not always coherent screenplay by the Epstein brothers), **Mr. Skeffington** found favour, and its lack of credibility mattered not a jot. Audiences loved the way Davis (centre) raised her voice a full octave higher than normal to achieve a youthful, girlish quality; they wallowed in her decline, and were thrilled by the grotesque make-up (foreshadowing her Blanche in *Whatever Happened to Baby Jane*, 1962) that Perc Westmore devised for her. The superb Claude Rains (left) lent dignity to the proceedings, particularly in a restaurant scene with his daughter (Gigi Perreau) which was one of the dramatic highlights of the film. Also cast were Walter Abel, Richard Waring, George Coulouris, Marjorie Riordan and Edward Fielding (right). The Epstein brothers also produced.

△

Two soldiers on sick leave (Robert Hutton and Dane Clark) spend a couple of memorable nights at the **Hollywood Canteen** before reporting back for active duty in New Guinea. That's about all there was to it, yet the film made an absolute fortune as part of Hollywood's war effort, and was Warner Bros.' top money-maker of the year. And with a plethora of guest stars such as (in alphabetical order) The Andrews Sisters, Jack Benny, Joe E. Brown, Eddie Cantor, Kitty Carlisle, Jack Carson, Joan Crawford, Helmut Dantine, Bette Davis, Faye Emerson, Victor Francen, John Garfield, Sydney Greenstreet, Alan Hale, Paul Henreid, Andrea King, Peter Lorre, Ida Lupino, Irene Manning, Nora Martin, Joan McCracken (centre), Dolores Moran, Dennis Morgan, Eleanor Parker, William Prince, Joyce Reynolds, John Ridgely, Roy Rogers and Trigger, S.Z. Sakall, Alexis Smith, Zachary Scott, Barbara Stanwyck, Craig Stevens, Joseph Szigeti, Donald Woods and Jane Wyman, plus Jimmy Dorsey and his Band and Carmen Cavallaro and his Orchestra, who cared about the plot? Today it's a fascinating piece of forties nostalgia and an interesting sociological document. But in 1942, to producer Alex Gottlieb and writer-director Delmer Daves, it was merely an entertainment designed to keep the boys at the front happy and the brothers Warner back home rich. Songs included: Don't Fence Me In (by Cole Porter), You Can Always Tell A Yank (by E.Y. Harburg and Burton Lane), What Are You Doing The Rest Of Your Life? (by Ted Koehler and Burton Lane), We're Having A Baby (My Baby And Me) (by Harold Adamson and Vernon Duke), and Sweet Dreams Sweetheart and Hollywood Canteen (by Ted Koehler and M.K. Jerome).

The Last Ride, a conventional gangster ▷ melodrama, starred Richard Travis as an incorruptible detective. He exposes the pernicious practices of a gang of blackmarket tyre-traffickers (secretly headed by police captain Cy Kendall) who steal good tyres off cars and replace them with inferior ones. It was written by Raymond Schrock and drearily directed by D. Ross Lederman with a cast that included Charles Lang (right), Harry Lewis (centre right), Eleanor Parker, Jack La Rue, Dolores Moran (centre), Virginia Patton (left) and Wade Boteler. Associate producer was William Jacobs.

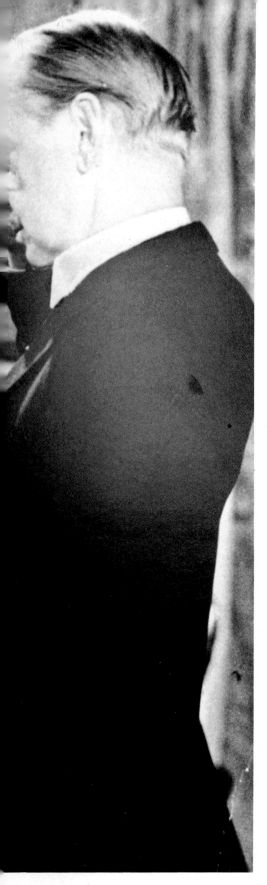

◁ **The Conspirators**, well-directed by Jean Negulesco, owed a great deal to *Casablanca* (1943), whose overall atmosphere it attempted to duplicate, after the success of the earlier film. Set in Lisbon during the Second World War, it starred a suave Paul Henreid as a guerrilla leader from Holland, and Hedy Lamarr (left), on loan from MGM, as a beautiful and mysterious woman whom he meets in bizarre circumstances and with whom he falls in love. Vladimir Pozner and Leo Rosten's screenplay, taken from a novel by Frederic Prokosh, didn't stand up to close examination, but the supporting performances by Sydney Greenstreet, Peter Lorre (centre), Victor Francen (right), Joseph Calleia, Carol Thurston and Vladimir Sokoloff were most agreeable. Jack Chertok produced.

△

The family around which Alvah Bessie and Delmer Daves structured their tiresome screenplay (story by Lionel Wiggam) for **The Very Thought of You**, were a pretty resistible bunch of folk — except, possibly, for Dad (Henry Travers) and his daughter (Eleanor Parker, right). The rest, including Mom (Beulah Bondi), were enough to give humanity a bad name. If the film had a *raison d'être* at all it could be found in its underlying theme: the pros and cons of war-time marriage. Reliable performances by Dane Clark and Andrea King in supporting roles were compensating factors, but it was heavy going just the same. Also cast were William Prince, Faye Emerson (left), John Alvin and Dick Erdman. It was produced by Jerry Wald, and the director was Delmer Daves.

1945

Mildred Pierce, Christmas In Connecticut, Pride Of The Marines, God Is My Co-Pilot, Objective Burma, To Have And Have Not, The Corn Is Green and Roughly Speaking were among the company's 19 feature releases that helped it to show a net profit of $9,901,563 for the year, a healthy improvement on the previous year. Mildred Pierce was nominated for the Best Picture Academy Award, but lost to The Lost Weekend (Paramount), although Joan Crawford (as Mildred) picked up the Oscar for Best Actress. Both Eve Arden and Ann Blyth were also nominated for Mildred Pierce in the Best supporting Actress category, and Joan Lorring in the same category for The Corn Is Green. The winner, however, was Anne Revere for National Velvet (MGM). A Warner two-reeler called Star In The Night won an Oscar for the Best Short Subject; while the best Documentary Short Subject was voted by the Academy to be Hitler Lives? The Pride Of The Marines was on the New York Times' Ten Best list.

Drenched in piety and weighed down with religious overtones, God is my Co-Pilot was a screen recreation of the best-seller by Colonel Robert Lee Scott in which a 34-year-old Georgia flyer, dismissed by the Army as too old for aerial combat, proves them wrong when he becomes a hero with General Claire Chennault's 'Flying Tigers'. Robert Florey's direction got off the ground only when the action did, but for most of the time, despite sincere performances from Dennis Morgan (as Scott), Dane Clark, Raymond Massey, Alan Hale, Andrea King, John Ridgely, Craig Stevens and Warren Douglas, the film failed to quicken the pulse. Still, it found favour with war-time audiences and cleaned up at the box office. The earnest, sometimes embarrassingly spiritual screenplay was written by Peter Milne and Abem Finkel, and the producer was Robert Buckner.

▽

After the spectacular success of *Grand Hotel*, novelist Vicki Baum came up with *Berlin Hotel, 1943*, which the studio purchased and retitled **Hotel Berlin**. Adapted by Jo Pagano and Alvah Bessie, the film chronicled the fates of a diverse group of people during the last days of the war. For example, Raymond Massey played a defecting Nazi general, Peter Lorre (left) a German scientist, Helmut Dantine (right) an underground leader fleeing for his life, and Andrea King an actress not to be trusted. It was about as convincing as a promise from Hitler, but its cast and director (Peter Godfrey) by refusing to take it too seriously, managed to squeeze a few entertaining moments from it. And if audiences found Alan Hale somewhat hard to take as a German sergeant, there were no complaints about the performances of Steven Geray, Henry Daniell and George Coulouris. The producer was Louis Edelman.

▽

A remake of *The Petrified Forest* (1936), ▷ **Escape in the Desert** did nothing for the studio's prestige, and even less for Robert E. Sherwood's play. Thomas Job's screenplay transmogrified Sherwood's intellectual hero into a Dutch flier hitch-hiking his way across America, and the villains of the piece into a band of Nazis on the run from a desert prison camp. What it all added up to was a less than convincing melodrama, directed by Edward A. Blatt and starring Philip Dorn (back left) as the flier and Helmut Dantine as the Nazi ringleader. Alan Hale (centre), Bill Kennedy (standing left), Jean Sullivan, Irene Manning (seated right) and Samuel S. Hinds (seated left) were also featured and the producer was Alex Gottlieb.

250

Roughly Speaking covered forty years in the life of Louise Randall Pierson, a delightful eccentric who pre-empted Women's Lib by over a quarter of a century. Starting in 1902, when Louise was twelve, and ending during World War II, the screenplay – written by Louise Randall Pierson herself – took viewers on an episodic journey involving the authoress' determination to overcome poverty, a bad first marriage (the second was more successful) and the problems inherent in bringing up five children. Rosalind Russell (left) was Louise, Jack Carson was Harold Pierson. Also cast were Alan Hale, Robert Hutton, Andrea King, Ann Doran (right), Craig Stevens and Donald Woods. The producer was Henry Blanke, and it was directed by Michael Curtiz, now making an average of two films a year for the studio.

Objective Burma was a grimly realistic, semi-documentary account of the hardships facing men in battle. The story of 50 American paratroopers (led by Errol Flynn) who locate and destroy a Japanese radar base, only to find themselves trapped in the Burmese jungle when their air rescue fails, was fictional, but there was nothing make-believe about the hellish situations in which Flynn and his men found themselves. The horrors of swamp warfare, the mental and physical deterioration of the men, and the sheer agony of battle, were brutally depicted in Ranald MacDougall and Lester Cole's realistic screenplay, James Wong Howe's uncompromising photography, and Raoul Walsh's masterly direction. Rising to the occasion with one of his most honest performances, Flynn (right) eschewed the 'cute' schoolboy heroics in which he often indulged, and delivered a performance of admirable restraint. So did James Brown, William Prince (left), George Tobias, Henry Hull (centre), Warner Anderson and John Alvin. Though well received in America, the film was withdrawn from British distribution one week after its London premiere because the English critics took severe exception to its American bias. They claimed that it gave the erroneous impression that the British played no part in the Burma campaign at all, and that Flynn seemed to have taken Burma single-handed. It was not until 1952 that the film re-surfaced in Britain, this time with an appeasing prologue appended. The producer was Jerry Wald.

The Horn Blows at Midnight, which starred Jack Benny the famous comedian (right), achieved the impossible: he failed to make people laugh. It was not his fault, but that of scenarists Sam Hellman and James Kern (story by Aubrey Wisberg) for concocting an unfunny screenplay about a trumpeter who falls asleep during a radio commercial for sleep-inducing coffee and dreams he is an angel with an earthly mission to preach Armageddon – or something vaguely resembling it. An unlucky dip of old gags and old situations, it insulted the talents of such notable performers as Allyn Joslyn, Reginald Gardiner, Guy Kibbee, John Alexander, Franklin Pangborn and Margaret Dumont. Alexis Smith (left) and Dolores Moran were also in it. It was directed by Raoul Walsh whose strong point was not humour; Mark Hellinger produced.

Zachary Scott (centre) played a two-timing ▷
swine in **Danger Signal**, veering indecisively
between his fiancee. Faye Emerson (seated)
and Mona Freeman (her younger and
wealthier sister). His indecision resolved
itself in a welter of melodramatics from
which no one emerged with any credit.
Adele Commandini and C. Graham Baker
wrote the anaemic screenplay (story by
Phyllis Bottome); it was produced by
William Jacobs with a cast that included
Dick Erdman, Rosemary De Camp (left),
Bruce Bennett (right) and John Ridgely, and
the director was Robert Florey. On this
occasion he should have chosen to shield his
reputation under his pseudonym Florian
Roberts.

◁ In one of his rare excursions into comedy
– and, alas, straining for the laughs –
director Vincent Sherman made the predictable plot of **Pillow to Post** rough going.
Starring Ida Lupino (left) as a young saleslady forced into finding a temporary husband if she is to be allowed to spend the
night in a motel that only caters for
marrieds, the movie offered no surprises and
little mirth. Scripted from Rose Simon
Kohn's stage play by Charles Hoffman, and
with a cast including William Prince (right)
as the husband, Stuart Erwin, Johnny
Mitchell, Ruth Donnelly, Sydney Greenstreet,
Stuart Erwin, Barbara Brown and Frank
Orth, it laid an egg. The producer was Alex
Gottlieb.

△
The trouble with **Rhapsody in Blue** was that
it came from a story by Sonya Levien and
not from its subject, George Gershwin.
Fanciful to the point of absurdity, the
Howard Koch-Elliot Paul screenplay was a
veritable sardine-tin of clichés (including the
one about it being lonely at the top) which
producer Jesse L. Lasky expected audiences
to swallow whole. The result was acutely
indigestible, with momentary relief supplied
by Oscar Levant (wryly playing himself) and
a complete performance of the title piece by
Paul Whiteman and his Orchestra. (The
work was also featured with Whiteman in
Universal's 1930 colour production, *King of
Jazz*), Robert Alda (for the second time on
celluloid) was woefully undercast as Gershwin, with indifferent performances coming
from Joan Leslie as Julie Adams (a figment of
Sonya Levien's imagination), and Alexis
Smith as a rich woman who loves Gershwin
but unselfishly relinquishes him. Irving
Rapper's direction reflected none of the
sparkle or originality that made Gershwin's
music unique. Also cast were Herbert Rudley
(as Ira Gershwin), Anne Brown, Charles
Coburn, George White, Hazel Scott, Al Jolson
(as himself), Julie Bishop, Albert Basserman
and Morris Carnovsky. Songs included:
The Man I Love, Fascinatin' Rhythm, Clap
Yo' Hands, I Got Rhythm, 'Swonderful,
Lady Be Good, Somebody Loves Me,
Swanee, Summertime, Yankee Doodle Blues,
Embraceable You, It Aint Necessarily So,
Love Walked In, Do It Again, I'll Build A
Stairway To Paradise, Liza, Someone To
Watch Over Me, Bidin' My Time, Delicious,
and I Got Plenty O' Nuttin'.

Producer William Jacobs was surely not too ▷
young to know that **Too Young To Know**
was a load of nonsense. The story (by
Harlan Ware, screenplay by Jo Pagano) of
an air-force captain (Robert Hutton, right)
who returns home from active service to be
greeted with the news that his ex-wife
(Joan Leslie, left) has literally given their
child away, didn't bear thinking about, a
fact very much in evidence in Frederick de
Cordova's direction. Also cast were Dolores
Moran, Harry Davenport, Rosemary De
Camp, Barbara Brown, Robert Lowell (centre), Arthur Shields, Craig Stevens, and,
making her first appearance at the studio,
Dorothy Malone.

Conflict found Humphrey Bogart (left)
wondering how to rid himself of his
shrewish wife (Rose Hobart) in order to pursue her attractive younger sister (Alexis
Smith, right). Simple: push her car over a
cliff, making quite sure she's inside it at the
time. Then, mission accomplished, return
home and report her missing. Which is just
what he does, except that a series of bizarre
incidents keep occurring to suggest that
maybe the victim isn't dead after all . . . It
could have been fun, and indeed, Sydney
Greenstreet's performance as a wily psychiatrist captured the spirit of the hokum to
perfection. But the rest of the cast (Charles
Drake, Grant Mitchell, Pat O'Moore, Ann
Shoemaker and Frank Wilcox) handled the
Arthur T. Horman – Dwight Taylor screenplay (story by Robert Siodmak and Alfred
Neuman) with obvious unease and failed to
prop up Curtis Bernhardt's enervated direction. William Jacobs produced.
▽

One of the great soap-operas of the forties, ▷
Mildred Pierce was turned down by both
Bette Davis, who was first choice for the
title role, and Barbara Stanwyck. It was
producer Jerry Wald who thought of Joan
Crawford, and his perspicacity resulted in a
five million dollar winner for the studio. It
also resulted in a first-class, highly literate
drama of a determined woman's rise from
waitress to restaurateur, the motivation for
success being her spoilt, indulged older
daughter (Ann Blyth) on whom she
lavishes (but does not receive in return) all
the love she can. Echoing the star's own
struggles, both private and professional, the
part clearly had personal reverberations for
Crawford (right) which she exploited to magnificent effect under Michael Curtiz's demanding direction. Based on the novel by
James M. Cain, with a screenplay by Ranald
MacDougall, **Mildred Pierce** also featured
Jack Carson (left), Zachary Scott, Eve Arden,
Bruce Bennett and George Tobias.

◁ A big money-maker for the studio, **Christmas in Connecticut** starred Barbara Stanwyck (now earning well over $100,000 a year) as a columnist for *Smart Housekeeping* whose talent, to judge from what she writes, would seem to embrace cooking, motherhood and housewifery. The snag is that the entire column is a piece of fiction – Stanwyck (left) is unmarried and the most undomesticated woman in the world. Her publisher (Sydney Greenstreet), however, doesn't know this, so when he unexpectedly asks her to entertain a war hero (Dennis Morgan) at her home, she has to find a husband, a baby, and a cook in order to remain employed. Miss Stanwyck's delightful flair for comedy was given ample scope in Lionel Houser and Adele Commandini's jolly screenplay (story by Aileen Hamilton); and an excellent cast, including Reginald Gardiner (as the 'husband' she finds), S.Z. Sakall (right) as the cook and Una O'Connor, provided strong support. The lively direction was by Peter Godfrey, and the producer was William Jacobs.

△
The exploration of anti-Fascist themes provided film-makers with an excuse to perpetrate all manner of rough-play – and **Confidential Agent** was a good example of exactly this sort of thing. A middle-aged Spanish Loyalist (Charles Boyer, left) attempts to prevent a Fascist-tinged business deal from taking place in England and, as a result of his efforts, is brutalized by a zoo-full of 'heavies'. Under Herman Shumlin's plodding direction, it was an uphill climb for much of the time, though Robert Buckner's cloak-and-dagger screenplay (from Graham Greene's novel) provided some effective moments for Katina Paxinou, Peter Lorre, Victor Francen, George Coulouris, Wanda Hendrix, George Zucco and John Warburton. Lauren Bacall (right) also starred, but failed, this time, to reinforce the the impact she made in *To Have And Have Not*. Buckner also produced.

Made by the Motion Picture Industry War Activities Committee and released by Warner Bros., **Appointment in Tokyo** was a 54-minute documentary whose purpose
◁ was to present a factual account of the war in the Pacific and the recapture of the Philippines. Vastly inferior to other war efforts, such as *Target for Tonight* (1941), its strength lay in its awesome action footage: its weakness in its often fictional approach to the material, redolent of Hollywood rather than the Theatre of War. Col. Emmanuel Cohen was the executive producer, it was written by Captain Jack Handley and Captain Jesse Lasky Jr, and the director was Major Jack Hively.

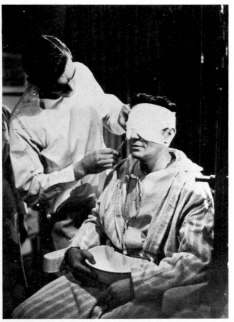

◁ The publicity poster for **Pride of the Marines**, showing its trio of stars – John Garfield, Eleanor Parker and Dane Clark – grinning broadly and walking arm-in-arm in the best musical comedy fashion, was clearly intended to tone down the more harrowing aspects of the true story. Al Schmid, a young Marine who loses his eyesight in the battle of Guadalcanal, returns home to his wife Ruth (Eleanor Parker) to face a new battle – that of adjusting to his affliction. The only excuse for the poster could be the optimism it exuded, for as brilliantly played by Garfield (right) the film, in the best studio tradition, was an optimistic and caring attempt to inspire returning servicemen with similar problems to cope with society and to serve it usefully. Albert Maltz's screenplay, though at times overpatriotic (forgiveable in the circumstances), was immensely moving; and Delmer Daves' direction sensitive to its demands. The producer was Jerry Wald.

△

Referring to himself as 'The rich man's Roy Rogers', Errol Flynn returned to Westerns in **San Antonio**, a handsome, Technicolored action picture that was always good to look at, but lacked the clout of *They Died With Their Boots On* (1942) or *Dodge City* (1939; whose main title music Max Steiner borrowed for **San Antonio**). The routine story of a Texas rustler (Flynn, right) who in 1877 tracks down a gang of well-organized cattle thieves, it was too full of clichés for there to have been any real element of surprise in it. Lifelessly directed by David Butler, who gave only as good as he got from the Alan Le May and W.R. Burnett screenplay, it also featured Alexis Smith, S.Z. Sakall, Victor Francen (left), Florence Bates, John Litel, Paul Kelly, Monte Blue and Robert Shayne. The producer was Robert Buckner.

◁ Emlyn Williams' play **The Corn is Green** was a hit when Sybil Thorndike first created the role of Miss Moffatt, the selfless English schoolmistress who takes a Welsh miner under her tutelage and prepares him for a university education. Ethel Barrymore played it over 450 times on Broadway, and Bette Davis (left), heavily padded to simulate middle-age, brought the role to life on the screen. The Welsh village of Glensarno was resurrected in the studio with the usual stagey results, but Frank Cavett and Casey Robinson's adaptation respected Williams' play, as did Irving Rapper's restrained and intelligent direction. As the miner, newcomer John Dall was totally convincing (Richard Waring, who created the role on Broadway, and impressed the studio with his work in the 1944 *Mr. Skeffington* was to have played it, but a draft notice made this impossible), and there was fine support from Mildred Dunnock, Joan Lorring, Nigel Bruce, Rosalind Ivan (right) and Rhys Williams. A miscalculation, however, was the Welsh vocalizing by a chorus of mining lads who produced sounds nearer in spirit to the Hollywood Hills than the Welsh valleys. To lend authenticity to designer Carl Jules Weyl's Welsh mock-up, cartloads of dirt were strewn about the set; so were some twenty tons of grass for the meadow scenes. Smoke machines were used to provide the 'haze' in which mining villages seemed perpetually bathed, and some ten thousand 'local' props were requisitioned for the sake of accuracy. The production of this undertaking was in the hands of Jack Chertok.

1946

Humphrey Bogart's contract was again reviewed in 1946 and upped to $5,000 a week. He was obliged to make at least one film a year, and had a choice of three scripts per film. For the second time in two years, there were no Oscar nominations for Warner Bros. features for Best Film, and this time none for Best Actor or Actress. The only Academy Awards won by the studio were for two short subjects, a one-reeler called **Facing Your Danger**, and a two-reeler called **A Boy And His Dog**. The Best Film Oscar was won by the Goldwyn-RKO release **The Best Years of Our Lives**. Still, the year ended with a mammoth profit for the company of $19,424,650.

△

Three oddly assorted individuals shared the lucrative benefits of a lucky sweepstake ticket in **Three Strangers**, a drama rich in irony and suspense. Sydney Greenstreet (left), on top of his usual scene-stealing form, played a lawyer desperately in need of cash to replace misused funds; Peter Lorre (right), was a small-time criminal who, in the service of the John Huston-Howard Koch screenplay, burns his sweepstake ticket, while Geraldine Fitzgerald (centre) was a deserted wife who meets a sorry end when she is struck over the head with a statue representing Fortune and Destiny, Life and Death. Not nearly as corny as it sounds, it was directed by Jean Negulesco with exemplary flair. Also cast were Joan Lorring, Robert Shayne, Marjorie Riordan, Arthur Shields and Rosalind Ivan. The producer was Wolfgang Reinhardt.

Actions spoke louder than words in **Burma Victory**, an impressive documentary chronicling the Burma Campaign in World War II. It was filmed by British Combat camera teams who redressed the balance that had been upset by Errol Flynn in *Objective Burma* (1945), by correctly crediting a major share of the victory to the British. Captain Roy Boulting directed from his own and Captain Frank Harvey's screenplay; it was produced by Lieut. Col. David MacDonald, and distributed in the US by Warner Bros. Educative, as well as gripping entertainment, it was a worthy successor to *Target For Tonight* (1941).

▽

Though elaborately mounted, **Saratoga Trunk**, based on Edna Ferber's novel, was a major artistic disappointment. Its credits were fine – both in front of and behind the cameras – but someone forgot to give the film the kiss of life. Ferber's probing story about the illegitimate Creole daughter (Ingrid Bergman, centre) of a New Orleans aristocrat, who returns from Paris in the 1890's, takes up with a gambler (Gary Cooper), and sets out to avenge the treatment suffered by her mother at the hands of her wealthy family, never took fire. Slow-moving and long (the film runs 135 minutes), and with Bergman and Cooper respectively miscast and wooden, the film also suffered from Sam Wood's turgid ▷ direction. Casey Robinson wrote the screenplay, failing completely to extract the essence or the drama of the Ferber novel. It was produced by Hal B. Wallis with a cast that also included Flora Robson (centre left), Jerry Austin (left), Florence Bates, Curt Bois, John Abbott (right) and John Warburton. However, despite the film's failings, the marquee value of Cooper and Bergman was potent enough to bring in American and Canadian rentals of over four and a half million dollars.

Originally intended as a small-scale 1944 ▷ war-time musical, **Cinderella Jones'** release was held up for two years in order to allow the studio to launch its male star, Robert Alda (centre right) in the more ambitious *Rhapsody in Blue* (1945). Unfortunately for both Alda and the studio, the Gershwin biopic was not Alda's springboard to instant stardom, and by mistiming the release of **Cinderella Jones**, many of its war-time references had to be edited out at the expense of the plot. What remained was the feeble story of a young woman (Joan Leslie, centre left) who stands to inherit ten million dollars on condition that she marries a man of unusual intelligence by a given date. Julie Bishop (left), William Prince (right), S.Z. Sakall (centre), Edward Everett Horton, Elisha Cook Jr, Ruth Donnelly (far left) and Hobart Cavanaugh were also in it. Charles Hoffman wrote it from a story by Philip Wylie, and Busby Berkeley, in the midst of an unhappy period in his personal life, directed it with none of the pezazz usually guaranteed by his name on the credits. Songs included: If You're Waitin' I'm Waitin' Too, Cinderella Jones, You Never Know Where You're Goin' Till You Get There and When The One You Love Simply Won't Come Back (by Sammy Cahn and Jule Styne).

In **Janie Gets Married**, the sequel to *Janie*, Joan Leslie (centre) replaced Joyce Reynolds as the eponymous heroine and did exactly what the title said she did – taking Robert Hutton (right) as her spouse. Agnes Christine Johnston's screenplay concentrated on the various domestic crises that befall young marrieds in their first year of togetherness, with parts for Robert Benchley (as the groom's stepfather), Edward Arnold (centre right), Ann Harding (centre left), Dorothy Malone (as a former flame of Mr Hutton's), Hattie McDaniel, Barbara Brown (left), Dick Erdman, Clare Foley and Donald Meek. Vincent Sherman did the best he could with very slender material. Alex Gottlieb produced.

Completed nearly three years before its release, **Devotion** was an absurdly romanticized biography of the Bronte sisters which, in many instances, turned fact into fiction. It starred Ida Lupino (left) as Charlotte, Olivia de Havilland (right) as Emily and Nancy Coleman (centre) as the youngest sister, Anne. Joan Fontaine, de Havilland's sister, was originally sought for the Lupino role, but her much-publicized feud with Olivia ruled out any possibility of their teaming. Also, because of Miss de Havilland's recalcitrant behaviour towards the studio and her virulent criticisms of its policies, she was given third billing below Lupino and Paul Henreid in the publicity campaign. Henreid was miscast as the Rev. Nichols, the Irish-born curate and the fabricated object of both Emily's and Charlotte's romantic yearnings. The best performance in an otherwise bogus film was by Arthur Kennedy as the tormented brother, Branwell. Keith Winter's screenplay refused to acknowledge that the unadorned facts were more dramatic than anything that emerged from his imagination; Curtis Bernhardt directed as if it were no more than pulp fiction which, in the circumstances, it was. Also cast were Dame May Whitty and Victor Francen. Erich Wolfgang Korngold wrote the score; Robert Buckner produced.

In **My Reputation**, Barbara Stanwyck (centre) played a widow from the upper echelons of society who, since the death of her husband, has lived a hermetically sealed existence, devoting her time to the demands of her two young sons (Bobby Cooper, left and Scotty Beckett, right) and her domineering mother (Lucile Watson). Then she meets a womanising bachelor (George Brent) and finds her unsullied reputation suddenly threatened. Stanwyck managed to make something of this soap-opera. Brent did not; and the result, despite James Wong Howe's glossy photography and Max Steiner's romantic score, was pretty mediocre. Catherine Turney wrote the screenplay, Henry Blanke produced and Curtis Bernhardt directed. Also in the cast were Eve Arden (right), Warner Anderson (left) and John Ridgely (far right). Critics gave it the thumbs down: audiences however, liked it, and it was a massive hit.

Bette Davis (left) not only doubled as the producer of **A Stolen Life**, she played identical twin sisters: sweet, kindly, introspective Kate Bosworth, and vivacious but thoroughly bitchy and unprincipled Patricia. After a boating accident in which Patricia is killed Kate takes her place and posing as her sister, attempts to win the love of Glenn Ford. Witless and self-indulgent to a degree, the film also featured Dane Clark (right), Walter Brennan and Charles Ruggles. Curtis Bernhardt directed the Catherine Turney screenplay (story by Karel J. Benes) and Max Steiner wrote the score. Audiences succumbed just as they had done when Elisabeth Bergner played the same role for Paramount in 1929, and it was a box-office success – because for all its nonsensical content, the film was quintessential Davis and her double exposure performance, particularly in the scenes in which she plays to herself, was a masterly example of her brilliant technique.

One More Tomorrow failed to convey the essence of the Philip Barry play *The Animal Kingdom* (first filmed by R.K.O. in 1932) on which it was based. The story of a wealthy playboy who marries a left-wing photographer and then buys up her magazine, its attempt to excavate from Charles Hoffman and Catherine Turney's screenplay the theme at the heart of the Barry original (radicalism v. conservatism) was totally abortive. Not even a cast which included Ann Sheridan, Dennis Morgan (left), Jack Carson, Alexis Smith (right), Jane Wyman, Reginal Gardiner and John Loder could animate the enterprise. Peter Godfrey directed and the producer was Henry Blanke.

Forget about the rather banal plot of **Two Guys From Milwaukee** (in which a Balkan prince, on a visit to America, befriends a cab-driver who helps him see the country through the eyes of a commoner), and concentrate instead on the performances of its attractive cast. Everyone else did. Dennis Morgan (right) was the Prince, Jack Carson (left) his cab-driver buddy – with Joan Leslie, Janis Paige, S.Z. Sakall, Patti Brady, Rosemary De Camp, and Franklin Pangborn in support. At the film's end Morgan gets to meet his dream girl Lauren Bacall, whom he sits next to on an aeroplane. His hopes of a romance, however, are soon dashed when a grim-faced Humphrey Bogart sourly claims his seat. David Butler directed from an original screenplay by I.A.L. Diamond and Charles Hoffman. The producer was Alex Gottlieb.

The second version of Somerset Maugham's **Of Human Bondage** found two fine performers, Paul Henreid (right) and Eleanor Parker, floundering embarrassingly in parts for which they were patently miscast. Henreid played the tortured, inward-looking cripple; Miss Parker the brashly insensitive waitress with whom he becomes obsessed. As they were both so at odds with their roles, the element of sexual conflict so germane to the story was missing, and boredom became the substitute. Apart from the stars, blame must also go to Catherine Turney for an unilluminating screenplay, and to Edmund Goulding for matching his direction to her words. Henry Blanke produced, and the cast included Alexis Smith, Edmund Gwenn (left), Janis Paige (centre), Patric Knowles, Henry Stephenson, Martin Lamont, Isobel Elsom and Una O'Connor.

A throwback to the studio's crime melo-dramas of the thirties, **Her Kind of Man** starred Zachary Scott (left) as a Prohibition gangster turned big-time gambler, Janis Paige (centre) as a singer who finds him irresistible, and Dane Clark (right) as a newspaper columnist attracted to Miss Paige. Gordon Kahn and Leopold Atlas' screenplay (from a story by Charles Hoffman and James Kern) came up with all the ingredients appropriate to the genre and a nice line in witty dialogue; but Frederick de Cordova's direction missed the essential no-nonsense toughness which characterized the era in which the film was set. Faye Emerson, George Tobias, Howard Smith, Harry Lewis and Sheldon Leonard were in it, too; and the producer was Alex Gottlieb. Songs included: Something To Remember You By (by Howard Dietz and Arthur Schwartz), Body And Soul (by Edward Heyman and Johnny Green) and Speak To Me Of Love (by Bruce Siever and Jean Lenoir).

'It's like grand opera, only the people are ▷ thinner,' remarked a perceptive critic of **Deception** – John Collier and Joseph Than's banal reworking of Louis Verneuil's play *Jealousy*. Telling the overblown story of a composer's fury when he discovers that the woman in his life (Bette Davis, right) loves another, director Irving Rapper, assisted by Erich Wolfgang Korngold's loudest, most flamboyant (and least successful) score, pulled out all the stops in a desperate attempt to pass off a phoney piece of flim-flam as high flying drama. Throwing restraint to the proverbial winds, Rapper allowed Davis to do precisely as she pleased, while he concentrated on Claude Rains as the composer and Paul Henreid (left) as his rival in love. It was Rains' film all the way. The rest of the cast included John Abbott, Benson Fong, Richard Walsh, Suzi Crandall and Richard Erdman. Henry Blanke produced.

Never Say Goodbye was the one in which a divorced couple realize that they are still in love and simply cannot live without each other. Five writers had a hand in the plot: screenplay by I.A.L. Diamond and James V. Kern, adaptation by Lewis R. Foster, original (!) story by Ben and Norma Barzman. In the event, the screenplay was no more than a collection of over-ripe situations which, for 97 contrived minutes gave new definition to the meaning of cliché. **Never Say Goodbye** should never have said hello. James V. Kern directed for producer William Jacobs, with a cast that included Errol Flynn (right), Eleanor Parker (left), Patti Brady, Lucile Watson, S.Z. Sakall, Forrest Tucker, Donald Woods, Peggy Knudsen and Tom D'Andrea.

▽

In accepting the directorial assignment on ▷ **Cloak and Dagger**, director Fritz Lang believed he would be able to use the film's basic story (in which nuclear physicist Gary Cooper is parachuted into Germany in an attempt to rescue an elderly Italian woman scientist kidnapped by the Nazis) to make some important statements about the uses and abuses of atomic energy. But the studio refused to release the film as shot, cut the final reel and substituted a happier, less doom-laden ending than the one originally intended. The result was a routine war adventure, with a few characteristically suspenseful Langian moments, but not much else. Even Gary Cooper (left) seemed ill at ease. Robert Alda played an Italian partisan; Lilli Palmer (right), making her American screen debut, was involved in the underground movement and Vladimir Sokoloff was an Italian scientist constantly in fear of his life. The screenplay (based on an original story by Boris Ingster and John Larkin, suggested, in turn, by the book by Cary Ford and Alastair McBain) was by Albert Maltz and Ring Lardner Jr. Milton Sperling, Jack Warner's nephew-in-law, produced.

Not even scriptwriters William Faulkner, Leigh Brackett and Jules Furthman could make head or tail of the screenplay they fashioned from Raymond Chandler's novel **The Big Sleep**. Under normal circumstances, this would have placed them and the prospective audiences at something of a disadvantage. But in one of the screen's greatest examples of style triumphing over content, disentangling the plot (Private Eye Philip Marlowe is hired by the father of a nymphomaniac daughter to rid him of a blackmailer, but it wasn't as simple as that) offered only an incidental pleasure next to the stylish performances of Humphrey Bogart (right) as Marlowe and Lauren ◁ Bacall (by now Mrs Bogart in real life) as a sexy young divorcée with whom he falls in love. The 'Big Sleep' of the title was death – a commodity the thriller was not short on – and producer-director Howard Hawks brilliantly choreographed the film's numerous killings with awesome inventiveness. Confusing it may have been, but dull it certainly wasn't. Aside from the film's visual elegance, Max Steiner's score contributed much to its overall success, as indeed did Sid Hickox's photography. If *Little Caesar* (1931) was the studio's quintessential crime melodrama, **The Big Sleep** was its most characteristic thriller with the look, the feel, and the sound of it unmistakably belonging to Warner Bros. Also cast were John Ridgely, Martha Vickers, Dorothy Malone (left), Peggy Knudsen, Regis Toomey and Elisha Cook Jr.

△
In **Humoresque**, John Garfield (front right), as a budding violinist, was upstaged by Joan Crawford (front left) as a wealthy patron of the arts, glamorous but unfortunately an alcoholic, who, after a stormy first encounter with the musician, agrees to sponsor his career in return for services rendered. Gradually she finds she cannot cope with his moods and becomes a prey to feelings of guilt exacerbated by Garfield's domineering mother (Ruth Nelson). It all ends in tears when Garfield decides that his music means more to him than Miss Crawford's love and attention, as a result of which, and to the strains of Wagner's *Liebestod*, she walks into the nearest ocean, never to return. Wisecrackingly scripted by Clifford Odets and Zachary Gold from Fannie Hurst's tear-jerking novel, it was directed with immense panache by Jean Negulesco, who clearly enjoyed contrasting the life-styles of the ghetto-born violinist

with his rich patron's assorted town and country estates, limousines and expensive clothes. And if you didn't know that Isaac Stern dubbed the violin solos, you could be forgiven for believing that Garfield had added another string to his bow. The illusion was achieved by having a large hole cut into the elbow of Garfield's coat through which passed a real violinist's hand to take care of the fingering. Meanwhile, hiding behind Garfield was a second violinist to take care of the bow. It worked brilliantly. Apart from these two unseen and unsung musical heroes, sturdy support was also lent to Jerry Wald's glossy production, filmed in Warners' most lavish style, by Oscar Levant as Garfield's cynical pianist friend, J. Carrol Naish, Joan Chandler, Craig Stevens (centre right) and Paul Cavanagh who remarks immortally of Garfield's music-making: 'It has fire. Rather like what you'd feel in a Van Gogh painting.'

Sydney Greenstreet (left) and Peter Lorre ▷ (right) were again paired for **The Verdict**, a feeble melodrama set in London in 1892, and involving disgraced Superintendent Greenstreet's attempts to plot the perfect murder after being relieved of his position in the force. Lorre played the super's oversuspicious friend whose inquisitiveness almost leads to his death. Director Don Siegel's idea of a fog-bound London provided some nice visual touches, but he was ultimately powerless against Peter Milne's vapid screenplay from a story by Israel Zangwill. Producer William Jacobs engaged Frederick Hollander to do the music, and a cast including Joan Lorring, George Coulburis, Rosalind Ivan and Arthur Shields.

Told in flashback, **Shadow of a Woman** was a woefully inept melodrama in which Andrea King (centre) marries Helmut Dantine, a phoney dietician, after a five-day courtship, only to discover that he is a divorcé and that, should his small son die, he will stand to inherit a fortune. Could that be the reason why he is starving the poor kid to death? A mere shadow of a thriller, it was written by Whitman Chambers and C. Graham Baker from a story by Virginia Perdue, directed by Joseph Santley for producer William Jacobs, and also featured Don McGuire, Dick Erdman, William Prince (right) and Elvira Curci (left).

▽

In **Nobody Lives Forever**, con-man John ◁ Garfield returns from the war to discover that his sweetheart has not only stolen his money, but has left him for another man. He heads out to California where he, in turn, swindles a rich widow (Geraldine Fitzgerald) out of *her* wealth. Fortunately he falls in love with her and at the final fade has not only redeemed himself, but is living happily ever after. Wisely, director Jean Negulesco, working from a screenplay by W.R. Burnett, decided to skim over the flimsy plot and concentrate instead on mood and atmosphere. Hence the opening of the film, which is set in New York, contrasts vividly with the more lyrical scenes (Pacific Beach, for example) in California. It was a stylish victory for all concerned and Garfield (right), working with material well below his capabilities, was given a chance to be both con-man (a role which by now fitted him to perfection) and a reformed lover, slightly uncomfortable in the classy West Coast society in which he is required to move. Faye Emerson, George Couloris, George Tobias and Walter Brennan (left) co-starred, and the producer was Robert Buckner.

A travesty of the great Cole Porter's life story, and a woebegone tribute to his immortal songs, **Night And Day** was a wretched musical whose failure to do justice to the dramatic and musical content of its subject was one of the great missed op- ▷ portunities in the history of the studio, but a box-office smash nonetheless. With the complete Porter catalogue at his disposal, Michael Curtiz, abetted by four writers (Jack Moffitt, Charles Hoffman, Leo Townsend and William Bowers) emerged with a garish non-starter, in Technicolor. Starting with the monumental miscasting of Cary Grant as Porter (behind right) and Alexis Smith as his wife Linda Lee (behind left), to LeRoy Prinz's unimaginative staging of the musical numbers, the film was a catalogue of disasters, only enlivened by Mary Martin's famous rendering of 'My Heart Belongs To Daddy' and Monty Woolley (left, playing himself)

△

The year ended with yet another 'let's-put-on-a-show' musical – a luke-warm Technicolored offering called **The Time, The Place And The Girl**. In it Jack Carson (left), Dennis Morgan, Janis Paige (centre) and Martha Vickers played show-folk looking for a buyer for their wares. Also cast were S.Z. Sakall (right), Alan Hale, Donald Woods and Florence Bates. It was written by Francis Swann, Agnes Christine Johnston and Lynn Starling (story by Leonard Lee); the director

talk-singing 'Miss Otis Regrets'. For the rest, Jane Wyman, Ginny Simms (right) and Eve Arden were simply not up to the Porter masterpieces they were called on to interpret; while the scene depicting the creation of the classic 'Night And Day', complete with the cliché 'Wait a minute, I think I've got it', has to be the most absurd in the history of a generally absurd genre – the musical biopic. The producer was Arthur Schwartz. Songs included: In The Still Of The Night, Old-Fashioned Garden, Let's Do It, You Do Something To Me, What Is This Thing Called Love, I've Got You Under My Skin, Just One Of Those Things, Begin The Beguine, You're The Top, I Get A Kick Out Of You and Easy To Love.

was David Butler (dance director LeRoy Prinz); Alex Gottlieb was the producer and the music, by Arthur Schwartz and Leo Robin, was adapted by Frederick Hollander. Luke-warm it may have been, but it turned out to be hot stuff at the box-office. Songs included: A Gal In Calico, What Do You Do On A Rainy Night In Rio? Through A Thousand Dreams, A Solid Citizen Of The Solid South and I Happened To Walk Down First Street.

1947

The year which saw the commencement of the Hollywood Communist witch-hunts was also the year in which Warner Bros.' net profit of $22,094,979 was the biggest in its history. Yet it was another undistinguished period for the studio as far as Academy Awards were concerned, with their only winner being a Tweetie Pie cartoon. The Best Film of the Year Award went to 20th Century-Fox's **Gentleman's Agreement**. William Powell was nominated as Best Actor for his performance in **Life With Father** and Joan Crawford as Best Actress for **Possessed**. They lost to Ronald Colman (**A Double Life**, Universal) and Loretta Young (**The Farmer's Daughter**, RKO). **Life With Father** was voted by the *New York Times* as one of the year's Ten Best, with the New York film critics voting for William Powell as best actor of the year.

Barbara Stanwyck's contract with the studio came to an end and, rather than renew it, she left to freelance. According to the US Treasury Department, Bette Davis was the highest paid female in America at $328,000 per year (Deanna Durbin was next at $323,477) and Humphrey Bogart the highest paid male at $467,361. The company's big money-makers for the year were **Humoresque, Life With Father, Nora Prentiss** and **The Time, The Place And The Girl** (released December 1946).

Melodrama reached the peak of absurdity with **The Two Mrs Carrolls**, director Peter Godfrey's thoroughly undistinguished screen version of the Martin Vale play. Humphrey Bogart (right) played a psychopathic artist who, after painting his numerous wives, kills them off by making them drink poisoned milk. Godfrey went all out for atmosphere (ominous weather, pealing bells, looming shadows, etc) and the climax, in all fairness, did have some exciting moments. But, despite a cast that included Barbara Stanwyck (left), Alexis Smith, Nigel Bruce and Isobel Elsom, and an impressively sinister score from Franz Waxman, Mark Hellinger's production made little impact. The screenplay was by Thomas Job.

▽

The only horror film made by the studio in the forties was the intermittently effective, but generally ludicrous **The Beast With Five Fingers**. It was based on William Fryer Harvey's story about a concert-pianist's hand which, severed from its owner after the man's violent death, takes on a life of its own and returns from the grave to seek its revenge. It starred Victor Francen as the pianist with Peter Lorre (at his most unrestrained) as his mentally disturbed secretary who, in his derangement, is the only one to see the severed limb. Director Robert Florey's inability to impose a sense of style onto the proceedings made Curt Siodmak's silly screenplay look even sillier. Also cast were Robert Alda (left), Andrea King (centre), J. Carrol Naish (right) and Pedro de Cordoba. William Jacobs produced.

▽

Adapted by N. Richard Nash from Paul Webster's original story, **Nora Prentiss** was a weepie which charted the downfall of a doctor who broke the law in his attempts to keep his wife from discovering his affair with a night-club singer. Kent Smith (right) was the doctor, Rosemary De Camp the wife and Ann Sheridan (left) the other woman. Relying on the melodramatics of the plot, and drawing atmosphere from tacky hotel rooms and seedy nightclubs, director Vincent Sherman milked the material for all it was worth, and delivered to producer William Jacobs a quintessential 'woman's film'. Also cast were Bruce Bennett, Robert Alda, Robert Arthur and John Ridgely. Songs included: Would You Like A Souvenir and Who Cares What People Say (by M.K. Jerome, Jack Scholl and Eddie Cherkose).

▽

◁ **Stallion Road**, which was originally to have been shot in Technicolor with Humphrey Bogart in the cast, was finally made in black-and-white with Zachary Scott replacing Bogart a week before shooting began. (It took an unheard-of 109 days to complete.) About a veterinary surgeon (Ronald Reagan, left), the lady horsebreeder (Alexis Smith, centre) who loves him and the other man (Zachary Scott, right) to whom Alexis turns after Reagan refuses to tend her ailing mare (he is busy vaccinating a herd of cows against anthrax), its chief virtue was the way it looked (it was photographed on location in the Madre Range, California). For the rest the film was average entertainment that did average business. It was written by Stephen Longstreet from his novel, produced by Alex Gottlieb and directed by James Kern with a cast that also featured Peggy Knudsen, Patti Brady, Harry Davenport and Angela Greene.

One of the studio's more ambitious forties ▷ Westerns, **Pursued** starred a laconic Robert Mitchum (left) as a Spanish-American war veteran who, as a result of his father having long ago had an illicit love affair, spends a large part of his adulthood bedevilled by disturbing and sinister events, the meanings of which are only made clear at the end of the film. Beautifully photographed by James Wong Howe, and with fine performances from Judith Anderson (right) and Teresa Wright (centre), the film relied on talk rather than on action for its impetus (screenplay and story by Niven Busch), though its violent climax went quite a way to redress the balance. Tough-guy director Raoul Walsh brought a rather grim aspect to it all (as well as an authentic sense of turn-of-the-century period) and drew fine performances from a supporting cast which included Dean Jagger, Alan Hale and Harry Carey Jr. The producer was Milton Sperling.

Probably one of the worst of the studio's forties comedies, **Love And Learn** was about a couple of impoverished song-writers who are snatched from the jaws of oblivion (where they clearly belonged) by a rich girl who feigns poverty. Jack Carson (right) and Robert Hutton (left) were the tunesmiths, Martha Vickers (centre left) their guardian angel, with other parts in this Eugene Conrad-Francis Swann-I.A.L. Diamond opus (story by Harry Sauber) going to Janis Paige (centre), Otto Kruger, Barbara Brown, Tom D'Andrea, Florence Bates and Craig Stevens. Frederick de Cordova directed and the producer was William Jacobs.

▽

Directed by Raoul Walsh, with a firm grip on shaky material, **The Man I Love** featured Ida Lupino (left) as a 'seen-it-all-and-I'm-still-here' nightclub singer who, on a visit to her sister (Andrea King) in California, becomes involved with a mobster club owner called Nicky Toresca (Robert Alda, right). Miss Lupino survived the many plot twists provided by the Catherine Turney-Jo Pagano screenplay from a novel by Maritta Wolff, and faced her numerous tribulations with enviable stoicism. She even got to sing a few standards courtesy of Peg LaCentra who ▷ supplied the voice. Audiences were less stoic and gave it the thumbs down. Still, thanks to craftsman Walsh who was vouchsafed sterling support from a cast that included Martha Vickers, Bruce Bennett, Alan Hale, Dolores Moran and John Ridgely, it wasn't as bad as it should have been. The producer was Arnold Albert. Songs included: The Man I Love and Liza (by George and Ira Gershwin), Why Was I Born? (by Jerome Kern and Oscar Hammerstein II), Bill (by Kern, Hammerstein II and P.G. Wodehouse) and Body And Soul (by Edward Heyman and Johnny Green).

△
That Way With Women was a remake of *The Millionaire* (1931) in which George Arliss had starred as a millionaire who, to assuage his boredom, went into partnership with a young man in a filling station venture. In the new version, the emphasis was switched from the millionaire (Sydney Greenstreet, left) to the younger man (Dane Clark), and his romance with the millionaire's daughter (Martha Vickers, right). Thus, with Dane Clark rather than Sydney Greenstreet as the star, and as written by Leo Townsend (original story by Earl Derr Biggers) and directed by Frederick de Cordova, its entertainment value was nil. Charles Hoffman produced, and the cast included Alan Hale, Craig Stevens and Barbara Brown.

△
A loose remake of Bette Davis' vehicle *The Letter* (1940) with Ann Sheridan in the Davis role, **The Unfaithful** emerged, if not with distinction, certainly with more credit than was expected of it, considering its illustrious antecedent. It was the story of a married woman (Sheridan) who deeply regrets having been unfaithful to her husband while he was abroad during the war — and who, since his return, finds herself implicated in a murder, the victim being the very man with whom she had the affair. It was rescued from mawkishness and total improbability by Sheridan's strong central performance, as well as by those of Lew Ayres as a lawyer friend, and Zachary Scott (left) as the unsuspecting husband. David Goodis and James Gunn's screenplay (based, without credit given, on the play by Somerset Maugham) skilfully handled the melodramatics of the plot, underlining it with some probing comments on the problems of divorce. Director Vincent Sherman's strong narrative sense kept it simmering, and he drew convincing performances from John Hoyt, Eve Arden (right) and Steven Geray. Jerry Wald produced.

Everyone appeared to be having an affair with someone else (mother of an illegitimate child marries a composer whose heart belongs to another) in Margaret Kennedy's **Escape Me Never** which starred Errol Flynn (left), Ida Lupino (right), Eleanor Parker and Gig Young. A remake of Herbert Wilcox's 1935 British version which featured Elisabeth Bergner in the Lupino role, and more or less a sequel to the same author's *The Constant Nymph* (1943), it was completed in 1946 and released almost two years later. A muddled screenplay by Thames Williamson and leaden direction by Peter Godfrey didn't help, though, as usual, Erich Wolfgang Korngold's score (his last for a Flynn film) was splendid. The producer was Henry Blanke, and the cast included Reginald Denny, Isobel Elsom, Albert Basserman and Ludwig Stossel.

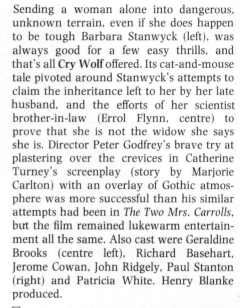

Hollywood's practice of filming biopics of obscure songwriters whose only claim to fame rested on one or two tunes, continued with **My Wild Irish Rose**. Its subject was singer-actor-composer Chauncey Olcott; its object, vague. On the evidence of Peter Milne's screenplay (story by Rita Olcott), Chauncey's life must have been depressingly moribund. And, as played by Dennis Morgan (left), he must have had a brogue as mystifying as any heard this side of Killarney. Wading through the clichés inherent in such distortions, were Andrea King (right) as Lillian Russell, George O'Brien as Iron Duke Muldoon and gorgeous newcomer Arlene Dahl who, in the course of the film, becomes Morgan's wife. Also in it were Ben Blue, Sara Allgood, William Frawley and Don McGuire. Dance specialities were provided by Igor Dega, Pierre Andre, The Three Dunhills, and Louis Willis Jr. They seemed to go on forever. The director was David Butler and the producer William Jacobs. Songs included: Wee Rose Of Killarney, Miss Lindy Lou, There's Room In My Heart For Them All, The Natchez And The Robert E. Lee, Come Down Ma Evenin' Star, One Little Sweet Little Girl, My Wild Irish Rose, A Little Bit Of Heaven and Mother Machree. The film was a hit at the box-office.

Sending a woman alone into dangerous, unknown terrain, even if she does happen to be tough Barbara Stanwyck (left), was always good for a few easy thrills, and that's all **Cry Wolf** offered. Its cat-and-mouse tale pivoted around Stanwyck's attempts to claim the inheritance left to her by her late husband, and the efforts of her scientist brother-in-law (Errol Flynn, centre) to prove that she is not the widow she says she is. Director Peter Godfrey's brave try at plastering over the crevices in Catherine Turney's screenplay (story by Marjorie Carlton) with an overlay of Gothic atmosphere was more successful than his similar attempts had been in *The Two Mrs. Carrolls*, but the film remained lukewarm entertainment all the same. Also cast were Geraldine Brooks (centre left), Richard Basehart, Jerome Cowan, John Ridgely, Paul Stanton (right) and Patricia White. Henry Blanke produced.

The screen version of Howard Lindsay and Russel Crouse's epoch-making stage play, **Life With Father** (3,224 performances on Broadway), respectfully adapted by Donald Ogden Stewart and directed with undisguised affection by Michael Curtiz, was a winner all the way. In Technicolored settings that meticulously evoked New York of the 1880s, its slender story — involving the Day household in general, and father's stubborn unwillingness to be baptised in particular — was full of quiet pleasures, not least of which was the felicitous casting of William Powell (right) as father, and Irene Dunne (left) as mother. Delightful, too, were James Lydon as the eldest son and ZaSu Pitts as Cousin Cora; with young Elizabeth Taylor and old Edmund Gwenn also in attendance. Wrapped up in an engagingly romantic score by Max Steiner, the package enchanted movie-goers and kept producer Robert Buckner busy counting the healthy returns.

Already the proud possessor of one Academy Award, Joan Crawford (right) clearly wished to gain a second for **Possessed**. Accordingly, and very effectively, she emoted in her role as a schizophrenic woman, overtaken by the intensity of her feelings and the frustration of her unrequited love for Van Heflin (left). She got neither the Oscar nor Van Heflin for her efforts in the highly charged Silvia Richards-Ranald MacDougall screenplay (from a story by Rita Weiman), with powerful direction to match by Curtis Bernhardt. Also cast were Raymond Massey (seated), Geraldine Brooks, Stanley Ridges, John Ridgely and Moroni Olsen. The producer was Jerry Wald.

The third teaming of Humphrey Bogart (left) and Lauren Bacall (right) in **Dark Passage** resulted in a fair-to-middling thriller. Bogart (now Hollywood's highest paid star at an annual salary of $467,361) played an escaped convict who, with the aid of plastic surgery changes his appearance and hides out in artist Lauren Bacall's apartment until he is able to track down the real murderer of his wife, thus clearing himself of the crime. The magical Bogart-Bacall chemistry, so effectively exploited in *To Have And Have Not* (1945) was underplayed here, surfacing only during a romantic dinner sequence with the background song 'Too Marvellous For Words' helping to express their sentiments. Neither star overstretched his or her dramatic abilities, and Agnes Moorehead, as the murderess, went way over the top. Based on the David Goodis novel, Delmer Daves' screenplay (he also directed) abounded in bizarre secondary characters, and Tom D'Andrea as a cab driver, Houseley Stevenson as the accommodating plastic surgeon, and Clifton Young as a small-time crook, attacked them *con brio*. The first 40 minutes of the film were photographed (by Sid Hickox) entirely from Bogart's point of view, an interesting device which established the star's presence without actually allowing audiences to see him. Also cast were Bruce Bennett, Douglas Kennedy and Rory Mallinson. The producer was Jerry Wald.

Director Michael Curtiz brought genuine style to **The Unsuspected**, the far-fetched story of a writer and producer of radio crime stories who, after committing what he considers to be the perfect murder, re-enacts it on the air. Claude Rains (centre) played the cool, calm, and ultimately collected killer and was, as usual, splendid. But that, alas, was it. Charlotte Armstrong wrote the story, Bess Meredyth adapted it, and Ranald MacDougall put some unconvincing words into the mouths of Joan Caulfield (left), Audrey Totter, Constance Bennett, Michael North (right), Hurd Hatfield and Fred Clark. The producer was Charles Hoffman.

The trouble with **Always Together** was that it wasn't. A comedy by Henry and Phoebe Ephron and I.A.L. Diamond, it was about a movie addict called Jane who inherits a million dollars from a multi-millionaire on his deathbed, only to have the cash reclaimed when he (Cecil Kellaway) recovers. Jane's addiction to the cinema manifested itself in interpreting certain incidents in her life as movie mythology. This gave numerous Warner Bros. stars a chance to make surprise appearances, among them Humphrey Bogart, Errol Flynn, Dennis Morgan, Janis Paige and Alexis Smith. The billed appearances were less stellar. Joyce Reynolds (right) played Jane and Robert Hutton (centre) the man she marries, with Ernest Truex, Don McGuire and Dewey Robinson (left) in support. Frederick de Cordova directed, Alex Gottlieb produced.

A traditional Western in which an erstwhile gambler joins the side of the law and apprehends a doggerel-spouting robber, known as 'The Poet', whose particular targets are stagecoach strong-boxes, **Cheyenne** starred Dennis Morgan (left) as the hero, Jane Wyman (far left) as the robber's wife (and the woman Morgan falls for), and Janis Paige as a dancehall girl. It was assembled from various horse-opera clichés by Alan Le May and Thames Williamson (story by Paul I. Wellman) and the surprisingly sluggish direction was by Raoul Walsh, with a cast that also featured Bruce Bennett as 'The Poet', Arthur Kennedy (far right), Alan Hale, John Ridgely, Barton MacLane and Tom Tyler. Songs included: I'm So In Love I Don't Know What I'm Doing (by Ted Koehler and M.K. Jerome) and Goin' Back To Old Cheyenne (by Koehler and Max Steiner).

Shirley Temple was **That Hagen Girl**. It was her first grown up role, though there was nothing adult about Charles Hoffman's screenplay based on a story by Edith Roberts. All about an illegitimate girl (Temple, left) whose life has become the butt of malicious, small-town gossip-mongering, it also starred Ronald Reagan (right, who tried his best to get out of doing the film) as a lawyer and war-hero, old enough to be Shirley's father (and suspected of being just that), but who turns out to be the man with whom she is romantically involved. Audiences weren't quite ready for the 'Lolita' aspect of the story; nor were they prepared to accept little Miss Moppet as a nubile young woman. It was directed by Peter Godfrey for producer Alex Gottlieb, and also featured Rory Calhoun, Penny Edwards, Lois Maxwell, Harry Davenport and Dorothy Peterson.

Some cynics saw **Deep Valley** as a cross between *Tobacco Road* (20th Century-Fox, 1941) and the novel *Cold Comfort Farm* with a soupçon of *High Sierra* (1941) thrown in as additional seasoning. It was, in fact, a superior melodrama which starred Ida Lupino (right) as a shy, parent-dominated farm girl who experiences a physical and mental awakening after a touching encounter with a headstrong convict (Dane Clark, centre) whom she shelters after his escape from a road-building work gang. Directed entirely on location in Big Sur and Big Bear by Jean Negulesco (there was a strike at the studio which prevented the use of the backlot) from a strangely affecting screenplay by Salka Viertel and Stephen Morehouse Avery (story by Dan Totheroh), it was certainly one of Miss Lupino's more notable dramatic achievements – though, unfortunately, few people made the journey to see it. The film also featured Wayne Morris, Fay Bainter (left), Henry Hull and Willard Robertson. The producer was Henry Blanke.

1948

Though the company's profits fell by $10,157,726 to $11,837,253 in 1948, two films – **The Treasure Of The Sierra Madre** and **Johnny Belinda** – helped Warner Bros. to regain some of the prestige it had lost in the preceding few years. Both films were nominated for Academy Awards and, although neither actually won the award in the end (the winner was Laurence Olivier's **Hamlet**), Jane Wyman received the Best Actress Oscar for **Johnny Belinda** and Walter Huston the Best Supporting Actor Oscar for **The Treasure Of The Sierra Madre**. John Huston received an Oscar for his direction of **The Treasure Of The Sierra Madre** as well as that for Best Screenplay for the same film. Claire Trevor took the Best Supporting Actress Oscar for **Key Largo**, Lew Ayres was nominated for Best Actor and Charles Bickford for Best Supporting Actor for **Johnny Belinda**. Both **The Treasure Of The Sierra Madre** and **Johnny Belinda** were on the *New York Times* Ten Best list; while **The Treasure Of The Sierra Madre** won the vote of the New York Film Critics as best film of the year and John Huston as best director.

In 1948 Bette Davis earned $364,000, and Henry Blanke $244,666. The highest paid man in America, however, was Louis B. Mayer at $733,024.

Warner Bros. top money-makers for the year were **Key Largo**, **My Wild Irish Rose** and **The Voice Of The Turtle**.

The story of three rogues who set out on an adventure to discover gold in Tampico, Mexico, **The Treasure of the Sierra Madre** was a psychological thriller with deeply moral overtones. A skilful dramatization of B. Traven's novel, John Huston's tough screenplay underlined the book's message about the evils of greed. It also offered Humphrey Bogart as Fred C. Dobbs the opportunity to give the greatest performance of his career in a role that allowed him to change from a fairly likeable drifter into a man capable of killing his best friend in cold blood. One of the first major postwar productions to be filmed entirely on location, it was, due to Huston's obsessive quest for

perfection (as obsessive in its own way as his trio of rogues' quest for gold), also one of the studio's most expensive productions at $3,000,000, and caused Jack Warner sufficient *angst* to demand that Bogart (right) should stay alive in the last reel. Huston, however, was adamant that Bogart should die, and he won his battle. Yet, despite the number of awards the film garnered throughout the year, it was a box-office disappointment. A fine supporting cast included Huston's father Walter, Tim Holt (left), Bruce Bennett, Barton MacLane and the superbly sinister Alfonso Bedoya. The celebrated score was by Max Steiner. The producer was Henry Blanke.

The screen version of **The Voice of the Turtle**. John Van Druten's sophisticated wartime comedy, opened in New York while the play was still running on Broadway, and confounded the sceptics whose prognostications were that the celluloid version would be no match for the real thing. Under Irving Rapper's solid, intelligent direction of Van Druten's screenplay, it matched the stage show line for line, and performance for performance. Ronald Reagan (left) starred as the lonely soldier on furlough who woos and wins Eleanor Parker (right), an actress in the throes of a broken romance. Eve Arden (in a typical Eve Arden role) was cast as the flinty, promiscuous, wise-cracking friend, with secondary roles going to Wayne Morris, Kent Smith, John Emery and Erskine Sanford. Charles Hoffman produced.

Drenched in nostalgia of the sickly, rather maudlin variety, **My Girl Tisa** related the adventures, some of them amorous, of an immigrant lass (Lilli Palmer, right) circa 1905, who despite her romantic dalliances, finds the time to bring her old dad to America ('the Beautiful', as the sound track reminds us). It was written by Allen Boretz from a play by Lucille S. Prumbs and Sara B. Smith, produced by Milton Sperling for United States Pictures and directed by Elliott Nugent. Also cast were Sam Wanamaker (centre) as Miss Palmer's aggressive beau, Akim Tamiroff, Alan Hale (left), Hugo Haas, Gale Robbins and Stella Adler.

Set in London's Soho district, **I Became A Criminal** (released in Britain as **They Made Me A Fugitive**) was the story of an R.A.F. officer (Trevor Howard) who abandons the straight and narrow to become a racketeer. In the end, however, he finds salvation with the help of an understanding Sally Gray (left). The villain of the piece was Griffith Jones (centre) with other parts going to Rene Ray, Mary Merrall, Charles Farrell, Cyril Smith, Maurice Denham and Vida Hope. The film was produced in England by N.A. Bronsten, the screenplay was written by Noel Langley (from a story by Jackson Budd) and the direction was left to Alberto Cavalcanti, who provided a sturdy, reliable, but uninspired film.

Jack Carson, himself a former vaudevillian, brought a certain extrovert panache to **April Showers**, a waterlogged backstage musical whose vaudeville setting had Carson (right), as Joe Tyme (known as Big Tyme) hitting the bottle. As a result, the family act ('The Three Happy Tymes') is forced to split up, each member going his separate way. But they get together again when Broadway beckons and, of course, are a smash. The same, however, could not be said for the film, churned out by director James Kern for producer William Jacobs, from a screenplay by Peter Milne and a story by Joe Laurie Jr. Ann Sothern (left) played Carson's wife, Robert Ellis (centre right) his upstaging son, with other parts going to Robert Alda (centre), S.Z. Sakall, Richard Rober, and Joseph Crehan. Songs included: Little Trouper (by Kim Gannon and Walter Kent), World's Most Beautiful Girl (by Gannon and Ted Fetter), Mr Lovejoy And Mr Jay (by Jack Scholl and Ray Heindorf), It's Tulip Time In Holland (by Dave Radford and Richard Whiting), April Showers (by B.G. DeSylva and Louis Silvers), and Carolina In The Morning (by Gus Kahn and Walter Donaldson).

A crime melodrama, **The Big Punch** made about as much impact as a gentle slap on the wrist. The story of a boxer (Gordon MacRae, left) who is framed for murder after refusing to throw a fight, it also starred Wayne Morris (centre right) as another boxer who deserts the ring for the Ministry, and Lois Maxwell (centre) as the girl both he and MacRae love. An uneasy blend of religion and fisticuffs, it resembled the John Garfield vehicle *Body and Soul* (Enterprise-United Artists, 1947) in content, but not in quality. It was written by Bernard Girard from a story by George C. Brown, directed by Sherry Shourds and also featured Mary Stuart, Anthony Warde, Jimmy Ames, Marc Logan and Eddie Dunn (right). The producer was Saul Elkins.

Audiences welcomed a new-look Bette Davis in **June Bride**, a snappy comedy about a high-powered magazine editor (Davis, left), her involvement with an ace reporter who is her former lover (Robert Montgomery), and her attempts to devote the June issue of her publication to an Indiana June wedding. The trouble is that the bride (Barbara Bates) and groom (Raymond Roe) are in love, but not with each other — a fact which Davis smartly sets out to turn to her advantage. Bretaigne Windust directed with the lightness of touch demanded from Ranald MacDougall's bantering screenplay, and Edith Head, working with Davis for the first time, clothed the star in a series of costumes that epitomised chic. Also cast were Fay Bainter, Betty Lynn, Tom Tully, Jerome Cowan (right) and Mary Wickes. The producer was Henry Blanke.

The role of Georgia Garrett in **Romance on the High Seas** (released in Britain as **It's Magic**) was originally intended for Judy Garland, but negotiations fell through when MGM, Garland's studio, and Warner Bros. failed to agree on terms. Betty Hutton was then offered it, but became pregnant. By chance the film's composer Jule Styne had recently heard a band-singer called Doris Day warbling 'Embraceable You' at one of his house parties, was impressed, and arranged for her to meet Michael Curtiz. Curtiz, the film's director, after screen-testing the newcomer, decided to take a chance on her, thus doing more for Miss Day's career than for the history of the screen musical. For **Romance on the High Seas**, with its Technicolored Caribbean cruise background, was a pretty average musical although graced by a pleasing Jule Styne-Sammy Cahn score, and the breezy personality of Doris Day (centre) who was given fourth billing to Jack Carson, Janis Paige and Don De Fore. Oscar Levant and S.Z. Sakall also had parts tailor-made to their distinctive personalities by writers Julius J. and Philip G. Epstein whose screenplay had additional dialogue by I.A.L. Diamond. The producer was Henry Blanke. Songs included: It's Magic, The Tourist Trade, Put 'Em In A Box, Tie 'Em With A Ribbon And Throw 'Em In The Deep Blue Sea and I'm In Love.

The hero and heroine of an earnest but misconceived drama called **To The Victor** were an American black-marketeer (Dennis Morgan, right) and the wife of an ex-collaborator (Viveca Lindfors, centre). They fall in love and, while attempting to readjust their lives to a peacetime situation, Lindfors gives evidence at her husband's trial — and in so doing condemns both her husband and herself. The contrived screenplay was by Richard Brooks, Delmer Daves was the director, and Jerry Wald produced. The cast included Victor Francen, Bruce Bennett, Dorothy Malone, Tom D'Andrea, Eduardo Cianelli, Konstantin Shayne (left), Douglas Kennedy and Joseph Buloff.

◁ After the exciting Civil War battle at the start of **Silver River**, it was tedium all the way. A 19th century reworking of the biblical David/Bathsheba/Uriah story, it starred Errol Flynn (right) as a ruthless gambler who, after being cashiered from the Union Army, becomes hell-bent on power-seeking. Always promising more than Stephen Longstreet and Harriet Frank Jr's screenplay (based on Longstreet's novel) delivered, it was a massive disappointment and the last film Raoul Walsh directed with Flynn. Also cast were Ann Sheridan, Thomas Mitchell (left), Bruce Bennett, Tom D'Andrea, Barton MacLane and Monte Blue. The producer was Owen Crump.

Wallflower, felicitously adapted from stage to screen, told the breezy story of a couple of determined sisters who are both after the same man. Joyce Reynolds (right) and Janis Paige were the sisters and Robert Hutton (left) the object of their aggressive desire. Phoebe and Henry Ephron's screenplay did well by Reginald Denham and Mary Orr's play, and Frederick De Cordova directed it with spirit. Also cast were Edward Arnold, Barbara Brown, Jerome Cowan, Ann Shoemaker and Don McGuire. Alex Gottlieb produced.

Bette Davis (right) received a decidedly wintry reception for Winter Meeting, one of the least successful films of her career. All about a poetess and her tentative romance with a naval hero who wants to become a Catholic priest but feels he is unworthy of the calling, the talky, turgid screenplay by Catherine Turney (from the novel by Ethel Vance) made its 104 minute running time seem treble that length. Also involved were Janis Paige, John Hoyt, Florence Bates and an inadequate James Davis (left) as Bette's leading man. Bretaigne Windust directed for producer Henry Blanke.

272

After spending more than a decade contributing very little to the prestige of the studio, Jane Wyman (left) sought employment elsewhere. She returned after impressive performances in *The Lost Weekend* (Paramount, 1945) and *The Yearling* (MGM, 1946) to star in her 28th film, Elmer Harris' harrowing Johnny Belinda, in which she portrayed, with heart-breaking conviction, a deaf-mute victim (called 'The Dummy') of a brutal rape. Charles Bickford (right) was her martinet fisherman father, Agnes Moorehead her tough but essentially kind aunt, and Lew Ayres the considerate young doctor who becomes her protector when, after giving birth as a result of the rape, she murders the baby's rapist father (Stephen McNally). Also cast were Jan Sterling, Rosalind Ivan, Alan Napier, Monte Blue and Dan Seymour. Although director Jean Negulesco couldn't always resist the temptation to overplay the melodrama and the sentimentality inherent in the story, he drew from Jane Wyman – who worked with deaf-mutes and perfected lip-reading by putting plastic plugs in her ears to shut out the sound – the performance of her career. Other memorable ingredients in the film were Ted McCord's stark black and white photography, and Max Steiner's brooding score. The producer was Jerry Wald who, with this one, enriched the studio's coffers by over $4,000,000.

◁ Richard Brooks and John Huston, in adapting Key Largo for the screen, changed the Civil War deserter at the centre of Maxwell Anderson's stage play, to a returning GI who has problems in adjusting to postwar life. Huston admired William Wyler's *The Best Years Of Our Lives* (Goldwyn, 1946) and the parable in his own film is as obvious as the similarity it also bears to Robert Sherwood's *The Petrified Forest* (1936). Basically the story of a group of hoods who take over a resort hotel and bully its inhabitants during a storm, its message, that we must fight evil (as personified in the cigar-chomping character of Johnny Rocco) for all we're worth, lest we find ourselves in the clutches of another Hitler, was, by 1948 a cliché which audiences hardly needed to be reminded of. Still, the film was a box-office success, due largely to Humphrey Bogart's (left) couldn't-give-a-damn approach, as effective as in *Casablanca*, Edward G. Robinson's (right) familiar *Little Caesar*-type characterization, Claire Trevor's alcoholic moll and Lauren Bacall's physically striking Nora. Others in the cast were Lionel Barrymore, Monte Blue, Thomas Gomez and Marc Lawrence. Max Steiner's score was a plus factor in a melodrama that needed all the help it could get. The producer was Jerry Wald.

Alfred Hitchcock's Rope was unusual in that it was his first film in colour, and that each of the eight camera set-ups lasted a full ten minutes without cutting away from the action – a technique which not only consolidated the film's theatrical origins, but emphasized the fact that all the events took place, uninterrupted, between seven-thirty and nine-fifteen on one specific evening. Inspired by the notorious Leopold-Loeb murder case, Rope was the ingenious story of two young homosexuals (John Dall, right and Farley Granger, left) who, just for kicks, strangle a college friend in a New York apartment, then hide his body in the very room that the dead man's parents and fiancée will be coming into for cocktails a short while later. Adapted by Hume Cronyn from Patrick Hamilton's play, and with a screenplay by Arthur Laurents, it was more of an interesting cinematic experiment than a fully effective thriller. Yet the master's name, coupled with that of James Stewart (centre) playing a former college professor whose constant probing results in the disclosure of the murder, was enough to ensure the success of Rope. The production cost $1,500,000 of which $300,000 went to Stewart. Also featured were Joan Chandler, Sir Cedric Hardwicke, Constance Collier, Edith Evanson, Douglas Dick, and William Hogan. Hitchcock also produced for Transatlantic Pictures.

Based on a play by Moss Hart, **The Decision of Christopher Blake** emerged, in Ranald MacDougall's screenplay, as a dehydrated drama with little of the play's point or purpose. Allegedly a study of the mental torment suffered by a young lad whose parents are forever at each other's throats, the film version, which depicted Ma and Pa Blake (Alexis Smith, and Robert Douglas, right) as rather average folk occasionally given to bickering, was, in a word, dreary. An actor's school performance, (all the right mannerisms, but never the right manner) from young Ted Donaldson (left) as the fraught son didn't help matters either. It was directed by Peter Godfrey, whose miscalculations in the dream sequence were ruinous, and produced by author MacDougall. The rest of the cast included Cecil Kellaway (first class as a judge), Harry Davenport, Mary Wickes, Art Baker, Lois Maxwell, Douglas Kennedy and Bert Hanlon.

Sydney Greenstreet (centre) without Peter Lorre seemed an unlikely idea, but it worked in **The Woman In White**, a Gothic nightmare (from the novel by Wilkie Collins) in which a villainous Count (Greenstreet at his most outrageous) sets out to kill a pair of twin sisters and appropriate their fortune. Good scenes abounded, with Greenstreet's death at the hands of his tormented wife (Agnes Moorehead, centre left) being one of them. Unfortunately, boring performances from Alexis Smith (centre right), Eleanor Parker (left) and Gig Young proved an insuperable liability which Peter Godfrey's neat but uninspired direction could not circumvent. Others in Henry Blanke's production were John Emery (right), Curt Bois, Emma Dunn, and John Abbott.

Fighter Squadron was the sort of picture that ▷ made one wish there was a Clichés Anonymous to which certain writers – Seton I. Miller and Martin Rackin in this instance – could have gone in an attempt to kick the habit. A World War II drama glorifying the Air Force and the men in it, it presented a series of well-worn situations in place of genuine dramatic action, and although some of the photography was stunning, the film as a whole was grounded by its script. Edmond O'Brien (right) starred as the hero of the piece, with other parts going to Robert Stack, John Rodney (left), Tom D'Andrea, Henry Hull, James Holden, Walter Reed, Shepperd Strudwick and a good-looking newcomer called Rock Hudson. The blood-and-guts direction was by Raoul Walsh, with author Seton I. Miller producing. It was filmed in Technicolor.

Dane Clark starred in **Embraceable You**, a romantic melodrama about a gangster (Clark, right) who fatally injures a girl (Geraldine Brooks, left) in an accident while driving a getaway car after a murder. Clark's guilt manifests itself in his providing victim Brooks with all the comforts he possibly can in the remaining weeks of her life but, in order to pay for them, he is forced into blackmailing the murderer. Edna Anhalt's screenplay achieved a certain degree of tension, which was neatly underlined by Felix Jacoves' direction. A fine performance from Wallace Ford as the detective assigned to track down the murderer, kept the film buoyant, with other roles going to S.Z. Sakall, Richard Rober, Lina Romay, Douglas Kennedy and Mary Stuart. The producer was Saul Elkins.

There was little, if anything, that was smart about **Smart Girls Don't Talk**, a gangster ◁ melodrama which starred Virginia Mayo as a beautiful but impecunious society woman who falsely claims she has lost some valuable jewellery when the night-club she frequents is robbed. Bruce Bennett (left) played the club owner (and the villain of the piece) who falls in love with Miss Mayo (centre), while at the same time arranging for her doctor-brother (Robert Hutton) to be murdered. It was pieced together by director Richard Bare (screenplay by William Sackheim); the producer was Saul Elkins, and the cast included Tom D'Andrea (right), Richard Rober, Helen Westcott and Richard Benedict.

The studio again paired Jack Carson (right) and Dennis Morgan (left) in **Two Guys From Texas**. They played a couple of vaudevillians who find themselves involved (pleasantly) with a couple of girls, and (unpleasantly) with some crooks. A formula musical (in Technicolor) written by I.A.L. Diamond and Allen Boretz from a play by Louis Pelletier Jr and Robert Sloane, its direction was by David Butler, whose cast included Dorothy Malone, Penny Edwards, Fred Clark, Gerald Mohr, Forrest Tucker and John Alvin. The Philharmonic Trio also appeared: so did Monte Blue. The producer was Alex Gottlieb. Songs included: Every Day I Love You A Little Bit More, Hankerin', I Don't Care If It Rains All Night, There's Music In The Land and I Wanna Be A Cowboy In The Movies (by Jule Styne and Sammy Cahn).
▽

1949

The Supreme Court ruling that gave the major studios a choice of remaining in two out of the three main spheres of the business (production, distribution and exhibition) came into force in 1949, with the consequence that Warner Bros. and 20th Century-Fox were forced to relinquish their lucrative cinema chains or fall foul of the Federal authorities. (MGM, because of its complex corporate structure did not follow suit until 1952.)

With the notable exception of **White Heat** (which went unheralded at the time of its release), for which Virginia Kellogg received an Oscar nomination for Best Motion Picture Story, 1949 was qualitatively the poorest year of the decade for Warner Bros. Richard Todd was nominated for an Academy Award for his performance in **The Hasty Heart** (the film, a British product, was released by Warner Bros. in January, 1950) but lost to Broderick Crawford in Columbia's **All the King's Men**, which also won the 1949 Academy Award for Best Film of the Year. Apart from two short subjects, one a cartoon called **For Scenti-Mental Reasons**, the other a Documentary Short Subject (also a cartoon) called **So Much For So Little**, the only Oscars awarded to a film from the studio in 1949 went to Leah Rhodes, Travilla, and Marjorie Best for their costumes for **The Adventures Of Don Juan**.

As the decade departed, so did two of Warner Bros.' major stars. Ann Sheridan, after 34 films, bought out what remained of her contract for $35,000; and during the shooting of **Beyond The Forest**, Bette Davis asked for her release and got it. The net profit for the year was $10,466,534. The studio's top grosses were **Flamingo Road**, **Johnny Belinda** (released in October, 1948) and **Look For The Silver Lining**.

Though both of them tried hard, there was very little that Joan Crawford or her director Michael Curtiz could do with the material offered by **Flamingo Road**, a steamy tale of political corruption in a small Southern town. Once again playing a woman of modest origins (in this instance a carnival dancer) who works her way to the top of the social scale, Crawford (illustrated, left) all but chewed up Leo K. Kuter's sets in an attempt to bring some dramatic verisimilitude to the proceedings – but to no avail. The role was too ill-defined for plausibility, and it was left to Sydney Greenstreet, in a portrayal of genuine malignancy as the town's thoroughly corrupt overseer, to pilfer whatever acting honours were going. The unworkable screenplay was by Robert Wilder (from a story by himself and Sally Wilder), with parts in it for Zachary Scott, David Brian, Gladys George, Virginia Huston, Fred Clark and Alice White. The producer was Jerry Wald.
▽

△
A Technicolored musical remake of *Strawberry Blonde* (1941), itself a remake of *One Sunday Afternoon* (Paramount, 1933), James Hagan's play surfaced for a third (and not so lucky) time, and was once again called **One Sunday Afternoon**. It starred Dennis Morgan (left) as the dentist out-manoeuvred in love by sharp-witted Don De Fore (centre right), with Janis Paige (right) as the strawberry blonde he loses, and Dorothy Malone (centre left) the more domesticated lass he marries on the rebound. Raoul Walsh, who also directed the 1941 James Cagney-Olivia de Havilland-Jack Carson-Rita Hayworth version, seemed to have lost interest in the warblings of his second cast, and his lack of enthusiasm showed. Robert L. Richards wrote the screenplay, leaving sufficient gaps to accommodate Ralph Blane's songs, and the producer was Jerry Wald. Also cast were Ben Blue, Oscar O'Shea, Alan Hale Jr and George Neise. Songs Included: Girls Were Made To Take Care Of Boys, One Sunday Afternoon, The Right To Vote and Johnny And Lucille.

Whiplash was a murky melodrama about a struggling artist (Dane Clark, front right) who has a brief affair with an attractive married woman (Alexis Smith, left). Her husband (Zachary Scott, seated left) is a physically and mentally crippled ex-prize fighter, and her liaison with the artist leads the latter to a brief career in the boxing ring. In the end he abandons both the woman and his boxing gloves and returns to the one true love of his life – painting. The unconvincing screenplay was the work of Maurice Geraghty and Harriet Frank Jr (from a story by Kenneth Earl); it was directed by Lewis Seiler for producer William Jacobs, and also featured Eve Arden, Jeffrey Lynn (centre left), S.Z. Sakall, Douglas Kennedy (right) and Ransom Sherman.
▽

Based on the play by Norman Krasna, **John Loves Mary** introduced Patricia Neal (left) but failed to utilize her special qualities. This inoffensive chestnut was about an American soldier who agrees to a marriage of convenience with a British girl only to find his life awash with complications when his fiancée gets to hear about it. Ronald Reagan (right) was the soldier, Virginia Field the girl he helped, and Patricia Neal the fiancée back home. Phoebe and Henry Ephron provided an entertaining and faithful adaptation, and David Butler directed it all with an appropriate and pleasing lightness of touch, also reflected in the performances of Jack Carson, Wayne Morris, Edward Arnold, Katherine Alexander and Paul Harvey. The producer was Jerry Wald.

The Adventures of Don Juan was originally ▷ scheduled for the spring of 1945, but was delayed by union problems involving the studio's set designers, and finally faced the Technicolor cameras in late 1947. This time the problem was its star, Errol Flynn, whose high living (which director Vincent Sherman, unlike Raoul Walsh, was unable to control) inevitably took its toll on his health, thus prolonging the production schedule and increasing the film's budget by a half a million dollars at a time when the studio was in the process of making drastic economies. Many of **Don Juan's** costumes were borrowed from *The Private Lives of Elizabeth and Essex* (1939) and entire scenes were lifted from *Robin Hood* (1938). Still, the film managed to override its numerous obstacles and, at the age of 39, Flynn (right) again proved his prowess as a swashbuckler. The George Oppenheimer-Harry Kurnitz screenplay was perfectly serviceable (an earlier version scripted by William Faulkner wasn't); so was Sherman's tongue-in-cheek direction. Because Flynn's powers of concentration were on the decline, it was Sherman's task to assemble a performance from bits and pieces. Elwood Bredell, the director of photography, had to make sure that Flynn's face, which betrayed his hedonistic life-style, was photographed in such a way as to disguise the fact that the star was as much Don Juan off the screen as he was on it. The story, as if it mattered, had Flynn saving Queen Margaret (Viveca Lindfors) and the King (Romney Brent) from the treacherous schemes of the wicked Duke de Lorca (Robert Douglas, left). A runaway success in Europe, the film did only moderate business in America, as a result of which the budgets on future Flynn vehicles at Warner Bros. were drastically reduced. The producer was Jerry Wald.

Having won an Oscar for her work in *Johnny Belinda*, Jane Wyman relaxed somewhat in her next assignment, **A Kiss in the Dark**. The real star was David Niven (centre) as a concert pianist who suddenly finds he has inherited a large apartment block. His proprietor/tenant associations with the inhabitants of the block was writer Harry Kurnitz's cue for the provision of amusing incidents, but the cue was missed and the result was a rather leaden comedy, sporadically enlivened by Niven's comic timing and the attractive presence of Miss Wyman (right) who played a photographer's model with whom Niven falls in love. Also in it were Wayne Morris (as Wyman's addle-brained sweetheart), Broderick Crawford (as a bellowing tenant), Victor Moore (left), and Maria Ouspenskaya as Maria Ouspenskaya. Delmer Daves directed it, with Harry Kurnitz doubling as producer.

South of St. Louis was a Technicolor action-crammed adventure with Joel McCrea, Zachary Scott and Douglas Kennedy as three joint ranch owners whose property has been burned down by Victor Jory and his Union guerillas at the start of the Civil War. Justice had to be done, so did a bit of romancing, and the feminine interest was supplied by Dorothy Malone and, as queen of the bar-rooms, Alexis Smith. Zachary Gold and James R. Webb's screenplay gave director Ray Enright every opportunity to kick up the proverbial dust, and as horse-operas went, this one had the lot. It was a United States Pictures Production, produced by Milton Sperling with a cast including Alan Hale, Bob Steele, Art Smith, Monte Blue and Nacho Galindo.

Colorado Territory – a remake of Raoul Walsh's *High Sierra* (1941) – became an effective Western, also directed by Walsh, which starred Joel McCrea (right) as the bandit who, though sprung from jail by his henchmen, was inextricably manacled to his inevitable fate. Dorothy Malone, and Virginia Mayo (left) as a half-breed squaw were the women in it, with other parts going to Henry Hull, John Archer, James Mitchell and Morris Ankrum. Though basically W.R. Burnett's story, screen credit was given to John Twist and Edmund H. North for providing both story and screenplay. The producer was Anthony Veiller. It was remade yet again in 1957 as *I Died A Thousand Times*. ▽

Virginia Mayo played the title role in **Flaxy Martin**, an entertaining gangster melodrama which demonstrated through the avaricious behaviour of its leading lady, the old adage about money being the root of all evil. Zachary Scott (centre) also starred, as an honest attorney whose association with a gangster syndicate results in his pleading guilty to a murder of which he is innocent in order to protect Miss Mayo (right), whom he loves. It was written by David Lang, capably directed by Richard Bare (for producer Saul Elkins) and also featured Dorothy Malone, Tom D'Andrea, Helen Westcott, Douglas Kennedy (left), Elisha Cook Jr, Douglas Fowley and Monte Blue.

Having firmly established herself as the girl-next-door type in *Romance on the High Seas* (1948), Doris Day (right) was cast in **My Dream Is Yours**, a Technicolor reworking of *20 Million Sweethearts* (1934), about a girl-next-door type of singer and her attempts to become a radio star. The burden of the musical numbers rested squarely on Doris' pretty shoulders (as they had done on Dick Powell's in the earlier version), but they lacked solid production values and were, ultimately, unmemorable. Co-starring were Jack Carson (left), Lee Bowman and Adolphe Menjou, with Eve Arden, S.Z. Sakall, Selena Royle, Edgar Kennedy, Sheldon Leonard and the animated talents of Bugs Bunny in support. Michael Curtiz (who also produced) directed a screenplay by Harry Kurnitz and Dane Lussier (from a story by Jerry Wald) that was less than scintillating. Songs included: My Dream Is Yours, Someone Like You, Tic Tic Tic and Love (by Harry Warren and Ralph Blane) and I'll String Along With You (by Al Dubin and Harry Warren).

276

An above average screenplay (by William Sackheim) gave **Homicide** an interest and entertainment value beyond the limits of its routine story. Robert Douglas (left) starred as a detective who poses as an insurance investigator, tracks down the killers of a young hitch-hiker (Warren Douglas), and discovers that they are a part of a sinister racing syndicate. Also cast were Helen Westcott (right), Robert Alda, Monte Blue, Richard Benedict, John Harmon and James Flavin. The director was Felix Jacoves, the producer Saul Elkins.

▽

△

An insipid June Haver (right) was cast as Marilyn Miller in **Look For The Silver Lining**, a musical biopic (in Technicolor) of the famous star. Far more successful was Ray Bolger (centre) as her mentor Jack Donahue, his rendering of Kern's immortal 'Who' being the highlight of a film singularly deficient in highlights. The screenplay, by Phoebe and Henry Ephron and Marian Spitzer from *The Life of Marilyn Miller* by Bert Kalmar and Harry Ruby, merely used the lady's life as an excuse (and not a very good one) on which to peg a familiar vaudeville-to-Broadway back-stage story. Gordon MacRae as Miss Miller's first husband was as anaemic as his co-star, with Charlie Ruggles, Rosemary De Camp (left), S.Z. Sakall and Walter Catlett in roles that were by now second nature to them. David Butler directed for producer William Jacobs, and the unimaginative musical numbers were staged by LeRoy Prinz. Songs included: Who and Sunny (by Otto Harbach, Oscar Hammerstein II and Jerome Kern), Look For The Silver Lining, Whip-Poor-Will and A Kiss In The Dark (by B.G. De Sylva and Kern), Pirouette (by Herman Frinck), Just A Memory (by B.G. De Sylva, Lew Brown and Ray Henderson), Time On My Hands (by Mack Gordon, Harold Adamson and Vincent Youmans), and Wild Rose (by Clifford Grey and Kern).

A Michael Curtiz-directed farce and a homage to Mack Sennett, **The Lady Takes A Sailor** was a scatter-brained affair which starred Jane Wyman (right) as the director of the Buyer's Research Institute. Her devotion to telling the truth, and nothing but, is challenged after her unorthodox meeting with top-secret government worker Dennis Morgan (left) and the wildly complicated, highly unlikely, but decidedly amusing incidents that follow. It was written by Everett Freeman from a story by Jerry Gruskin, but the film was funniest while it kept its mouth shut and, when it did, was a true valediction to the madcap era which inspired it. Also cast were Eve Arden, Robert Douglas, Allyn Joslyn, Tom Tully, Lina Romay, William Frawley, Fred Clark and Craig Stevens. Harry Kurnitz produced.
▽

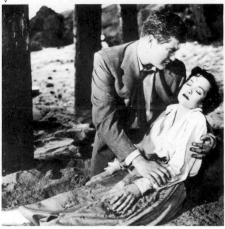

Returning to the studio after a seven-year ▷ absence, during which time his films had been released by United Artists and produced by his brother William, James Cagney was given **White Heat** which turned out to be one of the great crime films, and the apotheosis of his dazzling career. He played Cody Jarrett, who, in the studio's words was a 'homicidal paranoiac with a mother fixation', and under Raoul Walsh's *macho* direction, played it brilliantly, always resisting the temptation to descend into glossy histrionics. A scene in prison in which he hears of the death of his mother (Margaret Wycherley) and goes berserk, was shattering in its intensity and totally convincing. Basically the story of a ruthless killer who gets himself jailed on a minor charge to avoid a murder rap, it contained all the necessary ingredients of the genre, and quite a few more. Technically more proficient than the studio's raw but effective efforts of the early thirties, and with a screenplay (by Ivan Goff and Ben Roberts, based on a story by Virginia Kellogg) that catered as much for thrills as for character development, it was a solid winner. Its inferno-like climax in which Cagney bids the world adieu from the top of a blazing oil-tank with the words 'Made it, Ma! Top of the world!' gave the screen of the forties one of its most powerful images. Virginia Mayo (left) played Cagney's (right) sluttish wife, Steve Cochran was his two-timing henchman and Edmond O'Brien the undercover Treasury agent who deliberately sets out to win Cagney's confidence in prison, in order to betray him later. Others cast were John Archer, Wally Cassell, Mickey Knox and Fred Clark. The producer was Louis F. Edelman.

The notorious Younger brothers were at it again in **The Younger Brothers**, a Technicolor Western which posed the question: can the recently paroled brothers (Wayne Morris, left, Bruce Bennett, Robert Hutton, right, and James Brown), stay out of trouble for just two more weeks, and by so doing fulfil the terms of their parole? If they could, there'd be no film, so instead they are trapped by former enemies into a liaison with the fearless Shepherd gang who are planning a bank robbery with which the brothers become involved. Written by Edna Anhalt from a story by Morton Grant, it gave employment to Janis Paige and Geraldine Brooks (as the bad girl and the good), Alan Hale, Fred Clark, Monte Blue and Tom Tyler (centre). Edwin L. Marin directed, Saul Elkins produced.

By the time **Night Unto Night**, created as a showcase for the brooding talents of its star Viveca Lindfors (left) was released, Miss L. was no longer under contract to the studio, and this film was probably the reason why. She played a woman who spent most of her time mourning the death of her young husband, her grief being momentarily interrupted by co-star Ronald Reagan (centre left) as an epileptic scientist with troubles of his own. They meet somewhere along the Florida coast and spend a lot of time talking about love and life and generally trying to help each other with their respective problems. Ingmar Bergman might have managed to make something of it all, but as written by Kathryn Scola (from the novel by Philip Wylie) and directed by Don Siegel, all that emerged was a cataract of uninspiring chatter. Also cast were Broderick Crawford (centre right), Osa Massen, Rosemary De Camp (right), Craig Stevens and Erskine Sanford. The producer was Owen Crump.

A fictionalized account of the career of owner C.S. Howard's legendary thoroughbred, **The Story of Seabiscuit** was fine while it was concentrating on the horse in question, but less successful when it moved off into areas of romance – the niece of trainer Barry Fitzgerald (centre) played by Shirley Temple (left), complete with ill-fitting Irish brogue, falls for jockey Lon MacAllister (right). Filmed in Technicolor, with black-and-white newsreel footage showing Seabiscuit in action, it was an amiable little film with no pretensions. John Taintor Foote wrote it, David Butler was the director, William Jacobs the producer, and the cast included Rosemary De Camp and Pierre Watkin (as the Howards), William Forrest, 'Sugarfoot' Anderson and William J. Cartledge.

◁ Jack Carson (centre left) played a hammy, egotistical actor in **It's A Great Feeling**, an amiable, but only intermittently funny satire on Hollywood, written by Jack Rose and Melville Shavelson from an original story by I.A.L. Diamond. The Technicolor musical was chiefly interesting for its behind-the-scenes glimpses of the Warner Bros. lot, and of the several stars who played themselves, including Gary Cooper, Joan Crawford (centre right), Errol Flynn, Sydney Greenstreet, Danny Kaye, Patricia Neal, Eleanor Parker, Ronald Reagan, Edward G. Robinson and Jane Wyman. There were appearances too, by Michael Curtiz, King Vidor, Raoul Walsh and by David Butler who directed it all. Apart from the guest stars, the film also featured Dennis Morgan (right) and Doris Day (left). Alex Gottlieb produced. Songs included: It's A Great Feeling, There's Nothing Rougher Than Love, That Was A Big Fat Lie, Give Me A Song With A Beautiful Melody and Blame My Absent-Hearted Mind (by Jule Styne and Sammy Cahn).

In a bid to turn Patricia Neal into a major star, the studio cast her as architecture critic Dominique Franchon in their screen version of Ayn Rand's quasi-philosophical novel **The Fountainhead**. Had she been a movie critic, Miss Neal might have said a few unkind things about the taciturn way in which her co-star Gary Cooper (illustrated) somnambulated his way through the role of Howard Roark (modelled on Frank Lloyd Wright), a rebel who bucks big business concerns by refusing to lend his name to the creation of buildings that are merely functional. But she would also have had praise for director King Vidor's interesting attempts to impose (through Robert Burks' photography and Edward Carrere's designs) a look to the film very much in harmony with the simple, austere lines reflected in Roark's architecture. (Vidor wanted Lloyd Wright himself to design the film, but Jack Warner vetoed the idea). An unspoken subtext drenched the enterprise in Freudian symbols, the most striking of which were the phallic Winand Building at the end of the movie, and a scene in a quarry where Roark, in Miss Neal's presence, shatters the cliff face with a phallic drill. Not an artistic success, and a failure at the box office, **The Fountainhead** was nonetheless an ambitious attempt to say something about integrity and individuality, but in the end it was sabotaged by its pretentions. Ayn Rand wrote the screenplay, Henry Blanke produced, Max Steiner contributed the music, and Raymond Massey, Kent Smith, Robert Douglas and Henry Hull appeared in secondary roles.

▽

Delmer Daves wrote and directed **Task Force**, ▷ one of the few World War II films made by the studio that took to the sea. Unfortunately it never stayed afloat because of Daves' wordy screenplay. The story of a naval commander (Gary Cooper, right) and his effort to persuade the powers that be to invest in aircraft carriers, it was a windy bore, short on action (the little there was came courtesy of newsreel footage), and shorter on drama. There was plenty of sentimentality though, which torpedoed Jerry Wald's production and all who sailed in her. Those going under included Jane Wyatt (centre) as Cooper's faithful wife, Wayne Morris, Walter Brennan, Stanley Ridges (left), Julie London, Bruce Bennett, Moroni Olsen and John Ridgely.

△
Always Leave Them Laughing was tailored to fit the comic talents of Milton Berle (right). The Jack Rose-Mel Shavelson scripted comedy (from a story by Max Shulman and Richard Mealand) about the trials and tribulations of a comedian – from master of ceremonies at a summer resort to top laughter-maker on TV – succeeded admirably, despite its quota of clichés to which stories such as this were inescapably prone. Adding to the merry-making was the indefatigable Bert Lahr, with his famous and hilarious sketch about fountain pens that write underwater (first seen on stage in *Make Mine Manhattan*). Romantic interest was supplied by Ruth Roman, with Virginia Mayo as Lahr's partner, both on stage and off. Alan Hale, Grace Hayes, Jerome Cowan, Lloyd Gough and Max Showalter (left) were also in it: Roy Del Ruth did his best to take the title's advice; Jerry Wald produced.

Although there were elements of both *Rebecca* (United Artists, 1940) and *Notorious* (RKO, 1946) in Alfred Hitchcock's Transatlantic production, **Under Capricorn**, the film, weighing in at $2,500,000, was a catastrophe at the box-office. Adapted from Helen Simpson's novel by Hume Cronyn, and scripted by James Bridie, it featured Ingrid Bergman (right) as a dipsomaniac wife, Joseph Cotten as her husband, Margaret Leighton as a scheming housekeeper whose love for Cotten brings out the worst in her, and Michael Wilding (left) as a British immigrant (and cousin to Bergman) who exposes the housekeeper for the evil woman she is. Set in Sydney, Australia in 1830, it was misconceived from the outset, and suffered from a talkative, badly resolved screenplay, as well as from the miscasting of both Bergman and Cotten. Others involved were Jack Watling, Cecil Parker and Dennis O'Dea. It was the last costume drama Hitchcock (who also produced the film) was to make.

▽

In **The House Across The Street**, Wayne Morris (right) again portrayed that old standby, the newspaper reporter who gets a crack at solving a murder. (Remember *Gambling on the High Seas*, 1940?) He does so with the help of Janis Paige (centre), and although they made a fairly attractive team of sleuths, the screenplay, which was yet another remake of Roy Chanslor's *Hi Nellie!* was, as tapped out by Russell Hughes, a pretty guileless rehash that by now had gone decidedly stale. Richard Bare directed it, the producer was Saul Elkins, and the cast included Alan Hale, James Mitchell, Barbara Bates, James Holden (left), Bruce Bennett and Ray Montgomery.

The Girl From Jones Beach had many good points, two of which were owned by Virginia Mayo as a bathing suit model. Ronald Reagan was another of the film's plus factors, revealing himself to be a more than capable purveyor of such lightweight nonsense as that dished out by scenarist I.A.L. Diamond from a story by Allen Boretz. Reagan played a commercial artist in search of the perfect girl, and, after finding her in Miss Mayo (right), pretends to be an immigrant Czech lately arrived in the US and enrols in the night school where she teaches American history. An unlikely story, but likeably told, despite the excessive mugging of Eddie Bracken as a highly strung promotions man. Also cast were Donna Drake, Henry Travers (back left), Florence Bates, Lois Wilson, Jerome Cowan and Helen Westcott. Peter Godfrey directed and the producer was Alex Gottlieb.

There was nothing that Bette Davis (left) did not do in **Beyond The Forest** to bring unhappiness to the long-suffering Wisconsin country doctor (Joseph Cotten, right) to whom she happened to be married. In the course of 97 frenziedly dramatic minutes, Davis (billed as 'a twelve o'clock girl in a nine o'clock town') runs off to Chicago, commits adultery with a wealthy industrialist (David Brian), induces a miscarriage by jumping off a highway embankment, and even commits murder. Making no attempt whatsoever to underplay the sordid highjinks inherent in Lenore Coffee's ludicrous screenplay (story by Stuart Engstrandt), Davis' equally ludicrous caricature of herself (wearing an evil black wig) bulldozed its way through it all – and out of her 18-year association with the studio. Though she still had ten years to serve on her contract, she threatened to abandon the film mid-way if she was not released from her obligations on its completion. Jack Warner was happy to let her go. Her unfortunate last film for the studio under her present contract (she would not return until 1962 with *Whatever Happened To Baby Jane?*) was directed by King Vidor and co-starred Ruth Roman, Minor Watson, Donna Drake, and Regis Toomey. It was produced by Henry Blanke.

One Last Fling, a comedy about a bored housewife (Alexis Smith, left), who returns to the job she once had in her husband's musical store, only to have her composure ruffled with the appearance of a former WAC girlfriend of her husband, just wasn't worth the having. Zachary Scott (right) was the husband; Ann Doran the catalyst. Also cast were Ransom Sherman, Veda Ann Borg, Jim Backus Helen Westcott, Barbara Bates and Jody Gilbert. It was written by Richard Flournoy and William Sackheim from a story by Herbert Clyde Lewis; the director was Peter Godfrey and the producer Saul Elkins.

There was more laughter with **The Inspector General**, the studio's last film of the decade. A showcase for the inimitable talents of its star Danny Kaye, its script, by Phillip Rapp and Harry Kurnitz (very loosely based on Gogol's play) had Kaye as an illiterate buffoon being mistaken for an important Inspector General, with all the high-octane comic confusion the situation implied. At his very best in the musical numbers (by his wife, Sylvia Fine, and Johnny Mercer) Kaye (right) demonstrated his unique way with a complicated lyric – and brought to the songs a range of facial expressions, grimaces, and contortions that kept audiences equally contorted with laughter. Henry Koster, knowing a good thing when he saw it, kept his cameras glued to his star and didn't miss a trick. Doing the best they could in the face of overwhelming odds and unavoidable upstaging were Gene Lockhart as the town's crooked mayor, Elsa Lanchester (left) as his flirtatious wife, Walter Slezak, Alan Hale, Walter Catlett, Rhys Williams and Benny Baker. The producer was Jerry Wald. Songs included: Onward Onward, The Medicine Show, The Inspector General, Lonely Hearts, Gypsy Drinking Song, Soliloquy For Three Heads, Happy Times and Brodny.

THE FIFTIES

The fifties was Hollywood's decade of change. With television's continuing stronghold on the public, the film industry had to rethink itself into competing against the monster box and, in so doing, underwent a radical personality change. Instead of questioning a script's intrinsic worth and entertainment value, producers now had to ask themselves a new question; was it sufficiently different from what was being offered daily (and free) in the home? Clearly, the only way to lure audiences back into the cinema was to provide them with something that was unavailable on television. The alternatives soon became apparent: new projection ratios that could in no way be matched by the small screen, epics whose production costs were beyond the reach of TV, or a new sophistication in subject matter that would be deemed unsuitable for family viewing in the home and thus unacceptable to TV's commercial sponsors.

Most of the new projection techniques devised in the fifties were little more than gimmicks; **This Is Cinerama** (first shown on 30th September 1952) and 3-D (launched with United Artists' **Bwana Devil** on 27th November 1952) came and went as gimmicks do. 20th Century-Fox's CinemaScope made its first appearance in September 1953 (with **The Robe**), followed by Paramount's VistaVision and, in 1956 Michael Todd's 70mm Todd-AO process for **Around The World In Eighty Days.** 70mm projection equipment was not in fact new to the industry. As far back as 1930, it was used by MGM in selected cinemas to enhance the impact of **Billy The Kid.**

Of these, only CinemaScope survived for any length of time, its attendant distortions being ironed out in the early sixties with the appearance of the spherical Panavision lens.

The trouble with king-sized screens was that appropriate subject matter had to be found to fill them, hence such spectacles in the fifties as **The Ten Commandments** (Paramount), **Knights Of The Round Table** (MGM), **King Richard And The Crusaders** (Warner Bros.), **The Silver Chalice** (Warner Bros.), **War And Peace** (Paramount), **Land Of The Pharaohs** (Warner Bros.), and **Helen Of Troy** (Warner Bros.).

As an alternative to these lavish costume dramas, which were expensive to make and did not always recoup their costs, the fifties saw a succession of small-scale, black-and-white dramas with a refreshingly new adult approach that brought back to the cinema a realism and a vitality it had not experienced since the thirties. Largely responsible for the trend were two extraordinarily talented men: Lee Strasberg, who founded the Actor's Studio in New York, with its emphasis on 'naturalism' in acting (Marlon Brando and Montgomery Clift were two of its most celebrated exponents), and Elia Kazan, a director of genius who introduced this new style to Hollywood in such films as **Panic On The Streets** (20th Century-Fox), **A Streetcar Named Desire** (Warner Bros.), **On The Waterfront** (Columbia) and **Viva Zapata** (20th Century-Fox). Other naturalistic films dealing with major themes were 20th Century-Fox's **No Way Out** (bigotry), Paramount's **Come Back Little Sheba** (loneliness and alcoholism), Columbia's **Middle Of The Night** (romance between a young girl and an old man), Warner Bros.' **Baby Doll** (child sexuality), Columbia's **The Strange One** (implied homosexuality), Paramount's **Fear Strikes Out** (madness) and Columbia's moving screen adaptation of Arthur Miller's Pulitzer prize-winning play **Death Of A Salesman.**

Youth and its problems also featured prominently in the fifties in such films as **The Blackboard Jungle** (MGM), **High School Confidential** (MGM), **Rebel Without A Cause** (Warner Bros.), **Somebody Up There Likes Me** (MGM), **East Of Eden** (Warner Bros.) and **The Wild One** (Columbia).

The new permissiveness that would reach its peak in the cinema of the seventies began in the fifties with Otto Preminger's decision to release his 1954 comedy **The Moon Is Blue** (which dared to mention the word 'virgin') without the Production Code's Seal of Approval, and with the same office relaxing their provisions for Preminger's **The Man With The Golden Arm** (1955) which dealt with the hitherto taboo subject of drug addiction. (In 1957 20th Century-Fox, traversing similar territory, made **A Hatful Of Rain**).

Apart from the growth of television (by 1950 weekly cinema admissions were down to 60,000,000), the other major factors that contributed to the changing face of Hollywood in the fifties were the heavy US tax laws, the loss of cinema circuits, the restrictive conditions of the unions (who fought for and won a 44 hour, 5 day week), and the escalating cost of film production in Hollywood. All this resulted in a full-scale talent drain with many Hollywood-based film-makers taking advantage of a law passed by Congress (in December 1951) which stated that American citizens who had spent seventeen out of eighteen months abroad would be exempt from paying tax during that time. Added to this was the fact that most of the studios had 'frozen funds' in Europe (profits not allowed to leave the country) which could conveniently be used to finance films away from home. And as film production was cheaper in Europe, where there were no restrictive union practices, it was sensible for producers to take advantage of the facilities at their disposal there. Samuel Bronston even built a studio in Madrid offering Hollywood film-makers every modern amenity in return for a share of the profits. The production of American films in Europe eventually reached its peak in the sixties, with 30 per cent of all Hollywood productions being filmed outside the USA.

In March 1951, the House UnAmerican Activities Committee began their second series of hearings, and between 1951 and 1954, 212 people involved in the film industry – both in front of and behind the cameras – were blacklisted, and many careers were irrevocably ruined in the process.

The fifties was also the decade in which the monopolistic Technicolor became a victim of the 'consent decree' and had to make way for two major competitors – Eastmancolor and Ansco Color. The same decade saw both Republic and RKO Studios cease production, the TV rights of the latter's 740 feature films being sold by Howard Hughes for $15.2 million. (The first studio to sell to TV was Republic, who, in 1952 incurred the anger of theatre-owners across the country to such an extent that many refused to book Republic Pictures thereafter). The sale of the RKO catalogue resulted in other major studios (including Warner Bros.) selling off their product to TV for fairly insubstantial amounts of money compared with what they might have earned had they decided to hold onto them.

In 1957, United Artists bought out Mary Pickford's share in the company (she was one of its original founders), went public, and expanded their interests to take in TV and records; and the following year, which was not a very good one in Hollywood's chequered history (the cinema's weekly admissions dropped to a devastatingly low 39.5 million), Universal Studios, in financial difficulties, was saved from bankruptcy by The Music Corporation of America (MCA) who bought it from Decca (in 1962 MCA bought Decca as well).

Because of the decline of the studio system of the thirties and forties, several powerful independent producers emerged and rented space at major studios, in return for which the studio in question was given the distribution rights to the finished product. From Warner Bros., for example, Alfred Hitchcock operated his own production unit, Burt Lancaster his Norma Productions, and Charles K. Feldman his Charles K. Feldman Group Productions. Other independents on the lot included Jack Webb's Mark VII, Sid Luft and Judy Garland's Transcona, Doris Day's Arwin and John Wayne's Batjac. It was the beginning of a trend which, today, has become the rule rather than the exception.

Between 1950 and 1960, Warner Bros. made and/or released 246 feature films compared with 274 in the previous ten years, and 572 in the thirties. Qualitatively, it was the studio's least distinguished decade, despite several good films such as **A Streetcar Named Desire, A Star Is Born, Mr Roberts, Auntie Mame** and **The Nun's Story**, and the huge impact made by James Dean and the three films (**East of Eden, Rebel Without A Cause** and **Giant**) in which he appeared.

1950

Artistically, the decade opened unimpressively for the studio, and of the twenty-eight feature films Warner Bros. released during the year, only two titles were included in the annual Academy Awards presentation: **The Flame And The Arrow**, and **West Point Story**. (The winner of the Oscar for Best Picture was 20th Century-Fox's **All About Eve**.) Ernest Haller was nominated for Best Colour Photography for the first of these, but lost to Robert Surtees for MGM's **King Solomon's Mines**. In the second, Ray Heindorf was nominated for Best Scoring of a Musical Picture, but the winners were Adolph Deutsch and Roger Edens for MGM's **Annie Get Your Gun**. Eleanor Parker was nominated in the Best Actress Category for her work in **Caged**, but lost to Judy Holliday in **Born Yesterday** (Columbia). The only Oscar won by the studio was for a one-reel short subject called **Grandad Of Races**. Still, it was a good year financially, and several big money-makers, especially **Colt.45**, **The Flame And The Arrow**, **Task Force** and **Tea for Two** gave the company a net profit of $10,271,657.

Seemingly confined to portraying ambitious women bettering their lot in life, Joan Crawford (right), starred in **The Damned Don't Cry**, a turgid drama which had her forsaking her existence as a labourer's wife to become a gangster's moll. Unable to redeem the implausible Harold Medford-Jerome Weidman screenplay (from a story by Gertrude Walker), her performance, under Vincent Sherman's direction, was little more than a bag of tricks. Faring no better were David Brian (centre), Steve Cochran, Kent Smith (left), Hugh Sanders (centre left) and Selena Royle. The producer was Jerry Wald.

In its manner of telling how a young man (Gordon MacRae) sets out to prove that his best friend Edmond O'Brien (left) is not guilty of murdering a notorious gambler, **Backfire** certainly *did* backfire. Coincidence was the trademark of the Larry Marcus-Ivan Goff-Ben Roberts screenplay (story by Larry Marcus), robbing the piece of any credibility and suspense. Virginia Mayo, Dane Clark, Viveca Lindfors (right), Ed Begley, Francis Robinson, Monte Blue and John Ridgely were also in the film which was directed by Vincent Sherman and produced by Anthony Veiller.

Too old for his role as an ex-World War ▷ II pilot who agrees to test-fly a new jet which its manufacturer is hoping to sell to the Air Force, Humphrey Bogart (right) made far less of an impression in **Chain Lightning** than did Ernest Haller's splendid photography. Technically proficient, the film was dramatically dull. The general lethargy of Liam O'Brien and Vincent Evans' predictable screenplay (from a story by J. Redmond Prior) conveyed itself to co-stars Eleanor Parker (left), Raymond Massey, Richard Whorf and James Brown who, under Stuart Heisler's top-heavy direction kept the film grounded. The producer was Anthony Veiller, and his supporting cast included Roy Roberts, Morris Ankrum, Fay Baker and Fred Sherman. Song: The Long And The Short And The Tall.

Made in England as a co-production with Associated British Pictures, and utilizing some of the studio's 'frozen funds', John Patrick's stage play **The Hasty Heart**, (screenplay by Ranald MacDougall) was a notable success. It established an unknown English actor called Richard Todd (left) who, under Vincent Sherman's sensitive direction (Sherman also produced), became a star shortly after the film was released. He played an arrogant Scotsman in a Burma Army hospital unaware that he only has a short while to live. The men with whom he shares the ward, and the hospital's nurse (Patricia Neal, right), are aware of the young soldier's terminal illness, and the film's poignant strength derived from their relationship with him. Ronald Reagan played a plain-speaking wounded American, Howard Marion Crawford a Cockney and John Sherman an Australian, with other roles going to Anthony Nicholls, Ralph Michael and Alfie Bass.

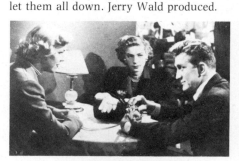

△

Perfect Strangers (released in Britain as **Too Dangerous To Love**) was a less than perfect comedy which starred Ginger Rogers (centre) and Dennis Morgan (left) as a single lady and a married man who fall in love with each other while doing a stint of jury duty together — the case in question being a love-nest murder. Director Bretaigne Windust got more out of his supporting cast than he did from his stars with Thelma Ritter in excellent laugh-a-line form playing a stupid housewife. Harry Bellaver (right) as a bailiff, Margalo Gillmore as a society lady and Alan Reed as a barber, enlivened the action whenever they appeared but the screenplay by Edith Sommer from a Hungarian play by Ladislaus Bus-Fekete (English version by Ben Hecht and Charles MacArthur) adapted by George Oppenheimer let them all down. Jerry Wald produced.

Violence and brutality were the main items on the agenda of **Barricade**, a fist-flying drama which starred Raymond Massey as a sadistic mine owner whose hard-pressed labourers work slavishly for him at the point of a gun. As an exercise in just how much physical punishment the human body can take, it was certainly effective. As entertainment, however, it was decidedly suspect. Dane Clark (standing) also starred, playing a fugitive from justice who sees to it that Massey dies as he lived i.e. he beats him to death. The film's mere smidgin of romance was supplied by Ruth Roman (left), with other parts going to Morgan Farley as a drunken judge, Robert Douglas (right) as a hostage given to spying and George Stern as a slave. Also cast were Walter Coy, Frank Marlowe and Tony Martinez. William Sackheim's screenplay didn't pack quite the same punch as some of its characters: neither did Peter Godfrey's direction. The film's overall resemblance to *The Sea Wolf* (1941) was unmistakeable. It was produced (in Technicolor) by Saul Elkins.

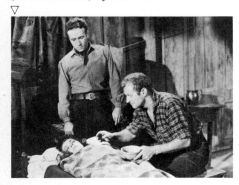

◁ Loosely based on the life of the great Bix Beiderbecke, **Young Man with a Horn** (released in Britain as **Young Man of Music**) was a musical drama starring Kirk Douglas (right) which charted the rise, fall and resurrection of a jazz musician. Lauren Bacall (centre) played a selfish society bitch and Doris Day (left) a sweet kid carrying a torch for Douglas. Other roles went to Juano Hernandez, Jerome Cowan and Mary Beth Hughes. Hoagy Carmichael provided the narration, and Harry James dubbed the Beiderbecke trumpet for Kirk Douglas. Carl Foreman and Edmund H. North fashioned the screenplay from Dorothy Baker's novel which the studio had purchased in 1945 as a vehicle for John Garfield. Michael Curtiz directed efficiently, and the producer was Jerry Wald. Songs included: The Very Thought Of You (by Ray Noble), I May Be Wrong (by Henry Sullivan and Harry Ruskin), The Man I Love (by George and Ira Gershwin), Too Marvellous For Words (by Johnny Mercer and Richard A. Whiting), Get Happy (by Harold Arlen and Ted Koehler), I Only Have Eyes For You (by Al Dubin and Harry Warren), Lullaby Of Broadway (by Al Dubin and Harry Warren) and With A Song In My Heart (by Richard Rodgers and Lorenz Hart).

What attracted Alfred Hitchcock to Selwyn Jepson's novel *Man Running* which was filmed as **Stage Fright**, was its theatrical ambience. The enjoyment that Hitchcock derived out of several key scenes, especially a theatrical garden party, as well as his light-hearted handling of such stalwart British character actors as Alastair Sim, Miles Malleson and Joyce Grenfell, was delightfully evident. But one major ingredient was missing: suspense. Whitfield Cook's screenplay (adapted by Alma Reville with additional dialogue by James Bridie) about a student actress's attempt to shield her boyfriend from a murder charge by taking a job as a maid to the musical comedy star who is allegedly the culprit, was both rambling and diffuse. Jane Wyman (right) played the student, Richard Todd her boyfriend, and Marlene Dietrich (left) the star who supposedly murdered her husband. It was, for the most part, told in flashback (a flashback which turns out to be a lie) and also featured Michael Wilding as a police inspector, Dame Sybil Thorndike as Miss Wyman's mother, and Hitchcock's daughter Patricia as a student at the Royal Academy of Dramatic Art. Of the principals, Richard Todd was the most convincing, with Dietrich, at her sexiest, running him a close second. Only Jane Wyman failed to jell. According to Hitchcock, she could not reconcile herself to the fact that – as a contrast to Dietrich – she was meant to look as plain as possible, and as filming progressed, would leave the set between takes to readjust her unglamorous make-up. Not one of the master's more distinguished efforts, it nevertheless had a certain English charm about it and, as was usual with Hitchcock, the set-pieces worked splendidly. The film was made in England at Associated British Pathe Studios.

Errol Flynn (right) portrayed an Australian (his true nationality), in **Montana**, one of his least memorable films. The story of a sheep herder who invades the cattle territory of Montana, it was photographed in Technicolor in the studio's Calabasas Ranch and ran a mere 76 minutes (a blessing in the circumstances). It co-starred Alexis Smith (left) with S.Z. Sakall, Douglas Kennedy, James Brown, Ian MacDonald, Charles Irwin and Monte Blue in support. Of what? Surely not the James R. Webb-Borden Chase-Charles O'Neal less than routine screenplay from an Ernest Haycox story. Ray Enright directed and the producer was William Jacobs.

Burt Lancaster's acrobatic training was very much in evidence in **The Flame and The Arrow**, an action-packed, Technicolored adventure. The film hardly paused for breath as it told the rather trite story of a Robin Hood-like peasant from the North of Italy who sets out, with a vengeance, to fell a land-grabbing tyrant. As was so often the case with such derring-do subjects, the story was secondary to the exploits of its hero whose physical prowess was positively awesome. Whether swinging from chandeliers, scampering across rooftops, leaping to and from balconies or demonstrating his ability with a bow and arrow, Lancaster (standing right), rose spectacularly to the occasion. Waldo Salt's screenplay, from his own story, was first-rate of its kind; so was Jacques Tourneur's zestful direction. The producers were Frank Ross and Harold Hecht (for Burt Lancaster's Norma F.R. Productions) and the cast they assembled included Virginia Mayo, Robert Douglas, Aline MacMahon (centre), Lynne Baggett, Robin Hughes (left), Norman Lloyd (foreground centre) and Lancaster's erstwhile partner from his circus days, Nick Cravat (right). It was all great fun.

The Messrs Scott – Randolph and Zachary – starred in **Colt .45**, a traditional Western (in Technicolor) with the forces of good and evil locked in deadly combat. Good, as represented by Randolph (right) finally triumphs against Bad, as represented by Zachary (left), but not before Thomas Blackburn's screenplay worked its way through the entire lexicon of sagebrush clichés. A demonstration of what can happen when a pair of Colt .45's fall into the wrong hands, it was directed, by Edwin L. Marin for the corn it was, and appropriately performed by a cast that also included Ruth Roman (as the obligatory romantic interest, and presumably Randolph's reward for siding with the angels), Lloyd Bridges, Ian MacDonald, Chief Thundercloud and Lute Crockett. Saul Elkins produced.

June Haver fell in love with Gordon MacRae in **The Daughter of Rosie O'Grady**, a Technicolor musical which drew its inspiration from the good old days of vaudeville, and its technique from sometime during the Dark Ages. Miss Haver (centre) played an Irish lass while Mr MacRae (right) was none other than the great Tony Pastor himself. James Barton was cast as Haver's father, and spent most of his time drunk and/or disapproving of his daughter's romance. It was written by Jack Rose, Melville Shavelson and Peter Milne (from a story by Rose and Shavelson) and flaccidly directed by David Butler for producer William Jacobs. Completing the cast were S.Z. Sakall, Gene Nelson, Jane Darwell and a very young Debbie Reynolds (left). Songs included: The Daughter Of Rosie O'Grady (by M.C. Brice and Walter Donaldson) and As We Are Today (by Charles Tobias and Ernesto Lecuona).

Though scenarist Virginia Kellogg spent a couple of months doing research in women's penitentiaries, **Caged** (which she wrote with Bernard C. Schoenfeld) added nothing new to the subject of women behind bars. What little impact it had was due entirely to John Cromwell's abrasive direction. Eleanor Parker (illustrated) played a 19-year-old girl jailed for a crime committed by her husband. Through her dehumanizing experiences (in the course of which she has a baby), the authors make a few harrowing points about the corrupting influence prison can have on people who are basically not criminals. Agnes Moorehead played a warden whose attempts to bestow a modicum of dignity on the inmates are thwarted by the interference of the governors, with other roles going to the Amazonian Hope Emerson, Ellen Corby, Betty Garden, Jan Sterling, Lee Patrick and Jane Darwell. The producer was Jerry Wald.

Having appeared together in *The Fountainhead* (1949), Gary Cooper and Patricia Neal were paired again in a romantic drama called **Bright Leaf**. Dispossessed of his land by cigar baron Donald Crisp, Cooper – hell-bent on revenge – borrows some money from an old flame (Lauren Bacall) to invest in a new cigarette-making machine, and before you can say tobacco he becomes wealthier and more powerful than his adversary, whose daughter (Patricia Neal) he makes the mistake of marrying. The shock of their marriage drives old Crisp to suicide after which Miss Neal (centre), who, ironically, only married Cooper (right) to save her father, sets about ruining him. Cooper did well enough by Ranald MacDougall's drawn-out screenplay (from the novel by Foster Fitz-Simons) but Patricia Neal, with her phoney Southern accent and wild over-acting, was a decided liability. Lauren Bacall wasn't much better. Director Michael Curtiz kept it moving as briskly as the material allowed, and his cast included Jack Carson (left), Gladys George, Elisabeth Patterson, Jeff Corey and Thurston Hall. Victor Young's score was excellent; so was Karl Freund's photography. Henry Blanke produced.

The prestige of American movies was enhanced not one iota by **This Side of The Law**. Kent Smith (left) starred as an impoverished young man who impersonates a missing millionaire to facilitate a scheme cunningly contrived by a crooked lawyer (Robert Douglas, centre) which involves an all-important will. Russell Hughes wrote the screenplay from a story by Richard Sale; Richard Bare directed for producer Saul Elkins, and the cast included Viveca Lindfors (right), Janis Paige, John Alvin and Monte Blue.

There was the germ of an amusing idea in **Pretty Baby**, but scenarists Everett Freeman and Harry Kurnitz (working from a story by Jules Furthman and John Klorer) might have been writing in baby talk for all the sense it made. It was about a young, unmarried woman (Betsy Drake) who, to ensure a seat on the subway, buys a toy doll, wraps it in a blanket and pretends it is real. She even gives the 'baby' a name, that of a well-known baby-food manufacturer. One day, while riding the subway, she gets into conversation with an elderly gentleman (Edmund Gwenn, right) who, after asking her what the 'baby's' name is, turns out to be none other than the food manufacturer himself. Not only that, but he is also the owner of the advertising agency at which Miss Drake (left) happens to be employed — and immediately secures a better job for her. Eventually the truth about the phoney 'baby' emerges, but not before Miss Drake has been drawn to the romantic attention of a couple of ad men in the shape of Zachary Scott and Dennis Morgan. Directed by Bretaigne Windust for producer Harry Kurnitz, it also featured William Frawley, Raymond Roe, Ransom Sherman and Sheila Stephens. Warner Bros. later remade the movie for television, calling it *Girl on the Subway*. It starred Natalie Wood, and was shown in British cinemas in 1958.

Having once already attempted to turn Hemingway's *To Have And Have Not* into a film, the studio tried again with **The Breaking Point**. The results were excellent. Under Michael Curtiz's expert direction, and with a screenplay by Ranald MacDougall whose fidelity to Hemingway's original novel was admirable (its new California setting in no way violating the book's intentions), the adventures of down-at-heel John Garfield (left) who hires out his fishing boat to wealthy businessmen (or anyone else who will pay his fee), made for compelling cinema. In this, his last film for the studio, Garfield, cast in a thoroughly disagreeable mould, was first-rate; so were his co-stars Patricia Neal (right) and Phyllis Thaxter. Juano Hernandez, Ralph Dumke, William Campbell, Sherry Jackson and Wallace Ford were in it, too, and the producer was Jerry Wald.

Fifty Years Before Your Eyes was a 70 minute compilation of newsreel footage (Lloyd George, left) which started with the funeral of Queen Victoria and ended with the threat of a possible third world war with Communist Russia. In between were such light-hearted vignettes as Mayor La Guardia's reading of the Sunday comics ▷ over the air. A prologue, containing clips from feature films, traced America's history from the landing of the Pilgrim fathers to the winning of the West. Superficial but enjoyable, the film was skilfully edited by Albert Helmes and Leonard C. Hein, directed by Robert G. Youngson, produced by Alfred Butterfield (who wrote it with Thomas H. Wolf), and narrated by Quentin Reynolds, H.V. Kaltenborn, Dwight Weist, Milton Cross, Norman Brokenshire, Andre Baruch, Clem McCarthy and Don Donaldson.

◁ **Kiss Tomorrow Goodbye** was more a case of kiss yesterday goodbye — for the criminal mayhem perpetrated in this Gordon Douglas-directed piece of hokum bore little relation to the classic crime films of the early thirties. It did, however, star James Cagney (right) whose characteristic mannerisms, while given full vent in Harry Brown's screenplay (from a novel by Horace McCoy), merely served to remind audiences that things weren't what they used to be. Even the rough-play directed at pretty Barbara Payton (centre) lacked the impact of Cagney's grapefruit-twisting scene in *The Public Enemy* (1931). The sordid story of a hood who frames two crooked cops and uses them for his own ends, it was gratuitously violent, poorly scripted and totally devoid of style. Luther Adler appeared as a shyster lawyer, with other parts going to Ward Bond (far right), Helena Carter, Steve Brodie, Rhys Williams, Barton MacLane (left) and John Litel. The producer was James' brother William.

Real-life robber Gerard Graham Dennis gave Warner Bros. permission to film his crooked exploits and the result was an entertaining caper called **The Great Jewel Robber**. David Brian (below left) was cast as Dennis and, although the message of the film was that crime does not pay, Brian presented Dennis as an attractive and charismatic villain whose Raffles-like escapades, stretching from Westchester to Beverly Hills, were not without glamour. Borden Chase wrote the screenplay, which was directed by Peter Godfrey and produced by Bryan Foy. Also cast were Marjorie Reynolds (as the robber's faithful girl-friend), John Archer, Jacqueline de Wit, Claudia Barrett, Fred Coby (above left), Alix Talton, Perdita Chandler and Mayor Stanley Church of New Rochelle as himself.

◁ Errol Flynn's last Western, **Rocky Mountain**, an indifferent story of a confederate officer (Flynn, left) determined to recruit outlaws in an attempt to bring the West under Confederate domination, was distinguished only in that it gave the word 'routine' new meaning. Patrice Wymore (centre, whom Flynn was later to make his third wife), Howard Petrie (right), Dick Jones, Slim Pickens, Peter Coe, Scott Forbes and Yakima Canutt were in it too; Winston Miller and Alan LeMay threw the screenplay together (and missed), and William Keighley directed for producer William Jacobs.

Doris Day (centre) proved herself to be an ▷ excellent dancer in **Tea for Two**, a delightful concoction of catchy tunes and energetic musical numbers which also starred Gordon MacRae, Gene Nelson, Patrice Wymore, Eve Arden (centre right), Virginia Gibson (centre left), Billy De Wolfe, Bill Goodwin (right) and S.Z. Sakall (left). Its slender story (screenplay by Harry Clork) which bore little resemblance to the Otto Harbach-Frank Mandell Broadway hit *No, No Nanette* (1924) which inspired it, had Doris agreeing to say 'no' to everything for 24 hours in order to win a bet which carried enough money for her to finance (and appear in) a Broadway show. David Butler directed agreeably, and gave the studio a solid hit. It was produced, in Technicolor, by William Jacobs. Songs included: I Know That You Know (by Anne Caldwell and Vincent Youmans), Crazy Rhythm (by Irving Caesar, Roger Wolf Kahn and Harry Warren), I Only Have Eyes For You (by Al Dubin and Harry Warren), Tea For Two and I Want To Be Happy (by Irving Caesar and Vincent Youmans), and Do Do Do (by George and Ira Gershwin).

△

The screen adaptation of Tennessee Williams' hauntingly beautiful drama, **The Glass Menagerie**, was almost irretrievably coarsened in director Irving Rapper's treatment of it (screenplay by Tennessee Williams and Peter Berneis.) Taking his cue from the central performance of Gertrude Lawrence as the mother, Rapper plumbed for laughter rather than tears, and several key scenes, including the climactic visit of the 'gentleman caller' (Kirk Douglas, left), failed to touch the heart as they had done in the stage play. Gertrude Lawrence, a comedienne and musical comedy artist of incomparable dazzle, tended to reduce the pathos at the centre of the play to the level of domestic comedy, and the optimistic ending tagged onto the film only helped to underline this misguided approach. Still, Jane Wyman (right) as the crippled Laura gave a touching and sensitive performance which echoed her work in *Johnny Belinda* (1948), Arthur Kennedy was fine as the poetic son aching to escape a claustrophobic existence with his doomed family, and Kirk Douglas was refreshingly 'normal' as the innocent gentleman caller who does not realize, until it is too late, that he has been invited to the Wingfield residence as a potential beau for the unfortunate Laura. The play was opened up to include several additional characters played, in the Jerry Wald-Charles K. Feldman Group Production, by Ralph Sanford, Ann Tyrrell, John Compton, Gertrude Graner, Sara Edwards, Louise Lorrimer, Cris Alcaide and Perdita Chandler.

James Cagney's (centre) first musical since *Yankee Doodle Dandy* (1942) was **The West Point Story** (released in Britain as **Fine and Dandy**) in which he played a run-down Broadway director who agrees to produce a musical spectacular for the famous military Academy. Half backstage musical, half West Point PR job, the film made the worst of both worlds, and despite a cast that included Doris Day (centre right), Gordon MacRae (right), Virginia Mayo (centre left), Gene Nelson (left) and Alan Hale Jr (far left), was tepid entertainment. John Monks Jr, Charles Hoffman and Irving Wallace wrote it. Roy Del Ruth directed, and the dull score was by Sammy Cahn and Jule Styne. Louis F. Edelman produced. Songs included: It Could Only Happen In Brooklyn, Military Polka, You Love Me and Ten Thousand Sheep.

▽

◁ In **Return of the Frontiersmen**, upstanding young son Gordon MacRae (centre) is blamed for a bank robbery in which he had absolutely no part. Not one to take injustice lying down, MacRae breaks jail, and the clichés which accompany his escape are laid to rest only when the real outlaws are finally apprehended. Apart from scenarist Edna Anhalt, the villain of the piece was Rory Calhoun, with other roles in this warmed-over oater going to Julie London (left), Fred Clark, Edwin Rand, Raymond Bond (right) and Matt McHugh. Richard Bare directed in Technicolor and Saul Elkins produced.

△

Three Secrets offered viewers two dramas for the price of one. Basically the story of a rescue attempt on a five-year-old boy – the only survivor of a plane crash on a Californian mountain which kills his foster parents – it also involved the plights of three women, each of whom, for secret reasons of their own, believes she is the real mother of the boy. The segments of the plot involving the rescue were undeniably gripping; the pulp-fiction interludes involving Eleanor Parker (left), Patricia Neal (right) and Ruth Roman as the three would-be mothers less so. Martin Rackin and Gina Kaus wrote it, director Robert Wise almost succeeded in welding the disparate elements of the story into a cohesive whole, and the producer was Milton Sperling. Also cast were Frank Lovejoy, Leif Erickson, Ted De Corsia, Edmond Ryan and Larry Keating. It was a United States Pictures Production.

△

Gary Cooper's sturdy presence was the chief virtue of **Dallas**, a Technicolor Western whose screenplay by John Twist kicked up a fair amount of dust in the telling of its story. It was about an ex-Confederate guerrilla (Cooper, left), who, pretending to be a marshal from the North, arrives at a frontier town in Texas and promptly proceeds to rid the town of the no-good Marlowe brothers. Steve Cochran and Raymond Massey were the brothers, with other parts going to Ruth Roman (right) as the love interest, Leif Erickson, Antonio Moreno and Reed Hadley. Stuart Heisler directed for producer Anthony Veiller.

Breakthrough was anything but as far as war films were concerned. In attempting to show both the good side of war (as if there were a good side) as well as the bad, writers Bernard Girard and Ted Sherdeman (from a story by Joseph I. Breen Jr), foundered in their general recounting of World War II's Normandy campaign and the experiences of one particular infantry platoon. By their misguided efforts to take a balanced view of the subject they weakened the film's impact, and nothing that its cast – David Brian, John Agar, Frank Lovejoy, Bill Campbell, Paul Picerni (left), Greg McClure (centre), Richard Monahan, Eddie Norris, Matt Willis, Dick Wesson (centre right) and Suzanne Dalbert – did, made much difference. It was directed by Lewis Seiler, and the producer was Bryan Foy.

▽

1951

A Streetcar Named Desire was nominated for ten Academy Awards: Best Film, Best Actor, Best Actress, Best Supporting Actress, Best Supporting Actor, Best Director, Best Screenplay, Best Black and White Photography, Best Black and White Art Direction, Best Sound Recording, Best Score for a Dramatic Picture and Best Black and White Costume Design. At the Oscar ceremony it received four of those Awards: Best Actress (Vivien Leigh), Best Supporting Actor (Karl Malden) – Gig Young was nominated in the same category for **Come Fill The Cup** – Best Supporting Actress (Kim Hunter) and Best Black and White Art Direction (Richard Day and George James Hopkins).

Marlon Brando, nominated for Best Actor, was beaten by Humphrey Bogart for **The African Queen** (Romulus-British Lion-United Artists), and Elia Kazan lost the Best Director Award to George Stevens for **A Place In The Sun** (Paramount). Tennessee Williams was pipped to the post by Michael Wilson and Harry Brown for Best Screenplay for **A Place In The Sun**. The Best Film of the Year Oscar went to MGM's **An American In Paris**.

The only other Academy Award won by the studio in 1951 was for a one-reel short called **World Of Kids**, though **I Was A Communist For The F.B.I.** was nominated as Best Feature Documentary. (The winner was R.K.O's **Kon-Tiki**.) Robert Burks was nominated in the Best Cinematography (Black-and-White) category for **Strangers on a Train**. **Streetcar** was voted one of the year's Ten Best films by the *New York Times*, while the New York Film Critics voted it the year's best film with Vivien Leigh and Elia Kazan as best actress and best director. The net profit for the year was $9,427,344, the big box-office success being **Captain Horatio Hornblower**, **On Moonlight Bay**, and **Operation Pacific**.

Made to appease the House UnAmerican Activities Committee, **I Was A Communist For The F.B.I.** starred Frank Lovejoy (right) as Matt Cvetic, a real-life investigator who infiltrated various Communist organizations in the guise of a Pittsburgh steelworker. Simplistic to the point of embarrassment, and dangerous in its implications that it is the school teachers, blacks and intellectuals of the country rather than 'ordinary' folk who are most susceptible to the Red menace, the film was propaganda of the most vicious kind, which, in the end, defeated its purposes by naively depicting the Communists as caricatures, or comic-strip heavies; the same tactics, in fact, used by the Nazis against the Jews. Crane Wilbur wrote the screenplay (from the story *I Posed As A Communist for the F.B.I.* by Cvetic and Pete Martin) and Gordon Douglas directed. The cast also included Dorothy Hart (left), Philip Carey, James Millican and Richard Webb. The producer was Bryan Foy.

Having made one of the definitive submarine films with *Destination Tokyo* (1944), the studio returned to the same subject in **Operation Pacific**, but couldn't quite make up its mind whether it wanted an all-out action film or a love story. George Waggner's screenplay settled for a bit of both, though the underwater sequences were definitely more successful than anything that took place on land. Waggner also directed for producer Louis F. Edelman and John Wayne (left) was the film's star who takes over the command of the US submarine *Thunderfish* when skipper Ward Bond (right) is wounded. Patricia Neal played the nurse Wayne marries, divorces, and still loves. Scott Forbes, Phil Carey, Paul Picerni and Kathryn Givney were also cast.

◁ Another conventional cops-'n-robbers thriller, **Highway 301** purported (via a prologue involving the real-life participation of the governors of Maryland, Virginia and North Carolina) to emphasize that crime does not pay (except for the manufacturers of synthetic items such as this) but was, in effect, a rather sadistic little shocker which revelled in the criminal activities of the Tri-State Gang and their various 'molls'. Steve Cochran (centre) was the ringleader in control of Robert Webber (right), Richard Egan (2nd left) and Wally Cassell. Virginia Grey (left) and Gaby Andre were the women in it. It was written and directed by Andrew Stone, and the producer was Bryan Foy.

In an attempt to recreate the same kind of wholesome nostalgia peddled seven years earlier by MGM in *Meet Me In St. Louis*, the studio signed Jack Rose and Melville Shavelson to turn some of Booth Tarkington's overworked Penrod stories into a musical as close in spirit to the MGM predecessor as possible. The result was **On Moonlight Bay** which starred Doris Day (left) in the Judy Garland role, Gordon MacRae (centre) as the boy next door, Leon Ames as father, Rosemary De Camp as a Mary Astorish mother, Eddie Muir (right) and, instead of Marjorie Main, Mary Wickes. But the magic was missing and nothing director Roy Del ▷ Ruth could do could supply it. It was produced by William Jacobs and photographed in Technicolor. Songs included: On Moonlight Bay (by Percy Wenrich and Edward Madden), Till We Meet Again (by Ray Egan and Richard Whiting), Pack Up Your Troubles (by Felix Powell and George Asaf), Cuddle Up A Little Closer and Every Little Movement Has A Meaning All Its Own (by Otto Harbach and Karl Hochna), and I'm Forever Blowing Bubbles (by Jean Kenbrovin and John W. Kellette).

Art Cohn and Guy Endore's screenplay for **Tomorrow is Another Day** reeked of scissors-and-paste treatment. The story of an ex-con (Steve Cochran, left) who, shortly after being released from prison, finds himself on the run for a crime he did not commit, it was formula film-making down to the final fade. Ruth Roman (right, as the girl Cochran marries), Lurene Tuttle and Bobby Hyatt (as a Californian farming couple who give the duo shelter), and Ray Teal were also in it; the director was Felix Feist, and the producer Henry Blanke.

△

Technicolor did little to alleviate the sense of *déjà vu* that permeated **Sugarfoot**. A tedious Western, the film starred Randolph Scott (centre right) and Raymond Massey (left) as two men who travel on the same wagon train to Prescott, Arizona, and arrive there each determined to make the town his own. Adele Jergens (right), S.Z. Sakall, Robert Warwick, Arthur Hunnicutt and Hugh Sanders (centre left) were also featured for producer Saul Elkins and director Edwin L. Marin. The screenplay was written by Russell Hughes from a novel by Clarence Budington Kelland, and was later re-titled *Swirl of Glory* for television, to distinguish it from the *Sugarfoot* TV series which it inspired.

A King Vidor-directed melodrama about a man (Richard Todd) accused of murdering his wife but found not guilty, **Lightning Strikes Twice**, with its convoluted screenplay by Lenore Coffee (from a novel by Margaret Echard) attempted to send chills up the spine. Standing in a draught would have achieved better results. Also starring was Ruth Roman (centre left) as an actress on a sabbatical who falls in love with Todd, despite the local gossip which proclaims him guilty of the crime. In the end the murderer was revealed as Mercedes McCambridge (right), who is conveniently killed in a car crash, and all ends happily. Zachary Scott, Rhys Williams (centre), Darryl Hickman (left) and Nacho Galindo were also cast. Henry Blanke produced.

▽

△

Made in the same year, and by the same studio as *A Streetcar Named Desire*, **Storm Warning**, in which a New York model (Ginger Rogers, right) travels South to visit her married sister (Doris Day, centre) and becomes involved with the Ku Klux Klan, bore more than a passing resemblance to Tennessee Williams' celebrated play. Under Stuart Heisler's taut direction, the film focused on violence and persecution, and was not without impact. Doris Day was excellent in her first non-musical role, but Ginger Rogers was not quite as convincing. Steve Cochran (left) was Day's husband, with other parts going to Ronald Reagan and Hugh Sanders. The film was written by Daniel Fuchs and Richard Brooks and produced by Jerry Wald.

△

A hard-hitting thriller, **The Enforcer** (released in Britain as **Murder Inc.**) starred Humphrey Bogart as a crusading District Attorney. According to the film's publicity blurb, the D.A. '. . . matched himself against a nationwide network of killers-for-hire . . . and tore apart the evil dynasty that peddled murder for a price'. Brutally tough, and sometimes uncompromisingly harrowing, Martin Rackin's original screenplay possessed all the classic elements of the genre – the first fifteen minutes were particularly effective – and with Bogart (making his last appearance for Warner Bros.) in brilliant form, it couldn't miss. The Milton Sperling–United States Pictures production was directed by Bretaigne Windust, with uncredited assistance from Raoul Walsh, and featured Zero Mostel, Ted de Corsia (centre), Everett Sloane, Roy Roberts (centre left), and King Donovan (centre right).

△

Cast in the role originally created by Madeleine Carroll in Fay Kanin's Broadway success, **Goodbye My Fancy**, Joan Crawford (left) played a Congresswoman who returns to her *alma mater* to receive an honorary degree and, in the process, finds herself involved in a romantic triangle with Robert Young (right) and Frank Lovejoy. Miss Crawford's interpretation of the role was too heavily histrionic for this flimsy romantic comedy, and director Vincent Sherman was unable to fillet any of the dramatic intensity from the star's performance. The film, which was written by Ivan Goff and Ben Roberts, suffered accordingly. Also featured were Eve Arden, Lurene Tuttle, Howard St. John, and pretty Janice Rule, to whose presence on the set Miss Crawford reacted with increasing resentment. Henry Blanke produced.

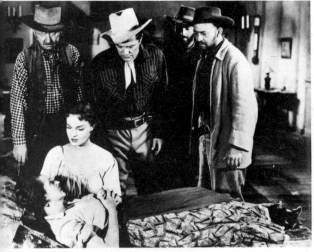

All the things that went on **Inside The Walls of Folsom Prison** had gone on inside the walls of several other prisons in several other Warner Bros. melodramas since the movies first learned to talk. All about the thwarted attempts of compassionate captain of the prison guards (David Brian) to make the penitentiary a more humane establishment, its screenplay, by Crane Wilbur, kept originality at bay, relying instead on the usual cliché conflicts, jailbreaks, and brutalities endemic to the genre. Steve Cochran (right), Ted de Corsia, Philip Carey (left), Scott Forbes, Lawrence Tolan, Dick Wesson (centre), Ed Norris and Dorothy Hart were in it too; it was directed by Crane Wilbur, and the production was in the capable hands of Bryan Foy.

By the time **The Tanks Are Coming** made its appearance, tanks had already come — and gone — in far better films than this one. A narrator assured us that the story about to unfold (i.e. the Third Armoured Division's encroachment on the German border from St. Lo in the summer of 1944) had never been told before. However, he omitted to mention that, in the telling of it, every platitude known to the genre would be placed in the service of the plot. Based on a story by Samuel Fuller, and written by Robert Hardy Andrews, it featured Steve Cochran as a sergeant, Paul Picerni as a tank driver, Mari Aldon as a photographer, Robert Boon as a gunner, Harry Bellaver as a mechanic and Philip Carey as a lieutenant. Lewis Seiler was responsible for the direction with D. Ross Lederman, and the producer was Bryan Foy.

◁ Sheer greed motivated Patricia Neal to try and get the better of her husband Dennis Morgan (centre) in **Raton Pass** (released in Britain as **Canyon Pass**), an above average Western. Husband and wife each own a half share in an enormous ranch which, to the avaricious Miss Neal, isn't good enough, believing as she does, that half a ranch is no substitute for a whole one. So she hires a bunch of renegades to help her keep what doesn't belong to her — and almost succeeds. Steve Cochran, Scott Forbes, Dorothy Hart (centre left), Basil Ruysdael and Louis Jean Heydt were also in it, Edwin L. Marin directed from a screenplay by Tom Blackburn and James Webb (story by Tom Blackburn) and the producer was Saul Elkins.

◁ After the disappointments of *Under Capricorn* (1949) and *Stage Fright* (1950), Hitchcock returned to form with **Strangers on a Train** in which two fellow passengers meet on a train and agree to an exchange of killings. It dazzled audiences both with its technical proficiency and its brilliantly structured moments of suspense, a particularly fine example being the justly celebrated tennis match towards the end of the film. Farley Granger (centre left) and Robert Walker starred as the two partners in crime, Laura Eliott was Granger's wife and Ruth Roman (centre right) his mistress. Also cast were Leo G. Carroll (left), Patricia Hitchcock (right), Marion Lorne and Jonathan Hale. Failing to see eye to eye with Raymond Chandler, who was engaged to turn Whitfield Cook's adaptation of Patricia Highsmith's novel, with its homosexual undertones, into a screenplay, Hitchcock hired Czenzi Ormonde with whom he worked on the final shooting script. The result was one of the best thrillers of the decade.

Gary Cooper remained laconic throughout ▷ practically all of **Distant Drums**, which was just as well as he would probably not have been heard above the gunfire, and other general noise which director Raoul Walsh imposed on the soundtrack of the film. It was a Technicolored adventure in which Cooper (centre) set out to track down a band of gun smugglers who were selling their illicit booty to Seminole Indians in the Everglades. The tired screenplay (by Niven Busch and Martin Rackin) was jollied along by Sid Hickox's excellent photography, and a score by Max Steiner that went some distance in disguising the story's lack of imagination. Mari Aldon, Richard Webb, Ray Teal, Arthur Hunnicutt, Robert Barrat and Clancy Cooper completed the cast. It was a United States Pictures production, and the producer was Milton Sperling.

The staging of the musical numbers (by Al White and LeRoy Prinz) for **Lullaby of Broadway** was not nearly as inventive as Busby Berkeley's had been for the *Gold Diggers* series in the thirties. White and Prinz even filched the opening of Berkeley's spellbinding 'Lullaby Of Broadway' sequence from *Gold Diggers of 1935*, but the finished routine was formula stuff. Still, the papiermaché story of a musical comedy star (Doris Day) who arrives in New York from London, unaware that her once famous actress mother (Gladys George) has become a drunken singer in a sleazy Greenwich Village club, was perfectly serviceable and gave enough openings for the many songs on offer. Stalwarts S.Z. Sakall (as a millionaire) and Billy De Wolfe (as his servant), played the friends who prevent the star being told the truth about her mother, and

Gene Nelson (centre with Miss Day) provided the love interest. David Butler directed from a screenplay by Earl Baldwin, while others in William Jacobs' Technicolor production were Florence Bates, Anne Triola, Hanley Stafford, The Page Cavanaugh Trio, and Carlo and Constance Da Mattiazzi. Songs included: Lullaby of Broadway and You're Getting To Be A Habit With Me (by Al Dubin and Harry Warren), Just One Of Those Things (by Cole Porter), Somebody Loves Me (by George Gershwin, B.G. De Sylva and Ballard MacDonald), I Love The Way You Say Goodnight by Eddie Pola and George Wyle), Please Don't Talk About Me When I'm Gone (by Sam Stept and Sidney Clare), In A Shanty In Old Shanty Town (by Little Jack Little, John Siras and Joe Young), and Zing Went The Strings Of My Heart (by James F. Hanley).

Despite its similarity in theme and content to Hemingway's World War I *A Farewell to Arms*, **Force of Arms**, directed by the ubiquitous Michael Curtiz, was a commendable romantic drama set during World War II. William Holden (right) starred as a war-weary G.I. who, during the Battle of San Pietro, meets and falls in love with a WAC (Nancy Olson, left). Because of the scars the war has already inflicted on her, Olson is at first reluctant to reciprocate Holden's love. But she does, and their relationship is almost as touching as Bogart and Bergman's was in *Casablanca* (1943). Fine performances from Frank Lovejoy as a major and from Gene Evans, Dick Wesson, Slats Taylor and Paul Picerni as Holden's colleagues, contributed solidly to Orin Jannings' intelligent screenplay (story by Richard Tregaskis); Max Steiner provided another of his workmanlike background scores and Anthony Veiller produced. The film was reissued in the US three years later as *A Girl for Joe*.

Fort Worth was another routine Randolph Scott Western. Hero Scott (centre) played a newspaper editor who takes the law into his own hands to stop David Brian from buying up the whole of Fort Worth and making himself unofficial dictator of the territory. Scott's endeavours weren't made any easier with the appearance of a group of prairie scavengers who give the locals more than their quota of unnecessary aggro. Phyllis Thaxter (left), Dick Jones, Emerson Treacy, Paul Picerni and Lawrence Tolan completed the cast; Edwin L. Marin directed from a screenplay by John Twist and the producer was Anthony Veiller. It was photographed in Technicolor.

Close To My Heart — an adroit soap-opera about a couple who discover that the orphaned child they wish to adopt had a murderer for a father — set out to prove that evil is not hereditary. Ray Milland (right) and Gene Tierney (centre) were the couple and Fay Bainter (left) the woman in charge of the orphanage, with other parts going to Howard St. John, Mary Beth Hughes, Ann Morrison, James Seay, Eddie Marr and Baby John Winslow. It was written by James R. Webb, directed by William Keighley, and produced by William Jacobs.

In **Only The Valiant** Gregory Peck, as the disciplinarian Captain of the US Cavalry had his hands full fighting several of his own men as well as the Apache Indians. Though patently brave in battle, Peck (left) lacked the common touch with his men, a deficiency which, in the circumstances, made life extremely difficult for him. In the end, however, his sterling qualities finally win through and his murderous white opponents forget their personal vendettas and offer him their valiant support when it is most needed. A conventional screenplay by Edmund H. North and Harry Brown (from a novel by Charles Marquis Warren) prevented the film from being anything more than a traditional Western, though Gordon Douglas' direction managed to bring a certain amount of excitement to it. It was produced by William Cagney for Cagney Productions, and the cast included Barbara Payton, Ward Bond, Gig Young, Lon Chaney, Neville Brand (centre) Jeff Corey and Warner Anderson.

295

Burt Lancaster (centre) was perfectly cast as **Jim Thorpe – All American** (released in Britain as **Man of Bronze**) which Michael Curtiz directed for producer Everett Freeman. Though the screenplay – by Freeman and Douglas Morrow (additional dialogue by Frank Davis) from the story by Morrow and Vincent X. Flaherty which, in turn, was based on the biography by Russell G. Birdwell and Thorpe himself – refrained from glamourizing the legendary athlete. It was routine in its telling, and failed to be more than just another hardship-to-triumph biopic. This was possibly because the sections of the film dealing with Red Indian Thorpe's private life, where he finds himself estranged from his wife (Phyllis Thaxter) and takes to drink, were less compelling than Curtiz's exciting recreation of the 1912 Olympics in which Thorpe wins the Pentathlon as well as the Decathlon. Still, it was entertaining enough, and in no way disgraced its remarkable subject. Also cast were Charles Bickford, Jack Big Head, Suni Warcloud, Al Mejia and Nestor Paiva.

▽

△

Hollywood's gesture in sending some of its stars to the Travis Air Base near San Francisco to entertain Korean-bound troops and wounded veterans was known as Operation Starlift. The musical fashioned from this gesture was called, quite simply, **Starlift**, and, despite its good intentions and a host of the studio's top stars in guest appearances, was a pretty feeble effort. Its credits were more impressive than its ultimate content, and those agreeing to do box office duty while a romance between a Hollywood star (Janice Rule) and an Air Force Corporal (Ron Haggerthy) slowly unfurled, were Doris Day (right), Gordon MacRae (left), Virginia Mayo, Gene Nelson, Ruth Roman, James Cagney, Gary Cooper, Virginia Gibson, Phil Harris, Frank Lovejoy, Lucille Norman, Louella Parsons, Randolph Scott, Jane Wyman and Patrice Wymore. It was written by John Klorer and Karl Kamb, directed by Roy Del Ruth, and produced by Robert Arthur. Songs included: Liza and S'Wonderful (by George and Ira Gershwin), You Do Something To Me and What Is This Thing Called Love? (by Cole Porter), It's Magic (by Sammy Cahn and Jule Styne), and I May Be Wrong But I Think You're Wonderful (by Harry Ruskin and Henry Sullivan).

The story of a newspaperman's attempts to overcome his drinking problem with the help of an ex-alcoholic friend, **Come Fill The Cup** brought a powerful performance from James Cagney (illustrated) whose craving for the bottle loses him his job. Not quite in the league of Paramount's *The Lost Weekend* (1945), it could have been much better than it was had the screenplay by Ivan Goff and Ben Roberts (from the novel by Harlan Ware) not made a midway descent into the maudlin and the implausible. James Gleason played the ex-alcoholic, with other roles going to Phyllis Thaxter, Raymond Massey, Gig Young, Selena Royle, Larry Keating, Charlita, and Sheldon Leonard. The director was Gordon Douglas who just missed making this an important film. The producer was Henry Blanke.

It cost $75,000 to turn Marlon Brando into an international star – that was the sum which the volatile performer received for appearing as Stanley Kowalski in the screen adaptation of Tennessee Williams' enduring masterpiece, **A Streetcar Named Desire**. Vivien Leigh (right), playing opposite Brando (left), gave a screen performance of consummate greatness as Blanche Dubois and, under the razor-edged direction of Elia Kazan, the two stars undoubtedly matched the stature of the play itself (in spite of the fact that in the early stages of the three month shooting schedule, Miss Leigh had 'artistic' disagreements with her director and social ones with her leading man). Working from Oscar Saul's adaptation of the play, Tennessee Williams fashioned a screenplay that retained the basic atmosphere and poetry of the original, but made ▷ two concessions to censorship: the homosexual references to Blanche's first husband were deleted, and the ending was rewritten to give the impression that Blanche's sister Stella had finally decided to leave the boorishly insensitive Kowalski after the shame and misery he had brought on Blanche, rather than (in Blanche's words to her) 'hang back with the brutes'. Both changes weakened the text, but not sufficiently to do it any serious damage. **A Streetcar Named Desire** remains a stunning cinematic experience, with invaluable contributions from Harry Stradling (photography), Alex North (music), and a brilliant supporting cast including Kim Hunter as Stella and Karl Malden as Mitch. An Elia Kazan production, produced by Charles K. Feldman for release by Warner Bros. it grossed $4,250,000 and was reissued by Twentieth Century-Fox.

◁ Yet another reworking of Avery Hopwood's *Gold Diggers* story, **Painting The Clouds With Sunshine** was a Technicolor musical in search of a single, original idea. The oft-told tale of a trio of 'golddiggers' out to marry wealth (but settling, instead, for true love), its Las Vegas setting, plus a clutch of excellent songs, did little to relieve the *ennui* engendered by the torpid Harry Clork – Roland Kibbee – Peter Milne screenplay. Virginia Mayo (right), Lucille Norman (left) and Virginia Gibson (centre left) were the girls; Gene Nelson (centre), Tom Conway and Dennis Morgan the guys, with S.Z. Sakall, Wallace Ford and Tom Dugan in it too. A remake of the 1929 *Gold Diggers of Broadway*, it was directed by David Butler, and the producer was William Jacobs. Songs included: Painting The Clouds With Sunshine and Tip-Toe Through The Tulips (by Al Dubin and Joe Burke), Vienna Dreams (by Irving Caesar and Rudolf Sieczy), With A Song In My Heart (by Richard Rodgers and Lorenz Hart), Birth Of The Blues (by De Sylva, Brown and Henderson), You're My Everything (by Harry Warren and Mort Dixon), Jealousy (by Vera Bloom and Jacob Gabe), Man Is A Necessary Evil, and Mambo Man (by Jack Elliott and Sonny Burke).

◁ Adapted by Ivan Goff, Ben Roberts and Aeneas Mackenzie from three C.S. Forester novels, **Captain Horatio Hornblower** (released in Britain as **Captain Horatio Hornblower R.N.**) was very much in the tradition of the studio's *Captain Blood* and *The Sea Hawk*, but not, alas, as good. Director Raoul Walsh brought the action to a simmer, rather than the boil, and never really breathed life into the tale of a 19th century British naval captain and his seagoing adventures with the French and the Spanish during the Napoleonic Wars. A taciturn, unflappable Gregory Peck (left) in the title role seemed embarrassed by it all and, without noticeable support from Virginia Mayo (right) as the admiral's widow he eventually marries, made little impact. Filmed in England (in Technicolor) amid phoney studio backdrops and on a specially constructed forty gun frigate, the film also featured James Robertson Justice, Robert Beatty, Terence Morgan and Denis O'Dea, and appealed mainly to young audiences.

△
Very little happened **Along the Great Divide** that audiences hadn't seen before. A Western, it starred Kirk Douglas (centre foreground) as a United States Marshal, whose current assignment is to deliver rustler Walter Brennan into the hands of the law, and Virginia Mayo (left) as the rustler's daughter. When Douglas wasn't running into trouble with Mayo, he was up against sandstorms and posses of cattlemen, but he came through in the end with justice being seen to be done. John Agar, Ray Teal, Hugh Sanders and Morris Ankrum helped to flesh out the Walter Doniger-Lewis Meltzer screenplay (from a story by Doniger); director Raoul Walsh did his best to disguise the film's hoary content, but Douglas seemed ill at ease. The producer was Anthony Veiller.

1952

Though the studio showed an overall net profit of $7,229,682 in 1952 – with the proceeds of the award-winning **A Streetcar Named Desire** (released in September 1951), as well as **The Miracle Of Fatima**, swelling the coffers – it was an undistinguished year for the company, with only two short subjects (a one-reeler and a two-reeler) being nominated for Academy Awards, and neither of them winning. The Best Film Oscar went to Paramount's **The Greatest Show On Earth**. The *New York Times*, in their Ten Best list, failed to cite a single Warner Bros. film for the year; as did the New York Film Critics, WarnerColor (Eastmancolor by another name) was introduced with the film **Carson City**, though this was in fact released after the second film made in the process, **The Lion And The Horse**.

I'll See You In My Dreams was an endearing and nicely scripted (by Melville Shavelson and Jack Rose) biopic of lyricist Gus Kahn that tugged at the proverbial heartstrings while setting the feet a-tapping. Danny Thomas (left) played Kahn, and Doris Day (right) his faithful ever-loving wife. Director Michael Curtiz brought a warmth and tenderness to it all and even LeRoy Prinz, not generally the most inspired of choreographers, contributed some well staged numbers. Deservedly a popular success, it also featured Frank Lovejoy, Patrice Wymore, James Gleason, Mary Wickes and Elsie Neft (centre). The producer was Louis F. Edelman. Songs included: Ain't We Got Fun and Ukelele Lady (by Gus Kahn and Richard Whiting), The One I Love Belongs To Somebody Else, I'll See You In My Dreams and It Had To Be You (by Kahn and Isham Jones), Makin' Whoopee, Yes, Sir, That's My Baby, Carolina In The Morning and Love Me Or Leave Me (by Gus Kahn and Walter Donaldson), and Pretty Baby (by Gus Kahn, Egbert Van Alstyne and Tony Jackson).

△

A warm-hearted, thoroughly engaging domestic comedy, **Room For One More** starred Cary Grant (left) and Betsy Drake (right, married in real life) as the parents of five children, three of them their own, two of them adopted. Jack Rose and Melville Shavelson's screenplay (from the novel by Anna Perrott Rose) piled on the kind of situations one would expect in a household of kids and, under Norman Taurog's direction, hit the target every time, especially in the scenes showing the natural suspicions and resentments of the adopted children (Iris Mann and Clifford Tatum Jr) towards their foster parents, and how these problems were finally laid to rest. Occasionally sentimentality intruded to the detriment of the film's generally pleasing tone, but not enough to mar the performances of Lurene Tuttle, Randy Stuart, George Winslow, Gay Gordon, Malcolm Cassell and John Ridgley. Henry Blanke was the producer.

Justifiably unhappy with the roles the studio ▷ had recently been tossing in her direction, Joan Crawford (left) parted company with Warner Bros. after appearing in **This Woman Is Dangerous**, a piece of arrant nonsense scripted by Geoffrey Homes and George Worthing Yates (from a story by Bernard Girard), and directed by Felix Feist. The story of a cold-blooded killer's equally cold-blooded mistress and her love affair with an eye-surgeon, it tested the loyalty of even Miss Crawford's most devoted fans. Dennis Morgan (right) and David Brian played the men in her life, with other roles going to Richard Webb, Mari Aldon, Philip Carey. Ian MacDonald and Kathleen Warren. The producer was Robert Sisk.

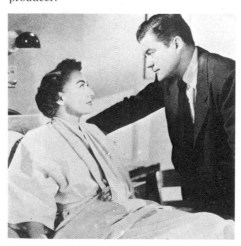

△

Retreat, Hell! was a well-made war drama, full of action and full of clichés. A tribute to the participation of the US Marine's First Battalion in the Korean War, it mixed newsreel footage with studio mock-ups in a successfully deceptive way, but what it was never able to disguise was the scissors-and-paste approach to its characters. All the familiar 'old faithfuls' germane to the genre were there, from Frank Lovejoy's tough, but humane captain, to Rusty (later Russ) Tamblyn's youngster out to prove himself a hero in battle (left); and not a line of the Milton Sperling – Ted Sherdeman screenplay added to our perception of the tensions and stresses on the battlefield. Still, it was directed in a suitably aggressive manner by Joseph H. Lewis, with performances to match by Richard Carlson, Ned Young (right), Lamont Johnson, Robert Ellis and Paul Smith. Anita Louise and Dorothy Patrick were also cast. It was a United States Pictures production and the producer was Milton Sperling.

◁ The studio chose picturesque Kanab in Utah and the awesome Zion National Park as locations for their second film in the dazzling new colour process, WarnerColor. (*Carson City*, released later, was their first). What it adorned, however, was a somewhat less colourful Western called **The Lion and the Horse**. A tale of devotion between a cowpoke and his stallion, it starred Steve Cochran (centre) as the horse-lover, and Wild Fire the Wonder Horse as the object of his affection, as well as the catalyst in Crane Wilbur's screenplay. For, just how Cochran endeavours to get Wildfire back after he is sold to a travelling rodeo, formed the basis of a film which, apart from the visual impact of its settings, offered very little to nourish the brain. It was directed by Louis King for producer Bryan Foy and featured Ray Teal, Bob Steele (right), Harry Antrim, Billy Dix (left) and George O'Hanlon, as well as the nameless lion of the title who misguidedly picks a fight with the horse.

Based on the tribulations of Grover Cleveland Alexander, a telephone linesman who rose to fame as one of America's greatest baseball players, **The Winning Team** was a fair-to-average biopic with Ronald Reagan (left) as the hero who secretly suffers from double vision and epilepsy. Doris Day (centre) played his wife who temporarily walks out on him believing, like everyone else, that he is an alcoholic. The indifferent screenplay was by Ted Sherdeman, Seelag Lester and Merwin Gerard (from a story by Lester and Gerard), it was directed by Lewis Seiler, and produced by Bryan Foy with a cast that included Frank Lovejoy, Eve ▷ Miller, James Millican, Rusty (Russ) Tamblyn, and Gordon Jones (right). Considering that the film was not a musical, quite a number of songs were featured. They included: Take Me Out To The Ball Game (by Albert von Tilzer and Jack Norworth), I'll String Along With You (by Al Dubin and Harry Warren), Lucky Day (by B.G. De Sylva, Lew Brown and Ray Henderson), and Aint We Got Fun (by Gus Kahn and Richard Whiting).

A familiar tale of political corruption in the big city, **The San Francisco Story**, set in 1856, starred Joel McCrea (right) as a miner-turned-vigilante, Sidney Blackmer as a crooked politician and Yvonne De Carlo (left) as the girl in the middle. Based on a novel by Richard Summers, and flaccidly written by D.D. Beauchamp, the film also featured Richard Erdman, Florence Bates, Onslow Stevens, Ralph E. Dumke and O.Z. Whitehead. A Fidelity-Vogue Production, it was produced by Howard Welsch and directed by Robert Parrish.

There were no fanfares for **Bugles in the Afternoon**, a Technicolored Western, and just one more tired variation on the cowboys-and-injuns formula with − instead of cowboys − a couple of cavalrymen in the shape of Ray Milland and Hugh Marlowe. This substitution was the brainchild of screenwriters Geoffrey Homes and Harry Brown, working from a novel by Ernest Haycox. Set on a frontier post, the narrative not only involved Milland (centre) in skirmishes with the warring Sioux, but also in a personal battle with Marlowe (as his commanding officer) whom he despises even more than he does the redskins. Helena Carter supplied the kisses whenever the dust settled long enough for her to do so, while additional masculine antics were the responsibility of Forrest Tucker, Barton MacLane, George Reeves and James Millican. A Cagney Production, the film was produced by William Cagney and directed by Roy Rowland.

◁ The real star of **Carson City** was the Studio's ultra-bright WarnerColor which made David Weisbart's production look better than it really was. Randolph Scott starred as a construction engineer involved in the building of a railroad between Virginia and Carson cities, with Raymond Massey as the villain of the piece and Lucille Norman (left) as the pretty girl whose initial aversion to Scott soon turns to love and admiration. Andre de Toth directed; the screenplay was written by Sloan Nibley and Winston Miller, and the cast included James Millican, Richard Webb (right), George Cleveland, William Haade, Don Beddoe, Thurston Hall and Vince Barnett.

Big Jim McLain was a shoddy effort centring uncritically on the Communist witchhunts of the time, with a commonplace love affair between John Wayne (left) and Nancy Olson (right) thrown in for good measure. Wayne's investigations into Communist activities in Hawaii were conducted with his fists rather than his brains. Edward Ludwig directed it and his cast included James Arness, Alan Napier, Veda Ann Borg, Gayne Whitman, Hal Baylor, Robert Keys and Hans Conried. A Wayne–Fellows production, it was produced by Robert Fellows from a screenplay by James Edward Grant, Richard English and Eric Taylor (story by English).

A Technicolor musical remake of the 1938 comedy *Brother Rat* (starring Ronald Reagan, Wayne Morris and Eddie Albert), **About Face** had none of the joyous spontaneity of the original, though Gordon MacRae (right), Dick Wesson (left) and Eddie Bracken (foreground left) as three cadets in a military academy – the latter being secretly married and terrified at the thought of approaching fatherhood – were likeable enough. So, indeed were the women in their lives, Virginia Gibson (centre left), Phyllis Kirk (foreground right) and Aileen Stanley Jr (centre right). The main trouble was Peter Milne's screenplay which managed to reduce the intelligence quotient of the principals to minus double figures. Newcomer Joel Grey made the best impression in a cast that also included Larry Keating, Cliff Ferre and John Baer. Roy Del Ruth's direction was dull, but it did fairly well at the box office. It was based on the successful 1936 play by John Monks Jr and Fred Finkelhoffe. William Jacobs was the producer. Songs included: If Someone Had Told Me, Piano, Bass And Drums, No Other Girl For Me, I'm Nobody, Spring Has Sprung, Wooden Indian, Reveille, Tar Heels and They Haven't Lost A Father Yet (by Charles Tobias and Peter de Rose).

Greed was the theme of **Mara Maru**, an Errol Flynn adventure about a deep-sea diver (Flynn, left) who alone knows how to retrieve a priceless diamond cross which sank with a PT boat in World War II. Basically a treasure hunt with all the attendant clichés, the film ended with Flynn heroically eschewing greed for decency and returning the coveted cross to its rightful place – the Church. It was extremely ordinary with Ruth Roman, Raymond Burr (right), Paul Picerni (centre), Richard Webb and Dan Seymour in supporting roles adding to the tedium. N. Richard Nash wrote the screenplay (based on a story by Philip Yordan, Sidney Harmon and Hollister Noble), and Gordon Douglas directed. The producer was David Weisbart.

Alan Ladd's first film for Warner Bros. was **The Iron Mistress** in which he played Jim Bowie whose main claim to fame was his design for the Bowie knife. In real life (and according to the book by Paul I. Wellman on which the movie was based), Bowie was something of a New Orleans thug who died heroically in the Alamo. In the screenplay, however, fashioned from Wellman's book by James R. Webb, Ladd (left) emerged as the archetypal romantic matinee idol who, for the love of an unworthy girl (Virginia Mayo, centre) resorts to gambling and land speculation. As he seems to be enemy-prone as well, Bowie designs a special knife with which to protect himself, and demonstrates its efficacy on several occasions. In the end he decides Miss Mayo isn't worth the effort and marries the Governor of Texas' daughter (Phyllis Kirk). It was directed with a flourish (in Technicolor) by Gordon Douglas, produced by Henry Blanke, and featured Joseph Calleia, Alf Kjellin, Douglas Dick, Richard Carlyle (right) and Anthony Caruso.

Operation Secret was based on a story by Alvin Josephy and John Twist from factual information supplied by Lt.-Col. Peter Ortiz. Cornel Wilde was cast as an American underground operator who has served in the French Foreign Legion, and now stands accused of murdering a Maquis officer in World War II. He's innocent, of course, the culprit being a bearded Steve Cochran. But before the true facts are revealed, Wilde (right), in flashback, proves himself to be a hero and incapable of such a deed. James R. Webb and Harold Medford's screenplay was serviceable; so was Lewis Seiler's direction. But the whole thing lacked impact and was simply a familiar story, told in workmanlike fashion. Token romantic interest was supplied by Phyllis Thaxter, with other parts going to Karl Malden (centre, excellent as a hard-boiled wino soldier), Paul Picerni (left), Lester Matthews and Dan O'Herlihy. The producer was Henry Blanke.

△
Set in California in 1900, **The Big Trees** was
an action adventure (in Technicolor) which
starred a determined Kirk Douglas who
arrives in the Northwest and immediately
sets about acquiring some Redwood territory
belonging to a group of settlers not unlike
Quakers in appearance and attitude. Similar
to *Valley of the Giants* (1938), John Twist and
James R. Webb's screenplay, adapted from
Kenneth Earl's story, traversed familiar
territory – even down to the scene in which
the heroine (Eve Miller) is trapped in the
caboose of a runaway train. However, if the
plot was well-worn, it was also efficiently
written. Patrice Wymore (right) played the
saloon-singer whom Douglas (centre) jilts
for Miss Miller (left), with other roles going
to Edgar Buchanan, John Archer, Alan Hale
Jr, Roy Roberts and Charles Meredith. Felix
Feist directed it, and the producer was Louis
F. Edelman.

◁ Aimed more at kids than at their parents,
the Bud Abbott (left) and Lou Costello
(centre) version of **Jack and the Beanstalk**
was played strictly for laughs, with only the
occasional moment of comedy suspense. A
protracted dream in which Costello finds
himself menaced by Buddy Baer (as the
giant), it was partly photographed in black
and white, and partly in SuperCinecolor.
Nat Curtis wrote the screenplay from a
treatment by Pat Costello, and Jean Yar-
brough directed. Only one thing was missing: a sense of wonderment. Also cast were
Dorothy Ford, Barbara Brown (centre right),
David Stollery, Patrick The Harp, and James
Alexander and Shaye Cogan as the romantic leads. The producer was Alex Gottlieb.
Songs included: He Never Looked Better
In His Life, I Fear Nothing, Darlene, and
Dreamer's Cloth (by Lester Lee and Bob
Russell).

1953

In the year in which Columbia's **From Here To Eternity** won eight Academy Awards, **Calamity Jane** was Warners' only Oscar winner. Sammy Fain and Paul Webster got it for their song 'Secret Love'. The company boarded the 3-D bandwagon with **House of Wax, The Charge At Feather River** and **The Moonlighter**, and had hits with the first two but not the third. The net profit for the year was $2,908,000. 1953 saw the death of Colonel Nathan Levinson, who first persuaded Sam Warner to try synchronized sound and film and was head of the Sound Department until he died.

Plot was of secondary importance to action in **The Man Behind The Gun**, a Technicolor Western that hardly rejuvenated an over-worked genre, but didn't disgrace it either. Randolph Scott (right), was the man behind the gun who, while pretending to be a school-teacher, was really a US Cavalry officer out to quell a rebellion in the early days of California's history. In the course of duty he meets and falls for school-mistress Patrice Wymore (left), thus ensuring the film its romantic interest. Dick Wesson, Philip Carey (centre), Lina Romay, Roy Roberts, Morris Ankrum, Alan Hale Jr, Douglas Fowley and Anthony Caruso completed the cast. It was written by John Twist from a story by Robert Buckner, produced by Robert Sisk and directed by Felix Feist.

Another backstage musical, **She's Back On Broadway** (in WarnerColor) starred Virginia Mayo as a Hollywood star who, at 27, feels her career will be over unless her new Broadway-bound musical *Breakfast In Bed* is a smash hit. Orin Jannings, who supplied both the story and the screenplay, hardly overtaxed his powers of invention, and despite a handful of amusing one-liners, gave a cast, which included Gene Nelson, Steve Cochran, Patrice Wymore and Frank Lovejoy, very little to sink their talents into. Nelson (right) played Miss Mayo's (left) leading man, Cochran was the show's director (and the man Miss Mayo sets her sights on), Wymore was Mayo's bitchy rival in love, and Lovejoy the show's harassed producer. Larry Keating, Paul Picerni, Condos and Brandow, Douglas Spencer and Jacqueline de Wit were in it too, and it was directed by Gordon Douglas for producer Henry Blanke. Songs included: I'll Take You As You Are, One Step Ahead Of Everybody, The Tie That Binds and Breakfast In Bed (by Bob Hilliard and Carl Sigman).

There was nothing epoch-making about the remake of **The Jazz Singer**. Apart from the requisite updating of the Samson Raphael-son play on which it was based, the Frank Davis-Leonard Stern-Lewis Meltzer screen-play was just as sentimental and tear-jerking as Alfred A. Cohn's version had been in 1927. This time Danny Thomas (right) played the cantor's son. An honourably discharged veteran of the Korean war, he returns home to Philadelphia where he comes to the conclusion that his heart belongs to show-business rather than to daddy or to God and, instead of the synagogue, seeks out the theatre. He is offered moral support, as well as romance, by Peggy Lee (left), and together they warble a clutch of standards by such com-posers as Rodgers and Hart, Cole Porter, Dubin and Warren and DeSylva, Brown and Henderson. It was directed by Michael Curtiz, who wisely made no attempt to disguise the schmaltzy, sentimental nature of the material, and produced by Louis F. Edelman. Also cast were Mildred Dunnock, Eduard Franz, Tom Tully, Alex Gerry, Allyn Joslyn and Harold Gordon. It was filmed in Technicolor. Songs included: I Hear The Music Now, This Is A Very Special Day (by Peggy Lee), Living The Life I Love, Just One Of Those Things, Four Leaf Clover, Birth Of The Blues and Just To Be With You.

Originally made in 1938 as *A Slight Case of Murder*, **Stop, You're Killing Me** traded the earlier version's deliciously satirical style for an all-out slapstick approach. The keynote of the film was struck by Broderick Crawford (right) who attacked the role originally played by Edward G. Robinson (ex-boot-legging beer baron attempting to go straight against overwhelming odds), with all the aggression of a man afraid that the role was going to attack back. The same unsubtle tone was in evidence in James O'Hanlon's screenplay, and it did irreparable violence to the play by Damon Runyon and Howard Lindsay on which it was based. Roy Del Ruth's direction didn't help, though Charles Cantor (centre), Joe Vitale (centre right) and Sheldon Leonard (centre left) made passable attempts to distil a Runyonesque essence from the characters they played. Less successfully cast were Claire Trevor (left), Louis Lettieri, Virginia Gibson, Bill Hayes and Howard St. John. Henry Morgan and Margaret Dumont were in it too. It was produced by Louis F. Edelman and photo-graphed in WarnerColor.

Relying on the premise that a Roman Catho-lic priest may not reveal, under any cir-cumstances, what he hears from a penitent during confession, Alfred Hitchcock's **I Confess**, based on a 1902 play by Paul Anthelme, explored the situation of a murderer who confesses his guilt to a priest in the knowledge that he will not be betrayed. ('Crushed Lips Don't Talk', pro-claimed the studio ads misleadingly!). Compounding the situation was the fact that the murdered man happened to be black-mailing the priest. Not one of Hitch's more successful thrillers (he feels, today, that it is heavy-handed, lacking in humour and subtlety, and that it should never have been made), it was nonetheless highlighted by some typical Hitchcockian moments, and Montgomery Clift's (right) performance as the tortured man of the cloth was especially fine. There was good work too from Anne Baxter, Karl Malden (left), Brian Aherne and O.E. Hasse. It was scripted by George Tabori and William Archibald and produced by Hitchcock for Alfred Hitchcock Productions.

The best thing about **The Blue Gardenia** was its professional gloss which, considering the banality of Charles Hoffman's screenplay (from a story by Vera Caspary), was an achievement not to be underestimated. It was about a girl (Anne Baxter, left) who, in defence of her honour, strikes her seducer over the head with a poker then flees. It also featured Richard Conte as a newspaper columnist who discovers that, although Baxter was indeed guilty of injuring the lecher, he was actually murdered by a completely different woman who happened to be hiding in the apartment at the same time. Ann Sothern (right), Raymond Burr, Jeff Donnell, Richard Erdman, George Reeves, Ruth Story and Ray Walker completed the cast. Responsible for the above-mentioned professional gloss was director Fritz Lang. A Blue Gardenia Production, it was produced by Alex Gottlieb. Song: Blue Gardenia (by Bob Russell and Lester Lee) – sung by Nat King Cole.

▽

Although twinkle-eyed Charles Coburn has taken a vow of poverty, as soon as he realizes that St. Anthony's College, of which he is rector, needs $170,000 to survive, he decides to engage a football coach for the purpose of creating a money-making team. Enter John Wayne – bookmaker, pool hustler, and star of **Trouble Along the Way**, who, to gain custody of his child, is happy to enter the relative seclusion of St. Anthony's where, in no time at all, he recruits, in a most unorthodox manner, a winning team. Donna Reed (right) also starred, as a probation officer who falls in love with Wayne (centre), with other parts going to Marie Windsor as Wayne's ex-wife, Sherry Jackson (left) as his daughter and Douglas Spencer, Leif Erickson and Dabbs Greer as members of the church. Melville Shavelson and Jack Rose, working from a story by Douglas Morrow and Robert Hardy Andrews, supplied a sparkling screenplay. Shavelson also produced, and the direction was by Michael Curtiz.

▽

△

A follow up to *On Moonlight Bay* (1951), **By The Light Of The Silvery Moon** (in Technicolor) was another 'good old days' wallow in nostalgia, with Doris Day (left) and Gordon MacRae (right) as the young lovers ever ready to burst into song. Again based on the Penrod stories of Booth Tarkington, it involved Miss Day's refusal to marry MacRae in order to keep herself free to protect her father (Leon Ames) from a bevy of glamorous actresses about to lease a local theatre. The corn was as high as an elephant's eye, but was harmless enough and quite enjoyable. David Butler directed from a screenplay by Robert O'Brien and Irving Elinson and, like its predecessor, it also featured Rosemary De Camp, Mary Wickes and Billy Gray. The producer was William Jacobs. Songs included: By The Light Of The Silvery Moon (by Gus Edwards and Edward Madden), I'll Forget You (by Ernest R. Ball and Annelu Burns), Your Eyes Have Told Me So (by Gus Kahn and Egbert Van Alstyne), Be My Little Baby Bumble Bee (by Stanley Murphy and Henry I. Marshall), If You Were The Only Girl In The World (by Clifford Grey and Nat D. Ayer), and Aint We Got Fun (by Gus Kahn and Richard Whiting).

The third version of Sigmund Romberg's ▷ 1926 operetta, **The Desert Song**, was also the least good and the least successful. Gordon MacRae (right) starred as The Red Shadow (here called El Khobar), Kathryn Grayson (left) was the general's daughter whom he woos, and Raymond Massey the dastardly Sheik Youssef whose nomadic army MacRae subdues in his guise as leader of the Riffs. Steve Cochran, Ray Collins, a tiresome Dick Wesson and an unrecognizable Allyn McLerie (as a houri) were also featured; the abysmal screenplay (based on the play by Lawrence Schwab, Otto Harbach, Frank Mandel, Sigmund Romberg and Oscar Hammerstein II) was by Roland Kibbee. Bruce Humberstone's direction was cumbersome and Rudi Fehr's Technicolor production a bore. Songs included: The Desert Song, Long Live The Night, The Riff Song, Romance, Gay Parisienne and One Alone.

A remake of *The Mystery of the Wax Museum* (1933), **House of Wax**, in WarnerColor and Natural Vision 3-D, covered the same territory as the earlier film without ever capturing its eerie atmosphere. Mainly an excuse to demonstrate, with the use of polaroid spectacles, the efficacy of 3-D, the film went all out for 'audience involving' effects, some of them genuinely impressive (such as boiling wax being tilted into the patrons' laps), others less so. A new sound process called 'directed sound' was also introduced, billed as WarnerPhonic sound, which meant that as well as pieces of the hardware shooting out from the screen, sound effects reverberated from various parts of the cinema at appropriate times. Vincent Price starred as the demented owner of the wax museum, with Frank Lovejoy, Phyllis Kirk (illustrated), Carolyn Jones, Paul Picerni, Roy Roberts and Charles Buchinsky (Bronson) in support. It was directed by Andre de Toth who, interestingly, only had one eye and was unable to see the 3-D effects himself. Crane Wilbur wrote the screenplay from a story by Charles Belden, and the producer was Bryan Foy.

▽

An undistinguished programmer, **The System** starred Frank Lovejoy (right) as a successful book-maker whose life collapses after an incident in which a young man is killed while robbing a shop in order to pay off his gambling debt to the bookmaker. Lovejoy's son (Bob Arthur) commits suicide,

◁ while Lovejoy himself is sent to jail with a promise from his sweetheart (Joan Weldon, left) that she'll be waiting to take him back on his release. Also featured were Paul Picerni, Donald Beddoe, Jerome Cowan, Dan Seymour and Sarah Selby; it was written by Jo Eisinger from a story by Edith and Samuel Grafton, directed by Lewis Seiler and produced by Sam Bischoff.

Filmed in 3-D, and WarnerColor. **The Charge** ▷
at Feather River was the oft-told tale of
the US Cavalry vs the Cheyenne Indians.
With attention squarely focused on the
range of 3-D effects devised by director
Gordon Douglas, what came out of the film
was far more important than what went
into it; and what came out of it, and straight
into the audiences' laps, were tomahawks,
arrows, spears, knives, pieces of furniture,
and even a mouthful of tobacco juice intended for a rattlesnake, but landing somewhere in the stalls. Guy Madison (centre
left) and Frank Lovejoy played a captain and
a sergeant who rescue Vera Miles and Helen
Westcott (centre right) from the Cheyenne
whose tepee-guests they have been for five
years! Dick Wesson, Onslow Stevens, Steve
Brodie and Ron Hagerthy (on ground) were
also cast. James R. Webb wrote it, David
Weisbart produced.

Errol Flynn's last film for Warner Bros. under
his present contract was **The Master of
Ballantrae**, based on Robert Louis Stevenson's novel about two brothers, one of
whom fights for the Stuarts in the Scottish
insurrection of 1745, while the other remains a loyal subject to his King (George II).
The film simplified the novel out of all recognition, eliminated any traces of wickedness
from the Flynn character, and changed the
ending to allow both brothers to survive.
Though Flynn (centre) was less glamorous
in this one than audiences remembered
him, and not quite so nimble on his feet, he
benefited from Jack Cardiff's superb colour
photography, and the picturesque locations
which ranged from the Scottish Highlands
to Palermo in Sicily. William Keighley directed (from a screenplay by Herb Meadow) and
his cast included Roger Livesey, Anthony Steel (as Flynn's brother), Beatrice
Campbell, Yvonne Furneaux, Felix Aylmer,
and Mervyn Johns. It was only a moderate
success in America, but fared better in
Europe, where it was made.
▽

▵
So This Is Love (released in Britain as **The
Grace Moore Story**) starred Kathryn Grayson as soprano Grace Moore, and traced
the operatic star's rise to fame from her
childhood in Tennessee to her debut at the
Metropolitan Opera House, New York. As
Miss Moore's life wasn't as dramatic as her
death (in a plane crash), it was simply an
entertaining account of a dedicated youngster's determination to succeed. Miss Grayson (left) was good in the central role and
vocally at home in both the popular and
operatic repertoires. Merv Griffin (making
his film debut) and Douglas Dick played
the men in her life whom she rejected in
favour of her career, with Joan Weldon
(right), Walter Abel (as Grace's father),
Rosemary de Camp, Jeff Donnell, Ann Doran
and Margaret Field (centre) also cast.
Gordon Douglas directed pleasingly; Henry
Blanke produced. Songs included: Time On
My Hands (by Harold Adamson and Mack
Gordon), Remember (by Irving Berlin), I
Wish I Could Shimmy Like My Sister Kate
(by Armand J. Peron), Ciribiribin (by Harry
James, Jack Lawrence and A. Pestalozza),
and extracts from *The Marriage of Figaro,
Faust and La Bohème.*

Ray Harryhausen's special effects for **The
Beast From 20,000 Fathoms** were not
especially effective in this Eugene Lourié-
directed horror movie which charted the
havoc caused by a prehistoric rhedosaurus
who, after being thawed out in the Arctic,
heads down the American East coast for
New York. The film's climax took place on
Coney Island where the hapless beast is
harpooned with a weapon containing a
lethal radioactive isotope. Competing with
the trick photography were Paul Christian,
Paula Raymond, Cecil Kellaway, Kenneth
Tobey, Donald Woods and Lee Van Cleef.
Lou Morheim and Fred Freiberger wrote it
from a story by Ray Bradbury. It was difficult to tell whether it or the beast was more
mechanical, but it made a good profit for
producers Hal Chester and Jack Dietz.

▽

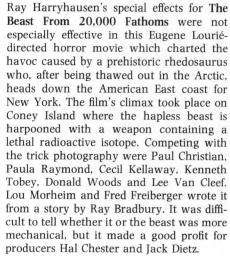

Though its title might understandably have
led one to believe otherwise, **South Sea
Woman** was a farce set in the Pacific
Islands in the early days of World War
II. It was all about the A.W.O.L. antics of
two high-spirited marines, Burt Lancaster
(left) and Chuck Connors (centre), with
female interest supplied by Virginia Mayo
(right) as an out-of-work showgirl who
◁ hitches up with the marines for a lark.
Other parts went to Arthur Shields, Barry
Kelley, Leon Askin, Veola Vonn and Robert
Sweeney. Lancaster had a field day tearing
apart Hong Kong bar rooms, pilfering
yachts from under German agents' noses,
and singlehandedly taking on the entire
Japanese fleet. But he seemed to enjoy himself more than audiences did, and the film
added nothing to the prestige of its star.
Adapted by Earl Baldwin and Stanley Shap-
iro from a play by William M. Rankin, (screenplay by Edwin Blum), it was directed by
Arthur Lubin and produced by Sam Bischoff.

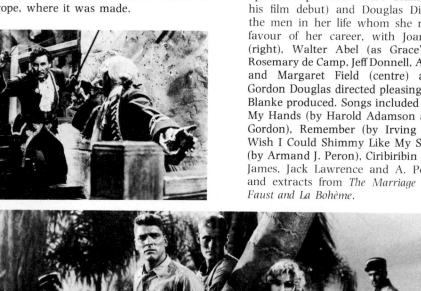

Exotic Oaxaca in Mexico, and its surrounding Zapotecan temples, were the chief sources of interest in **Plunder of the Sun**, a moderately diverting adventure in which a group of teasure-seekers set off in search of gold, silver and jade trinkets. Worth millions of dollars, the treasure was hidden some 350 years previously by the Zapotecans to prevent it falling into the hands of the Spanish. Glenn Ford (right) starred as an insurance adjuster out to make his fortune, with Diana Lynn as a blonde minx almost as much in love with Ford as she is with booze, Francis L. Sullivan (left) as a crooked collector, Sean McClory as an archaeologist, and Patricia Medina (centre) as a sultry Mexican beauty. It was written by Jonathan Latimer from a novel by David Dodge, directed by John Farrow and produced by Farrow and Robert Fellows for Wayne-Fellows Productions.

▽

John Wayne starred in, as well as produced (together with Robert Fellows, also for Wayne-Fellows Productions), **Island in the Sky**. He played a civilian pilot flying for the Army Transport Command who, together with his crew of four, is forced to crash-land in Labrador. At headquarters, Walter Abel instigates a search for Wayne (centre) and his crew, and sends out Andy Devine, James Arness, Lloyd Nolan and Allyn Joslyn to find them. It's a long haul, but in the end, they succeed. Written by Ernest K. Gann from his novel, the film made earnest and somewhat laboured attempts to philosophize about man and the elements, a miscalculation which almost sabotaged it. But a first rate cast, which also included Harry Carey Jr, Sean McClory (centre right), Hal Baylor (centre left), James Lydon (right), Wally Cassell (left) and Regis Toomey, overrode the pretensions, and the result was a suspenseful, well directed (by William A. Wellman) drama.

▽

△

John Gay's **The Beggar's Opera**, made in England and produced by Laurence Olivier and Herbert Wilcox, was a splendidly colourful blending of opera and film. The story of a highwayman, Macheath, (Olivier, right) who is betrayed for a £40 reward by the numerous women whose hearts he has broken in amorous forays, it was strongly cast with such heavyweight English character actors as Stanley Holloway, George Devine, Mary Clare, Athene Seyler and Hugh Griffith. Relative newcomer Dorothy Tutin (left) appeared as Macheath's pretty bride Polly Peachum, and Daphne Anderson as Lucy Locket, the jailer's alluring daughter. Adele Leigh, Jennifer Vyvyan, Joan Cross, John Cameron, Bruce Boyce and Edith Coates dubbed the singing voices, though Olivier sang for himself, in an adequate light baritone. Peter Brook's direction superbly captured the Hogarthian atmosphere of the period, as did Guy Green's beguiling Technicolor photography. It was written for the screen by Denis Cannan with additional dialogue by Christopher Fry.

Made in 3-D, **The Moonlighter**, from a screenplay by Niven Busch, and with Roy Rowland at the helm, was a sorry little Western about a cattle rustler who tries to mend his crooked ways. It starred Fred MacMurray (centre) as the rustler, Barbara Stanwyck and Ward Bond and, in secondary roles, featured William Ching, John Dierkes, Morris Ankrum, Jack Elam and Charles Halton. A J.B. Production, it was produced by Joseph Bernhard.

▽

With a cast that boasted Gary Cooper (right), Barbara Stanwyck, Anthony Quinn (left), Ruth Roman and Ward Bond, there were great expectations for **Blowing Wild**. But Philip Yordan's screenplay, involving banditry in the Mexican oilfields, as well as Miss Stanwyck's unrequited passion for 'Coop' (who sees through her wildcat ways and wants no part of them) was appalling. 'Why do you always fight against me?' asks Barbara, to which Cooper replies 'Because you're no good'. He might have been talking about the movie. It was directed by Hugo Fregonese and edited by Alan Crosland Jr, whose father directed the historic *Don Juan* in 1926. A United States Pictures Production, it was produced by Milton Sperling. Also cast were Ian MacDonald, Richard Karlan and Juan Garcia.

▽

◁ Clearly hoping for the kind of success MGM achieved with *Annie Get Your Gun* (1950), Doris Day was cast as the tomboy **Calamity Jane**, with Howard Keel co-starring as Wild Bill Hickok. Though at times too frenetic for comfort (Doris' performance came nearer to impersonating Betty Hutton than it did the legendary heroine of the title), it boasted a couple of good Sammy Fain-Paul Francis Webster songs and some eye-catching Technicolor photography (by Wilfrid M. Cline). David Butler directed from James O'Hanlon's screenplay, and the producer was William Jacobs. A popular success, it gave Doris Day (left) one of her biggest hit records ever with the Oscar-winning 'Secret Love'. Also in the cast were Allyn McLerie (right), Philip Carey, Dick Wesson, Paul Harvey, Chubby Johnson and Gale Robbins. Songs included: The Deadwood Stage, Higher Than A Hawk, Tis Harry I'm Plannin' To Marry, The Black Hills Of Dakota, Just Blew In From The Windy City and A Woman's Touch.

It takes a star to play a star, and as Keefe Brasselle (centre) was only an adequate performer who lacked star quality, his portrayal of Eddie Cantor in **The Eddie Cantor Story** was worthy but unconvincing. Caricature replaced characterization and the result was a routine rags-to-riches (or Henry Street-to-Hollywood) biopic which was more successful in its evocation of the golden age of vaudeville than in the reconstruction of Cantor's busy but undramatic life. Marilyn Erskine was cast as Cantor's wife Ida, whose only rival in love was the theatre, and Aline MacMahon was his grandmother. William Forrest played the ubiquitous Florenz Ziegfeld, Ann Doran and Hal March were Lillian and Gus Edwards, and Will Rogers Jr was Will Rogers Sr. Also in it were Arthur Franz, Gerald Mohr, Tristram Coffin (left) and Marie Windsor (right). It was written by Jerome Weidman, Ted Sherdeman and Sidney Skolsky (from a story by Skolsky, who also produced), and directed by Alfred E. Green. Songs included: Yes Sir, That's My Baby (by Joseph Meyer and B.G. De Sylva), If You Knew Susie and Making Whoopee (by Gus Kahn and Walter Donaldson), How Ya Gonna Keep 'Em Down On The Farm (by Walter Donaldson, Sam M. Lewis and Joe Young) and Now's The Time To Fall In Love (by Al Lewis and Al Shuman).

▽

△

A programme Western, **Thunder Over The Plains** starred a reliable Randolph Scott as the leader of a company of Texas cavalrymen. It's just after the Civil War, and Scott (right) is plagued by carpetbaggers on the one hand and by renegades on the other. His home life is equally fraught, with his wife (Phyllis Kirk) clearly not worthy of her man. And to make matters even worse, Lex Barker (left) as a rival captain, and Henry Hull as a colonel, are further thorns in his side. The thorn in the side of the film, however, was Russell Hughes' platitudinous screenplay which André de Toth's direction was unable to hide. The producer was David Weisbart. Charles McGraw, Elisha Cook Jr, Fess Parker, Hugh Sanders, Lane Chandler and James Brown were also in the cast.

A Lion Is In The Streets listed four Cagneys in the credits: James as star, sister Jeanne in a supporting role, and brothers William and Edward as producer and story editor respectively. Based on Adria Locke Langley's 1945 best-seller about an ambitious backwoods swamp-peddler turned politician who ruthlessly bestrides a corrupt path towards governorship, it gave Cagney (centre) ample opportunity to dominate the action which, despite a Southern accent that owed more to the Hudson than the Mississippi, he did. Raoul Walsh, directing from Luther Davis' screenplay, kept the narrative moving: Harry Stradling's Technicolor photography did much to evoke the atmosphere of the South, so did Franz Waxman's score. And making a favourable impression in a cast which also included Barbara Hale (right), Warner Anderson, Lon Chaney Jr, Frank McHugh and Mickey Simpson (left), was Anne Francis as a tempestuous blonde called Flamingo.

▽

◁ An adventure with a minuscule 'a', **The Diamond Queen** starred Fernando Lamas as a 17th century jeweller who braves India's 'swamps, savages and man-eating tigers' in his search for a blue diamond to adorn the crown of Louis XIV. Gilbert Roland appeared as Lamas' bodyguard, though the only body worth guarding belonged to Arlene Dahl (left) as Maya, the Queen of Nepal. Sheldon Leonard (right) was cast as Miss Dahl's evil husband, Great Mogul. Otto Englander wrote it and the director was John Brahm. A Melson Production, it was produced (in Super Cinecolor) by Frank Melford, with Edward L. Alperson Jr as associate.

Jane Wyman's (right) moving performance in the third screen version of Edna Ferber's Pulitzer prize-winning novel **So Big** alone justified the remake, and for at least three quarters of its running time, this celebrated story of a teacher in a country school who has devoted her life to her home and the raising of her adored son, was good, solid cinema. Only in the later Chicago sequences in which the son (Steve Forrest) now adult, detaches himself from his mother's influence and falls in love with an artist (Nancy Olson), did the film slip out of director Robert Wise's hitherto secure grasp. Sterling Hayden (left) was cast as Wyman's husband and Richard Beymer as a sensitive 12-year-old farm-boy pianist whom Wyman tenderly befriends. (Walter Coy took over the role after the pianist grows up). It was written by John Twist with roles for Elisabeth Fraser, Martha Hyer, Tommy Rettig, Jacques Aubuchon, Roland Winters and Ruth Swanson. Henry Blanke produced.

Hondo was an entertaining Western in 3-D and WarnerColor in which John Wayne (centre), riding dispatch for the US Cavalry circa 1874, comes across an abandoned wife (Geraldine Page, centre left) and her young son (Lee Aaker, left) at an isolated ranch. Against a background of Apache uprisings, the couple fall in love, but she refuses to desert her ranch for the safety of his arms. Reluctantly Wayne leaves her, but, on learning that the Apaches are up to their marauding tricks again, plans to return. On the way there he is ambushed by Page's husband (Leo Gordon) whom he kills. Moments later he himself is surrounded by Apaches... John Farrow directed it, and the screenplay was by James Edward Grant (from a story by Louis L'Amour). A Wayne-Fellows Production, it was produced by Robert Fellows with a cast that also included Ward Bond (right), Michael Pate, James Arness, Rodolfo Acosta, Paul Fix and Rayford Barnes.

Three Sailors And A Girl was an impoverished musical which attempted to marry off the Navy to Broadway in a story about the efforts of three sailors, an impecunious producer, and a singer to transform a nonentity of a revue into a Broadway smash. They succeed, of course, and the manner in which they do so formed the water-thin substance of Roland Kibbee and Devery Freeman's screenplay. It was based on George S. Kaufman's oft-filmed play *The Butter and Egg Man*, first transferred to the screen in 1928, then again in 1932 as *The Tenderfoot*, in 1937 as *Dance, Charlie, Dance* and in 1940 as *An Angel From Texas*. The film was directed — with a touch of desperation — by Roy Del Ruth, and produced by Sammy Cahn who, with Sammy Fain, also supplied the songs. Gene Nelson (centre left), Gordon MacRae (right) and Jack E. Leonard (left) were the sailors, Jane Powell (centre) was the girl, and Sam Levene (centre right) the impecunious producer. George Givot, Veda Ann Borg, Archer MacDonald and Raymond Greenleaf also appeared. It was photographed in Technicolor. Songs included: Show Me A Happy Woman And I'll Show You A Miserable Man, Kiss Me Or I'll Scream, I Made Myself A Promise, The Five Senses, Face To Face, You're But Oh So Right and I Got Butterflies.

1954

Despite the fact that eighteen of the year's twenty-one features were in colour – three in 3-D and eight in CinemaScope – Jack Warner realized that extra emphasis on production values was not the answer to the fast-encroaching menace of TV, now keeping people more at home. He believed in joining whatever he couldn't beat, and in 1954 entered TV production himself with a weekly, hour-long series of programmes called **Warner Bros. Presents.** His then son-in-law William T. Orr was in charge of production, and what the series amounted to was spin-offs of three earlier Warner Bros. features – **Casablanca, King's Row** and **Cheyenne**, the last-named proving to be so popular with viewers that it soon displaced the other two and became a series of its own which ran for seven successful seasons. On 19 January, Sydney Greenstreet, one of the studio's most stalwart character actors, died at the age of 74.

In one of the Academy of Motion Picture Arts and Science's major miscarriages of justice, they failed to award Judy Garland an Oscar for her extraordinary performance in **A Star Is Born**, giving it instead to Grace Kelly for **The Country Girl** (Paramount). James Mason was nominated for Best Actor in **A Star Is Born** but lost to Marlon Brando in **On The Waterfront** (Columbia), which was also voted Best Film of the year. Both Jan Sterling and Claire Trevor were nominated in the Best Supporting Actress category for their work in **The High And The Mighty**, but Eva Marie Saint won for **On The Waterfront. A Star Is Born** was nominated in three other categories – Best Art Director (Malcolm Bert, Gene Allen, Irene Sharaff and George James Hopkins), Best Scoring of a Musical Picture (Ray Heindorf) and Best Costume Design (Jean Louis, Mary Ann Nyberg and Irene Sharaff), but the only other Oscars won by the studio in 1954 were for Dimitri Tiomkin's score for **The High And The Mighty**, and for a one-reeler called **This Mechanical Age**. Tiomkin's theme song for **The High And The Mighty** was also nominated, but the winners were Jule Styne and Sammy Cahn for **Three Coins In The Fountain** (20th Century-Fox).

The New York Film Critics voted Grace Kelly actress of the year for her work in three films: **Rear Window** (Paramount), **The Country Girl** (Paramount) and **Dial M For Murder** (Warner Bros.). No Warner Bros. movies appeared on the *New York Times* Ten Best list, although their distinguished critic, Bosley Crowther, wrote that **A Star Is Born** would have made it if it had not been cut.

The studio's net profit for 1954 was $3,976,000, its big successes of the year being **Dial M For Murder**, **Hondo** and **The High And The Mighty**.

Gene Nelson (left) hung up his dancing shoes in **Crime Wave** and played an ex-con whose attempts to go straight are thwarted when, on discovering a former San Quentin inmate dying outside his home, he makes the mistake of telephoning his parole officer. Bernard Gordon and Richard Wormser's adaptation of John and Ward Hawkins' story *Criminal's Mark* (screenplay by Crane Wilbur) took a vivid and revealing look at the Los Angeles police force at work and the criminal environment in which they operate. The film's underlying theme – the difficulties and pressures experienced by ex-jailbirds in readjusting to civilian life – was forcefully conveyed under André de Toth's hard-hitting direction and in Nelson's surprisingly convincing central performance. Phyllis Kirk (centre) played Nelson's wife, and Sterling Hayden (right) was a sadistic sergeant, antagonistic to ex-cons on principle. Also cast were Ted de Corsia, Charles Buchinsky (Bronson), Jay Novello, James Bell, Ned Young and Dub Taylor. The producer was Bryan Foy.
▽

The studio's first film in CinemaScope was **The Command**, a par for the trail story which, on the elongated screen, looked bigger, better and bolder than it really was. The humdrum tale of a young medical recruit who finds himself in command of a troop-laden wagon train in dangerous Wyoming, it starred Guy Madison (right), with Joan Weldon (centre) as the woman in his life. James Whitmore (left), Carl Benton Reid, Ray Teal, Bob Nichols, Harvey Lembeck and Don Shelton were in it too; it was adapted from James Warner Bellah's novel by Samuel Fuller and written by Russell Hughes. David Butler directed the WarnerColor production, for producer David Weisbart.

◁ Tailor-made for the like-father-like-son talents of Will Rogers Jr, **The Boy From Oklahoma** was an easy-going, Michael Curtiz-directed Western. Rogers Jr (right) played a young law student who temporarily, and with surprising success, abandons his studies to become sheriff of a tough little town, in the process of which he unmasks the former sheriff's killer. Feminine interest came in the shape of Nancy Olson as the late sheriff's daughter, and Anthony Caruso (left) was the heavy, with other featured roles going to Lon Chaney, Wallace Ford, Clem Bevans, Merv Griffin. Louis Jean Heydt and Slim Pickens. The screenplay was written by Frank Davis and Winston Miller from a story by Michael Fessier, and the film was produced (in WarnerColor) by David Weisbart.

△

There was something comical rather than sinister about **Phantom of the Rue Morgue**, including Karl Malden's (centre) performance as the demented scientist-cum-zoo keeper who allows an equally demented ape to murder a few attractive women on his behalf. A remake of *Murders in the Rue Morgue* (Universal, 1932) it was scripted by Harold Medford and James R. Webb (from the story by Edgar Allan Poe) and featured Claude Dauphin (right) as a Police Inspector, Patricia Medina (as the one woman Malden's ape adores), and Steve Forrest (left) as her fiancé. Allyn McLerie, Veola Vonn, Dolores Dorn, Anthony Caruso, Merv Griffin and the Flying Zacchinis were also in it for director Roy Del Ruth, and Henry Blanke was responsible for the 3-D and WarnerColor production.

△

In **Riding Shotgun**, Randolph Scott faced the sort of situation which by now he could handle blindfolded. An inferior Western about a man (Scott, right) who, in order to prove he isn't the outlaw people say he is, singlehandedly has to stamp out the true villains of the piece, it was directed by André de Toth with a cast that included Wayne Morris, Joan Weldon (left), Joe Sawyer, James Millican, James Bell, Charles Buchinsky (Bronson) and Fritz Feld. Tom Blackburn wrote it (from a story by Kenneth Perkins) and it was produced (in Warner-Color) by Ted Sherdeman.

△

△

The incredible plot devised by Berman Swartz and Walter Doniger from Warden Clinton T. Duffy and Dean Jennings' *The San Quentin Story* and called **Duffy of San Quentin** (released in Britain as **Men Behind Bars**), had Louis Hayward (left) as a vicious, tough and thoroughly unmanageable con, being tamed by Joanne Dru (centre) as the prison's local nurse. Far-fetched to a degree, it lacked conviction on every level, with script, performances, and direction (by Walter Doniger) suffering from delusions of adequacy. Also featured were Paul Kelly (as Warden Duffy), Maureen O'Sullivan, George Macready, Horace MacMahon, Irving Bacon (right), Joel Fluellen, Joseph Turkel and Jonathan Hale. Berman Swartz and Walter Doniger produced.

In **Dial M For Murder**, director Alfred Hitchcock deliberately emphasized the property's stage origins by refusing to open out the action and, for the most part, confining events to a few rooms. The result was minor Hitchcock but gripping entertainment. All about a tennis player (Ray Milland, centre) who arranges to kill his wealthy wife (Grace Kelly, right) in order to inherit her money, it was stylishly performed by a cast that included Robert Cummings (left), John Williams, Anthony Dawson, Leo Britt, Patrick Allen and George Leigh. An Alfred Hitchcock Production, scripted by Frederick Knott from his own hit play, it was shot in 3-D and WarnerColor, but released almost everywhere in two dimensions.

Set on the Fijian island of Viti Levu, and photographed in Technicolor, **His Majesty O'Keefe**, loosely based on the derring-do escapades of a real-life South Sea island free-booter, gave Burt Lancaster (right) a marvellous opportunity to do all the things he did best. He played an American trader who, in 1870, journeys to the South Seas to teach the natives how to make the most of their natural resources. He introduces them to gunpowder, and plans to make his fortune by having the locals hand over the island's rich supply of copra to him. He doesn't have it all his own way though, and,
◁ in overcoming the obstacles created by Borden Chase and James Hill in their screenplay (from the novel by Lawrence Klingman and Gerald Green), is allowed to demonstrate, in vintage Lancaster fashion, that when it comes to looking after number one, no performer does it with more panache. Joan Rice co-starred as the half-caste woman he marries, with André Morell (left), Abraham Sofaer, Archie Savage, Benson Fong, Tessa Prendergast and Lloyd Berrell in other featured roles. It was energetically directed by Byron Haskin and the producer was Harold Hecht. Song: Esmerelda Isle.

The enervating story of a troupe of theatrical entertainers stranded in Miami, **Lucky Me**, the studio's first CinemaScope musical, was only partially redeemed by the gusto with which Doris Day (left) attacked her material. In the end, however, the material attacked back, leaving such talented performers as Robert Cummings, Phil Silvers (centre front), Eddie Foy Jr (centre), Nancy Walker (right) and Martha Hyer in search of a vehicle – preferably one which they could all use to make a quick getaway. The script was by James O'Hanlon, Robert O'Brien and Irving Elinson (from a story by O'Hanlon); Jack Donohue directed it, and the producer was Henry Blanke. It was filmed in WarnerColor. Songs included: Lucky Me, Superstition Song, I Speak To The Stars, Take A Memo To The Moon, Bluebells Of Broadway, High Hopes and Men (by Sammy Fain and Paul Francis Webster).

▽

△

△

Ring Of Fear was an indifferent circus melodrama in which a maniac ringmaster contrives a series of 'accidents' in order to terrorize Clyde Beatty and various members of his troupe. Mickey Spillane (right), playing Mickey Spillane, singlehandedly uncovered the villain, but as engineered by scenarists James Edward Grant, Paul Fix and Philip MacDonald, his sleuthing left audiences stonily unmoved. Sean McClory (left) was the evil ringmaster, with other roles going to Pat O'Brien, Marian Carr, John Bromfield, Gonzalez-Gonzalez, Jack Stang (centre) and Emmett Lynn. In addition, twelve of Clyde Beatty's Circus acts were featured, constituting the only real entertainment value in an otherwise ponderous effort. A Wayne-Fellows Production in CinemaScope and WarnerColor, it was produced by Robert Fellows and directed by James Edward Grant.

CinemaScope and WarnerColor were powerless against the numbing ineptitude of John Twist's screenplay for, and David Butler's clumsy direction of, **King Richard and the Crusaders**, a $3,000,000 excursion into medievalism in style as well as in content. George Sanders (lying down) played Richard the Lion Heart, relative newcomer Laurence Harvey (centre left) was the brave Scottish knight who warns the King of impending danger, an embarrassed-looking brown-faced Rex Harrison (centre) was cast as Saladin, and Virginia Mayo (second left) was Richard's cousin Lady Edith with whom Saladin, in disguise, falls in love. It was based on Sir Walter Scott's novel *The Talisman* but you would never have known it. Also in it were Robert Douglas, Michael Pate, Paula Raymond (fourth left), Antony Eustrel (third left), Henry Cordon and Wilton Graff. Henry Blake produced.

The High And The Mighty was the first ▷ CinemaScope film to demonstrate that the new process could work as well in confined spaces as it could in the great out-doors. It also preceded, by sixteen years, the air-borne disaster movies of the seventies and, as such, was ahead of its time. For the rest it was assembly-line entertainment in which an assorted group of passengers on a flight between Honolulu and San Francisco come perilously close to catastrophe when the plane loses an engine. John Wayne (centre) was the co-pilot, Robert Stack (right) the understandably jittery captain. Wally Brown (centre left) played an incompetent navigator; William Campbell (left) was the fourth member of the crew, and Doe Avedon (centre right) the stewardess. Passengers included Laraine Day and John Howard as a married couple about to get a divorce, Robert Newton as a theatrical impresario, David Brian as a faint-hearted playboy, Paul Kelly as an atomic scientist and Claire Trevor as a woman who has been around and seen it all. Also going along for the ride were Jan Sterling, Phil Harris, Sidney Blackmer, Julie Bishop, Ann Doran, John Qualen and Joy Kim. It was written, with all the clichés intact, by Ernest K. Gann (from his best-selling novel) and directed to formula by William A. Wellman. It was photographed in WarnerColor and was a Wayne-Fellows Production.

Played absolutely straight, as all self-respecting science-fiction efforts should be, **Them!** was a so-so chiller about an invasion of twelve-foot killer ants (illustrated). Edmund Gwenn was cast as a top entomologist; Joan Weldon as his researcher daughter. Written by Ted Sherdeman from a story by George Worthington Yates, and directed by Gordon Douglas for producer David Weisbart, it also featured James Whitmore, James Arness, Onslow Stevens, Sean McClory, Fess Parker and Olin Howland.

Duel in the Jungle, a safari melodrama, was ▷ a catalogue of missed opportunities. Apart from squandering the talents of its leading players, it failed to realize the potential of its African setting and was little more than another swampy romp in the Dark Continent. Dana Andrews (centre) played an insurance investigator who, learning of the death of a large policy holder (David Farrar), pursues the man's wife (Jeanne Crain, left) to Africa. Of course, Farrar isn't dead, and his presence supplied the film with what little conflict it had. Made on location in Rhodesia and at Elstree Studios in England, the film also featured Patrick Barr, Michael Mataka (right), George Coulouris and Mary Merrall. Written by Sam Marx and T.J. Morrison (from a story by S.K. Kennedy) for producers Marcel Hellman and Tony Owen, and directed by George Marshall, it was a Moulin Production, in Technicolor, released by Warner Bros. in the US.

Francis Webster and Sammy Fain), Someone To Watch Over Me (by George and Ira Gershwin), Just One Of Those Things (by Cole Porter), and One For My Baby (by Harold Arlen and Johnny Mercer).

One of the most impressive screen performances of the decade was James Dean's in **East Of Eden**. The film displayed a remarkable welding of actor to role, or vice versa, that was responsible for Dean's elevation from rebellious Broadway actor to spokesman for the 'generation-gap' youth of his era. Dean's performance as the un-loved Cal in Elia Kazan's penetrating film of John Steinbeck's novel, went (as far as his devout followers were concerned) beyond acting. To them Dean (right) was far more than an

Hall Bartlett wrote, produced and directed ▷ **Unchained**, based on Kenyon J. Scudder's book *Prisoners Are People*. Scudder was the supervisor of the California Institute for Men (Chino), a wall-less prison whose corrective methods were among the most lenient and advanced in the world. Dedicated to the 'honour system' practised within, the film combined fact with fiction, the former element being the more successful of the two. Several case-histories were offered as evidence of the prison's efficacy, the inmates being played by Elroy Hirsch (left), Todd Duncan, Johnny Johnston, Jerry Paris and John Qualen – stereotypes all. Still, for the glimpses it offered of a new approach to a continuing social problem (and one which has occupied Warner Bros. almost since the company's inception), it was certainly not without value. A Hall Bartlett production, it also featured Chester Morris, Barbara Hale, Peggy Knudsen, Tim Considine, Kathryn Grant and Bill Kennedy (right).

◁ Scenarists James Warner Bellah and John Twist bowdlerized Andrew Geer's World War II novel **The Sea Chase**, managing to

1955

For the first time since 1951 a Warner Bros. film, **Mister Roberts**, was nominated by the Academy for Best Picture of the year, but it lost to the modest but effective Hecht-Lancaster-United Artists production **Marty**. A charismatic newcomer named James Dean reached Hollywood, via the Broadway stage, and made a strong impression in **East Of Eden** and **Rebel Without A Cause** (**Giant** was released posthumously in 1956, after Dean's death on 30 September 1955, in a car accident on Route 466), and almost overnight became the mouthpiece for his generation. He was nominated for Best Actor for his performance in **East Of Eden**, but the award went to Ernest Borgnine for **Marty**. Jo Van Fleet, also in **East Of Eden**, was more fortunate, winning the Oscar for Best Supporting Actress. Peggy Lee was nominated for this award for **Pete Kelly's Blues**, as was Natalie Wood for **Rebel Without A Cause**. The Best Supporting Actor Oscar went to another newcomer from New York, Jack Lemmon, for **Mister Roberts**. Sal Mineo was also nominated for **Rebel Without A Cause**. Nicholas Ray was nominated for Best Motion Picture Story for **Rebel Without A Cause**, but lost to Daniel Fuchs for **Love Me Or Leave Me** (MGM), while Paul Osborn received a nomination in the Best Screenplay category for **East Of Eden**. The winner was Paddy Chayefsky for **Marty**. The Best Story and Screenplay Oscar went to William Ludwig and Sonya Levien for **Interrupted Melody** (MGM), though Milton Sperling and Emmet Lavery were nominated for **The Court Martial Of Billy Mitchell**, and Melville Shavelson and Jack Rose for **The Seven Little Foys**. The *New York Times* listed **Mister Roberts** as one of the Ten Best films of the year, but there were no New York Film Critics awards for the studio. **A Star Is Born** (released in October 1954), **Battle Cry**, **Dragnet** and **Mister Roberts** were the big moneymakers for 1955, contributing to the year's net profit of $4,002,000.

△

The New York City Anti-Crime Committee vouched for the overall authenticity of **New York Confidential**, and who are we to argue? A hard-hitting, informative, slightly unsavoury but thoroughly enjoyable gangster flick, its theme was the rise and fall of a ruthless crime syndicate. Not exactly a new concept in film-making, it was, nonetheless, expertly directed by Russell Rouse, who (working from a trenchant screenplay which he and Clarence Greene fashioned from a book by Jack Lait and Lee Mortimer), more than delivered the goods, turning a tired old plot into exciting, often vibrant cinema. Broderick Crawford played the Mr Big of the syndicate, Richard Conte (left) was his henchman and Anne Bancroft (right) his daughter. Also in it were Marilyn Maxwell, J. Carrol Naish, Onslow Stevens, Barry Kelley, Mike Mazurki and Ian Keith. A Challenge Production, it was produced by Clarence Greene.

Battle Cry, photographed in CinemaScope ▷ and WarnerColor, was a 147 minute long tribute to the US Marines in the Pacific. And what a fun-loving, likeable bunch of men most of them turned out to be! Raoul Walsh's direction omitted no clichés in the screenplay which Leon Uris fashioned from his own novel, and the result was a lavishly-mounted, predictable and thoroughly entertaining contribution to the guts-and-glory school of war drama, which its stellar cast turned into an $8,000,000 box-office winner. Van Heflin played the much loved colonel who is killed by the Japs, Aldo Ray (left) was the traditional ladies' man, Tab Hunter (centre right) the All-American college kid, and James Whitmore (right) the no-nonsense sergeant who

'55

△

There was as much drama off-screen as there was comedy on it in **Mister Roberts**. Assigned the task of recreating Joshua Logan and Thomas Heggen's Broadway hit about life on a small naval cargo vessel floating somewhere between the islands of Tedium and Ennui in the Pacific, director John Ford insisted that Henry Fonda (left), who created the role of Roberts on Broadway, repeat his characterization for the screen. Jack Warner wanted William Holden or Marlon Brando, but Ford was adamant and Fonda was signed. A week into shooting, however, Ford and Fonda feuded, resulting in Ford's being replaced by Mervyn LeRoy. After that it was plain sailing for *The Reluctant* and her crew and, on its release, the film opened to both critical and public

Jump Into Hell, the story of Dien Bien Phu, was another earnest, if uninspired, attempt to recreate history with the help of newsreel footage. Written by Irving Wallace, it starred Jacques Sernas (left), Kurt Kasznar, Peter Van Eyck and Norman Dupont as four officers who, for reasons of their own, decide to go to Dien Bien Phu at the height of hostilities. The director was David Butler who, despite the real-life film clips at his disposal, delivered a film that rarely conveyed the enormity of the Indo-Chinese battle, and gave the impression that only a mere handful of men (rather than the 12,000 who actually took part) were involved. Marcel Dalio, Lawrence Dobkin, Pat Blake, Joseph Waring (right), Irene Montwill and Alberto Morin were also in it, and it

△

John Wayne (illustrated) continued to wage a battle against the forces of Communism in **Blood Alley**, a vigorously directed (by William A. Wellman) action picture, in which hero Wayne, after being freed by local villagers from a Communist prison in Amoy, takes his rescuers (all 189 of them) aboard a ferry-boat on a 300-mile freedom voyage to Hong Kong. What befalls Wayne and his passengers formed the basis of A.S. Fleischman's screenplay (from his novel) which, while not without its incidental thrills and moments of suspense, hardly offered audiences a new experience in danger. Still, Wellman's approximation of the Formosa Straits (filmed at China Camp in San Rafael near San Francisco) lent just the right degree of authenticity, and with Lauren Bacall (at her most appealing as the daughter of a doctor killed by the Reds) providing the love interest, there was little cause for complaint. A Batjac Production, it was filmed in CinemaScope and WarnerColor, and also featured Paul Fix, Joy Kim, Berry Kroeger, Mike Mazurki and Anita Ekberg.

A British film, made in England by Associated British Picture Corporation, and released in the US by Warner Bros., **The Dam Busters** was a splendid war drama, based on Paul Brickhill's book of the same name and on Wing Commander Gibson's *Enemy Coast Ahead*. The stirring story of the circumstances leading to the R.A.F.'s historic assault on the Ruhr dams in 1943 (enhanced by actual newsreel footage of the raid itself), it combined exciting action sequences with a human story involving Richard Todd (illustrated) as the leader of the attack, and Michael Redgrave as the scientist-inventor whose idea it all was. Michael Anderson directed it, and his cast included Ursula Jeans, Basil Sydney, Patrick Barr, Ernest Clark and Derek Farr.

Director Howard Hawks employed 9,787 extras to appear in one of the many spectacular scenes that filled the Cinema-Scope screen in **Land of the Pharaohs** and, visually at any rate, he emerged with a stunner. He was less successful in his deployment of scenarists William Faulkner, Harry Kurnitz and Harold Jack Bloom whose screenplay, though literate enough, was basically commonplace. Jack Hawkins the British star (left), was top-cast as Khufu the Pharaoh, Joan Collins (right) appeared as Khufu's sexy second wife, and James Robertson Justice as Vashtar, the slave architect who agrees to design a pyramid for Khufu in return for the freedom of his people. Dewey Martin, Alexis Minotis, Luisa Boni, Sydney Chaplin, James Hayter and Piero Giagnoni were also featured in this sumptuous eye-catcher which was photographed in WarnerColor. A Continental Company Ltd. Production, it was also produced by Howard Hawks.

By signing Liberace for his screen starring debut in **Sincerely Yours**, a remake of the George Arliss vehicle *The Man Who Played God* (1932), Jack Warner fervently believed that he would be providing a service to the millions of middle-aged mums in America who had taken the flamboyant pianist to their bosoms. But he was wrong. Either there weren't as many fans as he had imagined, or an already larger-than-life personality was simply too much to take in close-up. Whichever it was, the result was a financial and artistic failure. The story of a concert-pianist who suddenly loses his hearing, it suffered from two serious drawbacks: (a) Liberace (left) was no Beethoven and (b) nor was he George Arliss. Director Gordon Douglas did his best to salvage what he could from Irving Wallace's absurd re-working of the Jules Eckert Goodman play, but to no avail. Joanne Dru co-starred as Liberace's faithful secretary; Dorothy Malone (right) was his fiancée. Others involved in the Henry Blanke production (for International Artists Ltd) were Alex Nicol, William Demarest, Lori Nelson and Lurene Tuttle.

A remake of *The Mouthpiece* (1932), ▷ **Illegal** heralded Edward G. Robinson's return to the studio (not counting a guest appearance in *It's A Great Feeling*, 1949) for the first time since 1948 in his starring role in *Key Largo*. In this not particularly auspicious come-back, he played a district attorney turned defence lawyer who finds himself vacillating between the right and wrong sides of the law. Robinson (left) was his usual, hard-bitten, impressive self, with Nina Foch (right), Hugh Marlowe, Robert Ellenstein, DeForest Kelley and Jayne Mansfield offering average support. W.R. Burnett and James R. Webb wrote the screenplay (based on Frank J. Collins' play *The Mouthpiece*), the director was Lewis Allen, and the producer was Frank P. Rosenberg.

The Qualities evinced by James Dean (illustrated) in *East of Eden* – lonely, misunderstood and discontented – reached their fullest expression in his second film. **Rebel Without A Cause**, directed by Nicholas Ray, whose distillation of the period's fashions, slang and mores was as much sociology as it was entertainment. A hitherto neglected subject – the problems of postwar youth and the very real generation gap that existed between parents and their children – it burst forcefully onto the screen and consolidated Dean's stature as the country's most important new young actor since Brando, as well as affirming his status as a cult hero. It also gave erstwhile child-star Natalie Wood a chance to show that she was no longer just a pretty little girl, but an attractive young woman with talent. And, as Dean's hero-worshipping friend Plato, Sal Mineo made quite an impression too. Dean's parents, however, (Jim Backus and Ann Doran), were treated (and played) as caricatures, which unbalanced the film slightly, though doubtless scenarist Stewart Stern deliberately intended the bias. Also featuring Corey Allen, William Hopper, Dennis Hopper, Rochelle Hudson and Edward Platt, **Rebel Without A Cause**, produced by David Weisbart in Cinema-Scope and Warner Color, was one of the year's big successes, and one of the decade's most powerful statements on contemporary youth.

The late Captain Joseph McConnell was a brave airman whose love of aviation resulted in his becoming America's first triple-jet ace in the Korean war. A pilot *extraordinaire*, his life-style was affectionately recreated in **The McConnell Story** (released in Britain as **Tiger In The Sky**), with Alan Ladd (left) cast as the titular hero, and June Allyson (centre), fixed into a mould she seemed unable to break at this stage of her career, playing his loving, understanding spouse. Ted Sherdeman and Sam Rolfe's screenplay, which showed McConnell as a navigator aboard a B-17 during World War II, as a peace-time white-collar worker with a desk job, and finally as an active participant in post-war jet aviation, was more at home when the action was above cloud-level than when it remained on terra firma, with CinemaScope and WarnerColor helping to turn the aerial photography into a thing of beauty. James Whitmore (right), Frank Faylen, Robert Ellis and Sarah Selby were also featured; it was directed by Gordon Douglas, and Henry Blanke produced.

A remake of *High Sierra* (1941), **I Died A Thousand Times** indeed died a thousand times. Stepping into Humphrey Bogart's shoes as the hunted gunman who meets a memorable end atop a mountain peak, Jack Palance seemed merely passé, while Shelley Winters (right), Lori Nelson, Gonzalez-Gonzalez, Lon Chaney and Earl Holliman (centre) were hardly supportive in other featured roles. CinemaScope and Warner-Color added little to W.R. Burnett's screenplay (from his novel), with Stuart Heisler's direction at odds with the dated material. It was produced by Willis Goldbeck, whose cast included Perry Lopez, Richard Davalos, Lee Marvin (left), Howard St. John, Olive Carey, Ralph Moody, James Millican, Bill Kennedy, Dennis Hopper and Mae Clarke.

In **Pete Kelly's Blues**, Jack Webb (left) was as tough and determined a trumpeter as ever pitted his wits against a few Prohibition-era gangsters. And although in the end he scored a victory against Kansas mobster Edmond O'Brien, it was at best a Pyrrhic victory for, in the process, he threw away the chance to direct, produce and star in what could have, on the evidence of the available talent, been an effective, hard-hitting musical drama. There was a great deal of violence for the sake of violence in Richard L. Breen's screenplay, and not nearly enough emphasis on the musical side of things — especially with such talents as Peggy Lee (right) and Ella Fitzgerald in attendance. Also cast were Janet Leigh, Andy Devine, Lee Marvin and Martin Milner. A Mark VII Ltd. Production, it was photographed in WarnerColor and Cinema-Scope, and had a catchy title song by Sammy Cahn and Ray Heindorf. Songs included: Pete Kelly's Blues (by Cahn and Heindorf), Sing A Rainbow and He Needs Me (by Arthur Hamilton), Somebody Loves Me, Sugar (by Maceo Pinkard, Sidney Mitchell and Edna Alexander), I Never Knew and Hard-Hearted Hannah (by Jack Yellen, Bob Bigelow and Charles Bates), Bye Bye Blackbird and What Can I Say After I Say I'm Sorry.

Target Zero was the story of a group of American soldiers (the usual bunch of stereotypes, as it turned out) plus three members of a British tank crew who, when their infantry patrol is cut off behind enemy lines, make their way to an isolated outpost and find the rest of their company killed. Sam Rolfe's screenplay, from a story by James Warner Bellah, contrived a romance between Lieutenant Richard Conte (left) and Peggie Castle (right), the latter tagging along for the ride in a really very unlikely piece of plotting. No more than a routine action picture, it also featured Charles Bronson, Richard Stapley, L.Q. Jones, Chuck Connors, John Anderson, Terence de Marney, Strother Martin (centre) and John Dennis. Harmon Jones directed it, and the producer was David Weisbart.

In 1925, General Billy Mitchell faced a military trial in Washington for his public pronouncements that the Army and the Navy were incompetent, criminally negligent and almost treasonable in their lackadaisical approach to the building up of air power after World War I. He was convicted of insubordination and suspended for five years. The highly dramatic trial formed the basis of **The Court Martial of Billy Mitchell** (released in Britain as **One-Man Mutiny**) which, like most trial films, was a sure-fire success especially with Gary Cooper (right) playing Mitchell. Away from the courtroom, however, the United States Pictures production (in CinemaScope and WarnerColor) suffered from a screenplay by Milton Sperling and Emmet Lavery which, though nominated for an Oscar, had more than its quota of longueurs and did little to characterize the central figure in the drama. Cooper's performance, while predictably sturdy, tended towards monotony, and Otto Preminger's direction lacked force. There were no complaints, however, about the strong supporting cast which included Rod Steiger as the prosecuting lawyer, Charles Bickford as the reactionary General Guthrie and Ralph Bellamy (centre) as a Congressman. Elizabeth Montgomery (the 22-year-old daughter of Robert) making her film debut, played the wife of a commander, with other roles going to Fred Clark, James Daly (left), Jack Lord, Peter Graves, Darren McGavin and Charles Dingle. The producer was Milton Sperling.

1956

After the success of their TV series *Cheyenne*, Warner Bros. added four more Western series to the list: *Maverick, Colt.45, Sugarfoot* and *Lawman*, and it would not be long before the other major studios would do the same. The Warner Bros. commitment to TV was complete, and in 1956 Jack Warner decided to sell all the films the studio had made up to 1949 to United Artists Television for $21,000,000. (Twentieth Century-Fox sold their library for $30,000,000, Paramount theirs for $50,000,000.)

Warner Bros. biggest film of the year was **Giant**, and it was nominated by the Academy for Best Picture. The winner, however, was **Around The World In Eighty Days** (Todd-United Artists). Both James Dean and Rock Hudson were nominated for an Oscar in the Best Actor category for their work in **Giant**, but Yul Brynner won for **The King And I** (20th Century-Fox). Mercedes McCambridge also received an Oscar nomination (Best Supporting Actress) for **Giant**, but lost to Dorothy Malone in **Written On The Wind** (Universal). In the same category Mildred Dunnock was nominated for **Baby Doll** and Eileen Heckart and Patty McCormack for **The Bad Seed**. Nancy Kelly was nominated as Best Actress for **The Bad Seed**, but the winner was Ingrid Bergman for **Anastasia** (20th Century-Fox). **Giant** received six other nominations: Best Director (George Stevens), Best Screenplay adaptation (Fred Guiol, Ivan Moffat), Best Art Direction for a Colour Film (Boris Leven, Ralph S. Hurst), Best Score for a Dramatic or Comedy Film (Dimitri Tiomkin), Best Editing (William Hornbeck, Philip W. Anderson and Fred Bohanan) and Best Costume Design for a Colour Film (Moss Mabry and Marjorie Best). George Stevens won for Best Director. Tennessee Williams was nominated for his screenplay for **Baby Doll**, but James Poe, John Farrow and S.J. Perelman won for **Around The World In Eighty Days**; and in the Best Cinematography (Black-and-White) category, Boris Kaufman was nominated for **Baby Doll** and Hal Rosson for **The Bad Seed** but the winner was Joseph Ruttenberg for **Somebody Up There Likes Me** (MGM). A short subject called **Crashing The Water Barrier** won an Oscar for Best One-Reeler.

Giant was considered one of the year's Ten Best by the *New York Times*, while the New York Film Critics named John Huston best director of the year for his work on **Moby Dick**.

The company's net profit for the year was $2,098,152, the studio's top money-makers being **The Court-Martial Of Billy Mitchell** (released December, 1955), **Moby Dick**, **Helen Of Troy**, **Rebel Without A Cause** (released October, 1955), and **The Searchers**.

In May, 1956, the majority of Warner holdings held by Jack, Harry and Albert Warner were sold to a group headed by Serge Semenenko of the First National Bank of Boston. The three brothers, however, remained directors of the Group, each holding 10% of the present stock with Jack continuing as studio chief. Some 800,000 shares changed hands for an estimated $20,000,000.

CinemaScope and WarnerColor came to the aid of **Helen of Troy**, whose edge-to-edge spectacle was its chief selling point. As long as the Greek and Trojan warriors were in full battle cry, hurling spears, scaling walls and assaulting the ramparts with balls of fire, the film justified its existence. Its more tranquil moments, however, evoked a comic strip rather than Homer's *Iliad*, with Jacques Sernas (centre right, as Paris), and Rossana Podesta (right, as Helen) worth their weight in eye-shadow. An inept screenplay by John Twist and Hugh Gray, from an adaptation by Gray and N. Richard Nash, in no way captured the epic sweep of the story, leaving experienced players such as Sir Cedric Hardwicke (Priam), Stanley Baker (Achilles), Niall MacGinnis (Menelaus), Nora Swinburne (left, as Hecuba), Robert Douglas (Agamemnon), Torin Thatcher (Ulysses) and Harry Andrews (Hector) stranded in search of some speakable dialogue. Also in the cast were Brigitte Bardot, Janette Scott (centre left), Ronald Lewis, Eduardo Ciannelli, Marc Lawrence and Maxwell Reed. Robert Wise was responsible for the indifferent direction of the film, which was made at the Cinecitta studios in Rome.
▽

△
A wordy TV spin-off, **Our Miss Brooks** starred Eve Arden (right) as a middle-aged school teacher who sets her sights on a biology professor (Robert Rockwell, left) but finds herself competing with the professor's mamma — to whose apron-strings he is firmly tied. Al Lewis (who also directed) and Joseph Quillan's screenplay (from an idea by Robert Mann) was all talk and little action; the cast included Gale Gordon, Don Porter, Jane Morgan, Richard Crenna and Nick Adams, and the producer was David Weisbart.

Little Tina Rona (Patty McCormack, illustrated), was more than just precocious. When, for example, she lost a writing award at school to a classmate, she took her revenge by cold-bloodedly murdering him during a picnic. And anyone who disagreed that it was simply an accident was bumped off too. Based on the play by Maxwell Anderson and with a screenplay by John Lee Mahin, **The Bad Seed** was a chilling study of evil and, like evil itself, totally mesmeric. The film's climax, in which the child's mother (Nancy Kelly), realizing that the monster she has spawned must, herself, die, was cleverly handled by Mervyn LeRoy, the director, who, in the film's closing credits, sweetened the pill somewhat by allowing his cast, as if in a stage production, to take a 'screen call', with young Patty being put across her mother's knee and soundly spanked. In the Broadway production, the child remains unpunished for her sins, an ending which the Johnston office (Eric Johnston succeeded censor Will Hays in 1945) would not tolerate in the screen version. The Mervyn LeRoy production also featured Eileen Heckart and Henry Jones (who, like Nancy Kelly and Patty McCormack, had played their roles on Broadway) as well as William Hopper, Paul Fix and Jesse White.

Hell On Frisco Bay was a crime melodrama given a patina of style by Edward G. Robinson (right) who, repeating some of his *Little Caesar* mannerisms, made a meal of his role as Victor Amato, a ruthless waterfront hood responsible for framing ex-cop Alan Ladd (left). The inevitable confrontation between the two men and the ensuing battle for survival, gave the film its main narrative thrust and, although Robinson's charisma made mincemeat of his popular co-star's attempts to assert his own personality, audiences didn't seem to mind one bit. Here was a rare chance to see vintage Robinson – in WarnerColor and CinemaScope yet! – and that was all that mattered. As for co-stars Joanne Dru, William Demarest, Paul Stewart (centre) and Fay Wray – they hardly got a look in. Frank Tuttle directed from a punchy screenplay by Sydney Boehm and Martin Rackin. The associate producer (for Jaguar Productions) was George C. Bertholon.

The events that occur when a group of mid-European border villagers find, to their dismay, that their river has changed its course, leaving them on the Communist-dominated side of the stream, formed the basis of **The River Changes**. The film was a virulent and highly emotional piece of anti-Communist propaganda written, produced and directed by Owen Crump, and made in Germany. The cast included Rosanna Rory (left) as a pretty young village girl and Harald Maresch (right) as the border guard with whom she becomes romantically involved. Renate Mannhardt, Henry Fisher, Jaspar V. Oertzen, Otto Friebel and Rene Magron were also in it.

An undistinguished prison melodrama, **The Steel Jungle** was just another glimpse at life behind bars, which featured Ted de Corsia as a powerful racketeer whose stay in the jail in no way diminishes his outside criminal activities. Also cast were Perry Lopez (centre) as one of his minions, and Leo Gordon, Kay Kuter and Richard Karlan as his evil henchmen inside. Beverly Garland, Walter Abel, Kenneth Tobey, Fred Graham (left), Charles Crane (right) and Allison Hayes were also in it; the script was by Walter Doniger who also directed, and the producer was David Weisbart.

Half of the 121 minute running-time of **Serenade** was devoted to star Mario Lanza (right) singing operatic arias, folk songs, and a couple of new Nicholas Brodszky-Sammy Cahn numbers designed for the hit parade; the other half was given over to the story (from the 1937 novel by James M. Cain) of a Californian vineyard worker's rise to operatic eminence and the two women – played by Joan Fontaine and Sarita Montiel – who occupy his private life. Miss Fontaine appeared as a wealthy society patroness who jilts the tenor when something better comes along; Miss Montiel was the Mexican señorita who weds him. Photographed in WarnerColor, the film was as good to look at as it was to listen to (the location shots of San Miguel de Allende in Mexico were particularly attractive), and found a ready and enthusiastic public. It was written by Ivan Goff, Ben Roberts and John Twist, who eliminated the more outspoken elements of Cain's novel, well directed by Anthony Mann, and given a solid production by Henry Blanke. Also featured were Vincent Price as a suave impresario, Harry Bellaver (left) as Lanza's manager and Joseph Calleia as his vocal coach. Songs included: Serenade, My Destiny, O Paradiso, Torna A Sorrento, Ave Maria and numerous operatic excerpts.

Goodbye, My Lady, a gentle drama, starred Brandon de Wilde (right) as a 14-year-old orphan who lives in the Mississippi swamps with an elderly uncle (Walter Brennan, left). De Wilde befriends a stray dog whom he calls Lady, only to find, after becoming strongly attached to the animal, that it belongs to someone else, and that there is a large reward on offer for its return. Young Brandon, torn between his love for Lady and his conscience, finally decides to return the hound to its rightful owner and, in the process, becomes a man. It was appealingly written by Sid Fleischman from a story by James Street, and featured Phil Harris (as a benevolent store-keeper), Sidney Poitier, William Hopper and Louise Beavers. William A. Wellman (who also produced for Batjac Productions), directed lovingly.

A leather-clad Clayton Moore (centre) starred as the Lone Ranger in **The Lone Ranger**, a Jack Wrather Production based on the TV and radio series. Jay Silverheels (foreground centre) played Tonto, with Lyle Bettger cast as the villain of the piece whose antisocial behaviour in pushing Red Indians off their reservation so he can lay his greedy hands on a mountain-full of ore, triggers off most of the action. Of which, incidentally, there was plenty. Stuart Heisler's direction kept Herb Meadow's screenplay moving briskly, and his cast included Bonita Granville (as Bettger's badly-treated wife) Perry Lopez, Robert Wilke, John Pickard (right) and Beverly Washburn. It was photographed in WarnerColor and Produced by Willis Goldbeck.

Two of Hollywood's best looking young ▷
stars, Tab Hunter (right) and Natalie Wood
(left), were teamed for **The Burning Hills**
(CinemaScope and WarnerColor), an entertaining Western which, under Stuart Heisler's resourceful direction traversed old
territory with a certain freshness. All about
a young rancher (Hunter) who clashes with
the son (Skip Homeier) of the cattle baron
who killed his brother, and is befriended by a
half-Mexican, half-Yankee girl (Wood), it
was written by Irving Wallace from a novel
by Louis L'Amour, and featured Eduard
Franz, Earl Holliman, Claude Akins, Ray Teal
and Frank Puglia. Richard Whorf produced.

△

A successor to *The Sea Around Us*, Irwin
Allen's **The Animal World** (illustrated) was a
vastly enjoyable documentary that successfully (if superficially) attempted to encapsu-
late two billion years of evolution into a
mere 80 minutes of screen time, from the
one-celled paramecium to a charging rhino.
Models of the Tyrannosaurus Rex and the
Brontosaurus were trotted out in a 12-
minute sequence to illustrate the prehistoric
era when such assertive creatures roamed
the earth. Writer-producer-director Allen
gathered his footage from 27 different
countries; the sequences requiring special
animation were the work of Ray Harryhausen; Arthur S. Rhoades was in charge of
special effects and the narrators were
Theodore von Eltz and John Storm. It was
photographed in Technicolor and was a
Windsor Production.

△

A lively adventure story which starred Alan
Ladd (left) and Lloyd Nolan (right) as a
couple of rival gun-runners *en route* to Cuba
prior to the Spanish-American war, **Santiago**
(released in Britain as **The Gun Runner**)
with its deft screenplay by Martin Rackin
and John Twist (story by Rackin), and
direction to match by Gordon Douglas, was
good clean fun. Also in the cast were Chill
Wills as the loquacious captain of the
paddle-wheel steamer on which the gun-
runners are travelling, Rossana Podesta
(centre), Paul Fix, L.Q. Jones, Frank De Kova
and George J. Lewis. It was photographed in
WarnerColor and WarnerScope and the
producer was Martin Rackin.

Jane Wyman gave her most affecting
performance since *Johnny Belinda* as a
rather plain Manhattan secretary in **Miracle
In The Rain**. The story, schmaltzy but
moving, tells of the brief but idyllic love
affair she has with Van Johnson (centre) a
reporter G.I. from Tennessee who, shortly
after the couple first meet (in the rain) is
killed in action. He 'returns', however,
when Wyman (left), seriously ill, makes her
way, again in the rain, to St. Patrick's
church, where her dead lover miraculously
materializes. Written by Ben Hecht from his
own story and sensitively directed (on
location in New York) by Rudolph Maté, it
suffered from too many sub-plots and an
over-abundance of sentimentality. But for
audiences who preferred their entertainment dewy-eyed it was a winner. Others in
the cast included Peggie Castle, Fred Clark,
Eileen Heckart (right), Josephine Hutchinson, Alan King, Paul Picerni and Arte
Johnson. The producer was Frank P.
Rosenberg.

▽

One of John Ford's best films, **The Searchers** ▷
eschewed the fast-developing trend towards
psychological Westerns and concentrated
instead on all the traditional elements of the
genre. It did, however, make a tentative
attempt to deal with the problem of racism
and, in that respect, was something of a
breakthrough for its aggressively right-wing
director. And, in a sense, for its star John
Wayne who, in the role of Ethan Edwards,
gave his most densely-conceived performance to date – better, even, than his work in
Howard Hawks' *Red River*. Wayne joins
forces with Jeffrey Hunter (a half-breed) in a
five-year search for his young niece (Natalie
Wood) who was abducted by Indians two
years after the Civil War. Although the basic
narrative line focused on the continuing
attempts of the two men to track down the
girl, on a more profound level it showed
how Wayne (right) gradually exorcised his
deep hatred of the Indian while, at the same
time, managing to remain true to his
beliefs. It was a moving, enigmatic performance and the film blossomed as a result
of it. Returning to the majestic Monument
Valley, Ford used his favourite location
brilliantly, relying on the seasonal changes
and their effects on the landscape, to indicate the slow passing of time. His handling
of all the relationships was subtler, more
economical than anything he had done
previously, and the performances he coaxed
out of Jeffrey Hunter, Natalie Wood, Vera
Miles and Ward Bond (left) were excellent.
Written by Frank S. Nugent (from the novel
by Alan Le May) and filmed in Vistavision
and Technicolor, the C.V. Whitney Production, under Merian C. Cooper's supervision,
was one of the great Westerns of the decade.

A hit at the 1954 Cannes Film Festival, the German-made drama **As Long As You're Near Me** (**Solange Du Da Bist**) was acquired for US distribution by Warner Bros. in 1956, and released in a new synchronized version (prepared by editor Rudi Fehr) as opposed to it merely being subtitled. The story of a film director's infatuation with an extra whom he builds into a star at the selfish risk of destroying her marriage, it starred O.W. Fischer as the director, Maria Schell (right) as his discovery, **Hardy Kruger** (left) as her husband and Brigitte Horney as the leading lady Miss Schell replaces in Fischer's affections. The film's underlying theme – that life and art are often inextricably bound – was eloquently expressed in Jochen Huth's screenplay (English version by Bert Reisfeld) and in Harald Braun's intensely felt direction. An N.D.F. Production, it was shot in Germany and also featured Mathias Wieman and Paul Bildt.

William Holden (right) starred in **Toward The Unknown** (released in Britain as **Brink Of Hell**) as a test pilot at the Edwards Air Force Base in California. His professional ambition is to test the Bell X-2 rocket plane, a machine capable of travelling at 1,900 miles per hour; his private ambition is to win the love of co-star Virginia Leith, and he succeeds on both counts. Mervyn LeRoy's production (he also directed) was full of technical information which never intruded on the narrative, devised and scripted by associate producer Bierne Lay Jr. On the contrary, it was the more personal element of the story that got in the way of the film's documentary-like approach to its absorbing subject. Lloyd Nolan (left) played the base commander, with Charles McGraw, Murray Hamilton, Paul Fix, James Garner, L.Q. Jones and Karen Steele in support. A Toluca production, it was photographed in WarnerColor and WarnerScope.

Satellite In The Sky's optical effects, shown off to splendid advantage by CinemaScope and WarnerColor, gave it a certain visual interest. For the rest, this British-made excursion into science-fiction (about a tritonium bomb which, instead of being lost in space, attaches itself to the rocket ship that is carrying it) was a wordy bore which featured Kieron Moore (right), Lois Maxwell, Alan Gifford, Donald Wolfit, Bryan Forbes, Jimmy Hanley (centre), Thea Gregory, Peter Neil (background centre), Barry Keegan, Walter Hudd (left) and Shirley Lawrence. It was written by John Mather, J.T. McIntosh and Edith Dell, directed by Paul Dickson and produced by Edward J. and Harry Lee Danziger.

325

Loudly condemned by the Roman Catholic Church who agreed with the Legion of Decency's verdict that 'it dwells almost without variation or relief upon carnal suggestiveness', **Baby Doll** – written by Tennessee Williams and directed by Elia Kazan (for Elia Kazan Productions) – was one of the most controversial films of the decade. Though tame by today's permissive standards, the sweaty story of a retarded, thumb-sucking, virgin child-bride's seduction by a virile young Sicilian, outraged the moralists, whose protests assured the film of box-office success. Carroll Baker (illustrated) as the mentally backward, but physically forward virgin created the cinema's newest sex object, the nymphet, at the same time as its latest fashion fad – the baby doll pyjama. It was a spectacular launching of a less than spectacular career for Miss Baker. Karl Malden played her ageing cotton-milling husband, and Eli Wallach his rival, both in and out of bed. Williams' trenchant screenplay was certainly bold for its time, and Kazan's direction as graphic as the Production Code would allow. Boris Kaufman's black-and-white photography brilliantly captured the steamy atmosphere of the Mississippi backwoods, as did the supporting performances of Mildred Dunnock, Lonny Chapman, Eades Hogue, Noah Williamson, and the participating townsfolk of Benoit, Mississippi.

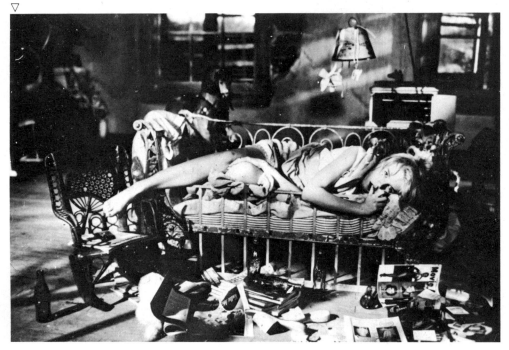

◁ Mainly for Randolph Scott (right) fans, **Seven Men From Now**, which was photographed in WarnerColor, was a better than average Western all about an ex-sheriff and the revenge he exacts from seven nasty varmints. A lot of dust was kicked up in the unfurling of Burt Kennedy's screenplay, but not enough to hide the clichés out of which the whole edifice was constructed. Still, it worked well enough, with Lee Marvin (centre right) excellently cast as the best of the heavies. Also in it were Walter Reed (centre), John Larch, Donald Barry (left) Fred Graham, John Barradino and Gail Russell (centre left). It was directed with the accent on action by Budd Boetticher and produced, for Batjac Productions, by Andrew V. McLaglen and Robert E. Morrison.

Tab Hunter (left) and Natalie Wood (right) were again teamed for **The Girl He Left Behind**, a comedy about the exploits of an insufferably spoilt young peacetime draftee, of whom the army finally makes a man. Wood, naturally, was his indulgent sweetheart. Guy Trosper's screenplay, from the novel by Marion Hargrove, had some extremely funny moments, most of them given to Murray Hamilton, Jim Backus and Alan King. However, as draftee Hunter was a real pain in the neck for most of 103 minutes, the film suffered accordingly. David Butler directed, Frank P. Rosenberg produced and the cast also included Jessie Royce Landis, Henry Jones, James Garner.

John Huston's version of Herman Melville's **Moby Dick**, the third to reach the screen, was by far the best of the trio. Captain Ahab's grim obsession to seek revenge for his previous encounter with the great white whale by killing him, unfolded with all the power and mysticism of Melville's novel intact, and with a surging sense of doom that was positively awesome. Huston had originally planned the role of Ahab for his father Walter who died in 1950. Instead, the director cast Gregory Peck (left) with Richard Basehart as Ishmael, Leo Genn (Starbuck, centre right), Harry Andrews (Stubb, right), James Robertson Justice (Captain Boomer), Friederich Ledebur (Queequeg) and Orson Welles (Father Mapple). Also among the distinguished cast were Bernard Miles, Gordon Jackson and Seamus Kelly (centre left). Huston and Anthony Veiller worked on the adaptation of the novel, with Ray Bradbury responsible for the screenplay. The film was shot in Portugal, the Canary Islands, the Azores and Wales, with real oceans and natural weather conditions taking the place of wind machines, studio tanks and back-projection, the only faking being in the deployment of latex whales. It was photographed by Oswald Morris in a colour process which combined black-and-white with Technicolor to give an unusual and effective sepia tint to the proceedings, and excellent music score was by Philip Stainton. The film, a Moulin Picture, was also produced by Huston.

By imposing his own highly individual cinematic style on the true-life case history of Manny Balastrero, a musician at New York's Stork Club who, after work one night, was arrested for a hold-up he did not commit, Alfred Hitchcock, with **The Wrong Man**, produced and directed something of a hybrid: a factual film he could not resist treating as fiction. The result was less satisfactory than it might have been had he opted for a purely documentary approach to the subject, especially since the film used several of the people actually involved in the case itself. The problem was a conflict between style and content, and it never really resolved itself. Still, as with most Hitchcock films, there was lots to admire in it, and both Henry Fonda (right, as Balastrero) and Vera Miles (left) as the wife whose mind snaps as a result of the nightmarish situation she and her husband find themselves in, were first rate. Though inspired by a report Hitchcock read in *Life* magazine, the film was based on Maxwell Anderson's *A Case of Identity* and scripted by Anderson and Angus MacPhail. Bernard Herrmann wrote the music for it, and the cast included Anthony Quayle (standing right, as Fonda's attorney), Harold J. Stone, Charles Cooper, John Heldabrand, Esther Minciotti and Doreen Lang.

Edna Ferber's sprawling novel **Giant** dealt with, among other things, the cataclysmic effects of the discovery of oil on everyone who came into contact with it. Synonymous with power and untold wealth, oil changed the Texas landscape just as surely as it changed a whole way of life. Always fascinated by progress and its consequences Ferber, in her novel, followed the fortunes of both Bick Benedict (Rock Hudson), a moneyed cattle baron married to a spoiled but beautiful Virginian called Leslie (Elizabeth Taylor, left); and Jett Rink (James Dean, right), a sullen farm-hand whose life-style undergoes a dramatic change after he discovers oil on his land and becomes a millionaire. In transferring the story to the cinema, director George Stevens, greatly helped by the use of the wide-screen to encompass the sweep of the landscape and a screenplay (by Fred Guiol and Ivan Moffat)

that skilfully compressed several decades into 201 minutes of playing time, gathered together a cast of heavyweights, drawing from them performances which rank among the best of their careers. Rock Hudson had certainly never been better, and James Dean confounded the sceptics who believed he was incapable of anything more than dramatizing inarticulacy. Only Elizabeth Taylor, in the last third of the film, failed to convey the passage of change so integral to the plot. Her earlier scenes, though, were

fine. Others in the large cast included Carroll Baker, Jane Withers, Chill Wills, Mercedes McCambridge, Dennis Hopper, Sal Mineo and Earl Holliman. The appropriately epic score was by Dimitri Tiomkin. It was photographed in WarnerColor by William C. Mellor and Edwin P. Du Par, and produced for George Stevens Productions by Stevens and Henry Ginsberg, turning in a massive profit of $12,000,000 to become one of the studio's biggest moneymakers of the fifties.

A Cry In The Night was a rather off-putting ▷ melodrama in which its young star (Natalie Wood) became the unfortunate victim of a violent sex maniac after being abducted from under her boyfriend's nose in a romantic spot known as Lover's Loop. Raymond Burr was the villain of the piece, Edmond O'Brien (left) was Natalie's police-official father, the hero. It was written by David Dortort from a novel by Whit Masterson, and directed by Frank Tuttle for associate producer George C. Bertholon. A Jaguar Production, the film also featured Brian Donlevy (right), Richard Anderson (centre), Irene Hervey, Carol Veazie, Herb Vigran (far right) and Anthony Caruso.

1957

The studio's most prestigious film for 1957 was **Sayonara**, which was nominated for ten Academy Awards and won three: Best Supporting Actor (Red Buttons), Best Supporting Actress (Miyoshi Umeki) and Best Sound Recording (Warner Bros. Sound Department under its director George Groves). The film's other nominations were for Best Film (won by Columbia's **The Bridge On The River Kwai**), Best Director (Joshua Logan, who lost to David Lean for **River Kwai**), Best Actor (Marlon Brando who lost to Alec Guinness for **River Kwai**), Best Screenplay (Paul Osborn, who also lost out to **River Kwai**, written by Pierre Boulle); Ellsworth Fredericks was nominated for Best Cinematography, and Arthur P. Schmidt and Phillip W. Anderson for Best Editing, and the film was considered one of the year's Ten Best by the *New York Times*. The studio also won an Oscar in 1957 for their cartoon, **Birds Anonymous**.

On 14 January Humphrey Bogart, who had been suffering from cancer, died in his sleep at the age of 56. A few months later, composer Erich Wolfgang Korngold, who had written a large number of marvellous scores for Warner Bros. films, died.

Net profit for the year was $3,415,367, the studio's top grossing films at the box office being **The Bad Seed** (released in September 1956) and **Giant** (released in October 1956).

△

Top Secret Affair (released in Britain as **Their Secret Affair**) was a slightly top-heavy affair with a larger-than-life Kirk Douglas (left) impersonating Major General Melville Goodwin, the hero of John P. Marquand's novel *Melville Goodwin U.S.A.*, and Susan Hayward (right) as the aggressive lady publisher who initially sets out to discredit him, but ends up romantically involved. It was written by Roland Kibbee and Allan Scott, directed by H.C. Potter, and produced, in association with Carrollton Inc., by Martin Rackin with Milton Sperling as supervising producer. Also in it were Paul Stewart, Jim Backus, John Cromwell and Roland Winters.

Paris Does Strange Things was a French-made curiosity starring Ingrid Bergman which Warner Bros. acquired, dubbed into English, cut, and released with disastrous results. A needlessly obtuse story about a Polish princess (Bergman, right) involved in a *coup d'état* in France, it diminished the considerable talents of Jean Renoir, its writer-producer-director, as well as those of its leading lady, and a cast that included Mel Ferrer (left), Jean Marais and Juliette Greco. The only redeeming feature was its dazzling Technicolor photography by master cameraman Claude Renoir. Its original French title was **Elena Et Les Hommes** (1956).
▽

◁ **The Big Land** (released in Britain as **Stampeded**) was a small Western which starred Alan Ladd (left) in a tale about cattlemen and wheat growers who join forces in building a railroad near their land in an attempt to quell the activities of ruthless cattle-buyers. Virginia Mayo was the love interest, Anthony Caruso the heavy, with other parts going to John Qualen, Edmond O'Brien (right), Don Castle and David Ladd. It was written by David Dortort (from the novel by Frank Gruber) and directed by Gordon Douglas. A Jaguar Production, the associate producer was George C. Bertholon.

△

The two stars of **The Spirit of St. Louis** were James Stewart (illustrated) as Charles Lindbergh, and composer Franz Waxman whose symphonic accompaniment to the 3,600-mile, 33½-hour, non-stop trip from New York to Paris in 1927 contributed incalculably to the film's overall atmosphere. Written by Billy Wilder and Wendell Mayes from a story by Charles Lindbergh and adapted for the screen by Charles Lederer, it effectively captured the pioneering spirit of the era it represented, and Lindbergh's ultimate achievement was suitably stirring. But the longueurs in the air prior to the historic landing left patrons restless, a fact which was reflected in the box-office returns of the multi-million-dollar Leland Hayward-Billy Wilder production (Wilder also directed). **The Spirit of St. Louis** was, in fact, one of the biggest financial failures in the history of the studio. Others in the cast were Murray Hamilton, Patricia Smith, Bartlett Robinson and Marc Connelly. It was filmed in WarnerColor and CinemaScope.

Made by Anglo Amalgamated's Merton Park Studios in England, and released in the US by Warner Bros., **The Counterfeit Plan** was a routine, albeit well-made crime melodrama which starred Zachary Scott (left) as a convicted murderer, who, after escaping from the French authorities, heads for England where he forces a reformed forger (Mervyn Johns, right) to set up premises for the printing of fake £5 notes. Complications arise when the forger's daughter (Peggie Castle) arrives from the Continent and is threatened with her life by Scott if she breathes a word of his operations to the police. It was written by James Eastwood, directed by Montgomery Tully and produced by Alec C. Snowden. Sidney Tafler, Lee Paterson, David Lodge, Mark Bellamy, Chili Bouchier and snooker champion Horace Lindrum also appeared in it.
▽

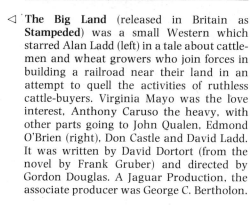

⊲ Mamie van Doren (centre) and Lori Nelson (with guitar) starred as sisters in **Untamed Youth**, a juvenile (in all senses of the word) melodrama in which the two well-shaped girls, having broken the law, find themselves in a prison-farm for rock 'n roll addicts. John Russell runs the establishment and his main activity, apart from rock 'n roll, is cotton picking. The script by John C. Higgins (story by Stephen Longstreet) was of no consequence at all, but then nothing much in director Howard W. Koch's film was, except, possibly, the way Miss Van Doren used her body as an accompaniment to Les Baxter's music. A Devonshire Production, it was produced by Aubrey Schenck and featured Don Burnett. Eddie Cochran, Lurene Tuttle and the Hollywood Rock and Rollers. Songs included: Oobala Baby, Salamander and Cotton Picker.

Another Randolph Scott Western, **Shoot-Out at Medicine Bend** was a sagebrush saga of revenge with Scott (centre) as the leader of a group of men who set out to avenge the murder of his brother at the hands of the Sioux. The tired screenplay was by John Tucker Battle and D.D. Beauchamp, with direction in the same league by Richard L. Bare. Richard Whorf produced and the cast included James Craig, Angie Dickinson, Dani Crayne, James Garner (right) and Gordon Jones (left).

⊲ After their triumphant collaboration for *On The Waterfront*, director Elia Kazan and writer Budd Schulberg teamed up again for **A Face In The Crowd**, a powerful indictment of the processes through which personalities are first manufactured by the media, then unquestionably accepted at face value by Mr and Mrs Public. In a highly impressive screen debut Andy Griffith (illustrated) played the role of Lonesome Rhodes, outwardly an 'aw shucks' hillbilly philosophizing on a local mid-Western TV station, but inwardly a power-crazy Frankenstein's monster, who is finally felled when his creator throws a switch on a microphone and catches him totally off-guard in the middle of a mocking tirade against the 'suckers' throughout the country who hang onto his every word. Dazzlingly directed by Kazan (who also produced), the film also featured Patricia Neal, Anthony Franciosa, Walter Matthau, Lee Remick (another impressive debut) and Marshall Neilan. For all its credentials, it failed to click at the box office. It was a Newton Production.

Terence Rattigan's flimsy stage play *The Sleeping Prince* became a vehicle for Marilyn Monroe and Laurence Olivier in Rattigan's own adaptation of it for the screen called **The Prince And The Showgirl**. A plot with about as much substance as vapour, had Olivier (right) playing a stuffy, monocled Balkan prince and wooing a tantalizingly gauche Monroe as a Gaiety Girl (left). Dame Sybil Thorndike appeared as the Regent's imperious mother, Jeremy Spenser as his priggish son and Richard Wattis as a prissy minister viewing it all with obvious disapproval. Monroe's soufflé-light performance was more engaging than Olivier's more stagey efforts at Teutonic grandeur, though the vehicle was worthy of neither of them. Set in the Carpathian Embassy, London, during the Coronation of George V, it looked much better than it sounded, with Jack Cardiff's luxurious Technicolor photography providing a dazzle appropriate to its time and place. A Marilyn Monroe Production, it was made in England, produced by Laurence Olivier (who also directed it), with Milton H.L. Green as executive producer. The music was composed by Richard Addinsell, and the cast included Esmond Knight, Paul Hardwick, Rosamund Greenwood, Aubrey Dexter, Maxine Audley and Jean Kent.

Another assertive vehicle for Jack Webb, **The D.I.** was a tribute of sorts to the exhaustive and exhausting training methods of the US Marines. Webb played a martinet drill-instructor who, in the course of 106 rather noisy minutes, turns Parris Island recruit Don Dubbins into the sort of man the Marines enjoy taking a pride in. A better-than-average bootcamp drama, it also featured Jackie Loughery, Lin McCarthy, Monica Lewis and Virginia Gregg. It was written by James Lee Barrett from his television play, and produced and directed by Jack Webb for his Mark VII Ltd Productions.

An exploitative follow-up to *The Quatermass Experiment* released the previous year, X **The Unknown**, produced by Anthony Hinds (executive producer, Michael Carreras), was minor league Sci-Fi and a variation on the Quatermass theme. All about a strange and unknown force feeding on radiation from a Scottish research centre, then turning into a malignant mass, it featured Dean Jagger (right), Edward Chapman, Leo McKern, William Lucas (left), John Harvey, Peter Hammond, Michael Ripper and Anthony Newley. It was written from his own story by Jimmy Sangster, and directed (in England) by Leslie Norman for Hammer Productions.

Ethel Barrymore (centre) brought a certain ▷ distinction to **Johnny Trouble**, an agreeable soap-opera in which she played a widowed invalid who lives for the day when her son, who walked out on her and her husband 27 years earlier, will return. It is only when she becomes the unofficial 'nanny' to a class of freshmen after the apartment block she lives in is sold off to a university, that her life takes on new meaning. For one of the freshmen, she firmly believes, is her grandson. Cecil Kellaway (left) co-starred as Miss Barrymore's chauffeur, with Stuart Whitman making his debut as the supposed grandson. Carolyn Jones, Jesse White, Jack Larson and Paul Wallace were in it too; it was written by Charles O'Neal and David Lord from the story by Ben Ames Williams and directed by John H. Auer. A Clarion Production, it was also produced by Auer, with John Carroll as executive producer.

The Rising Of The Moon, lovingly directed by John Ford, was a compilation of three Irish tales, each designed to demonstrate certain facets of the Irish temperament and personality. The first, called *The Majesty of the Law* and based on a story by Frank O'Connor, was a dialogue between an officer (Cyril Cusack) and a local worthy (Noel Purcell) who flatly refuses to pay the required fine for assaulting a neighbour. The second piece was by Martin J. McHugh, a farce called *A Minute's Wait*. Set in a busy country railway station, it featured Jimmy O'Dea, Tony Quinn, Paul Farrell, Maureen Potter, Michael Trubshawe, Anita Sharp and Harold Goldblatt. The last of the trio was based on Lady Gregory's cele- ◁ brated one-act play *The Rising of the Moon*, here called *1921*, the time to which the piece had been updated. All about the springing of a condemned patriot from a Galway prison during the troubles in Ireland, it featured Denis O'Dea, Eileen Crowe, Frank Lawton and Dennis Brennan. All the cast were Irish — even narrator Tyrone Power was of Irish descent: it was made in Ireland for Four Provinces Productions, the producer was Michael Killanin and it was scripted by Frank S. Nugent.

Arguably one of the silliest films of the decade, **The Story Of Mankind** attempted to tell the story of Mankind in 100 minutes flat. What emerged was 100 flat minutes of comic-strip history in which the Devil, as impersonated by Vincent Price (left), insists that Mankind is as evil as he is, and should be eliminated; while The Spirit of Man, as ◁ interpreted by Ronald Colman (right), claims the exact opposite. They put their respective cases to a court situated somewhere in outer space, illustrating their arguments with 'great moments' from history and, as it turned out, great moments from previous Warner Bros. films — themselves depicting great moments in our chequered development. The sort of film that grows more eccentric with each passing year, it may not be a great moment in the history of the cinema, but it was certainly one of its most curious. It was produced and directed (for Cambridge Productions) by Irwin Allen who, with Charles Bennett, co-authored the screenplay (from the book by Hendrik Willem van Loon). The large cast included Hedy Lamarr as Joan of Arc, Harpo Marx as Isaac Newton, Virginia Mayo as Cleopatra, Agnes Moorehead as Queen Elizabeth I, Peter Lorre as Nero, John Carradine as Khufu, Dennis Hopper as Napoleon, Marie Wilson as Marie Antoinette, Edward Everett Horton as Sir Walter Raleigh, Reginald Gardiner as Shakespeare, Francis X. Bushman as Moses and George E. Stone as a waiter!

The James Dean Story was an effective threnody for the late James Dean (illustrated) who died in a car crash in California in 1955 at the age of 24. George W. George and Robert Altman, who produced and directed this tribute to the young superstar, relied on photographs, film clips and interviews with Dean's friends, associates and relatives for their reconstruction and assessment of his life. It was narrated by Martin Gabel. Song: Let Me Be Loved (by Jay Livingston and Ray Evans).

A modest, and moderately entertaining Western, **Black Patch** starred George Montgomery (right) as a prairie marshal who, after jailing a former friend turned robber (Leo Gordon), is accused of murdering the man and keeping the swag for himself. Tom Pittman played a teenager with problems who has a climactic showdown with the marshal, with Diane Brewster (left), Sebastian Cabot and House Peters Jr in other roles. Leo Gordon wrote it and it was directed by Allen H. Miner, who also produced, for Montgomery Productions, Inc.

In the experienced directorial hands of George Abbott and Stanley Donen. **The Pajama Game**, adapted from the Broadway musical of the same name without too many changes, additions or subtractions, was a humdinger of a show. The story of a pajama factory and the $7\frac{1}{2}$ cents rise demanded by its employees, it had sufficient exuberance, vitality and good songs to keep box office cashiers fully employed for months. Originally purchased as a vehicle for Patti Page, the choice part of Kate Williams, head of the factory's grievance committee, finally went to Doris Day, who brought to it all the freshness, sparkle and full-throatedness audiences had come to expect of her. John Raitt repeated his Broadway role of workshop superintendent, with Thelma Pelish, Eddie Foy Jr, Reta Shaw and the late Carol Haney (all recruits from the original New York stage production) offering exuberant support. The screenplay was by George Abbott and Richard Bissell (from Bissell's novel $7\frac{1}{2}$ Cents), the memorable score by Richard Adler and Jerry Ross, and the all-enhancing choreography by Bob Fosse. An Abbott–Donen Production, it was produced by Abbott and Donen, with Fred Brisson, Robert E. Griffiths and Harold Prince as associate producers. Songs included: The Pajama Game, I'm Not At All In Love, Small Talk, Hernando's Hideaway, Hey There, Steam Heat, There Once Was A Man, I'll Never Be Jealous Again. This Is Our Once A Year Day and Seven And A Half Cents.

Another English-made Hammer production released in America by Warner Bros. was **The Curse of Frankenstein**, a conventional reworking of Mary Shelley's classic horror story, whose Gothic atmosphere was hardly enhanced by the addition of WarnerColor. (In Britain, Eastman Colour was used). Peter Cushing (centre) played Baron Frankenstein, Christopher Lee (foreground) was the monster he created out of a human cadaver. Robert Urquhart (right) played the Baron's uncomprehending associate, with the rest of the all-British cast being completed by Valerie Gaunt, Noel Hood, Marjorie Hume and Melvyn Hayes. Jimmy Sangster wrote it, it was directed by Terence Fisher and produced by Anthony Hinds, with Anthony Nelson Keys as his associate.

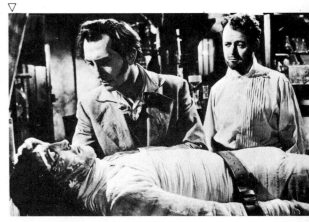

Aimed at the teenage rock 'n roll market, **Jamboree** (released in Britain as **Disc Jockey Jamboree**) sandwiched a meagre plot (about two 'singing sweethearts' and their formerly married agents) between no fewer than 21 songs. Kay Medford (centre) and Robert Pastine (left) – via Broadway and TV – played the agents; Freda Holloway (right) and Paul Carr (centre right) were their protegés. Leonard Kantor's screenplay played second fiddle to the musical numbers, with Fats Domino, Buddy Knox, Jodie Sands, Slim Whitman, Jerry Lee Lewis, The Four Coins, Lewis Lymon and the Teenchords, Connie Francis, Rocco and his Saints, Frankie Avalon, and Count Basie and his Orchestra the film's main centre of gravity. Roy Lockwood was the director, with Max J. Rosenberg and Milton Subotsky producing. Songs included: Jamboree, Great Balls of Fire, Record Hop Tonight, For Children Of All Ages, Glad All Over, Who Are We To Say, Teacher's Pet, Siempre, Cool Baby, Sayonara, Toreador, Your Last Chance, If Not For You, Unchain My Heart, A Broken Promise, One O'clock Jump, I Don't Like You No More, Cross Over, Hula Love, Wait And See and Twenty-four Hours A Day.

▽

Ann Blyth (illustrated) lacked vulnerability as well as star quality as the heroine of **The Helen Morgan Story** (released in Britain as **Both Ends Of The Candle**), a typical fifties biopic which it took four writers (Oscar Saul, Dean Riesner, Stephen Longstreet and Nelson Gidding) to fashion from the heart-rending facts of their subject's life. For all their combined efforts, it was a pale effort, in which one of the great torch singers of the twenties emerged as little more than a rather sad lady whose unhappy love affairs turned her to drink. Director Michael Curtiz did manage, however, to capture the essential mood and atmosphere of the period in which Miss Morgan came to prominence, which made one regret all the more that the essence of the subject itself eluded him so spectacularly. Paul Newman and Richard Carlson were cast as the men in her life (the former no good, the latter a kindly attorney, but already married), with Gene Evans, Walter Woolf King, Cara Williams and Virginia Vincent in support. Certainly the film was rich in its repertoire of well-known standards by first-rate composers. and Gogi Grant dubbed the vocals for Miss Blyth, whose soprano voice was not suitable. The musical numbers were staged by LeRoy Prinz. The producer was Martin Rackin. Songs included: Bill (by Jerome Kern and P.G. Wodehouse), Why Was I Born (by Kern and Oscar Hammerstein II), If You Were The Only Girl In The World (by Clifford Grey and Nat D. Ayer), I Can't Give You Anything But Love (by Dorothy Fields and Jimmy McHugh), Avalon (by Vincent Rose and Al Jolson) Do Do Do (by George and Ira Gershwin), Breezin' Along With The Breeze (by Haven Gillespie, Seymour Simons and Richard Whiting), Someone To Watch Over Me (by George and Ira Gershwin), Body And Soul (by Edward Heyman, Robert Souk, Frank Eyton and John Green), Can't Help Lovin' Dat Man (by Kern and Hammerstein), I've Got A Crush On You (by George and Ira Gershwin), and I'll Get By (by Fred E. Ahlert and Roy Turk).

▽

Bombers B-52 (released in Britain as **No Sleep Till Dawn**) was that rare thing: a tribute to the Air Force that was as appealing on the ground as it was in the air. For this, credit must go to Irving Wallace's intelligent screenplay (from a story by Sam Rolfe) and to Karl Malden as a veteran flyer and ground-crew chief whose dilemma – whether to continue doing the work he loves or leave aviation for a better-paid job in civvy street – concerned audiences almost as much as it did his own family (Marsha Hunt as mother, Natalie Wood as daughter.) Adding spice to the tale was a vendetta of sorts between Malden (left) and his daughter's commandant boyfriend, Efrem Zimbalist Jr (right). Photographed in CinemaScope and WarnerColor, and well-directed by Gordon Douglas, the film also featured Don Kelly, Nelson Leigh and Stuart Whitman. Richard Whorf produced.

▽

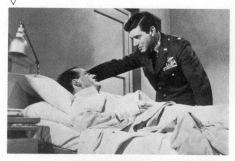

△

Although the special 'stop-motion' effects for **The Black Scorpion** were devised by Willis O'Brien, one of the key figures in the creation of the legendary King Kong, and were effectively repellent, the plot – about a volcanic explosion in Mexico activating a lair of giant, prehistoric scorpions – stung one into no more than numbness. The performances of Richard Denning (right), Mara Corday (centre), Carlos Rivas (left) and Mario Navarro were no antidote. David Duncan and Robert Blees wrote the screenplay (from a story by Paul Yawitz), Edward Ludwig directed for Amex Productions, and the producers were Frank Melford and Jack Dietz.

◁ A kitchen sink soap-opera *par excellence*, **Woman In A Dressing Gown**, naturalistically directed by J. Lee Thompson, was a downbeat British offering, released by Warner Bros. in the US, about a slovenly housewife who spends her day shuffling about in a dressing gown, her hair as un-combed as her bed is un-made. Her husband (Anthony Quayle, right), a soft-spoken, bear-like man who works as a clerk, is, understandably, disenchanted with his home-life, and adds a touch of glamour to his drab existence by having an affair with one of the women (Sylvia Syms) in his office. Hardly a commercial for marriage, it was, nonetheless, riveting material – thanks largely to Ted Willis' well-observed screenplay and the central performance of Yvonne Mitchell (left) as the unattractive wife who can't do anything right. Andrew Ray played their teenage son, with other parts going to Olga Lindo, Harry Locke, Marianne Stone and Melvyn Hayes. A Goodwin-Willis-Thompson Production, it was produced by Frank Goodwin and J. Lee Thompson.

A sort of contemporary *Madam Butterfly*, **Sayonara**, based on the best-selling novel by James A. Michener, made some sombre comments about two inter-racial love affairs, one of which ends in a parting, the other in suicide. Marlon Brando (left) starred as an American major riddled with racial prejudice until he meets and falls for a Matsubayashi actress (Miko Taka, right) in Japan; Red Buttons (superb) and Miyoshi Umeki were the doomed lovers. Paul Osborn's intelligent and sensitive screenplay gave director Joshua Logan (who originally acquired the rights in the hope of turning it into a stage musical with Irving Berlin) every opportunity to excel (which he did) and, as a bonus, Franz Waxman's score was augmented by a title song by Irving Berlin. The award winning Goetz-Pennebaker production (in Technirama and Technicolor) also featured Patricia Owens, James Garner, Martha Scott and Ricardo Montalban. It was both a financial and a prestigious success, grossing over $10,500,000.
▽

Set in an American reformatory for girls, **The Green-Eyed Blonde** was a somewhat squalid programmer in which several of the institution's inmates conceal an illegitimate baby from its delinquent mother. Produced by Martin Melcher and directed by Bernard Girard, its young cast included Susan Oliver, Norma Jean Nilsson and Tommie Moore. Linda Plowman, Beverly Long (right), Carla Merey (left), Sallie Brophy, Jean Inness and Olive Blakeney were also featured, and it was written by Sally Stubblefield who was also the associate producer for Arwin Productions.
▽

△
A burlesque of almost every pre-Civil War story ever filmed – complete with rambling Deep South mansions, spiritual-intoning negro slaves, exotic mulattos, powerful cotton barons from New Orleans, sadistic slave traders, etc. – **Band of Angels**, from the sprawling novel by Robert Penn Warren, starred Clark Gable, Yvonne de Carlo and Sidney Poitier. It was the story of a Kentucky belle (de Carlo) who, on the death of her father not only discovers she is penniless but, worse, that she has negro blood coursing through her veins! As a result, she is sold into slavery, bought by a New Orleans millionaire (Gable, illustrated) and becomes his mistress. Poitier was one of the slaves, with other roles in the John Twist-Ivan Goff-Ben Roberts screenplay going to Patric Knowles (as a Louisiana dude), Ray Teal (as a slave-trader), Torin Thatcher (as a sea captain) and Efrem Zimbalist Jr (as a Union officer). Andrea King, Russ Evans, Carolle Drake and Rex Reason were in it too. The wooden direction was by Raoul Walsh who was clearly not at home with stylized costume melodrama. It was photographed in WarnerColor by Lucien Ballard, and Max Steiner supplied the score. No producer was credited.

1958

Only two Warner Bros. films featured in the 1958 Academy Awards Presentations: **Marjorie Morningstar**, whose theme song 'A Very Special Love' by Sammy Fain and Paul Francis Webster was nominated in the Best Song category, and **Auntie Mame**, which received a total of six nominations: these were for Best Film (the winner was MGM's **Gigi**), Rosalind Russell for Best Actress (the winner was Susan Hayward for Figaro-United Artists' **I Want To Live**), Peggy Cass for Best Supporting Actress (the winner was Wendy Hiller for Hecht-Hill-Lancaster United Artists' **Separate Tables**), Malcolm Bert and George James Hopkins for Best Art Direction, Harry Stradling Sr for Best Colour Photography, and William Ziegler for Best Editing (none of whom won). The 1958 Irving G. Thalberg Memorial Award went to Jack Warner for his services to the cinema. No New York Critics awards were given to the studio, but **Damn Yankees** featured in the *New York Times* Ten Best list. On July 25th Harry Warner died at his home in Bel Air, and two weeks later Jack Warner was erroneously reported dead following a car smash in the South of France. After a lengthy period of convalescence he recovered and returned to work.

Although **Marjorie Morningstar, Indiscreet, No Time For Sergeants** and **Sayonara** (released December 1957) were considerable money-makers, the company showed a net loss of $1,023,000 – their first deficit since 1938.

A modest but effective little melodrama ▷ which warned of the evils of drug peddling, **Stakeout On Dope Street** was a well-made programmer about three teenagers who find a couple of pounds of heroin and start peddling it for cash. A cast of unknowns, including Yale Wexler (right), Jonathan Haze and Morris Miller, were sufficiently credible as the youngsters; it was directed in semi-documentary fashion by Irvin Kershner who wrote the taut screenplay with Irwin Schwartz and Andrew J. Fenady (who also produced), and featured Abby Dalton (left), Allen Kramer, Herman Rudin, Phillip Mansour, Frank Harding and Herschel Bernardi.

△

William A. Wellman surfaced again, but this time came a cropper with an ineffectual programmer called **Lafayette Escadrille** (released in Britain as **Hell Bent For Glory**), an unfocused drama about American pilots with the French Air Corps in World War I. A certain period atmosphere was conveyed, but little else in this dispiriting tale which A.S. Fleischman wrote from a story by Wellman himself, and in which handsome Tab Hunter (illustrated) was starred as the hero. Etchika Choureau was his sweetheart, Bill Wellman Jr, Jody McCrea, Dennis Devine, Marcel Dalio, David Janssen, Clint Eastwood and Veola Vonn were in it too. It was a William A. Wellman Production.

Clint Walker (centre), the star of TV's *Cheyenne* series, made a starring appearance in **Fort Dobbs**, a minor Western in which he played a fugitive on a murder charge who rescues a widow (Virginia Mayo, right) and her young son (Richard Eyer, left) from the Comanches against whom he also masterminds a successful stockade defence, thereby clearing his name. If it sounds familiar, it was. Gordon Douglas directed, it was written by George W. George and Burt Kennedy, and produced by Martin Rackin with a supporting cast that included Brian Keith, Russ Conway and Michael Dante.

▽

◁ **The Deep Six** was a World War II drama which starred Alan Ladd (left) as a gunnery officer whose pacifist Quaker beliefs were in direct contrast to his current role as a man of war. Unfortunately, what could have, and should have, been a deep psychological study with Ladd's moral dilemma as the first item on scriptwriters John Twist, Martin Rackin and Harry Brown's notepad, dissipated itself into a routine combat story with Diane Foster supplying the romance. Rudolph Maté's direction, however, capably steered it through the clichés, and there were fine performances from Keenan Wynn, James Whitmore, William Bendix (right) and Efrem Zimbalist Jr. Also cast were Joey Bishop, Barbara Eiler, Ross Bagdasarian, and Walter Reed. A Jaguar Production (photographed in WarnerColor), it was produced by Martin Rackin.

According to Jack Warner in his autobiography, when Errol Flynn returned to the studio for the very last time to portray John Barrymore in **Too Much Too Soon** he was 'one of the living dead'. A great admirer of Barrymore (on many counts their lives were similar), Flynn's own physical condition at the time, coupled with the fact that Art and Jo Napoleon's screenplay (based on the book by Diana Barrymore and Gerold Frank) took liberties with the truth, made it impossible for the actor to give a fully rounded characterization of the great romantic star. Nor was he helped by Art Napoleon's pedestrian direction. Diana Barrymore was played by Dorothy Malone (illustrated), with Efrem Zimbalist Jr, Ray Danton, Neva Patterson, Murray Hamilton and Martin Milner in featured roles. It was a sad exit for Flynn from the studio that made him famous, and which he in turn had helped to make rich. The producer was Henry Blanke.

▽

◁ The story of an American Commando unit's training programme in Britain before plunging into action in Europe and Africa, **Darby's Rangers** (released in Britain as **The Young Invaders**), as the special combat force of US soldiers was called during World War II, was more concerned with the men's extra-mural activities than with the war itself. Chasing women, rather than the enemy, was the order of the day (and night) as demonstrated by a cast that included James Garner (foreground left), fast making a name for himself in the TV series *Maverick*, Jack Warden, Edward Byrnes, Torin Thatcher, Peter Brown and Murray Hamilton (foreground right). The weaker sex were attractively represented by Etchika Choureau, Joan Elan, Andrea King and Venetia Stevenson. Guy Trosper wrote it from a book by Major James Altieri; it was produced by Martin Rackin and directed by William A. Wellman.

Based on a story by Jules Verne, **From The** ▷ **Earth To The Moon** starred Joseph Cotten (centre) as a wealthy scientist (circa 1868) who, contrary to prevailing opinion, insists that man can fly to the moon. He proves his point to the sceptics, but the film remained earthbound. Not surprising, really, as James Leicester and Robert Blees' leaden screenplay would have grounded a feather. Though the rocketship looked splendid, the special effects lacked imagination; so did Byron Haskin's humourless direction. Others involved were George Sanders (left, as the villain who sets out to wreck the great adventure), Debra Paget (centre left), Don Dubbins, Patric Knowles, Carl Esmond and Henry Daniell. An RKO Film in Technicolor, it was released in the US by Warner Bros., and produced by Benedict Bogeaus.

Frankie Vaughan (right) made his screen debut in **Dangerous Youth** (released in Britain as **These Dangerous Years**), and Anna Neagle her debut as a producer. A melodrama with a steady undercurrent of comedy, its well-worn story involved a tough young Liverpudlian (Vaughan) whose hobby is singing, but whose vocation is leading a local dockside gang, in a stint in the army. Predictably, military service makes a man of Vaughan, but at the cost of a friend's life. Jack Trevor Story's screenplay was nothing to shout about, but it gave Carole Lesley (centre, as Vaughan's girlfriend) and a cast which also included George Baker, Katherine Kath, Thora Hird, Jackie Lane (left), Eddie Byrnes, Kenneth Cope, John Le Mesurier and Reginald Beckwith a crack at a variety of recognizable English character types. Stanley Black provided the musical score; Richard Mullen, Peter Moreton and Bert Waller wrote the songs. Made in England by Associated British Pathe, it was an Anna Neagle Production directed by Herbert Wilcox, which Warner Bros. released in the US. Songs included: These Dangerous Years, Cold Cold Shower, and Isn't This A Lovely Evening.

▽

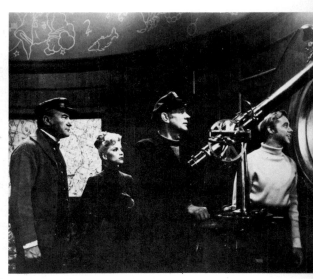

Manhunt In The Jungle, filmed entirely on location in Brazil, was based on the search undertaken in 1928, by Commander George M. Dyott, for explorer Colonel Percy H. Fawcett who mysteriously disappeared in the Amazon while on an expedition to seek out the remnants of an ancient white civilization, and the lost city from which it sprung. A routine jungle adventure with all the clichés of the genre emerging in mint condition, it featured Robin Hughes (left) as Dyott and James Wilson as Fawcett, with Luis Alvarez (centre), Jorge Montoro (right), John B. Symmes, Natalia Manzuelis and James Ryan among the supporting cast. Based on Dyott's book of the same name, its formula screenplay was by Sam Merwin Jr and Owen Crump, the director was Tom McGowan and the producer Cedric Francis.

▽

Chase a Crooked Shadow was a competent, sometimes engrossing thriller, which starred Anne Baxter (right) as an attractive and inordinately wealthy diamond heiress who finds her peace of mind invaded by the arrival of Richard Todd (left), a smoothie claiming to be the brother she supposedly lost in an automobile smash. The question ◁ is, is he the brother or isn't he? David Osborne and Charles Sinclair's screenplay, based on a TV play by Sinclair and William Fings (and re-made in 1975 as a TV film called *One Of My Wives Is Missing*), eventually reveals all, and if the denouement hardly shattered audiences, it kept them moderately satisfied. Herbert Lom (centre), Alexander Knox, Faith Brook and Alan Tilvern were in it too; it was competently directed by Michael Anderson in England and Spain for Associated Dragon Films, produced by Douglas Fairbanks Jr and released by Warner Bros. in the US.

Reminiscent of H.G. Clouzot's 1955 suspense masterpiece, *The Wages Of Fear*, **The Violent Road**, from a story by Don Martin, was an efficient programmer in which a group of men, while driving a dangerous cargo of explosives over bumpy terrain, reassess their lives and life styles. Directed by Howard W. Koch from a screenplay by Richard Landau, and produced by Aubrey Schenck, the film featured Brian Keith (centre right), Dick Foran, Efrem Zimbalist Jr (left), Merry Anders, Sean Garrison, Bob Alderette (centre), Ed Prentiss (right), Joanna Barnes, Perry Lopez and Ann Doran.

▽

Scenarist Orville H. Hampton took all ▷ sorts of liberties with history in **Badman's Country**, a fair-to-middling Western in which sheriff Pat Garrett, Wyatt Earp and Buffalo Bill pool their collective resources for a final showdown with Butch Cassidy. George Montgomery (left) was Garrett, Buster Crabbe Wyatt Earp, Malcolm Atterbury Buffalo Bill and Neville Brand Butch Cassidy. It was directed by Fred F. Sears with a cast that included Karin Booth (right), Gregory Walcott, Russell Johnson, Richard Devon and Morris Ankrum. A Peerless Production (not entirely true in this case!) it was produced by Robert E. Kent.

△

Based on Herman Melville's *Typee*, **Enchanted Island**, another RKO production released by Warner Bros. in the US, was easy on the eye, but was a patently silly adventure in which Dana Andrews (centre) and Don Dubbins (left) desert their whaling ship and find themselves keeping company with a tribe of South Sea Island cannibals. They're basically a friendly lot, however, with the Chief's daughter, Jane Powell, especially so towards Andrews. Ted de Corsia (as the captain of the whaling vessel), Arthur Shields, Friedrich Ledebur and Augustin Fernandez were in it too; it was written by James Leicester and Harold Jacob Smith, and directed by veteran Allan Dwan. A Waverly Production, it was photographed in Technicolor for producer Benedict Bogeaus.

In **Home Before Dark**, Jean Simmons (right) returns to her professor husband (Dan O'Herlihy, centre right) after a year in a mental institution and begins life afresh. All goes well until she discovers the delusions she thought she was having and for which she was committed, weren't delusions at all. By smoothing out the edges of the story and imbuing it all with a glossy surface, director Mervyn Le Roy robbed the drama of much of its impact but, fortunately, was unable to hinder Jean Simmons' powerful central performance. Written by Eileen and Robert Bassing (from a story by Eileen Bassing), and produced by Mervyn Le Roy for his own production company, the film also featured Efrem Zimbalist Jr (left), Mabel Albertson, Steven Dunne and Joan Weldon.

▽

Auntie Mame transferred most felicitously from Broadway to the screen and was a walloping, rip-roaring hit – as it deserved to be. With Rosalind Russell (right) repeating the role she had created on stage, it was a once-in-a-lifetime showcase which she made uniquely and entertainingly her own. Forrest Tucker was cast as Beauregard Burnside, the millionaire husband Mame finds for herself in South Carolina, and who leaves her all his money when he falls off the Matterhorn; Coral Browne (centre) was Vera Charles, Mame's bitchy actress friend, Fred Clark played Babcock the banker, whose chief occupation is trying to free Mame's young nephew (Jan Handzlick) from his eccentric aunt's influence, and Peggy Cass was Agnes Gooch, Mame's plain-Jane secretary who finds herself about to become an unmarried mother when she takes her employer's advice and 'lives a little'. Also cast were Roger Smith, Patric Knowles (left), Joanna Barnes, Pippa Scott, Lee Patrick, Willard Waterman, and Yuki Shimoda as Mame's Filipino houseboy, Ito. Betty Comden and Adolph Green clearly had a ball expanding Jerome Lawrence and Robert E. Lee's already cinematic stage play (from the best-seller by Patrick Dennis). It was gorgeously photographed in Techni-Color and Technirama by Harry Stradling, and the brisk, inventive direction was by Morton DaCosta who had steered the show to success on Broadway as well.

▽

◁ Andy Griffith (right) joyously repeated his Broadway success as the ingenuous Air Force draftee, Will Stockdale, in **No Time For Sergeants**, a delightful screen transfer of the Ira Levin play (from the novel by Mac Hyman). Myron McCormick, who was also in the New York production, again played Sergeant King. As in the play, most of the fun was derived from Griffith's naive belief that being drafted was the highest honour his country could bestow on him; and from his disarming attempts to treat McCormick as if he were nothing more than a new-found buddy. Under Mervyn Le Roy's buoyant direction (he also produced), it was as funny as the authors intended it to be. John Lee Mahin wrote the screenplay and the cast included Murray Hamilton, Howard Smith, Will Hutchins, Sydney Smith, Don Knotts and, in the role played on stage by Roddy McDowall (who turned down the chance to repeat his performance on film), Nick Adams (left). It was a Mervyn LeRoy production.

Director John Sturges' handling of Ernest Hemingway's interior monologue, **The Old Man And The Sea**, was more interesting for the nature of the exercise than its ultimate achievement. Magnificently photographed (in WarnerColor) by James Wong Howe, Floyd Crosby, Tom Tutwiler and Lamar Boren, effectively scored by Dimitri Tiomkin, and performed by Spencer Tracy (illustrated) with a dignity bordering on the tedious, the parable inherent in the story of an old fisherman and his battle against the forces of nature, failed to measure up to the stature of the novella on which it was based. Produced by Leland Hayward and scripted by Peter Viertel, it also featured Felipe Pazos and Harry Bellaver. It was not a financial success.

▽

△

Following his success in *No Time For Sergeants*, Andy Griffith was put into uniform once again in **Onionhead**. An entertaining if somewhat uneven comedy which Nelson Gidding scripted from a novel by Weldon Hill, it featured Griffith as a love-struck Oklahoman who deserts his college career for the Coast Guards when his romance with a local lass seems to be running out of mileage. Griffith (right) joins the *USS Periwinkle* as a cook, and his scenes with Walter Matthau (left) as the ship's chief cook, were the undoubted highlights of an uneven but enjoyable film. Norman Taurog directed for producer Jules Schermer, and the cast included Erin O'Brien as the girl Griffith leaves behind (and to whom he eventually returns), Felicia Farr as the interim object of his desires, Joe Mantell as a barber, Joey Bishop as a typical girl-chasing sailor, and James Gregory as the captain. Claude Akins, Ainslie Pryor, Ray Danton and Roscoe Karns were also in it.

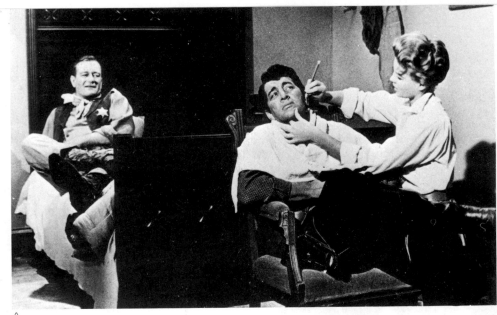

Another Western, and at 69 minutes running time, very much lower-case, **Westbound** starred Randolph Scott as a Union cavalry officer. He is assigned to re-establish the stagecoach line he once managed, for the purpose of shipping Californian gold to Federal banks at the time of the Civil War. Virginia Mayo and Karen Steele (centre) supplied the kisses, villain Andrew Duggan the hisses. Berne Giler wrote the screenplay from a story by Giler and Albert Shelby LeVino; it was directed by Budd Boetticher, produced by Henry Blanke (in WarnerColor), and also featured Michael Dante (left), Michael Pate. Wally Brown and Walter Barnes.

An absurd re-working of Max Reinhardt's celebrated production of Karl Vollmoeller's play, **The Miracle** starred Carroll Baker (centre) as a postulant nun who, during the Peninsular War, deserts the confines of her Spanish convent for an amorous encounter with a good-looking British officer (Roger Moore, left). At the same time, a statue of the Virgin Mary disappears, and takes her place in the convent in human form – hence the miracle of the title. When Baker's officer lover is believed to have been killed in the Napoleonic wars, she abandons herself to a series of romantic adventures with a gypsy (Vittorio Gassman), a bullfighter (Gustave Rojo), an elderly rake (Dennis King) and, once again, the handsome British officer who, it turns out, is still very much alive. In the end, though, she returns to the convent whereupon the drought which has been ravaging the countryside ceases, and the missing statue of the Virgin Mary miraculously re-appears. The one ingredient missing in Frank Butler's screenplay and Irving Rapper's direction was dignity, a fact which Technirama and Technicolor did little to conceal. Henry Blanke produced, and apart from Miss Baker, who did not see eye to eye with Rapper, the cast included Walter Slezak, Isobel Elsom, Katina Paxinou, Carlos Rivas, Torin Thatcher (right), Elspeth March and Daria Massey.

In Howard Hawks' own words, **Rio Bravo**, which he produced and directed, was 'the story of a friendship between a sheriff and his drunken deputy and how the deputy is rehabilitated'. Significantly, Hawks considered this aspect of the Jules Furthman–Leigh Brackett screenplay (from a short story by B.H. McCampbell) to be of more interest than the basic plot in which the sheriff (John Wayne, left) attempts to hold the killer (Claude Akins) in jail until the arrival of the US Marshal. Concentrating more on character than on the traditional situation, Hawks took 141 minutes to allow for the slow but marked development of his major characters. An answer of sorts to *High Noon* (United Artists, 1952), which he and Wayne disliked, **Rio Bravo** was conventional on the surface (it even had Dean Martin, centre, and Ricky Nelson proffering a musical interlude), but less pretentious than such contemporary Westerns as *Jubal* (Columbia, 1956) and *The Tin Star* (Paramount, 1957). Also cast were Angie Dickinson (right), Ward Bond, John Russell, and Walter Brennan as a crippled deputy. With **Rio Bravo** audiences re-discovered the traditional Western and liked it.

Another woebegone Sci-Fi thriller, **Teenagers From Outer Space** (released in Britain as **The Gargon Terror**) featured David Lowe (centre) and Dawn Anderson (right) in a way-out love story about an alien (accompanied by an unseen monster whose shadow suggests a giant crab) who is sent to Earth in order to destroy it. But he falls in love with a teenage girl, thus ensuring the continuation of the species. It was written, produced and directed by Tom Graeff for Topaz Films. The cast included Harvey B. Dunn, Ursula Hensen (left), Bryan Grant, Tom Lockyear and Robert King Moody.

-30- is the traditional sign-off used by journalists when they come to the end of their copy and it provided the title for producer, director and star Jack Webb's account of eight hours in the city-room of a metropolitan daily newspaper. (It was released in Britain as **Deadline Midnight**). Webb (right) played the tough night-managing editor, a man immune to crises, and regarded as a giant among his colleagues. The film's sub-plots, devised by scenarist William Bowers, involved a clash between Webb and his wife (Whitney Blake) over an adopted child, and re-write woman Louise Lorimer's setback when she learns that her grandson has died. But these happenings were mere appendages to the main business at hand: the production of the paper's next edition, whose front-page story is all about the rescue of a young child from a sewer. A moderately successful recreation of life on a busy newspaper (confined, for the most part, to one set) the film – a Mark VII Ltd. Production – also featured William Conrad (centre), John Nolan (left), David Nelson, James Bell, Nancy Valentine, Richard Bakalyan, Dick Whittinghill, Joe Flynn and Donna Sue Needham. -30-

59

A glossy soap-opera in the 1958 *Peyton Place* tradition and set in New England. **A Summer Place** was decidedly more outspoken than the former film in its attitude towards sex, virginity, divorce, pregnancy, etc. It was written and directed by Delmer Daves (from Sloan Wilson's best-seller) as if it were a commercial for illicit love, and it raked in the shekels, being a cannily crafted piece of work with mass audience appeal. For the grown-ups there was a steamy affair between a married woman, Dorothy McGuire, and her erstwhile lover Richard Egan, while the youngsters could identify with handsome newcomer Troy Donahue (left) and his female counterpart, Sandra Dee (right). Frank Lloyd Wright designed the 'summer place' of the title; Max Steiner wrote the lush score and haunting title song for Delmer Daves' hit production. Also in it were Arthur Kennedy, Beulah Bondi and Constance Ford.

Richard Burton (right) gave a blazing performance as Jimmy Porter – the horn-playing, working class candy-stall owner who wants to go places but can't think where – in **Look Back In Anger**, John Osborne's *cri de coeur* which heralded a *nouvelle vague* in the British Theatre when it was first presented at London's Royal Court Theatre in 1956. Intellectual and deeply sensitive, Jimmy Porter cannot stand the drabness of his life in the Midlands, is tortured by his failure as a husband, frustrated by his inability to make something of himself, and disgusted by the Establishment – which he holds responsible for most of his woes and unrealized dreams. Burton's performance, a reverberating howl of frustration, gave director Tony Richardson's film its centre of gravity, and was little short of mesmeric. Mary Ure (left) played Jimmy's middle-class wife Alison (and the butt of his numerous outbursts), with a weary but affecting resignation. Claire Bloom was his bitchy mistress, Gary Raymond his amiable best friend. Phyllis Neilson-Terry played Alison's haughty mother, with other parts taken by Glen Byam Shaw, Edith Evans, Donald Pleasence, Jane Eccles, and George Devine. Nigel Kneale wrote the screenplay (extra dialogue by John Osborne), it was photographed by Oswald Morris and produced by Harry Saltzman for Woodfall Productions.

The Cranes Are Flying, a prize-winning Russian film, shown in the United States under the cultural exchange programme presented by the USSR and the Department of State, and released by Warner Bros., was a propaganda-free World War II love story between a young hospital worker called Veronica (Tatyana Samoilova, centre) and Boris (Alexei Batalov, left), the man she hopes to marry. With the outbreak of war, Boris volunteers and is killed – a fact which Veronica refuses to believe. All the same, she allows herself to be seduced by Boris' pianist cousin (Alexander Shverin, right), whom she then marries despite her total lack of affection for him. Why Veronica should marry the cad after he has had his way with her, was the major flaw in Viktor Rozov's otherwise memorable and deeply moving screenplay. Still, Samoilova (the great-niece of Stanislavsky) gave a strong enough performance to prevent this plot point from marring the film irrevocably or drawing sympathy away from her and, under Mikhail Kalatozov's lyrical and expressive direction, helped the film to triumph. A Mosfilm Studios Production.

James Stewart divided his time equally between domesticity and operating as a successful federal agent in **The F.B.I. Story**. Weighing in at 149 minutes, the film was a tribute to marriage as well as to the F.B.I., both institutions being given top billing and both highly romanticized in director Mervyn LeRoy's entertaining, but overlong drama. As Stewart (illustrated) battled with Ku Klux Klan, 'Baby Face' Nelson, John Dillinger, 'Pretty Boy' Floyd and Nazi spy rings, Richard L. Breen and John Twist's screenplay (from the book by Don Whitehead) took a behind-the-scenes peek at the F.B.I. in order to show audiences how it all worked. Under LeRoy's breezy direction, it worked well enough, with Vera Miles cast as the epitome of the long-suffering but devoted spouse (was June Allyson on vacation?). Murray Hamilton, Larry Pennell, Nick Adams, Diane Jergens and Jean Willes were also in it. A Mervyn LeRoy Production with LeRoy producing, it was photographed in Technicolor and had a score by Max Steiner.

More interesting for the trends it set than for its artistic merits, **Hercules** was, in many respects, one of the decade's more important films. A cheaply made costume adventure about Hercules and his wife Iole, and their quest for the Golden Fleece, it was promoted by showman Joseph E. Levine (whose advertising budget far outdistanced the film's cost) into a multi-million dollar profit-maker. Levine, relying on TV and radio commercials rather than on newspaper promotion, gave the film saturation coverage, booking it into as many cinemas as he could for a week's run, then withdrawing it before poor word-of-mouth withdrew it for him. With only one famous name, Steve Reeves (illustrated) a former Mr America, to attract customers, the film had more than its quota of sex and violence and proved that, in the right venues, those two elements had as much pulling power as big-name stars. The right venues were the ever-popular drive-in cinemas, and the success of **Hercules** turned Levine into a major distributor, and later into an important film-maker as head of Avco-Embassy Productions. It more or less made a star of Steve Reeves, and turned Italy into a haven for many of Hollywood's beefy but aging glamour boys who were unable to find work nearer home but who were generally guaranteed employment in Rome in cheaply produced costume dramas and spaghetti westerns. **Hercules** clearly did not know his own strength! Filmed in Dyaliscope and Eastmancolor, it was directed by Pietro Francisci who, together with Ennio De Concini and Gaio Frattini, wrote the screenplay. Sylva Koscina played Iole, and Fabrizio Mioni was Jason.

In **Yellowstone Kelly**, Clint 'Cheyenne' Walker (right) playing a beefy fur-trapper, falls foul of both the Indians and the US Cavalry, but as he's the hero, he survives, and finds true love in the arms of Andrea Martin (left). Directed by Gordon Douglas from a screenplay by Burt Kennedy (book by Clay Fisher), the film also featured Edward Byrnes, John Russell, Ray Danton, Claude Akins and Warren Oates. It was photographed in Technicolor and consisted of 8,165 feet of celluloid clichés.

The Sixties

On 15 January 1960, the Screen section of the Writers' Guild of America went on strike for more equitable contracts and a share of the profits from films being sold to television; and in March of the same year, the Screen Actors' Guild of America demanded a raise in minimum salaries and a share of the TV residuals. In no time at all the IATSE and Directors' Guild followed suit, all with a degree of success, especially the actors, many of whom received an increase of up to 81 per cent on their salaries. As a result an economically teetering Hollywood, still reeling under the impact of TV, found itself in desperate need of financial assistance. Hence, Gulf and Western Oil stepped in to rescue Paramount; United Artists was taken over by the Transamerica Corporation – an insurance and investment combine; MGM shifted its emphasis from motion pictures to real-estate when it was bought by hotel tycoon and property speculator Kirk Kerkorian; and Warner Bros. became Warner Bros.-Seven Arts Ltd. through its affiliations with a Canadian-backed enterprise. At the end of the decade, Warner Bros.-Seven Arts Ltd. underwent a further change of management when the company was acquired by Kinney National, an outfit whose interests ranged from publishing to parking lots. The only studio to continue under the management of a group solely concerned with film making was 20th Century-Fox, even though, like MGM, it had sold off part of its backlot for real-estate. As far as the studios' new bosses were concerned, historical regard for the old Hollywood was of secondary importance to the business of making money, and, as there were vast profits to be tapped from TV, most of the major studios started making feature films especially for TV.

Universal (owned by MCA) was the first to enter this market in 1964 when, on October 7th, they premiered a made-for-TV feature film called **See How They Run**. In the next couple of years Columbia, MGM and Warner Bros. also entered the telefeature market. In addition to this, the networks were paying vast sums of money to the studios for their hit films (Columbia sold the screenrights of **The Bridge On The River Kwai**, 1957, to ABC for a limited period at a cost of $1,000,000) and, by 1965, the five-year embargo that prevented newly-made feature films from being shown on American TV was shortened to three. In 1965 there were well over 10,000 feature films available to the networks.

Hollywood in the sixties also saw the continuation of the rise in independent productions, with the main participants (star, writer, director, producer) sharing handsomely in the profits. Many of these productions were shot abroad – in 1962 30 per cent of all Hollywood product was filmed away from home, and productions like **Spartacus** (Universal, 1960), **King Of Kings** (MGM 1961), **El Cid** (Allied Artists/Rank 1961),

Barabbas (Columbia, 1962), **Taras Bulba** (United Artists 1962) and **Cleopatra** (20th Century-Fox 1963), were epic in scope as well as in cost. Other block-busters or 'road-shows' in the sixties, designed to lure audiences away from their TV sets, were **Exodus** (UA 1960), **Lawrence Of Arabia** (Columbia, 1962), **The Story Of Ruth** (20th Century-Fox, 1960), **It's A Mad Mad Mad Mad World** (UA 1965), **The Greatest Story Ever Told** (UA 1965), **The Great Race** (WB 1965), **Doctor Zhivago** (MGM 1965), **The Agony And The Ecstasy** (20th Century-Fox 1965), and **Grand Prix** (MGM 1965); and there was a spate of big budget Broadway musicals – filmed with admirable fidelity to the original stage shows such as **West Side Story** (UA 1961), **My Fair Lady** (WB 1964), **The Music Man** (WB 1962), **Gypsy** (WB 1962), **The Sound Of Music** (20th Century-Fox 1965), **Camelot** (WB 1965), **Bye Bye Birdie** (Columbia 1966), **Sweet Charity** (Universal 1969), and **Hello Dolly!** (20th Century-Fox 1969). The decade's original screen musicals included **Mary Poppins** (Disney 1964), **Doctor Dolittle** (20th Century-Fox 1967), **Star!** (20th Century-Fox 1968), and **Thoroughly Modern Millie** (Universal 1967). Both **Star!** and **Doctor Dolittle** were expensive failures.

Homosexuality and lesbianism, hitherto taboo subjects in the American cinema, featured prominently in the sixties. Examples include **The Children's Hour** (UA 1961), **A View From The Bridge** (1962), **A Walk On The Wild Side** (Columbia 1962) **The Best Man** (UA 1964), **Darling** (Anglo Amalgamated 1965), **The Group** (UA 1966), **Reflections In A Golden Eye** (WB 1967), **The Fox** (WB 1967), **The Detective** (20th Century-Fox 1968), **The Sergeant** (WB 1968), **If** (Paramount 1968), **The Lion In Winter** (Avco-Embassy 1968), **Midnight Cowboy** (UA 1969), and **The Killing Of Sister George** (Palomar, 1969).

Another minority group, the American blacks, also loomed large in films like **A Raisin In The Sun** (Columbia 1960), **Lilies Of The Field** (UA 1963), **Black Like Me** (1964), **A Patch Of Blue** (MGM 1965), **Duel At Diablo** (UA 1966), **One Potato, Two Potato** (Cinema V 1967) and **Guess Who's Coming To Dinner?** (Columbia 1967).

War films were a staple part of the sixties too, as they had been in the forties and fifties, but now, with films like **The Guns Of Navarone** (Columbia 1961), **The Great Escape** (UA 1963), **The Heroes Of Telemark** (Columbia 1965), **Von Ryan's Express** (20th Century-Fox 1965), **The Blue Max** (20th Century-Fox 1966), **Battle Of The Bulge** (WB 1966), **The Night Of The Generals** (Columbia 1967), and **The Bridge At Remagen** (UA 1968), they had an additional function as big-budget spectacles.

In 1968 Jack Valenti was appointed head of the Motion Picture Producers Association and did away with the censorship code to which Hollywood had for so many years adhered.

This was replaced with the present ratings system – from G. for general exhibition, to X for adults only, with M (later PG) and R between. Inevitably, this led to sex and violence being exploited in a way new to the American cinema. Suddenly there were fewer restrictions on what could be said, done or shown on the screen and film-makers, seeing the new-found freedom as a potent weapon in the ever more difficult battle against TV, were quick to take advantage of it.

The sixties also saw the Underground film (i.e. films shot on shoestring budgets, independently produced and released, and aimed at specialist audiences) emerging above ground as a viable alternative to the mass appeal, big-budget Hollywood product. Chief exponents of the genre were Andy Warhol (**The Chelsea Girls** 1966, **Bike Boy** and **The Nude Restaurant**, 1967), The Mekas Brothers (**The Brig** 1964) Kenneth Anger (**Scorpio Rising** 1963) and Shirley Clark, whose film **The Connection** (1961), was one of the first underground films to receive public recognition.

Another notable underground director to emerge in the sixties was Francis Ford Coppola, who, in 1967 at the age of 28, directed **You're A Big Boy Now** and, in 1968, **Finian's Rainbow** for Warner Bros.

Pornography surfaced publicly in the sixties with such titles as **Orgy At Lil's Place** (1962), **The Sadist** (1963), Paul Mart's **Sinderella and The Golden Bra** (1966) and Russ Meyer's **Faster Pussycat** and **Kill! Kill!** (1967).

In terms of technical innovation the sixties hardly matched the vigour of the previous decade as there was not much more that could be done with a strip of celluloid. Showman Mike Todd Jr introduced Smellovision which came (and went) in a film called **Scent Of Mystery** (1960); and Arch Oboler tried out a 3-D variation called Spacevision in **The Bubble** (1967). Three-strip Cinerama disappeared and was replaced by the one-strip 65mm. process known as Ultra-Panavision; and by the non-anamorphic, sharper 70mm. known as Super Panavision, seen in both **Lawrence Of Arabia** and **Doctor Zhivago.**

The sixties was also the decade of **The Graduate** (UA 1967) and **Bonnie And Clyde** (WB 1967); and introduced movie audiences to many of the super-stars of the 70s, including Dustin Hoffman, Warren Beatty, Robert Redford, Liza Minnelli, Faye Dunaway and Barbra Streisand.

Among the stars, writers, producers and directors who died during the decade were Alan Ladd, Gary Cooper, Judy Garland, Stan Laurel, Dick Powell, Marilyn Monroe, Clark Gable, Montgomery Clift, Clara Bow, Josef von Sternberg, Ben Hecht, Frank Borzage, Harpo and Chico Marx, Spencer Tracy, Peter Lorre, Buster Keaton, David O. Selznick, Boris Karloff, Charles Laughton, Michael Curtiz and Anthony Mann.

At the thirty-third annual Academy Awards presentation, **The Sundowners** was nominated for five Oscars, including Best Picture. The winner was United Artists' **The Apartment**. Fred Zinnemann was nominated for Best Director (Billy Wilder won for **The Apartment**); Deborah Kerr for Best Actress (Elizabeth Taylor won for MGM's **Butterfield 8**); Glynis Johns for Best Supporting Actress (the winner was Shirley Jones for UA's **Elmer Gantry**); and Isobel Lennart for Best Screenplay based on material from another source. (It went to Richard Brooks for **Elmer Gantry**.) Other nominees were Edward Carrere and George James Hopkins for **Sunrise at Campobello**'s Art Direction (Color), the Warner Bros. Sound Department for the same film, and Marjorie Best for Campobello's costume designs. In the Best Actress category, Greer Garson received a nomination for her performance in **Sunrise at Campobello**, and Shirley Knight was nominated as Best Supporting Actress in **The Dark at the Top of the Stairs**. The New York Film Critics voted Deborah Kerr's performance in **The Sundowners** as the best of the year; and **Sunrise at Campobello** was on the *New York Times* Ten Best list. The studio showed a net profit of $7,102,636.

For most of its 105 minute running time, **The Bramble Bush** was a superior soap-opera about a New England doctor who returns to his home town in order to save the life of a friend, falls for the dying man's wife, and indulges in a spot of mercy-killing. The ending, however, in which the doctor is accused of murder and has to face a trial, reduced the drama hitherto built-up in the Milton Sperling–Philip Yordan screenplay (from the novel by Charles Mergendahl) to potboiler level. Richard Burton (right) starred as the doctor, with Barbara Rush as the woman he falls for, Tom Drake as the ailing and bedridden friend, Jack Carson as a politico and Angie Dickinson (left) as a nurse in love with Burton. Also in it were James Dunn, Henry Jones, Frank Conroy and Carl Benton Reid. Daniel Petrie directed, and the producer was Milton Sperling. A United States Pictures Production, it was photographed by Lucien Ballard in Technicolor.

◁ James Garner (right) buried his *Maverick* image to play a financial and industrial whizz-kid (whose middle name could have been 'Finagling') in **Cash McCall**. One of his business ventures almost destroys the romance he is having with co-star Natalie Wood (left), but it all comes right in the end. It came right at the beginning too, thanks to a really crisp screenplay by Lenore Coffee and Marion Hargrove (from the novel by Cameron Hawley), with direction to match by Joseph Pevney, and a clutch of first-rate performances from its principals as well as Nina Foch, Dean Jagger, Henry Jones, E.G. Marshall and Otto Kruger. It was photographed in Technicolor, and produced by Henry Blanke.

Teenagers featured prominently in producer William Rowland's youth-orientated film **This Rebel Breed**. The two main items in Morris Lee Green's screenplay (from a story by William Rowland and Irma Berk) were narcotics and inter-racial tensions. Mark Damon played a detective with Mexican Negro blood in his veins, Rita Moreno appeared as a pregnant student and Richard Rust (left) and Diane (later Dyan) Cannon (right) were cast as a gang-leader and his moll. Director Richard L. Bare failed to come to grips with the problems posed by the scenario, but turned it into a fairly exciting drama just the same. An All God's Chillun Company Production, the executive producer was Robert H. Yamin.

Another United States Pictures Production with Milton Sperling as producer, **The Rise and Fall of Legs Diamond** was inspired by the TV success *The Untouchables*, and was an attempt, on behalf of the studio, to turn back the clock to their crime films of the thirties. It was a slick, well made, compulsively entertaining chronicle of the notorious underworld hood who shot his way up from petty thief to become one of New York's most notorious gangsters. Though the message underlying Joseph Landon's screenplay was that crime does not pay, director Budd Boetticher went all out to glamourize his eponymous hero and succeeded, despite the salutary ending, in giving the criminal activities of the roaring twenties a good name. Ray Danton (right) starred as Legs Diamond, with Karen Steele, Elaine Stewart (left), Jesse White and Simon Oakland in support.

▽

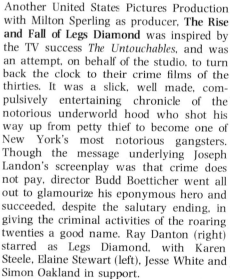

▽

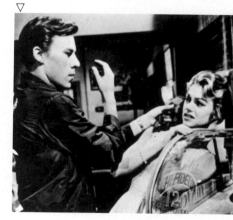

△

Alan Ladd and Jeanne Crain were teamed for **Guns of the Timberland**, an outdoor melodrama (in Technicolor) set against some spectacular scenery, all about a couple of partners in a timber concern (Ladd, left and Gilbert Roland, right) who not only fall out with local ranchers while tree-felling, but with each other as well. They shoot it out in the best sagebrush tradition, the winner's prize being an attractive horse trader (Crain). Ladd wins, and the romance he has with the pretty Jeanne sends sparks shooting all over the place, one of which was doubtless the cause of the forest fire which climaxed the film. There was little that was new in the Joseph Petracca–Aaron Spelling screenplay (story by Louis L'Amour), and under Robert D. Webb's direction, it was decidedly routine. Frankie Avalon, Lyle Bettger, Noah Beery, Alana Ladd and Regis Toomey were also in it, and the producer, for Jaguar Productions, was Aaron Spelling.

The only John Ford movie to feature a black ▷
man as hero was **Sergeant Rutledge**.
Pursuing the racist theme Ford had touched
on in *The Searchers* (1956) – though this
time it was negroes, not Indians who were
discriminated against – the James Warner
Bellah-Willis Goldbeck screenplay (from the
Bellah novel *Captain Buffalo*) told the story
of a black cavalryman called Rutledge who
finds himself on trial for a double murder
and for the rape of a white girl. Rutledge is
innocent, and is defended by a white
officer. Fearing, however, that prejudice
will jeopardize his chances of a fair trial, he
deserts his unit, returning only when he
learns that his fellow men are in danger.
Not one of the director's more memorable
Westerns, it was interesting for what it said
rather than for the way it said it. Woody
Strode (left) starred as Rutledge, with
Jeffrey Hunter (centre), Constance Towers
(right), Juano Hernandez and Billie Burke
(widow of showman Florenz Ziegfeld) also
cast. Willis Goldbeck and Patrick Ford
produced it in Technicolor.

△

Photographed in Italy and Yugoslavia,
Hannibal – with Victor Mature (right) as the
great Carthaginian conqueror – lumbered
its elephantine way across the Cinemascope screen and, apart from a couple of
well-staged battle scenes, was decidedly
heavy-going. Rita Gam co-starred as a
senator's niece (and the object of Hannibal's
affections), with Milly Vitale, Gabriele
Ferzetti, Rik Battaglia and Franco Silva
(left) – all of them dubbed – in other roles.
It was produced by Ottavio Poggi, written
by Mortimer Braus (from a story by
Poggi and an idea by Alessandro Conti-
nenza), and directed (in Technicolor) by
Edgar G. Ulmer.

Edna Ferber was nothing if not ambitious ▷
in her choice of subjects, and **Ice Palace**
was a perfect example of the power, sweep,
and fertility of imagination she brought to
bear on her work. But as adapted for the
screen by Harry Kleiner, her epic story
about the formation of Alaska was a
monumental bore. Running 143 minutes,
it starred Richard Burton (right) and
Robert Ryan (left) as antagonists in both
their private and professional lives (Burton
is a fish trapper and canner; Ryan dis-
approves), and Carolyn Jones as the woman
to whom they are both drawn. Directed
mainly against phoney studio backdrops by
Vincent Sherman, with a cast that included
Martha Hyer, Jim Backus, Ray Danton,
Diane McBain, Karl Swenson and Shirley
Knight, it received an icy reception from
press and public alike. Max Steiner wrote
the music and Henry Blanke produced (in
Technicolor).

One of the first of the 'heist' capers which
were to become such a staple part of the
cinema of the sixties and seventies, **Ocean's
Eleven** was a fun-filled – if decidedly
amoral – tale in which a group of ten
wartime buddies, under the beady eye of
Akim Tamiroff, successfully conspire to rob
five Las Vegas casinos one New Year's Eve.
The fact that circumstances prevent them
◁ from holding on to the swag was neither
here nor there. What mattered was the
mechanics of the heist, which an attractive,
if somewhat indulgent all-star cast under
Lewis Milestone's breezy direction, pulled
off with such disarming ingenuity that it
all looked as easy as losing at roulette. In
descending order of charm, the main
participants were Frank Sinatra (centre
left), Dean Martin (centre), Peter Lawford
(centre right), Sammy Davis Jr (left),
Richard Conte, Cesar Romero and Joey
Bishop. Angie Dickinson, Patrice Wymore
and Ilka Chase were also in it; so were Red
Skelton and George Raft appearing as
themselves. A Dorchester Production in
Cinemascope and Technicolor, Harry Brown
and Charles Lederer wrote it from a story
by George Clayton Johnson and Jack
Golden Russell; it was produced by Milestone and, box-office wise, broke the bank.

60

Jane Fonda (right) made her screen debut in **Tall Story** and was the freshest ingredient in an otherwise stale campus comedy which starred Anthony Perkins (left) as a basketball wizard who finds himself being bribed to lose a crucial match against a visiting Russian team. After being failed by college professor Ray Walston (who, responding to pressure, quickly manages to pass him), Perkins was romantically paired with Fonda for the final fade, and the couple seemed a lot happier with each other than audiences were with the film. Scripted by Julius J. Epstein from a play by Howard Lindsay and Russel Crouse (itself based on a novel by Howard Nemerov), and produced and directed by Joshua Logan (who also directed it on Broadway), it featured Marc Connelly (centre), Anne Jackson, Murray Hamilton, Bob Wright, Karl Lukas, Elizabeth Patterson and Tom Laughlin.

A decidedly arthritic relative of *The High and the Mighty* (1954), **The Crowded Sky** attempted to inject excitement into a situation involving a plane-load of passengers on a collision course with a Navy jet. Disaster was averted at the last moment when the jet was blown out of the sky, but not before a tedious succession of flashbacks filled us in on the sexual goings-on of a handful of passengers. However, there was no averting disaster for Michael Garrison's Technicolor production (screenplay by Charles Schnee from a novel by Hank Searls), directed by Joseph Pevney, in which Dana Andrews, Rhonda Fleming (left), Efrem Zimbalist Jr (right), John Kerr, Anne Francis, Keenan Wynn and Troy Donahue perished on impact with the script.

Hercules Unchained, one of the many sequels to Joseph E. Levine's money-making *Hercules* (1959), again starred muscleman Steve Reeves (centre) as the hero, involved this time with a kinky queen who kills her lovers, then stuffs and mounts them. Such a fate would have made little difference to Reeves' performance. Others involved in this juvenilia were Sylva Koscina (centre right), Primo Carnera and Sylvia Lopez. Pietro Francisci directed and also wrote (with Ennio De Concini) the story and screenplay (from 'the legends', or so said the credits).

In **Sunrise at Campobello**, Ralph Bellamy (centre left) repeated on screen the magnificent performance he had given on stage as Franklin D. Roosevelt. Basically concerned with the dark period in Roosevelt's life when he was stricken with poliomyelitis, Dore Schary's screenplay remained as faithful to his original stage treatment as the camera would allow, without betraying its origins. It opened out most effectively to show the President and his family in the Campobello summer residence prior to his illness, and for the climactic scene in which Roosevelt, with the aid of crutches, is able to stand in order to nominate Al Smith at the Democratic National Convention. Greer Garson (left) was not entirely at home as Eleanor Roosevelt, and filling her mouth with a set of protruding teeth hardly helped. Far better cast were Hume Cronyn (centre right) as Roosevelt's friend Louis McHenry Howe, Ann Shoemaker as Mrs Sara Delano Roosevelt, Jean Hagen (right), as secretary Missy Le Hand, and Alan Bunce as Al Smith. Though there were times when director Vincent J. Donehue (who also directed the play on Broadway) might profitably have toned down the two central performances which tended, on occasion, towards a certain theatricality, he managed to retain a dignified perspective on events without in any way detracting from the essentially heart-warming quality of the script. A Schary Production, it was produced by Dore Schary (in Technicolor) and had a score by Franz Waxman.

William Inge's Pulitzer Prize-winning play, **The Dark at the Top of the Stairs**, was less successful in its screen adaptation (by Harriet Frank Jr and Irving Ravetch) than it had been on Broadway, possibly as a result of the larger-than-life performance of Robert Preston as the head of the Flood household. More in scale with Inge's domestic drama were the performances of Dorothy McGuire as the wife Preston (centre) temporarily deserts, Angela Lansbury (right) as the woman he deserts her for, Eve Arden and Frank Overton as her sister and ineffectual brother-in-law, Robert Eyer as her adolescent son afraid of the dark at the top of the stairs, and Lee Kinsolving as a young Jewish lad driven to suicide by anti-semitism. Directed by Delbert Mann with all the sensitivity the subject demanded, it was a well-intentioned effort, but finally lacked conviction. Michael Garrison produced. (Technicolor.)

A 65 minute programmer, **The Threat** featured Robert Knapp (centre) as a policeman who sets out to prove that the reputation he has of being a sadist is a vile unfounded lie. In the process he discovers that the really mean member of his family is his brother (James Seay, left). A crime melodrama with little impact, it was produced and directed by Charles R. Rondeau, written by Jo Heims, and featured Linda Lawson, Lisabeth Hush (right), Mary Castle and Barney Phillips.

1961

William Inge won the studio's only Oscar in 1961 (Best Original Screenplay) for his work on **Splendor in the Grass**, though **Fanny** was nominated for five Academy Awards, including Best Picture. (The winner was United Artists' **West Side Story**.) Other **Fanny** nominees were Charles Boyer for Best Supporting Actor (Maximilian Schell won for UA's **Judgement at Nuremberg**), Jack Cardiff for Best Color Cinematography, Morris Stoloff and Harry Sukman for Best Scoring of a Dramatic or Comedy Picture, and William H. Reynolds for Best Editing. Natalie Wood received an Oscar nomination (Best Actress) for **Splendor in the Grass** but lost to Sophia Loren in the MGM release **Two Women**; so did Lotte Lenya for Best Supporting Actress in **The Roman Spring of Mrs Stone**. Rita Moreno won the award for **West Side Story**. **A Majority of One** received one nomination for Harry Stradling (Best Color Cinematography). The Studio's net profit was $7,209,822, with **Fanny** and **Splendor in the Grass** (voted one of the year's Ten Best by the *New York Times*) among the top money-makers of the year.

An unrecognizable Steve Reeves (right) ridiculously encumbered by an out-sized beard, appeared in and as **The White Warrior**, a poorly dubbed Italian spectacular about a tribal chieftain (Reeves) and his attempts to lead an attack against advancing Czarist troops in 19th century Russia. Based on Tolstoy's *Hadji Murad* it was written for the screen by Gino De Santis and Akos Tolnay, directed by Riccardo Freda, and featured Georgia Moll (left), Scilla Gabel, Gerard Herter and Renato Baldini. It was photographed in Dyaliscope and Technicolor and produced by Majestic-Lovcen in Italy.

A run-of-the-mill Western, **Gold of the Seven Saints** starred Roger Moore (centre) as an Irish cowboy whose lot it was to carry gold through the desert, and to prevent it from falling into the acquisitive hands of robbers, and every other marauder to which such plots are prone. His partner was Clint Walker (right), who didn't have a great deal to say for himself in the Leigh Brackett-Leonard Freeman screenplay (from a novel by Steve Frazee), with Leticia Roman (left), Robert Middleton, Chill Wills and Gene Evans in support. Gordon Douglas was responsible for the workmanlike direction, and Freeman also produced, in Warnerscope.

◁ A drama whose backbone (if it had had one) would have been politics, **A Fever in the Blood** featured Efrem Zimbalist Jr (right) as an incorruptible judge, and Jack Kelly (left) as an unscrupulous district attorney who thinks nothing of prosecuting an innocent man to advance his own political career. Also in the service of Roy Huggins and Harry Kleiner's routine screenplay (from the novel by William Pearson) were Don Ameche as a no-good senator, and Angie Dickinson (centre left) as his wife. Others in the cast were Herbert Marshall, Andrea Martin and Rhodes Reason, and it was directed by Vincent Sherman for producer Roy Huggins.

An off-the-peg melodrama, **Portrait of a Mobster** was also the portrait of a genre in deep decline. Set in the Prohibition era, it concerned a hood called Dutch Schultz (Vic Morrow, illustrated), but both the screenplay by Howard Brown (from the novel by Harry Grey) and the direction of Joseph Pevney had the taint of unintentional parody about them; a condition which infiltrated the performances of Leslie Parrish, Peter Breck, Norman Alden (on floor), Robert McQueeney, Ken Lynch, and, again playing Legs Diamond, Ray Danton.

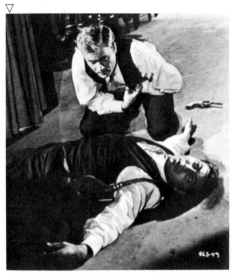

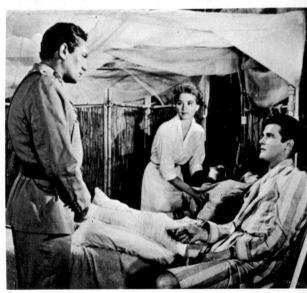

Angie Dickinson's sin in **The Sins of Rachel Cade** was having an illegitimate son by handsome Roger Moore (right), an American volunteer in the RAF whose plane happens to crash among the natives of the Belgian Congo at the very spot where the red-headed Angie (centre) is working as a missionary. As a result of her indiscretion, she decides to remain on in Africa rather than return to America with agnostic Dr Peter Finch (left, giving a replica of his 1959 *Nun's Story* performance), who is in love with her. A full-throated weepie designed to open the tear ducts of the ladies in the audience, it was written by Edward Anhalt from a novel by Charles Mercer, directed by Gordon Douglas, and produced by Henry Blanke. Also in it were Errol John, Woody Strode, Juano Hernandez, Frederick O'Neal and Mary Wickes. Max Steiner provided a lush and soupy score, and it was photographed in Technicolor.

George Montgomery (centre) produced, directed, co-wrote (with Ferde Grofé Jr and Malvin Wald) and starred in **The Steel Claw**. As if that were not enough, he lumbered himself with the loss of a hand as well. The story of an American marine captain (Montgomery) who, just as he is about to be discharged because of his disability, organizes an attack by Filipino guerrillas when the Japanese invade the Philippines, it reeked of phoney heroics and turned anorexic on its meagre diet of clichés. Also cast were Charito Luna (left), Mario Barri, Ben Perez (right), Paul Sorensen and Amelia De La Rama. A Ponderey Production (in Technicolor), its associate producers were Al Wyatt and Ferde Grofé Jr.

Like its heroine, producer Leonard Freeman's **Claudelle Inglish** (released in Britain as **Young and Eager**), was no good. The story of a pretty young farm-girl (Diane McBain, left), who goes completely to pieces when she is abandoned by her soldier boyfriend, and makes life hell for a number of her suitors, it had a trite and unconvincing screenplay (by Freeman from the Erskine Caldwell novel) which reduced all the characters to caricatures and the plot to soap-opera. Arthur Kennedy played Claudelle's farmer father, Constance Ford her pallid mother. Claude Akins (right), Frank Overton, Chad Everett and Robert Colbert were also in it; Gordon Douglas directed.

Produced in Czechoslovakia by Gottwaldor Film Studios and filmed in a process known as Mystimation, **The Fabulous World of Jules Verne** alternated tedium and invention in more or less equal proportions. Exploring a handful of Verne's favourite themes, the film combined live action and animation with mediocre results. The screenplay was by Karel Zeman, Francis Gross and Milan Vacca, with Zeman also directing. Joseph E. Levine presented it, and the cast included Louis Tock, Ernest Navara, Milo Holl and Francis Sherr (all anglicizations of Czech names).

Joshua Logan, working from a screenplay by Julius J. Epstein, and his own and S.N. Behrman's adaptation of part of the celebrated Marcel Pagnol *Marseilles Trilogy* (1931 and 1932), brought **Fanny** to the screen in superb Technicolor (the cameraman was Jack Cardiff), with a cast that included Charles Boyer, Leslie Caron and Maurice Chevalier. Based on Logan's Broadway presentation of the same material (where, in 1954, it surfaced as a musical with music and lyrics by Harold Rome), but with the songs omitted and the music relegated to the background, the gentle story of two elderly men who vie for the affections of an unmarried, but pregnant woman when her young lover leaves her to go to sea, had immense charm and style, thanks largely to the performances of Boyer (left) as Cesar, the proprietor of a waterfront bar, and Chevalier (right) as Panisse, the sailmaker. Leslie Caron (centre) as Fanny, and Horst Buchholz as Marius her lover, were fine; and there was colourful support from Baccaloni, Lionel Jeffries, Raymond Bussières and Victor Francen. A Mansfield Production, it was produced by Joshua Logan, with Ben Kadish as associate.

A long (140 minutes), and long-winded, tale about a young tobacco grower in the Connecticut River Valley and the problems he has with three sexy girls, **Parrish** was also the story of the young man's fight for acceptance by the snobbish yacht-club society in which he moves. Troy Donahue (left), his good looks in no way compensating for his almost total absence of talent, played Parrish in so stiff-jointed a manner that what he needed to guide him through his lines was an osteopath rather than a director; Claudette Colbert (right) co-starred as his gentle, solicitous mother, and Karl Malden as the avaricious landowner she marries. The screenplay (from the novel by Mildred Savage) was by Delmer Daves, who endowed it with the same synthetic gloss he brought to his direction, and the cast included Connie Stevens, Dean Jagger, Diane McBain, Sharon Hugueny, Dub Taylor and Hampton Fancher. It was produced by Daves, photographed (in Technicolor) by Harry Stradling, and had a score by Max Steiner.

The World by Night, dazzlingly photo- ▷
graphed in Technirama and Technicolor,
was a guided tour of some of the world's most
celebrated night-spots and the entertainment
on offer in them. Prominently featured were
Copenhagen's Tivoli Gardens, the Lido Show
in Paris, Harlem's Apollo Theatre, and The
Queen Bee Club in Tokyo, plus shows in
places as different in mood as Blackpool and
Las Vegas. Among those taking part were
The Nitwits, Kimio Lida, George Lee, Marco
(illustrated), female impersonator Ricky
Renee, Bob Williams and his dog, Wee Willie
Harris and Dora Pellettier. It was produced
(for Julia Films) by Francesco Mazzei and
Gianni Proia and directed by Luigi Vanzi.

A German programmer with a circus back-
drop, Bimbo the Great was about a trapeze
performer who, on learning that his step-
brother was the cause of his wife's death,
hits the bottle once too often, but successfully rehabilitates himself to his former
eminence. It featured a few speciality acts
that were diverting enough, but hardly
justified spending 88 minutes watching
them. Photographed in Eastman Color, its
cast included Claus Helm (right), Germaine
Damar (left), Elma Karlowa, Elke Aberle and
Marina Orschel. It was written by Hans
Raspotnik, Harald Philipp (who also directed) and Erich Kroehnke, produced for
Corona Film Productions, in Germany, by
Alexander Grüter, and presented by Joseph E.
Levine in the United States.
▽

◁ Another excursion into 3-D, The Mask was
a thriller about a mask which, when worn,
resulted in the wearer going insane. It
featured several hallucinatory sequences
(seen from the wearer of the mask's point
of view), but the biggest hallucination of all
was producer-director Julian Roffman's
belief that anyone would be interested. A
competent cast included Paul Stevens (right),
Claudette Nevins, Bill Walker, Norman Ett-
linger (left), Ann Collings and Martin Lavut.
The screenplay was by Frank Taubes and
Sandy Haber.

◁ Trebling as producer, director and writer,
Delmer Daves crammed a great deal of conventional soap-opera histrionics into Susan
Slade, but alas, not much emotional
honesty. Based on a novel by Doris Hume,
it starred Connie Stevens (left) as a young
woman who, after giving birth to an
illegitimate baby fathered by good-looking
mountaineer Grant Williams (he dies in a
climbing accident), attempts suicide. She
moves to Guatemala where she has her
baby, then, after the death of her father,
returns to California where she becomes
hitched to a shy horse-doctor (Troy
Donahue, right) in preference to wealthy
Bert Convy. A glossy cast, including
Dorothy McGuire and Lloyd Nolan (as
Susan's parents), Brian Aherne, Natalie
Schafer and Kent Smith splashed about to
little effect in Davies' sudsy screenplay,
which Lucien Ballard's Technicolor photography, and a score by Max Steiner were
powerless to elevate.

Working from an original screenplay by
William Inge, producer-director Elia Kazan
went all out for sweaty, grunting realism
in Splendor in the Grass, a drama of
repressed sexuality in a pair of adolescent
lovers in the Kansas of 1926 that was, and
still remains, vigorously powerful. Operating on maximum energy, Kazan's direction,
and the performances he coaxed out of
Natalie Wood (left), and a good-looking
newcomer called Warren Beatty (right),
gave Inge's story about a mid-Western
Romeo and Juliet a high-voltage charge that
left audiences reeling. Prevented by their
parents from marrying on the grounds that
they are too young, she goes mad and has
to be confined to a mental institution; he
hitches up with an incompatible floozy (Jan
Norris). Fred Stewart and Joanna Roos
played the parents responsible for wrecking
their children's lives. Unlike the adults in
Rebel Without a Cause (1955) they were in
no way caricatured, thus contributing an
emotional balance to the film which Rebel
lacked. Other roles went to Pat Hingle,
Audrey Christie, Zohra Lampert, Sandy
Dennis, Gary Lockwood, Barbara Loden,
Crystal Field, John McGovern, Sean Garrison and, making an appearance as a
minister, author William Inge.
▽

Vivien Leigh (right) ravished the senses to
such an extent in The Roman Spring of
Mrs Stone, Tennessee Williams' sensual
tale of a fading, middle-aged actress who
◁ retreats to Rome and buys love from a
handsome gigolo (Warren Beatty), that it
should have been Beatty (left) who was
paying for services rendered rather than
the other way round. Still, working from
an over-explicit screenplay by Gavin
Lambert, director José Quintero managed to
extract a few good moments, but in the end
couldn't conceal the fact that the finished
product was more Lambert than Williams.
(In the novella Williams unquestioningly
accepted his heroine's need to purchase
love; in the film Lambert ceaselessly dwelt
on it). The stunning Technicolor photography was by Harry Waxman, with
Richard Addinsell providing the music. An
impressive cast for the Seven Arts production
included Lotte Lenya (marvellous as a female
pimp), Jill St. John, Jeremy Spenser, Coral
Browne and Stella Bonheur, with other parts
going to Harold Kasket, Viola Keats, Cleo
Laine, Warren Mitchell, John Phillips, Ernest
Thesiger and Bessie Love.

1962

The Music Man was nominated for Best Picture by the Motion Picture Academy, but lost to Columbia's Lawrence of Arabia. It did, however, win an Oscar for Ray Heindorf for Best Scoring. Frank Perkins was nominated in the same category for Gypsy. Norma Koch received an Oscar for her costume designs (Black-and-White) for Whatever Happened to Baby Jane? and Don Feld was nominated in the same category for Days of Wine and Roses, released in January 1963. Other nominations were Henry Mancini and Johnny Mercer for the title song they wrote for Days of Wine and Roses; Ernest Haller for Best Black-and-White Cinematography (Whatever Happened to Baby Jane?); Harry Stradling for Best Color Photography (Gypsy); Joseph Wright and George James Hopkins for Best Black-and-White Art Direction (Days of Wine and Roses); Paul Groesse and George James Hopkins for Best Color Art Direction (The Music Man); the Warner Bros. and Glen Glenn Sound departments for The Music Man and Whatever Happened to Baby Jane?; William Ziegler for Best Editing (The Music Man); and Orry-Kelly and Dorothy Jeakins for Best Color Costume Design (Gypsy and The Music Man). Jack Lemmon won a Best Actor nomination for his work in Days of Wine and Roses, but lost to Gregory Peck in To Kill a Mockingbird (Universal), while Lee Remick (Best Actress nomination for Days of Wine and Roses), and Bette Davis (Best Actress nomination for Whatever Happened to Baby Jane?) lost to Anne Bancroft in United Artists' The Miracle Worker. Victor Buono was nominated as Best Supporting Actor for Whatever Happened to Baby Jane? but the winner was Ed Begley for MGM's Sweet Bird of Youth. The New York film critics gave no awards at all for 1962; while the New York Times Ten Best list did not include any Warner Bros. films. The studio showed a net profit of $7,565,763.

Director Claude Autant-Lara's re-telling of The Story of Monte Cristo was a waxwork affair which did scant justice to Dumas' celebrated tale in which one Edmond Dantes, falsely accused of being a Napoleonic sympathiser, is imprisoned, escapes, then makes the three men responsible for his incarceration pay for their misdeeds. Louis Jourdan brought a certain panache to the role of Edmond, but Jean Halain's screenplay (dubbed into English) was as old-fashioned as the direction, with Jourdan (left) the chief victim of its triteness. Jean-Claude Michel as the villainous Mortcerf fared somewhat better, but he was the only one in a cast that included Yvonne Furneaux (right), Pierre Mondy, Franco Silva and Bernard Dhéran, to do so. It was produced in France (in Dyaliscope and Technicolor) by Jean-Jacques Vital and René Modiano.

Good, as represented by a Catholic priest (John Mills, centre) and Bad, in the guise of a Mexican outlaw (a miscast Dirk Bogarde, right) clashed head-on in The Singer Not The Song, a pretentious, introspective, and lengthy (132 minutes) drama which developed into a curious triangle situation when a pretty rancher's daughter (Mylene Demongeot, left) is attracted to the priest, and is encouraged in her infatuation by the outlaw, whose own relationship with the man of the cloth has homosexual overtones. Based on the novel by Audrey Erskine Lindop, and written for the screen by Nigel Balchin, it was produced and directed by Roy Baker (associate producer Jack Hanbury) for the J. Arthur Rank Organisation. The film was made in Mexico (in Technicolor and Cinemascope), and also featured Laurence Naismith, John Bentley, Leslie French, Eric Pohlmann, Nyall Florenz and Roger Delgado.

An air of staleness pervaded Malaga, despite the authoritative presence of its star, Trevor Howard, playing a jewel thief who after being released from jail for a crime of passion, undertakes one more job to finance a trip to the South Sea Islands where he hopes to retire. Aided and abetted by Edmund Purdom (right) and Dorothy Dandridge (left), his scheme misfired and so did the film. David Osborn and Donald Ogden Stewart wrote it (from a novel by Donald MacKenzie); it was directed by Laslo Benedek and produced by Thomas Clyde. A Cavalcade Films Production (made in Britain, where it had already been released as Moment of Danger in 1960), it also featured Michael Hordern, Paul Stassino, John Bailey, Alfred Burke and Peter Illing.

The Couch was a workaday horror concoction about a psychopath who, while undergoing psychiatric treatment after being charged with homicide, embarks on a series of grisly ice-pick murders. Produced and directed by Owen Crump from a story he wrote with Blake Edwards, and flatly scripted by Robert Bloch, it starred Grant Williams (right), Shirley Knight (left) and Onslow Stevens, with William Leslie, Anne Helm, Simon Scott and Michael Bachus in the supporting cast.

◁ Similar in content to **Caged** (1950) but without any of the earlier film's dramatic impact or incisiveness, **House of Women** was a formula prison drama which starred Shirley Knight as a pregnant woman who is sent to prison for a robbery she did not commit. The film faltered, with scenarist Crane Wilbur unable to breathe life into the characters or the situations. Bryan Foy produced, Walter Doniger directed, and the cast included Andrew Duggan, Constance Ford, Barbara Nichols, Margaret Hayes, Jeanne Cooper and Virginia Gregg.

△

Delmer Daves was a three-time loser in **Rome Adventure** (released in Britain as **Lovers Must Learn**). He wrote it (from the novel by Irving Fineman), produced it and directed it (in Technicolor) and, as such, was entirely responsible for its failure. The slender story of an assistant librarian (Suzanne Pleshette, right) who goes to Rome to learn about love and, after a brief and unsatisfactory dalliance with Rossano Brazzi (left) falls for the more American charms of art student Troy Donahue, the plot thickened with the appearance of Angie Dickinson, one of Donahue's former flames. Also cast were Constance Ford, Al Hirt, Hampton Fancher, Iphigenie Castiglioni and Chad Everett.

Leonard Spigelgass' **A Majority of One** was ▷ a slender but disarming comedy about a widowed Yiddish Momma from Brooklyn and the unlikely romance she has with a widowed Japanese diplomat in Tokyo. As played by Gertrude Berg and Cedric Hardwicke on stage, it kept Broadway audiences delighted for 577 performances. Though faithful to the original, its transformation to the screen by Spigelgass (who wrote the screenplay) and Mervyn LeRoy (who produced and directed it) suffered heavily on two major counts: the miscasting of Rosalind Russell (left) and Alec Guinness (right) in the central roles; and its excessive running time (156 minutes). As Mr Asano, Guinness made little attempt to be anything more than inscrutable, though Russell, as Mrs Jacoby did at least attempt to deliver her lines with a tang of guefilte fish on her breath. But as talented a performer as she was, the role's ethnic origins defeated her. Madlyn Rhue and Ray Danton were amiable enough as her daughter and son-in-law, and there was colourful support from Marc Marno as a Japanese houseboy and Mae Questel as a nosey Brooklyn neighbour (both recruits from the original Broadway production). Also in it were Gary Vinson, Frank Wilcox, Harriet MacGibbon and Yuki Shimoda. Harry Stradling photographed it (in Technicolor) and Max Steiner wrote the score.

A tough, uncompromising tautly directed ▷ (by Samuel Fuller) World War II drama, **Merrill's Marauders** traversed familiar territory, but eschewed guts-and-glory heroics to make the point that there is nothing glamorous about war. All about an American volunteer group who, in Burma in 1942, assisted the British in preventing a Japanese invasion of India, it starred Jeff Chandler (illustrated) – in his last film – as a dying general determined to see his men succeed, and Ty Hardin as his likeable young lieutenant. Others cast were Peter Brown, Will Hutchins, Claude Akins, Charles Briggs, Luz Valdez and John Hoyt. It was written by Milton Sperling (who also produced for United States Pictures Productions) and Samuel Fuller from a story by Charlton Ogburn Jr. The film was eye-catchingly photographed by William Clothier (Second Unit, Higino J. Fallorina) in Technicolor and Technirama.

◁ UPA's animated feature **Gay Purr-ee** had a lot going for it, but it finally lacked the sheer sparkle and invention of a Disney equivalent despite the fact that many of the backgrounds — inspired by Matisse, Modigliani, Toulouse-Lautrec, Cézanne and Van Gogh — were enchanting. The story of a little cat from Provence called Mewsette, who finds true love in Paris when she is rescued from the clutches of undesirable city slickers by Juane-Tom, mouse-catcher *extraordinaire*, it featured the voices of Judy Garland (illustrated, with Mewsette!) and Robert Goulet, as well as Red Buttons, Hermione Gingold and Mel Blanc. Harold Arlen and E.Y. Harburg provided the score, it was written by Dorothy and Chuck Jones, and directed by Abe Levitow (in Technicolor) for executive producer Henry J. Saperstein. Songs included: Paris Is A Lonely Town, Take My Hand, Paree and The Money Cat.

△

Filmed at the Lyric Theatre in Hammersmith, London, in Technicolor and a process known as the Mitchell System 35, the screen version of the long-running Anthony Newley–Leslie Bricusse musical **Stop the World I Want to Get Off** was just as pretentious as its stage counterpart, but without the talents of its original stars, Anthony Newley and Anna Quayle, to give it the kiss of life. Set in a symbolic circus-ring (representing the world) the musical told the story of Mr Littlechap (Tony Tanner, left) whose one ambition in life, at the expense of everything else, is to improve his lot, regardless of the price or who he may hurt in the process. In the end, the person most hurt is none other than himself. It was produced by Bill Sargent, directed (resourcefully, considering the limitations) by Philip Saville, and co-starred Millicent Martin (right) in a variety of roles, with Leila and Valerie Croft, Neil Hawley, Georgina Allan, Natasha Ashton and Carlotta Barrow in support. Songs included: I Want To Be Rich, Typically English, Gonna Build A Mountain, Once In A Lifetime, Someone Nice Like You and What Kind Of Fool Am I?

△

A brave and important cinematic break-through in terms of its content and the rawness of its dialogue, **Who's Afraid of Virginia Woolf?**, skilfully adapted by Ernest Lehman from Edward Albee's prize-winning Broadway play, was a cathartic experience and one of the best American films of the decade. Its faults were the faults of the play (a sagging third act and the essentially contrived business regarding the protagonists' mythical son), but under Mike Nichols' solid, assured direction, they seemed minor in comparison to its virtues. Basically a boozy confrontation between history professor George, his wife Martha (daughter of the president of the New England college at which George lectures) and the young faculty couple, Nick and Honey, whom they invite back to their home, the film (as in the play) slowly, painfully and cruelly dissected the love-hate relationship between George and Martha that had been festering away for 20 years, while at the same time excavating tensions in the Nick-Honey relationship that were pretty explosive in themselves. In one of his best screen performances, Richard Burton as George (centre left) was brilliantly effective as a walking monument to self-loathing; while Elizabeth Taylor (right), bravely letting herself go in order to reach what she clearly hoped would be the apotheosis of her career, gave a dazzling display of histrionics as Martha, coming as near to achieving a great performance as she is ever likely to. As the traumatized young couple who are made privy to their marital secrets, George Segal (left) and Sandy Dennis (centre right) were superb. It was a Chenault production, produced by Ernest Lehman and photographed by Haskell Wexler, with a fine musical score by Alex North.

△

An enjoyable transfer from the Broadway stage to the Technicolor big screen, **Any Wednesday** (released in Britain as **Bachelor Girl Apartment**), was a featherweight comedy about a millionaire executive who sets up his mistress in a tax-deductible apartment (which he visits every Wednesday) and finds the course of infidelity running anything but smoothly when an associate of his is accidentally sent to the 'company' pied-a-terre. Jane Fonda (illustrated) was the mistress, Jason Robards the high-powered businessman, Rosemary Murphy (repeating the role she played on Broadway) the wife, and Dean Jones was Robards' associate. Julius J. Epstein's screenplay kept in all the best bits of Muriel Resnik's play, while director Robert Ellis Miller did his best to see that the laughter came in the right places. Julius J. Epstein produced.

66

Tony Curtis (left) and Virna Lisi (centre) starred as husband and wife (he's an air force officer, she's bored) in **Not With My Wife, You Don't!** with co-star George C. Scott (right), also of the air force, turning up and making a play for the lovely Virna who, since childhood, has always had a predilection for two of everything. There wasn't much mileage in the Norman Panama-Larry Gelbart-Peter Barnes screenplay (story by Panama and Melvin Frank), but what there was, was competently handled by the three principal players, their director (Norman Panama) and a supporting cast that included Carroll O'Connor, Richard Eastham, Eddie Ryder, George Tyne and Ann Doran. The producer was Norman Panama (for Fernwood-Reynard Productions) and it was photographed in Technicolor.

A really tacky treatment of Norman Mailer's novel on which it was based, **An American Dream** (released in Britain as **See You in Hell, Darling**) written by Mann Rubin, and starring Stuart Whitman (right) as a TV commentator who inadvertently causes the death of his impossible wife (Eleanor Parker) when, after a marital tiff, she falls thirty storeys to her death, left a decidedly nasty taste in the mouth. Whitman spent most of his time being pursued by the police, a gang of hoods, and his ex-mistress, Janet Leigh (left). The more sensitive members of the audience just wondered when and where it would all end. Barry Sullivan, Lloyd Nolan, Murray Hamilton and J.D. Cannon were also among the cast; it was produced by William Conrad (in Technicolor) and the director was Robert Gist.

A glossy Technicolor caper set in London and on the Riviera, and starring Warren Beatty (right) as a card-sharp who breaks into a European card factory, manages to mark the designs on the plates, cleans up as a result, then finds himself having to apprehend a narcotics smuggler during a decisive game of poker – or else go to jail for his nefarious activities, **Kaleidoscope** (also called **The Bank Breaker**) co-starred Susannah York (left) as the daughter of Scotland Yard inspector Clive Revill, with Eric Porter, Murray Melvin, George Sewell, Yootha Joyce, Larry Taylor and Jane Birkin in support. Robert and Jane-Howard Carrington wrote the screenplay, it was flashily directed by Jack Smight, garishly photographed by Christopher Challis and produced (in England) by Elliott Kastner for Winkast Productions. Stuff and nonsense, but not unamusing in parts.

Chamber of Horrors, originally intended for TV but withdrawn because of its excessively gruesome content, starred Patrick O'Neal (right) as a nutter who murders his unfaithful fiancée then 'marries' her corpse. A sort of House of Wax revisited (much of the action takes place in a wax museum in Baltimore), it was written by Stephen Kandel (from a story by Kandel and Ray Russell) and produced and directed in Technicolor by Hy Averback. Also cast were Cesare Danova, Wilfrid Hyde-White, Laura Devon, Inger Stratton (left), Patrice Wymore, Suzy Parker and, in a brief appearance, Tony Curtis. A 'Fear Flash' and 'Horror Horn' were introduced in order to alert audiences to the arrival of the film's four 'Supreme Fright Points'. Could it be that without them no one would have known whether they'd come or gone?

Photographed entirely on location in New York, **A Fine Madness**, adapted from his own novel by Elliott Baker, starred Sean Connery as an anarchic poet for whom life and its pressures become too much and who, after demonstrating that there is a violent streak in his nature, unwillingly has a lobotomy performed on him. Basically an old-fashioned screwball comedy with tragic overtones, the unusual mixture of ingredients resulted in a tastier brew than one might have imagined, made especially palatable by a superb cast that also included Joanne Woodward (as Connery's wife), Jean Seberg, Colleen Dewhurst, Clive Revill, Werner Peters, John Fiedler and, as a suave psychiatrist, Patrick O'Neal. It was slickly directed by Irvin Kershner and produced (in Technicolor) for Pan Arts by Jerome Hellman.

Returning to the depression years of the thirties, an era inextricably linked with Warner Bros., **Bonnie and Clyde** was arguably the best American film of the last 25 years. Director Arthur Penn's highly personal vision of the period melded with the grim story of the Barrow gang and their murderous exploits in a black comedy of startling power. Criticized for turning its protagonists into cult heroes and for glorifying violence (the climactic final scene in which Clyde Barrow and Bonnie Parker are reduced to marionettes as a thousand rounds of ammunition jerk their bodies into a grotesque dance of death, was as romantic as it was shocking), the film nevertheless appealed to a nostalgia-prone America and grossed over $23 million in domestic rentals alone. Apart from Faye Dunaway (right) and Warren Beatty (left) as Bonnie and Clyde, there were marvellous performances from Michael J. Pollard as C.W. Moss, Gene Hackman as Clyde's brother Buck, Estelle Parsons as his wife Blanche, Denver Pyle as a cop, and, making his movie debut, Gene Wilder as an innocent bystander whose car the Barrow gang requisition. David Newman and Robert Benton wrote the screenplay, Charles Strouse was responsible for the evocative period music, and Burnett Guffey's superb Technicolor photography captured to perfection the look, mood and feel of the era. Warren Beatty produced.

1967

Bonnie and Clyde was one of the nominations in the Best Film category in 1967, but lost to United Artists' **In the Heat of the Night.** The Clyde Barrow gang did, however, pick off two statuettes on their way to the bank: Estelle Parsons for Best Supporting Actress and Burnett Guffey for Best Cinematography. Warren Beatty was nominated for Best Actor for his work as Clyde, and Faye Dunaway for Best Actress as Bonnie. They lost to Rod Steiger in **In the Heat of the Night** and to Katharine Hepburn in Columbia's **Guess Who's Coming to Dinner**. Paul Newman was also nominated for Best Actor for **Cool Hand Luke**. Arthur Penn received a nomination for Best Director for **Bonnie and Clyde** but Mike Nichols won for the United Artists release, **The Graduate**. In the Best Screenplay From Another Source category, Donn Pearce and Frank R. Pierson were nominated for their work on **Cool Hand Luke**, and David Newman and Robert Benton for **Bonnie and Clyde**. The winner was Stirling Silliphant for **In the Heat of the Night. Camelot** received four nominations and won three: John Truscott, Edward Carrere and John W. Brown for Best Art Direction; Alfred Newman and Ken Darby for Best Musical Adaptation; and John Truscott for Best Costume Design, for which Theadora Van Runkle was also nominated for **Bonnie and Clyde**. Lalo Schifrin won an Oscar for his Original Scoring for **Cool Hand Luke**, and The Warner Bros.-Seven Arts Sound Department was nominated for **Camelot. Cool Hand Luke** was considered one of the year's Ten Best by the *New York Times*; While the New York Film Critics chose the Newman-Benton screenplay for **Bonnie and Clyde** as the best of the year. The year ended with a net profit of $9,145,000. In June, Warner Bros. became Warner Bros.-Seven Arts Ltd. On 24 November Albert Warner died at the age of 83.

67

There was a potentially good idea behind **A Covenant With Death**: a man, unjustly accused of murder, accidentally kills his hangman just as the real murderer confesses. It starred George Maharis (right) as a half-Mexican judge in a New Mexico community, on whose judgement of the case the film pivoted. Unfortunately, the Larry Marcus-Saul Levitt screenplay (from the novel by Stephen Becker) wasn't as good as its idea, and the end result was an uneasy *mélange* of melodrama and tedium. Lamont Johnson directed, the executive producer was William Conrad, and it featured Laura Devon, Katy Jurado (left), Earl Holliman, Sidney Blackmer, Arthur O'Connell, Gene Hackman, John Anderson, Emilio Fernandez and Wende Wagner. It was photographed in Technicolor.

The Corrupt Ones (released in Britain as **The Peking Medallion**), set in Macao and Hong Kong, was a Technicolored adventure whose chief asset was the way director James Hill kept it moving. The familiar story of an intrepid courier (Robert Stack, right) who finds the parcel in his charge is much sought after by a gang of hoods because it contains the key to hidden treasure, it featured Elke Sommer (left) as a beautiful widow, Nancy Kwan as a Tong belle, Werner Peters as a cunning police inspector and Christian Marquand as a crime syndicate's Mr Big. It was written by Brian Clemens from a story by Ladislaus Fodor and produced, in Techniscope, by Artur Brauner with Nat Wachsberger as executive producer.

The D'Oyly Carte Opera Company's production of Gilbert and Sullivan's **The Mikado** came to the screen as an unsatisfactory hybrid; it was not simply a photographed version of the operetta, nor was it freshly conceived for the cinema. The technique employed by screen director Stuart Burge fell somewhere in between. Nonetheless, as photographed by Gerry Fisher in Technicolor and on the wide screen, audiences were able to savour some of the good things from Anthony Besch's original stage production, and the singing was fine. Donald Adams played The Mikado and Philip Potter (left) was Nanki-Poo, with other roles sung by Kenneth Sandford, Thomas Lawlor, George Cook, John Reed (right), Valerie Masterson (centre) and Christian Palmer. A BHE Production, it was made in England with Anthony Havelock Allan and John Brabourne as executive producers.

The events that shaped the confused, adolescent life of newcomer Peter Kastner (left) and marked his progress from boyhood to manhood were the backbone of **You're A Big Boy Now**, an endearing comedy with a New York setting. Geraldine Page was marvellous as Kastner's possessive mother, with other splendid performances from Julie Harris, Karen Black (right) and, as the wicked little tease who becomes the most potent sexual turn-on in Mr. Kastner's innocent and inexperienced life, Elisabeth Hartman. Based on a story by David Benedictus, it was written and directed with a lively disregard for the routine by the up-and-coming Francis Ford Coppola and had a pleasing score by John Sebastian. Philip Feldman's Pathe-color production for Seven Arts was far better than the box-office returns indicated. Also cast were Rip Torn, Michael Dunn, Tony Bill and Dolph Sweet.

A patriotic World War II drama, no doubt churned out to remind the lads about to shuffle off to Vietnam that certain values in life were still worth fighting for, **First to Fight** starred Chad Everett (centre) as a marine hero who, after returning home and being decorated for his valour, marries, and takes a job as a bootcamp instructor. His heart is still at the Front though, and he arranges things so that he can rejoin his comrades in the Pacific; once there, however, he suffers an attack of nerves in battle. Being a red-blooded, all-American hero, he manages to pull himself together in time to save the day, but not, alas, the film. Marilyn Devin (left) played his wife, with other parts going to Dean Jagger (right), Gene Hackman, Bobby Troup, Claude Akins and Norman Alden. Christian Nyby directed it, William Conrad produced and it was written by Gene L. Coon. It was filmed in Technicolor and Panavision.

Eddie Chapman was a real-life double agent, and the only man to be hailed a hero in Britain while at the same time winning the Iron Cross in Germany. The possibilities inherent in such a story were, alas, dissipated in **Triple Cross**, a shoddy, anachronistic and unimaginatively directed (by Terence Young) attempt to recreate one of the most thrilling of all wartime adventure stories. Christopher Plummer (right, as Chapman) swaggered through the role with an air of arrogant indifference from which the film never quite recovered, with co-stars Romy Schneider, Trevor Howard, Gert Frobe, Claudine Auger and Yul Brynner (standing centre) all having been seen to better advantage elsewhere. René Hardy wrote the screenplay (from *The Eddie Chapman Story* by Chapman and Frank Owen) and it was produced in Technicolor for Cineurop Productions by Jacques-Paul Bertrand, with Fred Feldkamp as executive producer.

Trains, ships, aeroplanes, long-distance buses and hotels are a perpetual source of fascination to film-makers, as was once again demonstrated by **Hotel**. A competent, glossy, made-for-TV-type melodrama, it took a look at the hotel business in general and certain customers in particular at the plush (but fictitious) St Gregory in romantic New Orleans. A predictable plot combined with a series of one-dimensional characters to give the movie a two-star rating. It was produced and written by Wendell Mayes (from the Arthur Hailey novel) and directed by Richard Quine in Technicolor. It starred Rod Taylor (centre), Catharine Spaak, Merle Oberon (right), Karl Malden, Melvyn Douglas, Richard Conte and Michael Rennie.

After her Academy Award-winning role in *Who's Afraid of Virginia Woolf?* Sandy Dennis (illustrated) appeared in **Up The Down Staircase** as a schoolteacher initially unable to cope, either physically or emotionally, with the delinquent pupils who crowd the classrooms at the Calvin Coolidge High School on New York's West Side. How she finally adjusts to her problems, as well as the problems of some of her students — especially moody, good-looking, out on probation Jeff Howard — formed the basis of Tad Mosel's excellent screenplay (from the novel by Bel Kaufman). Without resorting to the pulpit, the film exposed certain deficiencies in an unsatisfactory education system, making the point that it is not the students who are always to blame, but the unenlightened, impatient teachers whose inability to handle the job is the fuse-paper to an already explosive situation. Apart from Miss Dennis (named Best Actress at the Moscow Film Festival for her work in the movie), the film featured Patrick Bedford, Eileen Heckart, Ruth White, Jean Stapleton, Sorrell Booke and Roy Poole. It was produced in Technicolor by Alan J. Pakula, and directed with great sensitivity by Robert Mulligan.

The Cool Ones was a youth-orientated comedy with a rock 'n' roll beat to it (but little else) in which impresario Roddy McDowall, for a publicity stunt, works hard to get two of his clients, a pop-singer on her way up (Debbie Watson) and a crooner on his way down (Gil Peterson) romantically involved. Phil Harris, Robert Coote, Nita Talbot, George Furth, Mrs Miller, Glen Campbell, The Bantams, The Leaves and T.J. and the Fourmations were in it; Gene Nelson directed from a story and screenplay by Joyce Geller, which he and Bob Kaufman adapted, and it was produced, in Technicolor and Panavision, by William Conrad. Songs included: Where Did I Go Wrong?, It's Magic, This Town, High, Tantrum, Hands, Baby, Baby, Your Love Is All I Need.

◁ A European co-production (involving West Germany, France, Spain and Italy), **The Viscount** was an irredeemable gangster melodrama about a 'viscount' named Clint de la Roche (Kerwin Matthews, left) who lends his services to uncovering a gang of dope dealers. Edmond O'Brien was the heavy, with scenarist Clarke Reynolds (working from a story by Jean Bruce), director Maurice Cloche and producer Nat Wachsberger having much to answer for. A Waterview Production in Technicolor, it also featured Jane Fleming (alias Silvia Sorente, right), Yvette Lebon, Jean Yanne and Fernando Rey.

The several strands of plot that comprised scenarist Stanley Mann's screenplay for **The Naked Runner** (from the novel by Francis Clifford), were left untied by the film's end, so that the story of a furniture designer, who once served as a crack shot in the Special Operations Forces in Germany, and who suddenly finds himself being pressed into service in order to eliminate an international top-level spy, confused more than it entertained. And not even Frank Sinatra (illustrated) as the designer could make it otherwise. Still, if you didn't probe too deeply into the logic of the narrative, and didn't mind director Sidney Furie's often infuriating habit of treating every camera set-up as if it were a work of modern art, the film was not entirely without its moments of genuine suspense. A Sinatra Enterprises Production, it was produced, in Technicolor, by Brad Dexter and featured Peter Vaughan, Derren Nesbitt, Nadia Gray, Toby Robins, Edward Fox and J.A.B. Dubin-Behrmann.

The Bobo was a booboo of a comedy which starred Peter Sellers (right) as a matador whose yearning to be a singer can only be fulfilled when he manages to seduce an attractive but impossibly choosy courtesan (Britt Ekland, left). Pretending to be an inordinately wealthy count, Sellers, in one of his least successful performances, sets out to woo the lady into his bed. Based on a play by David R. Schwartz (which, in turn, was based on a novel by Burt Cole) and with a screenplay by Schwartz that was sadly in need of a few good lines, it had nothing going for it, and not many people going to it. A Gershwin-Kastner production, directed by Robert Parrish in Technicolor, it was produced in England by Elliott Kastner and Jerry Gershwin, with David R. Schwartz as associate. Also cast were Rossano Brazzi, Adolfo Celi, Hattie Jacques, Ferdy Mayne, Kenneth Griffith and La Chana and the Los Tarantos Flamenco Company. Francis Lai provided the music, including a song written by himself, George Martin, Herbert Kretzmer and Sammy Cahn.

The Frozen Dead were a group of Nazi bodies, voluntarily frozen at the end of World War II. The German scientist (ineptly played by Dana Andrews) responsible for the experiment, decides the time has come to thaw the human blocks of ice in a lunatic attempt to revive the Third Reich. So much for the plot which, had it not been so clumsily handled by its originator Herbert J. Leder who also produced and directed the film, might have been fairly amusing. A Gold Star Production, it was produced in England in Eastmancolor (but shown in black-and-white in America), and featured Anna Palk (right), Philip Gilbert (centre), Kathleen Breck (left) and Karel Stepanek.
▽

A sex farce in the grand manner, The Birds, The Bees and The Italians was as Italian as ravioli without being as damaging to the figure. In fact, the only discomfort experienced was a slight pain in the sides as a result of an over-indulgence of laughter. The first of the movie's three segments involved a group of prominent citizens and their wives in a raucous party (a pair of suspenders proving vital to the story); the second item concerned a timid bank official who decides to leave hearth and home for the love of a shop girl; while the final (and most serious) tale told how several pillars of the community seduce an under-age country girl. Virna Lisi (left), Gastone Moschin (right), Nora Ricci, Alberto Lionello, Olga Villi, Franco Fabrizi, Beba Loncar and Gigi Ballista were in it; it was written by Age Scarpelli, Luciano Vincenzoni and Pietro Germi, the latter serving also as director and co-producer with Robert Haggiag. It was produced in Italy and photographed in Technicolor. Warner Bros. released it through an 'art' subsidiary, Claridge Pictures.
▽

Based on *All in Good Time*, Bill Naughton's observant play of working-class family life in Lancashire, **The Family Way** concentrated on the problem that newly married Hywel Bennett (centre left) has on his wedding night: his inability to consummate the marriage. His young wife, Hayley Mills (centre) thinks it's her fault, though the problem is in fact nothing more than their present circumstances. For they happen to be staying with Bennett's bullying father (John Mills, left) whose presence in the same house has an inhibiting effect on his sensitive son. As domestic dramas go, **The Family Way** was better than most, with Mills giving an especially compelling performance as the paterfamilias. Marjorie Rhodes played his wife, Murray Head (second left) his other son. The bride's family were represented by John Comer and Avril Angers, and Wilfred Pickles, Liz Frazer (centre right), Hazel Bainbridge, Diana Coupland, Ruth Gower, Fanny Carby and Barry Foster were also in it. Bill Naughton wrote the screenplay, and it was produced and directed, in Technicolor, by Roy and John Boulting for Lion International. The music was by Paul McCartney.

It took a bit of time for **Wait Until Dark** to find its form, but when it did, it was a gem of a thriller. Adapted by Robert and Jane-Howard Carrington from Frederick Knott's Broadway success, it told the chilling story of a blind woman whose apartment is invaded by three murderous thugs in search of a doll stuffed with heroin. How the sightless victim manages to save her skin in conditions that would have reduced a sighted person to a jibbering wreck, was the film's *raison d'etre*, and, as directed by Terence Young (whose bag of tricks included one single moment of shock that had audiences, quite literally, jumping out of their seats) was an effective excursion into suspense not unworthy of Hitchcock. Audrey Hepburn (right) starred as the put-upon heroine, with Alan Arkin (left), Jack Weston and Richard Crenna as the thugs. Efrem Zimbalist Jr was Miss Hepburn's husband, Julie Herrod her 14-year-old neighbour. Henry Mancini wrote the music and Mel Ferrer produced. It was filmed in Technicolor.

A horrid rather than horrifying horror film from the Gold Star stable, **It!** starred Roddy McDowall (illustrated) as the demented assistant curator of a museum who mysteriously brings to life an enormous rock statue only to discover that the piece of stone is cursed. The movie was cursed too, with McDowall's over-the-top performance no compensation for Herbert J. Leder's below par screenplay, production and direction. Also cast were Jill Haworth, Paul Maxwell, Aubrey Richards, Ernest Clark, Oliver Johnston and Noel Trevarthen.

Carson McCullers' superb novella **Reflections in a Golden Eye** was hardly ideal film material, as it concentrated more on the anguish of its hero's soul than on telling a solid story. Set in a peacetime army fort in Georgia – the centre of the drama being the home of a major (Marlon Brando, background) and his wife (Elizabeth Taylor, foreground) – McCullers' story probed their disastrous marriage (he is homosexual and she taunts him about his inability to make love to her), and ended in tragedy. Director John Huston made a bold stab at translating the novella's imagery and atmosphere to the screen (he tried unsuccessfully to have the film shown in desaturated Technicolor) but failed, as the quality of McCullers' prose was in no way matched by Chapman Mortimer and Gladys Hill's screenplay (an impossible task, anyway). The result was curious rather than satisfying or enlightening. The same could be said of Brando's performance which sounded most of the time like a man talking with his mouth full. Elizabeth Taylor was appropriately sensual and there were effective portrayals from Julie Harris, Brian Keith and Zorro David. Ray Stark produced.

All the glitter that $15,000,000 could buy was sprayed across King Arthur's mystical **Camelot**. Based on the Alan Jay Lerner and Frederick Loewe Broadway musical, adapted in turn from T.H. White's *The Once and Future King*, the 178-minute long film was no improvement on the already flawed stage show, but it did have Vanessa Redgrave (right) as Guinevere, the beautiful recipient of King Arthur's love. Richard Harris (left) was Arthur and Franco Nero the noble Lancelot du Lac, whose own love for Guinevere (and hers for him) disrupts the new order of chivalry as formulated by the Knights of the Round Table, and sends the unfortunate queen to the stake. Though director Joshua Logan brought a heavy hand to the proceedings, Lerner and Loewe's enchanting score, plus the three central performances, made it moderately worthwhile. David Hemmings played Mordred, Lionel Jeffries was King Pellinore and Laurence Naismith was cast as Merlin. Also in it were Pierre Olaf, Estelle Winwood, Gary Marshall, Anthony Rogers and Peter Bromilow. It was produced in Technicolor and Panavision by Jack Warner. Songs included: Camelot, If Ever I Would Leave You, Then You May Take Me To The Fair, C'est Moi, How To Handle A Woman, The Lusty Month Of May, Guinevere and What Do The Simple Folk Do?

Cool Hand Luke, coming 35 years after *I Am a Fugitive from a Chain Gang*, was more eloquent about prisoners and their problems than any of its screen predecessors. Starring Paul Newman (right) as a reticent, psychologically disturbed loner picked up by the police for decapitating parking meters, it charted the vicissitudes of his life in a correctional camp from outsider to camp hero as a result of eating fifty hard-boiled eggs in one uninterrupted session. Working from Donn Pearce and Frank R. Pierson's trenchant screenplay, Stuart Rosenberg's probing, intimate direction almost amounted to an invasion of the prisoners' privacy. The result was a tough, unsentimental drama which worked not only as social comment but as marvellous screen entertainment. Apart from Newman's powerful central performance, the film was expertly served by George Kennedy (left), J.D. Cannon, Lou Antonio, Robert Drivas, Strother Martin and Jo Van Fleet. It was produced in Technicolor and Panavision by Gordon Carroll for Jalem Productions with Carter De Haven Jr as associate producer.

The Young Girls of Rochefort starred Françoise Dorléac and Catherine Deneuve as a couple of girls who run a ballet school and constantly dream of meeting their ideal man. Their dreams materialize in the shape of Gene Kelly (illustrated) as a concert pianist, and Jacques Perrin. Director Jacques Demy, who also wrote it, turned the entire town of Rochefort-sur-Mer into one vast film set, gave it a pastel paint job from top to bottom, and set out to capture something of the dynamism of the classic MGM musical. But it didn't quite work out that way. Michel Legrand's score tinkled to little effect, the choreography (by Norman Maen) was effete, and the two leading ladies, neither of whom could sing or dance, were little more than attractive appendages to a basically soggy, albeit visually charming, entertainment. As for Kelly, he seemed to be employed merely for his image, to provide the film with an authentic face from the golden era of movie musicals to which **Rochefort** was paying homage. A Parc Film-Madeleine Production, it was produced in France by Mag Bodard and Gilbert de Goldschmidt and filmed in Technicolor.

1968

Warner Bros.-Seven Arts Ltd were awarded only one Oscar in 1968, and it was won by Frank P. Keller for his editing of **Bullitt**. There were several nominations, though, three of them – including that of Best Picture – going to **Rachel, Rachel. Oliver!** (Columbia) was named Best Picture, with Katharine Hepburn (Avco-Embassy's **The Lion in Winter**) and Barbra Streisand (Columbia's **Funny Girl**) jointly named as Best Actresses, while Joanne Woodward had to content herself with a nomination in the same category for her work in **Rachel, Rachel**. Alan Arkin was one of the Best Actor nominees for **The Heart is a Lonely Hunter**, but lost to Cliff Robertson in **Charly** (Selmur). Sondra Locke, also for **The Heart is a Lonely Hunter**, was nominated as Best Supporting Actress, but the winner was Ruth Gordon in Paramount's **Rosemary's Baby**. Stewart Stern's screenplay (from another medium) won him a nomination for **Rachel, Rachel**, but James Goldman beat him to it for **The Lion in Winter**. The Warner Bros.-Seven Arts Sound Department received nominations for **Bullitt** and **Finian's Rainbow**, with Ray Heindorf (also for **Finian's Rainbow**) being nominated for his musical scoring. Michel Legrand and Jacques Demy were similarly nominated for **The Young Girls of Rochefort** and Lalo Schifrin for his scoring of **The Fox**. The New York Film Critics voted Alan Arkin as the Year's Best Actor for **The Heart is a Lonely Hunter**, Joanne Woodward as Best Actress for **Rachel, Rachel** and Paul Newman, also for **Rachel, Rachel**, as Best Director. The *New York Times* named **Petulia** one of the Ten Best films of the year. **Rachel, Rachel** and **The Green Berets** were the studio's big money-earners. The year's net income was $10,350.000.

Originally made in Germany in 1965, ▷ **Flaming Frontier**, a Western, starred Stewart Granger (right) as Old Surehand and Pierre Brice as his Indian blood-brother Winnetou in a routine plot (by Karl May, screenplay by Fred Denger, Johanna Sibelius and Eberhard Keindorff) to foil a wicked white man's attempts to foment war between the Comanches and the Palefaces. A Rialto Film-Preben Philipsen (Berlin) and Jadran Film (Zagreb) Production, it was directed by Alfred Vohrer, produced by Horst Wendlandt, and featured Larry Pennell, Leticia Roman (left), Mario Girotti and Erik Schumann.

△

Though events have since overtaken the technology described in **Countdown**, Loring Mandel's screenplay (from a novel by Hank Searls) took a compelling look behind the scenes, both privately and professionally, at an astronaut's life and life-style. Newcomers James Caan (centre) and Robert Duvall (right) co-starred (as an astronaut and his hard-driving instructor), with Joanna Moore, Barbara Baxley, Charles Aidman and Steve Ihnat (left) in support. Under Robert Altman's intelligent direction, its plot, which had Caan attempting a solo space flight to the moon in a race against a Russian crew who are headed in the same direction, generated enough excitement to keep Sci-Fi addicts suitably engrossed. It was produced in Technicolor and Panavision by William Conrad.

◁ The third in a series of adventures based on characters created by Sax Rohmer, **The Vengeance of Fu Manchu**, in which the wily old Oriental decides to destroy Interpol by creating a double of his nemesis Inspector Nayland Smith, it suffered from a weak screenplay by Peter Welbeck, and flaccid direction by Jeremy Summers. Christopher Lee (as Fu, illustrated) and Douglas Wilmer (as Nayland Smith) starred, with Tsai Chin, Tony Ferrer, Horst Frank, Noel Trevarthen and Maria Rohm in support. A Babasdave Film, it was produced in colour by Harry Alan Towers but shown in the US in black and white.

Masturbation and lesbianism were prominently featured in **The Fox**, a striking adaptation (by Lewis John Carlino and Howard Koch) of the D.H. Lawrence novella of the same name. It told the story of two young women whose relationship is threatened, then destroyed, with the arrival at their farm of a virile young man who kills a marauding fox then symbolically takes its place. Sandy Dennis (right) and Anne Heywood (left) were the friends; Keir Dullea the outsider. Directed without the slightest trace of gratuitous sensationalism by Mark Rydell, whose approach to the work was only marginally more explicit than Lawrence's; and performed by the trio with appropriately Lawrentian ambivalence, the film, like the book, had the power to disturb – and did. A Stross Motion Picture International Production, it was produced in colour by Raymond Stross, and released by Warner Bros. through Claridge Pictures, a short-lived company dedicated to the production of films with a markedly adult content.

68

Updated to the 20th century, the Austrian-made **Heidi** with its authentic Alpine setting was a colourful re-telling of the famous Johanna Spyri story (screenplay by Richard Schweizer and English dubbing by Michael Haller) which worked extremely well. Eva Maria Singhammer (centre) played the title role without the 'cutesy-cutesy' quality Shirley Temple had brought to the same part for 20th Century-Fox in 1937, with Gustav Knuth (left) cast as her grandfather. Gertraud Mittermayr, Lotte Ledl, Ernst Schroder and Rolf Moebius were also in it; it was directed by Werner Jacobs and produced (in Technicolor) by Karl Schwetter and Richard Deitsche for Sascha Film.

▽

Apart from a segment in the 1948 comedy *On Our Merry Way*, James Stewart and Henry Fonda had never co-starred. **Firecreek**, a routine Western, rectified that and featured Stewart as a part-time sheriff in a dot-on-the-map town, with Fonda as the varmint who invades it. Needlessly sombre in its approach to such horse-play, Calvin Clements' screenplay did little to disguise the sheer predictability of it all, and although Messrs Stewart (illustrated) and Fonda were their reliable selves, the film offered nothing special apart from the novelty of seeing Fonda play a villain. TV recruit Vincent McEveety directed it in Technicolor and Panavision, with Philip Leacock producing in association with John Mantley. Also cast were Inger Stevens, Gary Lockwood, Dean Jagger, Eg Begley, Jay C. Flippen, Jack Elam and James Best.

▽

△

Two Yul Brynners for the price of one was about the best thing on offer in **The Double Man**, which cast its star (right) as a CIA agent as well as his double and which, like *Heidi*, was also set in the Austrian Tyrol. Unlike *Heidi*, however, it involved murder and mayhem, the unfortunate victim (he was pushed off an Alp) being CIA agent Brynner's son. Britt Ekland (left) was the love interest, with Clive Revill, Anton Diffring, Moira Lister, Lloyd Nolan, George Mikell, Brandon Brady and Julia Arnall in support. Frank Tarloff and Alfred Hayes wrote it from a novel by Henry S. Maxfield, it was directed by Franklin J. Schaffner and produced (in England, and in Technicolor) by Hal Chester and Albion Film Corp.

△

Bye Bye Braverman, director Sidney Lumet's screen adaptation of Wallace Markfield's novel *To an Early Grave*, used a funeral as an excuse to bring together four Jewish intellectuals whose diversion *en route* to the cemetery formed the substance of the film. An amusing satire on the behaviour and mores of the particular ethnic group with which the movie was concerned, it relied mainly on its performances for its comic impact, and with such actors as George Segal (illustrated), Jack Warden, Joseph Wiseman, Sorrell Booke, Jessica Walter, Phyllis Newman, Zohra Lampert, Godfrey Cambridge and Alan King in attendance, Herbert Sargent's screenplay had a verisimilitude about it that must surely have given a cross-section of the Jewish members of the audience an acute shock of recognition. It was shot in New York by Boris Kaufman (in Technicolor) and produced for his own company by Sidney Lumet.

Carol Lynley (right) and Oliver Reed starred in **The Shuttered Room**, a competently crafted spine-chiller set in New England and involving a deserted millhouse which, twenty years prior to the film's commencement, was the scene of several strange occurrences. Miss Lynley (the victim of these weird goings-on) returns to the millhouse with her husband (Gig Young, left) determined to get to the root of the mystery. A genuine miasma of evil permeated both David Greene's direction and the D.B. Ledrov-Nathaniel Tanchuck screenplay (from the story by August Derleth and H.P. Lovecraft) and, as Miss Lynley's sinister cousin Ethon, Oliver Reed oozed malignancy. Also cast were Flora Robson, Judith Arthy, William Devlin and Charles Lloyd Pack. Phillip Hazleton produced in Technicolor for Troy-Schenck productions.

▽

379

THE Seventies

An estimated 15 million Americans visited the cinema each week in 1970 compared with 43.5 million in 1960, 60 million in 1950, and 85 million in 1940. When there was something that people wanted to see, more of them went to see it than in previous decades, but at the beginning of the seventies, cinema-going was far from the national pastime it had once been. The result was that certain films, like **M.A.S.H.** (20th Century-Fox, 1970) grossed a fortune, but too many others barely recouped their print costs. Like the Broadway theatre, movies had become very much a hit-or-miss affair. With the dissolution of the studio system on which Hollywood had thrived, not only were fewer films being made, but independent producers hiring studio space were largely responsible for the product. Thus, there was no way in which the failures could be written off or balanced against the successes, as each effort was a separate undertaking, representing perhaps two years work, which had to stand or fall on its own merits. As there were no longer sufficient films being churned out each year to keep the picture palaces across the country equipped with a new feature each week (let alone two), a novel trend in cinema exhibition developed: the two, three or four-in-one movie-house complex in which a single attraction could run for several months and be enjoyed in intimate surroundings.

Escalating production costs led to far greater risks in film-making: in 1970 for instance, 20th Century-Fox, despite the success of **M.A.S.H.** and the previous year's **Butch Cassidy And The Sundance Kid**, showed a loss of $77 million. As a result of this, in the early part of the decade at any rate, there were fewer blockbuster 'road show' productions than there had been in the sixties.

As the seventies began, film-makers sought and followed trends initiated in the sixties. After the success of **Easy Rider** (Columbia, 1969) and **Alice's Restaurant** (United Artists, 1969) a deluge of anti-heroic, largely youth-oriented films flooded the market, the best of which were **Five Easy Pieces** (Columbia, 1970), **Two Lane Blacktop** (Universal, 1971), **Badlands** (Warner Bros., 1973), and **American Graffiti** (Universal, 1974). Pop music dominated the scene too, most notably with **Woodstock** (Warner Bros., 1970) and **Gimme Shelter** (Relpic-Maysles Film Inc., 1970).

Another trend that spilled over into the seventies was the spate of films about blacks. Notable examples were **Cotton Comes To Harlem** (United Artists, 1970), **The Great White Hope** (20th Century-Fox, 1970), **Lady Sings The Blues** (Paramount, 1972), **Black Girl** (Cinerama Releasing Corporation, 1972), **Sounder** (20th Century-Fox, 1972), **Uptown Saturday Night** (Warner Bros., 1974) and **A Piece Of The Action** (Warner Bros., 1978) plus several 'superspade' movies, including **Shaft** (MGM, 1971), **Superfly** (Warner Bros., 1972), **Cleopatra Jones** (Warner Bros., 1973) and **Cleopatra Jones And The Casino Of Gold** (Warner Bros., 1975).

The fast-changing social, moral and political values of the seventies were instantly reflected by the movie industry. For the first time the clear-cut lines of demarcation between good and bad and right and wrong began to blur. In certain circumstances crime could (and did) pay, while the hero was not necessarily good, wholesome, decent or clean-cut à la Gary Cooper or James Stewart, nor was he romantically dashing like Errol Flynn or Tyrone Power. Films no longer always passed moral judgements on their subjects, and instead often set out to disturb and provoke. Among those which succeeded in doing just that were **The Boys In The Band** (Cinema Center, 1970), **Carnal Knowledge** (Avco Embassy, 1971), **Sunday, Bloody Sunday** (United Artists, 1971), **The Conversation** (Paramount, 1974), **The Godfather I and II** (Paramount 1971 and 1974), **One Flew Over The Cuckoo's Nest** (United Artists, 1977), **Straight Time** (Warner Bros., 1978), **Network** (MGM/UA, 1977), and **An Unmarried Woman** (20th Century-Fox, 1978).

No sooner did MGM and 20th Century-Fox auction off their valuable collection of props, than a wave of nostalgia for the twenties and thirties swept over the movie capital, and resulted in such films as **The Last Picture Show** (Columbia, 1971), **Paper Moon** (Paramount, 1973), **The Sting** (Universal, 1973), **The Way We Were** (Columbia, 1973), **The Great Waldo Pepper** (Universal, 1975), **Thieves Like Us** (United Artists, 1972) and **At Long Last Love** (20th Century-Fox, 1975).

The industry enthused over its own past too, with such recent offerings as **That's Entertainment** (MGM, 1974), **Gable And Lombard** (Universal, 1976), **The Day Of The Locust** (Paramount, 1976), **W.C. Fields And Me** (Universal, 1976), **The Last Tycoon** (MGM, 1976), **Valentino** (United Artists, 1977), **Inserts** (United Artists, 1977), **Hearts Of The West** (MGM, 1977), **Won-Ton-Ton, The Dog That Saved Hollywood** (Paramount, 1977) and **Nickelodeon** (Columbia, 1977).

Another major and highly profitable trend in the seventies was the disaster movie, as represented by Universal's **Airport**

(1970) (and its sequels **Airport '75** and **Airport '77**), **The Towering Inferno** (20th Century-Fox–Warner Bros., 1974), **The Poseidon Adventure** (20th Century-Fox, 1972) **Earthquake** (Universal, 1974), **The Swarm** (Warner Bros., 1978) and the phenomenally successful **Jaws** (Universal, 1975) and **Jaws 2** (Universal, 1978).

The occult, another popular theme, also featured prominently in the seventies, with **The Exorcist** (Warner Bros., 1973), its sequel **The Exorcist Part 2: The Heretic** (1977), **The Omen** (20th Century-Fox, 1976), its sequel **Damien – Omen II** (1978) and **Carrie** (United Artists, 1977) heading the list.

For the first time, there was now nothing that could not be said or shown on the screen, particularly in matters sexual, as demonstrated by **The Music Lovers** (United Artists, 1970), **Myra Breckinridge** (20th Century-Fox, 1970), **Last Tango In Paris** (United Artists, 1972), the hard-core **Deep Throat** (Independent, 1973) – although in this instance, court cases and certain bannings followed on the grounds of obscenity – **Emmanuelle** (Trinacre Films, 1975), **The Night Porter** (Avco Embassy, 1975), **Shampoo** (Columbia, 1975), **Taxi Driver** (Columbia, 1976) and **Pretty Baby** (Paramount, 1978).

Violence was a prominent feature of the decade too, especially in such films as **Bloody Mama** (AIP, 1971), **A Clockwork Orange** (Warner Bros., 1971), **Deliverance** (Warner Bros., 1972), **Prime Cut** (Cinema Center, 1972), **Rollerball** (United Artists, 1975), **The Texas Chain Saw Massacre** (Excalibur Films, 1977), **Marathon Man** (Paramount, 1977), **Mandingo** (Paramount, 1977) and **Midnight Express** (Columbia, 1978).

The seventies was also the decade of the Kung Fu martial arts actioner instigated by Bruce Lee in such films as **Fist Of Fury** (Golden Harvest Productions, 1972), **Enter The Dragon** (Warner Bros., 1973), and **The Big Boss** (Golden Harvest Productions, 1972). Lee and his movies became a cult to certain audiences which continued after his death with literally dozens more, including **Dragon's Teeth** (1976), **Man From Hong Kong** (1976), **The Angry Dragon** (1976), and **Dragons Of Death** (1976).

Cop-movies proliferated in the seventies: **Dirty Harry** (Warner Bros., 1971), **Freebie And The Bean** (Warner Bros., 1975), **Hustle** (Paramount, 1975), **The Enforcer** (Warner Bros., 1976) and **The Choir Boys** (Lorrimar, 1978), representing a mere handful of them. The private-eye continued his investigations too, in films like **Klute** (Warner Bros., 1971),

The Long Goodbye (United Artists, 1973) **Chinatown** (Paramount, 1974), **The Drowning Pool** (Warner Bros., 1975), **Farewell My Lovely** (Avco Embassy, 1975), **The Late Show** (Warner Bros., 1977) and **The Big Sleep** (ITC, 1978).

Other notable and highly individual films outside these categories, included **Nashville** (Paramount, 1975), **The Apprenticeship of Duddy Kravitz** (International Cinemedia Center, 1974), **Mean Streets** (Warner Bros., 1973), **Annie Hall** (United Artists, 1977), **All The President's Men** (Warner Bros., 1976) and **California Split** (Columbia, 1974).

Foreign productions found a ready market in English-speaking countries in the seventies, especially the critically acclaimed **My Night At Maud's** (1970), directed by Eric Rohmer, de Sica's **The Garden Of The Finzi-Continis** (1970), Chabrol's **Le Boucher** (1971), Buñuel's **The Discreet Charm Of The Bourgeoisie** (1972), Jacques Tati's **Traffic** (1972), Bergman's **Cries and Whispers** (1972) and **The Emigrants** (1972), Truffaut's **Day For Night** (1973), Fassbinder's **Fear Eats The Soul** (1974), Fellini's **Amarcord** (1974), Bergman's **Scenes From A Marriage** (1976), and Buñuel's **That Obscure Object Of Desire** (1978).

With so much quality in evidence, movies were better than ever, and not even TV, with such audience-grabbing series as *Rich Man, Poor Man, Roots, Wheels, Seventh Avenue, The Moneychangers* and *Holocaust* could keep the public permanently at home. According to the trade paper Variety, in 1974 cinema admissions were 1 per cent higher than in 1973, 8 per cent up on 1972, and 23 per cent up on 1971. In February, 1977, the same journal stated that admissions were up 22 per cent on 1976. The upward trend continued in 1977 with **Star Wars** (20th Century-Fox) becoming not only the most financially successful film of the decade, but of all time; and 1978 the most profitable year in Hollywood's history. As the great majority of films are now in colour, they are not specifically listed as such in the entries for films in this decade.

As the seventies draw to an end, the major Hollywood studios, while continuing to keep their sound stages occupied, have surrendered their personalities completely as, indeed, they began to do in the sixties. There is now no longer a distinctive Warner Bros. look or an MGM look, or a Paramount look to characterize the product emerging from them. The great dream factories, together with the old star system, have gone for ever. At the age of 75, the American film industry has finally lost its innocence.

1970

In 1970 Kinney reorganized itself into Warner Communications Inc. (by which name the company continues to be known), a highly successful conglomerate whose interests, apart from theatrical and TV rentals, extend to music and book publishing as well as record making. **Woodstock** was the only Warner Bros. release to be featured in the 1970 Academy Awards presentation and it won an Oscar for the Best Feature Documentary, with nominations for Best Sound Recording and Best Editing. The Academy Award for Best Film of the Year went to 20th Century-Fox's **Patton**. The only Warner Bros. release to appear in the *New York Times* Ten Best list for 1970 was **The Ballad of Cable Hogue**. Net profit for the year was $27,713,000, the studio's top grossers being **Woodstock** and **Chisum**.

Described by its makers (Hammer Films) as a 'space Western', **Moon Zero Two**, set in the year 2021, was a low-budget Sci-Fi adventure which starred James Olson as a freelance spaceman (and the first man to reach Mars) employed by an autocratic tycoon to bring down an asteroid made of sapphire from an isolated section of the moon. Enter the baddies, together with a plot (by Gavin Lyall, Frank Hardman and Martin Davison; screenplay by producer Michael Carreras) of mind-crushing unoriginality and, after 100 minutes, exit the audience pummelled senseless by boredom. Roy Ward Baker directed, and the cast included Catherina Von Schell, Warren Mitchell (left), Adrienne Corri, Ori Levy, Dudley Foster (right), Bernard Bresslaw (centre) and Neil McCallum.

A Hammer Film Production, **Frankenstein** ▷ **Must Be Destroyed** deployed a minimum of chills as Peter Cushing (illustrated) attempted to perfect his experiments in brain transplants. Terence Fisher's direction held no surprises, but then neither did Bert Batt's screenplay from the story devised by Batt and Anthony Nelson Keys. It was produced by Keys, and featured Veronica Carlson, Freddie Jones, Simon Ward, Thorley Walters, Maxine Audley, Geoffrey Bayldon, George Pravda and Peter Copley.

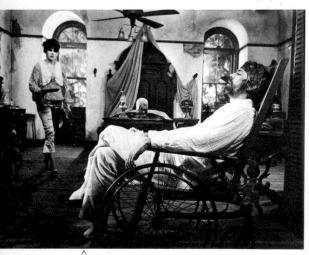

△

Director Sidney Lumet failed to make rhyme or reason out of **The Last of the Mobile Hot Shots**, an adaptation (by Gore Vidal) of Tennessee Williams' unsuccessful Broadway play *The Seven Descents of Myrtle*. In America, persons under 17 were not admitted, a stricture for which they should be eternally grateful. Set in a decrepit Southern plantation house called Waverley, it parodied the attempts of one Jeb Thorington (James Coburn, right) to acquire an heir before he is felled by terminal lung cancer. To this end, he marries Myrtle, a hooker on a TV show (Lynn Redgrave, left) who, when she isn't attempting to make love to the dying Jeb, is after his black half-brother Chicken (Robert Hooks). It all ends with the Mississippi flooding its banks and washing the whole sorry edifice away. Lumet's direction did nothing to help Redgrave and Coburn through the sweaty contrivances of the plot, with Perry Hayes and Reggie King two more of Myrtle's hapless victims. James Wong Howe photographed it, Quincy Jones provided the score, and Lumet also produced.

Despite its impressive list of cameo performances by such yesteryear stars as Joan Blondell, Xavier Cugat, Andy Devine, Fritz Feld, Leo Gorcey, Louis Hayward, George Jessel, Ruby Keeler, Patsy Kelly, Dorothy Lamour, Guy Lombardo, Joe Louis, Marilyn Maxwell, Butterfly McQueen, Pat O'Brien, Maureen O'Sullivan, Rudy Vallee and Johnny Weissmuller, **The Phynx** was an acute embarrassment to all concerned and, after a brief airing, was consigned to the shelf. All about the formation of a pop group whose only purpose is to rescue a clutch of show biz stalwarts from Communist captivity, it starred Lou Antonio (left), Mike Kellin (right), Michael Ansara and George Tobias. Lee H. Katzin directed it, and it was written by Stan Cornyn from a story by Bob Booker and George Foster (who was also the producer for Cinema Organization). R.I.P.

▽

△

A traditional, action-packed Western, **Chisum** starred a laconic John Wayne as a rancher who watches a New Mexican community fall under the villainous yoke of land baron Forrest Tucker. When he feels that Tucker has gone far enough, he galvanizes himself into action and the climax, involving a thunderous cattle stampede and an all-in shoot-out, was a beaut. Thanks to Wayne (left), good triumphed over evil and, in the process, an exciting time was had by all. Patric Knowles, Geoffrey Deuel as Billy the Kid (right), Pamela McMyler, Ben Johnson, Glenn Corbett and Christopher George were also cast. It was directed in fine sagebrush style by Andrew V. McLaglen, written by Andrew J. Fenady (who also produced), and beautifully photographed in Panavision by William A. Clothier. A Batjac Production (which grossed over $6,000,000), the executive producer was Michael Wayne.

An account of the already legendary rock festival that took place over a period of three days on a 600 acre farm near Bethel, N.Y. in August 1969, **Woodstock** was a definitive documentation of an era and its music. Half a million people flocked to the event, one of the best of its kind ever staged, including the director/cameraman Michael Wadleigh, who, with twelve other cameramen, recorded the occasion (on 16mm) for posterity, concentrating as much on the enthusiastic young audience as on the rock stars who comprised the once-in-a-lifetime line-up, most notably Richie Havens, Joan Baez, Crosby, Stills, Nash and Young, The Who, John Sebastian, Joe Cocker, Sha-Na-Na, Country Joe and the Fish, Arlo Guthrie, Santana, Sly and the Family Stone, Ten Years After, and the late Jimi Hendrix. In all, Wadleigh shot 315,000 feet of film (approximately 120 hours) which he, the producer Bob Maurice and a team of superbly creative editors, using a split-screen technique, finally managed to reduce to 184 minutes. The associate producer was P. Dale Bell. The bottom line of **Woodstock's** balance sheet totalled an impressive $13,500,000 in box office receipts, making it one of Warner Bros.' most successful films of the year. Musical items by the festival's numerous stars included: Long Time Gone, Wooden Ships, Going Up The Country, Joe Hill, Swing Low Sweet Chariot, Summertime Blues, At The Hop, With A Little Help From My Friends, Coming Into Los Angeles, Dance To The Music, Star-Spangled Banner and Purple Haze.

Start The Revolution Without Me was a ▷ disappointing farce which squandered the talents of its two leading players, Donald Sutherland (centre) and Gene Wilder (left). A tale of mistaken identity, it involved two sets of identical twins who, after being separated at birth (one twin from each pair) meet up 30 years later on the eve of the French Revolution. The undergraduate quality of the humour was reflected in the names of some of the characters invented by scenarists Fred Freeman and Lawrence J. Cohen (Duke d'Escargot, Count De Sisi, Claude Coupé, Mimi Montage) against which a host of good performers including Hugh Griffith (right), Jack MacGowran, Billie Whitelaw, Harry Fowler and, as narrator, Orson Welles, battled stalwartly but to little effect. A Bud Yorkin–Norman Lear Production, it was produced and directed by Yorkin with Lear as executive producer.

A heist caper aimed more at the funny bone than at the spine, **Sophie's Place** (released in Britain as **Crooks and Coronets**), had a limited showing in the States and was worth seeing solely for the sprightly performance of the octogenarian Dame Edith Evans (left). She played the owner of a stately home, ◁ which Telly Savalas (right) and Warren Oates, in cahoots with Cesar Romero, plan to rob of its ancestral treasures. But when the old girl endears herself to the hoods, the heist goes awry. So does the film. Apart from Dame Edith, there wasn't much in Jim Connolly's screenplay or direction that managed to appeal to audiences, and it sank without trace. Nicky Henson appeared as Dame Edith's titled grandson, with other parts going to several reliable British character actors including Harry H. Corbett, Hattie Jacques, Arthur Mullard, Frank Thornton, Thorley Walters and Clive Dunn. The producer was Herman Cohen.

A certain confusion and haziness permeated Robert Altman and Brian McKay's screenplay of **McCabe and Mrs Miller** from the novel by Edmund Naughton – and a certain pretentiousness and obscurity impeded Altman's symbol-seeking direction. Yet there was much to admire and enjoy in this North-Western frontier story, especially the fine performances of Warren Beatty (left) and Julie Christie (right) as the titular hero and heroine. He was a small-time gambler who, in 1902, in the guise of a notorious gunslinger, sets up a bordello in a zinc-mining town called Presbyterian Church; she was a frizzy-haired, hard-nosed madam who coerces him into setting her up in business in exchange for half of the profits. Their enterprise prospers and attracts the attention of 'The Company' – local mobsters who move in to take it over even though Beatty has no intention of selling. The film was awash with contemporary allusions, but its main strength lay in Altman's recreation of the mood of a mythical American frontier town at the turn of the century. If things weren't quite like the way he depicted them,

you felt they should have been. A deeply personal film in style more than in content, its quality was enhanced by Vilmos Zsigmond's atmospheric photography, Leonard Cohen's songs and the performances – all of them first rate – of Rene Auberjonois, Hugh Millais, John Schuck, Shelley Duvall, Corey Fisher, Michael Murphy, Keith Carradine, William Devane and Bert Remsen. A Robert Altman-Dave Foster Production, it was produced by Foster and Mitchell Brower with Robert Eggenweiler as associate producer, and filmed on location in Canada, in Panavision.

In **Man In The Wilderness** Richard Harris played an embittered, blasphemous frontiersman who, while out with a party of trappers in the uncharted Northwest of the 1820s, is mauled by a grizzly bear and left to die by his callous expedition leader (John Huston). His determination to survive and an understandable desire for revenge bring him into close contact with the unyielding forces of nature, in the course of which he relives (in flashback) incidents from his past life. Striving for an almost mystical experience in the telling of this Crusoe-like yarn, director Richard Sarafian concentrated more on the theme of man's ability to survive in impossible circumstances than on the credibility of Jack De Witt's hollow screenplay. What was said was less important than the images evoked by cameraman Gerry Fisher, whose depiction of man against his environment was extraordinarily powerful. Harris (illustrated) went through the film with an agonized expression on his face for most of the time which, considering his circumstances, was to be expected; though after 105 minutes it was hard to tell who was suffering more: he or the audience. John Bindon, Ben Carruthers, James Doohan, Bruce M. Fischer, Percy Herbert, Henry Wilcoxon, Bryan Marshall and Prunella Ransome were also in it, it was produced by Sanford Howard (who teamed with Harris in Cinema Center's 1970 release *A Man Called Horse*) for Sanford-Limbridge productions, with C.O. Erickson as associate producer.

Luchino Visconti's **Death In Venice** (from the novella by Thomas Mann) was visually exquisite, and at times profoundly moving, but it was not without its blemishes. The most damaging of these was the clumsy translation into tiresome flashbacks of Mann's inner monologues, with Aschenbach (now a composer rather than the writer Mann intended) endlessly discoursing on the nature of beauty and art with one of his students (Mark Burns). Also, the casting of Dirk Bogarde (right) as Aschenbach was not entirely successful. Too young, and already possessing an aura of decadence in the film's opening scenes, Bogarde did not have very far to fall, thus reducing the impact of Aschenbach's final loss of dignity as he lingers on in the disease-infected city, waiting to die. By overstressing the sexuality

of Bjorn Andresen's knowing Tadzio (left), Visconti deflected the emphasis of the novella away from the spiritual to the physical, which, while unfaithful to Mann's intentions, undeniably made for engrossing cinema. The film stunned the ear as well as the eye (the haunting background music was from Mahler's Third and Fifth Symphonies), and brilliantly evoked a particular period and place. It was written for the screen by Visconti and Nicola Badalucco, photographed by Pasquale de Santis, designed by Ferdinando Scarfiatti and costumed by Piero Tosi. Made in Italy for Alfa Cinematografica Productions, it also featured an exquisite Silvana Mangano as Tadzio's mother, Romolo Valli, Nora Ricci, a young Marisa Berenson, Carole Andre and Leslie French.

1972

The Emigrants, nominated as Best Foreign Film in 1971, was again nominated in 1972 – together with Deliverance – as the Best Film of the Year. The winner was Paramount's The Godfather. Other nominations for The Emigrants were Jan Troell for Best Director (Bob Fosse won for Allied Artists' Cabaret). Liv Ullmann for Best Actress (Liza Minnelli won for Cabaret) and Jan Troell and Bengt Forslund for Best Screenplay based on Material from Another Medium. (Mario Puzo won for The Godfather). The Best Original Screenplay Award went to Jeremy Larner for The Candidate. John Boorman received a Best Director nomination for Deliverence; and in the Best Sound Category Richard Portman and Gene Cantamessa were nominated for The Candidate. The New Land received an Oscar nomination for Best Foreign Language Film but the winner was The Discreet Charm of the Bourgeoisie (20th Century-Fox).

Edward G. Robinson 'who achieved greatness as a player, a patron of the arts and a dedicated citizen . . . in sum, a Renaissance man', was the recipient, in 1972, of an honorary Academy Award.

The *New York Times* failed to find a single Warner Bros. film for inclusion in their annual Ten Best list, though the New York Film Critics chose Liv Ullmann as Actress of the Year for her work in The Emigrants and Cries and Whispers (Gala). The top-grossing Warner Bros. films for 1972 were Dirty Harry (released in December 1971) and A Clockwork Orange (also released in December 1971).

Adam's Woman, an Australian film also known as Return of the Boomerang was briefly picked up for release by Warner Bros., but after a few initial screenings it was withdrawn. The net profit for the year was $23,066,000.

△

Dealing: Or The Berkeley-To-Boston Forty-Brick Lost-Bag Blues was produced by Edward R. Pressman and directed by Paul Williams who were both under thirty at the time, and starred Robert F. Lyons as a Harvard law student with no burning desire to join the Bar, but who doesn't mind acting as a marijuana carrier for campus dope king John Lithgow (right). On one of Lyons' trips to Berkeley to make a pick-up, he meets and falls in love with a kooky free-spirited girl (Barbara Hershey) whose good looks are secondary to the fact that she never wears underclothes, and who, in no time at all, gets herself arrested in Boston when the two suitcases of grass she happens to be carrying are confiscated by a detective in the narcotics squad. Lyons determines somehow to blackmail the detective who has kept one of the cases for himself, and how he goes about this provided director Williams with an opportunity to parody a typical cops-'n'-robbers chase whose main ingredients were laughter and suspense. He was only partially successful, due to the rambling nature of the screenplay he co-authored with David Odell and a rather lustreless performance from its leading man. Also in it were Charles Durning, Joy Bang (centre), Ellen Barber and Howard Gardner. It was a Pressman-Williams Production filmed in Panavision.

△

What director Jack Smight failed to do in his recreation of the forties world of the private-eye in *Harper*, Peter Bogdanovich failed to do for the screwball comedies of the thirties in What's Up Doc? Both directors reproduced rather than reinterpreted – particularly Bogdanovich whose affection for the period he parodied was never in doubt. Less obvious, though, was his sense of humour, and although the film (about an absent-minded musicologist whose unwanted involvement with a kook brings him into an unwanted involvement with a crook) had its amusing moments, it split its own sides rather than the audience's in trying to be funny. In the roles inspired by Cary Grant and Katharine Hepburn in *Bringing Up Baby* (RKO, 1938) Bogdanovich cast Ryan O'Neal (left) and Barbra Streisand (right), the former totally out of kilter with the frenzy of the proceedings, the latter more successful – eschewing impersonation and sticking to her own indomitable 'shtick'. There were nice bits, too, from Madeline Kahn, Sorrell Booke and Mabel Albertson. Bogdanovich produced it for his Saticoy Productions (associate producer Paul Lewis) and wrote the story on which the Buck Henry-David Newman-Robert Benton screenplay was based. The film grossed a walloping $28,000,000.

Tom Smothers (the blond member of the Smothers Brothers) played a top executive with a flashy sports car and a penthouse in Get To Know Your Rabbit. A disjointed comedy in which Smothers (illustrated) decides to break the executive habit by becoming a tap-dancing magician, it had a modicum of charm going for it but was sabotaged by its whimsy. John Astin co-starred as an ex-boss of Smothers who hits on an idea to institute an 'executive drop-out programme' (which in no time at all catches on and becomes a major business), with Katharine Ross, Suzanne Zenor, Samantha Jones, Allen Garfield and Hope Summers featured in other roles. Orson Welles was in it too playing the hero's magic instructor. It was produced by Steve Bernhardt and Paul Gaer (executive producer Peter Nelson) and directed by Brian De Palma who has since done far better work than this. Jordan Crittenden wrote it for Bernhardt-Gaer productions.

▽

△

Olympic ski champion Jean-Claude Killy (centre) proved to be as much of an actor in Snow Job (released in Britain as The Ski Raiders) as Olympic swimmer Johnny Weissmuller did in Tarzan. A caper in which Killy robs a ski resort, then sets off with the swag using his skis as transportation, it was partially redeemed by a deliciously hammy performance from Vittorio De Sica (right) as a supposed insurance investigator. Danièle Gaubert (left), Cliff Potts and Lelio Luttazzi appeared for director George Englund; it was written by Ken Kolb and Jeffrey Bloom from a story by Richard Gallagher, and produced by Edward L. Rissien in Panavision.

The Cowboys offered a violent version of the wild West as seen through the eyes of a group of 11 youngsters between the ages of 9 and 15 whom rancher John Wayne hires when his regular help deserts him to go prospecting for gold. Because of its conspicuous absence of bad language and explicit sex, the film was touted as ideal family entertainment (it even played at Radio City Music Hall in New York), regardless of the fact that the screenplay by Irving Ravetch, his wife Harriet Frank Jr and William Dale Jennings (on whose novel it was based) had the youngsters maturing from boyhood to manhood during a 400-mile cattle drive, by learning how to become cold-blooded killers after Wayne himself is killed by rustlers (illustrated). The admirable cast included Roscoe Lee Browne, Bruce Dern, Colleen Dewhurst and Slim Pickens. It was directed by Mark Rydell, who also produced in Panavision for Sanford Productions, with Tim Zinnemann as associate producer.

Adapted by Arnold Perl from *The Autobiography of Malcolm X*, **Malcolm X** was a moving, well-balanced documentary produced by Perl and Marvin Worth, which managed to delve beneath the stereotyped image of the controversial hate-preacher to reveal the sensitive, highly intelligent man who became one of the most dynamic leaders of America's black revolution. The film, relying largely on newsreel footage and photographs, traced its subject's life from hoodlum thief, dope peddler and pimp to his conversion to Elijah Muhammad's Nation of Islam, his dramatic rise to leadership in the black community, his break with Elijah Muhammad, his pilgrimage to Mecca, and his assassination during a meeting in New York, and ended with Ossie Davis supplying the funeral eulogy. It was narrated by James Earl Jones; technical assistance was supplied by Malcolm X's widow Betty Shabazz, and the music by Billie Holliday, The Last Poets, Slim and Slam, and Duke Ellington.

Maybe Philip Roth's brilliantly funny, yet underlyingly sad novel about a second generation Jew from New Jersey is simply unfilmable; or maybe Ernest Lehman, in his directorial debut, didn't have the skill or experience to crack it. Either way, **Portnoy's Complaint**, as it reached the screen, was a humourless travesty in which the central character's sexual hang-ups, fantasies and neuroses, so devastatingly explored in the novel, went for absolutely nothing on the Panavision screen. Richard Benjamin (centre) as the mother-dominated hero with a penchant for masturbation wandered through Lehman's abortive screenplay with a pained expression on his face (as well he might) leaving the acting honours to Karen Black who, as an upper East Side hillbilly, was the best thing in an otherwise lamentable effort. A miscast Lee Grant (far too young, far too attractive) appeared as Portnoy's mother, with other roles going to Jack Somack, Jeannie Berlin, Jill Clayburgh, D.P. Barnes, and Francesca De Sapio. A Chenault Production, it was produced by Ernest Lehman and Sidney Beckerman.

George C. Scott made his directorial debut with **Rage**, an uninvolving drama in which he appeared with Richard Basehart and Martin Sheen. Written by Philip Freedman and Dan Kleinman, it was the tale of a rancher (Scott, centre) and his son (Nicholas Beauvy, on bed), who are accidentally sprayed by a deadly nerve gas called MX-3, as a result of which the son dies and the father, on eventually learning the truth, goes berserk and destroys the chemical company where the toxic gas was manufactured. Director Scott tarted it up with a lot of fancy effects but to little purpose. Barnard Hughes, Paul Stevens, Stephen Young and Kenneth Tobey were also in it and it was produced by Fred Weintraub in Panavision with J. Ronald Getty and Leon Fromkess as executive producers.

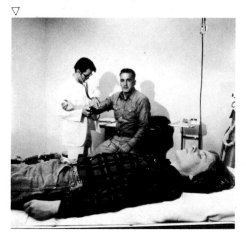

In **Come Back Charleston Blue** an actress called Jonelle Allen had a grapefruit rubbed into her face à la Mae Clarke, but any similarity to the classic gangster film *Public Enemy* (1931) ended right there. The story of two rival gangs (one black, the other white) competing to take control of the heroin trade in Harlem, it was a feeble successor to *Cotton Comes To Harlem* (1970) and again featured those ultra-hip black detectives Grave Digger Jones (Godfrey Cambridge, right), and Coffin Ed Johnson (Raymond St. Jacques). As written by Bontche Schweig (real name Ernest Kinoy) and Peggy Elliott from the novel *The Heat's On* by Chester Himes, the vernacular employed almost required subtitles for mass audience comprehension; so did the rather disjointed plot. Director Mark Warren, making his big-screen debut, tried to keep it all moving, but his efforts succeeded only in conveying a frenzied desperation with gunfights, car chases and someone masquerading as a nun on a motorbike passing for 'action'. Peter De Anda, Maxwell Glanville, Minnie Gentry, Dick Sabol and Leonardo Cimino were also in it, and the producer was Sam Goldwyn Jr.

Another black offering, **Superfly** cost less than $1 million to make, and grossed over $5 million in its first year. The story of Youngblood Priest (Ron O'Neal), a black cocaine dealer in New York (the title refers to the black ghetto's name for the drug) who plans one last sale before retiring on the profits, it was directed by Gordon Parks Jr who, in this his debut effort, revealed himself to be a man more at home with action than with words. How Priest parries the attempts of white police officials (one of whom is a cocaine supplier himself) to deprive him of his profits, gave Philip Fenty's screenplay its main narrative thrust, and audiences an immense amount of pleasure despite (or because of?) the dubious morality at its core. (In the end Priest is seen to have achieved his goal, his reward for perseverance being a Rolls Royce and lots of money on which to retire.) O'Neal played the role to the hilt; so did Carl Lee as his treacherous side kick. It was produced by Sig Shore and also featured Sheila Frazier, Julius W. Harris, Charles McGregor (centre), Nate Adams and Polly Niles.

△

The Candidate, which questioned certain aspects of American political life, starred Robert Redford (illustrated) as an idealistic apolitical Californian lawyer who, to his complete surprise, succeeds in becoming a senator only to find his lifestyle and treasured values undergoing a change. One of the best, most entertaining and informative films about power politics and the dirt it involves, it gave Redford an excellent opportunity to prove that he was more than just a pretty face. Directed by Michael Ritchie with an almost documentary-like obsession for the truth, and with a pungent screenplay by Jeremy Larner, the film also featured Karen Carlson as the wife Redford alienates in the course of his campaign, as well as Peter Boyle, Melvyn Douglas, Don Porter, Quinn Redeker and Morgan Upton. The producer of the Redford-Ritchie production was Walter Coblenz; the associate producer Nelson Rising.

Bob Hope made his 54th film, Cancel My ▷ Reservation, with an air of justifiable embarrassment on his well worn face. A comedy murder, it seemed obsessed with age, which considering that its 68-year-old star was palmed off as a mere youngster of 42, was understandable. Hope (right) played a famous TV personality who has to solve a murder mystery, thereby proving his own innocence in the affair, and also has to save his marriage (to Eva Marie Saint, centre) from disaster. The screenplay (by Arthur Marx and Robert Fisher based on a novel by Louis L'Amour) was strewn with deadweight gags (even to a quip about Bing Crosby's golfing prowess). Ralph Bellamy, Forrest Tucker, Anne Archer, Keenan Wynn, Herb Vigran (left) and Chief Dan George were other victims of its lack-lustre quality. A Naho Enterprises Production with Bob Hope as executive producer, it was directed by Paul Bogart and produced by Gordon Oliver.

405

needlessly complicated screenplay was by Walter Hill (from the novel by Terrence L. Smith), it was directed by Bud Yorkin with a score by Henry Mancini, and produced by Yorkin for the Tandem company.

Karate Tournament. After combating more than his fair share of foul play – most of it instigated by a rival karate expert – he not only wins the Tournament but also the love of Wang Ping. Patrons partial to the martial arts had a ball.

407

Jeremiah Johnson was a grass-roots story of an ex-soldier in the middle of the last century who has opted for a life of solitude and contemplation in the mountains. Not as easy a thing to do as he had anticipated, he

'74

◁ Swedish director Jan Troell's **Zandy's Bride** starred Gene Hackman (right) as a rugged rancher who, finding the female pickings in California's Big Sur Mountain country decidedly slim, acquires a mail order wife whom he savagely attempts to turn into a submissive all-purpose servant, at the same time expecting her to treat him with love and devotion. Liv Ullmann (left) was the wife, and the battle of wills between the two of them provided the film with its emotional conflict. More successful in the pioneering atmosphere it evoked than in the development of its narrative (screenplay by Marc Norman from a novel by Lillian Bos Ross) or its characters, it benefited greatly from Jordan Cronenweth's glorious photography and from Liv Ullmann's extraordinary presence which, even when not being particularly well-served by the text, illuminated the screen. Also cast were Eileen Heckart, Harry Dean Stanton, Joe Santos and Susan Tyrrell. Harvey Matofsky produced it in Panavision.

Jack Palance (left), Diana Dors, Julie Ege, Edith Evans, Hugh Griffith, Trevor Howard, Michael Jayston, Suzy Kendall and Martin Potter (right) sold their services to producer Herman Cohen and executive producer Gustave Berne for **Craze** — a British-made horror story based on a novel by Henry Seymour, and written by Cohen and Aben Kandel. All about an antique shop owner (Palance) who believes that the African idol, Chuku, which he keeps and worships in his cellar, will reward him with riches each time he (Palance) kills a woman as a sacrificial offering, it failed on almost every level, the only frightening aspect of it being that it was considered worth making at all. The director of this Harbor Production was Freddie Francis.

▽

Rockne Tarkington employed the ancient Japanese martial art of Kindo to defend himself and to rescue his kidnapped girlfriend in **Black Samson**. The shoddy story of a barkeeper (Tarkington) who stops at nothing to rid the street where he lives of dope pushers, it pretended to have its heart in the right place, but suffered a massive thrombosis in the crude way it condemned evil at the same time as revelling in it. William Smith, Connie Strickland, Carol Speed and Michael Payne were also in the Omni production written by Warren Hamilton Jr (story by Daniel B. Cady who also produced), and directed by Charles Bail.

The Abdication was a tedious costume-drama set in the 17th century in which Liv Ullmann was grossly misused as Queen Christina of Sweden, a woman of loose morals who renounces her Protestant kingdom, travels to Rome to embrace Catholicism and falls in love with a cardinal (Peter Finch, illustrated) who has been appointed to investigate the political and sexual intrigues of which she has been accused. But although her love is reciprocated there is no way they can make a life together, and the film ends with poor Christina facing the prospect of a bleak, lonely existence without a country, without power and, as Finch retreats into the Church, without love. Cyril Cusack, Paul Rogers, Graham Crowden, Michael Dunn, Kathleen Byron, Lewis Fiander and James Faulkner also featured in this turgid British-made drama; it was written by Ruth Wolff (from her play), directed by Anthony Harvey and produced by Robert Fryer and James Cresson.

▽

Those two talented actors Alan Arkin (right) and James Caan (left) co-starred with a fleet of motor cars in **Freebie and the Bean**, a comedy melodrama about a couple of cops, one Mexican (Arkin), the other all-American (Caan) who seem to care – in a platonic way, of course – more for each other than for the women in their lives. One of the plot points has Arkin suspecting his attractive wife (Valerie Harper) of infidelity, and, in the circumstances, it was not difficult to see why she might wish to cast her net elsewhere. Director Richard Rush was far too interested in the buddy-buddy relationship enjoyed by the two men to let the women ◁ intrude more than was necessary, and as such continued a pattern set by Robert Redford and Paul Newman in *Butch Cassidy and the Sundance Kid* (20th Century-Fox, 1969) and later in *The Sting* (Universal, 1973), Dustin Hoffman and Jon Voight in *Midnight Cowboy* (United Artists, 1969), Elliott Gould and Donald Sutherland in *M.A.S.H.* (20th Century-Fox, 1970) and Gene Hackman and Al Pacino in *Scarecrow* (1973). Basically the story of the two San Francisco cops and their attempts to track down the leader of a numbers racket, the film's contempt for personal and public property (mainly motor cars and human lives) was awesome, but at the same time, persuasively entertaining, thanks largely to Arkin's magnetic performance as the Chicano, some quite extraordinary stunt work, the 'anything goes' quality of Rush's direction (he also produced, in Panavision), and Robert Kaufman's trendily violent screenplay (story by executive producer Floyd Mutrux). Also in it were Alex Rocco, Loretta Swit, Jack Kruschen, Mike Kellin and Linda Marsh. The movie grossed $13,300,000.

1975

The studio's most prestigious film of the year was Stanley Kubrick's costly **Barry Lyndon** which was nominated for seven Academy Awards, including Best Picture of the Year, and won five: Best Cinematography (John Alcott); Best Art and Set Decoration (Ken Adam and Roy Walker; and Vernon Dixon); Best Costume Design (Ulla Britt Sonderlund and Milena Canonero); and Best Music Scoring and Adaptation (Leonard Rosenman). Kubrick was nominated for Best Director; so was Sidney Lumet, whose **Dog Day Afternoon** was also nominated in the Best Picture Category. (The winner was Milos Forman for United Artists' **One Flew Over the Cuckoo's Nest**, also voted by the Academy as Best Film of the Year.)

Al Pacino was nominated as Best Actor for **Dog Day Afternoon**, but Jack Nicholson was the winner for his performance in **Cuckoo's Nest**. Kubrick received one further nomination for **Barry Lyndon**: Best Screenplay from Another Source. He lost to Lawrence Hauben and Bo Goldman for **Cuckoo's Nest**.

Frank Pierson won the Best Original Screenplay Oscar for **Dog Day Afternoon** and, for the same film, Dede Allen was nominated for Best Editing.

The *New York Times* Ten Best list included **Alice Doesn't Live Here Any More**, **Barry Lyndon** and the documentary **Hearts and Minds**.

The studio's net-profit for the year was $41,704,000 and its box-office hits were **The Towering Inferno** (released December, 1974), **Alice Doesn't Live Here Any More** and **Dog Day Afternoon**.

Ellen Burstyn's vibrant, unsentimental performance in **Alice Doesn't Live Here Any More** was slightly out of kilter with Robert Getchell's conventional story of an impecunious 35-year-old widow who, after the death of her oppressive husband (Billy Green Bush) in a truck crash, gathers up her precocious 12-year-old son (Alfred Lutter) and hits the road. Her destination is California, and the object of her journey to find work as a singer (illustrated right) thus attempting (in vain, as it turns out) to make a childhood dream come true. The anger and frustration that informed practically everything Burstyn did were persuasive enough, but it was ultimately too emotionally charged for a fairy tale with a once-upon-a-time beginning and a happily-ever-after end. Still, it was directed at a terrific pace by Martin Scorsese, contained a gem of a scene in a Tucson diner where Burstyn finds a job as a waitress (illustrated left), and was always entertaining to listen to. Harvey Keitel — mean and macho — and Kris Kristofferson — rugged but caring — were the men Burstyn meets on her travels, with Diane Ladd, Lelia Goldoni, Lane Bradbury, Jodie Foster and Valerie Curtin excellent in supporting roles. The producers were David Susskind and Audrey Maas, and the film pulled in $7,800,000 at the box office.

▽

Rafferty and the Gold Dust Twins was a gentle, off-beat comedy in which Alan Arkin (left), this time playing a rather dim-witted driving instructor, is 'kidnapped' by Sally Kellerman (right) as another would-be singer and Mackenzie Phillips, a foul-tongued teenage breakaway who, at gunpoint, demand that he drives them from Los Angeles to Las Vegas. As they head inland, the structures of their relationships change, and by the time they reach a road-house in Tucson, three essentially lonely people have become friends, abandoning completely their kidnapper-victim status with which the film began. Directed with compassion, tenderness and an engaging freshness by Dick Richards and written with warmth by John Kaye whose screenplay, though slight in content, managed to bring out the best in Arkin, the film unfortunately failed to find a popular market and was sold to TV with its title changed to **Rafferty and the Highway Hustlers**. Whatever they called it, it was still a good movie. Alex Rocco (as a scrounger) and Harry Dean Stanton (as a pool shooter) were in it too; so were Charlie Martin Smith, John McLiam, Richard Hale and Louis Prima. The producers were Michael Gruskoff and Art Linson. It was filmed in Panavision.

▽

A Japanese-American co-production (Warner Bros. and Toei), **The Yakuza** transplanted American Mafioso techniques to the exotic Orient in a bloody, action-packed melodrama that starred Robert Mitchum as a perennial loner and private-eye manqué who journeys to Japan at the request of an old friend (shipping magnate Brian Keith), to rescue Keith's kidnapped daughter. Once in Japan Mitchum (right) enlists the help of 'the man who never smiles' (Takakura Ken, left), an erstwhile Yakuza (gangster) and a master of swordsmanship. The blood bath that followed hardly made for edifying viewing, with Paul Schrader and Robert Towne's discursive, perversely confusing screenplay emerging as the real villain of the piece. Mitchum took it all in his ample stride, supported by Kishi Keiko, Okada Eiji, James Shigeta, Herb Edelman and Richard Jordan. The uneven direction was by Sydney Pollack who produced it in Panavision with Michael Hamilburg, from a story by Leonard Schrader.

▷

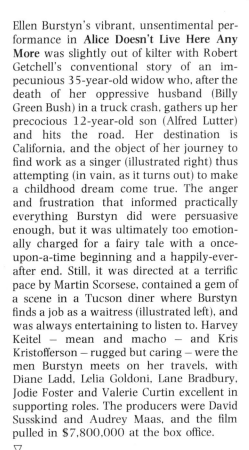

△

Bill Cosby (right) and Sidney Poitier made a return engagement after their successful *Uptown Saturday Night* (1974) in the appropriately titled **Let's Do It Again**. They did, playing two charitable members of the Sons and Daughters of Shaka Lodge who see a heaven-sent opportunity for raising money for that organization when, on running across a puny pugilist (J.J. Walker) in New Orleans, Poitier hypnotizes him (literally) into becoming champ. Lots of laughs and lots of action as supplied by the two engaging principals, plus a cast that also included John Amos and Calvin Lockhart (as a pair of gangsters), Ossie Davis, Paul Harris (left), Denise Nicholas and George Foreman. Poitier also directed it, the screenplay was by Richard Wesley (story by Timothy March) and the producer was Melville Tucker for Verdon-First Artists.

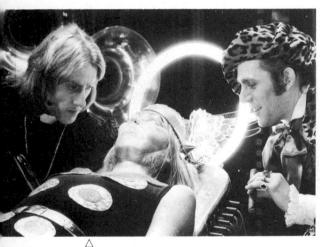

△

Ken Russell turned Franz Liszt into a 20th century Cockney pop star in **Lisztomania**, a formless piece of masturbatory cinema-making (which Russell wrote as well as directed) that set out, in sexually obsessed images, to diminish Liszt and Wagner but succeeded only in diminishing its director, whose undeniably inventive visual sense was here wasted in a welter of excess that refused to shock or outrage. And as to shock and outrage was clearly the film's intention, it must be considered a failure. Roger Daltrey (left) played Liszt, Paul Nicholas (right) was Wagner. Also cast were Sara Kestelman, Fiona Lewis, Veronica Quilligan, Nell Campbell, John Justin, and Ringo Starr as the Pope. Roy Baird produced with David Puttnam as co-producer for VPS/ Goodtimes Enterprises, and the executive producer was Sanford Lieberson.

418

Based on a true story, **Dog Day Afternoon** starred Al Pacino as an inept young man with problems: pressing debts, an unhappy wife, and a male lover hankering for a sex change operation. In the hope that money will alleviate these problems, he teams up with a friend (John Cazale, left) in order to rob a Brooklyn bank. But the hold-up misfires, and in an attempt to save their skins, the two men take refuge on the premises, using staff and clients as hostages. Frank Pierson's tautly written screenplay (based on an article by B.F. Kluge and Thomas Moore) concentrated on the relationships that developed between the gunmen and their hostages, eliciting sympathy for two basically unsympathetic characters. Director Sidney Lumet, as he had done in Paramount's 1973 release *Serpico*, again drew a stunning performance from Pacino (right) whose chaotic handling of the robbery situation and ultimate enjoyment of the instant notoriety it brings him, was mesmerically entertaining. Commendable too, was the director's sweaty evocation of a clammy summer afternoon and the effect it has on all concerned, including the crowds who gather outside the bank during Pacino's 'negotiations' with the cops for the release of his hostages. There were touching, well observed performances from Chris Sarandon (as Pacino's drag-queen lover) and Susan Peretz as his wife, with good work also from Penelope Allen, Sully Boyar, Beulah Garrick, Carol Kane, Sandra Kazan, James Broderick and Charles Durning. The producers of the Artists Entertainment Complex production were Martin Bregman and Martin Elfand. It grossed $22,300,000 at the box office.

△

The Prisoner of Second Avenue was a portrait of urban despair and the story of a nervous breakdown. But as it was based on a play by Neil Simon (who provided the screenplay) it was also extremely funny. Simon's love-hate relationship with the city of New York was nowhere better exploited than in this saga of an advertising executive who loses his job, has his apartment robbed and finds himself the victim of inconsiderate neighbours, domestic appliances that refuse to do as they're told, and a wife who suddenly becomes the breadwinner. Jack Lemmon (left) was the put-upon hero; Anne Bancroft (right) was his wife. Though Bancroft was far too attractive and sophisticated for the role (it was originally played on Broadway by the more suitably cast Lee Grant), Lemmon was fine, registering pain and suffering in a manner not altogether unpredictable by now. What mattered in the end was that both the stars firmly secured the laughs which playwright Simon had so carefully and skilfully plotted. So did Gene Saks, Elizabeth Wilson, Florence Stanley, Maxine Stuart and Ed Peck. Sylvester Stallone was in it too – as a youth in Central Park. It was produced and directed in Panavision, with a complete understanding of the genre, by Melvin Frank.

△

A moving and informative pacifist documentary about the American involvement in Vietnam, **Hearts and Minds** blended wartime footage with interviews to create an absorbing but by no means didactic statement on a national tragedy. The sensitive material was handled with lucidity and restraint by Peter Davis who conceived and directed the film, and it was expertly edited by Lynzee Klingman and Susan Martin, with Bert Schneider as executive producer for Touchstone Productions.

At six foot two, Tamara Dobson, a veritable one-woman task-force considered by some to make James Bond look meek and mild by comparison, followed her success in *Cleopatra Jones* (1973) with **Cleopatra Jones and the Casino of Gold**. This tepid espionage thriller found US government agent Jones off to Hong Kong and Macao to rout Dragon Princess (Stella Stevens), the feared leader of an international narcotics operation. Teaming up with a Chinese private eye (Tanny, left), Dobson (centre) enters the old walled city of Hong Kong to search for two of her cohorts who have mysteriously disappeared while trying to infiltrate the drug ring. Norman Fell (right), Albert Popwell, Caro Kenyatta, Chan Sen and Christopher Hunt were also in it; it was directed with an uncanny eye for a platitude by Chuck Bail, and produced by William Tennant (who also wrote it) and Run Run Shaw, whose Shaw Brothers company co-produced it with Warner Bros. as a US-Hong Kong co-production, in Panavision.

▽

Played absolutely for real and eschewing ▷ 'camp' in an attempt to capture authentic period detail (circa 1937) **Doc Savage**, or **The Man of Bronze** as it was sub-titled, was a po-faced but not unenjoyable resurrection of a thirties pulp-fiction superman who despatches himself to the Republic of Hidalgo to find out who killed his father, and why. A trip to the 'World's Edge' and the discovery of a 'lost' South American tribe firmly rooted the adventure in its comic-strip origins, with Ron Ely (sporting a chest more expansive than his talent) in splendid physical shape as the hero. Also cast were Pamela Hensley, Paul G. Wexler (left) Darrell Zwerling, Michael Miller, Robyn Hilton (right), Eldon Quick and Bill Lucking. Michael Anderson directed, and George Pal (who also produced) and Joseph Morhaim wrote it from a novel by Kenneth Robeson.

A treasure hunt with a prison background, **Inside Out**, filmed on location in Berlin, starred Telly Savalas (left) top-billed for the first time as an American ex-prisoner-of-◁ war, and James Mason (right) as the German ex-Commander of the camp in which Savalas was imprisoned. 31 years later, the two men join forces to smuggle a Nazi prisoner (played by Wolfgang Lukschy) out of Siegfried jail (and back again) as he is the only person alive who happens to know where six million dollars -worth of gold bullion, ambushed during the war by the Nazi élite, is hidden. Fanciful to a degree, but nonetheless entertaining and often tense, despite the sheer implausibility of it all, it was taken seriously by its stars who included Robert Culp (centre) and Aldo Ray; Doris Kunstmann, Guenter Meisner, Adrian Hoven, Lorna Dallas and Peter Schlesinger were in it too. The Kettledrum Production was competently crafted by writer-producer Judd Bernard, who scripted it with Stephen Schneck, and it was directed by Peter Duffell.

△

Timothy Bottoms (left) starred in **Operation Daybreak** as a World War II underground member of the Free Czech Forces who plotted the assassination of Hitler's confidant Reinhard Heydrich – the 'hangman' of the Czechs. Heydrich's murder resulted in the massacre of the Czech village of Lidice, harrowingly reconstructed in Ronald Harwood's screenplay (from Alan Burgess' *Seven Men At Daybreak*). The finale with the conspirators, betrayed from within, trapped in a church, their alternative to dying at the enemy's hand being suicide, was especially grim. Apart from Bottoms, the cast was primarily English, and included Joss Ackland, Nicola Pagett (centre), Anthony Andrews (right), Diana Coupland and, as Heydrich, Anton Diffring. Directed by Lewis Gilbert on location in Czechoslovakia, it was produced by Carter De Haven for Howard R. Schuster and American Allied Pictures.

Gene Hackman as a professional football ▷ star turned deeply moral shamus, was reunited with director Arthur Penn (for whom he made *Bonnie And Clyde* in 1967) in **Night Moves**, a complicated but intriguing thriller which divided its time equally between character and action. Hackman's seemingly simple assignment was to trace a film-star's vagrant daughter in the Florida Keys and return her to her mother, which he did without too much difficulty. But Alan Sharp's screenplay made quite sure there was more to it than that, and introduced a violent sub-plot (climaxing in a nasty beheading by a seaplane while scuba diving) that must have had Hackman (left) wishing he were back in the relative calm of the football field. Janet Ward and Melanie Griffith, as mother and daughter, were excellent in support, as were Edward Binns, Harris Yulin, Kenneth Mars (right), Susan Clark, Jennifer Warren and James Woods. The producer was Robert M. Sherman for Hiller-Layton productions.

Margot Kidder, Keir Dullea, Olivia Hussey ▷ (illustrated) and John Saxon starred in **Black Christmas** (also known as **Silent Night, Evil Night**) a macabre horror story which successfully piled on the tension as a ghoulish psychopathic killer terrorizes a college campus sorority house – first with obscene telephone calls, then with cold-blooded slaughter. A traditional whodunnit, and good of its kind, it was written by Roy Moore, produced and directed (in Canada) by Robin Clark for Film Funding and Vision IV Productions, and featured Andrea Martin, Marian Waldman, Art Hindle, Lunne Griffin and James Edmond.

◁ More explicit than anything shown in the Warner Bros. crime melodramas of the thirties, but not as effective, **Lepke** starred Tony Curtis as the notorious Jewish gangster Lepke Buchalter, the man who reorganized and operated Murder Inc. and masterminded more rackets in New York than any underworld baron before him. Echoing *The Public Enemy* (1931), the film traced Lepke's career from its humble lower East Side beginnings in 1912 to his execution by electric chair at the age of 47 in 1944, but failed to side-step the clichés en route. There was violence a-plenty, and with Curtis (left) giving a fair impersonation of the central character's complex behaviour, a certain entertainment value emerged amid the bloodshed. But after *The Godfather* (Parts I and II, Paramount, 1972 and 1974) there was little that was new to be said on the subject. Curtis' wife was played by attractive Anjanette Comer, with other parts going to Michael Callan, Warren Berlinger, Gianni Russo, Vic Tayback, Mary Wilcox (right), and Milton Berle as Curtis' disapproving father-in-law. It was written by Wesley Lau and Tamar Hoffs, and produced and directed, in Panavision, by Menahem Golan for AmeriEuro.

1978

The year which saw the death of Jack L. Warner (on Saturday, September 9th) happened, also, to be a record year in the history of the company he founded. With its vast spectrum of interests – including electronic toys, music and book publishing, records, as well as theatrical film rentals, Warner Communications reported a net profit of $87,106,000 – a rise of 23 per cent from the company's previous year's total of $70,766,000.

Superman was nominated for three Academy Awards: Best Editing, Best Original Score (John Williams) and Best Sound Recording; **Hooper** was also nominated in the Best Sound Recording category; **The Swarm** received a nomination for Best Costume Design, and **Bloodbrothers** for Best Screenplay (Walter Newman) based on material from another medium. At the Academy Award ceremony, the Warner Bros. special effects department received a special Oscar for the visual effects in **Superman**, an award which they well deserved for their ingenuity.

△

Lino Ventura made his British film debut in **The Medusa Touch**, an improbable but well-mounted thriller, in which he played a detective (French, due to French financial participation in the production) who sets out to discover why an unknown assailant murdered Richard Burton (left) by bashing in his skull. What he discovers is that although Burton's body is practically dead, his mind is still alive, and busy plotting all manner of grisly disasters from the destruction of a cathedral to the crashing of a jet into a London skyscraper. Lee Remick co-starred as a psychiatrist, with other roles going to Harry Andrews, Alan Badel, Marie-Christine Barrault (right), Michael Hordern, Gordon Jackson, Derek Jacobi, Michael Byrne and Jeremy Brett. It was written by John Briley from the novel by Peter van Greenaway, produced by Anne V. Coates and Jack Gold (with Arnon Milchan as executive producer), and presented by Sir Lew Grade (in association with Milchan and Elliot Kastner) for Coatesgold Films. Gold also directed.

△

Lina Wertmüller made her English-language debut with **The End of the World in Our Usual Bed in a Night Full of Rain**, a characteristic Wertmüller conversation-piece, whose all-pervading theme was, again, the battle of the sexes. It starred Candice Bergen (right) as an American photographer deeply entrenched in the feminist movement, and Giancarlo Giannini (left) as an Italian journalist whom she meets at a festival and who attempts to seduce her. The couple meet again in San Francisco, fall in love and decide to marry. But the marriage is hardly blissful and their differences (he being a male chauvinist Communist with a desire for hand-laundered shirts) formed the basis of Wertmüller's talky, often ponderous screenplay. A Liberty Film produced by Gil Shiva (executive producer Harry Colombo), it also featured Michael Tucker, Mario Scarpetta, Lucio Amelio, Massimo Wertmüller and Anna Papa.

△

That strange race of killer babies who did so much damage in *It's Alive*, surfaced for a second time in **It Lives Again**, this time inducing laughter rather than chills and definitely outstaying their welcome. Once again written, produced and directed by Larry Cohen, the further adventures of the bothersome little monsters were much the same as before, with John P. Ryan (centre) and Andrew Duggan (both recruits from the first film) joining forces with Frederic Forrest, Kathleen Lloyd, John Marley, Eddie Constantine and James Dixon to stop their anti-social behaviour.

◁ Doubling as both Prince and Pauper in **Crossed Swords** (released in Britain as **The Prince and the Pauper**), young Mark Lester (right) proved no match for the Mauch twins, who, in 1937, shared the two roles in the superior William Keighley version of Mark Twain's durable classic. The story of a pair of identical twins in medieval England, one a prince, the other a pauper, who exchange identities, it starred Oliver Reed (centre) in the role originally played by Errol Flynn, with Raquel Welch (centre left), Ernest Borgnine, George C. Scott, Rex Harrison, David Hemmings, Charlton Heston and Harry Andrews (left) lending sterling support to George MacDonald Fraser's re-working of an original screenplay by Berta Dominguez D. and Pierre Spengler. Spengler also produced, Ilya and Alexander Salkind were the executive producers, and Richard Fleischer directed in Panavision. A routine remake, it totally lacked the energy and excitement of the original.

△

Loosely based on a true story involving a sea trip from Jamaica to California undertaken by a group of actors and animal trainers, **The Sea Gypsies** (released in Britain as **Shipwreck!**) was ideal family entertainment about a father, his two daughters, a lady journalist and a stowaway who set out on a round-the-world voyage and find themselves stranded on a desert island off the coast of Alaska. Adventure abounded in Stewart Raffill's neatly constructed, agreeably written screenplay (Raffill also directed) with leading man Robert Logan (left) parrying all manner of dangers – from warding off an attack by a Kodiak bear to an encounter with a killer whale. The animal footage was particularly effective; so was Thomas McHugh's lush photography. Mikki Jamison-Olsen, Heather Rattray (right), Cjon Damitri Patterson and Shannon Saylor were in it too; it was produced by Joseph C. Raffill with Peter R. Simpson as executive producer.

◁ Though in content **Straight Time** was little more than a Warner Bros. melodrama circa 1933, its execution was decidedly contemporary, with the Alvin Sargent-Edward Bunker-Jeffrey Boam screenplay (from Bunker's novel *No Beast so Fierce*) hitting the screen with the impact of a devastating bodyblow. The story of an ex-con who, after serving six years in prison for burglary, finds on his release that going straight is a futile occupation and returns to his former criminal activities as a ruthless desperado, it starred a compulsively watchable Dustin Hoffman (illustrated) with Theresa Russell, Gary Busey, Harry Dean Stanton, M. Emmet Walsh, Rita Taggart, Kathy Bates and Sandy Baron in support. Though the film started out as social comment and charted the difficulties experienced by men on parole in adjusting to freedom, it developed into a routine heist thriller with Hoffman and his accomplices pulling off a series of jobs — from banks to jewellery shops in Beverly Hills. Fortunately, the abrasive quality of the screenplay, combined with the excellence of the performances, lifted it several notches above the ordinary, and under Ulu Grosbard's sturdy direction made quite an impact. A First Artists-Sweetwall film, it was produced by Stanley Beck and Tim Zinnemann with Howard B. Pine as executive producer.

△

A realistic, slice-of-life drama with an abundance of foul language for verisimilitude, **Bloodbrothers** probed the lives of the De Coco family and starred Tony Lo Bianco (right) as a construction worker and the head of the household. Paul Sorvino (left) played his brother, Lelia Goldoni his wife, and Michael Hershawe and Richard Gere (centre) his sons, the latter being undecided as to whether he should follow in his father's footsteps or settle for a job he really wants, viz working with small children. Written by Walter Newman (from the novel by Richard Price), the storyline was of less importance than the inter-relationships and behaviour of the leading characters and, had director Robert Mulligan's cast been less accomplished, it wouldn't have added up to very much. As it turned out though, all the performances were superb, including Kenneth McMillan's as a crippled bartender, and Marilu Henner's as a disco waitress. A Stephen Friedman-Kings Road Production, it was produced by Friedman and featured an effective rhythm-and-blues score by Elmer Bernstein.

The best thing about **Big Wednesday**, an arty and pretentious drama with a surfing background, were Greg MacGillivray's visually thrilling surfing sequences. For the rest, John Milius' phoney screenplay, which he wrote with Dennis Aaberg, about three surfing buddies from Malibu who, after growing from boyhood to manhood, are re-united in a climactic attempt to master the ocean, was a bore. Jan-Michael Vincent (centre right) was top-starred as the best surfer of the trio, with William Katt (centre left) and Gary Busey (centre) as his mates. An A-Team production, it was produced by Buzz Feitshans (executive producers Alex Rose and Tamara Asseyev), directed by Milius, and featured Patti D'Arbanville (left), Sam Melville, Lee Purcell (right), Robert Englund and Barbara Hale.

In **Capricorn One**, Elliott Gould played a reporter whose once-in-a-lifetime scoop pivoted on the fact that the first manned space-flight to Mars was an elaborate hoax and never actually took place. Just how Gould (left) happened upon this shattering information (and what he does with it) was the raison d'etre of a Sci-Fi thriller which took a hundred minutes to gather momentum before finally taking off in its last quarter of an hour. Peter Hyams' direction was fractionally better than his screenplay, with both relying on the film's stars to maintain interest. James Brolin, Sam Waterston and O.J. Simpson played a trio of intrepid astronauts, with Brenda Vaccaro, Hal Holbrook, Karen Black (right) and Telly Savalas (as a crop duster) in it too. An Associated General Films Production, it was produced by Paul N. Lazarus III in Panavision.

Premiered at the Montreal Festival 18 months after it was completed, Ibsen's **An Enemy of the People**, based on Arthur Miller's didactic stage adaptation of the play, and written for the screen by Alexander Jacobs, starred a heavily-bearded Steve McQueen (left) as Thomas Stockmann, a small-town doctor deeply concerned with his discovery that the town's hot-water spa has been contaminated by tannery effluent. Ignoring the advice of his brother, the town's mayor (played by Charles Durning, right), to keep his discovery to himself, Stockmann publicizes his findings at the cost of his career. Unfortunately, McQueen lacked the sheer weight of authority so prevalent in co-star Durning's charismatic performance, thus completely unbalancing Ibsen's dramatic structure. Bibi Andersson played McQueen's wife, Michael Cristofer was a far too contemporary newspaperman, with Eric Christmas, Richard A. Dysart, Michael Higgins, Richard Bradford, Ham Larsen, John Levin and Robin Pearson Rose completing the cast. A First Artists-Solar Production, it was produced and directed by George Schaefer, with McQueen as executive producer.

An excellent first feature by Claudia Weill, **Girlfriends** traversed much of the territory explored by Gail Parent in *Sheila Levine is Dead and Living in New York* (the book rather than the 1975 Paramount film) and, in atmosphere, was not entirely unlike *Annie Hall* (United Artists, 1977). The story of a Jewish girl photographer's search for identity (and a successful personal relationship) in New York, it concentrated on the insecurities she suffers after a flatmate of long standing leaves her to get married, and showed how mentally, as well as physically, she sets out to replace her. Melanie Mayron (right) played the photographer with a naturalness that belied the fact she was acting at all; Anita Skinner (left) was her erstwhile flat-mate and Christopher Guest and Bob Balaban were the men in their lives. Eli Wallach appeared briefly as a married rabbi with whom Mayron almost has an affair. Also cast were Viveca Lindfors, Gena Rogak, Amy Wright, Mike Kellin and Russell Horton. Refreshingly unsentimental in its approach to its material, it was written by Vicki Polon from a story by Polon and Weill and produced by Weill and Jan Saunders. **Girlfriends** began life with a $10,000 grant from the American Film Institute, and was augmented by friends of the director as the project expanded in size and scope. After the film was completed it was bought by Warner Bros.

Originally called **Who is Killing the Great Chefs of Europe?**, but released in Britain as **Too Many Chefs**, Peter Stone's suet pudding of a farce engaged the talents of George Segal (left), Jacqueline Bisset (right), Robert Morley, Jean-Pierre Cassel and Philippe Noiret, but to little avail. All about a portly gourmand (Morley) who learns from his doctor (John Le Mesurier) that unless he loses 140lb in weight he'll surely die, it centred around the bizarre murders of a group of Europe's top chefs, all of whom meet their end in the manner of their own specialities. (One, for example, is baked, another has his head crushed in a duck press, etc. etc.) The question is, whodunnit? All the evidence would seem to point to Morley who cannot contemplate going on a diet while his favourite chefs continue to produce all his favourite dishes. In the end it didn't really matter a sausage who the culprit was – for by the time all was revealed, audiences had already had a bellyfull of the tasteless tripe being offered them in the name of entertainment. It was directed with a heavy hand and none of the correct ingredients by Ted Kotcheff, and also featured Madge Ryan, Frank Windsor, Jean Rochefort and Luigi Proietti. An Aldrich Company-Lorimar Production, it was produced by William Aldrich with Merve Adelson and Lee Rich as executive producers.

Director Stanley Donen's **Movie Movie**, an affectionate recreation of a thirties-style double bill, parodied two favourite Warner Bros. genres of the period; the boxing melodrama and the Busby Berkeley musical. **Dynamite Hands**, the melodrama (in black and white) opened the programme and was the story of Joey Popchik (Harry Hamlin, centre) a poor young Hungarian law student who, in order to finance a trip to Vienna for his sister (Kathleen Beller) in the hope that her failing eyesight might be restored by an eminent surgeon there, unselfishly abandons his studies for the quick financial rewards of the boxing ring. A crack at the title is what he's after, but complications arise when a crooked promoter (Eli Wallach) takes an interest in him and orders him to throw a vital fight. Joey refuses and his stubbornness costs his faithful trainer (George C. Scott, left) his life. To avenge Scott's death the young Hungarian champ speedily completes his law studies and personally sees to it that Wallach pays for his villainy by burning in the electric chair. Stirring stuff, and as performed by a cast that also included Trish Van Devere, Michael Kidd, Jocelyn Brando, Ann Reinking, Art Carney, Barry Bostwick and Red Buttons (right), it was a wittily observed reworking of one of the cinema's most oft-told tales. The only thing missing was the word 'kid' from the title! The musical surfaced as **Baxter's Beauties of 1933** and was

the equally familiar one about the chorus girl who stands in for the leading lady and, before you can say *42nd Street*, becomes a star. Rebecca York (illustrated) was Ruby Keeler (here called Kitty Simpson), Barry Bostwick was Dick Powell (called Dick Cummings). The Warner Baxter role went to George C. Scott, Barbara Harris was an amalgam of Ginger Rogers, Una Merkel, Aline MacMahon and Joan Blondell, while Trish Van Devere was the Bebe Daniels-type leading lady who

breaks a leg an hour before curtain time. The rest of the cast was completed by Red Buttons and Eli Wallach. Lacking the kind of budget that would be required to recreate a typical Berkeley dance routine today, choreographer Michael Kidd resorted to one characteristic overhead kaleidoscope shot to convey something of the essence of the original. He was only partially successful, proving – as if proof were needed – that Berkeley is impossible to imitate convincingly. Far more faithful to the

period was the screenplay which Larry Gelbart and Sheldon Keller wrote (for both halves of the bill) but most nostalgic of all was the trailer sandwiched between the two features heralding a thirties war epic called *Zero Hour*. It captured the feel of the period to perfection. **Movie Movie** (which had an introduction by George Burns) was produced by Stanley Donen with Martin Starger as Executive producer. It was a box-office as well as a critical success.

An action-packed tribute to a group of the film capital's unsung heroes, **Hooper** focused on the trials and tribulations of stuntmen, without whose lunatic and daring antics movie-going would simply not be the same. Though Thomas Rickman and Bill Kerby's screenplay (from a story by Walt Green and Walter S. Herndon) concerned itself with stuntmen in general, their particular 'spokesman' was Burt Reynolds as Sonny Hooper (illustrated), one of the best and most experienced risk-takers in the business. Reynolds, his body marked with the scars of past stunts, is at last beginning to feel that there is a limit to the punishment he can go on inflicting on himself, and when the film opens, decides to take it easy. But the appearance on the scene of a charismatic newcomer called Ski (Jan-Michael Vincent) who has been highly touted as his only serious rival, has Reynolds (for a tidy $50,000) agreeing to perform the most spectacular and dangerous stunt of his career in order to assert his supremacy in the field. Engagingly performed by its two stars, and with effective support from Sally Field (as Reynolds' lover), Brian Keith, John Marley and Robert Klein (deliciously parodying director Peter Bogdanovich), **Hooper** hit the box-office jackpot and reinforced Reynolds' superstar status. The snappy direction was by Hal Needham and the film was produced by Hank Moonjean for Burt Reynolds-Lawrence Gord productions. Songs: A Player, A Pawn, A Hero, A King and Hooper.

◁ Clint Eastwood put down his Magnum 44 and relied on his fists for **Every Which Way But Loose**, a shapeless knockabout comedy which clicked at the box office – it was Eastwood's most profitable film to date – but failed to draw affirmatives from the critics. He played Philo Beddoe, a good-natured trucker whose penchant for bar-room brawls provided the film with most of its action. What little plot there was in Jeremy Joe Kronsberg's screenplay concerned Eastwood's search across the great South-West for the girl he loves – a Country-and-Western singer called Lynn Halsey-Taylor (Sondra Locke). Accompanying him are Orville (Geoffrey Lewis), whose function is to promote fights for money between Eastwood (left) and other heavy-weight brawlers; Orville's quick-witted girlfriend Echo (Beverly D'Angelo) and Clyde, a fully-grown male orang-utan (right) whom Eastwood has won in a bet. While the quartet team up to find Miss Locke, they themselves are being trailed by a mean-looking motorcycle gang called The Black Widows, and by an irate cop whose face Eastwood, in one of his numerous brawls, uses as a punchbag. It was directed by James Fargo (with assistant director Al Silvani, a trainer of professional boxers, advising on the brawl sequences), produced by Robert Daley for Malpaso, and featured Ruth Gordon (as Eastwood's octogenarian mother), Walter Barnes, George Chandler, Roy Jenson and James MacEachin. Songs included: Every Which Way But Loose, I'll Wake Up When I Get Home, Coco Cola Cowboy, Ain't Love Good Tonight, Don't Say You Don't Love Me No More and I Can't Say No To A Truck Drivin' Man.

A disaster movie in which a swarm of killer bees from Brazil devastates South East Texas, **The Swarm** (in Panavision) was one of the most unintentionally funny films of the year. Working from a novel by Arthur Herzog and a silly screenplay by Stirling Silliphant that positively buzzed with howlers, producer-director Irwin Allen and a cast that included Michael Caine (left), Katharine Ross (centre), Richard Widmark, Richard Chamberlain, Olivia de Havilland, Ben Johnson, Fred MacMurray, Jose Ferrer, Henry Fonda and Christian Juttner (right), floundered embarrassingly in what turned out to be a B picture in every sense of the word. And although in the course of the film nuclear plants were destroyed, trains overturned and the entire city of Houston, Texas reduced to ashes as the country's top entomologists and immunologists joined forces with the army to eliminate the killer insects, there was very little sting to the proceedings. All it succeeded in doing was putting one off honey.

Conceived by the father-and-son production team of Alexander and Ilya Salkind, and Pierre Spengler, in a sidewalk café in Paris, **Superman: The Movie** took two years to complete, with location work being done in New York City, Gallup, New Mexico, Alberta, Canada, and at Shepperton and Pinewood Studios in England. The first public intimation of the scope of the no-expense-spared undertaking (whose final budget topped a record $40,000,000) came with the announcement that Marlon Brando had been signed to play Superman's father Jor-El (a role with a thirteen day shooting schedule) for $3,000,000 dollars – which, calculated on a nine-hour day schedule – worked out at roughly $27,000 an hour, or $8 a second (generously, Brando offered to do an extra day of retakes without payment). For the key role of Superman himself, the Salkinds' first choice was Robert Redford, but he declined after failing to agree on money, and because of the absence, during negotiations, of a final shooting script. Paul Newman was then approached, but he too declined. (Newman was then offered the part of villain Lex Luthor but again said no. It finally went to Gene Hackman whose payment was a cool $2,000,000). Other stars initially sought or considered for the title role were Clint Eastwood, Steve McQueen, Charles Bronson, Ryan O'Neal, Sylvester Stallone, Burt Reynolds, Nick Nolte, Jan-Michael Vincent, David Soul, Kris Kristofferson and Robert Wagner. But with Brando and Hackman signed, a big name was no longer deemed essential. Salkind now actively sought an unknown whose personality would not be associated with an established superstar. The lucky contender was Christopher Reeve (illustrated), a stage actor who immediately embarked on a strenuous fitness programme that included two hours of weightlifting every day, road-work in the mornings, and ninety minutes on the trampoline! The part of *Daily Planet* girl reporter Lois Lane was won by Margot Kidder after a roster of stars such as Jill Clayburgh, Jessica Lange, Liza Minnelli, Shirley MacLaine, Natalie Wood and Carrie Fisher were either unavailable or rejected as unsuitable. Best-selling author Mario Puzo was paid $350,000 plus a promise of 5 per cent of the gross to devise the film's storyline (based on characters and concepts created way back in 1933 by Jerry Segal and Joe Shuster – though it wasn't until 1938 that the first *Superman* comic strip appeared) and came up with a plot that had the 'man of steel' pitting his Kryptonian wits against malignant Luthor's diabolical plan to create an earthquake which will cause everything west of California's San Andreas fault to sink into the ocean, but not before Luthor buys up all the arid land east of it in order to make a real-estate killing as the owner of a new coastline! Puzo also had a hand in the screenplay; so did David Newman, Leslie Newman and Robert Benton. The project's creative consultant was Tom Mankiewicz, the production was designed by John Barry, scored by John Williams, edited by Stuart Baird, photographed by the late Geoffrey Unsworth (to whom the movie is dedicated) and directed with not the slightest trace of 'camp' by Richard Donner. The associate producer was Charles F. Greenlaw. Block-buster entertainment guaranteed to appeal

to parents and children of all ages, it also featured Ned Beatty and Valerie Perrine as Hackman's useless assistants, Glenn Ford and Phyllis Thaxter as Ma and Pa Kent, (Superman's earthly parents), Jeff East as the young Clark Kent, Jackie Cooper as the editor of *The Daily Planet* and from the planet Krypton, Susannah York as Superman's real mother Lara, together with Trevor Howard, Jack O'Halloran, Maria Schell, Terence Stamp, Sarah Douglas, Marc McClure and Harry Andrews. Song: *Can You Read My Mind?* (by John Williams and Leslie Bricusse). **Superman** is, to date, the most profitable film in the history of Warner Bros.

The land had changed. They hadn't.
The earth had cooled. They couldn't.

A PHIL FELDMAN PRODUCTION

THE WILD BUNCH

Angels with Dirty Faces

STARRING JAMES CAGNEY & PAT O'BRIEN

...and happiness of the Broadway hit...

JAMES CAGNEY

BETTE DAVIS

having the time of their lives in the best picture of their lives,

"THE BRIDE CAME C.O.D."

Isn't it wonderful! ...both in the same picture!!

(Warner Bros. produced it)

OBJECTIVE BURMA

WARNER BROS.

...the girl who became the greatest show in show business.

ROSALIND RUSSELL NATALIE WOOD KARL MALDEN
as Gypsy Rose Lee

★★★★★ GYPSY ★★★★★

A MERVYN LeROY PRODUCTION

HERE'S THE SEASON'S PEPPIEST JITTERBUG RIOT!

BOGART

"PASSAGE TO MARSEILLE"

HAL B. WALLIS PRODUCTION
MICHAEL CURTIZ

WARNER BROS.

NAUGHTY BUT NICE

with
DICK POWELL ★ ANN SHERIDAN
GALE PAGE ★ RONALD REAGAN
HELEN BRODERICK

Warner Bros.-First National
TEDDINGTON

In 1931 Warner Bros. leased the Teddington Studios where, throughout the next 13 years they produced over 100 features, most of which were for home consumption only and never released in the United States. In 1934 Warner Bros. purchased the studios outright, and in 1936 added a new powerhouse and office block to the premises. On 5 July 1944 the studios were badly damaged in a bomb attack and it was not until 1948 that they were once again operative, though this time mainly providing facilities for independent producers. The last Warner Bros. film to be shot at the studio (interiors only) was **The Crimson Pirate** in 1952.

1931

Stranglehold. Isobel Elsom, Garry Marsh, Allan Jeayes; director: Henry Edwards. A Chinese half-caste ruins the marriage of a schoolmate who wronged his sweetheart. (Drama.)

1932

Murder on the Second Floor. John Longden, Pat Peterson, Sydney Fairbrother; director: William McGann. A novelist imagines a murder involving his fellow boarders. (Thriller.)

Help Yourself. Benita Hume, Martin Walker; director: John Daumery. A man throws a party in his rich aunt's absence during which crooks try to steal a necklace. (Comedy.)

Illegal. Isobel Elsom, D.A. Clark Smith, Margot Grahame; director: William McGann. A deserted wife is jailed for running a gambling club for the sake of her daughter. (Drama.)

Lucky Ladies. Sydney Fairbrother, Emily Fitzroy, Tracy Holmes; director: John Rawlings. Two sisters run an oyster bar with the £30,000 they won on the Irish sweepstakes and lose it all to a bogus count. (Comedy.)

The Silver Greyhound. Percy Marmont, Anthony Bushell, Janice Adair (illustrated); director: William McGann. The uncle of a King's Messenger recoups stolen papers from a female spy. (Crime.)

Blind Spot. Percy Marmont, Muriel Angelus, Warwick Ward; director: John Daumery. A gentleman thief's amnesiac daughter weds the KC who prosecutes him. (Crime.)

Her Night Out. Dorothy Bartlam, Lester Matthews, Joan Marion; director: William McGann. A golfer's jealous wife flirts with a bank robber. (Comedy.)

Little Fella. John Stuart, Joan Marion, Dodo Watts; director: William McGann. A baby helps a runaway orphan win a major from his fiancée. (Comedy.)

The River House Ghost. Florence Desmond, Hal Walters, Joan Marion; director: Frank Richardson. A Cockney girl unmasks crooks posing as ghosts. (Comedy.)

Don't be a Dummy. William Austin, Muriel Angelus, Garry Marsh; director: Frank Richardson. A lord, ruined through gambling, becomes a stage ventriloquist using a jockey as a dummy. (Comedy.)

1933

Mr Quincey of Monte Carlo. John Stuart, Rosemary Ames; director: John Daumery. A bank clerk uses his legacy to finance a film company. (Comedy.)

Naughty Cinderella. John Stuart, Winna Winifried, Betty Huntley Wright; director: John Daumery. A Danish girl fools her guardian by posing as a tomboy. (Comedy.)

Little Miss Nobody. Winna Winifried, Sebastian Shaw; director: John Daumery. A man's publicity stunt helps a girl win a film contract. (Comedy.)

The Stolen Necklace. Lester Matthews, Joan Marion; director: Leslie Hiscott. A gang seeks jewels already stolen by rivals. (Crime.)

Out of the Past. Lester Matthews, Joan Marion, Jack Raine; director: Leslie Hiscott. A manageress is blackmailed for posing as a co-respondent. (Crime.)

The Melody-Maker. Lester Matthews, Joan Marion; director: Leslie Hiscott. A composer re-writes his fiancée's sonata as a musical comedy. (Comedy.)

Double Wedding. Joan Marion, Jack Hobbs; director: Frank Richardson. The honeymoon troubles of two couples who have married in order to silence local gossips. (Comedy.)

Going Straight. Moira Lynd, Helen Ferrers; director: John Rawlings. A lady's ex-criminal servants try to save a novelist's son from falling in love with a secretary. (Comedy.)

Too Many Wives. Nora Swinburne, Jack Hobbs, Viola Keats; director: George King. A man persuades a maid to pose as his absent wife in order to entertain a foreign client. (Comedy.)

As Good as New. Winna Winifried, John Batten; director: Graham Cutts. A jilted girl turns gold-digger until her ex-fiancé is blinded. (Romance.)

The Thirteenth Candle. Isobel Elsom, Arthur Maude; director: John Daumery. Which of his many enemies killed the village squire? (Thriller.)

Long Live the King. Florence Desmond, Hal Walters; director: William McGann. A Cockney charlady on a prize holiday to Ruritania saves a baby prince from revolutionaries. (Comedy.)

Call Me Mame. Ethel Irving, John Batten; director: John Daumery. A man is about to inherit a peerage when his hard-drinking mother arrives from Mexico. (Comedy.)

High Finance. Ida Lupino, Gibb McLaughlin; director: George King. A selfish magnate is humanized by a jail sentence. (Drama.)

Strictly in Confidence. James Finlayson, Reginald Purdell; director: Clyde Cook. Reporters apprehend a confidence trickster. (Comedy.)

Head of the Family. Irene Vanbrugh, Arthur Maude; director: John Daumery. A bankrupt magnate becomes a nightwatchman for a rival, and catches his son attempting robbery. (Drama.)

Mayfair Girl. Sally Blane, John Stuart (centre right); director: George King. An American girl is framed for killing a cad while drunk. (Crime.)

Enemy of the Police. John Stuart, Viola Keats; director: George King. A reform guild's secretary is mistaken for a crook and given psychological treatment. (Comedy.)

Smithy. Edmund Gwenn, Peggy Novak; director: George King. A stockbroker decides to break the monotony of his existence with one night of freedom. (Comedy.)

Her Imaginary Lover (from A.E.W. Mason's *Green Stockings*). Laura La Plante (standing), Percy Marmont; director: George King. An heiress invents a fiancé to stave off fortune hunters. (Comedy.)

I Adore You. Margot Grahame, Harold French; director: George King. An old actor is mistaken for the owner of a new film studio. (Comedy.)

The Bermondsey Kid. Esmond Knight, Pat Peterson; director: Ralph Dawson. A boxing newsboy is forced to fight a sick friend for the championship. (Drama.)

The Acting Business. Hugh Williams, Wendy Barrie; director: John Daumery. Parents' interference causes newlywed actors to separate. (Comedy.)

1934

The Silver Spoon. Ian Hunter (right), Garry Marsh (left), Binnie Barnes, Cecil Parker; director: George King. Two gentlemen tramps confess to a lord's murder in order to shield a woman they both love. (Comedy.)

Trouble in Store. James Finlayson, Jack Hobbs; director: Clyde Cook. Store assistants catch burglars when they are accidentally locked in. (Comedy.)

Murder at the Inn. Wendy Barrie, Harold French; director: George King. Elopers are involved in the murder of a blackmailing landlord. (Crime.)

Guest of Honour. Henry Kendall, Miki Hood; director: George King. A lord posing as a dinner guest unmasks a blackmailer. (Comedy.)

The Girl in Possession. Laura La Plante, Henry Kendall, Claude Hulbert; director: Monty Banks. An American girl is tricked into thinking that she owns an estate in England. (Comedy.)

Nine Forty-Five. Binnie Barnes, Donald Calthrop; director: George King. A doctor proves that a crime to which three people confess was suicide. (Crime.)

No Escape. Binnie Barnes, Ralph Ince, Ian Hunter; director: Ralph Ince. The pursuit of a Malayan planter framed for poisoning his partner and suspected of carrying plague. (Melodrama.)

Something Always Happens. Ian Hunter, Nancy O'Neill; director: Michael Powell. A car salesman loves his secretary who turns out to be the daughter of a wealthy rival. (Comedy.)

The Life of the Party. Jerry Verno, Betty Astell; director: Ralph Dawson. A wife tries to hide drunken neighbours from her husband. (Comedy.)

The Office Wife. Nora Swinburne, Dorothy Bouchier, Cecil Parker; director: George King. A publisher's divorced wife eventually wins him back after he weds his secretary. (Romance.)

What Happened to Harkness? Robert Hale, James Finlayson; director: Milton Rosmer. A village policeman investigates the apparent murder of a miser. (Comedy.)

Leave it to Blanche. Henry Kendall, Olive Blakeney; director: Harold Young. A husband pretends to kill his wife's lover and is convinced he has succeeded. (Comedy.)

Too Many Millions. Betty Compton, John Garrick, Viola Keats; director: Harold Young. A millionairess poses as a maid to help, and woo, a poor artist. (Romance.)

The Blue Squadron. Esmond Knight, John Stuart; director: George King. A colonel loses a girl to his rival, but saves the rival's life in the Alps. (Romance.)

Father and Son. Edmund Gwenn, Esmond Knight, James Finlayson; director: Monty Banks. A bank clerk takes the blame for a theft he thinks was committed by his ex-convict father. (Crime.)

A Glimpse of Paradise. George Carney, Eve Lister; director: Ralph Ince. An ex-convict saves his daughter, who does not know him, from a blackmailer. (Crime.)

Big Business. Eve Gray, Claude Hulbert; director: Cyril Gardner. A businessman's unemployed double puts the firm back on its feet. (Comedy.)

Hyde Park. George Carney, Eve Lister; director: Randall Faye. A socialist refuses to let his daughter marry a lord's son but relents when he inherits £1,000. (Comedy.)

The Girl in the Crowd. Barrie Clifton, Googie Withers; director: Michael Powell. A man decides to wed a girl he picks at random, and lands in jail. (Comedy.)

What's in a Name? Carol Goodner, Barrie Clifton; director: Ralph Ince. A clerk posing as a foreign composer loves a girl posing as a film-star. (Comedy.)

1935

Widow's Might. Laura La Plante, Yvonne Arnaud, Garry Marsh; director: Cyril Gardner. Widows fake a burglary to win back ex-sweethearts. (Comedy.)

Murder at Monte Carlo. Errol Flynn, Eve Gray, Paul Graetz; director: Ralph Ince. A reporter in Monte Carlo solves the murder of a professor for his winning roulette system. (Crime.)

So You Won't Talk? Monty Banks, Claude Dampier, Ralph Ince; director: Monty Banks. An heir to £100,000 must not speak or write for one month. (Comedy.)

Mr What's-His-Name? Seymour Hicks, Olive Blakeney, Enid Stamp-Taylor, Martita Hunt; director: Ralph Ince. A married millionaire weds a beautician while suffering from amnesia. (Comedy.)

Full Circle. Rene Ray, Garry Marsh; director: George King. A burglar steals a will, then steals it again to return it to heiress. (Crime.)

Hello Sweetheart (from George Kaufman's play *The Butter and Egg Man*). Claude Hulbert, Gregory Ratoff, Jane Carr; director: Monty Banks. Americans persuade a farmer to use his inheritance to finance a film. (Comedy.)

Some Day. Esmond Knight, Margaret Lockwood; director: Michael Powell. A playboy helps a poor lift-operator to marry a cleaner. (Romance.)

Crime Unlimited. Esmond Knight, Lilli Palmer, Cecil Parker; director: Ralph Ince. A detective poses as a crook in order to unmask the leader of a gang of jewel thieves. (Crime.)

Man of the Moment. Douglas Fairbanks Jr, Laura La Plante, Claude Hulbert, Margaret Lockwood; director: Monty Banks. A prospective groom falls in love with a girl he saves from suicide. (Comedy.)

Get Off My Foot. Max Miller, Jane Carr, Chili Bouchier; director: William Beaudine. A major schemes to marry his daughter to his butler, an heir to a fortune. (Comedy.)

Mr Cohen Takes a Walk. Paul Graetz, Violet Farebrother, Chili Bouchier; director: William Beaudine. The founder of a store poses as a pedlar, but returns in time to save his business. (Drama.)

Black Mask. Wylie Watson, Aileen Marson; director: Ralph Ince. A gentleman crook who steals for charity is framed for the murder of a press knight. (Crime.)

1936

The Brown Wallet. Patric Knowles, Nancy O'Neill; director: Michael Powell. A bankrupt publisher is unjustly suspected of killing a rich aunt when he finds £200, but all turns out well in the end. (Crime.)

Faithful. Jean Muir, Gene Gerard; director: Paul Stein. A Viennese singer poses as a bachelor and is tempted by a socialite. (Musical.)

Gaol Break. Ralph Ince, Pat Fitzpatrick; director: Ralph Ince. A convict escapes gaol to save his son from being kidnapped by former associates. (Crime.)

Crown v. Stevens. Beatrix Thomson, Patric Knowles; director: Michael Powell. An ex-dancer kills a usurer and her husband, framing his employee. (Crime.)

Twelve Good Men. Nancy O'Neill (left), Henry Kendall (centre), Grace Lane (right), Ralph Roberts (in bed); director: Ralph Ince. An actor foils a convict who escapes to murder his jury. (Crime.)

Where's Sally? George Gerrard, Claude Hulbert, Chili Bouchier; director: Arthur Woods. A honeymoon wife learns of her husband's past and runs away. (Comedy.)

Fair Exchange. Patric Knowles, Roscoe Ates; director: Ralph Ince. A criminologist stages a picture theft in order to thwart his son's detective ambitions. (Comedy.)

Educated Evans. Max Miller, Nancy O'Neill; director: William Beaudine. A racing tipster becomes a trainer for a newly rich stable-owner. (Comedy.)

Hail and Farewell. Claude Hulbert, Reginald Purdell; director: Ralph Ince. The intertwined adventures of privates and officers while on a six-hour leave in Southampton. (Drama.)

Head Office. Owen Nares, Nancy O'Neill; director: Melville Brown. A clerk knows his employer's son died a coward, and blackmails him. (Drama.)

It's in the Bag. Jimmy Nervo (left), Teddy Knox (right); director: William Beaudine. Some Covent Garden porters find forged money with which they finance a night club. (Comedy.)

Irish for Luck. Athene Seyler, Margaret Lockwood, Patric Knowles; director: Arthur Woods. A poor duchess in Ireland, her orphan niece and a busker win fame on the BBC. (Comedy.)

1937

The Vulture. Claude Hulbert, Lesley Brook; director: Ralph Ince. A detective pretends to be Chinese in order to catch jewel thieves. (Comedy.)

Mayfair Melody. Keith Falkner, Joyce Kirby, Chili Bouchier; director: Arthur Woods. A car magnate's spoiled daughter helps a mechanic become an opera star. (Musical.)

Side Street Angel. Hugh Williams, Lesley Brook; director: Ralph Ince. A rich man poses as a gem thief to woo a girl who runs a reformatory. (Comedy.)

It's Not Cricket. Claude Hulbert, Henry Kendall; director: Ralph Ince. An affianced man tries to elope with his best friend's wife. (Comedy.)

Don't Get Me Wrong. Max Miller, George E. Stone; director: Arthur Woods and Reginald Purdell. A fairground entertainer promotes tabloid petrol substitute invented by a mad chemist. (Comedy.)

Patricia Gets Her Man. Hans Sonker, Lesley Brook; director: Reginald Purdell. A girl tries to make a star jealous by hiring a gigolo who is really a count. (Comedy.)

Gypsy. Roland Young (right), Chili Bouchier (left), Hugh Williams; director: Roy William Neill. A gypsy girl weds an ageing socialite believing her beloved lion-tamer is dead. (Romance.)

The Windmill. Hugh Williams, Glen Alyn; director: Arthur Woods. In the France of 1916, a spy blackmails an innkeeper's adopted German daughter. (War drama.)

The Compulsory Wife. Henry Kendall, Joyce Kirby; director: Arthur Woods. A burglar steals the clothes of a couple forced to spend the night together at a cottage. (Comedy.)

Ship's Concert. Claude Hulbert, Joyce Kirby; director: Leslie Hiscott. The passengers on a luxury cruise put on a show to aid stowaway actors. (Musical.)

The Perfect Crime. Hugh Williams, Glen Alyn; director: Ralph Ince. A clerk is framed for murder after he fakes his own suicide and robs his office. (Crime.)

The Man Who Made Diamonds. Noel Madison, James Stephenson, Wilfrid Lawson; director: Ralph Ince. An assistant kills a scientist to market his manufactured diamonds. (Crime.)

You Live and Learn. Glenda Farrell, Claude Hulbert; director: Arthur Woods. An American showgirl thinks she is marrying a rich landowner but finds that he is a widowed farmer with children. (Comedy.)

Change for a Sovereign. Seymour Hicks, Chili Bouchier; director: Maurice Elvey. A drunken double takes the place of a Ruritanian king while on holiday. (Comedy.)

Take It From Me (also known as **Transatlantic Trouble**). Max Miller, Betty Lynne, Buddy Baer; director: William Beaudine. A dud boxer elopes on a liner with a lady and his pursuing manager is mistaken for a millionaire. (Comedy.)

Who Killed John Savage? Nicholas Hannen, Barry Mackay, Edward Chapman; director: Maurice Elvey. The head of a chemical firm fakes his own murder to collect insurance. (Crime.)

1938

The Dark Stairway. Hugh Williams, Chili Bouchier, Garry Marsh; director: Arthur Woods. A hospital doctor is murdered for a new anaesthetic. (Crime.)

The Singing Cop. Keith Falkner, Marta Kabarr, Chili Bouchier; director: Arthur Woods. A policeman poses as an opera singer to expose a prima donna as a spy. (Musical.)

Quiet Please. Reginald Purdell, Lesley Brook; director: Roy William Neill. Buskers posing as a patient and a valet save a lady's gems from theft. (Crime.)

Mr Satan. Skeets Gallagher, James Stephenson, Chili Bouchier; director: Arthur Woods. A war correspondent falls in love with the agent of a supposedly dead armaments king. (Crime.)

Glamour Girl. Gene Gerrard, Lesley Brook; director: Arthur Woods. A conceited photographer is reformed by a loving secretary. (Comedy.)

Simply Terrific. Claude Hulbert, Reginald Purdell; director: Roy William Neill. Broke playboys promote a flower-seller's hangover cure. (Comedy.)

The Viper. Claude Hulbert, Betty Lynne; director: Roy William Neill. A detective dons numerous disguises to save a girl's diamond from an escaped convict. (Comedy.)

It's in the Blood. Claude Hulbert, Leslie Brook, James Stephenson; director: Gene Gerrard. A film fan, on a day trip to Boulogne, manages to catch a gang of jewel thieves. (Comedy.)

They Drive by Night. Emlyn Williams, Ernest Thesiger, Anna Konstam; director: Arthur Woods. A lorry driver and a girl help a fugitive ex-convict catch a silk-stocking strangler. (Crime.)

Thistledown. Aino Bergo, Keith Falkner; director: Arthur Woods. A Scottish laird believes his continental wife is unfaithful. (Musical.)

Thank Evans. Max Miller (right), Hal Walters (left); director: Roy William Neill. A broke tipster saves a lord's racehorse from a crooked trainer. (Comedy.)

Dangerous Medicine. Elizabeth Allan, Cyril Ritchard; director: Arthur Woods. A doctor helps a girl escape jail and traps the real murderer. (Crime.)

The Return of Carol Deane. Bebe Daniels, Arthur Margetson, Chili Bouchier; director: Arthur Woods. A female ex-convict marries a gambler to keep her secret from her son. (Crime.)

Many Tanks Mr Atkins. Claude Hulbert, Reginald Purdell; director: Roy William Neill. A cavalry trooper invents a tank super-charger and saves it from spies. (Comedy.)

Double or Quits. Patricia Medina, Hal Walters; director: Roy William Neill. A reporter is the double of a thief who steals rare stamps on a transatlantic liner. (Crime.)

Everything Happens To Me. Max Miller, Chili Bouchier; director: Roy William Neill. A cleaner salesman becomes an electioneer for both sides. (Comedy.)

1939

The Nursemaid Who Disappeared. Arthur Margetson, Peter Coke, Lesley Brook, Coral Browne; director: Arthur Woods. A playwright helps a detective to catch kidnappers posing as a domestic agency. (Crime.)

Too Dangerous To Live. Greta Gynt, Reginald Tate; director: Anthony Hankey, Leslie Norman. A French detective poses as a crook to unmask a leader of jewel thieves. (Crime.)

A Gentleman's Gentleman. Eric Blore, Marie Lohr, Peter Coke; director: Roy William Neill. A valet blackmails his master for supposed poisoning. (Comedy.)

The Good Old Days. Max Miller, Hal Walters; director: Roy William Neill. Persecuted players (*circa* 1840) save a lord's son from a chimney sweep. (Comedy.)

Confidential Lady. Ben Lyon, Jane Baxter; director: Arthur Woods. A jilted reporter helps a jilted girl thwart a press lord who ruined her father. (Romance.)

Murder Will Out. John Loder, Jane Baxter, Jack Hawkins; director: Roy William Neill. Crooks fake murder to blackmail a rich doctor's neglected wife. (Crime.)

His Brother's Keeper. Clifford Evans, Tamara Desni, Una O'Connor; director: Roy William Neill. Sharpshooting brothers quarrel over a gold-digging blues singer. (Drama.)

The Midas Touch. Barry K. Barnes (right), Judy Kelly (left); director: David Macdonald. A clairvoyant predicts that a faithless financier will die in a car accident involving his son. (Drama.)

Hoots Mon! Max Miller (left), Florence Desmond (centre), Hal Walters (right); director: Roy William Neill. Rivalry between a Cockney comedian and a Scots impressionist ends in love. (Comedy.'

1940

Dr O'Dowd. Shaun Glenville, Peggy Cummins; director: Herbert Mason. A drunken Irish doctor is reinstated after saving his engineer son from a diptheria epidemic. (Drama.)

George And Margaret. Judy Kelly, Marie Lohr (right), John Boxer (centre), Noel Howlett (left); director: George King. A suburban family's problems are sorted out by their maid. (Comedy.)

The Briggs Family. Edward Chapman, Jane Baxter; director: Herbert Mason. A lawyer's clerk defends his crippled son and exposes the real burglar. (Crime.)

That's The Ticket. Sid Field, Betty Lynne; director: Redd Davis. Cloakroom attendants' don disguises to save blueprints from spies in Paris. (Comedy.)

Two For Danger. Barry K. Barnes, Greta Gynt, Cecil Parker; director: George King. A barrister and his fiancé save a private art collection from international thieves. (Crime.)

Fingers. Clifford Evans, Leonora Corbett, Esmond Knight; director: Herbert Mason. An East End 'fence' falls for a socialite but returns to a girl of his own class. (Crime.)

1942

The Peterville Diamond. Ann Crawford, Donald Stewart, Oliver Wakefield; director: Walter Forde. A neglected wife flirts with a gentleman jewel thief in Mexico. (Comedy.)

1943

The Night Invader. Anne Crawford, David Farrar; director: Herbert Mason. An American girl helps a British agent capture a Nazi count. (War drama.)

The Dark Tower. Ben Lyon, David Farrar (left), Anne Crawford (centre), Herbert Lom (right); director: John Harlow. A hypnotist makes a circus girl perform trapeze stunts and tries to force her from her lover. (Drama.)

The Hundred-Pound Window. Anne Crawford, David Farrar; director: Brian Desmond Hurst. A clerk involved with crooked gamblers repents and exposes them as black-marketeers. (Crime.)

1945

Flight From Folly. Pat Kirkwood (left), A.E. Matthews (centre), Hugh Sinclair (right), Edmundo Ros and his Orchestra; director: Herbert Mason. A showgirl poses as a nurse to cure a playwright of amnesia. (Musical.)

Warner Bros. in Colour

Here is a selection of colourful moments from recent and not so recent Warner Bros. films, stretching back to **The Adventures of Robin Hood** (1938).

Richard Harris in **Camelot** (1967)

Robert Redford (left) and Will Geer in **Jeremiah Johnson** (1972)

James Dean in **Giant** (1956).

Below: Paul Newman in **The Towering Inferno** (1974)

Right: Burt Reynolds with (from left) Billy McKinney, Ronny Cox and Jon Voight in **Deliverance** (1972)

Dustin Hoffman (left) and Robert Redford in **All The President's Men** (1976)

Above: Clint Eastwood (left) and John Vernon in **The Outlaw Josey Wales** (1976)

Left: Errol Flynn in **The Adventures of Robin Hood** (1938)

Above right: Carroll Baker in **Cheyenne Autumn** (1964)

Right: Ward Bond (left) and John Wayne in **Rio Bravo** (1959)

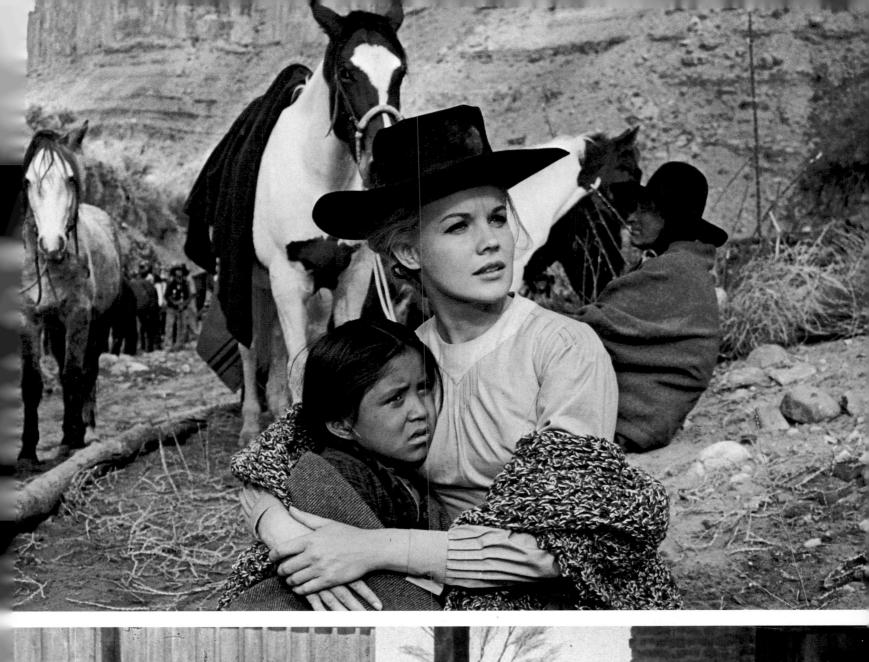

Michael J. Pollard, Gene Hackman, Warren
Beatty and Estelle Parsons (from left) in
Bonnie and Clyde (1967)

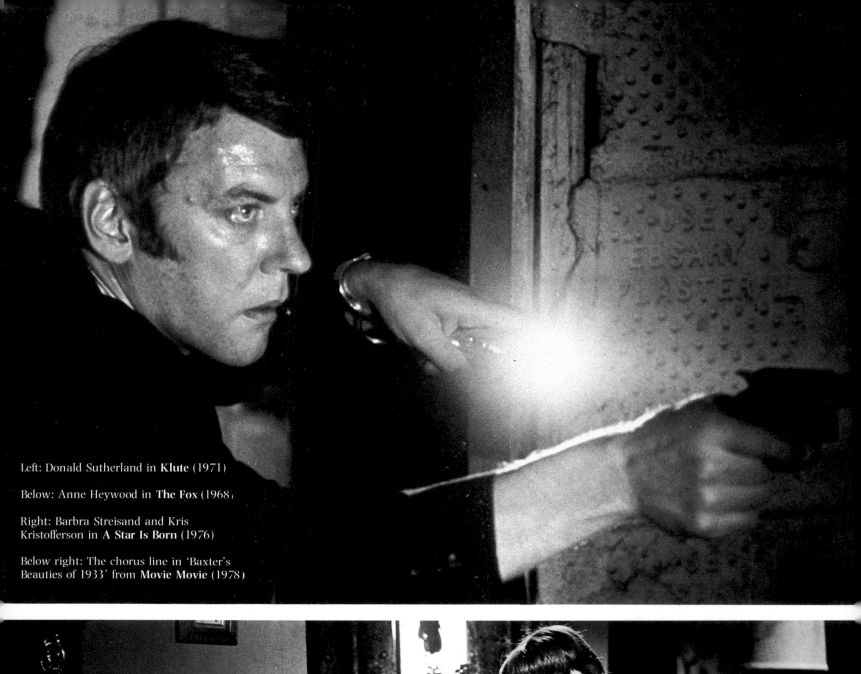

Left: Donald Sutherland in **Klute** (1971)

Below: Anne Heywood in **The Fox** (1968)

Right: Barbra Streisand and Kris Kristofferson in **A Star Is Born** (1976)

Below right: The chorus line in 'Baxter's Beauties of 1933' from **Movie Movie** (1978)

Christopher Reeve in **Superman** (1978)

James Cagney in **Captains of the Clouds** (1942).

INDEX

INDEX

INDEX